GOSPEL
PERSPECTIVES

The Jesus Tradition
Outside the Gospels

Volume 5

Edited by
David Wenham

jsot press
1985

Copyright © 1984 JSOT Press

ISBN 1 85075 006 8
1 85075 007 6 Pbk

Published by
JSOT Press
Department of Biblical Studies
The University of Sheffield
Sheffield S10 2TN
England

Printed in Great Britain
by Redwood Burn Limited
Trowbridge, Wiltshire

British Library Cataloguing in Publication Data

The Jesus tradition outside the Gospels.——
   (Gospel perspectives; v. 5)
   1. Jesus Christ——Biography——Sources
   I. Wenham, David   II. Series
   232.9'08   BT297

   ISBN 1-85075-006-8
   ISBN 1-85075-007-6 Pbk

CONTENTS

PREFACE

The canonical gospels are the main source of our knowledge about the person and work of Jesus, and the purpose of the *Gospel Perspectives* series has been to examine in a scholarly way and from various angles the question of the historicity of the gospels. This fifth *Gospel Perspectives* volume looks at the Jesus tradition *outside* the gospels; but it still rightly belongs in the series, since our concern has been to see what light is thrown on Matthew, Mark, Luke and John by other early Christian and non-Christian writings that refer to Jesus.

The potential of such an approach to the gospels was suggested by the previous volume in the series, vol. IV: *The Rediscovery of Jesus' Eschatological Discourse*, since that volume made extensive use of evidence from Paul's epistles and from the book of Revelation. It was argued not only that Paul and the author of Revelation knew tradition that we know as part of the synoptic tradition, but also that their evidence casts significant light on the form and history of the 'pre-synoptic' tradition. That volume examined one particular part of the gospel tradition; this volume looks more widely at Jesus traditions outside the gospels. It includes studies of New Testament writings other than the gospels; it looks at other early Christian writings, such as the Didache and the Gospel of Thomas; it also looks at some non-Christian traditions of Jesus, Jewish and classical.

The sorts of questions being addressed in the volume are quite complex. For example, a basic question is whether or not a particular writing contains quotations from, or allusions to, Jesus traditions. There is not usually any major problem in recognizing an explicit quotation. Recognizing allusions, on the other hand, is often a matter of very fine judgment: what looks like an allusion to the reader who is predisposed to see allusions may look like nothing of the sort to others. Critics have accordingly differed enormously in their conclusions: some, for example, believe Paul's letters to be permeated with Jesus traditions, whereas others recognize very few allusions. Given this situation, it is clearly important to try to avoid impressionistic judgments, and to see whether there is solid evidence for use and knowledge of Jesus traditions. Where there is a supposed parallel between a gospel tradition and a tradition outside the gospels, it is necessary to consider whether the parallelism is substantial enough to be significant, to realise that some similarities may simply be due to common background, and also to reckon with the possibility that the author of the particular gospel could have been influenced in his redaction by the non-gospel tradition, not vice-versa.

If it is established that a particular document contains or probably contains quotations from or allusions to Jesus traditions, the next and very important question to consider concerns the origin of those traditions and their relationship to the traditions of the canonical gospels. It is possible, certainly with some of the documents being examined, that the traditions concerned come directly or indirectly from the canonical gospels, and so throw very little light on the gospels. If, however, the wording, form or date of the quotation or allusion suggests that the author in question had a tradition independent of the gospels, then important light may be shed on the history of the gospel traditions.

Not only are the questions being examined complex, but the amount of evidence that could (and should) be examined is enormous. In this volume, inevitably, only a little of the relevant evidence has been explored. We had hoped to cover more than we have in fact covered; for example, we had hoped to include a discussion of Hebrews, but readers will have to wait for that study to be completed at a later date. Even where we have dealt with particular topics, we have not always done full justice to the material. For example two essays in the volume examine the Pauline evidence (and come to interestingly different conclusions), but a whole volume of essays or even several volumes could be devoted to an examination of the relevant Pauline material.

However, despite the limitations of the volume, we believe that it considers a useful sample of the evidence that needs to be discussed, and we hope that it may stimulate others to further research in this area. Further research is needed not only to cover the ground that we have failed to explore, but also to consider further some of the questions that we have discussed inconclusively. We have not reached unanimity on all points, and we are conscious of the need for ongoing study. At the end of the book Dr Richard Bauckham suggests some possible avenues for future research.

We are grateful to all those who have helped with the production of this volume - to those who have read and commented on articles, to the Council and staff of Tyndale House, Cambridge, for their practical support and to the JSOT Press.

PAUL'S USE OF THE JESUS TRADITION: THREE SAMPLES

David Wenham,
Wycliffe Hall,
Oxford OX2 6PW.

'Any suggestion that Paul was unfamiliar with or
uninterested in the Jesus tradition must be considered
improbable in view of the evidence for Paul's use of the
pre-synoptic eschatological traditions. It appears on the
contrary that Paul's teaching is very heavily dependent on the
teaching of Jesus, even though he does not often explicitly
acknowledge this dependence.' Such was the present author's
conclusion in the previous volume of the *Gospel Perspectives*
series on the basis of a study of the synoptic eschatological
traditions and of related material elsewhere in the New
Testament./l/ The Pauline evidence examined was principally
in 1 and 2 Thessalonians. The purpose of this paper is to see
whether the sort of picture that emerged in that study - of Paul
being familiar with what we called a 'pre-synoptic' form of the
gospel traditions (including traditions attested only in
Matthew or Luke) - can be confirmed by evidence from elsewhere
in the Pauline corpus. The paper will not attempt to be in any
way comprehensive, but will examine three selected passages from
three of Paul's other letters.

1. 1 Corinthians 7:10,11/2/

Most scholars are agreed that in 1 Cor 7:10,11 Paul is
quoting the teaching of Jesus, and that this quotation is
connected with the divorce sayings that we find in Mt 19:9,
Mk 10:10,11, Lk 16:18, Mt 5:32. But there is no agreement among
scholars about the exact relationship between Paul's citation
and the respective synoptic texts.

1.1. 1 Cor 7:10,11 parallel to Mk 10:9,11/Mt 19:6,9

The relevant Pauline text here is τοῖς δὲ γεγαμηκόσιν
παραγγέλλω, οὐκ ἐγὼ ἀλλὰ ὁ κύριος, γυναῖκα ἀπὸ ἀνδρὸς μὴ
χωρισθῆναι - ἐὰν δὲ καὶ χωρισθῇ, μενέτω ἄγαμος ἢ τῷ ἀνδρί
καταλλαγήτω - καὶ ἄνδρα γυναῖκα μὴ ἀφιέναι. τοῖς δὲ λοιποῖς
λέγω ἐγω, οὐχ ὁ κύριος......

The first thing to observe about this is that Paul puts his
citation of the Lord's words in the equivalent of inverted
commas: at the beginning of verse 10 he makes it clear that he
is quoting (οὐκ ἐγὼ ἀλλὰ ὁ κύριος) and at the beginning of
verse 11 he makes it clear that he has finished quoting (τοῖς δὲ
λοιποῖς λέγω ἐγώ, οὐχ ὁ κύριος).

The second thing to observe is that Paul's citation of the
Lord's words falls into two halves and that these two halves
correspond strikingly to the two sayings of Jesus about divorce
in Mark 10/Matthew 19. Thus compare:

   (a) 1 Cor 7:10a   with Mk 10:9/Mt 19:6

      γυναῖκα ἀπ' ἀνδρὸς   ὁ οὖν ὁ θεὸς συνέζευξεν
      μὴ χωρισθῆναι   ἄνθρωπος μὴ χωριζέτω

In both verses we have a straight prohibition of divorce or, to
be more accurate, of separation, and the wording used in both
places is very similar - μὴ χωρισθῆναι.... μὴ χωριζέτω./3/
There are differences between the respective sayings: Paul in
1 Corinthians 7 speaks particularly about the responsibility of
a married woman, probably because this was the immediate problem
in Corinth, whereas the synoptic saying is more general. The
similarities, however, remain striking.

   (b) 1 Cor 7:10b   with Mk 10:11 cf. Mt 19:9

      ἐὰν δὲ καὶ χωρισθῇ,   ὃς ἂν ἀπολύσῃ τὴν γυναῖκα
      μενέτω ἄγαμος.... καὶ   αὐτοῦ καὶ γαμήσῃ ἄλλην
      ἄνδρα γυναῖκα μὴ   μοιχᾶται ἐπ' αὐτὴν, καὶ
      ἀφιέναι   ἐάν ....

After the straight prohibition of separation, Paul adds a
further rider, 'But if (ἐάν) she separates .... let her remain
unmarried'. Similarly in the synoptic passage after the
straight prohibition of separation, Jesus goes on to explain to
the disciples that 'whoever (ὃς ἂν) divorces his wife and
marries another commits adultery, and if (καὶ ἐάν) .....'. The
similarity here between 1 Corinthians 7 and Mark 10 (cf. Matthew
19) is both in the ἂν/ἐάν type of construction used and in the
thought expressed, the focus now switching from divorce per se
to remarriage - this being the unthinkable thing.

The fact that 1 Cor 7:10 has these particular links with
the two synoptic sayings about divorce attested in Mk 10:9/
Mt 19:6 and in Mk 10:11/Mt 19:9 has not often been noted.

Given the links, there can be little doubt that we have common
tradition here, and it is at least reasonable to surmise that
Paul knew not just the two sayings, but also the dialogue
context which connects them in Matthew and Mark./4/

   *1.2. Other links between the sections in 1 Corinthians
         and Matthew 19/Mark 10/5/*
     The suggestion that Paul knew these sayings in their
synoptic context may be confirmed by further observations.
(a) In Matthew 19/Mark 10, the synoptic passage with which
Paul's saying seems connected, Jesus bases his comments on
divorce on an appeal to the 'one flesh' principle. It is, at
least, interesting that in 1 Corinthians Paul's discussion of
divorce is preceded by a discussion of the 'one flesh' principle
as it applies first to relations with a prostitute (6:12-20)
and then probably to relationships in marriage (7:1-6)./6/
(b) In Matthew 19 Jesus goes on after the divorce saying to the
difficult sayings about those who are eunuchs for the sake of
the kingdom of God. These sayings, as others have noted, are
somewhat reminiscent of Paul's teaching in 1 Corinthians 7 about
celibacy (for the Lord's sake and because of the shortness of
the time). Most notably 1 Cor 7:7 'I wish all men were as I am,
but each has his own gift from God' resembles Mt 19:11 'Not all
can receive this word, but those to whom it is given'./7/
Such 'M' tradition is commonly assumed to be late, and it might
therefore be thought improbable that Paul could here be drawing
on that tradition. But there is good reason for questioning
this view of 'M' tradition,/8/ and since Paul in 1 Corinthians 7
is certainly citing some elements found in Matthew 19 (i.e.
the divorce sayings), the possibility that he knew and is
reflecting the saying about eunuchs should be reckoned with.
(c) It is just possible that Paul's teaching about the
'holiness' of children in 1 Cor 7:14 could owe something to the
story of the children being brought to Jesus which follows the
divorce passage in Matthew and Mark, and that Paul's 'God has
called us to peace' (1 Cor 7:15) could be linked to Mk 9:50,
the verse preceding the divorce saying in Mark, 'Be at peace
among yourselves'./9/

     These possible links between the relevant synoptic
section and 1 Corinthians 7 are not all strong possibilities,
certainly when taken individually. But even if some of the
evidence is disregarded, the case for saying that Paul in
1 Corinthians 7 is drawing not just on the sayings of Jesus
about divorce, but more widely on the section of tradition in
which those sayings were found is plausible.

1.3 The synoptic problem posed by the divorce texts
Even if some of the possible links between 1 Corinthians 7
and the traditions of Matthew 19/Mark 10 are uncertain, the
link between the divorce texts (see section 1.1 above) is very
probable. And it is worth considering if the Pauline evidence
can help us to unravel the complex question of how the differing
synoptic divorce texts relate to each other.

The texts are as follows:

Mt 5:32   Lk 16:18

(a) ἐγὼ δὲ λέγω ὑμῖν ὅτι πᾶς   πᾶς ὁ ἀπολύων τὴν γυναῖκα
ὁ ἀπολύων τὴν γυναῖκα αὐτοῦ   αὐτοῦ καὶ γαμῶν ἑτέραν
παρεκτὸς λόγου πορνείας ποιεῖ   μοιχεύει, καὶ ὁ ἀπολελυμένην
αὐτὴν μοιχευθῆναι, (b) καὶ ὃς   ἀπὸ ἀνδρὸς γαμῶν μοιχεύει
ἐὰν ἀπολελυμένην γαμήσῃ, μοιχᾶται

Mt 19:6,9   Mk 10:9,11,12

..... μὴ χωριζέτω..........   ..... μὴ χωριζέτω............
9. λέγω δὲ ὑμῖν ὅτι ὃς ἂν   11. καὶ λέγει αὐτοῖς ὃς ἂν
ἀπολύσῃ τὴν γυναῖκα αὐτοῦ μὴ   ἀπολύσῃ τὴν γυναῖκα αὐτοῦ καὶ
ἐπὶ πορνείᾳ καὶ γαμήσῃ ἄλλην,   γαμήσῃ ἄλλην, μοιχᾶται ἐπ'
μοιχᾶται   αὐτήν. 12. καὶ ἐὰν αὐτὴ
                                     ἀπολύσασα τὸν ἄνδρα αὐτῆς
                                     γαμήσῃ ἄλλον, μοιχᾶται

The pattern of similarities and differences between the
gospels here is complex. But we can attempt to sum up the
situation as follows:

1.   There are four statements about the responsibility of
the man who divorces his wife. The most significant
similarities and differences between the four are these:
(a) Mt 5:32a speaks of the man making his divorced wife an
adulteress, whereas Mt 19:9, Mk 10:11 and Lk 16:18a all speak
of the man remarrying himself and so committing adultery.
(b) Mt 5:32a and Lk 16:18a both use a participial construction
πᾶς ὁ ἀπολύων and the verb μοιχεύειν, whereas Mt 19:9 and
Mk 10:11 use a ὃς ἂν construction and the verb μοιχᾶσθαι.

2.   There are three statements about the situation
of the divorced wife who remarries. The most
significant similarities and differences between them are
these: (a) Mt 5:32b and Lk 16:18b speak of the culpability of

the second husband and refer to the divorced wife as
ἀπολελυμένην, whereas Mk 10:12 speaks of the culpability of the
wife who divorces and remarries, referring to her as an active
party in the divorce - ἀπολύσασα. (b) Mt 5:32b and Mk 10:12
use an ἐὰν ... γαμήσῃ construction + the verb μοιχᾶσθαι.
Lk 16:18b (like 16:18a) has the participial ὁ... γαμῶν + the
verb μοιχεύειν. (c) Mk 10:12 and Lk 16:18b explicitly mention
the first husband (τὸν ἄνδρα, ἀπ' ἀνδρός) whereas Matthew does
not.

    Such is the synoptic evidence briefly summarized. But if
we are to make sense of it, we need to note some more
particular points:

    3. There is stylistic inconsistency within Mt 5:32. Thus
Mt 5:32a resembles Lk 16:18 in using the participial
construction πᾶς ὁ ..... + the verb μοιχεύειν, whereas
Mt 5:32b, while having some things in common with Lk 16:18,
resembles Mk 10:11,12 in using a ὃς ἐάν construction + the verb
μοιχᾶσθαι. Matthew's internal inconsistency and the way that
the two halves of his v 32 resemble different Markan and Lukan
traditions need explaining.

    4. There is a less obvious stylistic inconsistency in
Mk 10:11,12. Thus Mk 10:11 has ὃς ἂν ἀπολύσῃ καὶ γαμήσῃ, a
construction exactly paralleled in Mt 19:9. Mk 10:12, on the
other hand, does not link the divorcing and marrying verbs with
καί, but has a participial construction καὶ ἐὰν αὐτὴ ἀπολύσασα
... γαμήσῃ. This construction has some resemblances to
Mt 5:32b καὶ ὃς ἐὰν ἀπολελυμένην γαμήσῃ. The resemblances are
in (a) the use of ἐάν not ἄν, (b) the use of a participle of
ἀπολύειν. This last agreement in the use of a participle may
seem insignificant, since Matthew speaks of the responsibility
of a man marrying a divorced woman and uses a passive
participle ἀπολελυμένην, whereas Mark speaks of the
responsibility of a woman divorcing and remarrying and has an
active participle ἀπολύσασα. However, although at first sight
Matthew and Mark may seem to be addressing quite different
points, in fact both the Matthean and Markan statements are
speaking about the situation of the divorced wife who remarries
(whereas the other Matthean and Markan statements deal with the
culpability of the first husband when he divorces). And,
although at first sight, the active participle and the passive
participle of Matthew may seem unlikely to be connected, it is
in fact quite possible to see Mark's active participle as his
substitute for the Matthean passive (this passive being

paralleled in Lk 16:18) - Mark has his Gentile readership in
mind, and so speaks of a woman taking the initiative in divorce,
whereas Matthew reflects the Jewish practice according to which
the woman could only be on the receiving end of divorce - or,
less probably, to see Matthew's passive as his substitute for
the Markan active./10/ Either way the case for seeing
significance in the resemblances between Mk 10:12 and Mt 5:32b
is a good one, and so the puzzle posed by Mk 10:11,12 is not
just that there is a slight inconsistency between the Markan
verses, but also that the one verse seems closely paralleled
in one part of Matthew (19:9) and the other seems related to a
quite different Matthean verse (5:32b).

5. It is not possible to demonstrate any significant
stylistic inconsistency within Lk 16:18, unless it is arguable
that after the first clause πᾶς ὁ ἀπολύων τὴν γυναῖκα καὶ γαμῶν
ἑτέραν μοιχεύει we might perhaps have expected καὶ πᾶς ὁ γαμῶν
ἀπολελυμένην ἀπὸ ἀνδρὸς μοιχεύει rather than the present καὶ ὁ
ἀπολελυμένην ἀπὸ ἀνδρὸς γαμῶν μοιχεύει.

Such is some of the synoptic evidence that needs to be
explained in any account of the history of the relevant gospel
traditions. But what further evidence is contributed by Paul?

1. Paul appears to be using the tradition reflected in
Matthew 19 and Mark 10 with the two sayings ('Don't separate...
but if') and with the ἐάν construction.

2. Paul speaks in 1 Cor 7:10 of the woman separating
(χωρίζειν) and the man divorcing. Shortly afterwards in the
chapter he can refer to a man or a woman divorcing (vv 12,13)
and to a man separating (v 15). But in the specific citation
from Jesus, he does not put it both ways round. He has it
there the Jewish way with the *man* being able to divorce and the
woman only to separate herself (or could it be passive - to be
separated?)/11/ This may be the accidental consequence of his
preceding use of the verb χωρίζειν. But it is striking that in
this respect Paul agrees with Matthew and Luke against Mark. It
may well be that he has been careful to cite Jesus' teaching
accurately as he knew it (in the Matthean/Lukan form), and this
evidence may confirm that Mark's form is a modification of the
original saying for a Gentile audience.

3. Paul has the phrase ἀπ' ἀνδρός in his v 10, a phrase
paralleled in Lk 16:18 only (though Mark has τὸν ἄνδρα in his
10:12).

1.4. A solution to this synoptic problem
Given all this evidence from the synoptics and Paul, can
we solve the 'synoptic problem' of these texts? I suggest that
the solution is this: there were two quite distinct sayings of
Jesus about divorce in the tradition:

1. There was one tradition which resembled Mt 5:32a:

Tradition 1
ἐγὼ δὲ λέγω ὑμῖν ὅτι πᾶς ὁ ἀπολύων τὴν γυναῖκα αὐτοῦ παρεκτὸς
λόγου πορνείας ποιεῖ αὐτὴν μοιχευθῆναι.

2. There was the tradition utilized by Paul, which
resembled Mt 19:9/Mk 10:11 and Mt 5:32b.

Tradition 2
...... μὴ χωριζέτω........
ὃς ἂν ἀπολύσῃ τὴν γυναῖκα αὐτοῦ καὶ γαμήσῃ ἄλλην μοιχᾶται.
καὶ ὃς ἐὰν ἀπολελυμένην ἀπὸ ἀνδρὸς γαμήσῃ, μοιχᾶται

From this basis it is possible to explain all our texts:
Paul knew and has utilized tradition 2 in 1 Cor 7:10: he uses
it freely to address a particular problem, but he reflects its
thought and form./12/

Mark also used tradition 2, but he has turned the passive
Jewish woman of the second clause into an active divorcing
woman./13/

Matthew has tradition 1 in 5:32a, quite probably in its
original context. In support of this note that 5:32a follows
on very well from the preceding 5:28: compare:
  5:28 ἠκούσατε ὅτι ἐρρέθη οὐ μοιχεύσεις.
        ἐγὼ δὲ λέγω ὑμῖν ὅτι πᾶς ὁ βλέπων......
        ἐμοίχευσεν αὐτὴν ἐν τῇ καρδίᾳ........
  5:31,2   ἐρρέθη δὲ ὃς ἂν ἀπολύσῃ...δότω..ἀποστάσιου
        ἐγὼ δὲ λέγω ὑμῖν ὅτι πᾶς ὁ ἀπολύων......
        ποιεῖ αὐτὴν μοιχευθῆναι

The two verses have a common form and construction (ἐρρέθη...
ἐγὼ δὲ λέγω ὑμῖν ὅτι πᾶς ὁ.... αὐτήν), and both use the verb
μοιχεύειν. They probably belonged together in the tradition.
5:32b, however (καὶ ὃς ἐὰν ἀπολελυμένην γαμήσῃ, μοιχᾶται),
probably did not belong originally with 5:32a. This is
suggested by the following considerations: (a) the construction
and verb used are different. (b) 5:28 has only one clause in

its ἐγὼ δὲ λέγω ὅτι part-sentence. 5:32, though so obviously
parallel to 5:28, has two clauses: this is explicable if 5:32b
has been tacked on. (c) 5:32b introduces a different and
slightly alien thought into the context of 5:31,32: 5:31 and
5:32a both consider the responsibility of the man initiating a
divorce, whereas 5:32b introduces a quite different man and a
quite different thought. All these points suggest that 5:32b
may be an addition tacked on to 5:32a. The addition is unlikely
to have been Matthew's redactional creation, since he would
hardly have added a second clause different in form from the
first in all the respects mentioned. But the addition is very
well explained in terms of assimilation with the other divorce
tradition, i.e., our postulated tradition 2./14/

   In Mt 19:9 Matthew reproduces the first half of tradition
2, but he omits the second half of that tradition, having
already used it in 5:32, and he also introduces an 'exception'
phrase into tradition 2, which is probably to be understood as
a parenthetic reference back to the fuller exception phrase in
tradition 1./15/

Luke 16:18 is a mixture of traditions 1 and 2: Luke has
retained the form of tradition 1, but has used much of the
content of tradition 2./16/

1.5. Conclusions
   The proposed solution of this particular synoptic problem
seems to account for the relevant texts rather satisfactorily,
and may be considered probable. It evidently has significant
implications: it means that behind our gospels lies a pre-
synoptic form of the tradition reflected in Matthew 19 and
Mark 10, which was probably known independently by all the
evangelists and by Paul. It means that Matthew is not
exclusively or even very significantly dependent on Mark (at
least in this passage), which in turn means that Matthew's 'M'
material, including the eunuchs saying, which may perhaps lie
behind Paul's teaching about celibacy, must be taken seriously
as possibly primitive tradition. There was also another quite
distinct tradition of a divorce saying purporting to come from
Jesus that was known to Matthew and Luke (a 'Q' tradition, to
use the usual terminology). This was quite probably part of a
version of the Sermon on the Mount/Plain. So far as Paul is
concerned, the argument points to Paul's familiarity not just
with one synoptic saying (the divorce saying), but also with
another (the 'let not man put asunder' saying), and there is
some reason to believe that Paul may have known and have been

drawing on the whole block of tradition found in Mark 10/
Matthew 19, including the 'M' tradition concerning the eunuchs.
This situation is very much the situation we found in 1 and 2
Thessalonians.

2.   Romans 12.

2.1.   Introduction

The concluding chapters of Romans are full of possible
allusions to the Jesus tradition. In *The Rediscovery of Jesus'
Eschatological Discourse* it was seen that Rom 11:25 echoes the
saying of Jesus preserved in Lk 21:23,24 and that Rom 13:11-14
has a number of possible echoes of the eschatological discourse.
/17/ Other possible echoes of the Jesus tradition in the
closing chapters of Romans include Rom 13:7, where the command
to pay to all what you owe, including taxes, is reminiscent of
Jesus' injunction to pay to Caesar what is Caesar's and to God
what is God's (Mt 22:21 and parallels)./18/ That injunction is
followed in Matthew and Mark by the dispute over the
resurrection and by the debate over the greatest commands, the
second being 'You shall love your neighbour as yourself'.
Matthew concludes this section: 'On these two commands hang
all the law and the prophets' (22:40). Paul also follows
his instruction about paying taxes with a discussion of loving
one's neighbour and concludes that 'love is the fulfilling of
the law' (Rom 13:10). In Romans 14, where the question of eating
or not eating foods is discussed, there are further echoes of
the synoptics, notably in Rom 14:13,14, where the call not to
judge each other (cf. Mt 7:1) is followed by a call not to offend
a brother - Paul's use of the word σκάνδαλον here (in addition
to his own word πρόσκομμα) is a possible echo of the synoptic
usage (e.g., Mt 17:27, 18:6,7) - and then by Paul's statement
that 'I know and am persuaded in the Lord Jesus that nothing is
unclean of itself', this being strongly reminiscent of
Mt 15:1-20/Mk 7:1-23, where the same root κοινο-, used only here
in Paul, is found (cf. also Rom 14:20 with Mk 7:19 and Tit 1:15).

2.2.   Romans 12:14

But the particular echoes or possible echoes of the Jesus
tradition that will be studied here more closely are the echoes
of the Sermon on the Mount/Plain in Rom 12:14-21./19/ The first
of these is in Rom 12:14, where Paul urges εὐλογεῖτε τοὺς
διώκοντας, εὐλογεῖτε καὶ μὴ καταρᾶσθε. This is unmistakably
similar to Lk 6:28 εὐλογεῖτε τοὺς καταρωμένους, προσεύχεσθε
περὶ τῶν ἐπηρεαζόντων ὑμᾶς. It also has notable parallels in
1 Cor 4:12 λοιδορούμενοι εὐλογοῦμεν, διωκόμενοι ἀνεχόμεθα

and in 1 Pet 3:9 μὴ ἀποδιδόντες....λοιδορίαν ἀντὶ λοιδορίας,
τοὐναντίον δὲ εὐλογοῦντες. It is evident that we are dealing
with a well-known and early Christian hortatory tradition, and
Luke's evidence suggests that Jesus was the source of this
striking saying.

It could, of course, be the other way round. Luke could
have introduced the 'blessing' saying into the Jesus tradition
from the church tradition, and this possibility could claim some
support from Matthew's evidence, since in his parallel to
Lk 6:28, i.e., his 5:44, he has simply προσεύχεσθε ὑπὲρ τῶν
διωκόντων ὑμᾶς with no reference to blessing those who curse.
However, Matthew may betray his knowledge of the 'blessing'
clause in his following verse 'for... if you *greet* your brothers
only ....' (5:47).

Compare

A.	Mt 5:43 'Love your enemies and pray for those who persecute you'	Lk 6:27,28	'Love your enemies, do good to those who hate you, bless those who curse you, pray for those who despitefully treat you'
B.	46,47 'For if you love those who love you .... and if you greet your brothers only....'	32,33	'If you love those who love you... If you do good to those who do good to you.....'

In both Matthew and Luke section B picks up section A. But
Matthew's 'if you greet' (v 47) does not very obviously pick up
anything in his v 43. What it quite probably picks up is the
'bless those who curse you...' that Luke has./20/ We may
conclude that the Lukan phrase probably was in the 'Q' or pre-
synoptic tradition known to Matthew and Luke, and that it is not
Lukan redaction.

To trace the Lukan saying back to 'Q' is still not to prove
that it is Jesus-tradition. But there is no good reason for
doubting the 'Q' tradition in this respect, and it is entirely
likely that the phrase was well-known in the church precisely
because it was known to derive from Jesus.

It is probable then that Rom 12:14 is an echo of the
saying of Lk 6:27. Paul's repetition of the call to bless -
εὐλογεῖτε τοὺς διώκοντας εὐλογεῖτε καὶ μὴ καταρᾶσθε - is
explicable not just as effective rhetoric, but as a reflection
of the underlying tradition (i.e., Lk 6:27 εὐλογεῖτε τοὺς
καταρωμένους ὑμᾶς) with Paul adding his second phrase under the
influence of the tradition. It is possible that Paul's first
phrase (εὐλογεῖτε) τοὺς διώκοντας is also an echo of the
tradition, since Matthew in the same context says προσεύχεσθε
ὑπὲρ τῶν διωκόντων ὑμᾶς, and it is also found in 1 Cor 4:12
following the phrase λοιδορούμενοι εὐλογοῦμεν. If it is such
an echo, Paul may be seen as a witness to a pre-synoptic
tradition reflected partly in Luke (the blessing saying) and
partly in Matthew (the verb διώκειν)./21/

2.3. Romans 12:17-20
Rom 12:17-20 reads: μηδενὶ κακὸν ἀντὶ κακοῦ ἀποδιδόντες,
προνοούμενοι καλὰ ἐνώπιον πάντων ἀνθρώπων. εἰ δυνατόν, τὸ ἐξ
ὑμῶν, μετὰ πάντων ἀνθρώπων εἰρηνεύοντες μὴ ἑαυτοὺς ἐκδικοῦντες,
ἀγαπητοί, ἀλλὰ δότε τόπον τῇ ὀργῇ ...ἐὰν πεινᾷ ὁ ἐχθρός σου,
ψώμιζε αὐτόν .....

2.3.1. Connections with Mt 5:38-48
These verses may well be connected with Mt 5:38-48 (cf.
Lk 6:27-36).
Note (a) Paul has just a few verses previously drawn on this
section of the Sermon on the Mount/Plain, i.e., in the blessing
saying.
     (b) The thought of (not) returning evil for (ἀντί) evil in
Rom 12:17 is a similar idea and similarly expressed to the 'eye
for (ἀντί) eye, tooth for a tooth' phrase in Mt 5:38.
     (c) Immediately after the reference to 'eye for eye ...
tooth for tooth' Matthew has Jesus' words 'I tell you not to
resist evil' (μὴ ἀντιστῆναι τῷ πονηρῷ). This is a rather
similar instruction to the Pauline 'Do not pay back evil for
evil' (μηδενὶ κακὸν ἀντὶ κακοῦ ἀποδιδόντες) of Rom 12:17./22/
     (d) In the following verses, Rom 12:18,19, Paul urges that
'so far as it lies with you, live at peace with all men, not
taking revenge...'. This is saying in relatively abstract
terms exactly what Mt 5:39b-42/Lk 6:29-30 say in vivid
pictorial terms (i.e., about turning the other cheek and going
the second mile).
     (e) Paul goes on in Rom 12:20 to urge kindness to 'your
enemy', echoing Prov 25:21f. This is comparable to the synoptic
injunctions to love 'your enemy' and to 'do good to those who
hate you' (Mt 5:44, Lk 6:27,28).

The parallelism between the verses in Romans and
Mt 5:38-48 may be summarized thus:

| Mt 5:38 | Eye for eye tooth for)
tooth   )Rom 12:17 Do not return evil
)   for evil |
| 39a | Do not resist evil   ) |

| 39b
-42 | Whoever strikes you on
the right cheek..... | 18,19 Live at peace
with all, taking no
revenge, |

| 43 | Love your enemy | 20 Feed your enemy |

The verbal agreements are not numerous, but the sequence of
ideas is similar. And there is a reasonable probability of a
connection. But it is necessary to examine certain aspects of
the texts more closely before reaching definite conclusions.

2.3.2. 'Do not return evil for evil'

The phrase μηδενὶ κακὸν ἀντὶ κακοῦ ἀποδιδόντες in Rom 12:17
has close parallels in 1 Thess 5:15 μὴ τις κακὸν ἀντὶ κακοῦ τινι
ἀποδῷ and also in 1 Pet 3:9 μὴ ἀποδιδόντες κακὸν ἀντὶ κακοῦ ἢ
λοιδορίαν ἀντὶ λοιδορίας, τοὐναντίον δὲ εὐλογοῦντες./23/ The
recurrence of almost exactly the same phrase in these different
contexts is unlikely to be coincidental. The phrase probably has
a Jewish origin and background (being found on several
occasions in Joseph and Asenath);/24/ but it evidently became a
regular part of Christian parenesis. One possible explanation
of this is that the saying may have been known in the Jesus-
tradition.

Further to this possibility, it is notable that both in
Romans 12 and in 1 Pet 3:9 the saying is used in connection with
or in close proximity to the saying in the Sermon on the Mount
about returning cursing with blessing. In that section of the
Sermon, as has already been noted, the verses that most clearly
parallel the saying about not returning evil for evil are
Mt 5:38,39 'You have heard that it was said "Eye for eye and
tooth for tooth". But I tell you not to resist evil'.

In the light of this evidence the possibility that suggests
itself is that the Matthean 'I tell you not to resist evil'
should be connected with the Pauline/Petrine 'Do not return evil
for evil to anyone', and indeed that they should be seen as
differing versions of the same word of Jesus. It may in fact be

suggested that the Pauline/Petrine wording, which was well-known
in the church, is the more original, and that Matthew's 'not to
resist evil' is his paraphrase: certainly the term used by
Matthew πονηρός is a favourite of his, whereas κακός is
relatively infrequent in his gospel./25/ The sequence of thought
would be good:

> 'You have heard that it was said "Eye for eye and tooth
> for tooth".
> But I say to you: Do not return evil for evil....'

We may, tentatively at least, conclude that this was the
pre-synoptic wording.

2.3.3. 'But do good to all'

The proposal made may be taken a little further. It is
notable that on every occasion where the injunction not to
return evil for evil (or to resist evil) is found it is followed
by a positive counter-command. In Mt 5:39b there is *'but
whoever strikes you.....give him the other also'*; 1 Pet 3:9
reads 'Don't return evil for evil or abuse for abuse, *but on the
contrary* bless'; 1 Thess 5:15 has '*But* always pursue what is
good (τὸ ἀγαθόν) for each other and for all'; Rom 12:17 has
'Take thought for what is noble (καλά) in the sight of all. If
possible ... live peaceably with all'.

To draw conclusions from this divergent testimony may seem
rash. But it is interesting to note the similarity between the
two Pauline commands, both of which speak of doing or taking
thought for what is *good/noble* for/in the sight of *all*. In
Gal 6:10 Paul urges similarly 'Let us do good to all,
especially to the household of faith'. We may here be dealing
with a common and fairly obvious Pauline idea, which need be
traced back no further. But it is at least possible that Paul
is reflecting a tradition which spoke of doing good to all and
which both in 1 Thessalonians 5 and Galatians 6 he modifies or
supplements with a mention of the believer's particular
responsibility to fellow Christians. Such a tradition would fit
in very well after the negative command already discussed - 'Do
not return evil for evil, but do good to all...'.

To suggest that this was the original form of the Sermon
on the Mount is speculative. But it is to be noted that the
thought of 'doing good' even to one's enemies is present in the
relevant Lukan section of the Sermon (i.e., Lk 6:27,33,35) and
also in 1 Pet 2:20 and 3:17, both places where the author

appears to be drawing on the relevant section of the Sermon on
the Mount./26/

2.3.4. Making sense of the synoptic texts

But even granted this observation about Luke and 1 Peter,
how does the suggestion that the Sermon may originally have
read 'Do not return evil for evil, but do good to all' fit in
with the evidence of our present synoptic texts? Matthew has
the negative clause in the context of the eye for eye
antithesis, Luke a positive call to do good in connection with
the call to 'love your enemies'. How can their quite different
texts be explained given the proposal being made?

The relationship between the Matthean and Lukan traditions
at this point is complex, and has very frequently been
discussed. The relevant texts are these:

Mt 5:38-48	Lk 6:27-36
ἠκούσατε ὅτι ἐρρέθη· ὀφθαλμὸν ἀντὶ ὀφθαλμοῦ καὶ ὀδόντα ἀντὶ ὀδόντος. 38 ἐγὼ δὲ λέγω ὑμῖν μὴ ἀντιστῆναι τῷ πονηρῷ, ἀλλ' ὅστις σε ῥαπίζει εἰς τὴν δεξιὰν σιαγόνα σου, στρέφον αὐτῷ καὶ τὴν ἄλλην. 40 καὶ τῷ θέλοντί σοι κριθῆναι καὶ τὸν χιτῶνά σου λαβεῖν, ἄφες αὐτῷ καὶ τὸ ἱμάτιον. 41 καὶ ὅστις σε ἀγγαρεύσει μίλιον ἕν, ὕπαγε μετ' αὐτοῦ δύο. 42 τῷ αἰτοῦντί σε δός, καὶ τὸν θέλοντα ἀπὸ σοῦ δανείσασθαι μὴ ἀποστραφῇς. 43 ἠκούσατε ὅτι ἐρρέθη ἀγαπήσεις τὸν πλησίον σου καὶ μισήσεις τὸν ἐχθρόν σου. 44 ἐγὼ δὲ λέγω ὑμῖν· ἀγαπᾶτε τοὺς ἐχθροὺς ὑμῶν καὶ προσεύχεσθε ὑπὲρ τῶν διωκόντων ὑμᾶς. 45 ὅπως γε γένησθε υἱοὶ τοῦ πατρὸς ὑμῶν τοῦ ἐν οὐρανοῖς, ὅτι τὸν ἥλιον αὐτοῦ ἀνατέλλει ἐπὶ πονηροὺς καὶ ἀγαθοὺς καὶ βρέχει ἐπὶ δικαίους καὶ ἀδίκους. 46 ἐὰν γὰρ	ἀλλὰ ὑμῖν λέγω τοῖς ἀκούουσιν, ἀγαπᾶτε τοὺς ἐχθροὺς ὑμῶν, καλῶς ποιεῖτε τοῖς μισοῦσιν ὑμᾶς, 28 εὐλογεῖτε τοὺς καταρωμένους ὑμᾶς, προσεύχεσθε περὶ τῶν ἐπηρεαζόντων ὑμᾶς. 29 τῷ τύπτοντί σε ἐπὶ τὴν σιαγόνα πάρεχε καὶ τὴν ἄλλην, καὶ ἀπὸ τοῦ αἴροντός σου τὸ ἱμάτιον καὶ τὸν χιτῶνα μὴ κωλύσῃς. 30 παντὶ αἰτοῦντί σε δίδου, καὶ ἀπὸ τοῦ αἴροντος τὰ σὰ μὴ ἀπαίτει. 31 καὶ καθὼς θέλετε ἵνα ποιῶσιν ὑμῖν οἱ ἄνθρωποι, ποιεῖτε αὐτοῖς ὁμοίως. 32 καὶ εἰ ἀγαπᾶτε τοὺς ἀγαπῶντας ὑμᾶς, ποία ὑμῖν χάρις ἐστίν; καὶ γὰρ οἱ ἁμαρτωλοὶ τοὺς ἀγαπῶντας αὐτοὺς ἀγαπῶσιν. 33 καὶ γὰρ ἐὰν ἀγαθοποιῆτε τοὺς ἀγαθοποιοῦντας ὑμᾶς, ποία ὑμῖν χάρις ἐστίν; καὶ οἱ ἁμαρτωλοὶ τὸ αὐτὸ ποιοῦσιν. 34 καὶ ἐὰν δανίσητε παρ' ὧν ἐλπίζετε λαβεῖν, ποία ὑμῖν χάρις (ἐστίν); καὶ ἁμαρτωλοὶ ἁμαρτωλοῖς δανίζουσιν ἵνα

(Mt 5:38-48)

ἀγαπήσητε τοὺς ἀγαπῶντας ὑμᾶς,
τίνα μισθὸν ἔχετε; οὐχὶ καὶ οἱ
τελῶναι τὸ αὐτὸ ποιοῦσιν;
47 καὶ ἐὰν ἀσπάσησθε τοὺς
ἀδελφοὺς ὑμῶν μόνον, τί
περισσὸν ποιεῖτε; οὐχὶ καὶ
οἱ ἐθνικοὶ τὸ αὐτὸ ποιοῦσιν;
48 ἔσεσθε οὖν ὑμεῖς τέλειοι
ὡς ὁ πατὴρ ὑμῶν ὁ οὐράνιος
τέλειός ἐστιν.

(Lk 6:29-36)

ἀπολάβωσιν τὰ ἴσα. 35 πλὴν
ἀγαπᾶτε τοὺς ἐχθροὺς ὑμῶν καὶ
ἀγαθοποιεῖτε καὶ δανίζετε μηδὲν
ἀπελπίζοντες. καὶ ἔσται ὁ
μισθὸς ὑμῶν πολύς, καὶ ἔσεσθε
υἱοὶ ὑψίστου, ὅτι αὐτὸς
χρηστός ἐστιν ἐπὶ τοὺς
ἀχαρίστους καὶ πονηρους.
36 γίνεσθε οἰκτίρμονες, καθὼς
(καὶ) ὁ πατὴρ ὑμῶν οἰκτίρμων
ἐστίν.

It is not possible here to go into all the different possible
explanations of these texts. The possibilities are ably
summarized and discussed by J. Piper in his monograph 'Love
your enemies'./27/ He confesses to being unable finally to
choose between the view that Luke preserves the more original
'Q' form, Matthew having created his two antitheses out of the
Lukan form of tradition, and the view that Luke is less
original: on this latter view (which Piper appears slightly to
favour) Luke may be supposed to have known the two Matthean
antitheses - see the possible trace of the antithetical form in
Luke's ἀλλὰ ὑμῖν λέγω in his 6:27, cf. πλὴν in v 35 - and to
have conflated them into one non-antithetical section,
including in it the sayings about turning the other cheek etc.
(6:29,30).

    Although Piper's scholarly caution is wise, his apparent
preference for the view that Luke is dependent on something
like Matthew's form (rather than vice versa) may be supported
by the argument presented above concerning the 'Do not return
evil for evil' tradition. If this was correctly linked with
the Matthean antithesis, then some at least of that antithesis
is primitive, not Matthean. But it is possible to go much
further than this, and to suggest that the Pauline evidence may
be the clue to resolving the whole synoptic problem posed by
these particular synoptic texts.

    We suggest that the pre-synoptic (or 'Q') form of
tradition was approximately as follows:

    A. 'You have heard that it was said, Eye for eye and
       tooth for tooth. I say to you: do not pay back evil
       for evil, but do good to all. To the one who strikes

you on the right cheek............... To the one who
asks you to give, and the one who wishes to borrow from
you do not turn away.'

B. 'You have heard that it was said, You shall love your
neighbour and hate your enemy. I say to you: love your
enemies, bless those who curse/speak ill of you, pray
for those who ill-treat/persecute you, that you may be
children..........sends rain on righteous and
unrighteous. For if you love those who love you......
.... And if you greet your brothers only.........
But you shall be perfect/merciful.....'

The following points favour this proposal: (1) The
balanced pair of clauses in section A 'Do not pay back evil for
evil, but do good to all' is reflected in 1 Thess 5:15 and
Rom 12:17, though in Romans 12 the 'do good' clause has been
reexpressed in wording taken from Prov 3:4 LXX.

(2) The balanced clauses lead extremely well into the
following sayings about turning the other cheek: those sayings
do not just advocate a passive acceptance of insult, but a
positive response.

(3) In our reconstruction of section B there are three
positive commands 'love your enemies, bless.....pray for', but
not (in this context) 'do good'. It may possibly be significant
that *Did.* 1:3-5 and Justin, *Apol.* 1,15,9-13 also have the
injunctions to 'love...bless...pray', but not (in this context)
'do good'./28/

(4) Matthew's text is easily explicable given such a pre-
synoptic form: he retains the text for the most part. But
(a) he omits the 'Do good to all' clause from section A,
perhaps simply for the sake of brevity. That he has omitted
such a command is in any case likely enough, since Luke's call
to 'do good' has a strong claim to be traditional. (b) He also
then omits the exhortation to 'bless those who curse you' from
section B. But he betrays his knowledge of this clause in his
v 47 'If you *greet* your brothers...'.

(5) Luke's text is also explicable from the proposed pre-
synoptic form. He has conflated the two antitheses, dropping
the antithetical form (which does not fit in his version of the
Sermon). He achieves his conflation essentially by putting
elements from the first antithesis into the second antithesis.

Thus he first inserts the 'do good' command after the command
to 'love your enemies', adapting it to the new context by
saying 'do good to those who hate you' instead of the probably
original 'do good to all'. (The word 'hate' was ready to hand,
being found in the Matthean antithesis 'You shall love your
neighbour and hate your enemy', which Luke probably knew.)
Luke's second insertion is of the sayings about turning the
other cheek, which he places, quite appropriately, after the
call to 'pray for those who maltreat you'.

These two insertions lead on to the other Lukan divergences
from Matthew's form of the tradition: (a) Luke's insertion of
the sayings about turning the other cheek at the point where
Matthew has the saying about being children to your heavenly
Father leads Luke to postpone that saying until later (i.e.,
until his v 35b). But in reintroducing the saying in his v 35
Luke has to repeat the command to 'love your enemies...' to give
it its proper logical context. Luke's v 35a sounds like a
rather compressed recapitulation, and it is well explained as a
Lukan redactional lead into the saying of 35b./29/ (b) The
second result of Luke's insertion is to be seen in his vv 33,34
'If you do good....If you lend....' These phrases are absent
from the comparable passage in Matthew, who has a probably
original 'If you greet....', but they correspond exactly to
Luke's two insertions, i.e., to the 'do good' saying and to the
'turn the other cheek' sayings, the last of which speaks of
giving to one who asks and not turning away one who wishes to
borrow (Mt 5:42/Lk 6:30)./30/ Luke then has rewritten the
section of 'If you...' clauses (i.e., Mt 5:46,47 and Lk 6:32-34)
to fit in with his additions, and his vv 33,34 are largely
redactional, though expressing the same general thought as
Matthew's more original 5:47./31/

2.4. *Conclusions*
The proposed explanation of the synoptic differences with
the aid of evidence from Romans 12 seems more comprehensive and
satisfactory than other explanations that have been offered,
though we have only been able in this study to sketch out the
proposal, not to explore all the questions raised in detail.
/32/ If the explanation is correct, it is one more small piece
of evidence showing that the traditions behind the synoptic
gospels are primitive, being well-known to Paul, and showing
that both Matthew and Luke have preserved different parts of the
pre-synoptic tradition. Luke has been somewhat 'creative' in
his vv 33-35, but his redactional activity is necessitated by
his editorial conflation of the two adjacent traditions, not by

some theological Tendenz which made Luke sit lightly to received tradition. It is significant that once again Paul appears to have known, valued and drawn upon a substantial section of Jesus-tradition: the Jesus-tradition was evidently of fundamental importance to him in his teaching (as also to the author of 1 Peter).

3. Galatians 1 and 2/33/

3.1. Introduction

In an interesting article published in 1912 J. Chapman argued that in Galatians 1 and 2 Paul echoes the saying of Mt 16:17 about Peter the rock, which he accordingly ascribed to Q./34/ His article has received little attention from later scholars,/35/ no doubt partly because the *Revue Benedictine*, in which it was published, is not widely known, but perhaps also because the dominance of the Markan hypothesis has inclined scholars to regard material that is found only in Matthew and not in the parallel Markan and Lukan contexts as probably late and certainly suspect. (Mt 16:17 has in any case often been suspect to Protestants wary of the Papacy!) However, scholars have in recent years recognized that, even if the two source hypothesis is correct - a point that continues to be debated - this does not mean that Matthean or Lukan additions to Mark are necessarily late or redactional creations. And there have been scholars who have recognized the Semitic character of Mt 16:16-19 (as did Chapman) and have argued that it may well be a tradition that goes back to Jesus./36/ Given this changed climate of scholarly opinion and also our own conclusions about Paul's knowledge and use of some so-called 'M' traditions, Chapman's thesis at least deserves fresh and sympathetic consideration.

3.2. Paul's knowledge of Peter's commission

The first and obvious point to observe is that Paul in Galatians 1 and 2 betrays knowledge of Peter's call and, in some sense, of Peter's primacy. Although Paul refers to his dealings with the three 'pillars' of the Jerusalem church, i.e., James (the brother of Jesus), Peter and John, he and they acknowledge that Peter in a special way had been entrusted with the 'gospel of the circumcision' and with apostleship 'to the circumcision' (Gal 2:7,8). In arguing for his own apostleship, Paul takes Peter's apostleship as his point of departure and claims that his position is comparable to the undisputed position of Peter (2:7-9). In view of this evidence there can be no doubt that Paul knows that Jesus did specially commission Peter.

But that does not necessarily mean that Paul knows the
tradition of Peter's commissioning attested in Matthew 16.
J. Munck observes (in a note mentioning but not doing justice to
Chapman's argument/37/) that there are several gospel passages
where Jesus singles out Peter in a special way which Paul could
have known (e.g., Lk 22:32 'strengthen your brethren',
Jn 21:15-17 'feed my sheep' cf. 1:42). However, none of the
passages alluding to Peter's work so clearly suggests a
commissioning of Peter to leadership in mission as Matthew 16:
perhaps Lk 22:32 suggests that Peter is to act as the leading
'brother', and just possibly the implication of Jn 21:15-17
could be that Peter is to be the leading shepherd in the church.
But in neither passage is Peter's distinctive leading role very
explicitly expressed,and in neither is the theme of mission
explicit. Mt 16:18,19 scores more highly on both counts:
Peter's primacy is unambiguous, and the thought of mission is
clear in the reference to the building of the church and
perhaps in the following reference to wielding the keys of the
kingdom. If then Paul knew a tradition of Peter's commission
to mission it seems more likely that it was the tradition of
Mt 16:17-19 than any other gospel passage./38/ It is, of
course, possible that Paul knew a tradition not preserved in
the gospels. But to suggest that seems rather perverse, given a
perfectly suitable/tradition that is preserved.

It could be argued that neither Matthew 16 nor any of the
gospel passages suggest that Peter was specially commissioned
for mission to Jews (which is what Paul suggests), unless the
Johannine 'my sheep' is taken in that way. And this could be
taken to show that Paul is echoing a quite different tradition.
However, this point is hardly cogent: Peter's commission may
have been a general one, but, in seeking to evaluate Paul's
distinctive place and call, Paul and the pillar apostles may
have concluded that in God's design, as well as in practical
fact, Peter's ministry was intended primarily for Jews and
Paul's for Gentiles./39/ An alternative possible explanation is
that Jesus' command to the twelve to 'go only to the lost sheep
of the house of Israel' and not to the Gentiles (Mt 10:5,6) was
seen as setting limits to Peter's sphere of missionary
responsibility (because he was one of the twelve)./40/

3.3. Paul's call described like Peter's call
The case for seeing Mt 16:17-19 as the commissioning of
Peter known to Paul is strengthened by the observation that
Paul speaks of his own commissioning in terms that seem
reminiscent of Mt 16:17-19. Since Paul is quite deliberately

comparing his position and call with the position and call of
Peter - cf. Gal 2:8 'He who worked in Peter for apostleship to
the circumcision worked also in me for the Gentiles' - we might
expect to find Paul echoing Mt 16:17-19, if that was the
commissioning of Peter he knew. And this is in fact exactly
what we do find, especially in Gal 1:12-16.

Thus in Mt 16:16,17 Peter confesses Jesus as 'the Christ
the Son of the living God', and Jesus commends him 'Blessed are
you, Simon Barjona, because flesh and blood have not revealed
this to you, but my father who is in heaven'. Jesus goes on to
speak of Peter as the rock on which the church will be built.
In Galatians Paul speaks of his apostleship being 'not from men
nor through man, but through Jesus Christ and God the Father'
(1:1) and of his gospel being not 'from man ...nor was I taught,
but through a revelation of Jesus Christ' (1:12). He goes on
to speak of God's grace in calling him, and he says that, when
God chose 'to reveal his Son in me, that I might proclaim him
among the nations, I did not consult with flesh and blood, nor
did I go up to those who were apostles before me' (1:15-17).
The last phrase reminds us that Paul has in mind the comparison
of his own experience and the experience of those who were
apostles before him, and his description of his call parallels
the Matthean description of Peter's call to be a rock. Compare:

Mt 16:15	'You are the *Christ* the *Son of the living God*' (the content of the revelation)	Gal 1:12,15, 16	'a revelation of Jesus *Christ*', 'he was pleased to reveal *his Son* in me'
16:17	'Blessed are you .....'	1:15,16	'He was pleased.... through his grace ...'
	'because *flesh and blood* has *not*....'	1:1,12, 16	'Not from men, nor through man', 'Nor from man', 'I did *not* consult with *flesh and blood* ....'
	'*revealed*'	1:12,16	'But through *revelation*', 'to *reveal* his Son...'
	'by my father in heaven'	1:16	'to reveal his Son in me' (cf. 1:1)

```
Mt 16:18 'On this rock I        Gal 1:16 'that I might proclaim
         will build..'                   him'
```

The verbal parallels are only the references to 'flesh and
blood' (not a frequent phrase in Paul, cf. 1 Cor 15:50,
Eph 6:12) and to 'revelation'; but the substantial parallelism
is very considerable./41/

   Add together (a) the consideration that Paul knew of
Peter's commissioning and that the tradition of Mt 16:16-19 is
the most likely Petrine commissioning story known by Paul,
(b) the fact that Paul is in Galatians 1 and 2 deliberately
comparing himself and Peter (cf. Gal 2:18), and (c) the fact of
the notable parallelism between Gal 1:12-16 and Mt 16:16,17, and
the cumulative case for thinking that Paul is here drawing on
that Matthean tradition is strong./42/

3.4. Further observations

   Two small points noted by Chapman may perhaps strengthen
the case: (a) Paul's reference to James, Cephas and John as
so-called 'pillars' may perhaps be connected with the Matthean
description of Peter as the 'rock' on which the church will be
built. A pillar is, of course, not the same thing as a rock-
foundation (if this is how Matthew intends us to see Peter when
he speaks of him as a 'rock'), but with both terms we are
dealing with an analogy from building, and it is not hard to see
how the thought of Peter as the rock on which the church was to
be built might have led on to the thought of Peter and the
other apostles as all foundational (cf. Eph 2:20) and/or to the
idea of them as pillars within the fellowship./43/ (b) It is
striking that in Gal 2:7,8 Paul speaks of 'Peter', whereas
elsewhere in Galatians and elsewhere in his writings he always
uses the Aramaic 'Cephas'. This curious state of affairs may
prove nothing; but as good an explanation of the usage as any is
that Paul is here alluding to the tradition of Peter's call
attested in Matthew 16 and that he wishes to recall its play on
the word 'rock' (Cephas/Peter) - something that might easily be
missed in Greek if the Aramaic name Cephas was retained./44/

3.5. Conclusion

   Whether the last two points are considered substantial or
not, the whole case for Paul's use of the tradition of
Mt 16:17-19 is plausible. Whether Paul knew the tradition
within the context of the Caesarea Philippi incident or not is
uncertain, though it is quite possible that he did. But
whatever the truth on that is, the conclusion that Paul

probably knew this 'M' tradition confirms the impression gained
from other passages that much 'M' tradition is very primitive,
not Matthean redactional creation.

4. Conclusions

The three samples studied confirm and extend the
conclusions that we reached in *The Rediscovery of Jesus'
Eschatological Discourse* about Paul's extensive knowledge and
use of the Jesus-tradition. Not only did he know traditions of
Jesus' passion and resurrection - see 1 Corinthians 11 and 15 -
but also sections of the Sermon on tne Mount, Peter's
benediction, the dialogue about divorce and the eschatological
discourse. He may well have known the woes on the scribes and
Pharisees that precede the eschatological discourse in Matthew,
/45/ also the controversy stories that precede the woes,/46/ and
probably the mission discourse./47/ This list could be
extended,/48/ but even this amount of evidence makes it very
clear that Paul knew a considerable proportion of what we know
as the synoptic tradition (particularly of the material found
in Matthew 19-28 and parallels).

The evidence points to Paul's familiarity with a wide
range of gospel traditions - traditions attested in the
different synoptic strata (so-called 'Markan', 'Q', 'M' and 'L'
material) and traditions of different types, not just sayings
material./49/ It seems probable that Paul knew not simply
isolated sayings and traditions of Jesus, but also some
extended narratives and discourses, including sections of the
Sermon on the Mount, the mission discourse, the divorce
pericope, the eschatological discourse and the passion
narrative.

Paul cites the Jesus-tradition in various ways. Sometimes
he quotes the tradition explicitly and almost verbatim (as with
his account of the Last Supper). Sometimes he quotes the
tradition explicitly, but very freely, retaining relatively few
of the *ipsissima verba* of the tradition (as with the divorce
sayings). Most frequently he draws on the tradition freely and
incorporates Jesus' teaching into his own teaching without
explaining that he is doing so (as with the echoes of the
Sermon on the Mount in Romans).

Although Paul usually uses allusions to the Jesus-tradition
to justify or support a particular line of argument that he is
putting forward, his relationship to the tradition is

occasionally less obvious, as in Galatians where he appears to
be reacting with a known Jesus-tradition - the tradition about
Peter. It is not impossible that the relevant tradition about
Peter's supremacy had been used by Paul's detractors to
undermine Paul's authority, and that Paul is responding to them.
There are other places in Paul's letters where scholars have
suspected that Paul is responding to opponents who have quoted
Jesus-traditions against him./50/ If this is a correct reading
of the relevant passages, it is significant that the Jesus-
tradition was being used in this way. But in any case it seems
clear that Paul, his readers and his opponents saw the Jesus-
tradition as decisively authoritative for questions of faith and
conduct, so that it was necessary to justify any apparent
deviation from it.

If the Jesus-tradition was so regarded, why is it quoted
explicitly by Paul so infrequently?/51/ Many scholars have seen
this as a sign of Paul's lack of regard for the tradition.
However, the more plausible explanation is that Paul presupposes
knowledge of the tradition among his readers, and so does not
need to tell them every time he is drawing on that tradition.
It may be surmised that Paul passed on Jesus-traditions in a
relatively formal way to the churches that he founded.
1 Corinthians 11 is evidence that he passed on an account of the
Last Supper in this way, and he probably transmitted many other
traditions similarly, including those traditions that he later
alludes to rather indirectly in his letters (e.g., the divorce
traditions and the eschatological discourse). These traditions
will have been seen as having unquestionable authority and will
have become well-known in the Pauline churches./52/ Because of
this Paul normally has no need to repeat the traditions in his
epistles. He does so exceptionally when a particular situation
makes a reminder desirable (e.g., in 1 Corinthians 11). On
other occasions he refers explicitly to Jesus' words, but
without repeating those words verbatim; such repetition was
unnecessary. But more often he simply assumes familiarity with
the Jesus-tradition and draws on it or reacts with it in a way
that his well-taught readers will have understood and
appreciated./53/ Sometimes, as we have seen, there may
possibly have been a dialogue going on within the Pauline
churches and/or between Paul and his opponents about the
interpretation of certain sayings of Jesus.

The idea that the early church or the apostle Paul were
uninterested in, or uninformed about, the teaching and history
of Jesus is a priori improbable. It is true that Paul saw his

conversion experience on the Damascus Road as decisive for his
own understanding of the gospel, but that does not mean that he
was or remained ignorant of the earthly life of the Jesus, whom
he met there.   It is unlikely that someone of Paul's
intelligence who had been in Jerusalem so soon after Jesus'
ministry and who had so much contact with the followers of
Jesus (first hostile contact, then friendly) would have been
poorly informed; he could hardly have failed to hear and to
assimilate the gospel traditions.   It is hard to see how Paul
could have defended his conversion from Judaism to Christianity
or have proclaimed Jesus as Lord in missionary situations
without knowledge of Jesus.   But such a priori considerations
need to be supported with hard evidence.   I believe that the
sort of evidence examined in this article helps to show that
indeed the Jesus-tradition which came to be enshrined in the
gospels was well-known and was regarded as decisively important
by Paul himself and by the earliest Christian churches./54/

     This conclusion is of obvious importance for an assessment
of the gospels themselves.   They comprise traditions that were
known and respected at a very early date.   Our studies have also
shown (a) that the evangelists had access to the Jesus-tradition
independently of each other (whatever their mutual relationships
may have been), (b) that the special traditions of Matthew and
Luke are not infrequently primitive, and (c) that there has been
some redactional rearrangement of the traditions in the gospels,
but that the evangelists' redaction has been conservative
reapplication of the traditions, not innovative creation of
traditions.   There is a world of difference between Paul's use
of the Jesus-tradition in his epistles and the evangelists' use
of the tradition: he can take the tradition for granted most of
the time, and he alludes to it quite freely; they on the other
hand are trying to preserve and transmit the tradition (and
only secondarily to interpret or apply it), and so they are not
free to diverge substantially from the received tradition.

Notes

/1/ *The Rediscovery of Jesus' Eschatological Discourse*
(Sheffield: JSOT, 1984) 372.
/2/ For a broader and different look at the traditions of
1 Corinthians see Peter Richardson's and Peter Gooch's paper
in this volume 'Jesus-traditions in 1 Corinthians'.
/3/ The verb χωρίζειν is not especially common in the NT, being
used here only in the synoptic gospels (though three times in
Acts) and by Paul only three times outside 1 Corinthians 7.
/4/ It is just possible that Paul's understanding of the law as
added temporarily 'because of transgressions' (Gal 3:19) owes
something to Jesus' explanation of the divorce law as being 'for
your hardness of heart' (Mt 19:8 and par.).
/5/ On these points see D. Dungan, *The Sayings of Jesus in the
Churches of Paul* (Oxford: Blackwell, 1971) 132-134, and A.
Isaksson, *Marriage and Ministry in the New Temple* (Lund:
Gleerup, 1965) 106.
/6/ Note especially 7:4, cf. Eph 5:28.
/7/ J. Dupont (*Mariage et Divorce dans L'Evangile*, Bruges:
Abbaye de Saint-André, 1959, pp. 162-220) and Q. Quesnell
('"Made themselves eunuchs for the kingdom of heaven" (Mt 19,12)'
CBQ 30 (1968) 335-58) argue that the primary application of the
eunuchs saying in Matthew 19 is to the situation of the
divorcee whom Jesus prohibits to remarry - not to the situation
of the unmarried. The case for their interpretation is
uncertain: despite the arguments adduced, it is quite probable
that Mt 19:11 is a comment on the disciples' word in 19:10 and
means that not all are capable of celibacy. But even if their
interpretation of Mt 19:12 were correct, it is quite possible
that Paul's understanding of the saying (and perhaps the pre-
Matthean understanding, as Dupont suggests) was broader than
Matthew's, and it is quite possible that Paul was prompted by
the eunuch saying to his view of the gift of celibacy. Paul's
observation in 1 Cor 7:25 that he has no command of the Lord
about 'virgins' could seem to tell against the view that Paul
knew Mt 19:11,12 and that it is the basis of his view of
celibacy. However, (1) it is arguable that Paul is speaking
there about a special case (of betrothed virgins) not about the
unmarried generally, whom he has spoken about in 7:7-9 (which
is where he echoes Mt 19:11). (2) The enigmatic sayings of
Mt 19:11,12 could in any case hardly be described as a 'command'
of the Lord.
/8/ See the evidence for so-called 'M' material being in the
pre-synoptic pre-Pauline tradition in my *Rediscovery*.

/9/ C. F. D. Moule, *JTS* III (1952) 75-79, has suggested that
there is a link between 1 Cor 7:35 and Lk 10:38-42.

/10/ It has often been argued by commentators that Mark's
reference to the woman divorcing, and also his phrase 'against
her' in 10:11, which is not paralleled in Mt 19:9, are his
Gentile modifications of the more primitive Jewish tradition
which refers only to the man as the active partner in divorce.
It is true, as other commentators have observed, that there is
nothing impossible about Jesus in Palestine speaking about a
woman divorcing her husband: Herodias was a prominent example of
such divorce. However, given (a) that Jesus was speaking to
Jews about the Jewish law and (b) that Mark is evidently writing
for Gentiles and might well have translated the original into
Gentile terms, it does seem plausible that the direction of
change may have been to, not from, Mark.

/11/ Cf. D. Catchpole, 'The Synoptic Divorce Material as a
Tradition-Historical Problem', *BJRL* 57 (1974-5) 118.

/12/ Note the verb χωρίζειν, the ἐαν construction, the fact
that he speaks of the man divorcing and the wife separating.
Catchpole, *ibid.*, 107, recognizes that Paul knows something like
what we have proposed, though he does not note the synoptic
connection that we have suggested.

/13/ Paul also refers to the woman's responsibility, though he
speaks of her 'separating' not divorcing. C. M. Tuckett,
'I Corinthians and Q', *JBL* 102 (1983) 613, sees it as
significant that Paul and Mark both refer only to the
responsibilities of the husband and wife in the original
marriage, not to the position of the person marrying a divorcee,
as do Matthew and Luke. However, in 1 Cor 7:10,11 Paul quotes
the relevant teaching of Jesus in such a way as to address the
Corinthian situation, not word for word or in full; thus he
speaks first and most fully about the responsibility of wives,
only slipping in a brief remark about husbands (contrast the
synoptic order). This is no doubt because the problem in
Corinth in the first instance had to do with converted wives
who wished to know if they should continue to live with
unconverted husbands. The Corinthian question was not about the
position of third parties wishing to marry divorcees, and so
Paul's failure to cite the word of the Lord on this point does
not support Mark rather than Matthew or Luke.

/14/ R. A. Guelich, *The Sermon on the Mount* (Waco: Word, 1982),
in his thorough discussion of Mt 5:32 and related texts
(pp. 197-211) thinks that Matthew used μοιχεύειν in 5:32a to
create a bridge back to 5:27-28. But it is odd that Matthew
should deliberately create this link, and then revert to the
other verb in 5:32b. Guelich's objection to the view that

5:32b reflects the influence of Mk 10:11/Mt 19:9 is that it
overlooks the absence of such verbal 'influence' on the
different expressions of the 'except' clauses in 5:32a and
19:9.   But this argument is no objection to the proposal we
have offered.

/15/ Cf. Guelich, *ibid.*, 204-05. For discussion of the
exception see, as well as Guelich, Dupont, *Mariage*, 82-157.

/16/ It may not be accidental that the preceding verse in Luke
(16:17) has a parallel in the Matthean Sermon on the Mount (in
5:18) not very far removed from Matthew's first divorce saying
in 5:32.

/17/ For more detailed discussion of this eschatological
material, also of Rom 12:12, see my *Rediscovery*, passim.

/18/ Cf. C. E. B. Cranfield, *A Critical and Exegetical
Commentary on the Epistle to the Romans*, vol. 2 (Edinburgh:
T. and T. Clark, 1979) 669.

/19/ For some other recent discussion of these verses see J. P.
Brown, 'Synoptic Parallels in the Epistles and Form-History',
NTS 10 (1963) 27-48, C. H. Talbert, 'Tradition and Redaktion in
Romans XII.9-21', *NTS* 16 (1969/70) 83-93, U. Wilckens, *Der
Brief am die Römer (Röm 12-16)* (Zürich: Benziger, Neukirchen:
Neukirchener, 1982) 22,23.

/20/ Cf. J. Piper, *Love your enemies* (Cambridge: UP, 1979) 59;
see 2 Kings 4:29 for the word 'bless' used of a salutation.

/21/ A complication with this argument is that Luke's
ἐπηρεαζόντων is less usual and may be thought more primitive
than Matthew's διωκόντων (cf. 1 Pet 3:16). On the other hand,
Luke's καταρωμένους, being such an obvious contrast to the verb
'bless', might seem less primitive than the λοιδορούμενοι of
1 Cor 4:12 (cf. 1 Pet 3:9) if this is an echo of the same
saying. However, the complication is not a serious one: it may
well be that there were variant translations of the dominical
saying in circulation and that Paul knew more than one version.

/22/ Non-resistance is not necessarily the same thing as non-
retaliation. But the verb ἀνθιστάναι can have the sense of
actively 'standing up against' something (e.g., Gal 2:11), and
in the Matthean context the call for non-resistance implies
refraining from retaliation and reacting positively rather than
negatively to insult or injury.

/23/ For a discussion of the 1 Peter traditions see G. Maier's
'Jesustradition im 1. Petrusbrief'.

/24/ Cf. Piper, *Love your enemies*, 37-9.

/25/ The exact meaning of Matthew's τῷ πονηρῷ is debated. See,
e.g., Guelich, *Sermon*, 219,220. But the argument being
presented here is not affected by this question.

/26/ Compare 1 Pet 2:20 with Mt 5:46,47 and Lk 6:27-33, and
1 Pet 3:16,17 with Lk 6:27-28. Cf. 1 Pet 3:9.

/27/ pp. 54,55.

/28/ The Didache has an additional 'fast' after 'pray'. But
this may be seen simply as an expansion of the call to 'pray',
giving the combination 'pray/fast': having put 'pray for your
enemies' instead of the more original 'pray for *those who
persecute/maltreat you*', the Didache adds 'fast for *those who
persecute you*'.

/29/ The phrase 'And your reward shall be great' is part of
this redactional connection, picking up the thought of the
immediately preceding verses (cf. Mt 5:46,47), but also
echoing Mt 5:12/Lk 6:23.

/30/ Matthew's version of the last saying (5:42) refers
specifically to borrowing, whereas Luke has 'Do not refuse the
one who takes your things'. Matthew is probably more original
in referring to 'borrowing': Luke uses the verb αἴρειν instead,
a word he has used also in the immediately preceding saying
(Lk 6:29). But he shows his knowledge of the Matthean wording
in his v 34. So also Piper, *Love your enemies*, 191.

/31/ Luke's references to 'sinners' (6:32-34) for Matthew's
'tax-collectors.....Gentiles' (5:46,47) are probably his
redactional adaptation of the tradition for a Gentile
readership. His χάρις in the same verses may also be less
original than Matthew's μισθός, since Luke may show his
knowledge of the Matthean word in his 6:35. But 1 Pet 2:18-20
has the word χάρις, as well as the word κλέος, which could
correspond to μισθός. Again we may be dealing with differing
versions of the tradition.

/32/ For a broader discussion of the traditions of the Sermon
on the Mount see my review article on R. A. Guelich's *Sermon on
the Mount* in the *Trinity Journal* 5 (1983/4) 92-108.

/33/ I am grateful to the Rev. John Sweet for drawing my
attention to the possibilities explored in this section of my
article through a seminar paper presented in the Cambridge
University Divinity Faculty.

/34/ 'St Paul and the Revelation to St Peter, Matt. XVI, 17',
Revue Benedictine 29 (1912) 133-147.

/35/ Chapman's case is noted by A-M Denis in his article
'L'investiture de la fonction apostolique par "Apocalypse"
Étude thématique de *Gal.* 1,16' *RB* 64 (1957) 334-62 and 492-515
and by F. Refoulé, 'Primauté de Pierre dans les évangiles',
RevSR 38 (1964) 1-41. Both these authors consider that some of
the most distinctive links between Matthew 16 and Galatians 1
and 2 reflect Matthew's knowledge of Paul. Against this see
J. Dupont, 'La Révélation du Fils de Dieu en faveur de Pierre
(Mt 16,17) et de Paul (Ga 1,16)', *RSR* 52 (1964) 411-20, who
adduces weighty arguments to support Chapman's case. Also in

favour of Chapman's view (though not citing his article) see
B. Gerhardsson, *Memory and Manuscript* (Lund: Gleerup, 1961)
269-70, and 'Die Boten Gottes und die Apostel Christi', *SEA*
XXVII (1962) 120.

/36/ E.g., B. F. Meyer, *The Aims of Jesus* (London: SCM, 1979)
185-197.

/37/ *Paul and the Salvation of Mankind* (London: SCM, 1959)
63,64.

/38/ Paul does not speak of having the 'keys'. He does speak of
others seeking to 'shut him out' in Gal 4:17.

/39/ Cf. Rom 1:16 'to the Jew first and also to the Greek'.

/40/ For the primitive nature of Mt 10:5 see my *Rediscovery*,
chap. 5.

/41/ Dupont, *RSR* 52, pp. 417-19, argues that the use of 'flesh
and blood' in the rabbinic sense (contrasting the human and the
divine) and also the idea of God 'revealing' Jesus to someone
are unparalleled in Paul. This tells against those who
consider that these are Paulinisms borrowed by Matthew, and
favours the view that Paul is the borrower.

/42/ There is also discussion of Paul's and Peter's ministries
in 1 Corinthians 1-4. It may be significant that Paul speaks
here of God's revelation and of the church as a building with
Christ as the only foundation. He also speaks of himself and
Apollos as 'stewards' of God's mysteries, perhaps recalling the
parable of Mt 24:42-46/Lk 12:41-46 and again applying to himself
teaching originally addressed to Peter and the apostles. On
1 Corinthians 1-4 see B. Fjärstedt, *Synoptic Tradition in
1 Corinthians* (Uppsala: 1974) especially pp. 100-137, 154-168.
Gerhardsson, *Memory and Manuscript*, 269-70, notes how Paul in
other contexts speaks of himself having been given authority to
'build' (2 Cor 10:8, 13:10). This is a further possible point
of contact with the Petrine commissioning. Cf. also the
fascinating and important discussion of 1 Cor 15:8 by Peter
Jones, '1 Corinthians 15:8: Paul the Last Apostle', *TynB* 36 (1985)
forthcoming.

/43/ This idea is the more plausible if F. F. Bruce is correct
in proposing that the 'pillar' apostles were originally the
inner circle of Jesus' disciples, i.e., Peter, James and John
(the sons of Zebedee), and that when James was killed by Herod,
his place was taken within the inner circle by his name's sake,
the Lord's brother (*The Epistle of Paul to the Galatians*,
Exeter: Paternoster, 1982, p. 123). It is easy to see how, if
Peter was seen as the stone on which the church was to be built,
the sons of Zebedee (and hence James the Lord's brother) might
also have been called 'pillars'.

/44/ See H. D. Betz, *Galatians* (Philadelphia: Fortress, 1979),
97, for other explanations. He tends to favour the view that
Paul uses the Greek 'Peter' here because he is echoing the
Greek version of an official decree that arose out of Paul's
consultations with the apostles in Jerusalem. (Presumably on
this view we must suppose that Paul cites the Greek version,
rather than the Aramaic version (which will have spoken of
Cephas), because he wishes his Galatian readers, who will have
known the Greek version, to pick up the allusion.) This view is
possible, but there is no independent evidence of a decree in
Aramaic or Greek containing such wording, and it is at least as
plausible to think that Paul wishes his readers to pick up an
allusion to the tradition of Peter's commissioning, as this
seems to have been in Paul's mind. (For evidence which may
suggest that the Galatians were familiar with Jesus-traditions
see, e.g., 5:21 and 6:2.)
/45/ See my *Rediscovery*, pp. 351-353.
/46/ See Romans 13 and our brief discussion in section 2:1
above.
/47/ Cf. 1 Cor 9:14 with Mt 10:10/Lk 10:7. And see Dungan's
significant discussion of the mission discourses in his *Sayings*,
pp. 41-75. I failed to interact with Dungan when discussing the
mission discourses in my *Rediscovery* chapter 6; but I come to a
number of similar conclusions. For example, I agree with
Dungan that Matthew has preserved the most original form of the
discourse, though I consider that Luke has also preserved
original elements. I also consider Mt 10:8c, 'Freely you have
received, freely give', to be primitive tradition. Cf.
2 Cor 11:7, 2 Thess 3:8 and J. P. Brown, 'Synoptic Parallels',
pp. 37,38. A further substantial discussion of the mission
discourse is B. Fjärstedt's *Synoptic Tradition in 1 Corinthians*
(Uppsala, 1974) 66-99. He argues that Paul not only draws on
the mission discourse in 1 Cor 9:14, but also more widely in
1 Corinthians 9 (cf. my conclusions on the divorce material in
1 Corinthians 7). Some of Fjärstedt's suggested links between
1 Corinthians and the synoptic tradition are quite unimpressive.
But he is at his strongest when arguing for a link between the
mission discourse and 1 Corinthians 9 (cf. D. C. Allison, 'The
Pauline Epistles and the Synoptic Gospels', *NTS* 28 (1982) 6-10,
13). It may also be right to link 1 Corinthians 4 with the
eschatological discourse (Fjärstedt, 100-137).
/48/ See the very valuable article by D. C. Allison, 'The
Pauline Epistles and the Synoptic Gospels. The Pattern of
Parallels', *NTS* 28 (1982) 1-32. My conclusions overlap to a
considerable extent with his. He lists the following Pauline
texts as probable allusions to Jesus' teaching (uncertain

allusions in parentheses): Rom (8:15); 12:14,17,21; 13:7,
(8-10); 14:10-11, 13-14; (16:19); 1 Cor 4:14; 7:10; 8:13; 9:14;
11:23-27; 13:2; Col 3:5, (3:12,13; 4:6); 1 Thes 4:8; 5:2,4,13,15;
(2 Thes 3:3). See also J. W. Fraser, *Jesus and Paul* (Appleford:
Marcham, 1974); and for an older and unfortunately neglected
discussion see R. J. Knowling, *The Testimony of St Paul to
Christ* (London: Hodder, 1905). P. Stuhlmacher, 'Jesustradition
im Römerbrief', *Theologische Beiträge* 14 (1983) 240-50, also
sees Paul as significantly dependent on Jesus-tradition.
/49/ The mission discourse, the Petrine benediction and the
divorce sayings all probably had at least a narrative setting of
some sort. The passion traditions were presumably narrative,
including the Last Supper account with its opening 'On the
night that he was betrayed' (cf. Knowling, *Testimony*, 274).
/50/ Paul may be defending himself in connection with the words
of Jesus in 1 Cor 9:14 where he explains his failure to accept
support for missionary work (cf. Dungan, *Sayings*, 41-80) and in
2 Cor 1:17,18, where there is a probable echo of the saying of
Mt 5:37 (cf. Jas 5:12) and where Paul may be replying to
opponents who were accusing him of ignoring or misusing the
words of Jesus (cf. H. Chadwick, '"All Things to All Men"
(1 Cor IX.22)', *NTS* 1 (1972) 262).
/51/ Various scholars have noted that other early Christian
writers besides Paul (e.g., the authors of Acts, the Johannine
epistles and the Didache) all allude indirectly to the Jesus-
tradition, despite their knowledge of and interest in that
tradition (see, e.g., Allison, 'The Pauline Epistles', p. 22,
quoting L. Goppelt). It may seem odd that Paul explicitly
refers to the OT more than to the Jesus-tradition (though he
also uses the OT allusively). But it cannot be assumed that,
because he saw both the written OT and the probably oral Jesus-
tradition as authoritative, he must have used them in identical
ways. Part of the explanation could be that the OT was less
well-known in his churches than the Jesus-tradition. Paul cites
the OT particularly heavily when addressing questions about the
relationship of the old and new dispensations.
/52/ Although some of Paul's letters have more obvious
allusions to the Jesus-tradition than others, nearly all of
them have some possible allusions. No doubt all Paul's churches
were similarly instructed.
/53/ See Fjärstedt, *Synoptic Tradition*, 41-65, on the use of
allusion.
/54/ The recent volume *Das Evangelium und die Evangelien*, ed. P.
Stuhlmacher (Tübingen: Mohr, 1983), contains useful discussion
of the Jesus/Paul question, notably in the articles by B.
Gerhardsson and by P. Stuhlmacher.

LOGIA OF JESUS IN 1 CORINTHIANS

Peter Richardson and Peter Gooch
University College
University of Toronto
Toronto, Canada   M5S 1A1

> But is not such indifference [toward tradition about the
> life of Jesus] revealed by the extreme paucity of
> references in the Pauline epistles to what Jesus said and
> did? In answer to this question it must be admitted that
> direct citations in the Pauline Epistles of words of
> Jesus, and direct references to the details of Jesus'
> life are surprisingly few.... Undoubtedly, moreover, Paul
> knew far more about Jesus than he has seen fit, in the
> Epistles, to tell. It must always be remembered that the
> Epistles do not contain the missionary preaching of Paul;
> they are addressed to Christians.../1/

> But after the most liberal computation of such cases, it
> remains a matter of surprise that they are not more
> numerous and more unequivocal.... The assertion often
> advanced that in his oral teaching he made much more
> copious use of the evangelical narrative is one for which
> no proof can be given. We have no reason to believe that
> the Gospel as preached by Paul differed in any material
> respect from that unfolded in his Epistles./2/

Each of these two representatives of vastly different early
twentieth century views in his own way is surprised by Paul's
few references to *logia* of Jesus./3/ And both consolidate their
view by an argument from silence. Machen can argue from the
silence that Paul obviously knew much more, as is shown by
his appreciation of Jesus' character and the similarity between
Jesus' theology and Paul's. And Morgan can argue that Paul's
situation is different from Jesus' so that Paul thinks back
to Christ as redeemer (and here he is on the same ground as
Machen); Paul is on this side of the resurrection so he
proclaims the risen Christ; and Paul appeals to words of the
risen Lord, not the earthly Jesus.

Similar views continue to be strongly argued today, and both the maximalist and minimalist views still argue from silence. Each makes a quite different, and equally unproveable, argument. The one argues that Paul knows no more than we can find in his letters. The other argues that we are justified in filling in all the gaps with a full knowledge by Paul of Jesus' teaching; it is only his letters that skim quickly over Jesus' sayings.

The only sound way to proceed in the face of conflicting arguments from silence is to concentrate on the sources and evaluate as carefully as possible the recollections of Jesus' sayings in Paul. Such an examination, as Stanton properly observes, will not take us very far; nor, it should be added, will it allow us to verify the historicity of the traditions reflected. So we must go further if we are to make any headway, and assess two subordinate factors dealing with how Paul uses the material thus identified: a) how does he use sayings of Jesus in his letter as grounds for argument, and b) how strong are the indications of his concern to pass Jesus-traditions on to the church? The combination of these three investigations should give some better sense of Paul's attitude to *logia* of Jesus.

It goes without saying that Paul's letters are written at a crucial period in the formation of the Gospel traditions,/4/ and there are still many puzzles in the relation of Paul to the development of the Gospels./5/ It also goes without saying that Paul was acquainted with several of the key 'tradents,' Peter and James and John by Paul's own admission (Gal. 1:18-19; 2:9)./6/ Alongside these facts must also stand Paul's often noted assertion that he did not receive his gospel from man, it was a revelation (Gal. 1:11-12). That he had access to gospel traditions is altogether likely. That he might not have felt it appropriate to use those traditions extensively is also quite possible. The only way to resolve the question is to look at his actual use.

This paper on Jesus-traditions -- restricted to one Pauline letter -- addresses, then, three discrete questions:
  a) what traditions about Jesus' teaching can be shown to be known to Paul?
  b) how did Paul use those traditions he knew in 1 Corinthians?

c) to what extent did he hand on orally traditions he
     knew to the church in Corinth?
Answers to these questions should shed some light on the
historicity of the gospel traditions in two ways. In the
first place, by assessing the range of Paul's knowledge of
Jesus, we may be able to narrow the persistent gap between
Jesus and Paul. This gap continues to be an important factor
in New Testament studies, and even a modest narrowing of it
may be constructive./7/ In the second place, by attempting to
ascertain the source(s) which Paul is the nearest to in his
resemblances to the Jesus-traditions, we may help to underscore
the relative age of those sources./8/

     The paper concentrates on Jesus' *teaching* in Paul's first
letter to Corinth. There is, of course, indisputable evidence
of his reliance upon traditions about two *events* in Jesus'
life: the Lord's supper and the Lord's resurrection. These
two events are of crucial importance for Paul. Despite the
fact that he does not explicitly use traditions of Jesus'
crucifixion, which lies between the supper and the
resurrection, Paul does tell us that the cross is of
fundamental importance. So we should begin by affirming that
Paul is consciously dependent upon traditions about Jesus'
passion.

     Conversely, it is almost as clear that Paul does not
draw upon traditions about Jesus' actions during his ministry.
There are no occasions in 1 Corinthians -- or indeed anywhere
in Paul -- when he alludes to Jesus' healing, exorcising,
preaching, or miracles. This fact might be explicable by the
nature of the controversies Paul faces (especially in Corinth);
but since there is little room for disagreement with this
negative judgment we leave the question aside.

     It is with Paul's recollections of Jesus' teaching that
issues are least clear. In general we conclude that Paul
gives clear evidence of knowing traditions about Jesus'
teaching, even though he uses them in relatively limited ways.
Nevertheless, given the bulk of Paul's letters, the diversity
of the situations to which he wrote, and his overpowering
sense of obligation and commitment to Jesus, there are
surprisingly few explicit recollections about Jesus in his
letters. We would all be much more comfortable had he
demonstrated fuller knowledge of or greater dependence on or
more enthusiastic use of Jesus' teaching./9/ The debate on

these questions since F.C. Baur continues because of the
paucity of hard data.

Primary importance in this debate must be given to
1 Corinthians, for three reasons. First, it is the only
letter in which Paul makes explicit references to traditions
of Jesus' teaching that have clear links to the Synoptic
tradition. Second, it makes several allusions to
Synoptic-like traditions; despite this fact recent discussion,
most notably Dale C. Allison's recent article,/10/ tends to
neglect its evidence. Third, it sheds light on the degree to
which an early Pauline community knew Jesus-traditions, since
it allows more readily than any other letter a reconstruction
of earlier stages of Paul's preaching and teaching in the
community.

There are three kinds of evidence in 1 Corinthians:
explicit references to the Lord's commands and to the
traditions Paul passes on, possible allusions to
Jesus-traditions, and the indications in the letter of Paul's
earlier preaching and teaching.

Words and Traditions of the Lord

In four places in 1 Corinthians Paul directly refers
to traditions about Jesus: 15:3-8 'For I delivered to you ...
what I also received, that Christ died for our sins according
to the scriptures, that he was buried, that he was raised on
the third day...' and so on; 11:23-26 'For I received from the
Lord what I also delivered to you, that the Lord Jesus on
the night he was betrayed took bread...' and the rest of the
supper liturgy; 7:10 'To the married I give charge, not I
but the Lord, that the wife should not separate from her
husband ... and that the husband should not divorce his wife';
and 9:14 '...the Lord commanded that those who proclaim the
gospel should get their living by the gospel.'

The epitome of Paul's *paradosis* in chap. 15 begins not
with Jesus the healer and teacher but with the *Christos* who
died. This is unexceptional. Yet the point needs to be
noted, for it is entirely consonant with other indications in
1 Corinthians (and throughout the Pauline corpus) that Paul's
overriding concern with Jesus was his passion, resurrection
and presence in the community as God's *Christos*. This emphasis
is also seen in the supper liturgy *paradosis* in chap. 11.

These two passages will be more fully discussed below when we consider evidence for Paul's earlier preaching in Corinth. Taken together, the formal action of passing on these two basic traditions that enclose the passion may be taken as firm evidence of an interest by Paul in traditions about Jesus.

The other two references -- both cast as Lord's commands-- introduce us to the question of Jesus' teaching. The divorce saying in chap. 7 has clear links to the Synoptic tradition./11/ All three synoptic accounts have a tradition that Jesus viewed remarriage after divorce as adultery (Mark 10:11-12//Luke 16:18//Matt. 19:9; cf. Matt. 5:32); Mark has an absolute prohibition of divorce, while the Matthean tradition is not a prohibition of divorce but a rigorous limitation of valid grounds for divorce to adultery, and a prohibition of remarriage. Paul, like Mark, reports the Lord's command as an absolute prohibition of divorce.

Paul, however, without apology makes two applications of the absolute prohibition he reports. First, in 7:11, he allows for a case where the prohibition has been broken: 'If she does separate, let her remain single or be reconciled.' It is possible to see this 'Pauline exception' as an unstated working-out of the Matthean version of the saying; that is, Paul allows for separation on the grounds of adultery./12/ It is more plausible to view vs. 11 as simply addressing a *fait accompli* within the community -- 'it's better not to divorce, but since you have...', or making allowance for the human weakness which Paul recognizes in the Corinthian community. Second, and more significantly, Paul allows (in 7:15) the prohibition to be avoided in a case where a member of the community has a spouse who is *apistos* and wishes to end the marriage.

Further, though Paul seems in chap. 7 to make careful distinctions between levels of authority, especially emphasizing the greater authority of the command of the Lord, that distinction must be softened on closer examination. The whole chapter is a collection of *halakoth* on sexual matters, and is framed on Paul's own authoritative *halakah*: he states his principle, he states his commands, he makes clear his concessions to the community's weaknesses or to specific situations, his judgment is informed by the spirit of God and his judgment is *pistos*. Paul's focus does not rest on the Lord's command but his own principle; where he has no command

of the Lord he does not hesitate (vs. 25). /13/ The stress on
Paul's own authority is, no doubt unconsciously, reflected
clearly by the syntax of vs. 10:   'To those who are married
I command (*paraggelō*)--not I but the Lord...'./14/ The Lord's
command is not precisely an afterthought, but neither is
it foremost in Paul's mind as he writes. Indeed, the wider
context reinforces this sense with its succession of first
person singular verbs: *touto de legō* (v. 6), *thelo* (v. 7),
lego (v. 8), *paraggellō* (v. 10), *lego* (v. 12), *diatassomai*
(v. 17).

Paul argues in 9:14 that the Lord commanded that those
proclaiming the gospel should get their living by the gospel,
with which compare the mission-charges in Mark 6//Matt. 10//
Luke 9; cf. Luke 10./15/ As in 1 Cor. 7:10, though, the Lord's
command in 9:14 is not the foundation of Paul's case. There
it was buried in a sequence of words of personal authority;
here it is found only at the end of a long series of analogies
or arguments concerning work and wages. The arguments include
the practice of the other apostles, soldiers, vineyard keepers,
shepherds, an example from Torah, the practice of plowmen,
threshers, and the temple priests. D.L. Dungan argues that
the Jesus-tradition lies behind the whole of Paul's argument
since the mission-charge uses the workman-wage metaphor
(Matt. 10:10//Luke 10:7),/16/ but even if this is so, still
the command of the Lord functions as a cap-stone to the
argument and not its base./17/ The Corinthians are to be
persuaded by the analogies themselves, and all the more so
because the Lord said the same (*houtos kai*...).

Despite what the Lord commanded (*dietaxen*), Paul makes
no use (*ou kechrēmai oudeni touton*) of the right to support.
Paul has made the Lord's command (and it is a command both in
Paul's own words, and also in the mission-charges in the
Synoptic accounts: cf. Mark 6:8//Luke 9:3; Luke 10:4;
Matt. 9:9-10) into the Lord's concession--a concession which
in Corinth he chooses not to apply on his own behalf./18/

From these two explicit references to teachings of Jesus
in chaps. 7 and 9 several conclusions may be drawn. Paul
knows traditions concerning divorce and support of messengers
of the gospel that resemble traditions collected in the
Synoptic accounts. By referring to them as Lord's commands
rather than Jesus-traditions he underlines that they are
authoritative for him./19/ But in both places he uses them

only to support his argument, not to anchor it. Moreover, Paul
feels free to adapt the content of the divorce prohibition
to meet his communities' needs, and to claim a concession
from the command regarding support in what he judges to be the
overriding interests of the gospel and his relationship to a
particular church. Paul, then, knows synoptic-like traditions
of Jesus' teaching but applies them freely. They are neither
the acknowledged basis of his practice nor the chief source of
his *halakah* for his communities, despite the fact that he
stresses their authority as Lord's commands.

Paul also knows a Lord's command that cannot be rooted in
existing traditions about Jesus' teaching (1 Cor. 14:37).
After a section concerning questions of order in the meeting
Paul refers to the silence of women and claims that 'what I
am writing to you is a command of the Lord' (*kyriou entole*).
Since, so far as we know, Jesus did not in his lifetime give
rules for the ordering of Christian assemblies, and since
Jesus did not seem to demand the silence of women, this
'command' suggests another conclusion: Paul's understanding
of traditions of Jesus' teaching was fluid enough to allow a
command from the risen Lord to stand alongside those mediated
by tradition.

Allusions to Logia of Jesus

Given the clear evidence of Paul's knowledge of traditions
like those in the Synoptics (two of handing on tradition and
two of Lord's commands), an attempt to cull allusions in the
letter to other Jesus-traditions is warranted. The attempt
to find such allusions in Paul's letters has, of course, a long
and not very fruitful history, mainly because the allusions
have to be assessed on rather subjective criteria. Two main
difficulties hobble the attempt: one, the difficulty of
establishing valid criteria of what constitutes an allusion
as distinct from a coincidental turn of phrase, and two, the
difficulty of establishing that dependence on Jesus-tradition
is more likely than common dependence upon a stock of Jewish
or hellenistic materials.

Regarding the first difficulty, for example, Dale Allison
rightly criticizes Biörn Fjärstedt's work for depending upon
parallels of isolated words while the repetition of a phrase
(such as 'faith to move mountains') is a much more plausible
indication of an allusion;/20/ yet the great majority of

allusions which Allison allows show a verbal parallel limited
to one word only./21/

Regarding the second difficulty: W.D. Davies, who is
strongly committed to the claim that Paul knew and used
traditions of Jesus' teaching, feels constrained to note that
Paul's teaching may possibly derive 'from a non-Christian
Hellenistic-Jewish tradition, into which he introduced few,
if any, express words of Jesus.'/22/

With these cautions, then, we turn to an examination
of the likeliest allusions to Jesus' teaching in 1 Corinthians.
They fall into two groups: places where Paul uses an image
found in the Synoptic traditions to make the same point that
is made in the Synoptics, and places where Paul uses an idea
which may also be found in the Synoptic accounts. First,
parallel imagery.

a) *Faith to move mountains*
In 1 Cor. 13:2 Paul refers to one of the dramatic gifts
of faith: the ability to move mountains./23/ This resonates
clearly with the synoptic saying in Matt. 17:20//Luke 17:6
(and cf. Mark 11:23//Matt. 21:21).

1 Cor. 13:2	*kan echō pasan tēn pistin hōste orē methistanai*
Matt. 17:20	*ean echēte pistin hōs kokkon sinapeōs, ereite tōi orei toutōi, metaba enthen ekei kai metabēsetai...*
Mark 11:23	*echete pistin theou...hos an eipēi tōi orei toutōi; arthēti kai blethēti eis tēn thalassan...*

In form and wording Paul's comment in 1 Cor. 13:2 is closer
to the Q saying (and especially to the Matthean form of the
saying in 17:20)/24/ than to the Markan version or Matthean
doublet./25/ The sequence, *ean, echein, pistis, hōs (hoste),
ore, meta* (plus a verb of placement) creates a strong
presumption that the Pauline phrase and the synoptic passage
are related. The doublet in the synoptics, once in Q and
once in Mark, increases the presumption that these reflect an
authentic *logion* of Jesus. We may reasonably conclude that
here Paul is drawing upon a *logion*, though the point of each
is quite different./26/

b) *Skandalon*

In 1:23 Paul describes Jesus crucified as a *skandalon* to
the Jews; this resonates with the saying in Matt. 11:6//Luke
7:23 'Blessed is he who takes no offence of me' (*mē
skandalisthēi*). While it is clear that Mark and Matthew
emphasize the notion of a scandal more than Luke (see, for
example, Matt. 13:21//Mark 4:17), the saying in Matt. 11:6//
Luke 7:23 approximates very roughly Paul's explicit description
of Jesus as *skandalon*. In the same context in 1 Corinthians
Paul claims that the Jews seek signs (1:22); this in turn
resonates with the signs-sayings in Mark 8:11-12, where the
Pharisees seek a sign from Jesus (cf. also Luke 11:29-32//
Matt. 12:39-42; 16:4, the sign of Jonah).

1 Cor. 8:13 ('If food is a cause of my brother's falling
[*skandalizei ton adelphon mou*] I will never eat meat') is
strongly reminiscent of Mark 9:42//Matt. 18:6 ('whoever
causes one of these little ones to sin [*skandalisei*] it would
be better for him...'). It is also reminiscent of Matt. 18:7//
Luke 17:1 ('Temptations [*ta skandala*] are sure to come but woe
to him by whom they come!'). Allison argues that the
transitive use of *skandalizein* is very rare, and that since
both Mark 9:42//Matt. 18:6 and Paul use it to the same effect
we have telling evidence here of Paul's dependence on a Jesus
tradition./27/ It must be admitted however that all these
similarities involve the use of single words, words that can
be paralleled in other Jewish literature. It is by no means
certain that Paul's source is a *logion* of Jesus.

c) *Steward*

In 4:1-2 Paul develops a metaphor of stewardship. The
community is to regard Paul and Apollos and Cephas as servants
of Christ and stewards of God's mysteries; stewards are
required to be trustworthy (*hos huperetas Christou kai
oikonomous musterion theou....hina pistos tis heurethei*). This
metaphor is suggestive of the steward-parable in Matt.
24:45-51//Luke 12:41-46, whose point is different--to urge
faithful waiting for the delayed master--but whose main
character is, like Paul and Cephas and Apollos, set over his
master's household 'to give them their food at the proper time.'
Paul's vocabulary is somewhat closer to the Lukan parable: in
Matthew the main character is *ho pistos doulos kai phronimos*;
in Luke he is *ho pistos oikonomos ho phronimos*. It may also
be significant that in Luke the pericope is introduced by a
question of Peter's, whether the parable is to be applied

'to us' or 'to all' referring in the Lukan context to the
parable of watchfulness. It is also interesting to note other
pistos doulos stories in Luke and Matthew (e.g. Matt.
25:14-30//Luke 19:12-27), and other material found only in
Luke which expresses a general theme of stewardship (Luke
12:37, 'Blessed are the servants whom the master finds
awake...'; 13:6-9, the man and his vinedresser; 16:1-9, the
unjust *oikonomos*). The image of the steward applied to
Christian missionaries appears only here in Paul. The
resonance with Luke 12:41-42//Matt. 24:45 may suggest
dependence on a *logion* of Jesus.

d) *Sowing*
    In 3:6 Paul says that he 'planted' among the Corinthians,
Apollos 'watered' and God 'caused the growth'; in 9:7,11 he
returns to the sowing metaphor. It is not difficult to see a
link between this imagery and several sowing parables,
especially those in Mark 4:3-9//Matt. 13:3-9//Luke 8:5-8 and in
Mark 12:1-12//Matt. 21:33-46//Luke 20:9-19, where the relevant
words are a quotation from Isa. 51:1.

e) *Foundation*
    In 3:10-12 Paul calls himself a *sophos architektōn* laying
a foundation (*themelion*) on Jesus Christ, and he warns all to
take care how they build. This image and its point is
paralleled in the warning concerning building on the rock
(Matt. 7:24-27//Luke 6:47-49), the rock which is the teaching
of Jesus. Paul's allusion more closely resembles the Lukan
version of the warning, since Luke explicitly refers to a
foundation (*themelion*). In neither case is the similarity
very close.

    It would be well to note that this allusion to the 'wise
builder' tradition illustrates the problem of establishing
Paul's dependence on Jesus-tradition. In his assessment of
this passage, Allison argues that building imagery--and, more
significantly, the conjunction of building and planting
imagery as found in 1 Cor. 3--is well-known in Jewish tradition,
and cites examples from Jeremiah, Deuteronomy, and the
Community Rule of Qumran./28/ It may, therefore, be somewhat
likelier that Paul and Jesus were drawing on a common tradition
than that Paul was drawing on a saying of Jesus.

f) *Reign over the Enemies*
    In 1 Cor. 15:25 Paul notes that at the end *Christos* 'must

reign until he has put all his enemies under his feet.' This
is a *testimonium* from Ps. 110:1, similar to the Markan pericope
about David's son. The account in Mark 12:35-37//Matt.
22:41-46//Luke 20:41-44 belongs to the triple tradition, and
so is likely to be dependent on Mark. Here too there is a
possibility that Paul is not drawing on a Jesus-tradition,
since the contexts are quite different (in the one case a
reference to Adam, in the other to the Son of David).

   g) *Slave of all*
   There is one more image used by Paul which might be
connected to a Synoptic-like saying of Jesus, though not with
much confidence. In 9:19 Paul says he made himself a slave
to all (*pasin emauton edoulōsa*) that he might win the more;
this might be linked to the saying in Mark 10:43-44//Matt.
20:26-27// (with important differences) Luke 22:26-27 '...
whoever would be first among you must be slave of all (*pantōn
doulos*).' The point of Paul's claim in its context, however,
is to justify his missionary practice, and the imagery of
slavery is contrasted with freedom in connection with the
law and conscience, while in the Synoptic saying the point has
to do with true leadership with the image of slavery contrasted
to tyranny. This makes Paul's connection to such a
Jesus-tradition distant at best.

   There are also instances in 1 Corinthians where Paul
employs ideas which might be linked to Synoptic-like *logia*
of Jesus. The clearest of these are found at 1:17-21, 26-28
and 3:1 where Paul counters claims of wisdom, claims that
God chose the foolish (that is, the Corinthians) to shame the
wise, and calls the Corinthians children (*nēpioi*); this has
a startling parallel in the *Jubelruf* in Matt. 11:25-27//
Luke 10:21-22, 'I thank you, Father,...that you have hidden
these things from the wise...and have revealed them to
children (*nēpiois*)./29/

   It is possible that there is some connection between
Paul's clear preference for celibacy in 1 Cor. 7 and some of
the discipleship sayings in the Synoptics: 'anyone who loves
mother or father...sister or brother more than me...' (Matt.
10:37-39) or as Luke has it 'anyone who...does not hate his
own father and mother and wife and children and sisters and
brothers...' (Luke 14:25-27)' is interestingly comparable to
1 Cor. 7:1,7. The ideas are closest in the respective
conclusions that only some can accept (Matt. 19:11-12) and

that each has his own gift from God (1 Cor. 7:7).

Finally, Paul's exasperated question in 6:7, 'Why not rather be wronged? Why not rather be robbed?' may reflect the ideas behind the 'turn the other cheek' cluster of sayings in Matt. 5:38-42//Luke 6:29-30. Here, however, one reaches that point where the allusion is vague enough, and the content of Paul's question integral enough to its context that a dependence on a saying of Jesus can only be a weak possibility.

Paul's Knowledge of Logia of Jesus

From these allusions in 1 Corinthians to Synoptic-like *logia* several conclusions may be drawn. First, it is quite likely that Jesus-traditions inform Paul's treatment of some issues and that Paul is consciously using them in his letter. Second, those traditions centre on mission concerns--the son of David *testimonium*, the parable of the sower, the *skandalon* and sign sayings, the *Jubelruf*--or on moral concerns--the wise steward, the wise builder, and the celibacy sayings. Third, these sayings of Jesus do not appear in Paul's letter as traditions related to the church's Lord. We would not suspect a *logion* of Jesus underneath Paul's language if we did not already possess the sayings collected by the Synoptic authors, and if we did not have enough explicit references to sayings of the Lord to base the hypothesis that there might be more./30/ The meaning of Paul's letter where the allusions occur is quite intelligible without reference back to the Synoptic materials.

The final conclusion to be drawn from Paul's allusions to Jesus' sayings is that his awareness of those traditions derives very probably from a specific stratum of the development of those traditons--the collection of *logia*. The allusions we have described belong generally to the tradition shared by Matthew and Luke and not known or used by Mark, that is Q, with the few following exceptions. First, the parable of the sower belongs to the Markan account (it is found in virtually the same wording in Matthew; Luke's version is leaner but probably dependent on Mark since it is found in a Markan section of Luke); but certainly this parable would be at home in a collection of *logia*. Second, the Son of David *testimonium* belongs to the Markan material, but it was not clear that this saying was highly likely to rest on a Jesus-saying. Since *testimonia* to Jesus in the Old Testament

scriptures were collected early and independently its presence
in Paul may be unconnected with the saying of Jesus. The
third exception is the *skandalizein* saying in 1 Cor. 8:13
whose closest parallel is found in Mark 9:47. Here we may
appeal to Allison, who has carefully argued that Mark 9:33-50
(which includes our saying) is an early collection of *logia*
probably circulating independently, and that 1 Cor. 8 and
Rom. 14 show that Paul knew (at least parts of) this
collection./31/

The hypothesis that Paul's Jesus-traditions came from
a collection of *logia* is reinforced by Paul's explicit
references to Jesus-traditions. The tradition concerning
Jesus' commissioning instructions to which Paul probably
refers in 1 Cor. 9 is readily found in Q material: even though
Mark has a commissioning of the twelve which is parallel to
that found in Matthew and Luke, Luke has a doublet--the
commissioning of the seventy in Luke 10:1-12--which is entirely
Q material which has features very likely conflated by
Matthew into his commissioning of the twelve. Most
significantly the reference to a labourer deserving his
wages--Paul's point--is found only in Q material.

The Jesus-traditions regarding divorce are similar in this
respect: Mark 10:2-12 has a conflict-story regarding divorce
which is better told in Matt. 19:3-12, but this story is not
told by Luke. Rather, Luke reproduces a bald prohibition of
remarriage after divorce in the middle of the large central
section of Luke containing only Q and L material (Luke
9:51-18:14). Since Matthew also has a doublet of the
prohibition of remarriage (Matt. 5:31-32) in a context (the
Sermon on the Mount) where Q material is prominent, we must
conclude that the prohibition of remarriage was likely found
in the Q stratum. It is clear that 1 Cor. 7:10 as it stands
most closely resembles the Markan absolute prohibition in
Mark 10:9, but whatever the closest Synoptic parallel, it is
obvious that a divorce saying belongs in a collection of Jesus'
logia, and we may conclude that the two explicit references
to Jesus-traditions in 1 Corinthians support the hypothesis
that Paul drew on a collection of *logia*.

By making this claim, however, we do not imply that Paul's
knowledge of sayings of Jesus was restricted to one discrete
source, or that he must have known a written, or even a
relatively fixed oral, collection of Jesus-traditions. He may

have. But his very allusiveness cautions against identifying
too exactly the traditions he knew. The possibility of
references to traditions not found in Q cautions against any
too certain identification of the extent or source of Paul's
knowledge. In this our conclusions may be compatible with
Allison's, who argues after a consideration of Jesus-traditions
found in Rom. 12-14 and 1 Thess. 4-5 that the traditions Paul
knows cannot be traced to a single known source. Rather, he
claims, Paul knows *logia* later collected in both Q and
Mark./32/ Having said that, it does seem to be the case that
Paul has a strong tendency to reflect in 1 Corinthians material
that can also be traced in Q.

It is regrettable that Paul's allusions do not fall
neatly into one source. From Paul we get no clear indication
of an isolated development of one branch of the tradition. It
is also regrettable that the allusions in Paul are no real
help in evaluating the relative authenticity of the Matthean
or Lukan versions of Q material; we saw one allusion which
reflected a Matthean version of a saying (the faith to move
mountains) and another instance reflecting a Lukan version
(the wise steward)./33/ The Jesus-traditions which may be
recovered from Paul are good evidence, however, of an early
developing *Gattung* of *logia*-collections,/34/ and thus
indirectly support the Q hypothesis.

Paul's Use of Sayings of Jesus

While many have argued that Paul used the Jesus-traditions
available to him as a foundation for his paraenesis,/35/ the
evidence we have collected does not support this claim. Paul's
allusions to sayings of Jesus employ them chiefly as a source
of fruitful images: the sower, the steward and the rest.
Rarely do these allusions support a specific moral demand; the
only clear instance of this is Paul's demand that one not
skandalizein his brother, and even here Paul is ambivalent
toward this demand.

Another way of looking at this issue is to compare Paul's
use of scripture with his use of Jesus-traditions. A
comparison of two potential 'authorities' will shed light on
each. While we have seen that most of the Jesus-sayings in
1 Corinthians are referred to allusively and only a few
explicitly, we find the opposite in Paul's use of scripture.
For example, of the sixteen quotations of scripture in

1 Corinthians identified by the editors of Aland's 1966 Greek
New Testament only four are not introduced explicitly by
gegraptai or some other clear marker of a quotation (*phesin,
legei*); strictly speaking, moreover, these four instances are
not allusions but phrases lifted whole from scripture.
(Nestle's 1954 text notes in addition merely three or four
groups of what are more properly called allusions.) Further,
Paul consistently and explicitly attempts to ground his
paraenesis in scripture: for example, 5:13 'Drive out the
wicked person from among you!'; 6:17 (against *porneia*) 'The
two shall become one flesh'; 10:1-14, the *typoi* of the
Israelites; 11:7-9, concerning head coverings (Genesis 2);
14:21, Isaiah (concerning ecstatic speech). It is obvious
from Paul's explicit use of scripture, from the way he appeals
to it to gound his paraenesis, and from the number of citations
that he regards it as authoritative. In contrast, Paul's
allusions to sayings of Jesus do not usually ground his
paraenesis, and his explicit references to the Lord's commands
show a considerable degree of freedom in application. In only
two instances--both cases of handing on the *paradosis* in
1 Cor. 15:3 and in 1 Cor. 11:23--can Paul be said really to
ground an argument on Jesus-traditions generally. In the one
case it is a basis for church practice, in the other case for
belief. And in both cases the traditions are from the passion
narrative.

Paul's Handing On of Sayings of Jesus

We turn now to our third main question: given the
evidence that Paul knew and made use of traditions about Jesus'
teaching in the ways we have described, can it be concluded
that the Corinthian community also knew these traditions?/36/
Simply because Paul knew something he need not have taught it;
we must evaluate the evidence for Paul's preaching and teaching
in Corinth./37/

That Paul hands on tradition (*paradosis/paredōka*) is clear
from 15:1-9,11, and 11:23-26. Both traditions focus on the
events and meaning of Jesus' passion as God's *Christos*. This
focus is unremarkable in 1 Cor. 11 where the problem is conduct
at table-fellowship, but it is remarkable in 1 Cor. 15 where
Paul's epitome of his *euaggelion* stands without even a hint
of Jesus' actions or teachings. Paul's preaching concerns
Christ's death 'for our sins according to the scriptures.' In
1 Cor. 1:17-2:5, which is admittedly shaped by Paul's polemic

against wisdom, Paul's preaching is summarized in the words:
'We preach Christ crucified' (1 Cor. 1:23); 'For I decided
to know nothing among you except Jesus Christ and him
crucified' (1 Cor. 2:2); '...my kērygma was not in persuasive
speech of wisdom but in demonstration of spirit and power'
(1 Cor. 2:4). These explicit statements suggest that Paul's
core preaching concerning Jesus was not much about Jesus'
life. The interpretation of Jesus' death and resurrection
as the redemptive suffering of God's Christos was front and
centre.

Paul also says, however, that he did teach God's wisdom
(2:6-7) but not, apparently, to the Corinthians (3:1-2). This
raises the question whether the instructions Paul did give
in Corinth, as opposed to his kērygma, included traditions of
Jesus' teaching. W.D. Davies and Dale Allison both argue
that traditions concerning Jesus' teaching were an important
part of Paul's paraenesis; Davies supports this claim with a
series of arguments appealing to 1 Cor. 11:2; Phil. 4:9;
1 Thess. 4:1; 2 Thess. 2:15 and 3:6 where Paul refers to
maintaining traditions concerning conduct and community
rule,/38/ traditions derived from Jesus. But in these passages
Paul gives no indication of a link between the paraenetic
traditions and Jesus' teaching; rather in each case he links
those traditions explicitly with himself, with reference either
to his teaching (cf. 1 Cor. 4:6, tas hodous mou tas en
Christoi) or his practice./39/ Paul's general statements
concerning paraenetic traditions agree with the detailed
glimpses we have in 1 Corinthians of Paul's treatment of
specific moral problems; Paul pronounces to a very large extent
on his own authority.

Moreover, we are able to recover from 1 Corinthians some
indications of Paul's earlier instruction to his community.
The clearest evidence is found in Paul's responses to the
Corinthians' questions, which are themselves requests for
clarification of Paul's earlier teaching;/40/ these concern
questions of marriage, celibacy, food, head coverings,
charismata and order in community gatherings (as well as
queries concerning the collection, and Apollos). Only the
first of these topics is linked to a saying of Jesus, and
Paul's clarification of these questions does not centre on
Jesus-traditions.

Paul's earlier teaching may also be reconstructed from his
use of the formula *ouk oidate hoti*... ('Don't you know
that...'), which signifies either something that is obvious, or
has already been told to them./41/ The formula is used ten
times in 1 Corinthians. After removing two appeals to common
knowledge (9:13,24), the other eight instances indicate
concepts or applications of concepts which are not obvious,
yet which, Paul implies, the Corinthians ought to know:
3:16 '...that you are God's temple and that God's spirit dwells
in you?'; 5:6b '...that a little leaven leavens the dough?';
6:2 '...that the *hagioi* will judge the world?'; 6:3 '...that
we will judge angels?'; 6:9 '...that the unrighteous will not
inherit God's kingdom?'; 6:15 '...that your bodies are members
of Christ?'; 6:16 '...that he who joins himself to a *porne͞*
becomes one body?'; and 6:19 '...that your body is a temple
of the Holy Spirit in you?'.

Two instances--the leaven (5:6b) and the kingdom
(6:9)--are suggestive of Synoptic-like sayings of Jesus./42/
The kingdom saying in 6:9 is especially interesting because
it is one of the startlingly few references in Paul's writing
to the kingdom. But here Paul's link to Jesus' stress on the
kingdom is opaque. Similarly the leaven saying in Q likens
the kingdom to leaven while in Paul the image, though expressed
in similar vocabulary, is unambiguously turned instead to
moral use: leaven is malice and evil. These two instances
of the formula, then, do not suggest a close dependence of
Paul's earlier teaching on Jesus-traditions; the remaining
instances show almost no link to Synoptic-like traditions.

There are other arguments for Paul's dependence on
Jesus-traditions. Allison, following Goppelt, has argued that
Paul's relative silence concerning traditions of Jesus'
teaching is not the exception among early Christian sources
but the rule, and therefore that Paul's silence cannot be taken
to indicate that he rejected the authority of such traditions.
Goppelt notes that the author of Luke-Acts makes virtually no
reference to the traditions of Jesus' teaching in the Acts, and
that an analogous situation holds for the author of the gospel
and letters of John./43/ The phenomenon Goppelt notes in
Luke-Acts may be accounted for partly by the stress in Acts
on the *kerygma* (similar to Paul's) and partly by the nature of
those communities. They may have perceived no need of a
developed *halakah* based on traditions of Jesus' teaching, very
probably because they, like Paul, expected an imminent *parousia.*

Yet another argument is made by W.D. Davies,/44/ based on the observation that in 1 Cor. 10 Paul describes the Christian experience as a new Exodus, and that Paul employs elsewhere the related images of Passover, redemption and the presence of God in the Temple of his new people. Davies concludes that in this constellation of images is an implicit claim that Jesus' teachings are a new *Torah*. He is careful to admit that Paul never claims this explicitly, but offers the following as supporting evidence: 1 Cor. 11:2 where Paul commends the Corinthians for maintaining the traditions; 1 Cor. 9:21 (following C.H. Dodd)/45/ where Paul says he is not *anomos theou* but *ennomos Christou*; Gal. 6:2 where Paul speaks of fulfilling the law of Christ.

That evidence, however, will not bear the weight Davies puts on it. 1 Cor. 9:21 is part of a larger chiastically structured argument whose point is apologetic and Paul quite characteristically becomes a captive of his love of antithesis. It is clear that when Paul says he is not *anomos theou* (9:21) he is not equating *nomos* with *Torah*; but it is not clear what Paul does mean by *ennomos Christou*. In Gal. 6:2 Paul says 'Bear one another's burdens and so fulfil the law of Christ;' we see here not a new *halakah* based on a careful interpretation and development of Jesus' teachings but rather a variation of a theme common to Jesus and Jewish tradition, and echoed by Paul, that love of one's neighbour is the fulfilling of the whole *Torah* (Rom. 13:8-10). Paul's use of *nomos* is slippery; it cannot be shown that because Paul refers in 1 Cor. 9:21 and Gal. 6:2 to a law of Christ he therefore roots his *halakah* in the authoritative interpretation of Jesus' teaching.

What can be recovered of Paul's earlier preaching and teaching in Corinth shows very little connection to sayings material. Paul's explicit description of his *kerygma* shows an exclusive concern with the passion of *Christos*. Where he is aware of Jesus-traditions in his letters he uses them allusively. These three factors all point in a single direction: a dominant concern for preaching the crucified and risen Christ; little concern to teach about Jesus' teaching; and little inclination to use sayings of Jesus as decisive arguments in his paraenesis. While it is possible, of course, that Paul conveyed traditional sayings of Jesus to the Corinthians, the evidence we have tends against that claim.

Conclusion

In summary, then, Paul knows traditions of Jesus' teaching concerning divorce and the mission-charge. It is also likely that he knows traditions of Jesus' teaching concerning the faith to move mountains, the wise steward, the wise builder, the *Jubelruf*, and perhaps the son of David *testimonium*, and celibacy or abandonment of interfering attachment to family.

The large majority of these come from *logia* material, strengthening the Q hypothesis, but the shape of the traditions in Paul is so indistinct that unfortunately it contributes little to our understanding of the development of the Q stratum of the traditions. It is likely, however, that Paul himself knew and used one or another collection of *logia*.

There will always remain real uncertainty of how close Paul stood to traditions of Jesus' teaching, because Paul's *kerygma* stresses the meaning of Jesus' passion as *Christos*, because Paul uses traditions of Jesus' teaching only as auxiliary arguments or fruitful images, and because he is free to adapt those traditions to the communities' needs. Such Jesus-traditions seem not to be foundational to Paul's theory or his practice.

That may seem a negative conclusion in a volume such as this; nevertheless, we believe it to be a correct one. But such a conclusion strongly reinforces the extent to which Paul is committed to the crucified and risen Lord. That, as he himself tells us, forms the centre of his Christology.

Notes

/1/ J.G. Machen, *The Origin of Paul's Religion* (Grand Rapids: Eerdmans, 1965; reprint of 1925), 147, 151; cf. also 118.
/2/ W. Morgan, *The Religion and Theology of Paul* (Edinburgh: T. & T. Clark, 1917), 35.
/3/ See also G.N. Stanton, *Jesus of Nazareth in New Testament Preaching* (Cambridge: Cambridge University Press, 1974), 97; 115, n.1: '...the almost complete absence of references or allusions in the epistles to gospel traditions remains puzzling.' The whole of chap. 4 is a useful analysis of the problems.

/4/ See D.M. Stanley, S.J., 'Significance for Paul of Jesus'
Earthly History,' in Sin, Salvation and the Spirit
(Collegeville, Minn.: The Liturgical Press), 279-288,
especially 281: '...once the viewpoint of the recent techniques
in Gospel criticism be accepted, the too often repeated
assumption that Paul displayed little if any interest in Jesus'
earthly career should be subjected to radical revision...'
/5/ For a provocative treatment with respect to the
resurrection, see James M. Robinson, 'Jesus: From Easter to
Valentinus (or to the Apostles' Creed),' JBL 101 (1982), 5-37.
/6/ C.F.D. Moule, 'Jesus in New Testament Kerygma' in O. Böcher
and K. Haacher (eds.), Verborum Veritas: Festschrift für
G. Stählin (Wuppertal: 1970), 15-26, cites approvingly the
view that Paul took assistants such as Mark and Silas with him
in order to have a 'gospel source' with him, 'in the form of
a person acquainted with the facts' (25).
/7/ See P. Richardson and J.C. Hurd (eds.), From Jesus to
Paul: Studies in Honour of F.W. Beare (Waterloo: Wilfrid
Laurier Press, 1984), especially the essays by S.G. Wilson
('From Jesus to Paul: The Contours and Consequences of a
Debate') and by Hans Rollmann ('Paulus Alienus: William Wrede
on Comparing Jesus and Paul').
/8/ See P. Richardson, 'Streeter Revisited: Proto-Luke and the
Pauline Mission,' a paper delivered to the Canadian Society of
Biblical Studies in Ottawa, June 2, 1982 (to be published).
/9/ See C.F.D. Moule, 'Jesus in New Testament Kerygma;' more
recently he has dealt with the same question in an unpublished
paper, 'Paul as Interpreter of Jesus.'
/10/Dale C. Allison, Jr., 'The Pauline Epistles and the
Synoptic Gospels: The Pattern of the Parallels,' NTS 28 (1982),
1-32. See also, on 1 Thessalonians, J.C. Hurd, 'The Jesus Whom
Paul Preaches (Acts 19:13),' chap. 7 in P. Richardson and
J.C. Hurd (eds.), From Jesus to Paul; cf. P.J. Achtemeier,
'An Apocalyptic Shift in Early Christian Tradition: Reflections
on Some Canonical Evidence,' CBQ 45 (1983), 231-248.
/11/ For an extensive treatment of the links between 1 Cor.
7:10 and the Synoptic divorce sayings, see D.L. Dungan, The
Sayings of Jesus in the Churches of Paul: The Use of the
Synoptic Tradition in the Regulation of Early Church Life
(Philadelphia: Fortress Press, 1971), 83-135. See also
D.R. Catchpole, 'The Synoptic Divorce Material as a
Traditio-Historical Problem,' BJRL 57 (1974), 92-127.
/12/ Dungan holds that the Matthean form of the divorce-saying
is authentic, and that Paul's exception in 7:11 reflects Paul's
knowledge of this authentic tradition (Sayings, 102-131);

Catchpole argues against Paul's reliance on a Matthean
tradition ('Divorce Material,' 105-108).

/13/ See further Peter Richardson,'"I say, not the Lord":
Personal Opinion, Apostolic Authority and the Development of
Early Christian *Halakah*,' *Tyndale Bulletin* 31 (1980), 65-86.
See also Catchpole ('Divorce Material,' 120) concerning
Jesus' relation to Moses: 'What Moses commanded, the historical
Jesus rejects.'

/14/ Cf. 1 Cor. 4:17 '...who will remind you of my ways, the
ones *en Christoi*.'

/15/ The affinity is basically in sense; there is almost no
verbal overlap. The closest relationship is between Luke 9:6,
with its reference to the Twelve (9:1) 'going out...preaching'
(*dierchonto...euaggelizomenoi*), contrast Mark 6:12.
Nevertheless it seems likely that this tradition, for all its
complexity in the Synoptic Gospels, lies in some sense behind
Paul's 'command of the Lord.'

/16/ Dungan, *Sayings*, 79-80.

/17/ This impression is strengthened by the observation that Paul
begins this section not with a claim to a command but with an
appeal to a right (*exousian*).

/18/ Cf. Dungan (*Sayings*, 20), following B. Gerhardsson,
Memory and Manuscript (Uppsala: C.W.K. Gleerup, 1961), 319.
Dungan includes an illuminating discussion of the problems of
support in the early churches and the role Paul's denial of
support played in the tensions between him and the Corinthian
community (*Sayings*, 27-40, 76-77).

/19/ O. Cullmann has made much of Paul's description of
Jesus-traditions as Lord's commands, arguing for a
discontinuity in Paul's thought between the historical Jesus
and the exalted Lord in 'The Tradition,' in A.J.B. Higgins
(ed.), *The Early Church* (London: SCM, 1956), 59-104; per
contra W.D. Davies, *The Setting of the Sermon on the Mount*
(Cambridge: Cambridge University Press, 1964), 357-362.

/20/ Allison, 'Pattern,' 8, criticizing B. Fjärstedt,
*Synoptic Tradition in 1 Corinthians: Themes and Clusters of
Theme Words in 1 Corinthians 1-4 and 9* (Uppsala: Uppsala
Teologiska Institutionen, 1974).

/21/ Allison, 'Pattern,' 10; Allison is aware of this
difficulty and seeks to mitigate it by reference to parallel
ideas.

/22/ Davies, *Setting*, 366.

/23/ It is also, of course, a proverbial saying found in
Judaism and in secular literature. For the phrase 'move
mountains,' see Isa. 54:10.

/24/ G.Thom. 48 reinforces the Matthean reference to 'mountain,'
but it makes the protasis refer to 'peace...in the same house,'
not to 'faith.'
/25/ Contra Conzelmann, *1 Corinthians*, 222, n. 38, who
underlines the proverbial character of the phrase in Judaism
and refers only to Mark 11:23.
/26/ Contra C.K. Barrett, *1 Corinthians*, 301: 'He gives no
indication that he is quoting from Jesus, and was probably
not doing so.'
/27/ Allison, 'Pattern,' 15.
/28/ Allison, 'Pattern,' 7 and n. 39.
/29/ See Peter Richardson, 'The Thunderbolt in Q and the Wise
Man in Corinth,' in P. Richardson and J.C. Hurd (eds.),
From Jesus to Paul.
/30/ *Pace* Fjärstedt, *Synoptic Tradition*, who develops a
provocative but unconvincing argument that Paul's letter could
have been fully understood by the Corinthians only if they
knew the traditions to which Paul alludes.
/31/ Allison, 'Pattern,' 13-15.
/32/ Allison, 'Pattern,' 19.
/33/ It is very interesting to note, on the other hand, what
emerges when the question is asked the other way: can we
trace any influence from Paul to the redaction of the Q
materials, or to Jesus-traditions in general? The answer is
'yes,' in the case of Luke. There are six instances, listed
here in decreasing order of likelihood, where Paul (or Pauline
communities) may have influenced the redaction of Luke: 1.
Luke's supper liturgy, (Lk. 22:19-20) clearly resembles
1 Cor. 11:23-25, though the text of Luke is problematic
(see B.M. Metzger, *A Textual Commentary on the Greek New
Testament* [London/New York: United Bible Societies, 1971],
173-177). Metzger concludes that the similarity between the
passages 'arises from the familiarity of the evangelist with
the liturgical practice among Pauline churches.' 2.   The
Lukan introduction to the Q pericope about making friends with
one's accuser (Luke 12:57-59 'And why do you not judge for
yourselves what is right?'); compare 1 Cor. 6:1-8, esp. 6:5.
3.   The Lukan addition of Jesus' cry from the cross, 'Father,
forgive them for they know not what they do' (Luke 23:34);
compare 1 Cor. 2:7-8 'If [the rulers] had understood [the
wisdom of God] they would not have crucified the Lord...'
4.   The Lukan version of the commissioning of the seventy
(Luke 10:1-12), specifically vs. 7 '...eating and drinking
what is before you...'; compare 1 Cor. 10:27 '...eat whatever
is set before you...' 5.   The Lukan version of the 'Lord, Lord'

saying: Matt. 7:21 'Not everyone saying "Lord, Lord" will
enter the Kingdom...,' Luke 6:46 'Why do you call me
"Lord, Lord" and not do what I tell you?'; compare 1 Cor.
12:3, No-one can say 'Jesus is Lord' except by the Holy
Spirit. 6. The Lukan version of the Q saying re. loving
family more than me/hating family (Matt. 10:37-39//Luke 14:
25-27) includes a specific reference to wife and children,
absent from Matthew; compare 1 Cor. 7:32-35.
/34/ See J.M. Robinson, 'LOGOI SOPHON: On the Gattung of Q'
in J.M. Robinson and H. Koester, *Trajectories Through Early
Christianity* (Philadelphia: Fortress Press, 1971), 71-113.
/35/ For examples see V.P. Furnish, 'The Jesus-Paul Debate:
From Baur to Bultmann', *BJRL* 47 (1965), 342-381. For a
different view, see recently J. Murphy-O'Connor, 'The Divorced
Woman in 1 Cor. 7:10-11, *JBL* 100 (1981), 601-606.
/36/ See Catchpole, 'Synoptic Divorce Material,' 109.
/37/ For a suggestive but different type of analysis based on
1 Thessalonians see J.C. Hurd, 'The Jesus Whom Paul Preaches
(Acts 19:13).' His very important *The Origin of 1 Corinthians*
(London: SPCK, 1965), makes a major contribution to the
study of the pre-history of Paul's letters. See also Stanton,
Jesus of Nazareth, chap. 4.
/38/ Davies, *Setting*, 355-366; Allison, 'Pattern,' 21-23. This
is a position held by many scholars (see Furnish, 'Debate').
/39/ Rom. 6:17 (of which Davies makes much, *Setting*, 364-365)
is an exception to this statement, but the church in Rome was
not founded or visited by Paul before Romans and could not be
expected to know Paul's paraenetic tradition.
/40/ See Hurd, *Origin*.
/41/ In Stoic and Cynic parallels the formula 'prefaces ideas
with which the readers are presumed to be familiar and in
agreement.' (V.P. Furnish, *Theology and Ethics in Paul*
[Nashville and New York: Abingdon Press, 1968], 79).
J.C. Hurd has noted that 1 Cor. 3:16 ('Don't you know that
you are God's temple and that God's Spirit dwells in you?')
connects with 2 Cor. 6:16 ('For we are the temple of the
living God; as God said "I will live in them..."')
strengthening both the hypothesis that 2 Cor. 6:14-7:1 is a
fragment of Paul's earlier letter and that the *ouk oidate hoti*
formula points to Paul's earlier teaching (*Origin*, 237).
/42/ In a private communication (1 September, 1983)
David Wenham says: '...all the instances have possible links
with the Synoptic or Johannine Jesus-tradition. It seems to
me quite possible that Paul's basic teaching consisted of
Jesus-tradition--no doubt "translated" for his audience and

put into Paul's words--, and that what we see in his letters
is the apostle further applying the Jesus-tradition and
clarifying those things that were not explicit in it.'
/43/Allison, 'Pattern,' 22, following L. Goppelt, *Theologie
des Neuen Testaments: Erster Teil* (Göttingen: Vandenhoeck
& Ruprecht, 1976), 370.
/44/Davies, *Setting*, 363-366; *ibid.*, *Paul and Rabbinic
Judaism* (London: SPCK, 1948), 147-176.
/45/C.H. Dodd, 'ENNOMOS CHRISTOU,' in *Studia Paulina in
Honorem Johannis de Zwaan* (Haarlem: deErven F. Bohn N.V.,
1953), 96-110.

Appended Note

C. M. Tuckett, '1 Corinthians and Q,' *JBL* 102 (1983), 607-
619, argues that 'any link between 1 Corinthians and the
specific stratum of the synoptic tradition known as Q is very
difficult to establish' (619). He grants that Paul and the
Christians in Corinth knew Jesus-traditions. He implies that
there may be differences between the Corinthian Christians and
Paul concerning these traditions. Mostly, however, he is
concerned to show that the links between 1 Corinthians and
gospel-traditions are not specifically with Q.

A full treatment of his arguments will have to await
publication of the revised form of Peter Richardson, 'Streeter
Revisited' (as in note 8 above). This paper will argue that
Paul knew *logia*-traditions rather like Q (cf. the present
paper), that some of Paul's opponents in Corinth also knew
these traditions but valued them more highly than Paul did, and
that Proto-Luke is an attempt to write a more adequate gospel
for a Pauline church. In that stratum of the gospel-tradition
one is most closely in touch with Pauline emphases. One can
see certain important revisions to the overall content of a
logia-collection such as Q, and individual changes that might
well account for some of the evidence Tuckett presents. In
brief, the difficulties in Corinth can be attributed in part to
differing views of what constitutes an adequate 'gospel'.

Tuckett's concern for the relationship between Paul and
specific layers of gospel traditions is similar to ours. On
one specific point in his article, see Peter Richardson, 'The
Thunderbolt in Q' (as in note 29, above).

JAMES AND JESUS

Peter H. Davids,
Regent College,
2130 Wesbrook Mall,
Vancouver B.C. V6T 1W6,
Canada.

Only five years ago we discussed the transmission of the Jesus tradition in an article published in this series of volumes. In the conclusion of that article we concluded that the Jesus tradition had been deliberately transmitted from the beginning and was important to the early church from its earliest period, although the transmission was not as fixed or unredacted as B. Gerhardsson had apparently imagined./1/ Since that time there have been several helpful developments in this field. First, Gerhardsson himself has produced another work on the topic./2/ This has helped to clarify his position that the gospel traditions were transmitted by deliberate inculcation, memorization and notes, much as later rabbinic traditions were transmitted from rabbi to student, although it has not materially altered it.

Second, other scholars (principally British and German) have published works which demonstrate continuing interest in the historical Jesus and his teaching in the early church. Our earlier study in *Gospel Perspectives I* could have noted the work of G. Stanton; in that it focuses on the life of Jesus its relevance is somewhat tangential to a study of the teaching of Jesus, but in that he argues that the life of Jesus was important for the early kerygma, it suggests that his teaching might also have had a continuing value for the early church./3/ Since our earlier work, sociological studies of early Christianity have pointed to itinerant preachers as possible transmitters of the Jesus tradition, which would be an alternative to the rabbinic model proposed by Gerhardsson./4/ One need not agree with all the conclusions of, for example, Gerd Theissen about the life style of these preachers, their creativity, and their relationship to the more settled ministry

to give assent to the general result: the early preachers of the
gospel carried the Jesus tradition with them as they itinerated
proclaiming the good news. Furthermore, there has been Rainer
Riesner's study of the role of Jesus as a teacher deliberately
transmitting tradition by means of his disciples, although not
as formally as Gerhardsson thought, for Gerhardsson has
retrojected the later formal rabbinic schooling into the New
Testament period and Riesner has demonstrated a less organized
and institutionalized training situation, yet still one in which
the teacher deliberately passes on his teaching to others by
means of instructed disciples. The nuanced position of this
work is significant for the position taken in this present
article./5/

    Third, others have taken up the task of addressing the
issue which flows from the work done above: if Jesus was a
teacher and his teaching was so important to the earliest strata
of Christianity, why is there so little evidence of it before the
the gospels, except in the sources of the gospels themselves?
Why is this teaching not reflected in the pauline literature and
other early Christian works? In part this enters into a debate
of long standing. In 1967 W. D. Davies argued in his well-known
Paul and Rabbinic Judaism that there are more than 30 passages
in Paul where the apostle alludes to the teaching of Jesus./6/
This conclusion, naturally, did not go uncontested, although
even some of his critics allow at least 8 allusions to be added
to the 6 proved citations of Jesus in Paul./7/ Part of the
problem, of course, is determining where Paul *should* have used
the Jesus tradition. Whereas we with our history of interaction
with the gospels might feel that Paul should have cited Jesus in
numerous passages, Paul assuredly felt quite differently because
of the topic he was discussing, the audience he was addressing,
or the form of the tradition which he possessed. For example,
his letters are particularly concerned with topics such as the
reason for the cross, on which the gospel traditions provide
little helpful information (the sayings mainly indicating that
it was necessary and that Jesus' death was for others, not
reflecting on why it was necessary and in which way it was for
others, these things being Paul's burden). For this reason
C. F. D. Moule pointed out that since the words of Jesus are in
kerygmatic literature, *i.e.*, gospels, it was far more likely
that Paul transmitted such teaching as part of his basic
missionary preaching, which is not the subject of his epistles.
Indeed, it is only by chance (*i.e.*, a case of abuse) that we
know about Paul's concept of the eucharist, one of the topics of
the basic teaching for which the words of Jesus were relevant./8/

Since the work of Davies and Moule, however, there have been a number of studies which demonstrate that Paul's use of the Jesus tradition is far more extensive than was previously imagined. The latest of these, the work of D. C. Allison,/9/ points to the following facts: (1) the citations and allusions to Jesus in Paul fall into groups, (2) these sections are places in which Paul has added the Jesus material to the paraenetic tradition he has received, (3) this Jesus material itself is mined from blocks of presynoptic material, e.g., Luke 6:27-38, Luke 10, Mark 9:33-50, and the passion story, (4) this evidence shows that Paul knew not only isolated sayings of Jesus but whole blocks of Jesus material, and (5) when Paul refers to this material in his writings (e.g., 1 Thess 4-5), he refers to it as something his readers already know, i.e., a part of his foundation proclamation of the gospel. Therefore he purposely transmitted at least some blocks of Jesus material to his church during his first founding visit and thereafter presupposes that his readers know this material, i.e., have memorized it. This is in harmony with the method of Luke-Acts, where the second volume presupposes the teaching of Jesus in the first and never includes a citation of Jesus despite an obvious mastery of the tradition by the author./10/

It is not within the scope of this article to enter into the pauline debate (although it forms an important backdrop both historically and methodologically for this present study) or the continuing discussion of the nature of the transmission process behind the gospels themselves./11/ Rather, we shall leave for others to discuss the issue of the correctness of Allison's conclusions on Paul (although we believe that the points summarized above are in fact accurate observations), and instead sink a bore into the ground of the New Testament to see if the results obtained in a different body of literature are similar to those of Allison or otherwise. That is, if Allison is correct about Paul and Riesner about Jesus, then there should be evidence in the epistle of James that the author assumes that his readers have received and learned oral or written traditions about Jesus' teaching.

This epistle is appropriate for several reasons./12/ First, it is non-pauline, giving us a test case outside the pauline corpus. Second, James 5:12 contains a well-known citation of the Jesus tradition, which gives one a clear starting point for discussing the relationship of James to the gospels./13/ Finally, a proportionately larger number of suspected allusions to the Jesus tradition have been detected in James than in Paul.

If W. D. Davies finds allusions to Jesus in Paul, he finds
about the same number in James./14/ A composite listing of
suspected allusions indicates there are from 36 to 45 allusions
to the teaching of Jesus, some verbally close and other more
general parallels in thought, pointed out by various authors.
Therefore James is a promising area in which to carry out our
investigation.

The parallels between James and the Synoptic tradition may
be diagrammed as follows:/15/

James	Matthew	Luke	Source	Type
1:2	5:11-12	6:23	Q	close allusion
1:4	5:48			possible allusion
1:5	7:7f.	11:9	Q	close allusion
1:6	21:21f.		Mk.11:23f.	close allusion
1:9f.	18:4,23:12	14:11 22:26		basic concept
1:12	10:22			possible allusion
1:13	6:13			possible allusion
1:17	7:11	11:13	Q	close allusion
1:20	5:22			close allusion
1:21		8:8		basic concept?
1:22	7:24	6:46f.	Q	close allusion
1:23	7:26	6:49	Q	concept of parable
1:26f.	7:21-23			basic concept
2:5	5:3,5,11:5	6:20,7:22	Q	close allusion
2:6		18:3		concept of parable?
2:8	22:39f.		Mk.12:31	close allusion
2:10	5:19			close allusion
2:11	5:21f.			possible allusion
2:13	5:7			close allusion*
2:14ff.	7:21-23 25:31-46			possible allusion idea of parable
2:15	6:25			basic concept?
3:1ff.	12:36f.			possible allusion
3:12	7:16	6:44f.	Q	close allusion
3:13ff.	11:19			possible allusion
3:18	5:9			close allusion*
4:2	7:7			possible allusion
4:3	7:7f.,12:39			possible allusion
4:4	6:24	16:13	Q	close allusion
4:8	6:22			possible allusion
4:9	5:4	6:25		close allusion?

James	Matthew	Luke	Source	Type
4:10	23:12	14:11		close allusion
		18:14	Q	
4:11f.	7:1	6:37	Q	close allusion
4:13f.	6:34			possible allusion
4:17		12:47		possible allusion*
5:1		6:24f.		close allusion
5:2	6:19f.	6:37,12:33	Q	close allusion
5:5		16:19		possible allusion
5:6		6:37		possible allusion
5:7			Mk.4:26-29	idea of parable
5:8	24:3,27,39			basic concept
5:9	5:22,7:1, 24:33			close allusion
5:9b			Mk.13:29	possible allusion
5:10	5:11f.	6:23	Q	possible allusion
5:12	5:34-37			indirect citation*
5:14f.			Mk.6:13	idea of narrative
5:17		4:25		possible allusion?
5:19	18:15	17:3	Q	close allusion

This chart is, of course, incomplete, for many parables make
the same basic point that passages in James do and there are
often more gospel passages which could be cited as parallel to
passages in James, for the gospels themselves have a
redundancy of ideas. But enough has been included to provide
a picture of the data observed by commentators on James.

Given the data above, some analysis is called for. It is
significant that the allusions are not scattered all over the
gospels, but they focus on one large block, namely, the ethical
material contained in the Sermon on the Mount/Plain./16/ On the
one hand, this concentration should be expected, for the
paraenetic material collected in the Sermon is most suited to
the topics discussed in James. The fact that this material
appears in block form not only in Matthew and Luke (which may be
dependent on each other or may be independent redactions of a
previous collection) but also in James gives *prima facie*
evidence that there existed an early paraenetic collection of
the sayings of Jesus (oral or written) and that James knew a
version of that block of tradition. But two further
observations arise from the analysis of this information.

First, as critics have observed in connection with James
5:12,/17/ James is not dependent upon any particular gospel
redaction of this ethical tradition. While the numbers of
parallels show that Matthew is closer to James than is Luke,
in tone (for example, in his woes on the rich) and in language
James is far closer to Luke./18/ James is therefore using a
pre-gospel form of what we might loosely term the Q tradition
in a redaction (his own or someone else's) which differs from
both of the two canonical gospels. Thus James witnesses to a
third community for which the ethical teaching of Jesus was
important.

Second, Allison's work on Paul cited above shows that Paul
mines some of his ethical material from blocks of teaching
which are now part of the Sermon./19/ Thus the teaching of
Jesus had a continuing interest and authority for at least
these two groups of Christians (and possibly a third, if Q
represents a separate community) long before the gospels were
written. Since James probably reflects a Palestinian milieu
/20/ and Paul clearly places himself outside the Palestinian
church (Gal 1:15-2:10), this evidence demonstrates a knowledge
and use of the Jesus sayings-tradition in two quite different
areas of the church, suggesting a relatively widespread use in
the early church of this ethical material./21/

It is impossible to overlook the fact that neither James
nor Paul (with perhaps 6 exceptions) cite Jesus as the source
of their teaching. This fact, however, should not blind one to
their widespread use of allusion (*i.e.*, paraphrastic use of
phrases or ideas from a logion, with the probable intent of
reminding the reader of it), for allusive reference without
formal citation is consistent with later church usage. For
example, the Didache, which is filled with exact quotations of
or allusions to gospel material, only cites Jesus by name
twice, both times in liturgical contexts (*e.g.*, a eucharistic
context like Paul's in 1 Cor 11)./22/ The Shepherd of Hermas,
which is probably itself dependent upon James, never introduces
any of its allusions to the teaching of Jesus by using his
name. There is no reason to suspect that the visionary literary
genre should be the reason for this style, since by the time
Hermas was published (ca AD 96) the church was surely using
written gospels, especially in Rome (assuming a connection
between Mark and possibly Luke with Rome); and a reference to
such previous teaching would not appear any more inappropriate
than the angel's reference to Jeremiah in Daniel's discussion
of his 70 year prophecy./23/ The evidence of the Apostolic

Fathers demonstrates that even after the gospels were written
and circulating widely in the church it was not the custom to
refer to them by direct citation for the most part, but to
allude to them indirectly. A reasonable explanation for this
phenomenon is that each Christian had memorized the basic
teaching of Jesus as part of his or her initiation into the
church and thus allusion to this memorized body of data was more
fruitful than direct citation which would assume verbally
identical forms of oral tradition or a relatively fixed 'canon'
of written gospels. Everyone would recognize the authority
behind an allusion, whether or not their version of the
tradition had the exact verbal form./24/

Thus we can say that James knew the Jesus tradition and
assumed that his readers were also familiar with it (otherwise
the allusive references would fall on unknowing ears),/25/ but
we have not explained *how* James uses that tradition, nor its
importance for the argument of the epistle. Clearly a precise
description of James' use of Jesus' sayings is impossible, for
we do not know the exact limits of his contact with the Jesus
tradition; *e.g.*, there are some sayings in the epistle which are
suspected on the grounds of correspondence in style and subject
matter with known sayings of Jesus to be agrapha (*e.g.*, 3:18,
4:17), but which may or may not be included in lists of
allusions. If the saying is closely paralleled in a gospel but
is not an exact quotation of the gospel saying, it is listed as
an allusion, but should James have included a saying which
lacks such a parallel, it would not be included, despite its
similarity in style and tone./26/ Thus to the extent that James
knew a form of the Jesus tradition which differed from that
preserved in the gospels, the results of this study will be
distorted, *i.e.*, they will underestimate his use of the
tradition.

Given the assumption that we are probably underestimating
the evidence, we can make several observations on the basis of
the data presented in the chart above. First, the allusions to
the Jesus tradition are scattered relatively evenly throughout
the book,/27/ which means that they are not isolated phenomena
of one or even a few of the units (homilies or distribes,
proverbs, sayings) edited together to form the epistle.

Second, this even spread of the allusions means that they
not only occur in all parts of the epistle, but they fall into
every form-critically determined unit of the epistle, *i.e.*, of
22 sections in the epistle 15 have 'close' allusions, 5 others

'possible' allusions and the 2 remaining ones have less
verbally close parallels in the narrative and sayings tradition.
/28/ The following chart will illustrate:

James reference	Sermon	Other Q	Other non-Q	# not close or possible allus.
James 1:2-4	3			
James 1:5-8	1	1	1	
James 1:9-11			4	(4)
James 1:12			1	
James 1:13-15	1			
James 1:16-18	1	1		
James 1:19-21	1		1	(1)
James 1:22-25	4			(1)
James 1:26-27	1			(1)
James 2:1-13	6	2	3	(1)
James 2:14-26	2		1	(2)
James 3:1-12	2		1	
James 3:13-18	1		1	
James 4:1-10	6	4	1	
James 4:11-12	2			
James 4:13-17	1		1	
James 5:1-6	4	1	1	
James 5:7-11	4		6	(2)
James 5:12	1			
James 5:13-18			2	(1)
James 5:19-20		2		

If the argument above is correct, James displays a
knowledge of blocks of material in the Jesus tradition and has
spread allusions to this tradition throughout his epistle. The
issue which now arises is *how* this tradition functions in the
epistle. It is at this point that the full significance of the
previous observations becomes apparent. As the chart above
shows, each major paragraph in the epistle contains one or more
allusion, and further analysis would demonstrate that in every
paragraph the allusion(s) supports the main point. To fully
establish this assertion we would need to examine every
paragraph of the work, which is clearly impossible within the
limits of this article. Therefore a few examples given as
typical illustrations will have to suffice for the present. If
our hypothesis proves fruitful in these instances, it is at
least a useful working hypothesis for a later detailed
examination of the entire epistle.

In James 1:2-4 the major thrust, which is announced by
'Count it all joy. .. when you meet various trials', is to urge
the readers to endure suffering joyfully, *i.e.*, to see the
eschatological future in the midst of present evil or what J.
Thomas calls '*eschatologische Vorfreude*'./30/ This call to
anticipated joy is given in the form of a chain saying, which
James shares in common with Paul (Rom 5:2b-5) and 1 Peter
(1:6-7), although the basic paraenetic form has been used by
each writer for his own purposes. Matthew 5:11-12 or Luke
6:23/31/ is making precisely the same point: one should consider
oneself blessed when one suffers because one anticipates future
joy in the eschaton./32/ It is quite possible that this
dominical saying lies behind the chain-saying for all three
authors, but James at least is conscious of the connection.
First, one notices the amount of overlap between James and the
Beatitudes in general and thus would not anticipate one
exception. Second, James uses χαράν which is the one root that
both Matthew and Luke share. Third, in his summary James refers
to the example of the prophets as those whom we now congratulate
despite their former suffering, a concept which is assumed in
the Beatitude./33/ Thus anyone familiar with the Beatitude
would realize that James has restated and contemporized the
Jesus-saying in his epistle.

In James 1:21 a paragraph on pure speech (*i.e.*, speaking
without anger) is summed up with a call to receive the implanted
word which is able to save one's soul. The interesting fact is
that only in Luke 8:12 is the word (λόγος) said or implied to
have been able to save. Furthermore, the parable of the sower
may also be reflected in the idea of receiving the word (Luke
8:13) and in the strange use of ἔμφυτος which is probably
influenced by the use of φύω in the parable. The parable, of
course, supports James' call to put away evil (in this case
anger) by acting on (receiving) Jesus' instruction./34/

In James 1:22-25 the argument revolves around doing or
obeying the commands of God versus hearing them only. The
paragraph functions chiasticly with chapter 2, where the
theme is poverty and wealth/charity (which is the 'doing' under
discussion here and the 'works' of 2:14-26),/35/ and it is one
of the most semitic in the book, the phrase 'doer of the word'
being a most peculiar Greek usage./36/ The point James makes is
that simply knowing the gospel (assuming this is the same word
also mentioned in 1:18,21) is not enough. One must act on it or
obey it. Matthew 7:24,26 (paralleled in Luke 6:47-49) makes the
same point in parabolic form. One would be tempted to simply

cite the whole warnings section of the Sermon, Matthew 7:13-27,
as a general parallel, for the theme of the entire section (or
Luke 6:43-49, which contains most of the material) parallels
James' argument, but in this case the use of 'hears these words
of mine' and 'does them' is close enough to James' unusual Greek
usage that we believe that he had this particular parable in
mind.

In James 2:1-13 the author begins a two-part section on
charity, impartiality, and especially concern for the poor.
Each part opens with a thematic sentence (2:1; 2:14), then
develops with an illustration (2:2-4; 2:15-17), a 'theological'
argument (2:5-7; 2:18-19), and a two-part scriptural argument
(2:8-12; 2:20-25) before closing with a summary (2:13; 2:26).
The main point of the first part of this section is that the
church is counting the rich blessed and the poor despicable,
while God does just the opposite./37/ The church's action puts
it on the side of God's enemies and makes the Christians
oppressors of the poor (just like the church's persecutors) and
therefore breakers of God's law. This eschatological point-of-
view theme has already occurred earlier in James (e.g., 1:9-11),
and it will occur again in the reversal of fortunes of the rich
and poor in 5:1-6, 7-11./38/

The blessedness of the poor (reversal of fortunes) is, of
course, a major theme of the Sermon (Mt 5:3,5; Lk 6:20), as are
woes on the rich (e.g., Lk 6:24). What is particularly
significant in James is the fact that the author refers to a
promise of the kingdom to the poor (2:5). While the election
of the poor is a relatively well-known theme in Jewish
literature (e.g., Isa 61:1ff.; 4QpPs37), the language of the
promise of the kingdom together with the rejection of the rich
is particularly close to the Beatitudes, especially if one
believes James knew a form including the Lucan woes (and this
in turn depends on the disputed issue of whether these woes
reflect an original reversal of fortunes structure, whether
they arose in the tradition, or whether they are part of the
Lucan redaction)./39/ This promise, i.e., a saying of Jesus,
forms the foundation of James' whole theological argument.
Even his biblical argument (2:8ff.) may be dependent upon a
saying of Jesus, for having already referred to the kingdom he
now refers to the royal law, which is Leviticus 19:18, a
commandment which Jesus cites with approval several times in
the recorded sayings tradition. It may well be that this is
the royal law because it was so emphasised by the exalted Lord
of the kingdom. Thus allusions to the Jesus-tradition are the

basic authority behind this section, for otherwise an argument
based on a promise of the kingdom to the poor and a supposedly
royal law falls flat.

In James 3 the argument is for peace and unity in the
church. Teachers should not exalt themselves (3:1-2) and no one
should speak evilly of others (3:5-12). Consistent speech and
peacemaking are the marks of wisdom (= the Spirit, 3:13-18).
/40/ There is clearly a general contact with the teaching of
Jesus, for the Sermon tradition also includes sayings which
prohibit criticism of others (e.g., Mt 7:1-5), but then so did
other Jewish groups of the period (e.g., 1QS 7, where murmuring,
complaining, and slandering are among the infractions censured).
What is of specific interest in James is the fact that he
consistently draws the connection between lifestyle (fruit) and
genuineness or spirituality, using illustrations similar to
those Jesus used (Mt 7:16; Luke 6:44-45)./41/ Furthermore,
James sums up his argument in 3:18 with a saying which is so
close to Matthew 5:9 that many have taken it for an agraphon.
/42/ This stress on peace and peacemaking comes after a
previous reference to 'peaceable wisdom' in 3:17. It sums up
the theme of the tongue (no criticism of others, no factions)
and allows the argument to shift smoothly to the 'wars and
fightings' of the next chapter./43/ While it would be unwise
to insist that this is indeed an agraphon used to sum up the
whole argument of the chapter, it is at least a saying of James
which paraphrases the sense of the Beatitude, with its stress on
peacemaking. If this is the point towards which the whole
chapter is heading, then it is clear that a Beatitude underlies
James' whole argument.

A similar analysis could be carried on throughout the
book, whether for specific parallels or for the more general
structural and conceptual similarities, but the constraints of
space force us to leave the argument with these few
illustrations.

Several factors lead us to conclude that this pattern is
more than a case of our wishful thinking or circular reasoning.
First, the extent and shape of the contact with the Jesus
tradition argues that this pattern is more than the construction
of a modern mind foisted upon the text, for it would be hard to
construct so complex a set of relationships unless there were
some basis for it in reality. Second, in the examples discussed
it became clear that the allusions were not simply a large

number of similarities in thought between James and Jesus, but that the wording of sayings of Jesus had influenced the wording of James. The pattern is not simply global, but also extends to minor words and phrases. Third, the epistle can give the strongest of categorical commands to Christians 'in the diaspora' without any apparent self-consciousness. This is not like Paul giving commands to the churches he founded (although even there he was cautious),/44/ but an epistle sent to those neither James nor his community necessarily knew. This suggests that there was some pattern of traditional teaching (whether paraenesis or the sayings of Jesus) upon which the epistle is based./45/ Thus the evidence points away from a circumstantial explanation and towards an explanation which deals with the plan of James.

James is frequently at root an enlargement upon and application of the Jesus tradition in the light of community situations. If one wished to use the term loosely, one could term James a halakah based on the Jesus tradition in which the oral law (the tradition) is amplified and applied to concrete situations by means of argument and Old Testament exegesis (using both midrashic method and haggadic expansion). Two examples from Paul may suffice to illustrate./46/ In 1 Corinthians 7 Paul has a word of Jesus (7:10), which is enough to deal with the basic issue of divorce in the community, but he then goes on to amplify it in two ways, i.e., by giving permission for temporary separation to Christians and by dealing with the situation of mixed marriages in which only the Christian could possibly be bound by the law of Christ. Likewise in 1 Corinthians 9 he is likely alluding to the gospel tradition (e.g., Mt 10:5-10; cf. 1 Tim 5:17-18 where the Old Testament citation and the words of Jesus are combined, probably indicating an earlier fixed tradition), but now must explain why (1) it is a valid teaching (amplified by means of the Old Testament) and (2) he himself does not need to follow it, for his situation is different. In both cases the argument from the Jesus tradition is clarified and modified by both Old Testament citation and rational argument. In both it is applied to the community (and to Paul himself) as a type of halakah for the present situation.

The same phenomenon appears in James. James has the extant Jesus tradition, which both he and his community seem to know. But the tradition does not cover the exact situations in which he finds his community, and thus the community is able to ignore the implications of the tradition while giving verbal adherence to

Jesus as Lord. James' method is through allusion to the
tradition, at times very directly,/47/ to draw it into the
situation and then to show its applicability by argument or by
coupling it with Old Testament texts. In the process he
expands upon the tradition considerably.

At this point it would be helpful to go through the whole
epistle to show in what way this thesis applies in each
paragraph (e.g., does the Jesus tradition serve as a starting
point for the argument or as a summation of the argument or is
it perhaps ancillary?), but the limitations of an article of
this length do not allow for that. Two examples of critical
importance for James will suffice.

First, in James 2:1-13, which we have discussed in part
above, one has the hypothetical situation of a Christian
judicial assembly./48/ The illustration serves to give the
situation, i.e., discrimination, to which James wishes to
apply the tradition. In James 2:5 he alludes to the teaching
of Jesus and again in 2:6, pointing out how it fits the present
situation. Then he brings in first one supporting Old
Testament text (Lev 19:18, which is also important in the Jesus
tradition) and then a second Old Testament text (Exod 20:13-14).
His conclusion in 2:13 is at least an allusion to a saying like
Matthew 5:7 and perhaps itself a saying of Jesus, and it both
sums up the preceding argument and bridges to the following
discussion of charity. Whereas Jesus said nothing about
discrimination against the poor, James has through argument
extended the implications of the traditions to cover this
situation, making this teaching a binding rule for the
community.

Second, in James 2:14-26 a parallel phenomenon takes
place. There is first the illustration which is couched in
terms of the demand for charity, an important theme of the
Jesus tradition (e.g., Mt 6:25), and then in 2:17 (2:18 is a
most difficult verse, but probably is making the same point)
/49/ an allusion to teaching such as Matthew 7:21-23, 25:31-46.
The context of charity as a criterion for judgment would fit
both passages, but the faith-works contrast (i.e., hearing-
doing, cf. the comment on 1:22ff. above) points to Matthew
7:21-23./50/ This teaching is then applied and amplified by
use of two Old Testament texts (which may themselves have been
connected in the paraenetic tradition),/51/ i.e., the Abraham
and Rahab examples. The summary verse brings the reader back
to 2:17. Thus, whatever the situation which the author is

confronting in this passage (*e.g.*, a misunderstood paulinism
very early in Paul's ministry or at any rate before the author
had read any of Paul's epistles),/52/ he meets it through
statements which would remind the readers of the basic
Christian teaching they had received, extend its meaning, and
show them its applicability to the present situation using
both exegetical and rational argument.

    This explanation which we have advanced for the passages
discussed above appears most satisfactorily to clarify the
twin phenomena in the epistle of James of its closeness to the
Jesus tradition on the one hand and its lack of formal
citations of the tradition on the other. The epistle's method
is quite simple. The Jesus tradition, according to our
hypothesis, forms the underlying rule of life for the early
community. It is an oral rule, however, no specific verbal
form of which can be assumed in the communities 'in the
dispersion'. It is also a rule which provides general guide-
lines but does not cover every circumstance to which James
wishes to speak. Thus wherever possible the author alludes to
it and then shows its applicability in the present situation by
extending and amplifying it through argument and the other
authoritative standard which the early church had, namely the
Old Testament.

    We cannot claim to have demonstrated our hypothesis for
all of James, for we have dealt with a limited number of
passages. But we have shown that for these passages the
authority of the Jesus tradition underlies James' argument,
being part of either the main argument or the concluding
summary clinching statement. It is reasonable to believe that
since the allusions are spread throughout the book, this
hypothesis could likewise be demonstrated throughout the book,
but full demonstration would need a small monograph.

    To the extent we have established our hypothesis, the data
is consistent with the observations of others referred to
earlier on the apostle Paul. For example, Allison's point that
Paul mines his Jesus material from blocks of pre-synoptic
tradition and that this material was apparently already known
by his readers would also be true for James. On the other
hand, allusions to the Jesus tradition are more pervasive in
James than in Paul, and in James may be more the occasion of
the paraenesis than an addition to a previous paraenetic
tradition (although James fleshes out his paraenesis with
extensive use of biblical and post-biblical materials)./53/ At

least some of these differences may have to do with subject matter; the more important observation is the common knowledge of and reference to blocks of Jesus traditions even before the synoptic gospels were written.   Thus allusion to the Jesus tradition may well have been a general method of the early church, demonstrating the importance and binding nature of at least the ethical traditions assigned to Jesus for the life of the church during the first century of this era.

Notes

/1/ P. H. Davids, 'The Gospels and Jewish Tradition' in R. France and D. Wenham, eds., *Gospel Perspectives I* (Sheffield, 1980) 75-100.
/2/ B. Gerhardsson, *The Origins of the Gospel Traditions* (Philadelphia, 1979).
/3/ G. N. Stanton, *Jesus of Nazareth in New Testament Preaching* (Cambridge, 1974).
/4/ The principle stimulus has been the work of G. Theissen, especially *The Sociology of Early Palestinian Christianity* (Philadelphia, 1978), although his earliest discussion of this theme antedated this publication, *e.g.*, 'Wanderradikalismus', *ZTK* 70 (1973) 245-271.
/5/ R. Riesner, *Jesus als Lehrer* (Tuebingen, 1980). Cf. the abstract in *TLZ* 106 (Dec., 1981) col. 926.
/6/ Pp. 136-146.
/7/ V. P. Furnish, *Theology and Ethics in St. Paul* (Nashville, 1968) 51-59. Cf. his 'The Jesus-Paul Debate: From Baur to Bultmann', *BJRL* 47 (1965) 342-381, for the earlier background of this discussion.
/8/ 'Jesus in New Testament Kerygma' in O. Boecher and K. Haacker, eds., *Verborum Veritas* (Wuppertal, 1970) 15-26.
/9/ 'The Pauline Epistles and the Synoptic Gospels: The Pattern of the Parallels', *NTS* 28 (1982) 1-32. Cf. D. L. Dungan, *The Sayings of Jesus in the Churches of Paul* (Philadelphia, 1973), and B. Fjaerstedt, *Synoptic Traditions in 1 Corinthians. Themes and Clusters of Theme Words in 1 Corinthians 1-4 and 9* (Uppsala Theologiska Institutionen, 1974).

/10/ Allison, pp. 10-16,21-22; there is, of course, one citation
of Jesus in Acts ('It is more blessed to give than to receive',
Acts 20-35), but this exception fits the rule in that it does
not quote a saying already recorded in the gospel, but gives an
additional saying. The sayings included in the gospel are
assumed.

/11/ Although Allison's work is rather recent, there are already
indications of disagreement, e.g., P. Richardson and P. Gooch,
'Jesus-traditions in 1 Corinthians' in this volume.

/12/ Although there is an obvious importance of James for this
study, the size of the epistle in relationship to the limits of
space available to discuss it and the availability of our
previous exegetical discussion (P. H. Davids, The Epistle of
James (NIGTC) (Grand Rapids/Exeter, 1982)), which meant that
much of the digging had already been done, certainly predisposed
us to select this epistle for study.

/13/ E.g., P. S. Minear, 'Yes or No: the Demand for Honesty in
the Early Church', NovT 13 (1971) 1-13.

/14/ The Setting of the Sermon on the Mount (Cambridge, 1964)
402-403.

/15/ This chart is a modified version of one which appears in P.
Davids, The Epistle of James, 47-48; it is reproduced here by
permission. The 'Type' column should be interpreted thus: close
allusion = verbal parallels as well as same idea, possible
allusion = less convincing verbal similarity yet same idea,
basic concept = no verbal parallels, but similar idea,
* = suspected agraphon. The other remarks are self-explanatory.
Allusions have been included in some cases where James appears
to reverse the idea of some dominical teaching and attribute
this perverse attitude to those he criticises as an implicit
criticism. Obviously all these evaluations are by nature
subjective.

/16/ Twenty-nine out of 45 parallels come from the Sermon
tradition. Virtually all the rest come from Luke's central
section or the Matthean discourses. Contact with Mark is
slight (5 parallels), which is what one would expect if Jesus'
example were never cited. Ibid., 48. Cf. G. Maier's similar
independent conclusion about 1 Peter in 'Jesustradition im 1.
Petrusbrief' in this volume.

/17/ Cf. P. S. Minear, 'Yes or No', who argues that James is
closer to the original form of the tradition and that Matthew
has redacted this simple 'yes' in a legalistic direction, and
E. Kutsch, 'Eure Rede aber sei ja ja, nein nein', EvT 20 (1960)
206-218, who believes that the two sayings are essentially the
same (Matthew's version revealing a Jewish figure of speech for
an inward 'yes' being in harmony with an outward 'yes') and are

thus independent redactions of the core tradition. Neither
author sees any evidence for James' dependence upon the written
synoptic tradition. Each is a more satisfactory explanation
than that of M. H. Shepherd, 'The Epistle of James and the
Gospel of Matthew', *JBL* 75 (1956) 40-51, who argues that James
uses inaccurate memory quotations of Matthew, for, as S. S.
Laws, *A Commentary on the Epistle of James* (London: A. & C.
Black, 1980), 14, notes, there is no trace in James of Matthew's
redactional interests.
/18/ See J. B. Adamson, *An Inductive Approach to the Epistle of
James*, unpublished Ph.D. dissertation, Cambridge University,
1954, 293-295, who has collected impressive evidence for the
similarity of James and Luke, especially in vocabulary.
/19/ Allison, 11,21-22.
/20/ We have argued previously, P. Davids, *The Epistle of James*,
28-34, for a Palestinian milieu for James, even though we
believe that it is a two-stage work composed of an original
Jacobean tradition redacted by a later editor. However, even
should one accept S. S. Laws' contention that James was composed
in Rome (*A Commentary on the Epistle of James*, London, 1980,
24-26), one would have a witness to the use of the Jesus-
tradition in two areas of the church.
/21/ Since P. Richardson and P. Gooch, 'Jesus-traditions in
1 Corinthians', agree with Allison that Paul knew the Jesus-
tradition, this holds true even for those who accept their
argument that Paul did not necessarily pass on this tradition
to the churches he founded.
/22/ Didache 8:2, 9:5 are the two direct citations, which refer
to baptism and eucharist respectively. Didache 15:3-4 refers to
the teaching of the gospel in general and thus may be an
allusion to a known teaching of Jesus as a basic authority. It
is interesting that all of these citations come in the second
part of the Didache, not the ethical section. A parallel to
this situation is that of the Dead Sea Scrolls, for, excepting
the scrolls which he may have written, the Teacher of
Righteousness is mentioned but rarely cited, despite the fact
that his interpretation of the Old Testament was admitted to be
the foundation of the community. The analogy breaks down in
part, however, for the importance of the Teacher to Qumran
was certainly less than that of Jesus to the Church, for whom
Jesus was also eschatological judge.
/23/ Even if Mark were written as late as the 60's, by the late
90's gospels were certainly in use in Rome. In this regard
1 Clement provides mixed evidence, for most of his references
to Paul and to Jesus (*e.g.*, 24:5) are allusive. He knows, but
never cites Hebrews. But on two occasions he does cite Jesus

(in one case to provide a link to an Old Testament prophecy),
yet he does so in a catena form which does not match the written
gospels, but probably stems from catechesis (13:1ff., 46:7ff.).
/24/ If the words of Jesus were generally repeated at the
celebration of the eucharist and perhaps at baptism, this would
explain why citations first show up with reference to such
rites, for these texts would have taken on a certain fixity
relatively early.

Naturally one must assume some fixity in the tradition as
a whole, for otherwise allusive reference would have no basis
at all, but if a general outline of the sayings included in
the basic collection was a fixed part of the tradition, one
could have quite a variety in exact oral expression and still
have a recognizable tradition. This is especially true if a
Greek version of the tradition were known (which, as we argue
in *The Epistle of James*, 81, may be the case in 1:13). An
allusion might cover several Greek expressions of an Aramaic
saying.
/25/ While we refer to the author of the epistle as 'James', we
have previously argued (*The Epistle of James*, 12-13,21-22) that
the work is redacted, the product of Jacobean traditions edited
together by a redactor with fluent Greek, probably after the
death of James. This adds to the problem of agrapha, for they
might be (1) proverbial sayings of James, (2) sayings of Jesus,
or (3) proverbs from Jewish (or even Hellenistic) sources out
outside the tradition which serve to sum up the tradition.
/26/ Both 2:13 and 4:17 are good examples of the agrapha
problem. It is clear that 2:13 is a saying or proverb very
close in content to Matthew 5:7, 18:21ff., 25:34ff. (cf.
M. Dibelius, *James* (Philadelphia, 1976) 147-148). The verbal
closeness to Matthew 5:7 would make one at least list this as
an allusion, but, given that it is an isolated saying used to
sum up an argument, is it really a quotation, a variant of
Matthew 5:7? James 5:12 is almost verbally identical with
Matthew 5:34-37, although it is a condensed form of the saying.
But the difference in the case of James 2:13 is great enough to
leave doubt whether James or Jesus invented the saying.
James 4:17 is also an inserted saying of Jewish origin
(Dibelius, 231,235), but while it is congruent with the teaching
of Jesus (*e.g.*, Lk 12:13-21) it is not verbally similar. Thus
one must remain agnostic about whether it is a saying of
Jesus, a Jewish proverb, or a saying of James. The issue of
agrapha in non-canonical literature has been discussed by
J. Jeremias, *Unknown Sayings of Jesus* (London, 1964), and more
recently by M. Mees, *Ausserkonische Parallelstellen zu den
Herrenworten und ihre Bedeutung* (Bari, 1975). Jeremias deals

with later literature which normally cites Jesus explicitly,
making the author's intention easier to identify. Mees comes
closer to our study in that he includes parallels, *e.g.*, those
in the Didache, which do not cite Jesus directly. But his focus
is the transmission and use of forms in new settings, so he
does not help identify sayings of Jesus, although he does show
that the tradition was very much alive in communities which did
not use the 'Jesus said' form.

/27/ The one apparent exception is 5:13ff. The passage has
clear parallels in the actions of the apostles (Mk 6:13,
Lk 10:34) and so alludes to the narrative tradition, not sayings
of Jesus, but unless this is a practice which has been passed on
in the church separate from the narrative in which the
disciples practice healing at Jesus' command, it is hardly a
true exception to our rule.

/28/ The analysis of James into sections follows our previous
discussion in *The Epistle of James*, 22-29.

/29/ There has been an attempt to limit the parallels in
thought to those which a person would see as closely supporting
the argument in question; in some cases they are close to verbal
parallels. The sections are not entirely arbitrary, but this
division has been argued for in another place. See Davids,
Epistle of James, 22-29. However, similar results would be
obtained by other schemes of division.

/30/ 'Anfechtung und Vorfreude', *KD* 14 (1968) 183-206.

/31/ Cf. R. A. Guelich, *The Sermon on the Mount* (Waco, Texas,
1982) 95-97,107-109.

/32/ Here as in the chart each passage in the synoptic accounts
is enumerated separately, rather than counting parallels as a
single allusion. Obviously in the case of redactions of the
same saying it is likely that James knew only one form of the
saying, and this is probably the case in most instances. But
we have chosen not to argue whether any individual passage is
an independent tradition or a variant of another passage, for
it does not materially alter the conclusions.

/33/ In this study we must assume our earlier conclusions (*The
Epistle of James*, 25-26) based on the work of F. O. Francis,
'The Form and Function of the Opening and Closing Paragraphs of
James and I John', *ZNW* 61 (1970) 110-126, that James
recapitulates his three major themes in the summary paragraph,
5:7-11, and that it is thus proper to relate it to chapter 1 in
this way.

/34/ This connection was pointed out to me by a student,
R. Devans, in a class paper. See also J. M. Reese, 'The
Exegete as Sage: Hearing the Message of James', *Bib.Theol.Bul.*

12 (1982) 82-85, who briefly refers to this parallel.

The similarity of James to the Lucan redaction is an interesting facet of James research. There is a similarity in vocabulary, first pointed out by J. B. Adamson in *An Inductive Approach to the Epistle of James: Materials for a Fresh Study* (unpublished Ph.D. dissertation, Cambridge University, 1954), 293-294. There is also a conceptual similarity; *e.g.*, only James, Luke and 1 Enoch in Jewish and New Testament literature pronounce woes on the rich. James and Luke in general have intense concern about wealth and poverty. The similarity in vocabulary may be because both writers are among the most elevated styles in the New Testament. There could be independent choice of similar vocabulary. On the other hand, if the woes (mentioned below) are Lucan and the phrase in Luke 8:12c is a Lucan redactional explanation (noting the use of σώζω, a term which interests Luke), the James-Luke similarity might suggest a closer connection of James with Luke (or Proto-Luke?) than has been previously suspected.

What complicates this issue is that many, if not the majority, of the parallels between James and the synoptic tradition are to the content found in Matthew. Does this mean that James' similarity to Luke is simply independent selection of similar vocabulary and concepts? Or does it indicate that the Lucan tradition was originally larger than what is included in Luke? One notes that James 5:12 would fit nicely in a Lucan context, for there are no specifically Jewish references, as there are in the Matthean version. This is what Luke does, for example, to the divorce logion and to the saying on not resisting evil. Did Luke draw on a larger Lucan tradition or *lukanische Schule* in producing his gospel? This study has not been able to investigate such intriguing questions. But if the results of this study are accepted, then James, and perhaps other New Testament epistles, might be used as a tool in investigating the form and history of the pre-gospel synoptic tradition. Until such a systematic study is carried out, we can make observations of similarities, but we cannot establish the exact form of the tradition which James knew.

/35/ Cf. R. B. Ward, 'The Works of Abraham: James 2:14-26', *HTR* 61 (1968) 283-290, and A. Sisti, 'La parola e le opere (Giac. 1,22-27)', *BibOr* 6 (1964) 78-85, for a discussion of these two passages. Of course this same conclusion could be inferred from our own conclusions about James' structure.

/36/ In normal Greek this phrase would mean poet, as any Greek lexicon would show, but James' use is clearly semitic, parallel to the LXX's 'doer of the law' (Deut 28:58, 1 Macc 2:16, Sir 19:20, etc.). It was this semitic character that led Origen

(*Hom*. Gen 2:16) to argue that 1:22 was an agraphon of Jesus.
/37/ The basic theme of this section is not altered whether one
agrees with R. B. Ward, 'Partiality in the Assembly: James
2:2-4', *HTR* 62 (1969) 87-97 (cf. the support of this position in
P. Richardson, 'Judgment in Sexual Matters in 1 Corinthians
6:1-11', *NovT* 25 (1983) 50-51), that the assembly involved is a
judicial assembly of the church or not. It is still
discrimination against the poor, although Ward points to a rich
Old Testament background which may be involved.
/38/ Again one should see Thomas' article referred to above and
note that eschatological anticipated joy is dependent upon a
reversal of fortunes theology, for it is because one accepts the
reversal of fortunes that one anticipates future blessedness in
the face of present apparent reality.
/39/ On the origin of the Lucan woes (redactional expansion or
original component) see the debate between C. M. Tuckett and
M. D. Goulder, 'The Beatitudes: A Source-Critical Study', *NovT*
25 (1983) 193-216, or R. Guelich, *Sermon on the Mount* 112-118.
Either shows the tip of a much larger debate for which the issue
of what form of the tradition James knew has important
implications.
/40/ Cf. J. A. Kirk, 'The Meaning of Wisdom in James', *NTS*
16 (1969) 24-38.
/41/ Cf. R. Guelich, *Sermon on the Mount*, 394-396,409. James
does not use the same examples (*i.e.*, instead of figs on thorns
he speaks of figs on grapevines), but they are similar and have
the same meaning, *i.e.*, the two types of behavior do not mix
(just as a spring does not mix water and a tree does not mix
fruit).
/42/ While we do not want to discount the possibility of this
being a citation of Jesus, the stock language involved in 'the
fruit of righteousness' suggests that it could come from a
building upon a word of Jesus as well. Cf. E. Kamlah, *Die Form
der katalogischen Paraenese im Neuen Testament* (Tuebingen, 1964)
176-196. R. Hoppe, *Die theologische Hintergrund des
Jakobusbriefes* (Wuerzburg, 1977) 134, points out that the source
in Jesus' language is probable because of the uniqueness of this
Beatitude.
/43/ It is possible that the reference to Father in 3:9 might
already be betraying the presence of the Beatitude in James'
mind, but the argument for 3:18 stands on its own in any case.
The use of a verse to sum up an argument and refer forward as
well is not unusual in James (*e.g.*, 1:26-27; 2:13).
/44/ Cf. R. Banks, *Paul's Idea of Community* (Grand Rapids,
1980), 180ff., who argues that not even Paul used authority
freely.

/45/ Two subjective arguments might also be added. First, the
thesis of this article was not remotely in mind when the chart
containing the parallels was prepared for publication; but one
grants that there might have been some subconscious influence.
Second, a look at New Testament commentaries and monographs
would reveal parallels to the scriptures being discussed which
may have been intended by the author but which are not on the
major point of the passage. Rather they concern an interesting
word theme of subordinate value in the passage. Thus we note
that modern authors who are saturated with a topic also make
conscious and unconscious allusive references to the passage or
theme. There is no reason to believe James' psychology worked
otherwise.
/46/ While this is probably the least controversial illustration
which we could have chosen from Paul, we are aware that P.
Richardson and P. Gooch take a somewhat different approach in
'Jesus-traditions in 1 Corinthians' elsewhere in this volume.
/47/ James 2:5 is surely a rather direct allusion. Another may
well be James 1:12, especially if both it and Revelations 2:10
are based on a common gospel tradition, perhaps even an agraphon.
/48/ For an exposition of this position see Davids, *The Epistle
of James*, 107-110, or R. B. Ward, 'Partiality in the Assembly:
James 2:2-4', *HTR* 62 (1969) 87-97.
/49/ For a recent discussion of 2:18 see N. Heinz, 'Eine alte
crux interpretum im Jakobusbrief 2, 18', *ZNW* 73 (1982) 286-293.
/50/ We have ignored parallels in the Johannine tradition, but
one notes that F. O. Francis, cited above, sees
similarities between James and 1 John. The language of the two
epistles is dissimilar - neither has borrowed from the other.
But the content has considerable thematic overlap (*e.g.*, the
insistence that commandments be kept, the stress on charity and
love of the 'brother', the rejection of the world, and the
reference to healing). Thus James may be a parallel to 1 John
for the synoptic tradition, or there may have been overlap
between the two traditions at an earlier period with James
knowing some of the sayings ascribed to it. But space prevents
us examining these intriguing issues in more detail.
/51/ See H. Chadwick, 'Justification by Faith and Hospitality',
SP 4/2 = *TU* 79 (1961) 281.
/52/ For a fuller discussion of the relationship of James to
Paul see Davids, *The Epistle of James*, 50-51, and on the
relevant passages. There is obviously no attempt in this
article to give a full discussion of the passages mentioned, but
throughout the article only summaries of previously published
research by the author are offered. This method prevents
repetition and allows the focus to remain on the issue at hand.
/53/ Cf. our summary of Allison's work above (p. 65).

JESUSTRADITION IM 1. PETRUSBRIEF?

Gerhard Maier,
Albrecht-Bengel-Hans,
Ludwig-Krapf-Str.5,
7400 Tübingen,
West Germany.

Vorbemerkung
Die Frage der Beziehungen zwischen dem 1. Petr und der Jesustradition, vor allem den verba Christi, hat immer wieder Interesse gefunden. Insbesondere Selwyn hat mit seinem Nachweis der mannigfachen Beziehungen zwischen dem 1. Petr und den Evangelien/1/ einen forschungsgeschichtlichen Durchbruch erzielt./2/ Es fehlt auch nicht an speziellen Untersuchungen zu dieser Frage, z.B. von J. P. Brown, R. H. Gundry, C. Spicq und M. C. Tenney. Jedoch war man bisher auf die Verwendung von Jesustradition in der Einzelparänese konzentriert, was sich z.B. an den tabellarischen Vergleichen ablesen läßt. Außerdem wirkte sich die Vorstellung von einer besonderen Beziehung zwischen 1. Petr und einer Q-Form hemmend aus./3/

Formgeschichtlich müssen wir differenzieren zwischen a) der Jesustradition in der Einzelparänese und b) der Jesustradition in den kurzen katechismusartigen Stücken.

Bevor wir uns der Einzelparänese zuwenden, sei zunächst ein Wort zur Verfasserschaft erlaubt. Bekanntlich ist diese umstritten. Der Meinung vieler kritischer Forscher gibt W. Marxsen mit den Worten Ausdruck: 'Daß Petrus der Verfasser... sei, ist aus manchen Gründen mehr als unwahrscheinlich'./4/ Ganz ähnlich erklärt das gegenwärtige Standardwerk von W. G. Kümmel: '1 Pt ist ... ohne Zweifel (!) eine pseudonyme Schrift'./5/ Und auch H. Goldstein kommt in seiner Monografie über die Ekklesiologie des 1. Petr zu dem Urteil, der Brief sei 'pseudepigraph' und 'in nachapostolischer Zeit entstanden'./6/ Es ist hier nicht der Ort, die Verfasserfrage eingehend zu diskutieren. Interessanterweis nennt aber Kümmel mehr Verteidiger als Bestreiter der petrinischen Verfasserschaft./7/

Wir können uns Guthries nach gründlicher Diskussion gewonnenem
Ergebnis anschließen: 'The result of this survey ... leaves us
in no doubt that the traditional view which accepts the claims
of the Epistle to be apostolic is more reasonable than any
alternative hypothesis.'/8/ Deshalb gehen wir im Folgenden von
der Annahme aus, daß Petrus, der Apostel und Sprecher des
Zwölferkreises, der Verfasser des 1. Petrusbriefes war.

A. Die Einzelparänese

Vor einigen Jahren hat die Debatte zwischen Ernest Best
und Robert H. Gundry über die Jesuslogien im 1. Petrusbrief
erneut die Aufmerksamkeit für dieses Thema geweckt. Die
Differenzen zwischen Best und Gundry lassen sich auf folgende
Punkte bringen:
a) Gundry nimmt eine Verfasserschaft des Petrus an; Best lehnt
sie ab und setzt den 1. Petr in die Jahre 80 - 100 n. Chr./9/
b) Gundry findet im 1. Petr nicht nur einzelne Jesuslogien
wieder, sondern glaubt auch, daß der Brief auf Ereignisse und
Zusammenhänge Bezug nimmt, die uns die Evangelien ebenfalls
berichten, während Best die Berührungen zwischen dem Brief und
den Evangelien streng auf 'gospel logia' beschränken will./10/
c) Gundry notiert etwa zwanzig Parallelen zwischen dem 1. Petr
und den Evangelien, vorwiegend Lukas und Johannes; Best
vermindert die Parallelen auf ca. ein Drittel dieses
Bestandes./11/ d) Gundry sieht enge Beziehungen zu Teilen der
johanneischen Tradition, während Best solche Beziehungen
generell ausschließt./12/

Dennoch sollten wir nicht übersehen, daß es zumindest eine
Gemeinsamkeit zwischen Gundry und Best gibt: Beide nehmen
tatsächliche 'Kontakte' zwischen dem 1. Petr und der
Evangelientradition an. Offen bleibt die Frage, wieweit sie
reichen.

Im Folgenden sollen 1. noch einmal Stellen untersucht
werden, die in der Gundry-Best-Debatte zur Diskussion standen,
2. weitere Stellen des 1. Petr auf ihr Verhältnis zur
Evangelientradition geprüft werden, um 3. zu allgemeinen
Schlußfolgerungen hinsichtlich der petrinischen Einzelparänese
zu kommen.

Vielleicht ist es am Platz, eine weitere Vorüberlegung
deutlich zu machen. Die Paränese der ntlichen Briefe arbeitet

in der Regel mit kurzen Sätzen und kurzen Sinnabschnitten.
Wir dürfen also gar nicht erwarten, daß Anklänge an die
Evangelientradition oder, spezieller noch, an Jesuslogien *in
extenso* auftreten. Vielmehr ist auch dort, wo der Verfasser
bewußt an solche Jesustradition anknüpfen will, nur eine sehr
begrenzte Reminiszenz möglich. Das macht unsere Arbeit
schwierig und wird immer wieder zu unterschiedlichen
Beurteilungen führen.

I. *Umstrittene Stellen in der Diskussion zwischen Gundry
und Best*

1. *1. Petr 1,4*: Sachlich sprechen sowohl 1. Petr 1,4 als
auch Lk 12,33 von dem unzerstörbaren Erbe der
Gläubigen 'in dem Himmel'. Außerdem ist die
Gedankenführung beider Stellen miteinander verwandt.
Zweifellos ist diese Verwandtschaft auch enger als
diejenige, beispielsweise, zwischen 1. Petr 1,4 und
Kol 1,5.12. Dennoch reichen Gundrys Argumente für eine
'Adaptation' von Lk 12,33 in 1. Petr 1,4 nicht aus.
Es fehlen hier gegenüber Lk 12,33 die plastischen
Bilder vom 'Dieb' und von der 'Motte'. Auch sind
'Erbe' und 'Schatz' - gegen Gundry - nicht nur
Übersetzungsvariationen. Deshalb wird man Best darin
zustimmen müssen, daß 1. Petr 1,4 nicht unbedingt eine
Parallele zu Lk 12,33 darstellt, und es offen lassen,
ob hinter der Petrusbriefstelle ein Jesuslogion
steht./13/

2. Zu *1. Petr 1,8* urteilte Gundry: '*1 Pet. i.8 recalls
John XX.29*'. Best sieht nur eine gemeinsame 'idea' -
wie auch in 2. Kor 5,6-8 - und lehnt es ab, in 1. Petr
1,8 Reminiszenzen an den historischen Jesus oder an
Johannes zu entdecken. Das 'nicht sehen und doch
glauben' taucht aber an beiden Stellen unter Verwendung
derselben griechischen Worte auf. Ja, in 1. Petr 1,8
wird dieselbe Formel zweimal gebraucht, wobei in
geradezu johanneischer Redeweise 'glauben' durch
'lieben' ersetzt wird (vgl. dazu Joh 3,18f). Dabei
geht es beide Male um den Bezug zum auferstandenen
Jesus. Schließlich spiegelt sich die Seligpreisung aus
Joh 20,29 von ferne in der 'Freude' von 1. Petr 1,8.
Deshalb behält Gundry an diesem Punkt Recht./14/ In
dieselbe Richtung gehen Feuillet und Tenney./15/ Aber
vielleicht muß man ein Stück weiter ausholen. Es kann
ja nicht übersehen werden, daß die wichtigen Begriffe

'lieben' und 'Freude' auch im Kontext von Joh 15,9ff.
eng verbunden auftauchen. Und zwar so, daß sie sich
auf den Jesus beziehen, den die Jünger *nach* der
Auferstehung haben werden! Wir müssen also damit
rechnen, daß 1. Petr 1,8 nicht nur Joh 20,29 widerspie-
gelt, sondern auch Joh 15,11ff. Jedenfalls kann an der
Verbindung zur johanneischen Tradition kaum ein Zweifel
bestehen.

3. Kontrovers ist ferner die Beziehung von *1. Petr 1,10-12*
zu Lk 24,25-27. Nennen wir noch einmal das beiden
Stellen Gemeinsame: a) die Voraussage der Propheten,
b) das Thema 'Christus', c) die Begriffe 'leiden/
Leiden' und 'Herrlichkeit' (doxa allerdings in 1. Petr
1,11 im Plural), d) die Abfolge von Leiden und
Herrlichkeit, e) die Bezeichung 'tauta' für das
Christusleiden. Angesichts dieser relativ zahlreichen
Parallelen auf engem Raum mutet es künstlich an, wenn
Best meint, beide Stellen 'könnten' ganz unabhängig
voneinander entstanden sein. Die näherliegendere
Erklärung ist doch die, daß beide auf dasselbe Logion
(des auferstandenen Jesus) zurückgehen./16/ Auch
Goppelt sieht in seinem großen Petrusbrief-Kommentar
die Parallelität zwischen 1. Petr 1,10 und Lk 24,25
'Besonders ausgeprägt'./17/

     Nun genügt zwar für die Erklärung von 1. Petr
1,11 die Zusammenschau mit Lk 24,25ff., nicht jedoch
für die Erklärung von 1. Petr 1,10 und 1,12. Hier
muß der Blick auf Lk 10,24 bzw. Mt 13,17 und Joh 8,56
geweitet werden./18/ Nach diesen Jesuslogien sehnten
sich die Propheten und Gerechten danach, die
messianische Zeit zu 'sehen'. Von 'Propheten' ist in
Mt 13,17; Lk 10,24 und in 1. Petr 1,10 die Rede, von
'Gerechten' spricht Mt 13,17, und einen 'Gerechten' in
der konkreten Gestalt Abrahams nennt Joh 8,56. Von
'sehen' reden Mt 13,17; Lk 10,24 und Joh 8,56, während
dafür in 1. Petr 1,12 parakypsai steht. In Mt 13,17;
Lk 10,24 wird die messianische Zeit durch das Wirken
Jesu (das, was die Jünger 'sehen und hören', vgl. Mt
11,4!) bezeichnet, in Joh 8,56 durch den 'Tag' Jesu,
in 1. Petr 1,10ff. durch die Gnade und Verkündigung
im 'Jetzt'. Ja, in Mt 13,17 und in 1. Petr 1,12
finden wir in genau demselben Zusammenhang das Verb
epithymein. So scheint eine Parallelität von 1. Petr

1,10-12 nicht nur zu Lk 24,25ff., sondern auch zu Mt
13,17 par und Joh 8,56 gegeben. Der offensichtliche
Zusammenhang erklärt sich am besten, wenn man ein oder
evtl. mehrere verwandte Jesuslogien als die Quelle
betrachtet, aus der sowohl die Synoptiker als auch
Johannes und der 1. Petrusbrief schöpfen.

4. Die Parallelität vol *1. Petr 1,3.23; 2,2* und Joh 3,3ff.
hält Gundry für außerordentlich eng. Ähnlich Feuillet,
Goppelt und Selwyn./19/ Best jedoch sieht beide
Stellen unabhängig voneinander. Er möchte 1. Petr 1,
3.23 lieber mit der 'religious atmosphere of Asia
Minor' verbinden./20/ Ist jedoch die allgemeine
'Atmosphäre in Kleinasien' eine naheliegendere
Parallele als die Verbindung zu einem oder mehreren
Jesuslogien, die das Joh Ev bewahrt hat? Es ist ja
schon zweifelhaft, ob wir zur Zeit des 1. Petrusbriefes
die Wiedergeburtsvorstellung bereits als allgemeines
Gedankengut Kleinasiens voraussetzen dürfen./21/
Hingegen weist Goppelt - ausgehend von einer
nachpetrinischen Datierung zwischen 65 und 80 n. Chr.!
- nach, daß 'die Vorstellung der Wiedergeburt ... dem
hell. Christentum der nachpaulinischen Zeit in seiner
ganzen Breite geläufig' war./22/ Hieraus ergibt sich,
daß - wenn wir 1. Petr 1,3.23 nicht isoliert behandeln
wollen - Zusammenhänge zuerst im innerchristlichen bzw.
innerneutestamentlichen Raum untersucht werden müssen.
Auch Best gibt zu: in Joh 3,3ff. und 1. Petr 1,3.23;
2,2 'the conception is the same'./23/ Geringe
Unterschiede der Formulierung muß man geradezu
erwarten. Sie werden weit aufgewogen durch die Fülle
von Stichworten und Motiven, die der Kontext der
Petrusbriefstellen mit dem Joh Ev teilt. So ist die
nächstliegende Folgerung aus diesem Tatbestand, daß
Aussagen Jesu die gemeinsame Quelle für Joh 3,3ff. und
1. Petr 1,3.23; 2,2 bilden. Darüber hinaus ist es
interessant, daß sowohl Petrus als auch Johannes
dieselben Aussagen Jesu aufgreifen./24/

5. *1. Petr 1,13*: 'begürtet die Lenden eures Gemütes'
benutzt zunächst eine allgemeine Metapher und muß
nicht auf Lk 12,35 zurückgehen (cf. Prov 31,17; Jes
11,5; Jer 1,17). Darin ist Best zuzustimmen./25/
Allerdings hat das Begürten der Lenden in beiden
Stellen einen spezifischen eschatologischen Bezug, auf

ein und denselben Messias, der zur endgültigen
Offenbarung seiner Herrschaft erscheint, nämlich Jesus
Christus. Deshalb kann Goppelt sagen: 'Die nächste
sachliche Entsprechung zu 1. Petr 1,13 ist Lk 12,35.'
/26/ Daß 1. Petr 1,13 auf das Herrnwort in Lk 12,35
zurückgeht, läßt sich also vermuten./27/

6. Gundry glaubt, daß *1. Petr 1,22* und *4,8* auf Joh 13,34f.;
   15,12 zurückgehen. Best wendet ein, daß die Anweisung
   'liebet einander' auch in vielen paulinischen Stellen
   auftaucht. Besser als eine Herleitung von Joh 13,34f.;
   15,12 sei die Annahme, daß die frühe Kirche das Gebot
   'Liebe deinen Nächsten' zu dem Gebot 'Liebet einander'
   abgewandelt habe und eben Paulus, Petrus und Johannes
   gemeinsam Anteil an dieser frühchristlichen Tradition
   besäßen. Aber ist diese Annahme einfacher und
   näherliegender? Logisch kann man es sich leichter
   vorstellen, daß ein Wort Jesu von der Urgemeinde
   tradiert wurde und auf diese Weise sowohl zu Paulus als
   auch in den 1. Petr gelangte. Hinzu kommt eine weitere
   Überlegung. Die Wendung 'im Gehorsam der Wahrheit'
   (1. Petr 1,22) erinnert uns an das 'Gebot' des
   Christus, der 'die Wahrheit' ist (Joh 13,34; 14,6) und
   dem seine 'Jünger' folgen sollen (Joh 13,35); das
   anhypokritos erinnert uns an das Maß der Liebe, das
   Jesus nach Joh 13,1ff.,34; 15,12f. selbst gesetzt und
   verwirklicht hat; das 'reinigen' (hagnizein) von 1.
   Petr 1,22 erinnert uns an das 'heiligen' (hagiazein)
   von Joh 17,17.19. Hier haben wir tatsächlich auf
   engstem Raum mehrere Sachparallelen, ja sogar
   Wortparallelen zum Joh Ev vor uns, insbesondere zu Joh
   13. Die Meinung, daß das Jesuswort, das uns in Joh 13,
   34f.; 15,12 begegnet, die Wurzel für 1. Petr 1,22
   bildet, ist also gut begründet./28/

7. Zur Diskussion steht ferner *1. Petr 2,4ff.* Gundry geht
   davon aus, daß die Metapher vom 'Stein' = Jesus aus Mk
   12,10 parr stammt. Auch an dieser Stelle verweist Best
   auf die Tatsache, daß Ps 118 und damit die Rede vom
   messianischen 'Stein' im NT öfters begegnet (cf. Mt
   12,9; 23,39; Mk 11,9; Lk 13,35; 19,38; Joh 10,9; 12,13;
   Apg 4,11; Röm 8,31; 2. Kor 6,9; Hebr 13,6). Er
   bezweifelt, ob überhaupt eine Jesuswort den
   Ausgangspunkt bilde. 'Mark XII.10 reads much more like
   a comment of the early church.'/29/ Goppelt ist

ähnlicher Meinung: Mk 12,10 stamme 'schwerlich' von
Jesus. Über die aramäisch sprechende Gemeinde komme
man nicht zurück./30/ Anders J. Jeremias. Er führt Mk
12,10/Lk 20,18 auf 'Jesus selbst' zurück./31/ Aus
Raumgründen können wir hier nicht in die Erörterung der
verschiedenen Bedeutungen des 'Steines' sowie der
diesbezüglichen Aussagen des AT in Ps 118,22f.;
Jes 8,14; 28,16; Dan 2,31ff. eintreten. Wir lassen
auch die Frage aus dem Spiel, ob nicht die Bezeichnung
Petri als des 'Felsen' für 1. Petr 2,4ff. eine Rolle
spielt./32/ Den zweifellos kann die Paränese - wie es
ja tatsächlich in 1. Petr 2,4ff. geschieht - bei einem
eindrücklichen Bild verschiedene Assoziationen
anklingen lassen. Entscheidend ist vielmehr zunächst
die Frage, ob Jesus als der autoritative Lehrer der
Urgemeinde von sich selbst als dem 'Stein' gesprochen
hat. Und dies ist nach dem übereinstimmenden Zeugnis
des Matthäus, Markus und Lukas der Fall (Mk 12,10f.
parr). Es gibt keine durchschlagenden Argumente gegen
diese Behauptung der Evangelisten./33/ Dann aber ist
es auch wahrscheinlich, daß die weitgefächerte Rede vom
'Stein' = Christus im NT auf Jesus zurückzuführen ist,
und 1. Petr 2,4ff. in dieser von Jesus herkommenden
Tradition steht. 1. Petr 2,4ff. teilt mit dem
Jesuslogion von Mk 12,10ff. parr a) die Deutung des
'Steins' auf Jesus Christus, b) die Aussage seiner
Verwerfung durch Menschen, c) die Erwählung Jesu zum
'Eckstein', d) die Benutzung von Ps 118,22f./34/

8. Läßt sich *1. Petr 2,13-17* auf Mt 17,25ff. zurückführen?
Best erhebt dagegen einen 4-fachen Einwand: a) 1. Petr
2,13ff. redet von der 'Freiheit' des Christen, Mt
17,25ff. von der Freiheit der Kinder des Königs;
b) 1. Petr 2,13ff. spricht allgemein vom Verhältnis zum
Staat, Mt 17,25ff. speziell von der Steuerpflicht;
c) 1. Petr 2,13ff. stammt von einer Haustafel und nicht
aus der Jesustradition; d) Mt 17,25ff. ist in seiner
ursprünglichen Form nicht mehr zu eruieren. Ergebnis:
'there is little reason to detect any dependence of
I Peter on Matthew here'./35/ Demgegenüber ist zu
sagen: c) und d) wäre erst noch zu beweisen; a) stellt
sachlich keinen Unterschied dar./36/ Schwerer wiegt
das Bedenken unter b). Denn im Grunde greift 1. Petr
2,13-17 thematisch weit über Mt 17,24ff. hinaus. Es
gibt außerdem einen sachlichen Unterschied beider

Passagen, den Best freilich nicht geltend machte:
Mt 17,24ff. hat es mit dem Verhältnis Jesu zum Tempel
zu tun, 1. Petr 2,13ff. jedoch mit dem Verhältnis des
Jüngers zum heidnischen Staat. Deshalb ist es
angemessener, mit Goppelt den 'Ansatz' der Ausführungen
des 1. Petr 'in Jesu Wort zur Kaisersteuer, Mk 12,14-17
parr' zu suchen./37/ Wir notieren kurz die Parallelen:
a) Auch in Mt 22,15ff. geht es um das Verhältnis zum
heidnischen Staat; b) auch Mt 22,15ff. endet mit einer
generellen Anweisung; c) auch in Mt 22,15ff. wird eine
(begrenzte) Unterordnung unter diesen Staat vollzogen;
d) auch in Mt 22,15ff. wird unterschieden zwischen dem,
was Gott zukommt, und dem, was dem menschlichen
Herrscher zukommt. Das Verhältnis von 1. Petr 2,13ff.
zu Röm 13,1ff.; 1. Tim 2,1ff. und Tit 3,1ff. erklärt
sich außerdem am besten, wenn man alle diese ntlichen
Aussagen auf die Grundsatzentscheidung Jesu in
Mt 22,15ff. parr zurückführt. Bei dieser Erklärung
bleibt auch Raum für die - u.E. begründete - Vermutung,
daß Mt 17,25-27 eine der Wurzeln für die Aussage von
1. Petr 2,16 bildet. Nur ist eben Mt 17,25ff. zu
schmal, um das Ganze von 1. Petr 2,13-17 zu tragen./38/

9. Knüpft *1. Petr 3,9* an das Jesuslogion von Lk 6,27f. an?
   Gundry rechnet mit dieser Möglichkeit./39/ Best
   schließt sie nicht aus. Jedoch, 1. Petr 3,9 'probably
   depends on common catechetical tradition rather than
   directly on any saying of Jesus'./40/ Wieder zugegeben,
   daß eine gemein-christliche katechetische Tradition
   bestand - ist es dann nicht naheliegend, ihre
   gemeinsame Herkunft von verba Christi anzunehmen?
   Jedenfalls zeigen Mt 5,39ff. und Lk 6,27, welch tiefen
   Eindruck Jesu Aufruf zur Feindesliebe hinterließ.
   Zwar ist es zweifelhaft, ob der Verfasser des 1. Petr
   das Lk Ev oder das Mt Ev oder beide benutzt hat (das
   Stichwort eulogein ist sowohl in Lk 6,28 als auch in
   1. Petr 3,9 zu finden). Die Wortwahl erlaubt uns keine
   Entscheidung. Aber daß hier Jesustradition verarbeitet
   wurde, und dies in einer Form, die Lk 6,28 nahesteht,
   kann man doch annehmen./41/

10. In *1. Petr. 4,7f.* sieht Best ebenso wie Goppelt nur
    eine altkirchliche Tradition verarbeitet./42/ Gundry
    jedoch will Lk 21,31ff. und Mk 14,38 parr als Quelle
    ansehen, und 1. Petr 4,7f. damit von Herrnworten

ableiten./43/   Zunächst fallen die Parallelen zu
Matthäus auf. Dieser hat ἤγγικεν im Blick auf das neue
Zeitalter stark betont (3,2; 4,17; 10,7) und gibt
außerdem zum 'Ende aller Dinge' (1. Petr 4,7) eine
sachliche und wörtliche Entsprechung in der synteleia
tou aiōnos (Mt 13,39.40.49; 24,3; 28,20).   Er bietet in
dem 'Wachet und betet' (Mt 26,41), wie schon Gundry
bemerkte, eine weitere Parallele zu 1. Petr 4,7f.   Aber
mehr noch: In Mt 24,42ff. begegnet eine ganze Reihe von
sachlichen Entsprechungen zu 1. Petr 4,7f.   Cf. das
'wachet' (V. 42); die Ausrichtung auf den kommenden
Christus (vgl. 1. Petr 4,5!); das *klug* (V. 45); die
Unmäßigkeit und Unnüchternheit (V. 49).   Nur in
letzterer Beziehung steht Lukas (in 21,31ff.) etwas
näher bei 1. Petr 4,7.   Aufgrund dieser Beobachtungen
möchten wir annehmen, daß 1. Petr 4,7f. in Anknüpfung
an Herrnworte gebildet wurde, die uns heute vor allem
im Mt Ev (3,2; 4,17; 10,7; 13,49ff.; 24,3.42ff.; 26,41;
28,20) und teilweise auch im Lk Ev (21,31ff.) begegnen.
/44/

11. Gundry will auch *1. Petr 4,19* auf ein Herrnwort
    zurückführen, nämlich auf das Kreuzeswort von Lk 23,46.
    /45/   Obwohl die Gegengründe von Best/46/ nicht
    durchschlagen, sind die Argumente für eine
    Abhängigkeit von Lk 23,46 nicht stark genug, um mehr
    als eine vage Vermutung zu stützen.   'Leiden nach
    Gottes Willen' erinnert zwar an Mt 5,10f., das
    'anbefehlen ihrer Seelen' an Lk 23,46.   Aber beides
    kann auch direkt aus dem AT bzw. aus der Märtyrer-
    tradition (cf. 2. Makk 1,24; 7,1ff.) entnommen sein.
    /47/

12. Die Verse *1. Petr 5,3-5* gehen nach Gundry auf
    Lk 22,25-30; Mk 10,42-45 parr und Joh 13,4f. zurück.
    /48/   Best lehnt dies nicht ohne weiteres ab, meint
    aber: 'it is more probable that the common use of
    katakyrieuein is a mere matter of chance', und will
    lieber auf 'primitive tradition' als auf logia Jesu
    zurückgreifen./49/   Best stützt sich hier auf zwei
    Gegenargumente: a) katakyrieuein sei nicht typisch
    genug, um eine Verbindung zu Mk 10,45 parr herzustellen;
    Gundry entgegnet, daß das Wort nur in 1. Petr 5,3 und
    Mk 10,45/Mt 20,25 auf das Verhältnis der Führer des
    Volkes Gottes zu diesem Volk Gottes bezogen sei;

b) man müsse fragen, warum 1. Petr 5,3ff. nicht auch
Gebrauch von Mk 10,43-45a mache; Gundry weist
demgegenüber darauf hin, daß man von Petrus kein
übermäßig langes Zitat erwarten könne./50/

Betrachtet man 1. Petr 5,3-5 genauer, dann stellt
man wieder fest, daß eine Herleitung von einem
einzigen Logion bzw. von einer einzigen, präzisen
Evangelienstelle nicht möglich ist. Immer wieder
stießen wir auf die Tatsache, daß eine Art Kollektion
oder Konflation von Jesusworten hinter der
Petrusparänese steckt. Die Paränese versucht öfters,
möglichst viele Assoziationen mit Jesusworten
herzustellen. Dabei müssen wir voraussetzen, daß der
Katechumene mit diesen Logia Kyriou bekannt gemacht
wurde und deshalb solche Assoziationen sinnvoll sind.

Zuerst fällt die johanneische Prägung der V. 2ff.
auf. Das 'weiden' der 'Herde Gottes' ist schwerlich
ohne Beziehung zu Joh 21,15ff. Die Ältesten als
Hirten unter dem 'Erzhirten' Jesus erinnern außerdem an
Joh 10, die Ermahnung, 'Vorbilder der Herde zu werden',
an Joh 13,12-17. Und gerade auf diesen selben Kontext
von Joh 13 stößt uns das Hapaxlegomenon enkombōsasthe
in 1. Petr 5,5. Wenn es hier heißt: 'Bindet euch die
Demut um', so ist es außerordentlich naheliegend, an
die Tat Jesu in Joh 13,4f. zu denken. Mit Recht sagt
W. Grundmann, der diese Zusammenhänge dargestellt hat,
daß hier 'wie an anderen Stellen des 1. Pt das Bild des
Herrn hinter den Mahnungen erkennbar wird ... Es macht
sich also die joh - Petrustradition bemerkbar'./51/

Zweitens ist offensichtlich ein Bezug zu
Mt 20,20-28/Mk 10,35-45 gegeben: a) in dem
katakyrieuein, das nur noch Apg 19,16 auftaucht; b) in
dem Verweis auf die kommende Herrlichkeit (1. Petr
5,1.4 und Mt 20,20ff./Mk 10,35ff.); c) in der
Vorbildfunktion der leitenden Persönlichkeit (1. Petr
5,3 und Mt 20,28/Mk 10,45)./52/

Schließlich könnte man erwägen, ob nicht auch eine
Beziehung zu den Jesusworten in Mt 18,1-5 gegeben ist.
Auch dort geht es um die Ordnung der Verhältnisse
innerhalb der Jüngerschaft; um Demut; um Unterordnung;

um die eschatologische Belohnung./53/

Es erscheint gerade angesichts der Verwandtschaft
von 1. Petr 5,1-5 mit Apg 20,17ff.; 1. Tim 3,1-13;
Tit 1,5-9 als sehr wahrscheinlich, daß Petrus in diesem
Abschnitt von den Worten und dem Bild des Herrn
ausgeht, die Joh 13,4ff.; 21,15ff. einerseits und
Mt 20,20ff. parr (Lukas hier am wenigsten) andrerseits
- vielleicht auch Mt 18,1-5 parr - überliefern./54/

13. Für Gundry sind die eschatologischen Diskurse,
Lk 22,31f. und Mk 14,38 par, die Quellen, aus denen
Petrus in *1. Petr 5,8f.* schöpft./55/ Feuillet,
Schelkle, Brown, Selwyn, Goppelt und Spicq suchen
ebenfalls Parallelen bzw. Ausgangsorte in den
Evangelien (Feuillet in Joh 8,44; Schelkle in
Mt 5,25/26,41; Brown in Mt 5,39/Lk 12,11; Selwyn in
Lk 21,36; Mk 13,13; Mt 7,24-27; Goppelt in den
Parusiegleichnissen, der Gethsemaneperikope,
Mt 12,25ff. par und Lk 22,31-36; Spicq in Lk 22,31f.
und Joh 15,18f.; 16,8.33)./56/ Best hingegen erklärt
bezüglich Mk 14,38 par: 'There is ... no direct link
here between 1 Peter and Mark or 1 Peter and a logion
of Jesus', und bezüglich Lk 22,31f., 'that I Peter did
not know this logion'. 1. Thes 5,6.8 sei eher als
Quelle für 1 Petr 5,8f. denkbar./57/ Demgegenüber
stellt Gundry die Gegenfrage: 'may not both Paul and
Peter draw their exhortations from a common source, a
dominical saying...?'/58/ Wenn wir Jesuswort(e) haben,
die die Entstehung sowohl von 1. Petr 5,8f. als auch von
1. Thes 5,6.8 oder anderer Stellen in der apostolischen
Literatur erklären können, dann ist es in der Tat die
nächstliegende Lösung, die Herkunft von solchen
Herrnworten anzunehmen.

'Seid nüchtern, wachet!' (1. Petr 5,8a) hat seine
nächste Parallele in den Parusiegleichnissen bzw. der
eschatologischen Mahnung zur Wachsamkeit. Die
Gethsemaneperikope mag ebenfalls im Hintergrund stehen.
Jedoch sitzt das 'Wachet und betet!' von Mt 26,41 parr
in der Evangelienüberlieferung so fest, daß kaum
einzusehen wäre, weshalb der 1. Petr in 'Seid nüchtern,
wachet!' hätte ändern sollen - und dies umso weniger,
als auch die Gethsemaneworte sehr sinnvoll in den
Kontext gepaßt hätten. Mustert man die Evangelien

genauer, dann scheidet Mk 13,33ff. bald aus. Denn nur
in Mt 24,42ff. und Lk 21,34-36 sind beide Elemente
vorhanden: das Wachen und das Nüchternsein. Ja,
vielleicht muß man sogar Mt 24,42ff. favorisieren.
Denn nur hier steht das grēgoreite von 1. Petr 5,8,
während Lk stattdessen agrypneite hat. Erst wenn wir
Lk 12,35ff. heranziehen, rückt auch Lukas wieder gleich
nahe an 1. Petr 5,8 heran. Übrigens haben wir schon
unter 10. in Mt 24,42ff. die nächste Parallele zu dem
mit 5,8 verwandten 1. Petr 4,7f. beobachtet./59/

Für 1. Petr 5,8b f. aber scheint tatsächlich
Lk 22,31f. die nächstliegende Parallele und ein
Ursprungsort zu sein: der diabolos entspricht dem
Satanas; dem zētein entspricht das exētēsato; es geht
beide Male um die pistis; beide Male attackiert der
Böse die Jünger Jesu. Man könnte diesem von Gundry/60/
genannten Gesichtspunkt einen weiteren hinzufügen: der
'brüllende Löwe' von 1. Petr 5,8b entstammt einem der
Leidenspsalmen Jesu (Ps 22,14) und gehört daher
ebenfalls zum Kontext von Lk 22,31f. als einem
Passionsereignis.

Schwierig bleibt es jedoch, einzelne Stichworte
(antidikos) oder Motive (der Teufel als eschatologische
Macht) auf bestimmte Stellen der Evangelien zurückzuführen. Deshalb sollte man Mt 5,25.39; 7,24ff.;
12,25ff.; Mk 13,13; Lk 12,11 oder Joh 8,44 nicht
unbedingt als Parallelen oder gar als Quellen
ansprechen. So reizvoll es anmutet, das stereoi von
1. Petr 5,9 mit Lk 22,32: sterizein zu verbinden,
bleibt man besser auch an diesem Punkt vorsichtig./61/

Wir haben unseren - allerdings nicht erschöpfenden! - Durchgang
durch Stellen, die zwischen Gundry und Best umstritten sind,
beendet, und wenden uns anderen Stellen der Paränese des
1. Petr zu.

II. Weitere Stellen in der petrinischen Paränese

Wieder verdeutlichen wir uns, daß a) nicht jeder Anklang
oder jede Ähnlichkeit der Begriffe und Vorstellungen einen
Traditionszusammenhang begründet,/62/ und b) an einer Stelle
mehrere Traditionen bzw. Herrnworte verarbeitet sein können.

1. In *1. Petr 1,7* tritt mit der Apokalypsis Jesu Christi
   ein gemeinchristliches Motiv auf. Der Kontext erinnert
   jedoch an Lk 17,26ff. Auch dort wird das apokalyptes-
   thai Jesu mit dem pyr verbunden (17,29f.); auch dort
   geht es um die Rettung der psychē (cf. Lk 17,33 mit
   1. Petr 1,9); auch dort wird die versuchliche Zeit vor
   der Offenbarung Jesu Christi angesprochen (cf.
   Lk 17,26ff. mit 1. Petr 1,6). Da jedoch das "Feuer" in
   einen anderen Bedeutungszusammenhang eingeordnet ist
   und auch die peirasmoi verschieden sind, läßt sich
   höchstens vermuten, daß Jesusworte in einer Zusammen-
   stellung, wie sie Lk 17,26ff. entspricht, im
   Hintergrund von 1. Petr 1,6-9 stehen. Mehr als eine
   Möglichkeit läßt sich nicht behaupten.

2. G. Dautzenberg sah *1. Petr 1,9* in einem inneren Zusammenhang mit Mk 8,36f. und Lk 21,19./63/ W. Foerster
   notierte zu sōtēria psychōn: 'Dieser Ausdruck kann
   Bekanntschaft mit Mk 8,35 par ... voraussetzen'./64/
   Halten wir die Übereinstimmungen fest: a) dem
   petrinischen komizein entspricht sachlich das
   kerdainein in Mt 16,26/Mk 8,36/Lk 9,25; b) dem 'Ziel
   des Glaubens' in 1. Petr 1,9 entspricht sachlich der
   Blick auf das Ziel der Nachfolge in Mt 16,24ff. par;
   c) dem sōtēria entspricht das sōsai in Mt 16,25 parr;
   d) dem psychōn entspricht das mehrfache psychē in
   Mt 16,25f. parr. Das sind auf engem Raum überraschend
   viele Parallelen in Aufbau und Wortwahl. Von da her
   besteht eine gewisse Wahrscheinlichkeit, daß die
   Jesusworte in Mt 16,24ff. parr wenigstens eine der
   traditionsgeschichtlichen Quellen von 1. Petr 1,9
   bilden.

3. Ernstlich zu erwägen ist, ob nicht *1. Petr 1,15* auf das
   Jesuswort in Mt 5,48 parr zurückzuführen ist. Im
   Grundgedanken: wie Gott als Vater, so sollen auch die
   Jünger als seine Kinder handeln und sein, entsprechen
   sich jedenfalls beide Stellen. Der Kontext deutet
   ebenfalls in diese Richtung: cf. die Begriffe 'Kinder'
   und 'Vater' in 1. Petr 1,14.17 mit 'eurem Vater im
   Himmel' in Mt 5,48./65/ Eine weitere Unterstützung
   erfährt diese Überlegung durch die Tatsache, daß hinter
   Mt 5,48 Lev 19,2 steht, und daß dieselbe atliche
   Bezugsstelle (Lev 19,2) in 1. Petr 1,16 ausdrücklich
   und begründend zitiert wird./66/ Ferner läßt sich

zugunsten dieser Überlegung anführen, daß die Wendung
'als Vater anrufen' ebenfalls in die Bergpredigt Jesu
führt, nämlich zum Vaterunser (Mt 6,9). Schließlich
bildet eine weitere Stelle aus der Bergpredigt, nämlich
Mt 5,16, noch einmal eine sachliche Parallele zu. 1.
Petr 1,14-17. So ergibt sich eine begründete Vermutung
- wenn auch keine letzte Gewißheit -, daß 1. Petr
1,14-17 u.a. auf die Bergpredigt Jesu zurückgeht, und
insbesondere 1. Petr 1,15 auch von dem Jesuslogion in
Mt 5,48 ausgeht./67/ Die Abwandlung von 'vollkommen'
(Mt 5,48) zu 'heilig' (1. Petr 1,15) erklärt sich leicht
daraus, daß 1. Petr 1,15 ja Lev. 19,2 ausdrücklich
zitiert.

4. Läßt sich *1. Petr 1,23* auf die Saatgleichnisse Jesu
   zurückführen? 1. Petr 1,23 spricht von der Wiedergeburt
   'aus unvergänglichem Samen, (nämlich) durch das
   lebendige und bleibende Wort Gottes'. In Lk 8,11 sagt
   Jesus: 'Der Same ist das Wort Gottes'. Sachlich
   besagen Mt 13,18ff./Mk 4,13ff. dasselbe. Für eine
   Ableitung von 1. Petr 1,23 aus Mt 13,18ff. parr
   sprechen folgende Gründe: a) der Vergleich des Wortes
   Gottes mit dem Samen, b) der Vergleich der Hörer mit
   Pflanzen - ein Vergleich, der durch das Jesajazitat
   (Jes 40,6-8) in 1. Petr 1,24 noch verstärkt wird; c) die
   sprachlichen Parallelen: speirein/sporos/spora und logos
   tēs basileias (Mt 13,19)/logos (tou) theou (Lk 8,11;
   1. Petr 1,23); d) die Seltenheit des Vergleichs des
   Wortes Gottes mit dem Samen im Judentum, trotz der
   atlichen Wurzel in Jes 55,10f.; Jer 4,3;/68/ e) die
   Bedeutung des Bleibens sowohl in Mt 13,18ff. par
   (besonders Lk 8,15) als auch in 1. Petr 1,23 (hier
   allerdings auf das Wort bezogen). An diesem Punkt
   könnte man auch einen Einfluß von Mt 24,35 erwägen.
   /69/ Insgesamt ergibt sich also eine Wahrscheinlichkeit, daß 1 Petr 1,23 auf Mt 13,18ff. parr, vielleicht
   speziell auf Lk 8,11-15, zurückgeht, oder genauer
   formuliert: auf die dort aufbewahrten Jesuslogien.

5. 'Daß der Herr gütig ist', drückt *1. Petr 2,3* durch ein
   Zitat von Ps 34(33),9 aus. Möglicherweise stehen auch
   hier jesuanische Aussagen über die Güte Gottes im
   Hintergrund. Vor allem die Bergpredigt, speziell in
   der lukanischen Form, weist eine Nähe zu 1. Petr 2,3

auf (cf. Lk 6,35 und Mt 5,45ff.; aber auch Mt 20,1ff.).
Die Übertragung auf Jesus könnte durch das Jesuswort
von Mt 11,30 erleichtert worden sein. Wenn Gundry und
Best recht haben mit ihrer Annahme, daß die Beziehung
zwischen dem 1. Petr und Lk 6,22ff. besonders eng ist,
/70/ wäre ein Einfluß von Lk 6,35 auf 1. Petr 2,3 noch
leichter vorstellbar. Aber hier kommen wir über eine
gewisse Möglichkeit nicht hinaus.

6. Selwyn hat *1. Petr 2,9* mit Mt 5,14.16; Lk 16,8 und
11,35f. in Zusammenhang gebracht./71/ Auch Brown
dachte an Mt 5,16./72/ Solche Zusammenhänge sind
erwägenswert, solange man mit Goppelt die Versetzung
aus der Finsternis ins Licht als 'Berufung zum Glauben'
versteht./73/ Da aber der Kontext vorher vom Herrn und
Christus spricht, läßt sich das 'Licht' in 1. Petr 2,9
auch als die Sphäre Gottes bzw. Christi verstehen. Die
'Nächste Entsprechung'/74/ ist ja Apg 26,18, und dort
ist das 'Licht' nicht mit dem Glauben, sondern mit Gott
in Parallele gesetzt. Versteht man also das 'Licht'
von 1. Petr 2,9 analog zu Apg 26,18 und Kol 1,13 als
den Herrschaftsbereich Jesu als des Messias Gottes,
dann ergibt sich ein sachlicher Zusammenhang mit
denjenigen Jesuslogien und Jesusdeutungen der
Evangelien, die Jesus als das 'Licht' bezeichnen. Vor
allem Mt 4,14ff. und Joh 8,12 kommen hier in Frage.
Sie sind wie 1. Petr 2,9 von dem Gegensatz skotos/
skotia und phōs geprägt (cf. als atlichen Hintergrund
Jes 8,23f.; 42,6; 49,6; 60,1ff.). Sie sind auch -
wieder wie 1. Petr 2,9 - bestimmt von dem Gedanken,
daß durch das 'Licht' Jesus das ntliche Gottes - 'Volk'
erlöst und gesammelt wird (cf. den Begriff laos in
Mt 4,16 und 1. Petr 2,9; der kosmos in Joh 8,12
entspricht ihm sachlich). Die Beifügung 'wunderbar'
(thaumastos) in 1. Petr 2,9 verstärkt diesen Bezug.
Denn 'thaumastos' wird in Mt 21,33/Mk 12,11 Christus
als der 'Stein' genannt, und gerade von diesem
Christus=Stein war ja im Kontext von 1. Petr 2,9 die
Rede./75/ So ergibt sich wiederum eine Wahrscheinlichkeit, daß 1. Petr 2,9 von der Jesustradition in
Mt 4,14ff. und Joh 8,12 zumindest mit-geprägt ist.

7. In *1 Petr 2,19ff.*geht es um das 'Verfolgungsleiden' der
Christen. Schon deshalb sollte man nicht mit Brown
/76/ die Verbindung mit den von der Feindesliebe

handelnden Stellen (z.B. Lk 6,28.33) suchen. Vielmehr
verschlingen sich in 1. Petr 2,19ff. zwei Grundmotive,
die wir aus der Jesusverkündigung der Evangelien kennen:
a) das Leiden um des Guten willen, und b) das Leiden
als Teil der Jesusnachfolge. Das erste Grundmotiv
führt uns zur Bergpredigt, und zwar vor allem zu
Mt 5,10f. Man beachte die Entsprechungen: a) von charis
(1. Petr 2,19f.) und makarios (Mt 5,10f.); b) von lypē/
paschein/kolaphizein (1. Petr 2,19f.) und 'verfolgen'/
'schmähen'/'Übles reden' (Mt 5,10f.); c) von
agathopoiein und adikōs (1. Petr 2,19f.) und
diakaiosynē (Mt 5,10). Das zweite Grundmotiv führt uns
zu Mt 16,24 parr. Hier entsprechen sich: a) die Spuren
Jesu bzw. das epakolouthein (1. Petr 2,21) und das
akolouthein (Mk 8,34); b) die Verbindung von 'leiden'
und Christusnachfolge; c) die Ähnlichkeit des
Christusweges und der Jüngernachfolge, konkret
ausgedrückt im hypogrammos bzw. in 'seinen Fußspuren'
(1. Petr 2,21) und im Kreuz (Mk 8,34 parr); d) das
'berufen' (1. Petr 2,21) und der Ruf in die Nachfolge
(Mk 8,34 parr). Interessant ist, daß (ep) akolouthein
außerhalb der Evangelien nur in Apk 14,4 und 1. Petr
2,21 auftaucht./77/ Auch dies weist auf eine
Herleitung von 1. Petr 2,21 aus der Jesustradition hin.
Im Blick auf paschein in 1. Petr 2,21 schrieb Goppelt:
'diese ganze terminologische Tradition geht sehr
wahrscheinlich auf die palästinische Kirche,
möglicherweise auf Jesus selbst zurück'./78/
Berücksichtigt man, daß das kolaphizomenoi in 1. Petr
2,20 evtl. aus der Passionserzählung (Mt 26,67 parr!)
stammt, dann läßt sich wiederum eine Wahrscheinlichkeit
formulieren, wonach in 1. Petr 2,19-21 die Herrnworte
von Mt 5,10f. und 16,24 parr verarbeitet wurden./79/

8. Hängt das Stichwort prays in *1. Petr 3,4* ebenfalls mit
der Jesustradition zusammen? Best meinte im Gegensatz
zu Spicq: 'there is no need to see direct dependence on
Matt V.5'./80/ Es gibt aber erhebliche Gründe, 1. Petr
3,4 und Mt 5,5 in einem engeren Zusammenhang zu sehen:
a) Im ganzen NT findet sich der Begriff prays außer in
1. Petr 3,4 nur noch in den Jesuslogien Mt 5,5; 11,29
und in dem atlichen Zitat aus Sach 9,9 in Mt 21,5;/81/
b) dem 'kostbar vor Gott' in 1. Petr 3,4 entspricht die
eschatologische Belohnung in Mt 5,5. Daß Jesus das
prays betonte, würde die weite Verbreitung der Weisung

zur Sanftmut in der frühen Kirche gut erklären (cf. hier
auch 1. Petr 3,16). Ohne daß wir hier zu einer letzten
Gewißheit kommen, können wir doch vermuten, daß
1. Petr 3,4 in der Seligpreisung von Mt 5,5 gründet.
Dann haben wir hier den interessanten Fall vor uns, daß
der 1. Petr mit dem matthäischen Sondergut bekannt
ist./82/

9. Sowohl Goppelt als auch Michel rechnen damit, daß
    1. Petr 4,10 letzten Endes auf Lk 12,42ff. par
    zurückgeht./83/ In beiden Stellen findet sich der
    Begriff oikonomos; beide Male geht es um die Einsetzung
    und Beauftragung von Gott her; beide Male um den Dienst
    des oikonomos in der Gemeinde und zwar entsprechend
    seinem Auftrag. Man wird also Lk 12,42 par mindestens
    als eine Wurzel der Aussage in 1. Petr 4,10 betrachten
    müssen. Evtl. war auch Mt 20,25ff. par von Einfluß,
    eine Parallele, die uns schon bei 1. Petr 5,1-5
    wichtig geworden war.

10. In *1. Petr 4,12-16* begegnet uns wieder das für den
    ganzen Brief charakteristische Thema vom 'Verfolgungs-
    leiden'. Mehrfach wurde schon auf eine Herkunft von
    Jesuslogien hingewiesen. Deshalb beschränken wir uns
    hier auf eine knappe Zusammenfassung: a) Die Verbindung
    des peirasmos in V. 12 mit dem Leiden Christi in V. 13
    legt die Annahme nahe, daß das Gethsemanewort Mt 26,41
    par auf 1. Petr 4,12 eingewirkt hat./84/ b) Das
    chairete in V. 13 geht sehr wahrscheinlich direkt auf
    Mt 5,12 zurück; das ergibt sich ebensowohl aus der
    präsentischen Form wie aus dem Zusammenhang mit V. 14,
    der Mt 5,11 widerspiegelt./85/ Die Gemeinschaft mit
    den Leiden Christi kann überdies durch Mt 10,24f. und
    16,24 par mitbestimmt sein. Ob die 'Offenbarung seiner
    Herrlichkeit' auf Mt 25,31 zurückgeht? Jedenfalls ist
    die Aussage: 'freut euch, damit ihr euch auch bei der
    Offenbarung seiner Herrlichkeit jubelnd freut' (V. 13),
    nicht nur durch das chairein, sondern auch durch das
    agalliasthai und die eschatologische Belohnung
    unmittelbar mit Mt 5,12 verknüpft. c) 1. Petr 4,14
    'knüpft eindeutig an die letzte Seligpreisung Jesu' in
    Mt 5,11f.an./86/Oneidizein 'wird in vergleichbarer Weise
    nur an diesen beiden Stellen verwendet' (Mt 5,11 par;
    1. Petr 4,14);/87/ das makarioi entspricht sich ebenso
    wie das Leiden 'um meinetwillen' und 'um des Namens

Christi willen'. Goppelt meinte: 'Möglicherweise geht
... die zweite Hälfte unseres Satzes (= 1. Petr 4,14)
ebenso wie die erste von einer Jesusüberlieferung aus',
und denkt dabei an die Geistverheißung für die
verfolgten Jünger in Mt 10,19f. par./88/ d) Das
'Leiden als ein Christ' in V. 16 entspricht sachlich
dem Leiden 'um des Namens Christi willen' in V. 14./89/
So stoßen wir hier auf eine verifizierbare Abhängigkeit
des 1. Petr von Herrnworten, wie sie uns gerade
Matthäus bewahrt.

11. Es frägt sich, ob der 'Zeuge' in *1. Petr 5,1* auf ein
Logion des auferstandenen Jesus zurückgeht (Lk 24,48;
Apg 1,8)./90/ Auch der Petrus der Apg benutzt diesen
Begriff für sich (Apg 5,32). Die Antwort auf die
gestellte Frage ist deshalb nicht leicht, weil uns der
Begriff auch in die Nähe der johanneischen Tradition
bringt, einer Tradition, die auch in der Bezeichnung
Petri als presbyteros anklingt (cf. 2. Joh 1; 3. Joh 1
und Apk 11,3). Wir müssen die Antwort hier offen
lassen.

12. Die Paränese 'Alle eure Sorge werfet auf ihn, denn er
sorgt für euch' in *1. Petr 5,7* geht wahrscheinlich auf
die Jesusworte in Mt 6,25ff. par zurück. 'Sie nimmt in
paränetischer Formulierung auf, was Jesu Logion gegen
das Sorgen um das Lebensnotwendige samt seiner
Begründung meint'./91/ Nicht nur das Stichwort
merimnan und die Warnung vor der Sorge um alles
Lebensnotwendige, sondern auch die Sachaussage 'er sorgt
für euch (oder: kümmert sich um euch)' finden sich in
Mt 6,25ff. par wieder.

Es fragt sich jetzt, welche Schlüsse aus den genannten
Beobachtungen zur petrinischen Paränese zu ziehen sind.

III. *Schlüsse aus den bisherigen Beobachtungen zur Paränese*

1. Die Häufigkeit der Berührungen zwischen der
petrinischen Paränese und den Aussagen Jesu in den
Evangelien überrascht. Sie ist weit größer, als z.B.
Best annahm./92/ Dies gilt selbst dann, wenn man
mehrere der oben festgestellten Parallelen ausscheidet.

2. Diese Parallelen beziehen sich *überwiegend* - wie bei der
   Paränese naturgemäß anzunehmen - auf *Jesuslogien.* Aber
   sie schließen Gleichnisse, Gleichnishandlungen und
   geschichtliche Vorgänge wie z.B. die Passion Jesu ein.
   Der 1. Petr fußt also nicht nur auf Logientradition,
   sondern auch auf Erzähltradition (Beispiele: Mt 17,25ff.,
   26,41; Lk 22,31f.; Joh 13 und 21)./93/

3. Überblickt man die Vergleichsstellen in den Evangelien,
   dann lassen sich vorwiegend drei 'Blöcke' ausmachen,
   die dem 1. Petr besonders nahestehen: a) die
   Bergpredigt (z.B. Mt 5,5.10ff.48; 6,25ff. parr), b) die
   eschatologischen Reden und Abschiedsreden (z.B.
   Mt 24,42ff.; 25,31; Lk 12,35ff.42; 21,31ff.,34ff.;
   Joh 13,34f.; 15,11ff.), c) die Passions- und
   Auferstehungsberichte (z.B. Mt 26,41.67; Lk 22,31f.;
   24,25ff.; Joh 13,4ff.; 20,29; 21,15ff.)./94/

4. Die Jesustradition, die der 1. Petr verarbeitet, läßt
   sich aber nicht auf synoptische Überlieferungen
   begrenzen. Sie enthält vielmehr überraschend viele
   Berührungen, ja sogar Gemeinsamkeiten, mit der
   johanneischen Tradition (z.B. Joh 3,3ff.; 8,12.56;
   10,1ff.; 13,4ff.34f.; 15,11ff.; 20,29; 21,15ff.).
   Wenn Goppelt einmal bemerkte: 'Das Joh Ev wird nirgends
   wahrnehmbar',/95/ so ist dieses Urteil korrektur-
   bedürftig. Dagegen erwiesen sich diejenigen Forscher als
   im Recht, die wie Gundry, Spicq und Tenney gerade auf
   die Parallelen zwischen dem 1. Petr und dem Joh Ev
   hingewiesen haben./96/

5. Dann aber war die christliche Traditionsbildung schon
   vor der Abfassung des 1. Petr in reichem Maße
   ausgeprägt./97/ Ja, man kann mit Spicq und Feuillet
   noch einen Schritt weitergehen und vermuten, daß alle
   vier Evangelien auf eine annähernd gleich alte
   Überlieferung zurückgreifen konnten./98/

6. Eine außerordentlich schwierige Frage ist diejenige
   nach dem Ursprung der vom 1. Petr benutzten Jesus-
   tradition. Wir wollen uns dieser Frage eingehender
   zuwenden, sobald wir die Kurzkatechismen behandelt
   haben. Drei grundsätzliche Möglichkeiten zeichnen sich
   jedoch jetzt schon ab: a) Petrus hat als Augenzeuge

weder aus Büchern noch aus mündlicher Tradition,
sondern aus eigener Erfahrung geschöpft. Diese Ansicht
vertreten z.B. Spicq und Tenney./99/ Dann muß man
voraussetzen, daß der Brief authentisch und kein
Pseudepigraph ist. b) Der Verfasser des 1. Petr. schöpft
aus mündlicher Überlieferung oder aus schriftlichen
Quellen, wie sie auch den Evangelisten zur Verfügung
standen. Dann wären wir hier gewissermaßen Zeugen
eines 'vor-evangelischen' Prozesses./100/ c) Der
Verfasser stützt sich auf fixierte (kanonische)
Evangelien. Dann muß entweder der 1. Petr zeitlich
später angesetzt oder die Datierung der Evangelien im
Verhältnis zur heutigen kritischen Forschung früher
angesetzt werden.

7. Die Einzelparänese des 1. Petr modifiziert Jesus-
tradition und Jesuslogien in vielfältiger Weise.
Hätten wir nicht die Evangelien, denn könnten wir die
ursprüngliche Form der Jesusworte nicht mehr mit
genügender Wahrscheinlichkeit feststellen. Oder, um es
vom Standpunkt der Evangelien her zu formulieren: Wir
finden auffallenderweise kein Direktzitat! Damit
stehen wir vor einem forschungsgeschichtlichen Rätsel.
Spicq hat dieses Rätsel so zu lösen versucht, daß er
Petrus als 'Zeugen' und 'Begleiter' Jesu kennzeichnet,
der gerade als solcher die Möglichkeit freier Zitation
besitzt./101/ Aber dem steht die Beobachtung B.
Gerhardssons entgegen, wonach man in allen Briefen des
NT 'fast niemals direkt' zitiert./102/ Wollte man
Spicqs These folgen, dann müßte auch Paulus ein 'Zeuge'
und 'Begleiter' Jesu gewesen sein! Die Lösung muß also
in anderer Richtung gesucht werden.

8. Man kann die Frage aufwerfen: Weshalb benutzt Petrus
überhaupt eine bestimmte Tradition, wenn er doch
Augenzeuge ist? Diese Frage läßt sich mit dem Hinweis
beantworten, daß Petrus kein isolierter Zeuge war,
sondern einen Teil der Schule bildete, die Jesus in
seinem Jüngerkreis begründete und die vermutlich schon
vor Ostern eine gemeinsame Logientradition aufbewahrte.
/103/ Als Teil dieser Schule kannte und schätzte
Petrus diese Tradition und hatte er keinen Grund,
stets neu zu formulieren - selbst wenn er Augenzeuge
gewesen ist. Im Gegenteil: Es mußte ihm daran liegen,
die gemeinsame Tradition auch in der Paränese anklingen
zu lassen und zu unterstreichen.

9. Insgesamt erweist sich die ganze Paränese des 1. Petr
als durchtränkt von Anspielungen auf die Jesusüberlieferung./104/ Damit ist klar, daß die Worte des
historischen Jesus für Petrus einen einmaligen und
autoritären Rang hatten.

Wir wenden uns jetzt den Kurzkatechismen zu.

B. Die Kurzkatechismen

I. Die Kurzkatechismen und die Evangelientradition
Solche Kurzkatechismen, die Goppelt 'Christusformeln'
nennt,/105/ die man aber besser als heilsgeschichtliche
Kurzkatechismen bezeichnet,/106/ finden sich an drei Stellen im
1. Petr: In 1,18-21; in 2,21-25; und in 3,18-22. Die
Abgrenzung im einzelnen ist freilich umstritten./107/
Thematisch geht es um folgende Gedankenkreise: die Präexistenz,
Passion, Auferstehung, Erhöhung und ausschließliche
Heilsmittlerschaft Jesu Christi.

Sehen wir uns diese Aussagen genauer an:
1. Die *Präexistenz* Christi bringt vermutlich 1,20 zum
Ausdruck: 'der vorhererersehen wurde vor Grundlegung der Welt'.
Dahin deutet u.a. die Verwandtschaft mit Apg 2,23; 3,18./108/
Jedenfalls ist der Heilsplan Gottes, durch Christus die Welt zu
retten, schon vor der Schöpfung gefaßt, also suprakreatianisch.
Vorsichtigerweise muß man aber anmerken, daß die Präexistenz
Jesu aus 1. Petr 1,20 nicht zweifelsfrei zu erschließen ist.
/109/ Es könnte sich auch um die Erwählung einer menschlichen
Persönlichkeit handeln, die erst im Laufe der Geschichte
hervorgebracht wird, so wie das erwählte Israel erst im Lauf
dieser Geschichte entstand.

2. Am reichsten sind die *Passionsaussagen.* Ohne Zweifel
steht die Passion Jesu christologisch im Mittelpunkt sowohl des
ganzen Briefes als auch der Kurzkatechismen.

1,19 erinnert uns an 'das kostbare Blut Christi', und zwar
in einer Art und Weise, die ihre nächsten Parallelen bei
Paulus (Röm 3,25), beim Hebräerbrief (9,14ff.) und bei der
Johannesoffenbarung (1,5; 5,9) hat. Doch die weitere Frage
muß lauten: Besteht auch eine Verbindung zu den verba Christi?
1,19 verknüpft mit der Betrachtung des Blutes Christi den
Vergleich mit einem 'fehllosen und unbefleckten Lamm'.
Traditionsgeschichtlich ist diese Aussage in den atlichen

Opferbestimmungen verankert (z.B. Lev 1-6). Noch präziser
werden wir hier an die Vorschriften für das Passalamm erinnert
(Ex 12,3ff.). In Jes 53,7ff. erreichen wir eine weitere Stufe
im Offenbarungsgeschehen. Der Gottesknecht wird hier mit einem
Lamm verglichen, das zum Schuldopfer dient (cf. Lev 5,14ff. mit
Jes 53,7.10). Schöpft 1. Petr 1,19 direkt aus Ex 12 oder
Jes 53? Eine solche Annahme bleibt möglich. Mindestens
genauso naheliegend ist aber eine andere Annahme: daß nämlich
der Täufer und Jesus dem Verfasser des 1. Petr die in 1,19
ausgesprochene Sicht vermittelt haben. Zum Täufer cf. Joh 1
Joh 1,29.36. Petrus war sowohl ein Schüler des Täufers
(Joh 1,40ff.) als auch Jesu. Bei Jesus macht der Lösegeldspruch
in Mt 20,28/Mk 10,45 deutlich, daß er als der leidende
Gottesknecht auch das Lamm von Jes 53,7 sein will./110/ Und
beim Abendmahl tritt er selbst an die Stelle des geschlachteten
Lammes (Mt 26,28 parr)./111/ Ferner wird Jesus im Verlauf
seines Wirkens seine Sündlosigkeit mehrfach bestätigt (cf.
Mt 22,16; 27,19.23; Lk 22,22; Joh 8,46; 18,38; 19,4.6). Die
Tatsache, daß die Bezeichnung Jesu als des 'Lammes' und die
Überzeugung von seiner Sündlosigkeit verschiedenen Schichten
des NT angehört, erklärt sich am besten, wenn dahinter die
Ereignisse des irdischen Lebens Jesu als gemeinsamer Quellgrund
stehen (cf. Joh 19,36; 1 Kor 5,7; 1. Petr.1,19; Apk 5,6ff.;
19,7ff.; 21,9 einerseits und Mt 22,16; 27,19.23; Lk 22,22;
Joh 8,46; 18,38; 19,4.6; Apg 3,14; 13,28; 2 Kor 5,21; 1.Petr
1,19; 2,22; 3,18; 1 Joh 3,15; Hebr 4,15; 7,26 andrerseits).
Immerhin fällt auf, daß 1. Petr 1,19 im Blick auf den
Sprachgebrauch vom Lamm am engsten mit johanneischen
Parallelen verbunden ist./112/

    Kehren wir noch einmal zurück zu 1,18f. Die Wirkung des
Blutes Jesu besteht darin, 'daß ihr losgekauft wurdet aus
eurem eitlen, von den Vätern überkommenen Wandel'. Nicht leicht
zu verstehen ist hier das elytrōthēte. Die Kommentare denken
an Jes 52,3 als atliche Quelle. Aber das hebr. g'l setzt nicht
unbedingt ein Gegenüber voraus, das einen Kaufpreis fordern
kann. Im Gegenteil: Ägypten oder Assur erhielten gerade kein
Lösegeld! So müßte man eher mit 'erlösen' übersetzen. Diese
Übersetzung wird aber dadurch problematisch, daß 1. Petr 1,18f.
das Blut eben mit einem Kaufpreis vergleicht./113/ Wieder
erhebt sich die Frage: Kommen wir durch einen Vergleich mit der
Jesusüberlieferung weiter? Nach Mt 20,28; Mk 10,45 will Jesus
sein Leben als 'Lösegeld für viele' geben. Dabei denkt Jesus
offensichtlich an Jes 53,10ff. Bei Jesus also läßt sich das
'Lösegeld' definieren. Es meint das Auslösen aus der
Gerichtsverfallenheit, aus dem kommenden Zorn Gottes. D.i.

nichts anderes als der Gedanke des stellvertretenden Sühne-
leidens./114/ Damit ist aber der Bedeutungsgehalt von
Mt 20,28 par noch nicht ausgeschöpft. Vielmehr ist im
gesamtneutestamentlichen Horizont zu bedenken, daß der von Gott
getrennte sündige Mensch von bösen Machten beherrscht und in
die Verdammnis getrieben wird. Das ist ebensogut die
Auffassung Jesu (cf. Mt 9,36) wie die der Apostel (cf. Röm 6 - 7;
1 Kor 15,56; Eph 6,11ff.; 1. Petr 5,8f.; Jak 4,7; Apk 12,12).
Die in Mt 20,28 par gemeinte Erlösung schließt also das
Auslösen aus der Gewalt der Sünde, des Todes und des Teufels
ein. Und genau diese umfassende Sicht spiegelt sich auch in
1. Petr 1,18. Denn es kann kein Zweifel sein, daß der Ausdruck
'eitler Wandel' auf den der Sünde, den Lüsten und dem Tod
verfallenen Wandel anspielt (cf. V. 13ff.,22ff.). Jesu
Sühnetod erlöst uns, indem er uns nicht nur vom kommenden Zorn
Gottes erlöst, sondern auch aus der Gewalt jener Mächte
loskauft. Das verborgene Subjekt des Passivs elythrōthēte ist
also Jesus Christus, nicht Gott der Vater./115/ Diese
Beobachtungen machen es wahrscheinlich, daß der 1. Petr das
Jesuswort von Mt 20,28 par aufnimmt und verarbeitet./116/

     Nun läßt sich der Stellvertretungsgedanke nicht nur
indirekt aus 1. Petr 1,18 erschließen. Vielmehr ist er in
2,21ff. direkt ausgesprochen. Und zwar zunächst in 2,21:
'Christus hat für euch gelitten', was sachlich einem: 'Christus
ist für euch (uns) gestorben' entspricht./117/ Sodann aber
durch den im NT beispiellos dichten Rückbezug auf Jes 53./118/
Nicht weniger als sechs Mal wird Jes 53 in 2,22 -25 zitiert
(Jes 53,9 in V. 22; Jes 53,4.12.11.5 in V. 24; Jes 53,6 in
V. 25). Jesus ist also der leidende Gottesknecht, der uns
durch seinem Sühnetod erlöst. 1. Petr 3,18 wiederholt genau
dies. Wieder könnte man erwägen, ob Petrus durch eine
originelle Auswertung von Jes 53 zu diesen Aussagen gekommen
ist, um durch seine theologische Reflexion das Sterben Jesu zu
interpretieren. Aber auch hier ist ein traditionsgeschichtlicher Sprung über die Jesuslogien hinweg wenig wahrscheinlich.
Näher liegt es, daß Petrus an die Jesajadeutung anschließt,
die Jesus selbst in den Abendmahlsworten und in Mt 20,28 par
vorgenommen und nach dem Bericht der Evangelien in seiner
Taufe von der himmlischen Stimme vernommen hat (cf. Mt 3,17 parr
mit Jes 42,1)./119/

     Bisher erfuhren wir rein faktisch nur die Tatsache des
Sterbens Jesu. 1. Petr 2,21ff. liefert aber darüberhinaus eine
Reihe von Angaben, die in faszinierender Weise an die
Passionserzählungen der Evangelien erinnern. Dazu gehört die

Verurteilung eines Schuldlosen. Sowohl die Widersprüche der
Zeugen als auch der römische Statthalter bestätigen nach den
Evangelienberichten, daß Jesus unschuldig hingerichtet wurde
(Mt 26,59ff.; 27,18ff.; Joh 18,38; 19,4.6). Auf den Prozeß
bezieht sich wohl auch 2,23: 'Als er geschmäht wurde, schmähte
er nicht wieder, als er litt, drohte er nicht'. Alle Evangelien
berichten von dem merkwürdigen Schweigen des angeklagten Jesus
(Mt 26,62f.; 27,12.14; Mk 14,60f.; 15,4f.; Lk 23,9; Joh 19,9).
Jesus hat hier durch sein Verhalten Jes 53,7 - offenbar sehr
bewußt - realisiert. Daß man Jesus 'schmähte', läßt sich
sowohl auf seine Verhöhnung durch die Juden (cf. Mt 26,67f.;
Joh 18,22) als auch auf seine Verhöhnung durch die römischen
Soldaten (cf. Mt 27,27ff.) beziehen. Zugleich erinnert jedoch
die Formulierung von 2,23 auffallend an Mt 5,39ff. V. 24
informiert uns darüber, daß Jesus am 'Holz' = Kreuz starb, und
zeichnet durch die Stichworte 'an seinem Leib' und 'Wunden'
ein realistisches Bild seiner Hinrichtung. 3,18 erweitert das
Bild um die Feststellung, daß er 'dem Fleische nach' wirklich
'getötet wurde'. Das Bild rundet sich vollends, wenn man die
zahlreichen Stellen vom 'leiden' Jesu ins Auge faßt: 'Im
1. Petr tritt πάσχω ... so dicht wie in keiner anderen Schrift
des NT auf; es begegnet 12 mal, während es im ganzen übrigen
NT 30 mal steht'./120/

    Wieder stehen wir vor der Frage: Gibt es eine Beziehung
zur Evangelientradition oder ist Petrus völlig unabhängig von
dieser zu denken? Gundry formulierte einst den Eindruck des
Auslegers 'as if the scene of the crucifixion had left an
indelible impression on the author's mind'./121/ Aber auch
wenn wir uns Petrus als Augenzeugen der Kreuzigung bzw. der
Passion denken, ist es nicht ausgeschlossen, ja sogar naheliegend, daß er an Worte Jesu oder allgemeinchristliche
Überlieferung anknüpft. Goppelt meinte, die Aussagen über die
Leiden Jesu gingen 'möglicherweise auf Jesus selbst zurück',
/122/ nämlich auf die Leidensweissagungen Jesu (cf. Mt 16,21;
Mk 8,31; 9,12; Lk 9,22; 17,25). Diese Vermutung wird noch
verstärkt durch die Beobachtung, daß dem 1. Petr gerade die
Weissagungen auf das Christusleiden wichtig sind (cf. 1,11 und
die Jesajazitate in 2,22ff.)./123/ Jedoch reicht es nicht aus,
nur die verba Christi ins Auge zu fassen. Dort, wo die Passion
in den Kurzkatechismen des 1. Petr eine konkrete Farbe gewinnt
(Schuldlosigkeit, Schmähung, Schweigen, Kreuzholz), wird
vielmehr eine solche Übereinstimmung mit den Evangelienerzäh-
lungen erreicht, daß die nächstliegende Erklärung dieses
Tatbestandes diejenige ist, daß Petrus als Traditionsträger
Anteil an einer gemeinsamen Erzähl-Tradition hatte, die dann
auch in die Evangelien eingegangen ist.

3. Nach der Passion bildet die Auferstehung Jesu das
herausragende Ereignis des in den Kurzkatechismen aufgezeich-
neten 'Christusweges'./124/ Gott 'hat ihn von den Toten
auferweckt' heißt es in 1,21. In 3,18 wird gesagt: 'der
lebendig gemacht wurde dem Geiste nach', oder: 'durch den
Geist'. In 3,21 ist die Rede von der 'Auferstehung Jesu
Christi' (dieselbe Wendung in 1,3). Die Auferweckung Jesu
begründet die christliche Hoffnung, vor allem die
Heilsgewißheit.

Zunächst fällt hier die Nähe zu paulinischen Aussagen auf
(cf. Röm 1,4; 4,24; 8,11; 10,9; 2 Kor 4,14; Gal 1,1; Eph 1,20;
Kol 2,12; 1 Thes 1,10). Liegt darin ein Hinweis auf den
'Ausstrahlungsbereich paulinischer Gedanken', den man immer
wieder für den 1. Petr reklamiert?/125/ Dieser Annahme stehen
zwei gewichtige Bedenken gegenüber: a) sind die o.g.
paulinischen Aussagen mindestens teilweise aus vorpaulinischer
Bekenntnistradition geschöpft, b) gibt Paulus in 1 Kor 15,1ff.
expressis verbis zu verstehen, daß er die Nachricht von der
Auferstehung Jesu aus urchristlicher Paradosis übernommen hat
(was keinen Einwand gegen das Damaskuserlebnis bedeutet!).
Eine Abhängigkeit der Auferstehungsaussagen der petrinischen
Kurzkatechismen von Paulus ist also nicht anzunehmen.
Andrerseits liegt der Zielpunkt aller Evangelien und des
apostolischen Kerygmas nach der Apostelgeschichte in der
Auferstehung und Erhöhung Jesu. So ergibt sich auch an dieser
Stelle die Vermutung, daß Petrus an einer allgemeinen
urchristlichen Tradition partizipiert, die einerseits in die
Briefe, andrerseits in die Evangelien eingegangen ist.
Darüberhinaus läßt sich legitim fragen, ob nicht die
Voraussage Jesu von seiner künftigen Erweckung einer der
Ausgangspunkte der Kurzkatechismen gewesen ist (cf. die sog.
Leidensweissagungen sowie Mt 12,39f.; 19,28f.; 21,42; 26,64;
Joh 14,1ff.; 16,16ff.)./126/

Ein Punkt, der uns später noch beschäftigen soll, sei hier
vorweg notiert. Gerade bei den Aussagen zur Auferstehung Jesu
fällt auf, daß sie so knapp formuliert sind. Sie muten an wie
Kürzel. Man bekommt den Eindruck: Die Leser des 1. Petr
wissen schon darüber Bescheid, was es mit der Auferstehung Jesu
auf sich hat.

4. Keiner der drei petrinischen Kurzkatechismen endet bei
der Auferstehung. Alle münden sie in die Erhöhung Jesu ein.
In 1,21 folgt der Auferstehung die doxa, die ihm Gott 'gegeben
hat'. In 2,25 beschreiben 'Hirte' und 'Episkopos'

offensichtlich Funktionen des Erhöhten (cf. 5,4). Die
ausführlichsten Angaben sind in 3,22 enthalten: 'der zur
Rechten Gottes ist, nachdem er in den Himmel gegangen ist,
wobei ihm die Engel, Mächte und Kräfte untergeordnet sind.'
Die Beobachtung, daß 'Nirgends so viele Stücke des 2. Artikels
des Apostolikums präformiert sind',/127/ könnte darauf
schließen lassen, daß der Verfasser des 1. Petr diese Aussagen
eigenschöpferisch geformt hat. Nun wird man ja nicht leugnen,
daß er sie gelehrt und teilweise auch selbständig formuliert
hat. Dennoch weisen uns zwei weitere Beobachtungen darauf hin,
daß Petrus auch hier weitgehend am Strom der gemeinchrist-
lichen Überlieferung partizipiert: a) Sachlich und
terminologisch finden sich in den Evangelien und in der
Apostelgeschichte ganz ähnliche Aussagen (cf. Mt 26,64; 28,18;
Joh 14,2f.; 17,24; 20,17; Apg 1,10; 3,21; 7,55). Es ist aber
äußerst unwahrscheinlich, daß Matthäus, Johannes und Lukas
hierin nur von Petrus oder gar noch spezieller vom 1. Petr
abhängig sein sollten. b) Wie bei der Auferstehung braucht
Petrus die Aussagen über die Erhöhung Jesu nicht zu erläutern.
Die Leser wissen offenbar schon Bescheid, sodaß knappe
Formulierungen genügen.

Partizipiert hier Petrus erneut an allgemeiner urchristlicher Tradition, so muß weiter nach deren Quellen gefragt
werden. Ähnlich wie oben kommen grundsätzlich zwei
Überlieferungsorte in Betracht: einmal die von den Augenzeugen
erlebten Begebenheiten bzw. die Erzählungen darüber, und zum
andern die verba Christi./128/ Gehen wir letzteren noch ein
wenig nach. Gundry sah den 'Hirten' und 'Bischof' von 1. Petr
2,25 in Parallele zu Joh 10,11ff./129/ Geht man davon aus,
daß sich der irdische Jesus den Jüngern gegenüber als der
messianische 'Hirte' zu erkennen gab, was nicht nur durch
Joh 10,11ff., sondern auch durch Mt 9,36; 25,32; 26,31; Mk 6,34
und 14,27 bezeugt wird, dann liegt tatsächlich die Vermutung
nahe, daß 1. Petr 2,25 auf Jesus selbst zurückgeht. Sind wir
hierbei schon auf eine johanneische Parallele gestoßen, so
tritt nun eine weitere johanneische Parallele in unser
Blickfeld. Es handelt sich darum, daß vor allem das Joh Ev die
Existenz Jesu nach seiner Auferstehung mit dem Begriff der doxa
kennzeichnet (cf. Joh 7,39; 12,16.23; 13,31f.; 17,1.5.22.24).
Ja, der Ausdruck: 'die Herrlichkeit geben' (1. Petr 1,21) ist
sogar typisch johanneisch (cf. Joh 17,22.24). Darin scheint
also Gundry recht zu behalten, daß er eine besondere Nähe des
1. Petr zur johanneischen Tradition annimmt./130/ Man muß
allerdings hinzufügen, daß auch der synoptische Jesus öfters
von seiner zukünftigen doxa spricht (Mt 16,27 parr; 19,28;

25,31; 24,30 parr).   Alles in allem ist festzustellen, daß sich
im Munde des Jesus der Evangelien alle Aussagen wiederfinden,
die die Kurzkatechismen des 1.Petr über den Erhöhten machen:
daß ihm der Vater die Herrlichkeit gibt (Joh 17,22.24); daß er
der Hirte ist (Joh 10,11ff. und die o.g. synoptischen Stellen);
daß er zur Rechten Gottes ist (Mt 26,64); daß er in den Himmel
geht (Joh 14,2f.; 20,17); daß ihm die Engel und Mächte untertan
sind (Mt 13,41; 24,30f.; 25,31; 28,18).   Die Vermutung drängt
sich deshalb auf, daß die Kurzkatechismen auch dann auf
Jesusworte zurückgehen, wenn sie vom erhöhten Jesus sprechen.

     5.   Schließlich bringen die Kurzkatechismen die
ausschließliche Heilsmittlerschaft Jesu zum Ausdruck.   In 1,21
wird von den Lesern gesagt: 'die ihr durch ihn an Gott glaubt'.
/131/ Nach 3,18 hat Christus gelitten, 'um euch zu Gott
hinzuführen'.   Dabei ist der Grundgedanke zweifellos der, daß
nur Jesus uns zu Gott hinführen kann.   Es geht also
tatsächlich um die ausschließliche Heilsmittlerschaft.
Letztlich wurzelt diese Aussage in der Überzeugung vom
stellvertretenden Sühnetod Jesu (cf. den Kontext von 3,18).   Sie
ist nicht erst in der Auseinandersetzung mit der orientalischen
oder hellenistischen Umwelt, sondern schon in der Auseinandersetzung mit dem priesterlichen und synagogalen Judentum betont
worden.   Interessanterweise legt gerade der Petrus der Apg Wert
auf sie (Apg 4,12).

     Haben wir auch hier wieder eine allgemeine urchristliche
Überzeugung vor uns, so öffnet sich ein weiteres Mal der Weg
der Rückfrage nach den Jesusworten.   Schon die Sendungsinstruk-
tionen des irdischen Jesus setzen im Grunde die Heilsmittlerschaft voraus (cf. Mt 10,11ff.; Lk 10,5ff.16), erst recht dann
die Missionsbefehle des Auferstandenen (cf. Mt 28,18ff.;
Lk 24,47; Joh 20,23).   Speziell zu 1.Petr 3,18 liegt nun in
Joh 14,6 eine nahe Parallele vor. Denn der exklusive 'Weg', den
der Christus dort zu sein beansprucht, auf dem jedermann 'zum
Vater kommen' kann, entspricht sachlich dem 'zu Gott hinführen'
von 1.Petr 3,18 und steht auch sprachlich in der Nähe dieser
Petrusstelle (unter den paulinischen Parallelen cf. Röm 5,2;
Eph 2,18; 3,12; im Hebräerbrief cf. 10,19ff.)./132/

     II.   *Die Kurzkatechismen und die Apostelgeschichte*
     Bevor wir aus den in I. genannten Beobachtungen weitere
Schlüsse ziehen, wenden wir uns der Apostelgeschichte zu. Denn
die Apg enthält in Kap 2, Kap 3 und Kap 10 offenbar als typisch
betrachtete Petruspredigten.   Sie dürfen für eine Untersuchung
zu unserem Thema nicht außer Acht gelassen werden.   Zwar nannte

Zahn die Petrusausführungen in der Apg und im 1. Petr 'zwei
schwer zu vergleichende Dinge'./133/ Dennoch notierte er nicht
nur 'das Zusammentreffen von 1 Pt 2,7 mit AG 4,11... und von
1 Pt 4,5 mit AG 10,42', sondern auch die beiderseits
festzustellende 'Koncentration... auf den Kreuzestod, die
Auferstehung und die Wiederkunft Christi'./134/   Selwyn hat
dann die Parallen zwischen dem 1. Petr und den Petruspredigten
der Apg kräftig betont./135/ Er vermutete, die petrinischen
Actapredigten seien wenigstens teilweise 'dependent on written
sources or oral information'./136 Was läßt sich von den
Kurzkatechismen ausgehend dazu erheben?

    1. In Apg 2 beginnt die petrinische Pfingstpredigt
eigentlich mit V. 22./137/ Sie nimmt ihren Ausgang bei Jesus
Christus (V. 22) und sie endet auch bei Jesus Christus (V. 36).
Man könnte sagen, daß sie den 'Christusweg' unter missionarisch-
paränetischer Zielsetzung nachzeichnet. Zuerst erwähnt sie
die 'Taten und Wunder und Zeichen', d.h. das Wunderwirken Jesu
vor der Passion (2,22), dann die Vorausersehung Gottes (2,23),
die Passion und den Kreuzestod Jesu (2,23.32; cf. 2,36), die
Auferweckung durch Gott (2,24), wie sie prophetisch im AT
angekündigt ist (2,25-31), die Erhöhung zur Rechten Gottes und
seine Himmelfahrt (2,33-35), und schließlich seine Stellung
als Herr und Messias (2,36). Vor allem die letztgenannte
Aussage schließt die alleinige Heilsmittlerschaft Jesu ein.

    Vergleicht man die Darstellung des Christusweges in Apg
2,22-36 mit den Kurzkatechismen des 1. Petrusbriefes, dann
ergibt sich eine frappierende Ähnlichkeit im Aufriß. Abgesehen
von den irdischen Wundertaten Jesu finden sich alle Themata von
Apg 2,22ff. in den Kurzkatechismen wieder. Drittens gibt es
terminologische Berührungen. Man vergleiche die prognōsis von
Apg 2,23 mit dem prognōsmenon von 1. Petr 1,20,/138/ die
Begriffe thanatos und sarx in Apg 2,24.26.31 mit 1. Petr 3,18;
oder das tē dexiā tou theou in Apg 2,33 mit dem en dexiā tou
theou in 1. Petr 3,22./139/

    2. Kürzer als in Apg 2 ist die petrinische Predigt in
Apg 3,12-26. Sie ist weniger eine Darstellung des
Christusweges als vielmehr eine missionarische Konfrontation
der Hörer mit dem Handeln des Gottes Israels. Dennoch schlägt
auch diese Predigt den Weg einer geschichtlichen Erzählung ein.
Dabei schreitet sie von der Passion des sündlosen Jesus (3,13f.)
weiter zu dessen Tod und Auferweckung (3,15), betont Gottes
Vorherbestimmung bezüglich des Christusleidens (3,18.22ff.),

die Heilsmittlerschaft und Messianität Jesu (3,19f.) und endet
mit dem Hinweis auf die Erhöhung Jesu und die Vollendung der
Heilsgeschichte (3,21).

Wiederum ergibt der Vergleich mit den Kurzkatechismen im
1. Petrusbrief eine eindrucksvolle Ähnlichkeit im Aufbau. Hier
wie dort ist der geschichtliche Ablauf die Grundlage dieses
Aufbaus. Abgesehen von der Apokatastasis pantōn (Apg 3,21)
finden sich beiderseits alle Themen wieder. Und auch an
terminologischen Berührungen mangelt es nicht: cf. das
doxazein von Apg 3,13 mit dem doxan didonai in 1. Petr 1,21;
/140/ die Verknüpfung der Begriffe doxazein bzw doxan didonai
und egeirein ek nekrōn in Apg 3,13.15 und 1. Petr 1,21; das
dikaios in Apg 3,14 und 1. Petr 3,18;/141/ das paschein des
Christus in Apg 3,18 und 1. Petr 2,21; 3,18; das Sein Jesu im
ouranos nach Apg 3,21 und 1. Petr 3,22. Außerdem hat Selwyn
beobachtet, daß sowohl in Apg 3 als auch im 1. Petrusbrief
(2,22ff.!) auf Jes 53 Bezug genommen wird./142/

3. Im Blick auf Apg 10,34 - 43 sah Selwyn die größte Nähe
zum 1. Petr gegeben./143/ Wie in Apg 2,22ff. beginnt Petrus
hier mit der irdischen Tätigkeit Jesu, spricht aber nicht nur
von den Wundertaten, sondern auch von der Predigt Jesu Christi
(10,36 - 38). Danach spricht er in äußerst knappen
Formulierungen von der Passion und dem Kreuzestod (10,39). Es
folgen die Aussagen von der Auferweckung (10,40f.), vom
Missionsbefehl, vom Richteramt (10,42), von der Ankündigung
durch die Propheten und von der Heilsmittlerschaft Jesu (10,43).
Berücksichtigt man, daß Missionsbefehl und Richteramt
Tätigkeiten des Erhöhten darstellen, dann kann man erneut
feststellen, daß außer der Erwähnung der Tätigkeit Jesu vor der
Passion alle Themen der Petruspredigt von Apg 10,34ff. in den
Kurzkatechismen des 1. Petrusbriefes wiederkehren. Beiderseits
liegt derselbe historisch-chronologische Aufriß vor. Erneut
gibt es auch terminologische Berührungen: Xylon findet sich
sowohl in Apg 10,39 als auch in 1. Petr 2,24 (auch in Apg 5,30
redet Petrus vom xylon!); egeirein und didonai, von Gott
ausgesagt, sowohl in Apg 10,40 als auch in 1. Petr 1,21./144/

4. Das Ergebnis des Vergleichs zwischen den Petruspredigten der Apg und den Kurzkatechismen des 1. Petrusbriefes
läßt sich nun wie folgt zusammenfassen: Beide lassen denselben
Aufbau erkennen. Wesentlich für diesen Aufbau ist der
geschichtliche Ablauf des Christusweges. D.h. man verkündet
Jesus so, daß man den Weg seines Wirkens, den 'Christusweg',
darstellt. Beiderseits begegnen mit wenigen Ausnahmen

dieselben Themen, teilweise sogar dieselben Formulierungen.
D.h. Lukas läßt Petrus fast genauso predigen, wie es der
Verfasser des 1. Petrusbriefes in den zentralen Passagen seiner
Kurzkatechismen tatsächlich tut.

III. Schlüsse aus den bisherigen Beobachtungen zu den Kurzkatechismen

Im Folgenden versuchen wir mit der gebotenen Vorsicht
einige Schlüsse aus dem zu ziehen, was sich uns bei der
Beobachtung der Beziehungen zwischen den Kurzkatechismen des
1. Petr und der Evangelienüberlieferung bzw. der Apg dargeboten
hat.

1. Die Kurzkatechismen sind im Verhältnis zur Fülle ihrer
Aussagen so ungeheuer knapp formuliert, daß man kaum dem Schluß
entrinnen kann, daß sie Dinge ansprechen, die den Lesern schon
in wesentlichen Zügen bekannt gewesen sind. Sie gleichen
geradezu Anamnesen, die Bekanntes in die Erinnerung zurück-
rufen. Der 1. Petr selbst bietet keine Erläuterung an. Deshalb
muß die Bekanntschaft der Leser mit den Aussagen der
Kurzkatechismen schon vor der Absendung des Briefes bestanden
haben. Sie mußten wissen, was das ist: Christi Leiden und
Kreuz, seine Auferstehung, Himmelfahrt, Erhöhung usw. Woher
wußten sie es? Diese Frage wird später noch einmal
aufzugreifen sein.

2. Die Kurzkatechismen stellen zweifellos *Selektionen*
dar. Ein 'Katechismus' bedeutet Konzentration. Daß es sich
um Selektionen handelt, merkt man z.B. an der Art, wie einmal
in dem einen, dann in dem andern Stück sozusagen en passant
konkrete Züge auftauchen können, die sonst fehlen: 'Als er
geschmäht wurde, schmähte er nicht wieder' (2,23) - 'nachdem
er in den Himmel gegangen ist' (3,22) o.a. Wohl stehen wir
insgesamt vor einer Fülle von Einzelaussagen: Jesus ist der
Messias; er ist die vor Erschaffung der Welt vorgesehene
eschatologische Erlösergestalt; im Prozeß schwieg er in
auffallender Weise, obwohl ihn die Gegner schmähten; die
Verurteilung traf einen Sünd- und Schuldlosen; er starb am
Kreuzesholz; dabei hat er stellvertretend den Sühnetod für uns
erlitten; der tote Jesus wurde von Gott durch eine
Schöpfungstat im Heiligen Geist auferweckt; der Auferweckte hat
den Toten gepredigt; er ist in den Himmel gegangen und herrscht
zur Rechten Gottes über die Mächte; er ist der alleinige
Heilsmittler für die Menschen; in alledem erfüllte sich das
prophetische Wort (Jes 53!). Man darf aber den Charakter des
Selektiven nicht außer Acht lassen. Er zeigt sich ein

weiteres Mal am Thema der Wiederkunft. Der 1. Petr teilt mit
dem übrigen NT durchaus die Hoffnung auf den wiederkehrenden
Christus (1,7.13; 4,5.13; 5,4). Aber in keinem der drei
Kurzkatechismen ist von der Wiederkunft die Rede! Eine
Konsequenz aus dieser Beachtung des selektiven Charakters der
Kurzkatechismen ist also die, daß fehlende Aussagen nicht ohne
weiteres als unwichtig oder unbekannt oder abgelehnt betrachtet
werden dürfen. Das betrifft neben der Wiederkunft z.B. das
irdische Wirken Jesu, seine Präexistenz oder seine wunderbare
Geburt.

   3. Eines der hervorragendsten Merkmale der Kurzkatechismen ist *ihr geschichtlich chronologischer Aufbau.* Wie wir
sahen, teilen sie diesen mit den Petruspredigten der
Apostelgeschichte. Jetzt ist hinzuzufügen: Sie teilen ihn
auch mit den Evangelien. Die Abfolge Passion - Auferstehung -
Erhöhung, eine heilsgeschichtliche Ordnung gewissermaßen, ist
konstitutiv für alle kanonischen Evangelien. Das Joh Ev macht
hier keine Ausnahme. Schaltet man der Passion den Bericht von
der irdischen Tätigkeit Jesu in Worten und Wundern vor, dann
hat man tatsächlich den Evangeliengrundriß vor sich. D.h. die
Kurzkatechismen und die Petruspredigten der Apg sind Evangelien
in nuce! Die früheste Christenheit verkündigt Jesus in der
Gemeinde (Paränese und Kurzkatechismen), in der Missionspredigt
(Apostelgeschichte) und in den Evangelien stets so, daß sie
seinen Weg darstellt. D.h. sie verkündigt Jesus geschichtlich.
Es ist außerordentlich interessant, daß das aus den Kurzkatechismen des NT - nicht zuletzt des 1. Petr!/145/ -
herausgewachsene spätere apostolische Glaubensbekenntnis an
diesem geschichtlichen Aufriß festhält.

   4. Sprachen wir eben vom geschichtlichen Charakter der
petrinischen Kurzkatechismen, so ist jetzt zu betonen, daß es
sich um *gedeutete Geschichte* handelt. Wenige Beispiele
genügen, um dies zu erhellen. So ist in 1,19 nicht nur vom
Blut Jesu Christi die Rede, sondern vom 'kostbaren Blut'. In
2,21 ist nicht nur das Leiden Christi erwähnt, sondern auch
sofort dieses Leiden als ein stellvertretendes gekennzeichnet:
'Christus hat für euch gelitten'. Ähnliches gilt für 3,18.
Wir beobachten genau dasselbe bei den Evangelien. Stets wird
dort die Geschichte, von der berichtet wird, auch gedeutet, sei
es durch Zitate aus dem AT, sei es durch Bemerkungen des
Evangelisten oder in sonstiger Weise. Man darf allerdings
nicht in den Fehler verfallen, gedeutete Geschichte mit
fragwürdiger Geschichte zu verwechseln. Vielmehr setzt

gedeutete Geschichte Fakten voraus, die in ihrer Bedeutung
erschlossen werden können. So ergibt sich sowohl für die
petrinischen Kurzkatechismen als auch für die Evangelien ein
doppeltes Interesse, nämlich an bestimmten Geschichtstatsachen
einerseits, und an ihrer geistlich legitimierten Deutung
andererseits.

   5. An mehreren Stellen ergab sich bei der Untersuchung
der Kurzkatechismen die Vermutung, *daß deren Formulierungen
durch Jesuslogien beeinflußt* sind. Man muß es deutlich
aussprechen: Es handelt sich nur um Vermutungen; ein voller
Beweis ist hier nicht zu führen. Dennoch gewinnen diese
Vermutungen durch zwei Überlegungen ein besonderes Gewicht:
a) die traditionsgeschichtliche Verbindung mit Jesuslogien ist
öfters die naheliegendste Annahme (cf. zum 'Blut' und zum
'Lamm' 1. Petr 1,19: Mt 20,28; 26,28 parr; zum 'loskaufen'
1. Petr 1,18: Mt 20,28 par; zum stellvertretenden Sühnetod
1. Petr 2,21ff.: Mt 20,28 par; zu 1. Petr 2,23: Mt 5,39ff.; zum
'leiden' 1. Petr 2,21; 3,18: die Leidensweissagungen Jesu in
Mt 16,21; Mk 8,31; 9,12; Lk 9,22; 17,25; zum 'Hirten' 1. Petr
2,25: Mt 9,36; 25,32; 26,31; Mk 6,34; 14,27; Joh 10,11ff.; zum
'Herrlichkeit geben' 1. Petr 1,21: Joh 17,22.24 sowie Mt 16,27
parr; 19,28; 24,30 parr; 25,31; zum Sein 'zur Rechten Gottes'
1. Petr 3,22: Mt 26,64; zum 'gehen in den Himmel' 1. Petr 3,22:
Joh 14,2f.; 20,17; zum 'unterworfen sind die Engel und Mächte
und Kräfte' 1. Petr 3,22: Mt 13,41 24,30f.; 25,31; zum 'zu
Gott hinführen' 1. Petr 3,18: Joh 14,6), b) für die
Einzelparänese nimmt heute eine große Zahl von Exegeten eine
Verarbeitung von verba Christi an./146/ Dann aber liegt ein
solcher Rückgriff auf Jesuslogien auch für die Kurzkatechismen
nahe.

   6. Es erhebt sich nun ein schwieriges Problem. Voraus-
gesetzt, die Kurzkatechismen gehen wie die Einzelparänese des 1.
Petr wenigstens teilweise auf Jesuslogien bzw. auf Überlieferungen zurück, die auch in die Evangelien eingegangen sind,
wie ist dann die gegenseitige Beziehung näher zu bestimmen?
Präziser gefragt: *In welcher Form lagen z.B. die Jesuslogien
dem Verfasser des 1. Petr vor?* Schöpfte er aus Q oder einer
Frühform von Q, wie manche geneigt sind anzunehmen?/147/ Oder
greift er schon auf fertige Evangelienschriften zurück?

   Unweigerlich spielt hier zunächst das Datum der Abfassung
des 1. Petr eine Rolle. Es handelt sich geradezu um ein
Schulbeispiel für die Bedeutung, die Einleitungsfragen für die
ntliche Exegese haben können. Wie eingangs dargelegt, gehen

wir von der Authentizität des Briefes aus, d.h. von der
Verfasserschaft des Apostels Petrus, gleich, wie der Vorgang
der Niederschrift im Einzelnen verlaufen ist. Die Parallelen,
die wir zwischen den Petruspredigten der Apg und den
Kurzkatechismen des 1. Petr festgestellt haben, sprechen
übrigens für eine petrinische Verfasserschaft des 1. Petr./148/
Dann wäre der Brief also etwa 60-64 n.Chr. anzusetzen.

In dieser Zeit um 60-64 n.Chr. kann das Mt Ev schon als
fertige Evangelienschrift vorgelegen haben./149/ Bei Mk ist
eine solche Annahme jedenfalls angesichts der ältesten
kirchlichen Nachrichten wenig wahrscheinlich;/150/ bei Lk ist
sie möglich, wenn man mit Harnack, Guthrie u.a./151/ das
lukanische Werk auf den Anfang der 60er Jahre des 1. Jh.
datiert; bei Joh ist sie ausgeschlossen. Die Frage, ob der
Verfasser des 1 Petr kanonische Evangelien benutzt hat, kann
also von den Kurzkatechismen her definitiv nicht beantwortet
werden. Sie muß vorläufig offen bleiben. Und es ist außerdem
zu beachten, daß eine Benutzung bei dem einen Evangelium
gegeben sein kann, während sie bei einem anderen ausscheidet.

7. Das ist jedoch nicht alles, was hier zu sagen ist.
Vielmehr fordern jetzt die *johanneischen Parallelen* unsere
Aufmerksamkeit. Wir haben im I. Teil 24 solche johanneische
Parallelstellen zu den Kurzkatechismen notiert. Selbst wenn
deren Zahl eingeschränkt werden müßte, bleibt die Tatsache
bestehen, daß der 1. Petr eine auffallende Nähe zum Joh Ev -
und nicht nur zu den Synoptikern - aufweist. Wir erinnern uns
hier auch an Gundry's Urteil: 'Almost as striking is the
support for parts of the Johannine tradition...'/152/ sowie an
die Tatsache, daß sowohl Gundry als auch Selwyn und Spicq eine
beträchtliche Reihe von Parallelstellen aus dem Joh Ev
zusammengestellt haben./153/ Hier, im Falle der johanneischen
Parallelen, kommt eine Herleitung aus dem kanonischen
Evengelium eindeutig nicht in Frage. Das kanonische Joh Ev
ist erst nach 64 n.Chr., dem Todesjahr Petri, vollendet worden.
/154/ Somit bleibt nur eine Erklärung übrig: Der Verfasser de
des 1. Petr kennt 'johanneische' Jesuslogien entweder aus
mündlicher Tradition oder aus vorläufigen schriftlichen Notizen.
Insofern liegt bezüglich der petrinischen Kurzkatechismen ein
Fall von Jesustradition vor, die grundsätzlich von den uns
bekannten Evangelien unabhängig ist.

8. Einige weitere Konsequenzen seien nur kurz angedeutet:
a) Waren unsere bisherigen Ergebnisse richtig, dann steht
Petrus in der Mitte zwischen den sog. Synoptikern und Johannes.

Er teilt Traditionen sowohl mit den Synoptikern als auch mit
Johannes. Der forschungsgeschichtlich oft so quälend
empfundene Abstand zwischen den Synoptikern und Johannes würde
sich erneut ein Stück weit verringern./155/ b) Sind im
Zeitraum 60 -64 n.Chr. bereits johanneische Traditionen im
1. Petr aufweisbar, dann spricht dies für das Alter und letzten
Endes auch für die geschichtliche Zuverlässigkeit dieser
'johanneischen' Traditionen. c) Ist der 1. Petr im Blick auf
die johanneischen Traditionen unabhängig vom kanonischen
Evangelium, dann neigt sich die Waage bezüglich aller Jesuslogien zugunsten der *Annahme, daß Petrus unabhängig von den
kanonischen Evangelien Jesustradition - mündlich oder in
vorläufigen Notizen - zur Verfügung hatte.* Damit soll
allerdings nicht aufgehoben werden, was oben gesagt wurde, daß
nämlich eine letztgültige Entscheidung hinsichtlich der Frage,
ob Petrus synoptische Evangelien benutzt habe, nicht möglich
ist. d) Für verfehlt halte ich allerdings das Unterfangen,
Beziehungen zwischen dem 1. Petr und 'Q' herzustellen, wie das
schon versucht wurde./156/ Denn 'Q' ist eine viel zu
verschwommene und letztlich vielleicht gar nicht vorhandene
Größe. Besser ist es, mit einer Mehrheit von schriftlichen
Notizen zu rechnen./157/ Jedenfalls sind für den 1. Petr die
Berichte vom Geschick Jesu ebenso wichtig wie die verba
Christi.

    9. Angesichts der petrinischen Kurzkatechismen soll eine
letzte Frage aufgegriffen werden: *Woher stammt die Form
dieser Kurzkatechismen?* Gibt uns das AT eine Antwort? Dies
ist in der Tat der Fall. Gerhard von Rad nannte einst den
Abschnitt Dt 26,5ff. ein 'heilsgeschichtliches Credo' oder ein
'heilsgeschichtliches Summarium'. Hartmut Gese spricht im
Blick auf Dt 6 von der literarischen 'Gattung der Sohnesfrage
mit der katechismusartigen Antwort des Vaters'./158/
Heilsgeschichtliche, katechismusartige Zusammenfassungen
ähnlicher Art liegen z.B. in Dt 6,21 -23; Jos 24,2 - 13; 1 Chr 16,
15 - 22 und in erweiterter Form in den Psalmen 78; 105 und
136 vor. Ja, eine erweiterte Form dieser Gattung läßt sich
sogar noch im NT aufweisen, nämlich in Apg 7, 2 - 50, der sog.
Stephanusrede. Wie bei den petrinischen Kurzkatechismen
liegt das Typische dieser atlichen Stücke in der Verbindung von
Glaubensbekenntnis und Geschichte, im geschichtlich -
chronologischen Aufriß, in der Selektion jeweils bedeutsamer
Tatbestände und der Verknüpfung von Geschichte und
Geschichtsdeutung. Außerdem werden sie funktional ebenso
eingesetzt wie in 1. Petr: nämlich um konkretes Verhalten zu
motivieren und zu normieren. Ja, die Ähnlichkeit reicht noch

weiter. Die Psalmen 78; 105 und 136 zeigen, daß diese
heilsgeschichtlichen, katechismusartigen Bekenntnisse leicht
in Hymnen umgesetzt werden konnten. Und gerade die
petrinischen Kurzkatechismen werden immer wieder als Teile von
Christushymnen betrachtet./159/ Man kann hier also den Weg vom
Psalm zum Christushymnus nachzeichnen. Mehr noch: die Form des
Kurzkatechismus erweist sich als genuin alttestamentlich.
Präziser müßte man 1.Petr 1,18-21; 2,21-25; 3,18-22 sogar als
'heilsgeschichtliche Kurzkatechismen' bezeichnen. Vermutlich
sind solche heilsgeschichtlichen Kurzkatechismen aufgrund der
atlichen Vorbilder unmittelbar nach der Himmelfahrt Jesu
entwickelt (cf. die Stephanusrede Apg 7,2ff.!) und zum
Grundriß apostolischer Predigt und Lehre gemacht worden. Ein
solcher Prozeß würde das Verhältnis der Petruspredigten der
Apg zu den petrinischen Kurzkatechismen des 1.Petr jedenfalls
ausgezeichnet erklären. Die Evangelien haben, so darf man
weiter vermuten, diesen Grundriß der heilsgeschichtlichen
Kurzkatechismen aufgenommen, und entfaltet, was im 'Katechismus'
angelegt war (cf. Lk 1, 1 - 4). So würde noch einmal bestätigt,
daß a) die heilsgeschichtlichen Kurzkatechismen Evangelien in
nuce sind, und b) die Jesustradition dieser Kurzkatechismen
eine frühere Stufe der Tradition darstellt als das, was
schließlich in den kanonischen Evangelien fixiert wurde.

Literaturverzeichnis

Best, E.   'I Peter and the Gospel Tradition', *NTS*, 16,
                    1969/70, S. 95 - 113
                    abgek.: Best

Brown, J. P.,   'Synoptic Parallels in the Epistles and Form-
                    History', *NTS*, 10, 1963/64, S. 27 - 48
                    abgek.: Brown

Cothenet, E.,   *Les orientations actuelles de l'exegèse de la
                    première lettre de Pierre, Études sur la
                    première lettre de Pierre*, Lectio divina,
                    102, Paris, 1980, S. 13 - 42
                    abgek.: Cothenet

Cranfield, C. E. B., 'The Interpretation of I Peter iii. 19
                    and IV.6', *ExpT* 69, 1957/58, S. 369 - 372
                    abgek.: Cranfield

Dautzenberg, G.,   'Σωτηρία ψυχῶν (1 Petr 1,9)', *BZ*, 8, 1964,
                    S. 262 - 276
                    abgek.: Dautzenberg

Elliott, J. H.,   'The Rehabilitation of an Exegetical Step-
                       Child: 1 Peter in Recent Research', *JBL*, 95,
                       1976, S. 243 - 254
                       abgek.: Elliott

Feuillet, A.,   'Quelques reflexions sur le quatrième évangile
                       à propos d'un livre récent, l'apôtre Pierre,
                       garant de la tradition évangelique', Compagnie
                       de Saint - Sulpice, *Bulletin du Comité des
                       Études*, 57/58, 1969, S. 235 - 247
                       abgek.: Feuillet

Gese, H.,   *Zur biblischen Theologie*, München, 1977
                       abgek.: Gese

Gerhardsson, B.,   *Die Anfänge der Evangelien-Tradition*,
                       Wuppertal, 1977
                       abgek.: Gerhardsson

Goldstein, H.,   *Paulinische Gemeinde im Ersten Petrusbrief*,
                       SBS, 80, Stuttgart, 1975
                       abgek.: Goldstein

Goppelt, L.,   *Der Erste Petrusbrief*, KEK, II/1, 8.Aufl.,
                       Göttingen, 1978
                       abgek.: Goppelt Petr

Goppelt, L.,   *Theologie des Neuen Testaments, II*, Göttingen,
                       1976
                       abgek.: Goppelt NT

Grundmann, W.,   Art: 'ταπεινός' usw., *ThWNT*, 8, 1969, S. 1 - 27
                       abgek.: Grundmann

Gundry, R. H.,   'Verba Christi in I Peter: Their
                       Implications Concerning the Authorship of I
                       Peter and the Authenticity of the Gospel
                       Tradition', *NTS*, 1966/67, S. 336 - 350
                       abgek.: Gundry

Gundry, R. H.,   'Further Verba on Verba Christi in First
                       Peter', *Bib.*, 55, 1974, S. 211 - 232
                       abgek.: Gundry Bib.

Guthrie, D.,   *New Testament Introduction*, 7.Aufl., 1978
                       abgek.: Guthrie

Leaney, A. R. C.,   *The Letters of Peter and Jude*, CNEB, 1967
                       abgek.: Leaney

Lohse, E.,   'Paranëse and Kerygma im 1. Petrusbrief', *ZNW*,
                       45, 1954, S. 68 - 89
                       abgek.: Lohse

Riesner, R.,   *Jesus als Lehrer*, WUNT, 2. Reihe, 7, Tübingen,
                1981
                abgek.: Riesner

Robinson, J. A. T., *Redating the New Testament*, Philadelphia,
                1976
                abgek.: Robinson

Scharfe, E.,   *Die petrinische Strömung der neutestamentlichen
                Literatur*, Berlin, 1893
                abgek.: Scharfe

Schelkle, K. H., *Die Petrusbriefe, der Judasbrief*, HThK, 13,2,
                5. Aufl., 1980
                abgek.: Schelkle

Schlosser, J., 'Ancien Testament et christologie dans la prima
                Petri', *Études sur la première lettre de Pierre*,
                Lectio divina, 102, Paris, 1980, S. 65 - 96
                abgek.: Schlosser

Schrage, W.,   Der erste Petrusbrief, in: NTD, 10, *Die
                katholischen Briefe*, 11. Aufl., 1973, S. 59 - 117
                abgek.: Schrage

Seeberg, A.,   *Der Katechismus der Urchristenheit*, Leipzig, 1903
                abgek.: Seeberg

Selwyn, E. G., *The First Epistle of St. Peter*, London, 1949
                (Reprinted)
                abgek.: Selwyn

Spicq, C.,   *Les Epitres de Saint Pierre*, SBi, 1966
                abgek.: Spicq

Spicq, C.,   'La I[a] Petri et la témoignage évangélique de
                saint Pierre', *Studia Theologica* (Scandinavian
                Journal of Theology), 20, 1966, S. 37 - 61
                abgek.: Spicq StTh

Stibbs, A. M., *The First Epistle General of Peter*, TNTC, 9.
                Aufl., Grand Rapids, 1979 (Introduction by
                Andrew F. Walls)
                abgek.: Stibbs

Tenney, M. C., 'Some Possible Parallels Between 1 Peter and
                John', *New Dimensions in New Testament Study*,
                Grand Rapids, 1974, S. 370 - 377
                abgek.: Tenney

Vanhoye, A.,   'l Pierre au carrefour des théologies du Nouveau
                  Testament', *Études sur la première lettre de
                  Pierre*, Lectio divina, 102, Paris, 1980, S. 97 -
                  128
                  abgek.: Vanhoye

Zahn, Th.,   *Einleitung in das Neue Testament, II*, Leipzig,
                  1899
                  abgek.: Zahn

Anmerkungen

/1/ Selwyn S. 17ff., 363ff.
/2/ Cf. u.a. Schelkle S. 6f.; Dautzenberg S. 262; Lohse S. 71;
Vanhoye S. 108.
/3/ Brown sah z.B. hinter den Episteln einen 'Catechism as one
traditional edition of Q' (S. 28); cf. ferner Selwyn S. 24.
/4/ W. Marxsen, *Einleitung in das Neue Testament*, 2. Aufl.,
Gütersloh, 1964, S. 201.
/5/ W. G. Kümmel, *Einleitung in das Neue Testament*, 20. Aufl.,
Heidelberg, 1980, S. 374.
/6/ Goldstein S. 12.
/7/ L.c.S. 373,34 und 372,21. Dabei fehlen u.a. Feuillet,
Tenney und Zahn.
/8/ S. 790
/9/ Gundry S. 348ff.; Best S. 112.
/10/ Gundry S. 345ff.; Best S. 111.
/11/ Gundry S. 337ff.; Best S. 111 und S. 96ff.
/12/ Gundry S. 350; Best S. 99.
/13/ Cf. Best S. 103f. mit Gundry S. 337; Bib. S. 223f.
/14/ Cf. Best S. 98 mit Gundry S. 337f.; Bib. S. 218.
/15/ Feuillet S. 244; Tenney S. 373.
/16/ Cf. Best S. 108; Gundry S. 338; Bib. S. 228; Spicq StTh
S. 39,9.
/17/ Goppelt Petr S. 106,72.
/18/ So schon F. J. A. Hort 1898, auf den Gundry S. 338
hinweist, und neuerdings Goppelt Petr S. 109,90; Schelkle S. 6.
/19/ Cf. Feuillet S. 244; Goppelt Petr S. 92; Selwyn S. 391.
/20/ Cf. Best S. 98.
/21/ Cf. Goppelt Petr S. 93.
/22/ A.a.O. S. 92.
/23/ A.a.O.
/24/ Cf. Gundry S. 338f.; Bib. S. 218f.
/25/ Cf. Best S. 104.

/26/ Goppelt Petr S. 116,23.
/27/ Cf. Gundry S. 339; Bib. S. 224; Selwyn S. 447.
/28/ Cf. Gundry S. 340; Bib. S. 215f.; Feuillet S. 244; Goppelt
Petr S. 128; Tenney S. 374.
/29/ Best S. 101.
/30/ Goppelt Petr S. 142.
/31/ J. Jeremias in *ThWNT*, 4, 1942, S. 277.
/32/ Hier ist Gundry in Bib. S. 222 selbst vorsichtiger
geworden.
/33/ Cf. Jeremias a.a.O. und Gundry Bib. S. 221f., der sich
u.a. auf Cranfield, Fiebig und Snodgrass beruft. Cf. auch
Schelkle S. 6.
/34/ Cf. Gundry S. 340; Spicq StTh S. 56f.
/35/ Best S. 110f.
/36/ Gundry Bib. S. 230.
/37/ Goppelt Petr S. 180 (dort auch der Hinweis auf Selwyn S.
423-433); ebenso Spicq StTh S. 50f.
/38/ Cf. Goppelt Petr a.a.O. und S. 187,47. Anders Gundry Bib.
S. 222.
/39/ Gundry S. 342.
/40/ Best S. 105.
/41/ Gundry Bib. S. 226 kommt zu einem ähnlichen Ergebnis. Cf.
Brown S. 34; Goppelt Petr S. 225ff. (ausführliche Begründung!);
Schelkle S. 6; Schrage S. 60; Spicq StTh S. 42.
/42/ Best S. 104; Goppelt Petr S. 278ff.
/43/ Gundry S. 343; Bib. S. 225; Selwyn S. 446 unterstützt ihn.
/44/ Spicq StTh S. 42f. weist auf Mt 5,7; 6,14f.; 18,23 - 25;
Lk 6,37 als Parallelen zu 1.Petr 4,8 hin.
/45/ Gundry S. 343f.; ebenso Spicq StTh S. 43.
/46/ Best S. 108.
/47/ Vorsichtig mit einer Herleitung von Lk 23,46 auch Goppelt
Petr S. 316.
/48/ Gundry S. 344f.; ebenso Spicq StTh S. 45.
/49/ Best S. 100.
/50/ Gundry Bib. S. 220.
/51/ Grundmann S. 24,75. Cf. Gundry a.a.O.; Feuillet S. 244;
Spicq StTh S. 39,9.45.47f. Zurückhaltender Goppelt Petr
S. 332f.
/52/ Cf. wieder Gundry a.a.O. sowie Goppelt Petr S. 321.327f.
/53/ Über weitere Zusammenhänge mit den Evangelien cf. Goppelt
Petr S. 321ff.
/54/ Tenney notiert S. 375f. weitere johanneische Parallelen:
Joh 1,31; 2,11; 7,4; 9,3; 21,1.14.22.
/55/ Gundry S. 344.
/56/ Cf. Feuillet S. 244; Schelkle S. 6; Brown S. 33; Selwyn
S. 377.448; Goppelt Petr S. 339; Spicq StTh S. 46.

/57/ Best S. 100.107.

/58/ Gundry Bib. S. 220f.

/59/ Cf. Goppelt Petr S. 339,10.

/60/ Gundry S. 344.

/61/ Tenney nennt neben Joh 8,44 noch Joh 6,70; 13,2.24.27 als
vergleichbare johanneische Stellen.

/62/ Zu den Maßstäben traditionsgeschichtlicher Vergleichung
cf. Goppelt Petr S. 47f.

/63/ Dautzenberg S. 267ff.; cf. Goppelt Petr S. 104.

/64/ ThWNT, 7, 1964, S. 996,134.

/65/ Cf. Spicq StTh S. 39,9.

/66/ Cf. hier G. Delling in ThWNT, 8, 1969, S. 75.

/67/ Ähnlich Schelkle S. 6, während Selwyn S. 403 auf die
Verwandtschaft von 1. Petr 1,14.17 mit Joh 4,23f. hinweist.
Stibbs S. 87 verweist ebenfalls auf Mt 5,48.

/68/ Cf. G. Quell und S. Schulz in ThWNT, 7, 1964, S. 537ff.
sowie J. Jeremias, Die Gleichnisse Jesu, 6. Aufl., Göttingen,
1962, S. 77.

/69/ Cf. Goppelt Petr S. 132,29.

/70/ Gundry S. 345; Best S. 106.

/71/ Selwyn S. 377.

/72/ Brown S. 31.

/73/ Goppelt Petr S. 153.

/74/ A.a.O. S. 153,68.

/75/ Cf. Goppelt Petr S. 154.

/76/ Brown S. 34; ähnlich Gundry S. 341; Bib. S. 226; Best S. 106.

/77/ Cf. Goppelt Petr S. 202.

/78/ A.a.O. S. 200; cf. überhaupt S. 199ff.

/79/ Ähnlich Spicq StTh S. 41, der noch auf Joh 13,15 hinweist
(S. 54).

/80/ Best S. 108.

/81/ Cf. Goppelt Petr S. 217; F. Hauck und S. Schulz in ThWNT,
6, 1959, S. 649f.

/82/ Spicq StTh S. 45 zieht außerdem die Verbindung zu Mt 11,29;
12,19; 21,5.

/83/ Goppelt Petr S. 287; O. Michel in ThWNT, 5, 1954, S. 153.

/84/ Cf. H. Seesemann in ThWNT, 6, 1959, S. 23ff.

/85/ Cf. Goppelt Petr S. 301.

/86/ Goppelt Petr S. 305; cf. Schelkle S. 6. Nicht einmal Best
S. 109 lehnt dies ganz ab. Cf. auch J. Schneider, ThWNT, 5,
1954, S. 240; Best S. 105; Gundry S. 342f.; Brown S. 30; Spicq
StTh S. 41.

/87/ Goppelt a.a.O.

/88/ A.a.O. S. 306.

/89/ Goppelt a.a.O. S. 305.

/90/ Cf. Goppelt Petr S. 322.
/91/ Goppelt Petr S. 337; vgl. Spicq StTh S. 43.
/92/ Cf. Best S. 111.
/93/ Gegen Best a.a.O.
/94/ Ähnlich Gundry S. 345; Spicq StTh S. 39.
/95/ Petr S. 53; ähnlich Best S. 99.
/96/ Gundry S. 350; Spicq StTh S. 39; Tenney S. 370; cf.
Feuillet S. 243; Grundmann S. 24,75.
/97/ Cf. Selwyn S. 366.
/98/ Feuillet S. 247; Spicq StTh S. 39,9.
/99/ Spicq S. 39; Tenney S. 377.
/100/ Cf. Walls bei Stibbs S. 42f.
/101/ StTh S. 39.
/102/ S. 47.
/103/ Cf. z.B. Gerhardsson S. 48ff.; Riesner S. 500ff.
/104/ Cf. Feuillet S. 242.
/105/ Goppelt NT S. 505ff.; von 'primitiver Katechese' spricht
Spicq S. 16.
/106/ Damit nähern wir uns Spicq, der von 'résumés dogmatiques'
oder 'énoncés du credo' spricht (StTh S. 38).
/107/ Cf. zu 3,18ff. die Erörterung bei Cranfield S. 369, sowie
allgemein Seeberg S. 86ff.
/108/ Cf. die Diskussion bei Selwyn S. 33,35; sowie Spicq S. 17.
/109/ Cf. die Diskussion bei Goppelt Petr S. 124f.
/110/ Mit Goppelt (NT, I, 1975, S. 241ff.) und P. Stuhlmacher
(*Vom Verstehen des Neuen Testaments*, Göttingen, 1979, S. 230)
nehmen wir an, daß Mk 10,45 par auf Jesus selbst zurückgeht, und
auch Jesus selbst seinen weg von Jes 53 her gedeutet hat.
/111/ Cf. hierzu Gese S. 113, der im übrigen eine andere Sicht
vertritt.
/112/ Cf. Spicq S. 17; StTh S. 40.44.53; Tenney S. 373f.
/113/ Goppelt Petr S. 121f.: 'Den Sinn des Verbums oszilliert
an unserer Stelle... (es) bleibt in seiner Bedeutung ambivalent'.
/114/ Cf. Gese S. 105f.
/115/ Anders Goppelt Petr S. 121.
/116/ Ähnlich Walls bei Stibbs S. 35; Spicq StTh S. 40.53.
/117/ So auch Goppelt Petr S. 199.
/118/ Cf. Schlosser S. 83ff.
/119/ Ebenso Goppelt Petr S. 206; cf. Spicq StTh S. 53.
/120/ Goppelt Petr S. 200.
/121/ S. 347.
/122/ A.a.O.
/123/ Gundry verbindet S. 338,1. Petr 1,10-12 mit Lk 24,25f.
/124/ Zum Begriff des 'Christusweges' cf. Goppelt NT S. 415. 507.
/125/ Zuletzt Goldstein S. 12 und Schrage S. 59; cf. auch die
Diskussion zwischen Elliott und Beare (Elliott S. 246) sowie
Lohse S. 83; Walls bei Stibbs S. 39; Spicq StTh S. 61.

/126/ Interessanterweise benutzt auch der Jesus des Joh Ev den
Begriff zōopoiein, dem wir in l. Petr 3,18 (aber auch einige
Male bei Paulus) begegnen. Über die Echtheit der Leidens- und
Auferstehungsweissagungen vgl. Goppelt (NT, I, 1975, S. 235ff.)
und Stuhlmacher (L.c.).
/127/ Goppelt Petr S. 240.
/128/ Selwyn erinnert hier an die Unterscheidung von
halachischer und haggadischer Überlieferung (S. 24).
/129/ S. 341f.; ebenso Spicq S. 17; cf. Tenney S. 374.
/130/ S. 350; ebenso Spicq StTh S. 39,9 und vor allem Tenney
S. 370ff.
/131/ Cf. Goppelt Petr S. 126.
/132/ Eine besondere Ausprägung findet die Aussage von der
ausschließlichen Heilsmittlerschaft Jesu im l.Petr dort, wo von
der Predigt an die Toten die Rede ist (3,19f.; 4,6). Diese
Stellen sind aber besonders umstritten, sodaß sich eine
Einbeziehung in unsere Untersuchung nicht empfiehlt.
/133/ S. 28.
/134/ S. 36.28.
/135/ S. 33ff. Cf. Lohse S. 70; Walls bei Stibbs S. 36; Spicq
StTh S. 53ff. (unter Berufung auf J. W. C. Wand).
/136/ S. 33.
/137/ In V. 14 - 21 wird die 'Zungenrede' erklärt.
/138/ Cf. Selwyn S. 33; Spicq StTh S. 60,67.
/139/ Cf. Selwyn S. 34; Spicq StTh S. 54.
/140/ Cf. Spicq StTh S. 54.
/141/ Cf. Spicq StTh S. 53.
/142/ S. 35; ebenso Spicq StTh S. 53ff.
/143/ S. 33.
/144/ Weitere terminologische Berührungen zwischen Apg 10,34ff.
und dem l.Petr überhaupt bei Selwyn S. 35; cf. auch Walls bei
Stibbs S. 35f.; Scharfe passim und Spicq StTh S. 53ff.
/145/ Cf. Goppelt Petr S. 240: 'Nirgends sind so viele Stücke
des 2. Artikels des Apostolikums präformiert'.
/146/ Cf. Brown S. 28ff.; Dautzenberg S. 267ff.; Elliott S. 254;
Gundry S. 337; Schelkle S. 6; Schrage S. 60; Selwyn S. 23f.
366ff.; Lohse S. 70.85; Walls bei Stibbs S. 34ff.; Cothenet
S. 29f.; Spicq StTh passim; Tenney passim.
/147/ Cf. Brown S. 28; Selwyn S. 24.
/148/ Cf. die Diskussion bei Guthrie S. 806.
/149/ Cf. Irenäus Adv. haer. III,1,1 und Robinson S. 116.
/150/ Cf. die Diskussion bei Robinson S. 95ff.
/151/ Cf. Guthrie S. 110ff.
/152/ S. 350; cf. auch S. 339: 'I Peter is clearly moving
within the circle of Johannine thought'.

/153/ Gundry zuletzt in Bib. S. 214ff.; cf. Spicq S. 16f.;
StTh S. 39ff.; Cothenet S. 30.
/154/ Dies gilt für 'the final form of the Gospel' sogar nach
Robinson S. 307.
/155/ Cf. auch meinen Beitrag zu *Gospel Perspectives II*,
S. 267ff., bezüglich des Verhältnisses von Mt und Joh, sowie
Feuillet S. 247.
/156/ Z.B. bei Brown S. 28ff.; Selwyn S. 24.
/157/ Ähnlich Lohse S. 85.
/158/ Gese S. 66; v. Rad, *Theologie des Alten Testaments, I*,
1962, S. 135.
/159/ Cf. hierzu Goppelt Petr S. 204ff.

Anhang

Wahrscheinliche und mögliche Parallelen von 1. Petr und
Evangelienüberlieferung in der *Einzelparänese*

1. Petrusbrief	*Synoptiker*	*Johannes*	*Art der Parallele*
1,3.23; 2,2		Joh 3,3ff.	wahrscheinlich
1,4	Lk 12,33		möglich
1,6 - 9	Lk 17,26ff.		möglich
1,8		Joh 15,11ff.; 20,29	wahrscheinlich
1,9	Mt 16,24ff. par		wahrscheinlich
1,10 - 12	Lk 24,25ff. Mt 13,17 par	Joh 8,56	wahrscheinlich
1,13	Lk 12,35		möglich
1,15	Mt 5,48		wahrscheinlich
1,22		Joh 13,34f.; 15,12	wahrscheinlich
1,23	Mt 13,18ff. par Lk 8,11 - 15		wahrscheinlich
2,3	Lk 6,35 Mt 5,45ff.		möglich
2,4 - 8	Mk 12,10ff. parr		wahrscheinlich
2,9	Mt 4,14ff.	Joh 8,12	wahrscheinlich

1. Petrusbrief	Synoptiker	Johannes	Art der Parallele
2,13 – 17	Mt 17,25ff. 22,15ff. parr		wahrscheinlich
2,19ff.	Mt 5,10f.; 16,24 parr		wahrscheinlich
3,4	Mt 5,5		möglich
3,9	Lk 6,27f. Mt 5,39ff.		möglich
4,7 – 8	Mt 3,2; 4,17; 10,7;13,49ff.; 24,3.42ff.; 26,41; 28,20 Lk 21,31ff.		wahrscheinlich
4,8		Joh 13,34f.; 15,12	wahrscheinlich
4,10	Lk 12,42ff. (evtl. Mt 20, 25ff. par)		wahrscheinlich
4,12 – 16	Mt 5,11f.; 26,41 (evtl. 10,19f. par; 10,24f.; 16,24 par; 25,31)		wahrscheinlich
4,19	Lk 23,46		möglich
5,1	Lk 24,48; Apg 1,8		möglich
5,3 – 5	Mt 20,20ff. parr (evtl. Mt 18,1 – 5 parr)	Joh 13,4ff.; 21,15ff.	wahrscheinlich
5,7	Mt 6,25ff. par		wahrscheinlich
5,8 – 9	Mt 24,42ff.; Lk 12,35ff.; 22,31ff.		wahrscheinlich

Eine Tabelle der Stellen aus den Kurzkatechismen ist wenig
sinnvoll, da hier jeweils umfangreiche Traditionen aufgenommen
und verarbeitet sind.

THE USE OF DANIEL IN THE SYNOPTIC ESCHATOLOGICAL DISCOURSE AND
IN THE BOOK OF REVELATION

G. K. Beale,
Department of New Testament,
Gordon-Conwell Theological Seminary,
South Hamilton, Mass.

I. Introduction

The purpose of this article is to demonstrate that the
Book of Revelation develops the Danielic 'midrash'/1/ of the
synoptic eschatological discourse, especially that in Mark 13.
This development does not show strict adherence to the
synoptic material, an observation which may point to an
independent knowledge of a Danielic tradition perhaps even
underlying the gospel narratives.

II. Recent Proposals Concerning the Danielic Midrash of the Synoptics and its Relation to Revelation

Lars Hartman in his *Prophecy Interpreted* has presented the
most convincing case that Mark 13 and its parallels (Mt 24 and
Lk 21) are based on the apocalyptic chapters of Daniel./2/ He
sees 'that the main part of the eschatological discourse [in
Mark 13 and Matthew 24] is based on a coherent exposition of or
meditation on' texts from Daniel 7-9, 11-12./3/ His thesis is
supported by a trenchant and detailed, inductive exegetical
argument and copious comparisons with the relevant Daniel
texts./4/ Hartman's work has received some criticism,/5/ but
the essence of his argument concerning the influence of Daniel
still appears persuasive. Although some of Hartman's allusive
alignments with Daniel may be questioned, the cumulative force
of his exegesis is strong. It may also be questioned whether
Hartman's use of the term 'midrash' is appropriate. Nevertheless the fact of a predominant influence from Daniel in the
eschatological discourse appears to have been established.

At the conclusion of his work Hartman speculated that the
midrash on Daniel represented a tradition traceable to the
historical Jesus. He also asserted that there are significant
eschatological parallels between Mark 13 and the Thessalonian
epistles, which point to Paul's acquaintance with the Daniel
midrashic tradition represented in Mark./6/ He suggested the
same thing for the Johannine epistles/7/ and speculated that
there may also be fruitful comparisons with Revelation
(primarily Rev 13)./8/

Austin Farrer and John Sweet have also discussed the use of
Daniel in Mark 13, although not to the extent of Hartman.
Their primary purpose has been to point out that the material
and ideas from Daniel in Mark 13 have been re-used in
Revelation. Farrer has seen the influence in Mark essentially
in terms of Daniel's eschatological time scheme, which is taken
up again by the author of Revelation as a governing motif
throughout the book. According to Farrer, the Apocalypse has
been broadly patterned after the form of Daniel's eschatological
half-week./9/ For Sweet, Mark 13 represents Jesus' own
purported use of Daniel, which has been reshaped by Matthew and
Luke. In addition, John's Revelation is to be viewed as an
'updating' of Christ's supposed reference to Daniel in the
Marcan apocalypse./10/ Others have also seen the same
relationship between Mark 13 and Revelation./11/ Most recently
Desmond Ford has re-affirmed the connection generally/12/ and
has specifically traced the presence of the 'abomination of
desolation' theme (Dan 8:13; 9:27; 11:31) in Mark 13 and
throughout Revelation./13/ Thus broad connections have been
established between Daniel and Mark 13 on the one hand, and
between Mark 13 and Revelation on the other. In the following
discussion we will especially be assuming the validity of
Hartman's conclusions concerning the predominant influence of
Daniel in the synoptic eschatological discourse.

III. Evidence of a Daniel Midrash in Revelation 4-5

A. *Introduction*
All of the above proposals of a synoptic-Revelation
connection in terms of Daniel have been of a rather general
nature. While these proposals have plausibility, more detailed
argument from the data in Revelation would add to their
probability. The following discussion will attempt to show that
the broad segment of Revelation 4-5 is based on Daniel,/14/ and
that this further augments the above suggestions of a synoptic-
Revelation link, as well as possibly pointing to the

apocalyptist's knowledge of a Jesus tradition independent of the synoptic form.

The few works dedicated only to studying the use of the OT in Revelation fail to give proper attention to chapters 4-5, much less to the use of Daniel therein. The most thorough study of the OT influence in these two chapters is by H. P. Müller. Müller attributes the origin of the two chapters to the dominant influence of certain OT texts, of which he regards Daniel 7 to be one of the most prominent, though he sees it as the primary influence only in the last half of chapter 5./15/ Apparently there has been no suggestion that the whole of Revelation 4-5 is modelled primarily on Daniel, especially Daniel 7. The initial goal of the present study is to establish just this point.

> B. *Survey of OT Allusions in Revelation 4-5*
> B.1. Preview of the Structure of Chapters 4-5

An overview of the structural outline of chapters 4-5 may be helpful in establishing a framework within which to carry out our brief exegetical survey. In fact, through such an overview of the two chapters *together a unified* structure is revealed which corresponds more to the structure of Daniel 7 than with any other vision structure in the OT. If we begin with Daniel 7:9ff. and observe the elements and order of their presentation which are in common with Revelation 4-5, a striking resemblance is discernible:

1.) Introductory vision phraseology (Dan 7:9 [cf. 7:2,6-7]; Rev 4:1)
2.) The setting of a throne(s) in heaven (Dan 7:9a; Rev 4:2a [cf. 4:4a])
3.) God sitting on a throne (Dan 7:9b; Rev 4:2b)
4.) The description of God's appearance on the throne (Dan 7:9c; Rev 4:3a)
5.) Fire before the throne (Dan 7:9d-10a; Rev 4:5)
6.) Heavenly servants surrounding the throne (Dan 7:10b; Rev 4:4b, 6b-10; 5:8,11,14)
7.) Book(s) before the throne (Dan 7:10c; Rev 5:1ff.)
8.) The 'opening' of the book(s) (Dan 7:10d; Rev 5:2-5,9)
9.) The approach of a divine (messianic) figure before God's throne in order to receive authority to reign forever over a kingdom (Dan 7:13-14a; Rev 5:5b-7, 9a, 12-13)
10.) This 'kingdom' includes 'all peoples, nations and tongues' (Dan 7:14a [MT]; Rev 5:9b)

11.) The seer's emotional distress on account of the vision
     (Dan 7:15; Rev 5:4)
12.) The seer's reception of heavenly counsel concerning the
     vision from one among the heavenly throne servants
     (Dan 7:16; Rev 5:5a)
13.) The saints are also given divine authority to reign over a
     kingdom (Dan 7:18, 22, 27a; Rev 5:10)
14.) A concluding mention of God's eternal reign (Dan 7:27b;
     Rev 5:13-14).

From the comparison Revelation 4-5 can be seen to include
the same fourteen elements as Daniel 7:9ff. in the same basic
order, but with small variations which result from the
expansion of images. For example, Revelation 4-5 contains more
description of the heavenly throne servants than Daniel 7 and
repeatedly portrays their presence around the throne, while they
are mentioned only three times in Daniel. That both visions
contain the image of a sea may also be noteworthy (Dan 7:2-3;
Rev 4:6).

However, if one considers only the first section of the
vision in 4:1-5:1, then Ezekiel 1-2 appears to be the source of
an even larger number of allusions and has many of the same
elements as in the above outline. Therefore, Ezekiel 1-2 has
been held to be the dominant influence in chapters 4-5. But
there are more variations in order, and five important elements
are lacking (cf. elements #8, #9, #10, #13, #14 in above
parallels between Daniel 7 and Revelation 4-5). Therefore, the
structure of Daniel 7 dominates the whole of the Revelation 4-5
vision, even if the structures of Daniel 7 and Ezekiel 1-2 are
equally present from 4:1 to 5:1. In 5:2ff. the structure of
Ezekiel 1-2 and allusions to it fade out. If only 4:1-5:1 were
viewed, apart from 5:2ff., Ezekiel would be considered more
dominant than Daniel, but this is not the case when the two
chapters are properly seen as a *unified* vision./16/

Within such an overall Danielic framework we present a
survey of the OT allusions in these two chapters. That is, a
second line of evidence pointing to a Daniel midrash in
Revelation 4-5 is the number of *verbal* allusions to Daniel which
can be observed there. Because of space limitations these
allusions will not be discussed, but only an abbreviated
summary can be shown in order that more discussion can be
dedicated to the crucial issue of the relationship between the
Daniel traditions in Mark and Revelation. The following survey
is an abridgement of a detailed exegetical analysis of

Revelation 4-5, which is to appear in my forthcoming book, *The Use of Daniel in Jewish Apocalyptic Literature and in the Revelation of St. John.*/17/ Those who are interested in seeking exegetical validation for the following list of allusive alignments should consult the more thorough discussion of my book, since here I am assuming the validity of the arguments and conclusions found there. I will make the same assumptions in my following discussions of the Danielic nature of Revelation 1 and 13.

Only allusions to Daniel will be listed here./18/ The allusions can be broken down into three categories and are as follows: (1) *clear allusion* - Rev 4:1d-Dan 2:45; (θ; cf. 2:28-29 of LXX, θ); 4:9b-Dan 4:34 (θ) and 12:7 (θ; cf. LXX; cf. also 6:27 [θ]); 4:10b-Dan 4:34 (θ) and 12:7 (θ; cf. LXX and 6:27 [θ]); 5:11d-Dan 7:10; (2) *probable allusion* (with more varied wording) - Rev 4:1a-Dan 7:6a,7a; 4:11b-Dan 4:35 (θ) and 4 4:37 (LXX); 5:1c-Dan 12:4,9 (θ);/19/ 5:2a-Dan 4:13-14, 23 (LXX) and 4:14 (θ); 5:2b-Dan 7:10; 5:2c-Dan 12:4,9; 5:3a-Dan 7:10; 5:4a-Dan 7:10; 5:5d-Dan 7:10; 5:5e-Dan 12:4,9; 5:7-Dan 7:13; 5:9b-Dan 7:10 and 12:4,9; 5:9d - coined phrase from Dan 3-7; 5:10-7:18,22,27 (LXX); (3) *possible allusion* (or echo) - Rev 4:2b-Dan 7:9a; 4:4a-Dan 7:9; 4:6a-Dan 7:2-3; 4:11a-Dan 3:52 -55ff. (LXX); 5:8c-Dan 7:18ff.; 5:12b-Dan 2:20,37 (LXX) and 4:30 (LXX, θ; cf. 4:31 of LXX); 5:13b-Dan 2:37 (LXX), 4:30 (LXX, θ) and 4:31 (LXX).

To cite two or three particular examples of my method would be appropriate in discussing these above allusions, but there is unfortunately not space.

C. Conclusion of the Revelation 4-5 Study
We conclude that Daniel 7 is the model which lies behind the chapter 4-5 vision because of the same basic structure of common ideas and images, which is supplemented by numerous phrases having varying degrees of allusion to the text of Daniel. Of the various allusive references from Daniel, about half are from Daniel 7 and half from other chapters in Daniel. When the latter are studied they are seen to have parallels and themes associated with Daniel 7 and, therefore, they may have been employed to supplement the interpretative significance of Daniel 7 in the scene. When Daniel 7 is *not* seen as the *Vorbild* for chapters 4-5, one can perhaps understand why many references from similar OT theophanies have been combined with references from Daniel 7, but how does one account for so much material from the non-theophanic contexts of Daniel 2, 4 and 12? A

possible answer is that throughout Revelation John draws on the
whole of Daniel, and its language colours the book throughout.
But because of such a concentration of this material in so
small a section (primarily 4:9-5:13), our proposal of a Daniel 7
model would seem to be the best answer. If Daniel 7 was the
controlling pattern of John's thought, other Danielic material
would have lain close in the field of association and would
have been convenient to draw on for supplementary purposes.

The same supplementary approach was probably taken with
respect to the other OT allusions outside Daniel which were
drawn into the portrayal (cf. Ezek 1, Isa 6, Exod 19).

Ezekiel 1 should not be seen as the model for chapters 4-5,
but more probably has been used because of its many parallels to
Daniel 7. As has been said, its influence is more dominant than
Daniel's in 4:1-5:1 if seen in isolation from 5:2ff.; but when
chapters 4-5 are considered as *one* vision, the structure and
allusiveness of Ezekiel 1-2 fades in 5:2ff. and the structure of
Daniel 7 appears as the overall pattern. The universal cosmic
significance that Daniel 7 has in common with Revelation 4-5
points to a theological dominance of Daniel over Ezekiel 1-2,
since the latter's message is concerned primarily with the
nation of Israel.

Very possibly the picture existing in the writer's mind
throughout chapters 4-5 is a result of his acquaintance with a
liturgical or more probably an eschatological tradition based on
Daniel 7, which may have had some of its exegetical links with
the *Ausgangstext* cut, so that clear connections with Daniel 7
are not as evident as before./20/ This could explain why there
is such a cluster of clear and subtle associations with
Daniel 2,4,7 and 12 in 4:9-5:13 and why so little of Daniel is
evident in the first part of the vision, and yet why there is
also a clear structural similarity with Daniel 7. What better
Danielic eschatological tradition should be identified behind
Revelation 4-5 than that represented in Mark 13 (and its
parallels)? A positive answer to this question may be supported
from the above-mentioned proposals of a Daniel midrash in
Mark 13 and its subsequent general connection with the same
Danielic tendency in the Apocalypse. This linkage is made
stronger by noticing that the Daniel traditions in both the
synoptics and Revelation are based on the apocalyptic chapters
of Daniel (chaps. 2,7-8, 11-12), and not the sections of
historical narrative. In fact, each of the three synoptic
discourses and Revelation 4-5 have the same Daniel 2:28-29,45

allusion in their introductory sections (cf. Rev 4:1 with
Mt 24:6, Lk 21:9 and Mk 13:7), which brings them even closer
together.

The probability is that more than a coincidental broad
connection exists between the Daniel midrash of the synoptics
and that of Revelation 4-5. However, such a link might be
argued against on the grounds that the content of the two
midrashim are different both in terms of *specific* OT allusive
material and themes. While the former is true for the most
part,/21/ there are some important common themes:
(1) a depiction of the fulfillment of the Daniel 7:13 enthronement prophecy of the Son of Man in direct relation to
(2) his role in judgement. Although it is likely that John has
knowledge of the synoptics, perhaps the clear difference of
content within the two Daniel midrashim point to the possibility that he has not been influenced directly by Mark, but by
an apocalyptic Daniel tradition underlying it, which was
circulating within the early Christian community. However,
this latter suggestion *is* speculative.

In this light it is perhaps not coincidental that the
enthronement of Christ in Revelation 5 issues immediately into
the beginning judgements of Revelation 6:2-17. Concerning
Revelation 6 R. H. Charles first observed that the 'seal'
judgements mentioned there have definitely been modelled on the
synoptic eschatological discourse, but the Revelation passage
does not betray dependence on any one of the synoptic accounts,
but seems to combine elements from all three. Charles
concluded that John was not directly influenced by the
synoptics, but by a 'document behind the Gospels',/22/ 'a
pre-existing eschatological scheme',/23/ which has been 'recast
under new forms' and with *new material inserted.*/24/ This view
of Revelation 6 fits in with and lends some verification to our
speculation that Revelation 4-5 is a midrash broadly based on a
pre-synoptic eschatological tradition inspired by Daniel, which
has been taken and recast with different content.

Subsequent commentators since Charles have agreed with his
contention, the most recent being David Wenham in his
Rediscovery of Jesus' Eschatological Discourse./25/ Wenham not
only draws the same conclusion as Charles about the relation of
the woes in Revelation 6:2-8 to the synoptic discourse, but
also observes other connections elsewhere in Revelation 6. He
sees the following allusive connections between Revelation 6
and Luke 21: Revelation 6:11-Luke 21:24c,/26/ Revelation

6:12-Luke 21:11/28/ and Revelation 6:14-Luke 21:25b./29/ If our
theory about Revelation 4-5 is accurate, then how logical and
natural that the author would append in Chapter 6 a list of woes
and other allusions linked to the same eschatological tradition
as that of the preceding two chapters. Hence, just as in the
synoptics (or pre-synoptic tradition?), so also in
Revelation 4-6 the enthronement depiction of the Son of Man is
directly related to earthly woes which man is to suffer. That
there would be more focus on the enthronement scene (i.e.,
Rev 4-5) than in the synoptics is understandable since from
John's viewpoint Jesus was enthroned at God's right hand after
the resurrection. In fact, this may be the reason the content
of the two Daniel models is so different: John developed the
Daniel tradition with which he was familiar in the direction of
the heavenly enthronement scene, since he wanted to explain
more about the heavenly status of Jesus.

    While John could have had acquaintance with a synoptic
or independent pre-synoptic Daniel tradition, he seems also to
have had direct knowledge of the texts of Daniel/30/ and may
have been conscious of Daniel 7 itself as a framework./31/ In
this respect, John may have turned his attention to the OT text
of Daniel 7 both as a result of being spurred on by his
knowledge of a Daniel-synoptic tradition and because of his
attempt to describe a vision which was beyond description in
human words but corresponded in his mind to the theophany
visions of the OT, especially to that of Daniel 7. Now Daniel 7
is a text referred to by other NT writers. That the NT authors,
including John, appealed to many of the same OT contexts is
likely because they were all working with a common tradition
handed to them which pointed them to these text plots. Such a
point is made by C. H. Dodd, who sees this early tradition as
having its ultimate source with Jesus./32/ Dodd's idea appears
applicable also to Revelation.

    Perhaps then Revelation 4-5 is explainable on the
supposition of John's initial acquaintance with a synoptic
(pre-synoptic?) eschatological tradition based on Daniel, which
he may also then have developed through his further reflection
on the book of Daniel itself./33/ If our speculation about a
pre-synoptic form of the tradition is correct, then the Danielic
nature of the synoptic eschatological discourse antedates the
final writing down of that narrative. This would not provide a
proof of the historicity of that discourse, but it would imply
that the gospel writers did not impose the Danielic material on
the pre-existing tradition they were using, but that this

material was already an inherent part of that circulating
tradition. The further back a tradition can be traced, the
more credible becomes the assertion that it has its derivation
in the teaching of Jesus of history. In the following sections
of this essay, we will look at several other points in the
Apocalypse which lend further weight to our general conclusion
about Revelation 4-5.

IV. Evidence of a Daniel Midrash in Revelation 1 and
    Revelation 13

A. Introduction
In this section we cannot be as detailed, but will give a
brief outline of proposals for Revelation 1 and 13 which are
very similar to that of Revelation 4-5.

B. Revelation 1
Most commentators have agreed that the Son of Man vision
of Revelation 1:13-17 is based on chapters seven and ten of
Daniel. This influence may extend even from 1:13 to 1:20. In
order to show this we present a summary survey of the OT
allusions similar to that of the preceding section:/34/:

(1) *clear allusion* - Rev 1:13b-Dan 7:13 (ϑ, LXX) and 10:6 (LXX),
16 (ϑ), 18 (LXX, ϑ); 1:13c-Dan 10:5 (LXX, ϑ); 1:14a-Dan 7:9
(LXX, ϑ); 1:14b-Dan 7:9b (LXX, ϑ); 1:15a-Dan 10:6 (LXX, ϑ);
1:19-20a - Dan 2:28-29,45-47 (LXX, ϑ); (2) *probable allusion*
(with more varied wording) - Rev 1:12a-Dan 7:11 (LXX); 1:13a-
Dan 3:25 (92) of ϑ (cf. Dan 10:5 [LXX]); 1:15c-Dan 10:6 (cf.
also Ezek 1:24 and 43:2); 1:17a-Dan 10:8-20 (esp. vv. 9-10,
12,17-19) and 8:17-18; (3) *possible allusion* (echo) - Rev.
Rev 1:15b-Dan 3:25 (92) of ϑ (cf. also Ezek 1:27); 1:16a-Dan
8:10 and 12:3; 1:18a-Dan 4:34 (ϑ), 6:21-22,27 (LXX) and 12:7.

Verses 1-7 appear to serve as a kind of introduction to
this Daniel framework, since allusions to Daniel are found in
vv. 1-3/35/ and the general structure of images in vv. 4-20 is
like that of Daniel 7:

1.) God sitting on a throne (Rev 1:4; Dan 7:9a)
2.) Plurality of heavenly beings surrounding the throne
    (Rev 1:4; Dan 7:10b)
3.) Mention of a son of man's (Christ's) universal rule
    (Rev 1:5; Dan 7:13-14)
4.) The saints are given or made a kingdom (Rev 1:6,9;
    Dan 7:18,22,27a)

5.) The coming of a son of man on clouds with authority
     (Rev 1:7a; Dan 7:13)
6.) Image of a book associated with judgement (Rev 1:11;
     Dan 7:10)
7.) Detailed description of a heavenly figure and His
     environment (Rev 1:12-16; Dan 7:9-10)
8.) The seer expresses emotional distress because of the
     vision (Rev 1:17a; Dan 7:15)
9.) The seer receives heavenly counsel consisting of an
     interpretation of part of the vision (Rev 1:17-20;
     Dan 7:16-17ff.)

In light of the introductory role of vv. 1-6 perhaps even
the whole of Revelation 1 can be viewed as being encompassed
by a Daniel 7 and 10 *Vorlage*, and especially the former. This
is highlighted by observing that the same allusions to
Dan 2:28-29ff introduce and conclude Revelation 1 (cf. 1:1;
1:19b-20a).

Again, there is the possibility that the Daniel framework
of Revelation 1 has the same kind of relationship to the Daniel
tradition represented in the synoptics as we have concluded
above for Revelation 4-5. However, in contrast to Revelation
4-5, there are some clear allusions in chapter 1 to the
synoptic eschatological midrash, which strengthen its proposed
link with that section. These allusions act as 'tips of the
iceberg', betraying an association with the synoptic discourse
or a tradition connected with the discourse. We will look at
each of these allusions and in so doing we will rely primarily
on the foundational work of L. A. Vos, *The Synoptic Traditions
in the Apocalypse.*/36/

B.1. Rev 1:7
Revelation 1:7 reads, 'Behold, He is coming with the
clouds, and every eye will see Him, even those who pierced Him;
and all the tribes of the earth will mourn over Him.' This
text is distinctive in that it is a combined allusion to
Dan 7:13 and Zech 12:10. These two OT texts are also combined
in the eschatological narrative of Matthew 24, where v. 30
reads: 'and then shall appear the sign of the Son of Man in
heaven; and then shall all the tribes of the earth mourn, and
they shall see the Son of Man coming on the clouds of heaven
with power and great glory' (cf. also Apocalypse of Peter 6).

Vos has a particularly comprehensive study of Rev 1:7,
which can only be summarized here. He expresses certainty that
Rev 1:7 is associated in some way with Matthew 24:30 because of
the uniqueness of the combined OT texts. However, there are
differences between the two which show that Revelation was not
totally dependent on Matthew. The allusion in Matthew is
closer to Daniel 7, whereas that in Revelation is more faithful
to Zechariah. For example, Revelation includes the Zechariah 12
idea of 'piercing' ἐξεκέντησαν), which is absent in Matthew.
This inclusion reflects some degree of independence from
Matthew's text, yet does not mean John was absolutely
independent from the influence of a tradition that may be
traceable behind Matthew. The addition may be due to the
writer's 'familiarity with the Zech. text'/37/ or, just as
possibly may come from part of the pre-synoptic tradition not
picked up by Matthew. Therefore, Vos says that the textual
form of Rev 1:7 points not to a strict dependence on Matthew
but 'adheres to the tradition as recorded in Matthew'./38/
'This adherence is also evident by the similar interpretation
which both Matthew and the apocalyptist give'/39/ of Zechariah,
especially in terms of universalizing the prophecy of the
parousia from Israel to the world. Vos concludes his
discussion in the following manner:

> Our study has shown that Rev 1:7 is very closely aligned
> with this saying as it is found in Matt 24:30.
> *Independent use of the Old Testament* passages by both
> Matthew and the Apocalyptist respectively is definitely
> improbable. *A collection of Old Testament 'proof-texts'*
> *is likewise an improbable source* of the saying in
> Matt 24:30 and Rev 1:7. Stendahl's alternative
> suggestion, which finds the source of this saying in the
> *Verbum Christi* must be seriously considered, in which case
> the Apocalyptist witnesses to the very tradition itself,
> and often with remarkable identity in wording and
> interpretation. The many and diverse facets of this
> saying in Rev 1:7 can best be accounted for by recognizing
> John's thorough knowledge and skillful employment of the
> Old Testament text...and by a definite relationship with
> and dependence upon the *logion* tradition which, in this
> case, is unique with Matthew (my italics)./40/

More recently Wenham has come to the same conclusion as
Vos./41/ The combined allusion may possibly derive from early
Christian eschatological tradition in general or from a
collection of proof texts in particular. Nevertheless, this is
improbable as Stendahl and Vos especially have shown (as has
C. H. Dodd more generally)./42/ Revelation 1:7 may also be
dependent only on the Matthean form of the synoptic apocalypse;
this could be supported by Apocalypse of Peter 6, where almost
the same Daniel-Zechariah allusion is found as part of a larger
context based on Matthew 24./43/ But it is just as possible
that Revelation 1:7 is derived from a larger pre-synoptic Daniel
tradition because of its appearance within the broader Danielic
framework of Revelation 1. This observation may even point to
the probability of a link between Revelation and such a
tradition, since the Daniel framework is *not* as apparent in the
Matthean version, as it *is* in Mark and especially as it is when
all three of the synoptics are seen together as part of one
discourse./44/

This conclusion about Revelation 1:7 lends plausibility to
our own proposal that Revelation 1 as a Daniel midrash is
loosely linked to a similar Daniel tradition lying behind the
gospels. It would appear to be more than chance that the
allusion in Revelation 1:7 should occur in this particular
Danielic framework. Our general conclusion would still be valid
even if the proposed influence of Daniel in Revelation 1 were
limited to vv. 13-20, since v. 7 would still serve as an
introduction to the following section.

B.2. Rev 1:3
Vos observes that Revelation 1:3b (ὁ γὰρ καιρὸς ἐγγύς) has
been linked by commentators with Matthew 26:18 (ὁ καιρός μου
ἐγγύς ἐστιν) or Mark 13:28 (ὅτι ἐγγὺς τὸ θέρος ἐστίν). Vos,
however, decides against a link with either of these passages
because they differ too much in textual form and especially in
interpretation./45/ He then proposes that a more probable
connection is with Luke 21:8 (ὁ καιρὸς ἤγγικεν), which has
essentially identical phraseology and the same theological
meaning. Vos notes the following parallel themes in the two
texts: (1) an overt *eschatological* period (2) which includes
a number of apocalyptic events preceding the coming of Christ;
(3) Luke stresses that men should not be deceived by an
unauthoritative announcement concerning an end-time fulfillment
by a pseudo-messiah, and Revelation 1:3 is intent on
emphasizing that the eschatological fulfillment now announced
is a *truly* authoritative one arising from 'Jesus', the

legitimate 'Christ' (Rev 1:1)./46/ In response to those saying
that such phrases like Revelation 1:3 and Luke 21:8 are mere
'commonplaces of primitive Christianity' - so Romans 13:11,
1 Corinthians 7:29, Philippians 4:5, etc. - Vos counters by
suggesting that their interpretations are markedly different
from that which is common to Luke and Revelation. Therefore,
such stock-in-trade texts are not on the same level as the
texts in Luke and Revelation./47/

The Matthew-Mark parallels to Luke 21:8 omit the phrase.
Perhaps Luke at this point is picking up a part of the
pre-synoptic tradition omitted by Matthew-Mark, but which is
further attested to by Revelation 1:3.

B3. Revelation 1:1 and 1:19
Although Vos does not discuss these verses, they appear
also to have reference to the Daniel tradition of the synoptics.
Commentators have recognized that Revelation 1:1 (ἃ δεῖ
γενέσθαι) and 1:19 (ἃ μέλλει γενέσθαι μετὰ ταῦτα) are allusions
to the same basic phrase in Daniel 2:28-29,45 (cf. Dan 2:45
(Theod), ἃ δεῖ γενέσθαι μετὰ ταῦτα)./48/ Most commentators
(including the margin editors of the standard Greek texts)
recognize these allusions in Revelation. A significant number
of commentators have also recognized that almost the same phrase
in the synoptic eschatological discourse is dependent on these
Daniel texts (cf. Luke 21:9 [δεῖ γὰρ ταῦτα γενέσθαι]; so Matthew
24:6 and Mark 13:7, the only significant change being the
absence of ταῦτα)./49/ This synoptic-Revelation link may be
further confirmed by recognizing that Luke 21:7 (μελλη ταῦτα
γινέσθαι) reflects the same Daniel 2 allusion and is probably to
be seen together with 21:9 as standing behind the phrase in
Revelation 1:19 (ἃ μέλλει γενέσθαι μετὰ ταῦτα).

In each of the synoptic passages the Daniel 2 phrase forms
part of the introduction, and this is the case also, both in
Revelation 1:1 and in Revelation 4:1 (where the Daniel 2
allusion occurs in even fuller form)! This evidence links up
Revelation 1 (and 4) further with the synoptic discourse and
shows even a partial similarity of midrashic pattern./50/

B.4. Conclusion
This discussion of Revelation 1 points to the same
conclusion as reached in the Revelation 4-5 study. Among the
allusive references to the synoptics, Revelation 1:7 and
1:1,19 are the most probable, while 1:3 may well be in the same
category.

C. Revelation 13

The same phenomenon of a Daniel midrashic framework already observed in Revelation 4-5 and Revelation 1 can likewise be seen in Revelation 13. For lack of space there will be no attempt to demonstrate this./51/ Vos argues for the possibility that Revelation 13 echoes Matthew 24:24 and cites the following parallels: (1) appearance of pseudo-messianic and pseudo-prophetic figures who are closely related; (2) these two figures have the role of deceiving many on earth; (3) the employment of 'great signs' (σημεῖα μεγάλα) to carry out the goal of deception./52/ David Wenham generally endorses Vos' idea and also proposes that Revelation 13:7,10 specifically parallels Luke 21:23-24, while the idea of the beast's blasphemy and the second beast's deceptive signs have unique affinity with the Matthew/Mark version of the eschatological discourse. He concludes that such a combination of synoptic ideas could represent an early harmonization of the synoptics or, more simple to understand, they were already found together in a pre-synoptic form known to the author of Revelation./53/

In addition, Wenham argues that Revelation 13:7 reflects the *combined* motifs of Matthew/Mark and of Luke concerning 'first an attack on Jerusalem and then a distress affecting all flesh, including the elect'./54/ Indeed, the motifs in Revelation 13:7 of the beast (1) waging war and conquering the saints, (2) gaining authority over 'every tribe, people, tongue and nation', (3) resulting in earth's inhabitants worshipping the beast (except for the elect) is not merely connected with the synoptic discourse, but also with Daniel. In fact, Revelation 13:7-8 contain *three* distinct verbal allusions to Daniel (v. 7a - Dan 7:21; v. 7b-8a - Dan 7:13-14; v. 8b - Dan 12:1b-2)./55/ This may be accounted for in several ways. (1) Daniel may have been part and parcel of a synoptic tradition - most likely pre-synoptic because of the *combined motifs*, as Wenham argues - and John is reflecting such a tradition. (2) Or perhaps these motifs were associated with some kind of Daniel tradition which then inspired John to develop the tradition by adding more Daniel material to it. (3) That John *independently* adds the Daniel material to these synoptic motifs is possible, but unlikely. The fact that the Daniel allusions were not part of the written synoptics could then point to one or other of the first two alternatives.

When it is remembered that Revelation 13 is modelled broadly on Daniel, the likelihood of a synoptic-Revelation 13 link becomes more probable, since the eschatological discourse was likewise modelled.

V. Conclusion

In the preceding we have attempted to show not only that
a link exists between the Daniel midrashic framework of the
synoptics and that of Revelation, but that there is some
evidence which may indicate that both were dependent on a common
pre-synoptic Daniel tradition./56/

Again, Vos has made a suggestion which adds weight to this
conclusion. After examining the repeated expression 'the word of
God and the testimony of Jesus' (and suchlike phrases),/57/ he
asserts that it refers to the tradition or 'testimony' which is
none other than the 'deposit of material, sayings, deeds,
explanations, etc. which derives from Jesus Himself", and which
was imparted to His followers./58/ Two primary points are
adduced to support this understanding: (1) The use of the
phrase 'word of God' by Paul designates an early Christian
tradition./59/ (2) If the phrase 'the word of God and ... the
testimony of Jesus' in Revelation 1:2 refers to Jesus' *heavenly*
message to John, then the subsequent similar phrases in the book
must refer to Jesus' *earthly* message or 'tradition' imparted to
the apostolic community (*e.g.*, 1:9)./60/ For John and other
Christians to hold to 'the word of God and the testimony of
Jesus' is to be faithful in passing on and living according to
the oral tradition ultimately derived from Jesus./61/

The significance of this phrase would then be to show even
further the connection of Revelation with the gospel tradition,
and would point specifically to further links with Revelation 1
and Revelation 4-6, since the phrase appears in both these
sections.

Our overall discussion has attempted to show that John's
use of Daniel was not done independently, being broadly similar
to that of the synoptic eschatological discourse. In fact, even
if there were not specific allusions to the synoptic discourse
(or tradition) found in the Daniel models of Revelation 1, 4-6
and 13 (see *infra*), the presence of the models themselves hints
at a linkage. Of course, the possibility exists that John is
independently responsible for creating these Daniel models,
especially since Daniel would have been one of the most
obvious sources for early Christian apocalyptists. However, the
likelihood is that the Daniel material has arisen in connection
with a Daniel-synoptic tradition for the following reasons:
(1) it is true that whole sections of Jewish apocalyptic writings
are modelled on chapters of Daniel,/62/ and that this suggests

that Daniel would be an obvious source for Christian writers.
But this need not have been the case, and appears not to have
been the case, since Daniel is not so used as a *broad model* in
any early Christian writings *except* the Apocalypse and, of
course, the synoptic eschatological discourse. If it were an
obvious source, one would expect at least *some* of the
historical and epistolary literature to *use* Daniel similarly to
some *significant* degree. It is noteworthy that even allusions
to Daniel 7:13 are found only in the synoptics and Revelation .
(although cf. perhaps Acts 7:56 and Apocalypse of Peter 6).
Indeed, mere individual allusions to Daniel are rare outside the
gospels and Revelation; of the 133 allusions to Daniel cited in
the UBS text, only 17 are found outside the gospel-Revelation
corpus (only 4 come from John). Such evidence seems to point to
some kind of link between Revelation and the Daniel-synoptic
tradition in general, and between Revelation and the synoptic
eschatological discourse in particular. It has even been
suggested that some of the significant uses of Daniel in
Jewish apocalyptic may have arisen as a result of or in
response to prior Christian usage rather than the other way
around./63/

   (2) In view of the already accumulated evidence that John
was not only familiar with the synoptics (so Vos *passim*) and
especially Mark 13 par. (cf. Wenham), but probably also with a
pre-synoptic tradition behind Mark 13 (cf. Vos on Revelation 1
and Wenham on Revelation 1,6,13 and 11),/64/ it is not mere
speculation that the Danielic models of Revelation 1,4-5 and
13 are also related in *some way* to Mark 13 par.. General
links proposed by Farrer, Sweet and Ford between the use of
Daniel in Mark 13 and the use throughout Revelation may lend
more credence to the above suggestion. Although our
discussion has not presented absolute proof, it has provided
reasonable grounds for considering that the author of
Revelation knew the eschatological discourse tradition in its
Danielic framework and reused this traditional framework in
chapter 1,4-6 and 13. (3) The 'word of God' and 'testimony of
Jesus' phrases in Revelation 1 and 6 are more formal indicators
supporting our theory of such an identification with a Jesus
tradition in Mark 13 par..

   At the very least then, the study points to an association
of John's work with that of the synoptic eschatological
discourse. We also have observed that while there is a broad
similarity in terms of a midrashic model of the apocalyptic
portions of Daniel, a significant degree of difference exists

in specific content. This has led us to speculate that the
dissimilarity was perhaps due to John not being directly
dependent on the synoptics themselves, but on a pre-synoptic
tradition. No doubt, the dissimilarity is *also* to be
attributed to John's own interpretative creativity.

Possibly the various non-synoptic Daniel allusions found
within the Daniel models of Revelation could represent *part* of
the original content of the pre-synoptic discourse which was
not picked up by the synoptic writers, but was preserved and
alluded to by John (but this is surely unprovable). Wenham
makes the same speculation about material in Revelation 6./65/
However, this is unlikely on a very large scale, since such a
large amount of material in these Daniel-Revelation models has
not survived anywhere else in the form of a Jesus eschatological
tradition. Furthermore, it would be difficult, if not
impossible, to distinguish between the Daniel material from the
synoptic eschatological tradition and that resulting from
John's own creative interpretation of Daniel itself. *The more
probable theory better accounting for the Daniel material in
Revelation is that John's acquaintance with the Danielic
framework of the synoptic eschatological tradition generally
influenced him in the framing of his own visions and also
sparked off a train of thought in which he directly alluded to
Daniel and filled the Daniel models with different material
than found in the Daniel tradition associated with Mark 13 par..
The author of Revelation seems to have known something very
like the Daniel-synoptic tradition, but he adapted it quite
freely to his own purposes bringing in all sorts of extra OT
allusions, both from Daniel and elsewhere.* This is to say
that John adopts the method of speaking of Christian truth
through the lens of Daniel because he was following the
precedent set by the author(s) of the eschatological tradition
in Mark 13 par.. In view of this it is a little difficult to
know whether John has been broadly influenced by the tradition
as represented in the synoptics or a pre-synoptic form of it.
However, it can at least be known that this common tradition
was saturated with Daniel material and that John has been
influenced to some significant degree by it.

It could perhaps still be argued that the similarity of
Daniel frameworks is not enough to link the synoptic discourse
and Revelation, but that more specific allusions to the
Danielic parts of the discourse are needed to confirm the
connection. While I have already argued above that such a
broad similarity of frameworks is enough to establish a

discernible link, the issue of specific allusions deserves
more comment. Are the specific allusions cited in Revelation
1,4-5 and 13 enough to lend any confirmation to our theory?
In these sections of Revelation the following allusions have
been argued for: (1) 1:1 - Luke 21:9 par. (Dan 2:28-29,45);
(2) 1:7 - Mt 24:30 (Dan 7:13-Zech 12); (3) 1:13 - Mt 24:30
Dan 7:13)?   (4) 1:19 - Luke 21:9 par. (Dan 2:28-29,45);
(5) *perhaps* Rev 5:7-Mt 24:30 par. (Dan 7:13).   In addition to
these shared Daniel allusions, there are other references to
the eschatological discourse in these sections of Revelation:
(1) 1:3 - Luke 21:8; (2) 6:2-8 - parallel to woes in Mark 13
par.; (3) 6:11 - Luke 21:24c; (4) 6:12 - Luke 21:11; (5) 6:14 -
Luke 21:25b; (6) 6:14b-16 - Luke 21:25-26; (7) 13:7,10 - Luke 21:
23-24./66/ The Revelation 6 references can legitimately be
included in this list, since chapter 6 can be seen as either a
continuation of or appendix to chapters 4-5, *i.e.*,
Revelation 4-6 can be seen as a block of material influenced by
the synoptic eschatological discourse.

    Even if half of these above references were questioned,
there would still be significant evidence in the category of
specific allusions to give weight to our proposals concerning
the identification of Daniel models. In the above list the
most important category is that of the shared Daniel
references. The allusions in Revelation 1:1, 7 and 19 can
stand on their own, while 1:13 and 5:7 are more questionable,
since the Daniel 7:13 Son of Man figure is such a prominent
part of the synoptic tradition in general quite apart from the
eschatological discourse. Although this is certainly true *in
general,* the combination of the Son of Man's (1) coming and
exaltation together with his (2) role of future *judgement* does
not occur so often in the gospels. It occurs clearly only
five times outside the synoptic apocalypse/67/ and six times
within it./68/ Therefore, when the Daniel 7:13 allusions are
found in Revelation 1 and 5, there is a good possibility that
they derive from the synoptic discourse, and when they are
seen within their Danielic frameworks, this becomes more
likely. The second category of non-Daniel allusions to the
synoptic discourse are important enough to add cogency to our
proposed synoptic-Revelation connection.

    Therefore, our proposal seems to be a reasonable
explanation for the repeated pattern in Revelation of whole
chapters being subsumed within frameworks based on sections of
Daniel, as well as for the fact that within these frameworks
there are verbal allusions to specific verses from Daniel.

The hypothesis that the phenomena are derived from John's acquaintance with the *similar phenomenon* in some form of the eschatological discourse tradition accounts better for the data than does the idea that John created this material *ex nihilo* or from *only* his *own* reinterpretation of the OT (Daniel). It would account particularly for the otherwise unparalleled use of Daniel 2:28ff. as an introductory device, a common feature in *all three* of the synoptic apocalypses and in Revelation 1 and 4-5 (indeed, the only occurrences of the Dan 2:28-29, 45 allusion in the NT appear in Mt 24:6, Mk 13:7, Lk 21:9, Rev 1:1, 1:19, 4:1 and 22:6). The likelihood of this conclusion is enhanced when the studies of Vos and Wenham are also considered.

The phrases 'word of God' and 'testimony of Jesus' mentioned by Vos may be significant since they would seem to point not merely to the synoptic form of a Jesus tradition, but also to a circulating tradition (more likely oral than written) independent of both the synoptics/69/ and John./70/ Lars Hartman has come to the same conclusion about Paul's λόγῳ Κυρίου phrase in 1 Thessalonians 4:15/71/ on the basis of similar observations to those which we have also made about Revelation. From the overall context of Vos' discussion concerning specific synoptic allusions in Revelation,/72/ it can be deduced that he came to similar conclusions as Hartman about the almost identical phrases in Revelation 1:9 and 6:9. Both Hartman and Vos allow for influence from an independent tradition, as well as the writers' own interpretative development./73/

Therefore, if we concede a more flexible and natural understanding of the 'traditional' significance of the 'word of God'--"testimony of Jesus' phrases, the likelihood of a pre-synoptic tradition would seem to increase, as would the probability that the Daniel material was not superimposed by the synoptic writers, but was part of a tradition handed to them. In light of the *traditional* significance of these phrases it is also more plausible to suggest that the allusions to Matthew 24:30 and Luke 21:8 in Revelation 1 (cf. vv. 7 and 3) come from a circulating, quite probably pre-synoptic tradition rather than a more formal, written form of the gospels. The same may also be true of the synoptic discourse allusions in Revelation 13 and 6, as Wenham has attempted to show. Even if a pre-synoptic tradition cannot be discerned, it would still be significant that John is generally depending on the synoptic discourse. This would hint at the authority the discourse had already come to have in the latter part of the first century.

Notes

/1/ The term 'midrash' is used loosely to refer to the dominant
influence of an OT passage on a NT writer and to that writer's
interpretative development of the same OT text, so that we are
not using the word in its generic sense. For the non-generic
and generic sense of 'midrash' see the discussion of B. Chilton,
'Varieties and Tendencies of Midrash: Rabbinic Interpretations of
Isaiah 24:3', *Gospel Perspectives III*, edd. R. T. France and
D. Wenham (Sheffield: JSOT, 1983), 9-11.
/2/ *Prophecy Interpreted* (Lund: C. W. K. Gleerup, 1966), *e.g.*,
207.
/3/ *Ibid.*, 158.
/4/ For Hartman's complete discussion see *Prophecy Interpreted*,
145-252.
/5/ *E.g.*, see the varying critical evaluations of Morna Hooker,
JTS 19 (1968), 263-265; J. Lambrecht, *Biblica* 49 (1968),
254-270; T. Holtz, *ThLZ* 92 (1967), cols. 910-912.
/6/ Hartman, *Prophecy Interpreted*, 178-205.
/7/ *Ibid.*, 237-238.
/8/ *Ibid.*, 250.
/9/ Farrer, *The Revelation of St. John The Divine* (Oxford:
Clarendon, 1964) 6-13.
/10/ Sweet, *Revelation* (London: SCM, 1979) 19-21.
/11/ *E.g.*, see G. R. Beasley-Murray, *Revelation* (Grand Rapids:
Eerdmans, 1978) 41-42; P. Carrington, *The Meaning of Revelation*
(London: SPCK, 1931) 54-56. Cf. similarly W. G. Moorhead,
Studies in the Book of Revelation (Pittsburgh: United
Presbyterian Board, 1908) 18-19, who understands Revelation to
be a development of Daniel *and* the Olivet discourse.
/12/ *Crisis!* I (Newcastle, CA: Desmond Ford, 1982) 86-94; see
also Ford's *The Abomination of Desolation in Biblical
Eschatology* (Washington: University Press of America, 1982)
129-131, where he discusses the overarching influence of Daniel
in Mark 13.
/13/ Ford, *Abomination of Desolation in Biblical Eschatology*,
129-192, 243-306.
/14/ The following discussion of Revelation 4-5 is based on a
much more indepth exegetical analysis which will appear
forthcoming in *The Use of Daniel in Jewish Apocalyptic
Literature and in the Revelation of St. John* (Washington, DC:
University Press of America, 1984).
/15/ Müller, 'Formgeschichtliche Untersuchungen zu Apc. 4F.',
I (doctoral diss.: Univ. of Heidelberg, 1962); see a summary
of his work on Revelation 5:1-5 in 'Die himmlische
Ratsversammlung', *ZNW* 54 (1963) 254-267.

/16/ There have also been various proposals that a liturgical
tradition stands behind Rev 4-5. Perhaps the most cogent
proposal is that of Prigent, *Apocalypse et Liturgie* (Neuchatel:
Delachaux et Niestlé, 1964) 46-79.

/17/ This forthcoming book is a minor revision of my 1981
Cambridge Ph.D. dissertation.

/18/ Other OT allusions and parallels can be found in my *Use of
Daniel in Jewish Apocalyptic and in Revelation*. Among these
references, Ezekiel 1-2 is especially significant (cf.
Rev 4:3a, 3b, 5b, 6-8; 5:1, 6a, 8a).

/19/ This allusion to Daniel may also be combined with a
reference to Isa 29:11.

/20/ Cf. A. Bludau, 'Die Apokalypse und Theodotions
Danielübersetzung', *TQ* (1897) 17, who sees that Dan 7:10 (θ)
influenced early Christian liturgy since it is found already
quoted in 1 Clement 34:6, a work which has been shown to
contain much liturgical influence. Cf. Piper, 'Liturgy', 12,
who makes the same general conclusion based on 1 Clement 34:5-7,
especially since there 'the heavenly worship is set forth as
forming the example of the earthly worship'. But see W. C. van
Unnik, '1 Clement 34 and the "sanctus"', *VC* 5 (1951) 204-248,
who gives a thorough summary of all those arguing for a
liturgical background in 1 Clement 34:6 and then points out the
problems of such a view. He concludes that 1 Clement 34:6 was
taken from 'the stock of eschatological tradition' (p. 227) and
was associated with 'a prayer-meeting' of 'the early Christian
church-service', 'which may be, but is not necessarily
connected with the eucharist' (p. 248). So R. M. Grant and
H. H. Graham, *The Apostolic Fathers* (New York: T. Nelson and
Sons, 1965) 60-61. This qualification also fits within the
framework of our proposal. The fact that Isa 6:3 and Dan 7:10
are combined in 1 Clement 34:6 and in 1 Enoch 39:12-40:1 may
show further that Daniel 7 was associated with early Jewish
and Christian eschatological tradition.

/21/ However, note our above comment about the use of
Dan 2:28ff. in Rev 4:1 and the synoptic discourse. For further
discussion see *infra*.

/22/ Charles, *The Revelation of St. John I* (Edinburgh: T. and
T. Clark, 1963) 159; so also G. R. Beasley-Murray, *Revelation*
(London: Marshall, Morgan and Scott, 1981) 128-131.

/23/ Charles, *Revelation I*, 159.

/24/ *Ibid.*, 159-160; so Beasley-Murray, *Revelation*, 128-131.

/25/ In *Gospel Perspectives IV* (Sheffield: JSOT, 1984), cf.
296-297 with respect to Rev 6:2-8.

/26/ *Ibid.*, 208-209.

/27/ *Ibid.*, 311.

/28/ *Ibid.*, 313.

/29/ *Ibid.*, 313.

/30/ This is pointed to by the fact that Daniel, in proportion
to its length, yields more allusions in Revelation than any
other OT book (so H. B. Swete, *Commentary on Revelation* (Grand
Rapids: Kregal, 1980) cliii).

/31/ Few have seen the whole of chaps. 4-5 as a Daniel 7 model,
but cf. G. H. Lang, *The Revelation of Jesus Christ* (London:
pub. by author, 1945) 109-139 and P. Mauro, *The Patmos Visions*
(Boston: Hamilton Brothers, 1925) 145,176, although they
only state the idea generally and present no detailed
exegetical support. Müller, 'Formgeschichtliche
Untersuchungen', 86, 144 sees Dan 7:13ff. as the dominant
influence in 5:6-14; so M. Kiddle, *The Revelation of St. John*
(London: Harper, 1947) 77-78. Cf. more generally J. Comblin,
'Le Christ dans l'Apocalypse in Bibliothèque de Théologie,
Théologie Biblique, Série 3, Vol. 6 (Tournai: Desclée, 1965) 67.
J. M. Ford, *Revelation* (Garden City: Doubleday and Co., 1975)
88, sees I Enoch and Daniel 7 as key influences in chap. 5,
especially with respect to the 'figure who is both "lion" and
"lamb" who stands in a position analogous to that of one like a
son of man'.

/32/ See Dodd, *According to the Scriptures* (New York: Scribner,
1953) 60, 110. In fact, Dodd concludes that Daniel 7 and 12
were specific contextual plots often drawn from by NT writers
because they had been under the influence of Jesus or a Jesus
tradition which had repeatedly made use of this context
(*ibid.*, 67-70).

/33/ Although other broad segments of Jewish apocalyptic
literature are also based on Daniel (*i.e.*, 1QM 1, I Enoch
90:9-27, I Enoch 46-47, IV Ezra 11-12, IV Ezra 13, 2 Baruch
38-39), Revelation 4-5 should be seen as dependent on a
circulating Christian tradition based on Daniel because of its
obvious and specific Christian content. However, this is not to
say that the original tradition behind Mark 13 was not also
associated with a tradition linked to these Jewish texts (on
this issue see further *infra*).

/34/ For discussion of this see my forthcoming *Use of Daniel in
Jewish Apocalyptic and in Revelation*.

/35/ See *infra* and my *Use of Daniel in Jewish Apocalyptic and
in Revelation*. *E.g.*, note the use of ἀποκάλυψις and σημαίνω
in Rev 1:1, which has its background in Daniel 2 (where
ἀποκάλυψις appears repeatedly; cf. Dan 2:28,29,45). For other
OT influences see my book.

/36/ Vos, *Synoptic Traditions* (Kampen: J. H. Kok N.V., 1965).
/37/ *Ibid.*, 68.
/38/ *Ibid.*, 68.
/39/ *Ibid.*, 69.
/40/ *Ibid.*, 71.
/41/ Wenham, *Rediscovery*, 314-315.
/42/ Dodd, *According to the Scriptures, passim, e.g.*, 60).
/43/ I am indebted to Richard Bauckham for bringing Apoc. of Peter 6 to my attention.
/44/ See Hartman, *Prophecy Interpreted*, 145-252.
/45/ Vos, *Synoptic Traditions*, 178-179.
/46/ *Ibid.*, 180.
/47/ *Ibid.*, 181. It is also quite possible that Mark 1:15 is related to Rev 1:3. This would be significant since Mark 1:15 is likely an echo of Dan 7:22. In fact, the standard Greek testaments cite Dan 7:22 as an allusion in Luke 21:8 itself, which is quite possible in light of the Daniel material elsewhere in the eschatological discourse.
/48/ For further arguments in favor of the validity of the Daniel allusion in 1:19 and 1:1 see my forthcoming *Use of Daniel in Jewish Apocalyptic and in Revelation*, where I also show that the Daniel allusions in Revelation introduce the major sections of the book and, therefore, are formative on its overall structure.
/49/ Hartman, *Prophecy Interpreted*, 147-150, has observed these Daniel 2 allusions in the synoptics, which is also acknowledged by others (see Lambrecht, *Biblica* 49 [1968], 260; J. Bowman, *The Gospel of Mark* [Leiden: Brill, 1965], 241-242; R. H. Gundry, *The Use of the Old Testament in St. Matthew's Gospel* [Leiden: Brill, 1967], 46; T. F. Glasson, 'Mark xiii. and the Greek Old Testament', *ET* 69 [1957-58], 214; H. B. Swete, *The Gospel According to Mark* [London: Macmillan and Co., 1898], 281; J. Schniewind, *Das Evangelium nach Markus* [Göttingen: Vandenhoek and Ruprecht, 1952], 168; R. Grob, *Einführung in das Markus Evangelium* [Stuttgart: Zwingli, 1965], 209; *The Greek New Testament*, ed. G. D. Kilpatrick [London: British and Foreign Bible Society, 1958], 77, 256; *The Greek New Testament*, edd. K. Aland, M. Black, C. M. Martini, B. M. Metzger and A. Wikgren [New York: United Bible Societies, 1968], 92. 298; *Novum Testamentum Graece*, edd. E. Nestle and E. Nestle [Stuttgart: Deutsche Bibelstiftung, 1979], 68, 133, 229]. Cf. also W. Grundmann, 'δεῖ', *TDNT* II, 23. These phrases in the synoptics not only show allusion to Daniel's ἃ δεῖ γενέσθαι but also appear to be developing the following clause 'επ' ἐσχάτων τῶν ἡμερῶν, the τέλος of which Daniel predicted will not occur until the sequence of events mentioned in the discourse first take place.

/50/ See L. Goppelt, *Typos* (Grand Rapids: Eerdmans, 1982) 197
(n.81), who apparently is the only one who has come close to
recognizing this Daniel 2 linkage: he says in a footnote, 'Mark
13 par., like Revelation, stands under the guiding principle of
the apocalyptic prophecy in Dan 2:28; Mt 24:6 par.; Rev 1:1;
cf. v. 19; 4:1; 22:6'.
/51/ See my *Use of Daniel in Jewish Apocalyptic and in
Revelation*. We are giving the least amount of discussion to
Revelation 13, since most commentators agree that the
apocalyptic chapters of Daniel (e.g., chapters 7-8) are the
predominant influence in vv. 1-12.
/52/ Vos, *Synoptic Traditions*, 133-136.
/53/ Wenham, *Rediscovery*, 205-206.
/54/ *Ibid.*, 212-213.
/55/ Cf. Beale, *The Use of Daniel in Jewish Apocalyptic and
in Revelation*.
/56/ It is germane that D. Guthrie can say that the idea that
Mark 13 is based on 'a previously existing Jewish Christian
apocalypse...has come to be regarded almost as a fact of
Synoptic criticism', *New Testament Introduction* [Downers Grove:
Inter-Varsity, 1970], 139. He also lists those holding the
position, who do not trace the tradition back to Jesus, but it
is just as likely that it is derived from Him (in this regard,
see further Guthrie, *Introduction*, 140).
/57/ Cf. Rev 1:9; 6:9; 12:17; 19:10; 20:4.
/58/ Vos, *Synoptic Traditions*, 208.
/59/ *Ibid.*, 199-200. Vos likewise points out that the same
phrase in the Gospels and Acts designates an early Jesus
tradition (*ibid.*, 199).
/60/ *Ibid.*, 208-209.
/61/ See *ibid.*, 196-209 for the full discussion.
/62/ *E.g.*, see the references *supra* in footnote #33.
/63/ *E.g.*, it is thought by some that IV Ezra 13:2-3 is a
polemic against the Christian interpretation of Daniel. So
F. T. Tillman, *Der Menschensohn, Jesu Selbtzeugnis für seine
messianische Würde, Biblische Studien* 14 (1907), 105-106; M. J.
Lagrange, 'Notes sur le messianisme au temps de Jésus", *RB* 2
(1905), 498.
/64/ For these discussions on Revelation 1,4-5 and 13 see
supra. For Revelation 11 see Wenham, *Rediscovery*, 207-208.
/65/ Wenham, *Rediscovery*, 312-314.
/66/ Cf. Wenham, *supra*.
/67/ Cf. Mt 13:41; 16:27; 25:31ff.; Luke 17:26, 30; John
5:27-29.
/68/ Mt 24:27; 24:30; 24:37ff.; Mark 13:24-27; Luke 21:25-27.

/69/ *E.g.*, cf. Guthrie, *Introduction*, 956 and J. A. T. Robinson, *Redating the New Testament* (Phil.: Westminster Press, 1976), 239, who do not see the gospel parallels in Revelation as literarily dependent on the synoptics, but see them as reflecting an acquaintance with a common, oral tradition.

/70/ The force of this statement perhaps becomes stronger *if* the date of Revelation were to be moved back about twenty-five years to 68-70 AD (*e.g.*, see the argument for such a date in J. A. T. Robinson, *Redating the New Testament*, 221-253).

/71/ Hartman, *Prophecy Interpreted*, 182, 188-189, 246.

/72/ See *supra*.

/73/ See also Hartman's discussion of the same phenomenon from the viewpoint of Luke's relationship to the antecedent form of the Daniel midrash in Mark 13 (*Prophecy Interpreted*, 229, 233).

THE GOSPEL ACCORDING TO THOMAS AS A SOURCE OF JESUS' TEACHING

Bruce Chilton
Department of Biblical Studies
The University
Sheffield   S1O 2TN

I   Is *Thomas* an Eastern "Q"?

The Gospel according to Thomas consists of some 114
sayings of Jesus, and has no narrative element which can
compare with what we find in the canonical Gospels. Should
we take these sayings seriously as representing the teaching
of Jesus? The document is found in the so-called library of
Nag Hammadi, a collection of thirteen codices, which was
discovered in Egypt in 1945. Datable records associated with
the collection, as well as the Coptic dialect in which *Thomas*
is written (Sahidic, with elements of Subachmimic), permit us
to place the writing of the manuscript in the fourth century /1/.
Some of the sayings in *Thomas* are paralleled in certain Greek
fragments (numbered I, 654 and 655) discovered at Oxyrhynchus
and datable within the third century /2/.   The time lapse
between Jesus and *Thomas* is therefore far greater than that
involved in the canonical Gospels, and the transition of
language involved is far more radical.   Nonetheless, a strong
case has been made for the antiquity of the substance of *Thomas*.

Helmut Koester has been the boldest proponent of this
point of view. "Thomas" is identified in the Gospel as "Didumus
Judas Thomas", that is: Judas Thomas, the "twin". *The Acts of
Thomas,* written in Syriac in the third century, shows signs of
contact with the Gospel and clearly identifies this "Thomas"
with Judas the brother of Jesus. Indeed, Judas Thomas is
unequivocally made out to be the twin brother of Jesus in the
Acts. Koester argues that this identification is "primitive",
and that *Thomas* reflects the stream of tradition associated
with this disciple. As such, it is the eastern branch of the
sayings tradition whose western branch we know as "Q" /3/.   On
Koester's understanding, Jesus had stressed the presence of the

kingdom in his teaching, and the "Gnosticism of the Gospel of
Thomas appears to be a direct continuation of Jesus'
eschatology," while "Q" reverted to a more conventional,
apocalyptic style /4/.

Certain reservations in respect of these claims need
immediately to be offered. First - and obviously - the
relatively late date of the claim that Judas was Jesus' twin
makes it unlikely to be true, if that is what Koester means by
"primitive" /5/. "Thomas" indeed means "twin" in Aramaic, and
is translated as such in *The Gospel of Thomas,* the *Acts,* and
even in the New Testament (John 11.16; cf. John 14.22 in OS^C).
The explicit assertion of the *Acts* that the twin brother of
Jesus is meant is only a third century development, so far as
is known. In other words, "Thomas" may originally have been
the cognomen of any disciple. "Judas", of course, was a common
name in Jewish antiquity, and "Thomas" might be as useful a
cognomen as "Iscariot" or "Zealot". But even *if* the disciple
in question were named Judas, he need not have been a brother
of Jesus. And if he were a brother of Jesus, that does not
prove Jesus was the twin in mind, as he had four brothers
(cf. Mark 6.4). The way in which the meaning of "twin" seems
to dissolve into a series of options when it is taken literally
reminds us that certain cognomens, such as Cephas and Boanerges,
can only be understood as metaphors. In this case, Thomas -
Didumos would no more imply genetic identity than Cephas - Peter
means Simon was actually made of stone. "Thomas" in the context
of other cognomens might imply no more than that the person so
named was similar, or wish to be seen as similar, to someone
else. However "Thomas" is taken, the failure of the New
Testament and the *Gospel of Thomas* to portray the disciple as
Jesus' twin makes the literalistic claim in the *Acts* appear to
be an apocryphal legend spawned by a misunderstanding.

Koester creates a difficulty for himself by assuming that
in pre-Christian Judaism there was an apocalyptic understanding
of the kingdom. He then has to argue that Jesus departed from
this understanding, while the compilers of "Q" reverted to it.
His refusal to accept the contention of Albert Schweitzer that
Jesus held to a purely futuristic vision of the kingdom is to
be welcomed, but he fails to observe that the very difficulty
with Schweitzer's position is that he supposes apocalyptic
eschatology was part and parcel of the religion of Jesus' day /6/.
Finally, Koester treats of "Q" as if it were a known document,
and not a hypothesis, and to this extent the foundation he lays
is not stable /7/.

Some of the kingdom sayings in the Gospel can be compared
with witnesses to the text of the New Testament.   Such
comparison is necessary in order to determine whether *Thomas*
in fact manifests the "primitive" traits which Koester claims
it does.   Analysis along these lines has been carried out,
particularly by Wolfgang Schrage /8/, Richard L. Arthur /9/,
and Gilles Quispel /10/.   Of course, not all of the sayings
can be compared to New Testament texts; some of them are
unique.   Nonetheless, a clear picture does emerge when
comparable passages are considered.

In one case (*logion* 46), a saying departs so markedly from
a "Q" saying (Mt 11.11/Lk 7.28), while agreeing with it in
substance, that it may seem to reflect an independent recension
of the same basic tradition:

> From Adam until John the Baptist there is among those
> born of women none higher than John the Baptist, so
> that his eyes will not be broken.   But I have said
> that whoever among you becomes as a child shall know
> the kingdom, and he shall become greater than John.

The statement that John's eyes will not be broken is a way of
saying he will not see death /11/, and serves as a specification
of the reward of John's greatness, which is not spelled out in
"Q".   In a similar fashion, the last clause in the saying might
be taken as an explanatory addition to a logion such as Matthew
and Luke hand on.   If such additions are seen as explanatory in
respect of a saying such as we have in "Q", Koester's hypothesis
cannot be commended fully in this instance.   Although *Thomas* at
least could not be said here to depend absolutely on the
Synoptic Gospels, it nonetheless represents a developed, far
from primitive, form of the "Q" tradition.

There are three instances in which *Thomas* appears to
present a harmonized version of "Q" material.   *Logion*
(hereafter: *l*.) 54 agrees with Matthew 5.3 in the reading "of
the heavens" instead of "of God", but with Luke 6.20 in omitting
the phrase "in spirit":

> Blessed are the poor, for yours is the kingdom...

The saying also presents a mixture of the Matthean third person
and the Lukan second person; while Luke's οἱ πεινῶντες is to
be read in context as a vocative, the noun NϩHKE in *Thomas* with
the copula (NE) should be taken as a third person form, agreeing

with Matthew /12/. The tendency to mix Matthean and Lukan
elements is also evident in *1.* 96:

> The kingdom of the father is like a woman who has
> taken a little leaven and hidden it in dough and
> has made large loaves of it.

Schrage observes that *Thomas* is closer to Matthew (13.13) than
to Luke (13.20-21) in using the form of introduction, "the
kingdom is like," /13/ although it should be observed that
the adjective "like" (Sahidic ΕΣΤΝΤΩΝ) is also present in the
Coptic text of Lk. 13.21 (as in Sahidic Matthew and *Thomas*).
The impression that we are dealing with a harmonized version
of the saying is confirmed when we observe that the Venetian
Diatessaron and the Pepysian Harmony also insist that a "little"
leaven is in question, and the specification of "three measures"
is also omitted in some harmonizing witnesses /14/. The case
is similar when we consider *1.* 107:

> The kingdom is like a shepherd who had a hundred
> sheep. One of them went astray, the largest. He
> left behind ninety-nine, he sought for the one
> until he found it. Having tired himself out, he
> said to the sheep, I love you more than the ninety-
> nine.

Thomas here agrees both with Luke 15.4 (in the reference to the
shepherd who "had" sheep and to the search "until he found it")
and with Matthew 18.12 (in omitting the question, "Who among
you?" and including the verb "to seek"). Notably, the Sahidic
Luke also has the reference to the search for (not merely the
loss of) the "one" sheep, as does the Persian Diatessaron /15/
and *The Gospel of Truth* (31.35-32.17).

Thomas and "Q" are similar, but Koester's hypothesis that
Thomas is an independent recension of "Q" appears untenable,
even supposing "Q" was an actual document. More accurately,
the Gospel might be described as a harmonizing version of
Jesus' sayings. Its harmonizing tendency at times (cf. above,
on *1.* 107 and n. 12) accords with the Sahidic New Testament,
and this serves to confirm that the document was copied in the
fourth century. But the bulk of the instances of harmonization
either parallel overtly harmonizing textual witness of the
Gospels or represent (so far as we know) independent developments
in the tradition of Jesus' words. The nature of this
harmonization will concern us in the next section; for the
moment, only the fact of its harmonizing tendency is at issue.
A textual consideration must conclude that *Thomas* is, tradition

critically, not comparable with "Q", even if we think of "Q"
as a loose collection of sayings and not a document. Further
indications to the same effect may be given more briefly. In
l. 20 /16/ and *l*. 99 /17/ Thomas presents harmonized versions
of Synoptic triple tradition, and *l*. 57 /18/ and *l*. 76 /19/
parallel peculiarly Matthean material as presented in
harmonizing versions. The impression is quite unavoidable
that *Thomas'* relation to "Q" is incidental, simply an aspect
of the relation to gospel tradition generally, and this
impression is strengthened by observing the eleven cases
(*ll*. 3, 22, 27, 46, 49, 82, 97, 98, 109, 113, 114) of kingdom
sayings with elements which are not paralleled in the canonical
Gospels. *Thomas* is a harmony of canonical and non-canonical
tradition, not a version of "Q".

II   *Thomas* as a Structured Harmony

       No scholar has pursued the question of the nature of
Thomas' harmonization more thoroughly than Quispel. Our
observation of agreements between *Thomas* and harmonizing
manuscripts is largely dependent on his careful and extensive
collations. These collations have led Quispel to the conclusion
that there is a specific relationship between *Thomas* and the
Diatessaron of Tatian /20/. He admits that the agreement
between the two is not perfect, and on this basis he posits
their common reliance on a tradition he calls "the Gospel of
the Hebrews" /21/. Because this tradition is not attested in
western witnesses, he considers that it is of eastern
provenience, and he believes that it is authentic /22/. We
are again faced with a bold hypothesis, or rather a sequence
of bold hypotheses, which requires to be assessed as an account
of the evidence to hand.

       That Tatian compiled a Diatessaron is not to be doubted,
but his work has been lost. The extant harmonies, whose
readings are extremely diverse, may have some relationship to
his work, but just what this relationship is has not been
determined, so that the text of Tatian's *Diatessaron* has not
even been established. There is, then, a necessarily large
degree of speculation involved in speaking of any specific
connection between *Thomas* and "Tatian". To give examples of
the diversity of manuscripts to which he appeals in order to
justify his assertions, we refer (in addition to our remarks
above) to Quispel's citation of the Persian Diatessaron and the

Armenian Ephraem in respect of *l*. 20 /23/, of the Liège
Diatessaron in respect of *l*. 57 /21/, and of the Venetian
Diatessaron in respect of *l*. 96 /25/. Which, if any, of these
harmonistic witnesses best evidences the work of "Tatian"?
Does none of them, and no collection of them, consistently
present the readings of "the *Diatessaron*"? If not, then we
cannot speak of a relationship between *Thomas* and "Tatian",
but only of sporadic affinity between the Gospel and harmonizing
manuscripts. The large number of non-canonical, and perhaps
non-"Tatianic", sayings in *Thomas* must be considered also, as
well as the contacts with such sources as the Clementines /26/,
The Gospel of Truth /27/, and Clement of Alexandria /28/.
"Tatian" might just be a link that joins these sources together
and relates them to *Thomas,* but at the present stage that is a
very bold inference, not a deduction.

"The Gospel of the Hebrews" is, if anything, a more
unknown quantity than even Tatian's *Diatessaron,* so that
comparison with *Thomas* is again problematic. So far as can
be determined from extant sources, *Thomas* shares traditions
with several documents; "the Gospel of the Hebrews" might be
among them, but the relationship between the two cannot be
established as closer than that. This observation, in addition
to our remarks on the alleged contact with "Tatian", cast doubt
on Quispel's finding that *Thomas* consists substantively of
authentic, "Jewish Christian Gospel tradition" /29/.

Our reservations in respect of what Quispel deduces from
his collations of agreements in no way diminishes the
importance of those collations themselves. *Thomas* displays
contact with ancient, harmonizing sources, some of them from
the second century. This fact, taken in conjunction with the
apparent knowledge of the Gospel in the third century *Acts of
Thomas* and the parallels offered by the Oxyrhynchus Papyri,
confirms that the Gospel is in substance a second century work.
Nonetheless, there is some indication that the Thomas tradition
continued to be shaped and modified after that time: the
agreement with the Oxyrhynchus fragments is not complete, even
allowing for variants in translation, and there are some
agreements (as we have seen) between *Thomas* and the later
Sahidic Gospels.

Between the second century and the fourth century, the
substance of the Thomas tradition was structured into
essentially its present form. The prominent place given to

Thomas as a tradent of Jesus' words in post-apostolic
literature would suggest that crucial structuring occurred
during the second century, although the process may have
continued into the third (and even the fourth) century /30/.
The present collection of some 114 sayings is by no means a
random selection. Association by catchword and by subject is,
of course, a feature /31/, but there is a far more positive
instrument of structure evident in the Gospel. H.E.W. Turner
observed that the questions asked by the disciples give an
indication of leading themes in the work /32/. Actually, not
only questions, but also statements, serve as occasions on
which Jesus speaks. They provide the framework within which
sayings are presented. The structural importance of what the
interlocutors have to say explains why the principle of
association by catchword can be overridden (cf., for example,
the distance between the verbally similar *l*. 3 and *l*. 113,
and between *l*. 56 and *l*. 111). Of course, sometimes sayings
are grouped according to their traditional associations, which
are in tension with the framework imposed by the interlocutors,
and this gives the document an uneven appearance. But the
following interlocutions (here paraphrased) may be taken to
highlight major themes in *Thomas,* themes which influence the
order of the sayings:

> Superscription - the secret words of Jesus
>
> *l*. 12 - the question of right leadership
>
> *l*. 18 - the demand to know the end of discipleship
>
> *l*. 24 - the question of where Jesus can be found
>
> *l*. 51 - the question of "rest", or the new world
>
> *l*. 61b - the relation between master and disciple
>
> *l*. 99 - the way of discipleship
>
> *l*. 113 - the time of the kingdom.

As has already been intimated, these interlocutions merely
provide the framework for sayings, groups of sayings and
subsidiary questions. The redactor does not seem to atomize
traditional complexes altogether, and the interlocutory
framework is less strict than apocryphal Gospels of the
discourse type. Nonetheless, the principal concerns of the
redactor stand out clearly: the interpretation of the "secret
words" is applied especially to the questions of how the

community is to be ordered and how the kingdom, the end, or
rest is to be understood.

III   Can we trust *The Gospel according to Thomas*?

Koester's contribution focussed our attention at the
beginning of this paper on the kingdom in *Thomas*. "Kingdom"
is here used nineteen times in purported sayings of Jesus,
each usage is not separated by more than eighteen sayings from
the next, and the term appears both in the introductory logia
complex (*ll*. 1-3) and in the last clause of the entire work
(*l*. 114). That the kingdom is of central importance to the
understanding of the Gospel is obvious. Indeed, the density
and distribution of its occurrences make the kingdom more
prominent in *Thomas* than it is even in Matthew, the most
kingdom-absorbed book in the New Testament /33/. The general
reliability of *Thomas* can therefore be tested in respect of
the kingdom sayings. The parables in *Thomas* are to be considered
elsewhere in the present volume; only non-parabolic kingdom
sayings will be dealt with here. The first of these appears in
l. 3:
        If those who lead you say to you,
        See, the kingdom is in heaven,
        then the birds of heaven will precede you.
        If they say to you,
        It is in the sea,
        then the fish will precede you.
        But the kingdom is within you and without you.
        Contextually, the meaning of *l*. 3 is clear; the first two
sayings promise eternal life for whoever seeks and finds the
interpretation of Jesus' words, and the present kingdom logion
serves to explain the mystery of the kingdom. Because *Thomas*
prefers to use "kingdom" in the absolute (as here), or qualified
by "of the heavens" or "of the father", rather than with "of
God", it has been argued that a Gnostic dualism is evident /34/.
Given that Matthew has a similar preference, and that "kingdom"
unqualified appears in Targum Ezekiel 7.7, 10, this finding is
rather incautious, especially in the light of contacts between
Thomas and Jewish Christian documents, since there is a
well-known reluctance in Judaism to speak of God directly.
On the other hand, it must be openly stated that the kingdom
in *l*. 3 is spoken of in terms of knowledge: the saying goes on
to refer to knowing oneself and being known by God. Because
the kingdom is seen as associated with a relationship of

knowledge, we may describe it as interpreted in a gnostic
direction.

L. 3 is "gnostic", however, only in the very general sense
of the word, not because it is dualistic /35/. It is no more
heterodox, say, than Clement of Alexandria, and is far removed
from the elaborate cosmology of *The Gospel of Truth*. Moreover,
the kingdom saying within *1*. 3 need not be taken in the
direction of *1*. 3b, and in itself may well be authentic. The
primary parallel is with Lk. 17.20-21, although there is the
additional feature that the kingdom is said to be "without you".
That is, the statement that the kingdom is immanent ("within
you") is immediately qualified by the statement that it is
transcendent ("without you"). Jacques Ménard has argued that
this feature corresponds to a Gnostic motif of the resolution
of all earthly duality /36/. L. 22 indeed expresses such a
theme (whether or not it is actually "Gnostic"), but the
language there is different, and it appears to be the first
occurrence of the idea. Moreover, T.F. Glasson has shown that
1. 3 is in line with aspects of Jewish and Christian exegesis /37/.
Deuteronomy 30.11-14 maintains that the commandment is neither
"in heaven" nor "beyond the sea", but "in your mouth and in
your heart". The passage is applied to Wisdom in Baruch
3.29-30 and to Christ in Romans 10.6-8. Even more tellingly,
Tertullian expounds Luke 17.20-21 in terms of Deuteronomy
30.11-13. As he does so in *Adversus Marcionem* (4.35), he may
have been surprised to hear the suggestion that such an
exegesis is "Gnostic".

Taking the hint from Tertullian, Glasson suggests that
Thomas consciously expounds Luke 17.20,21 in terms of
Deuteronomy 30.11-14. Against this finding, one must observe
that the Old Testament is not used as a source, or even as a
harmonizing influence, in the Gospel /38/. The possibility
should be considered that we have here, as elsewhere in the
document /39/, what is substantively a saying of Jesus. Aside
from the coherence with Luke 17.20, 21, the conception of the
kingdom in *1*. 3 lends support to this point of view. Elsewhere
in the tradition of Jesus' words, the kingdom is presented as
the saving activity of God himself, an understanding that
accords with the Prophetic Targum /40/. The case would seem
to be the same in *1*. 3: God alone can be said to be
unconditioned by space, within and yet without us. Just as
Jesus said the kingdom is neither "here" nor "there" (Luke
17.20, 21), so he may have observed that it is "within you"

(Luke and *Thomas*) in the sense that it is not to be seen
cosmologically, as simply in heaven or beneath the sea (*Thomas*).
Limitations of space are therefore excluded, and - if *1. 3* is
authentic - the idea of the kingdom as a purely interior
possession is also rejected. The divine reality, in its call
for a human response, is not limited by that response; it
remains eschatological, *extra nos*. This coincides with Jesus'
preaching of the kingdom as we know it from the New Testament,
where the demand to respond by repentance is accompanied by an
insistence that the divine initiative is unconditional, and is
not merely an aspect of repentance (cf. Mark 1.15 above all).

     If, as seems possible, *1. 3* is in substance a saying of
Jesus, it is so as *ipsissima vox,* not *ipsissima verba*. We are
dealing with a Coptic version of a Greek tradition whose
ultimate source, in the case of authentic sayings, was Aramaic.
We are confronting the result of a strong harmonizing tendency
and of an interlocutory structure which emphasizes the need to
interpret Jesus' words in the search for knowledge about the
way of discipleship and the nature of the kingdom. The road
from Jesus to *Thomas* is demonstrably convoluted, but the journey
back is neither impossible nor unrewarding.

     In this journey backwards, there are two methodological
short cuts which are tempting, but they can only mislead us.
Koester's short cut is sign-posted by the claim that *Thomas*
represents the Jesus tradition as well as the canonical Gospels
do /41/. Such a supposition does no justice to the fact that the
tradition history of *Thomas* is demonstrably more complex than
what we usually find in the New Testament. For this reason, each
saying in *Thomas* must be typed in respect of redaction and tradition before the possibility that it is authentic can reasonably
be considered. The other short cut is sign-posted by the assumption that *Thomas* is so thoroughly "Gnostic" that everything in it
is to be read with suspicion, as the distortion of a tendentious
theology /42/. But the fact that a document has an argument to
make by no means implies that everything contained in it has been
created to express that argument. (Such suppositions have given
a bad name to some redaction critical approaches to the New
Testament.) Indeed, tensions between individual logia in *Thomas*
and its overall themes provide the starting point of a redaction
critical and tradition critical investigation.

Of course, the fact that a tradition seems relatively
"primitive" as compared to the document in which it is contained
does not necessarily mean that it is authentic: all Aramaic
interpreters of Jesus' words, for example, cannot be held *a
priori* to have been less creative than Greek interpreters. In
the case of *1*. 3a, although the conception of the kingdom and the
use of the Old Testament are consistent with Jesus' preaching as
reflected in the New Testament, there are signs of secondary
interpretation as well. The first of these is that the saying
seems to be directed against false expectations among religious
leaders (cf. Mark 13.6, 21-23 and parallels, where such expectations are not explicitly attributed to leaders). Unless these
leaders were active in the period *after* Jesus' ministry, it is
difficult to see how they could have threatened to seduce his
followers with their apocalyptic speculation. Second, the kingdom saying outside its Lukan context lacks a sense of the dynamic
coming of the kingdom. (Although "is" appears repeatedly in the
translation of the Coptic text, the term should not be pressed.
The verb is at first only implied, and then the copula is used;
it is Luke who uses the emphatic ἐστιν.) As we will see in the
treatment of *1*. 113, a diminution of the eschatological aspect of
the kingdom seems to be part of Thomas' programme. In other words,
the tradition critical judgement that a saying is primitive does
not prove that every element in it is authentic. Tradition
criticism should never replace historical judgement: it merely
gives an occasion on which historical consideration can begin.

Saying 113 picks up the idea expressed in *1*. 3 and applies
it in a new way. The disciples ask when the kingdom will come
(*1*. 113a), and Jesus first of all (*1*. 113b) replies in terms
strongly reminiscent of the Lukan parallel (17.20-21) to *1*. 3:

It will not come by expectation.
They will not say, See--here, or, See--there.

The last part of this saying (*1*. 113c), however, is innovative as
compared to the New Testament:

But the kingdom of the father is spread
upon the earth and men do not see it.

The assertion that the kingdom is spread upon the earth goes
beyond the statement of *1*. 3 that it is "within you and without
you". Even more importantly, a radical explanation is given for
men's ignorance of the kingdom: it is a veiled reality which
people generally do not perceive (cf. *1*. 51) /43/.

The addition is clearly interpretative, but the question is: whose interpretation is it? Two features suggest it was added at the stage when *l*. 3 was brought into the Gospel. As we saw in the previous discussion, *l*. 3b appears to be a gnostic addition which explicates the kingdom as a relationship of saving knowledge. *L*. 113c has precisely the same effect, which suggests it was added at the same (relatively late) stage. The introductory "but", moreover, corresponds to the kingdom saying in *l*. 3, which strengthens the suspicion that it is intended to serve as an explanatory restatement of the same idea. Finally, the position of this interpretation, at the close of the document and after the final interlocution, alerts us to the presence of a greater degree of reformulation than we might find elsewhere. In the end, *l*. 113a, b confirms the provenience of the tradition contained in *l*. 3 (as parallel to Luke 17.20-21), but *l*. 113c seems to be an expansive and late addition. In its expansion, it corresponds to the later elements in *l*. 3 (the emphasis on knowledge above all, but also the reference to the false expectations of leaders, and the diminution of the eschatological aspect of the kingdom).

We confront radically more surprising material when we come to *l*. 27:

>   If you do not fast to the world,
>   you will not see the kingdom.
>   If you do not keep the sabbath as sabbath,
>   you will not see the father.

There is no question here of any dependence on a tradition reflected in the New Testament. Nonetheless, the coordination between seeing the kingdom and seeing the father corresponds, not with the gnostic explication of the kingdom in *Thomas* (manifest in *l*. 113), but with the conception in *l*. 3: the kingdom is strongly identified with God himself. Joseph A. Fitzmyer has argued that the saying bears another mark of authenticity: the phrase "fast to the world" appears to represent a Syriac idiom /44/. The Syriac provenience of the saying is also suggested by its ideology of abstinence, for which the Eastern Church is well known /45/. In just this regard, the saying stands in some tension with the ideology of *Thomas*. *L*. 14 has Jesus condemn fasting, prayer and almsgiving in even more unqualified terms than he does in Matthew 6.1-6. This condemnation comes soon after the major interlocution concerning community leadership (*l*. 12), and therefore should be taken to represent the ethical teaching of the document better than *l*. 27 does.

Although the Syrian provenience of this tradition is probable, the authenticity of the saying is doubtful. Jesus is
scarcely known to us from the Gospels as a notable ascetic (cf.
Matthew 11.16-18 and Luke 7.31-35). The conception of the kingdom
is admittedly primitive, in the sense that it accords with that
of Jesus, and this tends to confirm that the tradition was circulated among those who were in touch with the earliest understanding of kingdom language. But the link between the kingdom and
abstinence is so untypical of Jesus, and so consistent with the
ethos of Syrian Christianity, that it should be seen as a
secondary (but pre-redactional) elaboration. Indeed, this saying
ought seriously to be considered by every reader of the New Testament
who believes that the presence of formal parallelism is an
infallible sign of the *ipsissima verba Jesu*.

One of the few cases in which *Thomas* appears to reflect a
saying also known in "Q" is *1*. 46b:

And I have said that whoever among you becomes a child
shall know the kingdom, and he shall be greater than John.

Comparison with Matthew 11.11b and Luke 7.28b shows that the
saying is basically as authentic as what the New Testament presents. For that matter, *1*. 46a corresponds to Matthew 11.11a and
Luke 7.28a. But to the saying about John, a crucial addition is
made ("his eyes will not be broken", cf. above and note 11) which
seems to promise immortality to John. The secondary nature of
this addition is suggested by its appearance elsewhere, both in
so many words and in other language. This makes us suspicious of
the innovative phrase in *1*. 46b ("whoever among you becomes as a
child shall know the kingdom"), which looks very much like an
explanatory paraphrase of a difficult phrase ("the least in the
kingdom") which appears in "Q". In fact, Thomas himself gives us
a clue that he is paraphrasing in the introduction "I have said".
This refers back to the very elaborate parable of childhood in
1. 22. In that parable, becoming a child (and entering the kingdom) is explained as the process of identifying oneself with one's
heavenly counterpart (cf. *11*. 11, 18). The notion of having some
sort of counterpart in heaven does appear in Matthew 18.10, but in
Thomas Jesus is made to offer an account of salvation as union with
one's heavenly image /46/. In *1*. 46, a basically authentic saying
has been explicated by a back reference to this gnostic ideology.

Indeed, within this section of *Thomas* gnostic ideas of salvation come clearly to the fore. This is hardly surprising, as
the major interlocution (*1*. 24) concerning the "place" of Jesus

has led in *1.* 43 to a sub-question concerning Jesus' authority.
Jesus answers in a series of statements which emphasize that one
is either against him (and with "the Jews") or on his side (and
with the kingdom). *L.* 49 is the climax of this series:

> Blessed are the solitary and elect,
>   for you shall find the kingdom;
> because you come from it, you shall go there again.

This saying amounts to a thorough redefinition of the kingdom:
it is now no longer the saving activity of God himself, but the
source and goal of the saved few. The terms in which the idea is
expressed are themselves remiscent of the classic description of
gnosis in the *Excerpta ex Theodota* (78): "the knowledge of who
we have been and what we have become, where we have been..." /47/.
Instead of the kingdom being in the midst of the disciples, as in
11. 3, 113, the disciples are portrayed as from the midst of the
kingdom. Although this sort of macarism was, of course, a standard form for the transmission of Jesus' teaching, the present
saying appears quite inauthentic. Once again, we must acknowledge
that a purely form critical approach to the saying would have led
us astray.

Once the next interlocutory section has been entered (with
1. 51), the authenticity of the kingdom sayings seems to improve.
It has already been observed that *1.* 54 parallels Matthew 5.3 and
Luke 6.20, and the omission of "in spirit" (with Luke) is an indication that the wording is relatively more primitive than what we
have in Matthew, where the phrase appears to be an explanatory
gloss which was added in the course of transmission /48/.

L. 82 in *Thomas* reads:

> Whoever is near to me is near to the fire;
> whoever is far from me is far from the kingdom.

If this saying was ascribed to Jesus in the New Testament, few
voices would be raised against its authenticity. The antithetical
parallelism, the use of the imagery of fire (cf. Mark 9.49; Luke
12.49; *1.* 10), and even the conception of the kingdom in relation
to Jesus (cf. Matthew 12.28 and Luke 11.20) are all characteristic
of the dominical *ipsissima vox*. These considerations, as well as
the attestation of the saying as dominical in Patristic sources
/49/, have led to the consensus that, at this point, *Thomas* provides us with an authentic saying of Jesus. It is notable also
that the saying appears in the same major interlocutory section
in which the undoubtedly authentic *1.* 54 is included.

L. 99 begins a new interlocutory section, which is designed

to explain the way of discipleship. The disciples say here, as
they do in the Synoptics (cf. Mark 3.32 and parallels) that Jesus'
brothers and mother are standing outside. Jesus replies in *l*. 99b:

> Those here who do the will of my father
>   are my brothers and my mother;
> these are they who shall enter the kingdom of my father.

In *l*. 99bα, we have an excellent parallel to what we read in the
Synoptics /50/, although the adverb "here" is probably an explanatory addition. Its insertion results from the lack of a definite
narrative context in *Thomas*, and may betray the awareness that the
saying ought to have (or once did have) such a context. But what
of *l*. 99bβ? The parallelism between doing God's will as Jesus'
brother or mother and entering the kingdom is very immediate; there
is no fresh start to introduce the kingdom material, signalled
by "but" or "and", which marks an elaborative addition elsewhere
(cf. *ll*. 3b, 46b, 113c). Also, the language of entering the
kingdom, rather than "knowing" it (cf. *l*. 46b), is probably not
a preferred usage in *Thomas*. The kingdom here refers, not to
the source and goal of the gnostic believer (cf. *ll*. 27, 49, 113c),
but to God's own activity (cf. *ll*. 3a, 46b, 82) and relates the
kingdom to Jesus in the same direct way that *l*. 82 does. In this
case, what might seem to be an addition when one compares *Thomas*
to the Synoptics unreflectively should rather be viewed as a
probably authentic statement. This conclusion does not
necessarily involve the supposition that the Synoptic traditions
excised a statement such as *l*. 99bβ. They may have done so,
since their narrative contexts lay all the stress on relationship
to Jesus rather than on entering the kingdom. But it is equally
possible that Jesus said something in the nature of Matthew 12.49-
50; Mark 3.34-35; Luke 8.21; *Thomas l*. 99b on more than one
occasion, and did not consistently include the kingdom reference
embodied in *l*. 99bβ every time he did so.

Having found a rather rich vein of authentically dominical
material in *ll*. 54, 82, 99, it comes as a disappointment to read
l. 114c:

> For every woman who makes herself male
> will enter the kingdom of heaven.

Thomas is notoriously anti-sexual; within this Gospel, sexual
polarities are part of the evil which it is the business of salvation to overcome (cf. *ll*. 15, 22, 37, 79). The present saying
complements the view that men should make eunuchs of themselves
for the sake of the kingdom (Matthew 19.12) /51/, but in doing so
it sounds an explicitly ascetical note at the very close of the
Gospel. The saying corrects the anti-feminine statement of Peter

in *1*. 114a, however, so that it is not wisely dismissed as an
expression of purely heterodox Gnostic dualism. More probably, we
have here another testimony to the Syrian provenience of the tradition in *Thomas*, but it seems to be the result of elaboration as
tendentious as we have seen in *1*. 113c.

   The non-parabolic kingdom sayings in *Thomas* fall into three
categories:

inauthentic	partially authentic	authentic
27	3 (cf. Luke 17.20-21)	54 (cf. Matthew 5.3; Luke 6.20)
49	46b (cf. Matthew 11.11; Luke 7.28)	82
113c	113a, b (cf. Luke 17.20-21)	99 (cf. Matthew 12.48; Mark 3.33; Luke 8.21).
114c		

Among the inauthentic sayings, *1*. 27 appears to be of Syrian provenience and reflects an ascetical ethos. The same ethos comes
to expression in *1*. 49, where the kingdom concept acquires a gnostic
meaning, being protrayed as the domain of the elect. *Ll*. 113c,
114c share the same conception. The radical shift in the understanding of the kingdom may reflect a difference in provenience,
in which case *ll*. 49, 113c, 114c would stem from a later,
Egyptian stage of the tradition. *L*. 46b is partially authentic,
but presents a similarly gnostic understanding of the kingdom as
something which the believer, who becomes a "child" at unity with
his divine counterpart (cf. *1*. 22), alone can know. *Ll*. 3, 113a,
b have been interpreted in that direction as well, but--as in the
case of *1*. 46b--there is enough material left when the interpretation is removed as to suggest they are paritally authentic.
Notably, the inauthentic sayings include simple creations (*ll*.
27, 49) and elaborative additions (*ll*. 113c, 114c), and the
method of elaboration is also evident in *1*. 3, a partially
authentic saying. *L*. 46b presents us with a case of elaboration
achieved by a back reference. Aside from observing signs of
elaboration and back reference, we have also profited from
observing the interlocutory contexts of sayings. This has helped
to alert us to what is highly interpretative and inauthentic
(cf. *ll*. 3b, 46b, 49, 113c, 114c). Nonetheless, the presence
of an interlocution before *1*. 99b was certainly not a proof of
its secondary nature. It joins *1*. 54 as witnessing a primitive,
authentic saying such as we have in the Synoptic Gospels, and
belongs to the same category as *1*. 82, which is no less authentic

for being unattested in the New Testament.

In practice, *Thomas* can only be trusted as a witness to the sayings of Jesus to a limited extent. In this document, the interpretation of Jesus' teaching did on occasion result in the creation of new sayings, although probably in the Syrian and (early) Egyptian phases of the tradition. But the force of the interlocutory structure and the back reference in *l.* 46b suggest that interpretative activity was also substantive at the level of redaction. When *Thomas* does present authentic sayings, this is demonstrably the case only because comparison with the New Testament (and Patristica, as in the case of *l.* 82) is possible. Such comparison may involve an actual collation between the wording of *Thomas* and that of the Synoptics, or--where collation is impossible--an assessment of the concepts in *Thomas* against the background of the Synoptic presentation of Jesus. In either case, there can be no presumption that *Thomas* is a good or a bad witness. The document is a structured presentation of harmonized traditions: some of those traditions are authentic, and some are not. Generalizations to the effect that *Thomas* and "Q" are somehow to be identified, or that *Thomas* is to be ignored as an instance of heterodox "Gnosticism", are beside the point. The application of form critical "criteria of authenticity" are also misleading, as we have seen above. What is needed is simply historical judgement exercised within a sound tradition critical framework. If we are equal to that task, we will find that in some measure we can indeed trust *The Gospel according to Thomas*.

Notes

/1/   The standard edition was published in 1959 by E.J. Brill in Leiden. Many introductions are available, cf. the articles by J.-É. Ménard ("Thomas, Gospel of"), G. MacRae ("Nag Hammadi") and B. Layton ("Coptic Language") in: *The Interpreter's Dictionary of the Bible.* Supplementary Volume (Nashville: Abingdon, 1976).
/2/   Cf. M. Marcovich, "Textual Criticism and the Gospel of Thomas" in: *JTS* 20 (1969) 53-74 and J.A. Fitzmyer, "The Oxyrhynchus *logoi* of Jesus and the Coptic Gospel according to Thomas" in: *Essays on the Semitic Background of the New Testament* (London: Chapman, 1971) 355-433.

/3/   H. Koester, "ΓΝΩΜΑΙ ΔΙΑΦΟΡΟΙ: The Origin and Nature of
Diversification in the History of Early Christianity" in: *HTR*
58 (1965) 279-318 (also available in his joint work with
J.M. Robinson, *Trajectories through Early Christianity*
[Philadelphia, Fortress, 1977, 114-157]).
/4/   H. Koester, "One Jesus and Four Primitive Gospels" in:
HTR 61 (1968) 203-247, 219 and *op. cit.*, 158-204, 175.
/5/   Cf. J.D. Turner, "A New Link in the Syrian Judas Thomas
Tradition" in: *Essays on the Nag Hammadi Texts* (ed. M. Krause;
Leiden: Brill, 1972) 109-119.
/6/   For the most vigorous recent statement of this observation,
cf. T.F. Glasson, "Schweitzer's Influence - Blessing or Bane?"
in: *JTS* 28 (1977) 289-302.
/7/   Koester continues to express his position, albeit in a
guarded way, cf. *Introduction to the New Testament* II
(Philadelphia: Fortress, 1982) 49, 247.
/8/   W. Schrage, *Das Verhältnis des Thomas-Evangeliums zur
synoptischen Tradition und zu den koptischen Evangelienüber-
setzungen* (Berlin: Töpelmann, 1964); "Evangelienzitate in den
Oxyrhynchus-Logien und im koptischen Thomas-Evangelium" in:
Apophoreta (ed. W. Eltester and F.H. Kettler; Berlin: Töpelmann,
1964) 251-268.
/9/   R.L. Arthur, *The Gospel of Thomas and the Coptic New
Testament* (unpublished Ph.D. thesis from the Graduate
Theological Union in California: 1976).
/10/   Among his many publications, cf. *Tatian and the Gospel
of Thomas* (Leiden: Brill, 1975).
/11/   Cf. B.D. Chilton, "'Not to taste death': a Jewish,
Christian and Gnostic Usage" in: *Studia Biblica 1978* II
(Sheffield: JOST, 1980) 29-36.
/12/   As Schrage (*Das Verhältnis,* 119) points out, however,
the Sahidic text of Luke is even more harmonized.
/13/   *Op. cit.*, 184.
/14/   Quispel, *op. cit.*, 188.
/15/   Quispel, *op. cit.*, 189.
/16/   Cf. Quispel, *op. cit.*, 178; Schrage, *op. cit.*, 63; Arthur,
op. cit., 64.
/17/   Quispel, *op. cit.*, 188; Schrage, *op. cit.*, 186-188. Cf.
J.-É. Ménard, *L'Évangile selon Thomas* (Leiden: Brill, 1975) 199.
/18/   Quispel, *op. cit.*, 183; Ménard, *op. cit.*, 159.
/19/   Quispel, *op. cit.*, 185. This agreement might warn us
away from the opinion of Jeremias and Hünzinger that Thomas'
version of the saying is more primitive than Matthew's (cf.
Ménard, *op. cit.*, 176).

/20/ Quispel, "L'Évangile selon Thomas et le Diatessaron" in: *Gnostic Studies*. II (Istanbul: Nederlands Historisch-Archaeologisch Institut, 1975) 31-55, 38.

/21/ Quispel, "L'Évangile selon Thomas", 54-55; "The Gospel of Thomas and the Western Text: A Reappraisal" from the same volume cited in n. 20, 56-69, 57; "The Gospel of Thomas and the New Testament," from the same volume, 3-16, 7.

/22/ Quispel, "The Gospel of Thomas", 57.

/23/ Quispel, *Tatian*, 178.

/24/ Quispel, *Tatian*, 183.

/25/ Quispel, *Tatian*, 188.

/26/ Cf. Quispel, "L'Évangile selon Thomas et les Clémentines" in: *Gnostic Studies* II, 17-29. Now, cf. "The *Gospel of Thomas* Revisited" in: *Colloque International sur les textes de Nag Hammadi* (ed. B. Barc; Québec: Université Laval, 1981) 218-266.

/27/ Mention has already been made of this document in connection with *l*. 107; cf. also Ménard, *op. cit.*, 197. There are two further instances in which *The Gospel of Truth* expresses in an abstract way what is more concretely said in *Thomas*: 22.16-19 cf. *l*. 28 and 37.34-38.4 cf. *l*. 18.

/28/ Cf. Ménard, *op. cit.*, 199.

/29/ Quispel, "The Gospel of Thomas and the Western Text", 57.

/30/ Cf. in particular *The Book of Thomas the Contender, The Acts of Thomas, The Infancy Gospel of Thomas* and *Pistis Sophia* 42, 43.

/31/ Cf. Rodolphe Kasser, *L'Évangile selon Thomas* (Neuchâtel: Delachoux et Niestlé, 1961) 19.

/32/ H.E.W. Turner, "The Theology of the Gospel of Thomas" in: *Thomas and the Evangelists* (written with H. Montefiore; Naperville: Allenson, 1962) 79-116, 80-82.

/33/ Cf. A. Kretzer, *Die Herrschaft der Himmel und die Söhne des Reiches* (Stuttgart: KBW, 1971).

/34/ Cf. J.-D. Kaestli, "L'Évangile de Thomas: son importance pour l'étude des parole de Jesus et du gnosticisme chretien" in: *ETR* 54 (1979) 375-396, 392; Ménard, *op. cit.*, 201.

/35/ Cf. R. McL. Wilson, *Studies in the Gospel of Thomas* (London: Mowbray, 1960) 21; G. MacRae, "Gnosis in Messina" in: *CBQ* 28 (1966) 322-333; U. Bianchi (ed.), *The Origins of Gnosticism*. *Numen* Supplements XII (Leiden: Brill, 1967); H.A. Green, "Gnosis and Gnosticism: A study in methodology" in: *Numen* 24 (1977) 95-134.

/36/ Ménard, *op. cit.*, 81.

/37/ T.F. Glasson, "The Gospel of Thomas, Saying 3 and Deuteronomy xxx.11-14" in: *ExT* 78 (1976-1977) 151-152.

/38/ Cf. *l.* 52. In the three cases (*ll.* 25, 37, 111) in
which there may possibly be an allusion to the Old Testament,
it probably derives from the traditional saying, not the
redactor.

/39/ Cf. Wilson, *op. cit.*, 151.

/40/ Cf. B.D. Chilton, "Regnum Dei Deus Est" in: *SJT* 31 (1978)
361-370; *God in Strength: Jesus' Announcement of the Kingdom.*
Studien zum Neuen Testament und seiner Umwelt 1 (Friestadt:
Plöchl, 1979); K. Koch, "Offenbaren wird sich das Reich Gottes"
in: *NTS* 25 (1979) 158-165.

/41/ Cf. Charles W. Hedrick, "Kingdom Sayings and Parables of
Jesus in the *Apocalypse of James*" in: *NTS* 24 (1983) 1-24.
Applying the criteria of authenticity developed by Perrin for
the New Testament, Hedrick opens the possibility that there might
be authentic sayings in the *Apocalypse*. His contribution is
valuable, but he ignores the consideration that such criteria may
only be used when we are confident that a document has some claim
to historicity in the first place. Even when we do think so (as
when the criteria are applied to the canonical Gospels), criteria
of authenticity are no more than rough rules of thumb for
assessing the provenience of traditions. When possible, finer
tools of tradition criticism should be used.

/42/ Cf. H.E.W. Turner, *op. cit.*

/43/ So Kasser, *op. cit.*, 119. It is quite possible to interpret
this saying (as well as *l.* 3) in terms of dualistic Gnosticism, cf.
Bertil Gärtner, *The Theology of the Gospel of Thomas* (London:
Collins, 1961) 213-217. But this view involves exaggerating the
gnostic tendency of the text and applying the saying in a way the
redactor himself did not. Even to insist on the interiority of
the kingdom here, as does Ménard, *op. cit.*, 209, is tendentious.
The point of view here developed appears generally to agree with
that of S.L. Davies, *The Gospel of Thomas and Christian Wisdom*
(New York: Seabury, 1983), but neither the U.K. distributors nor
the Universities' Inter-Library Loan service could make this
volume available to me.

/44/ Fitzmyer, *op. cit.*, 391-392. The argument (accepted from
A. Guillaumont and A. Baker) is that the Syriac accusative
particle stands behind the Greek τὸν κόσμον (*Ox. P.* I.5, 6) and
the Coptic ΕΠΚΟΣΜΟΣ. There are, however, other explanations, cf.
Ménard, *op. cit.*, 120 and C. Tuckett, "Synoptic Tradition in
Some Nag Hammadi and Related Texts" in: *Vigiliae Christianae* 36
(1982) 173-190.

/45/ Cf. A.F.J. Klijn, "Christianity in Edessa and the Gospel of
Thomas" in: *NovT.* 14 (1972) 70-77; H.W.J. Drijvers, *Bardaisan of
Edessa*: Studia Semitica Neerlandica (Assen: Van Gorcum, 1966) and
"Facts and Problems in Early Syriac-Speaking Christianity" in:

The Second Century 2 (1982) 157-175.
/46/ Cf. Ménard, *op. cit.,* 113-115. The verbal similarity
between *1.* 22 and Matthew 18.1-10 may betray the source of the
saying, in which case the traditional development it represents
is extremely elaborative.
/47/ Cf. Ménard, *op. cit.,* 151; A.F.J. Klijn, "The 'Single One'
in the Gospel of Thomas" in: *JBL* 81 (1982) 271-278.
/48/ Cf. Wilson, *op. cit.,* 55-56.
/49/ Cf. Ménard, *op. cit.,* 182-183.
/50/ Cf. Wilson, *op. cit.,* 115-116; Ménard, *op. cit.,* 199-200.
/51/ Cf. Philippe de Suarez, *L'Evangile selon Thomas* (Marsanne:
Métanoia, 1975) 315.

TRADITION AND REDACTION IN THE PARABLES OF THE GOSPEL OF THOMAS

Craig L. Blomberg
Palm Beach Atlantic College
1101 S. Olive Avenue
West Palm Beach, FL 33401

The Gnostic Gospel of Thomas/1/ affords many unique insights into the nature of the tradition history of Jesus' teachings outside the canonical gospels. Of all the writings broadly referred to as apocryphal gospels/2/, no other document contains nearly as many sayings attributed to Jesus which so resemble those of the Synoptics. From very early on in Nag Hammadi research, scholars have recognized the tremendous potential that Thomas has for illustrating Synoptic *Traditions-geschichte* where parallel processes have been at work at both form- and redaction-critical levels/3/. Of the 114 logia in Thomas/4/, over half resemble at least one canonical text to some extent or another/5/. Most notably Thomas presents 13 parables of Jesus, 11 of which have clear parallels in the New Testament. These logia, therefore, provide a good sample for studying tradition history in Thomas and the Synoptics, at least for one major form of gospel pericope.

Research on the relationship between Thomas and the New Testament Gospels has so far tended to fall into two main categories. Early study of the Nag Hammadi finds raised hopes that Thomas might provide an important independent witness to the Synoptic traditions, and several scholars even argued that Thomas had regularly preserved a more primitive form of the sayings of Jesus/6/. The strongest champion of this position was G. Quispel, who defended a pre-Synoptic origin for much of Thomas in a series of important articles/7/. Quispel's principal arguments included: (1) Thomas frequently agrees with Tatian's Diatessaron, the pseudo-Clementine literature, Western textual variants, or the Heiland (a medieval Saxon poem derived from the Diatessaron) against the wording of the Synoptic accounts/8/, (2) in many instances these variant readings may represent alternate translations from an Aramaic original/9/, and (3) Thomas displays other Semitic features,

especially traces of *parallelismus membrorum*/10/. Additionally
though perhaps less significantly, (4) certain logia closely
parallel extant fragments or citations from the so-called
Jewish-Christian gospels/11/, and (5) Thomas' interest in James
the 'Just' parallels his prominence in early Jewish-Christian
circles/12/.

Other arguments which early studies put forward to support
the independence and/or primitive nature of Thomas *vis-à-vis* the
Synoptics included (6) the greatly altered order of the Synoptic
material in Thomas, (7) the Palestinian and non-Gnostic nature
of some of the unparalleled logia (among the parables, see
Thomas 97 and 98), (8) Thomas's non-use of key Synoptic sayings
easily taken to support Gnostic doctrine (most notably the
μυστήριον passages of Mark 4:11 pars.), (9) the less Gnostic
nature of some of the parallel Greek sayings in the fragments of
the Oxyrhynchus papyri (cf. e.g. Thos. 77 with pOx 1), (10)
Thomas' frequent separation of passages found together in the
Synoptics, (11) Thomas's lack of narrative, and (12) Thomas's lack
of secondary elements like 'apocalyptic imagery, allegorical
interpretation, and generalizing conclusions'/13/.

In 1964, however, Wolfgang Schrage published his thorough
comparison of the relationship of Thomas both with the Synoptic
tradition and with the Coptic translations of the canonical
gospels. Schrage accounted for many of Thomas' minor
distinctives by arguing that he consistently depended on the
Sahidic and Bohairic Coptic renderings of the Synoptics for his
text, concluding that 'die erstaunlich zahlreichen Fälle, in
denen wir einen von sekundären Paralleleinflüssen durchsetzten
Text antreffen werden, durchkreuzen energisch alle Thesen von
der Unabhängigkeit des Th'/14/. Although most feel Schrage's
case to be overstated, the trend since his work has been growing
more and more to view Thomas as dependent on the Synoptic
tradition at least for the bulk of his paralleled material/15/.
Thus J.-D. Kaestli, despite his view which finds a greater
amount of independent tradition behind Thomas, admits that
'aujourd'hui, la thèse la plus largement acceptée est celle de
la dépendance de l'*ETh* par rapport aux Évangiles canoniques:
loin de disposer d'une source originale, *Thomas* ne donnerait
qu'un reflet déformé des paroles de Jésus telles qu'elles sont
transmises par Mt, Mc et Lc'/16/.

The scholarly world remains polarized on this issue,
however, as many still advocate the independence of Thomas,
often without acknowledging or interacting with dissenting

views/17/. But after thoroughly surveying the literature on
Thomas, one is baffled as to how a recent article on 'The
Present State of Gnostic Studies,' can declare that this gospel
'is now mostly interpreted as an originally non-gnostic work
which in its present form is only slightly gnosticized'/18/.
The most extreme example of this one-sided approach to Thomas
appears in Stevan Davies's important new monograph, *The Gospel
of Thomas and Christian Wisdom*. *In nuce*, Davies argues that
Thomas is not in any meaningful sense Gnostic, but reflects a
Jewish-Christian background of Wisdom Christology and ought to
be dated along with or even prior to Q between 50 and 70 A.D.
/19/.

    Davies's discussion does warn one against too readily
reading this enigmatic gospel from a uniformly Gnostic viewpoint.
It also offers plausible suggestions on several side-issues,
including the likelihood of a baptismal *Sitz im Leben* for at
least some of the logia and the possibility of an indirect link
between Paul's opposition at Corinth and the community which
produced Thomas/20/. But Davies errs to the opposite extreme
of reading everything in light of Jewish Wisdom literature,
even to the extent of equating the terms 'kingdom,' 'light,'
'image,' and the 'living one' all with Wisdom/21/! He ignores,
retranslates, or attributes to a glossator the most obviously
Gnostic terminology/22/ and makes no allowance for the
possibility that the strong Wisdom overtones in Thomas stem
from an implicit Gnostic Sophia-mythology rather than from the
parallels he adduces in Old Testament and intertestamental
Wisdom literature. He rightly argues that the trajectories of
early Christianity need not have developed uniformly so that
what seems to be most clearly Gnostic need not be late, but
then he contradicts this logic by demanding that the non-
titular Christology of Thomas must be early or primitive/23/.
But the most serious problem of all with Davies's thesis is
with his initial premise: he begins by assuming without any
argument Thomas's independence from the Synoptics, claiming it
as consensus opinion/24/. If this assumption proves groundless
then much of his thesis collapses.

    The case for independence does seem less persuasive. All
of Quispel's arguments presuppose an early Jewish-Christian
provenance for Thomas which is difficult to defend for more
than a handful of his sayings. Much of Thomas's unparalleled
material clearly reflects a Gnostic milieu very different
from early Jewish Christianity (cf. esp. Thos. 1-3, 22-23, 27-
28, 37, 52, 67, 75, 77, 108, and 114)/25/. The Diatessaron,

pseudo-Clementines, and Western variants all generally
represent later developments of the gospel tradition, while
apparent Semitisms can often be explained in other ways as
well/26/. The issue parallels the question of Semitisms in the
Synoptics, which often turn out to be Septuagintalisms. Thomas
has so imbibed the flavor of the New Testament gospels that
many of his Semitisms may simply reflect the Aramaicized Greek
found there. A. Guillaumont has recently pointed out a few
genuine Semitisms which cannot be explained away, but these
prove more the exception than the rule and do not much affect
the Synoptic-like parables which Thomas presents/27/.

   The other arguments for independence fare little better.
Argument (6) proves nothing; R. M. Grant uses the observation
that Thomas so consistently changes Synoptic order to suggest
that he employs 'purposeful non-correlation' (an equally
speculative conclusion)/28/. Argument (7) seems to reflect the
exception rather than the rule, once again, as the Gnostic
character of much of Thomas demonstrates. Argument (8) is
balanced by the plethora of Synoptic sayings patient of Gnostic
interpretation which Thomas does utilize. Argument (9) is
offset by the observation that even the Greek version of Thomas
seems dependent on the Synoptics/29/. Argument (10) is balanced
by the fact that Thomas frequently combines or conflates sayings
which are separate in the Synoptics/30/. The non-narrative
nature of Thomas, argument (11), is indeed striking, but it is
difficult to know what conclusions to draw from it. Y. O. Kim
argues that 'the lack of narrative accounts of the actual deeds
of Jesus can probably be explained as a consequence of the
author's views according to which the salvation of man does not
depend upon the deeds of Jesus in his earthly ministry, but
man's attainment of this secret knowledge He imparts as the
Revealer'/31/. Finally, argument (12) presupposes more
certainty about the tendencies of the tradition than the
evidence warrants. Apocalyptic imagery, *pace* Montefiore, is
usually taken as a sign of more primitive Jesus-tradition, and
recent parable research has shown that neither allegory nor
generalizing conclusions are necessary signs of inauthenticity
/32/.

   On the other hand, at least four additional arguments
favor Thomas's dependence on the Synoptics. First, the fact
that Thomas contains material parallel to all four canonical
gospels and to all the Synoptic strata (triple tradition,
double tradition, and material peculiar to each of the three)

better supports a hypothesis of Thomas's secondary use of the
Synoptics rather than vice-versa. Even material unique to Mark
(a rare commodity indeed) seems to appear at the end of Thos. 21
(cf. Mark 4:29), leading R. McL. Wilson to remark that here is
'final proof that if Thomas used our gospels he employed all
three Synoptics'/33/. Second, some sayings reflect a
development from Synoptic to Gnostic tradition within Thomas
itself. Thos. 73-75, for example, present in sequence a saying
closely parallel to Luke 10:2, an unparalleled saying of similar
significance, and a clearly Gnostic adaptation of the same idea
(the laborers and harvest become drinkers and cistern and then
'solitaries' and bridal chamber). Third, some sayings in Thomas
follow each other for no apparent reason other than that they
appear in that sequence in the Synoptics. For example, Thos. 66
follows 65 (the cornerstone quotation following the parable of
the wicked husbandmen) even though Thomas has omitted the
intervening material from the Synoptic versions. Finally, some
sayings exhibit interruptions which make little sense apart from
their Synoptic contexts. Thus Thos. 14, with its intrusive
phrase 'heal the sick among them,' likely stems from Luke 10:9
following the parallel between the previous part of the saying
and Luke 10:8/34/.

     Thomas's relationship to the Synoptics no doubt defies
simple description. Wilson's conclusion that he has combined
gospel harmonization, free quotation of the Synoptics, and
independent tradition seems quite sane/35/. Yet there appears
to remain enough evidence both of Thomas's use of the Synoptics
for his paralleled material and of his use of unorthodox Gnostic
/36/ theology for his unparalleled material to place the burden
of proof on the person who would argue for the authenticity of
any of his sayings, *pace* the approach appropriate for the
Synoptics/37/. With respect to the parables, A. Lindemann has
recently defended in some detail the claim that 'alle im ThEv
erzählten Gleichnisse repräsentieren eine gegenüber den
synoptischen Evangelien sekundäre Stufe der Überlieferung'/38/.
Lindemann's case seems weakest for the two parables peculiar to
Thomas (log. 97 and 98), which lay as much claim to authenticity
as any of Thomas's logia/39/, although they too may have been
retouched slightly by Gnostic redaction/40/. But his case seems
quite convincing for the paralleled parables.

     If the parables of Thomas thus represent for the most part
a later stage in the gospel tradition than the Synoptics,
important new conclusions begin to emerge. For until now,

scholars have tended to draw one of two main conclusions
concerning the significance of Thomas for Synoptic research.
Those viewing Thomas as independent and primitive have
interpreted his parables as the earliest versions of those
teachings of Jesus now extant. Those viewing Thomas as dependent
and secondary have interpreted his parables almost exclusively
in terms of their Gnostic tendencies. An important third
approach remains unexamined. If at least for his paralleled
parables Thomas is dependent on and later than the Synoptic
tradition, then the versions in which his parables appear should
reveal something not only about Gnostic theology but also
something of the pre-Gnostic stages of the tradition as it
continued to develop from its canonical versions.

From this perspective, one aspect of Thomas's paralleled
parables stands out dramatically. In eight of eleven instances,
Thomas's versions are abbreviated--shorter and less detailed.
The tradition seems to have continued to develop as it had
already begun to do in moving from Mark to Luke (and less
consistently from Mark to Matthew)/41/. For a word count of
parallel passages reveals that of 92 pericopae common to Mark
and Luke, Luke is shorter in 71 instances (and of 104 pericopae
common to Mark and Matthew, Matthew is shorter in 63 instances)
/42/. Significantly, Thomas is closer to Luke's versions of his
Synoptic-like sayings more often than to either of the other
gospels/43/. That Thomas discloses this continuation of the
tendency to abbreviate not only further demolishes Bultmann's
so-called 'law of increasing distinctness'/44/, but even
suggests that for relatively detailed forms such as parables,
the more frequent tendency of the tradition was in the direction
of abbreviation. This tendency has already been suggested by
various studies of oral tradition/45/; exceptions to this in the
parables of Thomas may virtually all be explained in light of
conscious editorial redaction and therefore pose no threat to
the thesis of this study. Our next task must therefore be an
examination, in turn, of each of the paralleled parables of
Thomas. The sequence of parables discussed will roughly
correspond to the amount of abbreviation displayed, proceeding
in decreasing order.

> *The Wheat and the Tares (Thos. 57, Matt. 13:24-30)*
> Jesus said, 'The kingdom of the Father is like a man who
> had (good) seed. His enemy came by night and sowed weeds
> among the good seed. The man did not allow them to pull up
> the weeds; he said to them, "I am afraid that you will go

intending to pull up the weeds and pull up the wheat along
with them." For on the day of the harvest the weeds will
be plainly visible, and they will be pulled up and burned.'

By far the most abbreviated parable in Thomas is this
version of the parable of the wheat and tares. As in Matthew,
Thomas presents the narrative as a kingdom parable, but like
frequently elsewhere in his gospel (cf. Thos. 76, 96, 97, and
98), the kingdom is 'of the Father'. This expression probably
stems from Thos. 2-3 where Thomas describes 'the kingdom'
(unqualified) as 'inside of you. . .when you come to know
yourselves. . .and you will realize that it is you who are the
sons of the living Father.' As L. Cerfaux explains, 'On
comprendra cette notion comme une disposition intérieure du
chrétien,' and again, 'Le "regnum" s'est clairement intériorisé;
il est la vie profonde de l'âme chrétienne et son contact avec
Dieu'/46/. Throughout the Nag Hammadi library, eschatology is
presented as almost entirely realized, and the concept of the
kingdom as internalized or spiritualized/47/. The rest of the
parable is then stripped of all but the bare essentials of the
narrative, yet without any obvious distortion/48/.

The secondary character is clear from the plural pronouns
'them' and 'you' which refer to the servants in Matthew's
version but appear without antecedent in Thomas, thus
presupposing a version more like Matthew's/49/. The enemy
comes 'by night,' an obvious inference from Matthew's 'while men
were sleeping,' although Schoedel suggests that it emphasizes
the psychological significance of the seed/50/. Thomas's
conclusion differs from Matthew, and may suggest that the
Gnostics placed more confidence in their ability to grow into a
type of people visibly distinguishable from everyone else than
did most orthodox Christians (cf. e.g. the famous passage of the
Epistle to Diognetus V). Separatistic tendencies reappear
throughout the Nag Hammadi literature; a striking example of
similar imagery occurs in Authoritative Teaching 25.12-26: 'For
if the chaff is mixed with the wheat, it is not the chaff that
is contaminated, but the wheat. For they are mixed with each
other. . . . But a pure seed is kept in storehouses that are
secure.' The most obvious characteristic of Thomas's parable
nevertheless remains its condensed form, which can scarcely be
due entirely to de-allegorizing or de-eschatologizing tendencies
/51/, since these affect only the conclusion of the parable.
It is much more likely that the parable has already undergone
compression in the tradition.

The Rich Fool (Thos. 63, Luke 12:16-21)
Jesus said, 'There was a rich man who had much money. He
said, "I shall put my money to use so that I may sow, reap,
plant, and fill my storehouse with produce, with the result
that I shall lack nothing." Such were his intentions, but
that same night he died. Let him who has ears hear.'

Thomas's version of the parable of the rich fool offers the
second most dramatic example of abbreviation in his gospel. The
narrative is somewhat ambiguous without knowledge of the longer
Lucan form and not surprisingly has proved difficult to
interpret. But it preserves just enough detail to stand on its
own--the description of the man as rich in goods or 'useful
things,' his soliloquy (without the rhetorical question) with
the triad 'eat, drink, and be merry,' replaced by 'sow, reap,
and plant,' the references to filling his barns and lacking
nothing, and his sudden, tragic fate. God's address to the
rich man, specifically calling him a fool, disappears, leaving
open the possibility that the parable is to be interpreted as a
positive example-story. This possibility is enhanced by the
omission of the pejorative introduction of Luke 12:13-15. But
Thomas presents a gnosticized version of these verses in Thos.
72, which is equally negative/52/. Moreover, the conclusion of
the parable contradicts a positive interpretation. Lindemann's
explanation that Thomas has transformed the portrait of the rich
man from a 'kleinbürglicher' to a 'kapitalistischer' one seems
more plausible/53/. The entire Nag Hammadi library contains
many strong ascetic injunctions, and the very next parable in
Thomas stresses the renunciation of all forms of business or
merchandising (Thos. 64--cf. the discussion below)/54/. Yet a
Gnostic redactor would scarcely have left out all the detail of
the Lucan form, especially not God's rebuke, which only serves
to enhance the rich man's condemnation. Most likely oral
tradition had already abbreviated the parable just about as much
as it could without altogether destroying its intelligibility,
before it reached its final editor. The concluding call to hear
is a 'floating logion' often added in both Thomas and the
Synoptics, and with this parable it may well be due to early
lectionary usage/55/.

The Parable of the Sower (Thos. 9, Mark 4:3-8, Matt. 13:3-9,
Luke 8:4-8)
Jesus said, 'Now the sower went out, took a handful (of
seeds), and scattered them. Some fell on the road; the

birds came and gathered them up. Others fell on rock, did
not take root in the soil, and did not produce ears. And
others fell on thorns; they choked the seed(s) and worms
ate them. And others fell on the good soil and produced
good fruit; it bore sixty per measure and a hundred and
twenty per measure.'

Here Thomas reproduces a triple-tradition parable, even
more abbreviated than the shortest Synoptic form (Luke), which
in turn already abbreviated the fuller original (Mark)/56/.
Specifically, Thomas omits the superfluous verb 'to sow' after
'the sower went out,' and the similarly unnecessary phrase 'the
thorns grew.' He also lacks the concluding call for having ears
to hear, which Thomas had added to the parable of the rich fool.
As with the parable of the wheat and tares, Thomas omits Jesus'
subsequent interpretation. The concluding call is again a
'floating logion' in both Thomas and the Synoptics/57/, while
the lack of interpretation is no ground for rejecting the
authenticity of it in the canonical texts/58/.

More noteworthy than the omissions in Thomas are his
alterations of detail: (a) the sower *fills his hand* to scatter
the seed, (b) the first seed falls *on* the road, (c) the second
seed 'did not produce ears,' (d) the third seed is eaten by
worms, and (e) the final seed bears 120-fold. Although several
of these alterations at first glance look like vivid, authentic
details/59/, all turn out to be easily understood as secondary
changes. Fullness is a key Gnostic concept, not only in the
well-known myth of the divine Pleroma but also in the maturity
expected of the 'believer' (cf. esp. Apocryphon of James 2.28-
4.19)/60/. At the same time W. H. C. Frend points to the
parallel in 1 Clement 24.11, 12-18, which suggests that this
change may also be a product of the earlier (but still post-
Synoptic) tradition/61/. The reading 'on the road' has already
been discussed above/62/; it needs only to be added that Schrage
suggests that παρά in the Synoptics can bear the translation 'on,'
so perhaps this is not a modification at all (cf. BGD, s.v.).
The reference to ears not going forth up to heaven seems surely
to reflect the doctrine of the heavenward ascent of the good
seed, the true Gnostic. Hippolytus, for example, describes the
Naassene ritual initiation in which converts contemplate 'a
green ear of corn reaped in silence,' an ear which was then
lifted heavenward and waved in the air to symbolize the promised
life after death/63/. This imagery reappears in a parable
attributed to the Risen Lord in Apoc. Jas. 12.22-30: 'The

kingdom of heaven is like an ear of grain after it had sprouted
in a field. And when it had ripened, it scattered its fruit and
again filled the field with ears for another year. You also
hasten to reap an ear of life for yourselves that you may be
filled with the kingdom'/64/. Hedrick has recently argued that
ll. 22-26 may reflect an authentic parable, but that ll. 27-30
(the concluding sentence) are a secondary interpretation/65/,
and it is the latter that the Thomas parable more closely
parallels.

The addition of the worm parallels Thomas's redaction
elsewhere (cf. Thos. 76) and probably symbolizes the evil,
corrupting influence of the world. Thus the Gospel of Truth
33.16-21 enjoins its readers: 'Do not be moths, do not be
worms. . .do not become a (dwelling) place for the devil, for
you have already destroyed him.' Or as Asclepius 66.14-25
remarks: 'But if there is ignorance. . .evil comes with them
(the passions) in the form of an incurable sore. And the sore
constantly gnaws at the soul and through it the soul produces
worms from the evil and stinks'/66/. Finally, the addition of
120-fold, not one of the various numbers used in the Synoptic
versions, appears to have come from the symbolic value of the
number. At least in the Concept of Our Great Power 43.21-22,
based on the number of years Noah preached before the flood,
120 is called 'the perfect number that is highly exalted'.

Thomas's parable may thus represent the results of the
Gnostic's proselytizing, or more probably the response of the
Gnostic to his Father's call. In any event, Thomas's redaction,
coupled with his agreements with each of the Synoptics in
various places against the others/67/, seems to confirm the
secondary nature of this parable, which again stands out for its
shortened form.

*The Parable of the Mustard Seed (Thos. 20, Mark 4:30-32,
Matt. 13:31-32, Luke 13:18-19)*
The disciples said to Jesus, 'Tell us what the Kingdom of
Heaven is like.' He said to them, 'It is like a mustard
seed, the smallest of all seeds. But when it falls on
tilled soil, it produces a great plant and becomes a
shelter for birds of the sky.'

Again Thomas draws upon all three Synoptic versions/68/;
again Thomas presents an abbreviated form. Thomas adopts
Matthew's unique introductory 'kingdom of heaven' against his

usual tendency to speak of the 'kingdom of the Father'/69/. He
also specifically attributes the start of the discussion to the
disciples, as frequently elsewhere (cf. Thos. 6, 12, 18, 20, 24,
37, 43, 51, 52, 53, 99, 100, 113, and 114), but omits Jesus'
introductory formula--easily understandable as the result of the
tradition eliminating extra details. Thomas preserves Mark's
reference to the mustard seed as smallest of all seeds, since
this is crucial to his understanding of the parable, which may
similarly contrast the small size of his community then (cf.
Thos. 23: 'one out of a thousand, and two out of ten thousand')
with the impact which he believed it would one day have/70/.
In this case, Lindemann would be correct to highlight how this
parable shows 'mit welch geringen Mitteln ein auf das Reich
Gottes bezogenes Gleichnis Jesu gnostisiert werden konnte'/71/.
On the other hand the metaphor may have a more individualized
referent, depicting the projected maturity of the individual
Gnostic from his initial divine spark/72/. The rest of the
parable merely condenses the Synoptic accounts, with the sole
exception of the phrase 'when it falls on tilled soil,' which
probably emphasizes the fact that 'die göttliche Abstammung des
Gnostikers ist keine Garantie, sonder eine Verpflichtung'/73/.
This phrase also harks back to the parable of the sower; compare
the very remarkable parable of the grapevine in Thomas the
Contender 144.19-36 which offers reminiscences of both sower and
mustard seed/74/.

> *The Great Dinner (Thos. 64, Matt. 22:2-14, Luke 14:16-24)*
> Jesus said, 'A man had received visitors. And when he had
> prepared the dinner, he sent his servant to invite the
> guests. He went to the first one and said to him, "My
> master invites you." He said, "I have claims against some
> merchants. They are coming to me this evening. I must go
> and give them my orders. I ask to be excused from the
> dinner." He went to another and said to him, "My master
> has invited you." He said to him, "I have just bought a
> house and am required for the day. I shall not have any
> spare time." He went to another and said to him, "My
> master invites you." He said to him, "My friend is going
> to get married, and I am to prepare the banquet. I shall
> not be able to come. I ask to be excused from the dinner."
> He went to another and said, "My master invites you." He
> said to him, "I have just bought a farm, and I am on my way
> to collect the rent. I shall not be able to come. I ask
> to be excused." The servant returned and said to his
> master, "Those whom you invited to the dinner have asked to

be excused." The master said to his servant, "Go outside
to the streets and bring back those whom you happen to
meet, so that they may dine." Businessmen and merchants
will not enter the Places of My Father.'

Several important differences set Thomas's version apart
from both Matthew and Luke in what is again the shortest of the
narratives. The double invitation becomes the somewhat unclear
'A man had received visitors. . .he sent his servant to invite
the guests.' The dinner is not 'great,' much less a wedding
feast. The servant's invitation is in each case phrased, 'My
master invites you,' and the responses of a full four of the
guests are described with slightly altered excuses. The rest of
the parable is greatly abbreviated, with no reference to the
king's anger and destruction (Matthew), to the second invitation
to the outcasts (Luke), or to the man without a wedding garment
(Matthew). The conclusion parallels neither Matthew nor Luke
but depicts the master proclaiming an anathema against all
traders in commerce. Overall the parable is much closer to the
Lucan version than to the Matthean, if it is even proper to
speak of these passages as 'versions' of the same parable/75/.

At first glance, however, Thomas's parable seems to
represent, as F. W. Beare puts it, 'precisely what modern
scholars would generally regard as the original form created by
Jesus'/76/. The conclusion, though, reveals obvious Gnostic
redaction, as already noted above. Compare Thos. 110: 'Whoever
finds the world and becomes rich, let him renounce the world.'
Each of the four excuses given probably illustrates this dislike
for worldly affairs, and the fact that there are four of them,
each narrated in some detail, may well underline their
condemnation. Three of the excuses are business-related and
not obviously exaggerated, as in the Synoptics; even apparently
legitimate excuses are rejected if commercially oriented. The
other excuse has shifted from the man having just married a
wife to one of having to prepare the banquet for a friend's
wedding. This transformation may reflect a strong aversion to
marriage current in many Gnostic circles (cf. esp. Hippolytus's
discussion of the Naassene attitude in *Philosophumena* V, 2)/77/,
and at the same time a conservative tendency reluctant to
abolish the motif altogether. On the other hand, it may be
designed to bring the excuse in line with the others, if it be
assumed that the man received remuneration for his service.
The phrase 'Places of My Father' resembles expressions for other
holy 'places' in Thomas (cf. Thos. 4, 24, 60, 68); frequent

similar references in other Gnostic literature consistently link
up with the concept of 'rest' (άνάπαυσις)/78/. The major
omissions of the allegorical details in the Synoptic accounts
may reflect Thomas's disinterest in their eschatological
implications/79/. However, they may equally reflect the
abbreviating tendency of the tradition, since they enhance the
master's condemnation of the originally invited guests--a point
as important to Thomas as to Matthew and Luke. At any rate,
the strong ascetic atmosphere and renunciation of all forms of
business or merchandising, so characteristic of much of the Nag
Hammadi library, shines through even in Thomas's more subdued
comments, and ensures the secondary nature of this narrative/80/.

> *The Wicked Husbandmen (Thos. 65, Mark 12:1-11, Matt.*
> *21:33-44, Luke 20:9-18)*
> He said, 'There was a good man who owned a vineyard. He
> leased it to tenant farmers so that they might work it and
> he might collect the produce from them. He sent his
> servant so that the tenants might give him the produce of
> the vineyard. They seized his servant and beat him, all
> but killing him. The servant went back and told his master.
> The master said, "Perhaps 'they' did not recognize 'him'?."
> He sent another servant. The tenants beat this one as well.
> Then the owner sent his son and said, "Perhaps they will
> show respect to my son." Because the tenants knew that it
> was he who was the heir to the vineyard, they seized him
> and killed him. Let him who has ears hear.'

This parable follows immediately upon the previous one
discussed in Thomas's gospel, and with the rich fool of Thos. 63
completes a triad of parables which present characters who miss
the true meaning of the Christian revelation (whether
interpreted in orthodox or Gnostic fashion). As with all of the
parables so far discussed, Thomas offers the shortest account
and seems closest to Luke (again the shortest of the three
Synoptic versions)/81/. As with the parable of the great dinner,
Thomas's version somewhat parallels certain modern
reconstructions of the parable's most primitive form. But again
secondary alterations betray the influence of later processes
at work.

Thomas begins by calling the parable's protagonist a 'good'
man/82/, probably because the landlord symbolizes God, whom the
Gnostics repeatedly emphasized as good (even to the occasional
exclusion of his justice)/83/. Thomas adds that the tenants'

lease required them to work the farm that 'he might collect the produce of the vineyard,' probably reflecting the Gnostic emphasis on man's participation in salvation/84/. In the description of the sending of the servants, the tradition follows the trend already visible in Luke of reducing their number (Mark has three + 'many others' + the son, Luke has three + the son, and Thomas has two + the son). This phenomenon seems much more likely to reflect form-critical rather than redaction-critical processes, as both Luke and Thomas fit the classical pattern for oral storytelling with their climactic triads/85/. The master's comment that 'perhaps <they> did not recognize [literally, 'know' <him>]'/86/, unambiguously displays the Gnostic emphasis on knowledge/87/.

Finally, the conclusion is stripped of all but the most essential detail. The eschatological implications of the Synoptic versions may not have appealed to Thomas, but the destruction of the man's enemies and the transfer of the vineyard to others would have also fit Gnostic designs very suitably. Gnostics, probably much more than their orthodox counterparts, viewed themselves as aloof from unbelievers and saw God at war with the spiritual forces holding them captive. Again the tendencies of the developing tradition seemed to have worked to condense and compress/88/.

> *The Lost Sheep (Thos. 107, Matt. 18:12-14, Luke 15:4-7)*
> Jesus said, 'The Kingdom is like a shepherd who had a hundred sheep. One of them, the largest, went astray. He left the ninety-nine and looked for that one until he found it. When he had gone to such trouble, he said to the sheep, "I care for you more than the ninety-nine."'

Here Thomas's abbreviated version for the first time parallels Matthew more closely than Luke; significantly Matthew also presents (again for the first time) the shorter of the Synoptic accounts/89/. The parable of the lost sheep seems to have been a favorite with the Gnostics. Irenaeus explains its interpretation in Valentinian circles; the lost sheep is the Gnostic (or his heavenly prototype), while the shepherd is the Gnostic mother Sophia (also called Achamoth)/90/. The Gospel of Truth discloses a slightly different understanding in 31.35-32.4, which reads, 'He [the Son] is the shepherd who left behind the ninety-nine sheep which were not lost. He went searching for the one which was lost. He rejoiced when he found it.' But after this bare summary of the parable, the Gospel of Truth goes

on to give a detailed interpretation (showing that Gnostics did
interpret and allegorize parables, even if Thomas did not),
explaining that the ninety-nine are deficient without the one
which completes the hundred. 32.18-25, with ll.38-39 inserted
between 23 and 24, continues, apparently with reference to
Matt. 12:11: 'Even on the Sabbath, he labored for the sheep,
having brought it up from the pit in order that you might know
interiorly--you the sons of interior knowledge--what is the
Sabbath, on which it is not fitting for salvation to be idle'
/91/.

     William Petersen wisely warns against too quickly
interpreting Thomas in light of the Gospel of Truth here, as
many have done. Petersen points out that the main changes in
Thomas can readily be understood against an ordinary Jewish
background. That the lost sheep is the largest and that the
shepherd loves him the most represent the fact that God
preferred his people Israel. That the shepherd tires himself in
the search reflects God's longsuffering for his chosen nation.
Moreover, sheep and shepherd were very popular metaphors for
Israel and her God throughout the Old Testament, intertestamental
and Rabbinic literature/92/. On the other hand, the parable
fits Gnostic teaching equally well, so that in light of Thomas's
demonstrably tendential redaction in every other passage so far
examined, it seems more appropriate to assume similar forces at
work here. The Gnostic also believed that God loved him more
than the non-Gnostic (cf. esp. Gospel of Mary 18.14-15), and the
conclusion of Thomas's parable is in fact only a small step from
the interpretations of the Synoptic versions in Matt. 18:13 and
Luke 15:7/93/.

     Thomas's version of the parable of the dragnet provides a
striking parallel with its reference to the fisherman choosing
to keep only 'a fine large fish'. At the same time, the
omissions of geographical location, explanatory conclusion, and
interrogative form prove less easy to explain as deliberate
excisions; whatever their origin, the end product is once again
streamlined in comparison to Matthew and Luke. Nor is the
addition of 'The kingdom is like. . .' obviously Gnostic, but
may just as easily represent assimilation to stereotypic parable
form/94/.

     The Parable of the Dragnet (Thos. 8, Matt. 13:47-50)
     And he said, "The man is like a wise fisherman who cast his
     net into the sea and drew it up from the sea full of small

fish. Among them the wise fisherman found a fine large
fish. He threw all the small fish back into the sea and
chose the large fish without difficulty. Whoever has ears
to hear, let him hear.'

This is the final parable to show marked abbreviation from
its Synoptic parallel(s). Apart from the condensation, the
major substantive change is the shift from the contrast between
good and bad fish to one between many small fish and one large
good fish. In addition, Thomas changes the comparison of the
kingdom of heaven with a dragnet to that of a man with a wise
fisherman, although only the insertion of the term 'wise' seems
theologically motivated. The wise person chooses gnosis (cf.
the reference to choice in 34.1), or else the Gnostic redeemer
chooses the Gnostic/95/. The Authoritative Teaching 29.3-30.25
provides an interesting parallel from an opposite perspective:
"For this reason, then, we do not sleep, nor do we forget [the]
nets that are spread out in hiding, lying in wait for us to
catch us. . .And we will be taken down into the dragnet. For
man-eaters will seize us and swallow us, rejoicing like a
fisherman casting a hook into the water. . . . In this very way
we exist in the world, like fish. . .' Perhaps the Gnostic
envisaged both good and bad fishermen, hoping that he would be
hooked by his Savior rather than his adversary.

Other alterations prove more minor. The details of
judgment have all vanished, again perhaps due to the Gnostics'
eschatological perspective/96/, or perhaps due to a traditional
tendency to abbreviate. On the other hand, Thomas adds the call
to hearing (paralleled in Matt. 13:9, 43), which appears
scattered elsewhere throughout his gospel (cf. esp. Thos. 63,
65, and 96)/97/. The omission of the reference to the kingdom
is better explained as a Gnostic 'interiorization' than as the
mistake of a scribe/98/. And the addition of 'without
difficulty' links nicely with the Gnostic concept of rest which
the truly redeemed enjoy/99/. As Schrage concludes, 'Wir werden
also wieder darauf hingewiesen, dass die Worte Jesu einen
verborgenen Sinn haben und sich nur dem Gnostiker erschliessen,
der durch seine pneumatische Qualität zum Hörer und damit zum
Heil prädestiniert ist'/100/.

The remaining three parables display no abbreviation when
compared with their Synoptic parallels. The first two are
roughly the same length as their parallels, and the third is
noticeably expanded.

The Parable of the Pearl (Thos. 76, Matt. 13:45-46)
Jesus said, 'The Kingdom of the Father is like a merchant
who had a consignment of merchandise and who discovered a
pearl.   That merchant was shrewd.   He sold his merchandise
and bought the pearl alone for himself.   You, too, seek his
unfailing and enduring treasure where no moth comes near to
devour and no worm destroys.'

The significance of the parable of the pearl closely
matches that of its Synoptic twin, the parable of the dragnet,
in both Matthew and Thomas.   It also presents the same ambiguity
in interpretation; the pearl is either the Gnostic or gnosis, or
both/101/.   In the Gospel of Philip 62.17-26, the pearl is
explicitly compared with the sons of God who have great value in
the eyes of their Father.   On the other hand, in the Acts of
Peter and the Twelve Apostles 2.10-5.1, the pearl represents a
heavenly prize which the disciples cannot afford but receive
free of charge/102/.   The parable in Matthew requires few
modifications for a Gnostic interpretation; those which Thomas
makes have all been previously discussed.   The kingdom of heaven
becomes his more common 'kingdom of the Father'.   The fact that
the man is a 'merchant' and therefore almost by definition non-
Gnostic until he abandons his 'merchandise' is highlighted by
the repetition of both terms.   The merchant is again specifically
called wise/103/.   Interestingly, Thomas omits the description
of the pearl as of great price; perhaps that bordered too
closely on the very concept of commercialism which he so
abhorred.   Finally, Thomas juxtaposes a variation on Matt.
6:19-20 (par. Luke 12:33) linked undoubtedly by the catchword
'treasure'/104/.   But instead of moth and rust as the enemies,
Thomas speaks of moth and worms.   This is precisely the imagery
which is combined in Gospel of Truth 33.16-17, as noted above
/105/.

*The Parable of the Leaven (Thos. 96, Matt. 13:33, Luke
13:20-21)*
Jesus [said] , 'The Kingdom of the Father is like a certain
woman.   She took a little leaven, [concealed] it in some
dough, and made it into large loaves.   Let him who has ears
hear.'

Perhaps the shortest of all gospel parables, the parable of
the leaven remains equally brief in Thomas.   He again describes
the kingdom as 'of the Father,' compares it directly with the

woman, rather than with the leaven, omits the description of
three measures quantity, and adds that she made it into 'large
loaves'. Again Thomas attaches the call to hear. Each of these
changes parallels previously discussed tendencies. One need add
only that the omission of the amount of meal seems more likely
due to traditional abbreviation, for it enhances the small/large
contrast which Thomas otherwise stresses with his addition of
'large loaves' (cf. the large fish and large sheep of Thos. 8
and 107). To see in the shift of *tertium comparationis* 'nicht
die Selbsttätigkeit, mit der der Sauerteig den ganzen Teig
durchsäuert, sondern die Aktivität der Frau, die die grossen
Brote herstellt'/106/, may be reading too much into a type of
change frequently found without theological import in the
Synoptics as well/107/. The overall interpretation, however,
undoubtedly involved the symbolism of the true Gnostic guarding
his 'substance pneumatique' which 'détermine toute l'existence'
/108/ from the world's corruption/108/.

> *The Treasure in the Field (Thos. 109, Matt. 13:44)*
> Jesus said, 'The Kingdom is like a man who had a [hidden]
> treasure in his field without knowing it. And [after] he
> died, he left it to his son. The son did not know (about
> the treasure). He inherited the field and sold it. And
> the one who bought it went plowing and found the treasure.
> He began to lend money at interest to whomever he wished.'

Here is the one exception to Thomas's pattern of presenting
parables at least as short as, and usually shorter than, the
Synoptic versions. Whereas Matthew's parable has only one
'act,' Thomas offers three. The emphasis falls on the repeated
ignorance (or lack of gnosis) of both the original field-owner
and his son about the treasure hidden in their land. Finally,
a third man who buys the field discovers the treasure while
plowing. Haenchen undoubtedly grasps the main point here, 'dass
die meisten Menschen gar nicht ahnen, welcher Schatz in ihnen
angelegt ist'/109/. On the other hand, Lindemann places the
emphasis on the first part of the parable, viewing it as a
'Warngleichnis' against the mistakes of the first two men/110/.
It is possible that Thomas's expansion reflects conflation with
similar Rabbinic and Aesopic fables/111/, although the entire
story remains wholly intelligible in Gnostic categories/112/.
The conclusion, however, seems to contradict Thos. 95: 'If you
have money, do not lend it at interest, but give [it] to one
from whom you will not get it back.' It may be, though, that
Thomas's community would have interpreted that logion fairly

literally, while taking the end of saying 109 primarily in a
spiritual or symbolic sense/113/. One might argue that the rich
man's lending is simply typical behavior, but granted the
biblical stance against collecting interest, it is doubtful that
this is original.

   Thomas's parables display an intricate interweaving of
traditional and redactional elements. The types of differences
between his versions and their Synoptic parallels fall broadly
into two categories: (a) abbreviation and omission of
unnecessary detail in ways which suggest that the tradition
streamlined and compressed relatively full narratives as it
developed, and (b) redactional additions and alterations which
almost always reflect important Gnostic themes. Yet even here
Thomas prefers to alter as little of the wording as possible;
the Gnostics no doubt realized that the more they could merely
superimpose their own interpretations on otherwise unchanged
tradition, the more they could mount a credible alternative to
that orthodoxy which accepted only the New Testament canon as
authoritative. Neither of these two types of differences should
cause great surprise. Thomas merely displays the continuation
of the same processes that Luke (or his tradition) consistently
applied to Mark. A 'law' of *decreasing* distinctness or detail
seems to characterize the transmission of relatively lengthy
popular stories more frequently than does one of increasing
distinctness or detail. Bultmann's 'law' to the contrary should
therefore be laid to rest once and for all, and studies of
Synoptic parallels (especially of Q material, where neither
Matthew nor Luke shows a consistent trend to be longer or
shorter) should proceed extremely cautiously whenever
attributing apparent expansion, embellishment, or allegorizing
to the natural tendencies of tradition. These alleged
tendencies, if allowed to operate over three-quarters of a
century (i.e. even presuming a late first-century date for the
Synoptics and a mid-second century one for Thomas), should have
rendered the gospel parables all but unrecognizable. Instead,
J. A. Baird's claim that 'as the teaching of Jesus circulated
in the community, both processes were at work with the tendency
to shorten predominant over that to expand'/114/ finds detailed
confirmation.

   As for the likelihood of Thomas having preserved pre-
Synoptic versions of these parables, the probability seems slim.
A detailed examination of each passage does not overthrow our

initial presupposition of Thomas's post-Synoptic nature, but
rather reinforces it strongly. To be sure, a few unparalleled
logia may be new, relatively authentic agrapha/115/, but the
focus of this study has been on the paralleled material,
because of its implications for the historicity of the Synoptic
accounts. As R. McL. Wilson explains, if Thomas's material
pre-dates his Synoptic parallels, then this document 'can
contribute to discovering the history and the motivation behind
the development of a particular saying,' and no study of the
Synoptic passages dare ignore Thomas's versions as potentially
more primitive/116/. At the very least, this study should place
a question mark before the need to adopt this approach. At
least for the paralleled parables surveyed here, Matthew, Mark,
and Luke still put us much closer to the original words of Jesus.
As indicated in the introduction to this study, a very sizable
and still-growing number of scholars concurs/117/.

Notes

/1/ Thus entitled so as to distinguish it from the infancy
gospel by the same name. No presuppositions about the
theological character of the document are thereby indicated.
Hereafter the title will be abbreviated simply to 'Thomas'. All
quotations are taken from T. O. Lambdin's translation in *The
Nag Hammadi Library* (ed. J. M. Robinson; San Francisco: Harper
& Row, 1977). Other important English translations which should
be consulted include A. Guillaumont, H. Ch. Puech, G. Quispel,
W. C. Till, and Y. 'abd al Masih, *The Gospel according to Thomas*
(New York: Harper & Bros., 1959); R. McL. Wilson, in *New
Testament Apocrypha*, vol. 1 (ed. E. Hennecke and W.
Schneemelcher; Philadelphia: Westminster, 1963); W. R. Schoedel,
in R. M. Grant and D. N. Freedman, *The Secret Sayings of Jesus*
(New York: Doubleday, 1960); Leonard Johnston, in Jean Doresse,
The Secret Books of the Egyptian Gnostics (New York: Viking
Press, 1960); and Ray Summers, in *The Secret Sayings of the
Living Jesus* (Waco: Word, 1968).
/2/ See primarily the two collections of Robinson, *Library*; and
Hennecke-Schneemelcher, *Apocrypha*.
/3/ The literature on Thomas is enormous. The fullest
bibliographic sources are D. M. Scholer, *Nag Hammadi
Bibliography 1948-1969* (Leiden: Brill, 1971); with annual
supplements in the final fascicle of each volume of *NovT*,
excluding 1976.
/4/ Enumeration varies from one translation to the next. We
are following Lambdin, in Robinson, *Library*.
/5/ Summers, *Sayings*, provides a good synopsis of parallels.

/6/ See esp. C.-H. Hunzinger, 'Unbekannte Gleichnisse Jesu aus dem Thomasevangelium,' in *Judentum, Urchristentum, Kirche* (ed. W. Eltester; Berlin: Töpelmann, 1960) 209-20; H. Montefiore, in *Thomas and the Evangelists* (with H. E. W. Turner; Naperville: Allenson, 1962); J. Jeremias, *Unknown Sayings of Jesus* (London: SPCK, 1957); A. J. B. Higgins, 'Non-Gnostic Sayings in the Gospel of Thomas, *NovT* 4 (1960) 298-99; and somewhat more cautiously, H.-W. Bartsch, 'Das Thomas-Evangelium und die synoptische Evangelien,' *NTS* 16 (1965) 449-54; and S. M. Iglesias, 'El evangelio de Tomás y algunos aspectos de la cuestión sinóptica,' *EstEcl* 24 (1960) 883-94. This approach was developed in later books on New Testament parables, esp. J. Jeremias, *The Parables of Jesus* (London: SCM, 1972); N. Perrin, *Rediscovering the Teaching of Jesus* (London: SCM, 1967); J. D. Crossan, *In Parables: The Challenge of the Historical Jesus* (New York: Harper & Row, 1973). But already at this early date there were dissenting views. Cf. esp. G. Garrité and L. Cerfaux, 'Les paraboles du royaume dans l'évangile de Thomas,' *Le Museon* 70 (1957) 307-27; H. K. McArthur, 'The Dependence of the Gospel of Thomas on the Synoptics,' *ExpT* 71 (1959-60) 286-87; A. L. Nations, 'A Critical Study of the Gospel according to Thomas,' (Ph.D. Diss.: Vanderbilt, 1960); and E. Haenchen, *Die Botschaft des Thomas-Evangeliums* (Berlin: Töpelmann, 1961).

/7/ Esp. G. Quispel, 'The Gospel of Thomas and the New Testament,' *VC* 11 (1957) 189-207; idem, 'Some Remarks on the Gospel of Thomas,' *NTS* 5 (1958-59) 276-90; idem, 'L'évangile selon Thomas et la Diatessaron,' *VC* 13 (1959) 87-117; idem, 'The "Gospel of Thomas" and the "Gospel of the Hebrews",' *NTS* 12 (1965-66) 371-82.

/8/ Quispel's most famous example compares the canonical 'by the road' (παρὰ τὴν ὁδόν) in the parable of the sower with the reading 'on the road' attested to in several of the above sources along with Thomas, as the place where the sower sowed the first portion of his seed. Cf. Mark 4:4=Matt. 13:4=Luke 8:5 with Thos. 9.

/9/ In the example from the parable of the sower, 'on' and 'by' would both reflect an original על.

/10/ E.g. Luke 11:40 is the converse of Thos. 89; Quispel, 'Thomas and the NT,' 199, suggests that both drew independently from an original saying of Jesus containing both members.

/11/ Cf. e.g. Thos. 2 with Clement, *Strom.* II 9.45,5 and V 14.96,3.

/12/ Cf. e.g. Thos. 12 with the role of James in Acts 15. Quispel's current views, now more carefully nuanced, appear in 'The *Gospel of Thomas* Revisited,' in *Colloque International sur*

les textes de Nag Hammadi (ed. B. Barc; Québec: Les Presses de
l'Université Laval, 1981) 218-66. Quispel now assigns each of
the logia to one of four sources--an Encratite author, the
Gospel of the Nazorenes (or some other Jewish-Christian gospel),
the Gospel of the Egyptians (or something similar), and a
Hermetic anthology. I am grateful to Prof. E. Yamauchi for
providing me with a synopsis of this article.
/13/ Montefiore, in *Thomas*, 78; cf. Perrin, *Rediscovering*, 36-
37.
/14/ W. Schrage, *Das Verhältnis des Thomas-Evangeliums zur
synoptischen Tradition und zu den koptischen Evangelien-
Übersetzungen* (Berlin: Töpelmann, 1964) 18. E. P. Sanders, *The
Tendencies of the Synoptic Tradition* (London: CUP, 1969) 42-43,
concludes that Schrage's study 'now probably sets the pattern
for future work in this area.'
/15/ See e.g. J. B. Sheppard, 'A Study of the Parables Common to
the Synoptic Gospels and the Coptic Gospel of Thomas' (Ph.D.
Diss.: Emory, 1965); Summers, *Sayings*; Y. O. Kim, 'The Gospel of
Thomas and the Historical Jesus,' *NEAJT* 2 (1969) 17-30; J.
Finegan, *Hidden Records of the Life of Jesus* (Philadelphia:
Pilgrim, 1969); B. Dehandschutter, 'Les paraboles de l'évangile
selon Thomas,' *ETL* 47 (1971) 199-219; idem, 'L'Évangile selon
Thomas: témoin d'une tradition prélucanienne?' in *L'Évangile de
Luc* (ed. F. Neirynck; Gembloux: Duculot, 1973) 287-97; W. R.
Schoedel, 'Parables in the Gospel of Thomas,' *CTM* 43 (1972)
548-60; Klyne R. Snodgrass, 'The Parable of the Wicked
Husbandmen: Is the Gospel of Thomas Version the Original?' *NTS*
21 (1974-75) 142-44; P. B. Payne, 'The Authenticity of the
Parable of the Sower and Its Interpretation,' in *Gospel
Perspectives*, vol. 1 (ed. R. T. France and D. Wenham; Sheffield:
JSOT, 1980) 187-93 (an appendix); and above all, A. Lindemann,
'Zur Gleichnisinterpretation im Thomas-Evangelium,' *ZNW* 71
(1980) 214-43. J.-É. Ménard's major commentary, *L'Évangile
selon Thomas* (Leiden: Brill, 1975) takes no strong stand on the
issue overall but recognizes most of Thomas's paralleled
parables as secondary.
/16/ J.-D. Kaestli, 'L'Évangile de Thomas,' *ETR* 54 (1979) 384.
Cf. the similar verdict of B. Dehandschutter, 'The Gospel of
Thomas and the Synoptics: The Status Quaestionis,' *TU* 126 (1982)
160.
/17/ H. Köster remains the most prolific proponent of Thomas's
independence, but at least he argues his case. See esp.
'ΓΝΩΜΑΙ ΔΙΑΦΟΡΟΙ ,' and 'One Jesus and Four Primitive Gospels,'
in *Trajectories through Early Christianity* (with J. M. Robinson;
Philadelphia: Fortress, 1971) 114-57, 158-204; 'Gnostic Writings

as Witnesses for the Development of the Sayings Tradition,' in
The Rediscovery of Gnosticism, vol. 1 (ed. B. Layton; Leiden:
Brill, 1980) 238-56. Less balanced treatments include John
Horman, 'The Source of the Version of the Parable of the Sower
in the Gospel of Thomas,' *NovT* 21 (1979) 326-43; W. L. Petersen,
'The Parable of the Lost Sheep in the Gospel of Thomas and the
Synoptics,' *NovT* 23 (1981) 128-47; and esp. P. de Suarez,
L'Evangile selon Thomas (Marsanne: Metanoia, 1975).

/18/ R. van den Broek, *VC* 37 (1983) 49.

/19/ (New York: Seabury, 1983).

/20/ Ibid., 117-47.

/21/ Ibid., 56, 68, 82. Davies admits there is no precedent for
such undifferentiation of terms: 'it is a new move, a creative
shift of the tradition' (p. 45).

/22/ On the 'solitaries,' see p. 60; on the 'All,' p. 66; on
the negative view of the flesh, p. 73; on additional scribal
'fatigue,' pp. 153-54.

/23/ Ibid., 48, 81, 146. The absence of titles for Jesus,
however, is more plausibly explained by the genre of Thomas.
Even in the NT, Jesus seldom uses titles for himself in his
sayings, save for the 'Son of man' which is scarcely used
anywhere outside the canon.

/24/ Ibid., 5.

/25/ The most likely provenance for Thomas is Syria (possibly
Edessa), and while some pre-Synoptic tradition may have been
preserved there, analogies with the textual history of canonical
Syriac versions suggest that most distinctives will prove
secondary. See esp. B. Lincoln, 'Thomas-Gospel and Thomas-
Community: A New Approach to a Familiar Text,' *NovT* 19 (1977)
65-76; H. J. W. Drijvers, 'Facts and Problems in Early Syriac-
Speaking Christianity,' *Second Century* 2 (1982) 157-75; J. D.
Turner, 'A New Link in the Syrian Judas Thomas Tradition,' in
Essays on the Nag Hammadi Texts (ed. M. Krause; Leiden: Brill,
1972) 109-19; A. F. J. Klijn, 'Christianity in Edessa and the
Gospel of Thomas,' *NovT* 14 (1972) 70-77. On the Gnostic flavor
of Thomas's theology more generally, see esp. B. Gärtner, *The
Theology of the Gospel according to Thomas* (New York: Harper &
Bros., 1961); Haenchen, *Botschaft*; R. McL. Wilson, *Studies in
the Gospel of Thomas* (London: Mowbray, 1960); and now in more
popular form, Elaine Pagels, *The Gnostic Gospels* (New York:
Random House, 1979).

/26/ E.g. Bartsch, 'Thomas-Evangelium,' 250, turns Quispel's
argument from the parable of the sower on its head, maintaining
that Thomas's 'on the road' reflects an attempt to erase the
apparent Synoptic contradiction in which seed sown 'by the road'

becomes trampled by those walking 'on the road'!

/27/ A. Guillaumont, 'Les sémitismes dans l'Évangile selon Thomas,' in *Studies in Gnosticism and Hellenistic Religions* (ed. R. van den Broek and M. J. Vermaseren; Leiden: Brill, 1981) 190-204.

/28/ Grant and Freedman, *Sayings*, 3.

/29/ See esp. H. K. McArthur, 'The Gospel according to Thomas,' in *New Testament Sidelights* (Hartford: Seminary Foundation, 1960) 68-69.

/30/ For possible Gnostic motivation for this phenomenon, see Schrage, *Verhältnis*, 6-7.

/31/ Kim, 'Thomas,' 23. D. H. Tripp, 'The Aim of the Gospel of Thomas,' *ExpT* 92 (1980) 41-44, explains the character and structure of Thomas's sayings by appealing to a liturgical origin for the document. Cf. the approach of Bruce Chilton elsewhere in this volume.

/32/ See my 'New Horizons in Parable Research,' *Trinity Journal* n.s. 3 (1981) 3-17.

/33/ Wilson, *Studies*, 73.

/34/ On this passage, see esp. Grant and Freedman, *Sayings*, 106.

/35/ Wilson, *Studies*, 115-16. Cf. idem, *Gnosis and the New Testament* (Philadelphia: Fortress, 1968) 113-14.

/36/ These terms are used strictly descriptively to refer to certain religious groups and their distinctive ideas which were eventually rejected by the main Christian councils. They are not intended pejoratively and do not presuppose any particular view on the controversy concerning the origins of orthodoxy and heresy in early Christianity.

/37/ Cf. Stewart C. Goetz's and my 'The Burden of Proof,' *JSNT* 11 (1981) 39-63.

/38/ Lindemann, 'Gleichnisinterpretation,' 213.

/39/ See e.g. Summers, *Sayings*, 74; Kaestli, 'Thomas,' 387; Higgins, 'Sayings,' 304.

/40/ G. C. Stead, 'Some Reflections on the Gospel of Thomas,' *TU* 88 (1964) 392-93.

/41/ Markan priority is hereby presupposed; despite its various challenges, this hypothesis still seems to pose the fewest problems. Cf. esp. K. Uchida, 'The Study of the Synoptic Problem in the Twentieth Century: A Critical Assessment' (Ph.D. Diss.: Aberdeen, 1981).

/42/ For a chart displaying the relevant data, see my 'The Tradition History of the Parables Peculiar to Luke's Central Section' (Ph.D. Diss.: Aberdeen, 1982) 25-27.

/43/ Cf. H. Schürmann, 'Das Thomasevangelium und das lukanische Sondergut,' *BZ* 7 (1963) 236-60.

/44/ R. Bultmann, 'The New Approach to the Synoptic Problem,' in
Existence and Faith (ed. S. M. Ogden; London: Collins, 1964) 47:
'Whenever narratives pass from mouth to mouth the central point
of the narrative and general structure are well-preserved; but
in the incidental details changes take place, for imagination
paints such details with increasing distinctness.' Cf. the
criticisms of this approach by L. R. Keylock, 'Bultmann's Law
of Increasing Distinctness,' in *Current Issues in Biblical and
Patristic Interpretation* (ed. G. F. Hawthorne; Grand Rapids:
Eerdmans, 1975) 193-210; and the voluminous data amassed against
this 'law' by Sanders, *Tendencies*.
/45/ See V. Taylor, *The Formation of the Gospel Tradition*
(London: Macmillan, 1933) appendix B, 202-9; W. S. Taylor,
'Memory and the Gospel Tradition,' *TToday* 15 (1958): 470-87;
F. C. Bartlett, *Remembering* (Cambridge: CUP, 1932); T. W. Manson,
'The Life of Jesus: Some Tendencies in Present-Day Research,' in
The Background of the New Testament and Its Eschatology (ed.
W. D. Davies and D. Daube; Cambridge: CUP, 1950) 213; J. Vansina,
Oral Tradition: A Study in Historical Methodology (London:
Routledge & Kegan Paul, 1965) 26; G. Stanton, *Jesus of Nazareth
in New Testament Preaching* (London: CUP, 1974) 178; M. D. Hooker,
'On Using the Wrong Tool,' *Theology* 75 (1972) 572.
/46/ G. Garrite and L. Cerfaux, 'paraboles,' 317.
/47/ See Bruce Chilton's article elsewhere in this volume.
/48/ Even Montefiore, *Thomas*, 51, recognizes the secondary
nature of Thomas's parable here, which he terms 'a striking
instance of compression to the point of absurdity.'
/49/ Cf. Schrage, *Verhältnis*, 124.
/50/ Schoedel, 'Parables,' 551.
/51/ The question of Thomas's knowledge of Matthew's
interpretation of the parable (attributed to Jesus) is a
separate issue, and the problem of the authenticity of that
interpretation is not solved by an appeal to Thomas's shorter
form, since he and other Gnostic writers frequently omit any
explanation of enigmatic passages.
/52/ No conclusion about the original context of these verses in
Luke is justified from their separation in Thomas. For a
thorough tradition-critical analysis of Luke 12:13-15 and its
'offspring,' see T. Baarda, 'Luke 12, 13-14, Text and
Transmission from Marcion to Augustine,' in *Christianity,
Judaism and Other Greco-Roman Cults* (ed. J. Neusner; Leiden:
Brill, 1975) 107-62.
/53/ Lindemann, 'Gleichnisinterpretation,' 228.
/54/ Cf. also Thos. 110 and Authoritative Teaching 27.12-21 and
32.20-23.

/55/ J. N. Birdsall, 'Luke XII, 16ff. and the Gospel of Thomas,'
JTS 13 (1962) 332-36.
/56/ A few scholars have argued that Luke reflects a simpler
pre-Markan form of the parable, but all of the differences
between Luke and Mark are readily explicable via the standard
two document hypothesis. Cf. my 'Tradition History,' 273-78.
/57/ See esp. Iglesias, 'Tomás,' 887.
/58/ See esp. Payne, 'Authenticity,' 163-207.
/59/ Thus Horman, 'Sower,' argues that Thomas's version is the
earliest of the four.
/60/ Grant and Freedman, *Sayings*, 128, suggest that the filling
of the sower's hand symbolizes the fullness or completion of the
sowing of souls or spirits.
/61/ W. H. C. Frend, 'The Gospel of Thomas: Is Rehabilitation
Possible?' *JTS* 18 (1967) 13-26. Cf. also the fragmentary
parallel in Papyrus Egerton 2.67-69.
/62/ See nn. 8, 9, 26.
/63/ Hippolytus, *Philosophumena* V.8,41; cf. the discussion in
Ménard, *Thomas*, 92-93.
/64/ Cf. the similar imagery in Apoc. Jas. 8.16-27.
/65/ C. W. Hedrick, 'Kingdom Sayings and Parables of Jesus in
The Apocryphon of James: Tradition and Redaction,' *NTS* 29 (1983)
9-13.
/66/ Yet another possibility is that this variant arose from a
Coptic copyist's error; see Schrage, *Verhältnis*, 47.
/67/ Ibid., 44.   /68/ Ménard, *Thomas*, 109.
/69/ 'Kingdom of heaven' appears elsewhere in Thomas only in
sayings 54 and 114.
/70/ Cf. Grant and Freedman, *Sayings*, 140.
/71/ Lindemann, 'Gleichnisinterpretation,' 225.
/72/ Cf. Ménard, *Thomas*, 110: 'L'opposition est entre le
caractère présent caché du gnostique et l'immense gloire ou
l'immense pouvoir dont il jouit.'
/73/ Schrage, *Verhältnis*, 65.
/74/ Very abbreviated references to the mustard seed also appear
in Dialogue of the Saviour 144.1-8 and to the sower in
Interpretation of Knowledge 5.16-21.
/75/ On the question of the relationship between these texts,
see my 'When Is A Parallel Really A Parallel? A Test Case--The
Lucan Parables,' *WTJ* 46 (1984): forthcoming.
/76/ F. W. Beare, 'The Gospel according to Thomas: A Gnostic
Manual,' *CJT* 6 (1960) 108. Cf. Jeremias, *Parables*, 176; Perrin,
Rediscovering, 113; Crossan, *Parables*, 72-73.
/77/ Cf. Schrage, *Verhältnis*, 136; Haenchen, *Botschaft*, 56;
Lindemann, 'Gleichnisinterpretation,' 230-31; K. E. Bailey,

Through Peasant Eyes: More Lucan Parables (Grand Rapids:
Eerdmans, 1980) 95-99.
/78/ Not all Gnostics were ascetics, but the milieu which
produced Thomas clearly leaned strongly in this direction.   No
certainty as to the specific sect involved exists, but the
Naassenes represent a strong candidate.   See esp. W. R. Schoedel,
'Naassene Themes in the Coptic Gospel of Thomas,' *VC* 14 (1960)
225-34.
/79/ Ménard, *Thomas*, 165-66.
/80/ Cf. Gärtner, *Theology*, 47; Schrage, *Verhältnis*, 135.
/81/ For Lucan redaction of this parable, see my 'Tradition
History,' 278-83.
/82/ For the view that the lacuna here should be restored so as
to make the man a 'usurer,' see B. Dehandschutter, 'La parabole
des vignerons homicides (Mc., XII, 1-12) et l'évangile selon
Thomas,' in *L'Évangile selon Marc* (ed. M. Saabe; Leuven: LUP,
1974) 218.
/83/ Cf. Schoedel, 'Parables,' 560.   Ménard, *Thomas*, 166, on the
other hand, attributes this detail to the influence of the
'good man' in Thos. 8.
/84/ Schoedel, 'Parables,' 559.
/85/ R. Bultmann, *The History of the Synoptic Tradition* (Oxford:
Blackwell, 1963) 188.   Snodgrass, 'Husbandmen,' moreover, notes
that Mark 12:4 and Luke 20:12 were already omitted from sy[S] and
sy[C], respectively, so that with Syrian provenance likely for
Thomas, a pre-Thomas origin of this development seems certain.
/86/ The words enclosed in angular brackets are Lambdin's
emendation of the text which actually reads 'he. . .them,' but
which many view as a scribal error.   On the other hand, this
construction could reflect knowledge of the Synoptic versions
in which more than one servant was sent before the master's
reaction is narrated.
/87/ Cf. esp. Gospel of Truth 31.1-4:   'For the material ones
were strangers and did not see his likeness and had not known
him' (i.e. the Son).
/88/ Dehandschutter, 'homicides' 212-16, presents in full the
evidence that 'une rédaction propre à l'ET dérivant du texte
de Luc et influencée par la formulation des paraboles du
contexte, nous semble plus plausible.'
/89/ Again direct literary dependence may not be involved.
Cf. my 'Parallel,' forthcoming.
/90/ *Libros quinque adversos haereses* I.7,1 and I.8,4.   For
additional references, see Schrage, *Verhältnis*, 195.
/91/ Cf. further references to the Gnostics' shepherd
(undoubtedly also drawing on Johannine imagery) in Authoritative

Teaching 32.33-33.3; Concept of Our Great Power 40.14; and
Teaching of Silvanus 106.21-30.
/92/ Petersen, 'Parable,' esp. *pace* F. Schnider, 'Das Gleichnis
vom verlorenen Schaf und seine Redaktoren,' *Kairos* 19 (1977)
150-53.
/93/ Which are probably not to be taken ironically! See my
'Tradition History,' 203-4.
/94/ *Pace* Wilson, *Studies*, 95; Grant and Freedman, *Sayings*, 192.
/95/ Schrage, *Verhältnis*, 41, cautions against setting these
interpretations against one another in an either/or fashion, a
caution which applies to several of the parables above as well.
/96/ Schoedel, 'Parables,' 557.
/97/ See above, n. 57
/98/ Köster, 'ΓΝΟΜΑΙ ,' 132; *pace* Davies, *Thomas*,
/99/ Ménard, *Thomas*, 89.
/100/ Schrage, *Verhältnis*, 42.
/101/ Thus, again, 'il n'y a que peu de différence entre ces
deux possibilités: la gnose est la "gnose de soi-même" en
premier lieu.' B. Dehandschutter, 'La parabole de la perle (Mt
13, 45-46) et l'évangile selon Thomas,' *ETL* 55 (1979) 260.
/102/ For Gnostic use of the pearl metaphor outside the Nag
Hammadi literature, see G. Quispel, *Makarius, das
Thomasevangelium und das Lied von der Perle* (Leiden: Brill, 1967.
/103/ On the preponderance of this theme in Thomas, see
Dehandschutter, 'perle,' 253-54.
/104/ Lindemann, 'Gleichnisinterpretation,' 220.
/105/ See the discussion of the parable of the sower.
/106/ Lindemann, 'Gleichnisinterpretation,' 226; cf. also
Gärtner, *Thomas*, 230.
/107/ Cf. Jeremias, *Parables*, 100, 147.
/108/ Ménard, *Thomas*, 197.
/109/ Haenchen, *Botschaft*, 47. For less probable views, see
Grant and Freedman, *Sayings*, 194; Gärtner, *Theology*, 238.
/110/ Lindemann, 'Gleichnisinterpretation,' 234.
/111/ See Midr. Cant. 4:12, and cf. G. Garitte & L. Cerfaux,
'paraboles,' 315. Even Davies, *Thomas*, 10, agrees that here
Thomas is secondary.
/112/ See esp. Dehandschutter, 'paraboles,' 215-18.
/113/ J. B. Bauer, 'Echte Jesusworte?' in *Evangelien aus dem
Nilsland* (ed. W. C. van Unnik; Frankfurt a. M.: Heinrich
Scheffler, 1960) 143.
/114/ J. A. Baird, *Audience Criticism and the Historical Jesus*
(Philadelphia: Westminster, 1969) 167.
/115/ On criteria for locating these, see W. L. Lane, 'A
Critique of Purportedly Authentic Agrapha,' *JETS* 18 (1975) 29-35.

/116/ R. McL. Wilson, 'Nag Hammadi and the New Testament,' *NTS*
28 (1982) 297.
/117/ See esp. n. 15 above.

APOCRYPHAL GOSPELS: THE 'UNKNOWN GOSPEL' (PAP. EGERTON 2) AND
THE *GOSPEL OF PETER*

David F. Wright,
Department of Ecclesiastical History,
New College,
Edinburgh EH1 2LU.

The chief historical value of the apocryphal gospels has
traditionally been held to lie in the light they throw on
popular Christian piety in the second and subsequent centuries,
especially in strongly ascetic fringe circles.   Their
significance for the ministry of Jesus has rarely rated more
than a cursory dismissal.   A recent verdict starts with a
qualification but reflects a long standing consensus:

> By and large, the apocryphal gospels are secondary
> composition, manifestly dependent upon the four traditional
> Gospels, but otherwise abounding in legendary details and
> anachronisms...   The doctrinal and apologetic interests of
> the apocryphal gospels are painfully apparent./1/

The Coptic *Gospel of Thomas* now constitutes a conspicuous
exception to such an evaluation.   That it preserves, at least in
part, traditions of the teaching of Jesus independent of and
perhaps more primitive than the Synoptic Gospels is probably now
the judgment of a clear majority of scholars.   But of no other
apocryphal gospel could it be claimed that its historical
importance for the Jesus-tradition is even a matter of widespread
debate.

In an article published in 1980 Helmut Koester challenged
the sharp dichotomy usually drawn between apocryphal and
canonical gospels,/2/ arguing that 'five of these apocryphal
gospels ... are perhaps at least as old and as valuable as the
canonical gospels as sources for the earliest developments of
the traditions about Jesus.   They are significant witnesses for
the formation of the gospel literature in its formative stages'.
They belong to a stage in its development 'comparable to the

sources which were used by the gospels of the NT'./3/ Koester's
five candidates are the *Gospel of Thomas*, the *Gospel of Peter*,
the fragments of Papyrus Egerton 2 known from its *editio
princeps* as the 'Unknown Gospel', and the *Apocryphon of James*
and the *Dialogue of the Saviour* from the Nag-Hammadi collection.
This study will concentrate upon the Egerton papyrus gospel
(hereafter *UG*) and the *Gospel of Peter* (*EvP*)./4/

       First, however, comments are in order on the initial pages
of Koester's study. Here he sets out to show that the external
evidence of surviving manuscripts to the end of the third
century and of quotations in Christian writers of the first two
centuries reveals no preponderance of canonical over apocryphal
gospels and warrants no distinction between the two. Since
this introductory section is obviously intended to predispose
the reader to a favourable reception of the theses he
subsequently defends, an assessment of it is appropriate at the
beginning of a critical examination of some of these theses.

Gospels: External Evidence

       To Koester's list of extant gospel MSS from the second and
third centuries three or four more should probably be added,/5/
but such minor adjustments would not alter the general picture.
The catalogue comprises seventeen MSS containing one or more
canonical gospels (twenty-one in all), and six manuscripts each
containing one apocryphal gospel (three being copies of the
Gospel of Thomas). Thus all four canonical and four apocryphal
gospels are attested, although one of the latter, the so-called
Fayoum Gospel (P. Vindob. G. 2325), is hardly more than an
abridged version of Mark 14:27ff./6/ In total numbers copies of
the former outweigh the latter by between three and four to one,
which constitutes a clear preponderance, despite Koester's
claim to the contrary. Yet whether much significance should be
attached to such statistics is doubtful. The only copy of Mark
to survive is in the four-gospel P 45. The Fourth Gospel
accounts for ten of the twenty-one canonical copies. Since all
of these MSS come from Egypt where Christianity is known to
have had a particularly strong heterodox character for much of
the second century, their evidence can scarcely be held to be
representative.

       It is often difficult to determine with certainty whether
an early Christian writer has used one or more of the canonical
gospels. Koester explains that he has been deliberately

conservative in cataloguing usage, along the minimising lines
argued in his influential study *Synoptische Überlieferung bei
den Apostolischen Vätern*./7/ However, before questioning some
of the conclusions incorporated into his table, more basic
deficiencies need to be pointed out.

(i)   At the outset Koester seems to restrict his survey to
'use' of gospels, but soon broadens it into 'knowledge' of
gospels. The difference could be important. In the end it is
not clear whether 'use' or 'knowledge' is the criterion for
inclusion. For example, Irenaeus is listed for the four
canonical gospels, but also for the *Gospel of the Ebionites*.
But in no sense did Irenaeus 'use' or accept the latter, and
his 'knowledge' of it was at best second-hand./8/ The *Secret
Gospel of Mark* is listed twice, under the Carpocratians and
under Clement of Alexandria. If one and the same entity is
intended, it must be the Carpocratians' *Secret Gospel* which
Clement condemned as a 'tissue of falsehoods'. If, however,
the mention under Clement denotes the mystical version of
canonical Mark which he alleged the Carpocratians had
adulterated, we are dealing with a gospel whose existence is
attested solely by the new letter of Clement, on the basis of
which it is not at all certain that we should conceive of an
'alternative Mark' differentiated from its canonical original,
rather than the latter decked out with allegorizing
interpretations./9/ Or again, where for Marcion Koester lists
only Luke, with Matthew as a possibility, should we conclude
that he did not *know* of, say, John's Gospel, or merely that he
did not *use* any others?/10/ Likewise, under Papias only Mark
is listed along with 'Free sayings of Jesus' and '*Sayings of
Matthew* (= Q?)'./11/ Papias' extant fragments do not, of course,
mention Luke or John, but many scholars hold that Papias'
comments on Mark imply a comparison with, and therefore a
'knowledge' of, John.

(ii)   The table shows some surprising omissions. Melito is
referred to in the text as attesting the knowledge of John in
Asia Minor but is not tabulated. The same holds for 'the
Montanists'. The *Didache* is missing altogether. Koester had
earlier accepted that *Did.* 1:3ff. include logia which derive
from Matthew and Luke but were drawn by the *Didache*'s compiler
from some intermediate collection of logia./12/ Silence also
shrouds the *Epistle of Barnabas*, whose possible 'knowledge'
of at least Matthew is more likely than his direct literary
dependence on it./13/ Other second-century writers should
be added, such as Polycrates of Ephesus (John), the

anti-Montanist Apollonius (Matthew), and the letter of the
Gallic churches on the persecution at Lyons (Luke and John).

(iii) Despite the uncertainties in this area of study,
Koester's judgments should be challenged at some points. It is
particularly bold to assert that evidence is lacking for the
knowledge of John in Asia Minor until late in the second
century./14/ Irenaeus' assertion that John wrote his Gospel at
Ephesus is scarcely conceivable without a knowledge of the
Gospel in Asia going back to at least mid-century. Other
traditions point to the early currency of the Gospel in this
region, and if Ignatius knew it, as is most likely, *pace*
Koester,/13/ this would also be relevant. *2 Clement* is credited
by Koester with use of solely 'Free sayings of Jesus' and 'Non-
canonical materials', but a footnote records that its source for
the sayings of Jesus 'shows influence from the canonical Gospels
of Matthew and Luke', thus making it an indirect witness to
these Gospels. Even this is most probably too cautious a
judgment./16/

    The impression of second-century use or knowledge of
gospels conveyed by Koester's table should, therefore, not be
taken too seriously. It requires supplementation and probably
correction at several points, and is altogether too blunt an
instrument to measure gospel use. In particular, some entries
conceal that very drawing of explicit distinctions by early
Christian writers between canonical and apocryphal gospels
which Koester is concerned to deny.

The 'Unknown Gospel' (*UG*)

    For his evaluation of the significance of these three
papyrus fragments first published in 1935, Koester relies on a
Marburg dissertation by a Japanese scholar, Goro Mayeda,
published in 1946./17/ He endorses Mayeda's conclusion that
UG was compiled independently of the canonical gospels, and goes
beyond this to argue that 'the author of the Fourth Gospel seems
to have utilised pieces from the much more tightly composed
Unknown Gospel in order to construct his elaborate discourses'.
/18/ Mayeda's judgment is that *UG* and the Fourth Gospel depend
on a common tradition or source (p. 75). It is worth noting
that Koester's view accords closely with the judgment of the
first editors of *UG* in 1935, a judgment one of them had
abandoned two years later./19/

Other scholars have not been so convinced by Mayeda.
Jeremias's verdict is that the Egerton compiler 'knew all and
every one of the canonical Gospels' but was reproducing their
content from memory rather than text./20/ Philipp Vielhauer's
judgment is fairly similar. The fragments display some
relation to all four canonical works, although there is no
question of direct literary use of any of them. Rather *UG*
constitutes 'ein deutlicher Beleg für die gegenseitige
Beeinflussung von mündlicher und schriftlicher Tradition',
since the composition of our four gospels did not bring the
oral Jesus-tradition to a halt./21/ None of these scholars
mentions the fullest discussion of the fragments since Mayeda -
two long articles published in 1956 by the Italian Ugo Gallizia
of Turin./22/ His study advances some pertinent criticisms of
Mayeda's arguments.

The special fascination of *UG* arises from the interweaving
of Johannine and Synoptic elements. If the first two pericope
may be characterized as Johannine and the next two as Synoptic,
'the Johannine material is shot through with Synoptic phrases
and the Synoptic with Johannine usage' - although, as we shall
see, this judgment by Jeremias somewhat overstates the case./23/
But in addition, the Synoptic passages contain parallels with
at least two of the Synoptic gospels. Taken together, these
factors seem to exclude the possibility that we are dealing with
a literary pastiche compiled directly from the canonical
gospels.

The text of the first pericope is as follows, in the
reconstruction accepted by Mayeda:

```
                        ]ι. [ὁ δὲ]
              ['Ι(ησοῦς) εἶπεν] τοῖς νομικο[ῖς· κολά-]
              [ζετε πά]ντα τὸν παραπράσσ[οντα]
              [καὶ ἄνο]μον καὶ μὴ ἐμέ· [ὅτι] ἀ[ν]ε[ξ-
      5       [έταστον] ὃ ποιεῖ, πῶς ποιε[ῖ·] Πρὸς
              [δὲ τοὺς] ἄ[ρ]χοντας τοῦ λαοῦ [στ]ρα-
              [φεὶς εἶ]πεν τὸν λόγον τοῦτο[ν·] ἐραυ-
              [νᾶτε τ]ὰς γραφάς· ἐν αἶς ὑμεῖς δο-
              [κεῖτε] ζωὴν ἔχειν· ἐκεῖναί εἰ[σ]ιν
      10      [αἱ μαρτ]υροῦσαι περὶ ἐμοῦ · μὴ δ[ο-]
              [κεῖτε ὅ]τι ἐγὼ ἦλθον κατηγο[ρ]ῆσαι
              [ὑμῶν] πρὸς τὸν π(ατέ)ρα μου· ἔστιν
              [ὁ κατη]γορῶν ὑμῶν Μω(ϋσῆς) εἰς ὃν
              [ὑμεῖς] ἠλπίκατε· α[ὐ]τῶν δὲ λε-
      15      [γόντω]ν· ε[ἶ] οἴδαμεν ὅτι Μω(ϋσεῖ) ἐλά-
```

[λησεν] ὁ θ(εὁ)ς[˙] σὲ δὲ οὐκ οἴδαμεν
[πόθεν εἷ]˙ ἀποκριθεὶς ὁ Ἰη(σοῦς) εἷ-
[πεν αὐτο]ῖς˙ νῦν κατηγορεῖται
[ὑμῶν ἡ ἀ]πιστεί[α
20   ? ἄ]λλο. [

No agreement has been reached about the original form of lines
1-5. Jeremias briefly discussed whether κολάζετε .... μὴ ἐμέ
and the utterance in lines 18-19 should be regarded as genuine
agrapha, but concluded that they are 'secondary transitional
links'./24/ The interest centres on lines 5-18. Koester is
impressed by the careful construction of the unit, by the
continuity between (the parallels to) John 5:39 and 5:45, which
in John's Gospel have been separated by an interposed discourse
on another theme, and by the obvious connection with lines
15-17, which John has used elsewhere to supplement a statement
he has himself composed (John 9:28). Not only is the
composition here 'more original', but vocabulary and style are
less typically Johannine and more typically Synoptic. Some
instances of the evidence gathered by Mayeda are noted by
Koester.

     Before looking at this case in any detail, a general
argument needs to be laid out of special relevance to this
pericope but of some general relevance also. Given that the
three substantive sentences in lines 5-18 agree 'almost
verbatim' (Koester's words)/26/ with the verses in John, and
given other, almost incontrovertible circumstances, such as the
priority of John to these papyrus fragments, its currency in
Egypt at the time they were written (proved by P 52, the famous
Rylands fragment of John, and perhaps confirmed by the new
second-century fragment referred to in n. 5), and the general
'knownness' of John compared with the obscurity of the 'Unknown
Gospel' (which contrasts markedly with the situation of the
*Gospel of Thomas), a powerful initial presumption exists that
the latter is dependent on the former.* While we must heed
Morton Smith's warning against the 'naive assumption that any
occurrence in early Christian literature of an expression found
in one of the canonical gospels is to be explained as a
borrowing from the gospel',/27/ gospel criticism runs the
opposite danger of reaching hazardous conclusions by
discounting, for inadequate reasons, normal historical
probabilities. It is not a standard historical procedure to
approach the question of the relation between *UG* and the Fourth
Gospel as though all of the possible explanations were of
equal standing. The question therefore becomes this: are the

considerations advanced by Mayeda and Koester strong enough to
override the undoubted *a priori* probability in this case?

Koester exaggerates the cohesion of the first *UG* pericope.
The separate address to 'lawyers' and 'rulers of the people' is
awkward, and without parallel in the canonical gospels./28/
Although John 5:45 and 9:29 are linked by their common
reference to Moses, the connection between 5:39 and 5:45 is by
no means so obvious. The witness of the Scriptures before men
is scarcely parallel to the role of Moses as the accuser before
God. The content of the two verses is so different that they
would not have been brought together unless *UG*'s compiler had
found them in the same context - e.g. in John 5. Even 5:45 and
9:29 have little in common apart from Moses. While 9:29 fits
in well in its context in 9:27-33 (his disciple(s) - disciples
of Moses - well known that God spoke to Moses but not where he
(Jesus) comes from - yet he opened my eyes - unheard of - if he
were not from God he could do nothing), its allusion to the
question of Jesus' origin occurs without preparation in *UG*.
Koester's strongest argument is the interruption of 5:39 and
5:45 by 5:41-44 (not 40-44). Nevertheless, in John's Gospel
5:39 relates well to what precedes it, and 5:45 to what
follows it, as Dodd points out./29/

That these lines contain aspects of vocabulary and style
that align them at some points more with the Synoptics than
with John is undeniable. In particular, 'lawyers' (νομικοί)
occurs only in the Synoptics (in fact almost always in Luke -
once in Matthew and never in Mark), and so too does 'unbelief'
(ἀπιστία), but too rarely (once in Matthew and twice in Mark)
for its occurrence here to be conclusively significant. Where
John 5:29 has 'eternal life' and *UG* only 'life', this is not a
preference for Synoptic over Johannine as has often been
claimed. Not only do the Synoptics have 'eternal life' more
often than 'life', John has 'life' almost as often as 'eternal
life' and in any case so much more frequently than the
Synoptics that we must regard 'life' alone as more
characteristic of John than of the Synoptics. Gallizia
(pp. 59-60) effectively criticises Mayeda's attempt (p. 22) to
interpret ζωή simply as 'Lebenskraft' without reference to the
specifically Christian content it has in John, and to dispute
also the specifically Johannine character of μαρτυρεῖν
(line 10).

Patently Synoptic rather than Johannine is the participle
ἀποκριθείς with εἶπεν rather than ἀπεκρίθη καὶ εἶπεν. But such

a variation is of little significance if the author of *UG* was
working from memory rather than directly from the gospel texts.
It is characteristic of most users of the gospels in every age
not to observe differences between them in such a common and
unimportant matter of style as this. The construction ἦλθον
+ infinitive, which is also Synoptic rather than Johannine,
falls into the same category./30/

Mayeda (pp. 19-21) makes much of the fact that *UG* 7ff. has
ἐραυνᾶτε as an imperative, which he regards as more primitive
than John's indicative. He fails to note that all the ancient
commentators except Cyril of Alexandria read John's ἐραυνᾶτε as
an imperative, as Gallizia points out (pp. 215-216). The
confusion in the early versions, which Mayeda does record, is
best explained as arising from different readings of John's
Greek. So *UG*'s imperative is no index of the priority of his
text over John's.

It is doubtful whether the accumulative weight of the
evidence discussed above, even when reinforced by other minor
points analysed by Mayeda, is sufficient to overthrow or even
seriously challenge the *a priori* presumption of *UG*'s dependence
on the canonical gospels. The fact that *UG*, in using
Johannine material, has inserted elements of Synoptic
vocabulary and style, even if only by memory, is not surprising
for the second century, when most Christian writers were not at
all interested in distinguishing the gospels from each other.
The diversity of the gospels was liable to be as much a source
of embarrassment as a matter for differentiated appreciation.
/31/ As Campenhausen notes, it was a distinctive practice of
early Christianity lasting at least until Clement of
Alexandria and abandoned perhaps first by Marcion, not to make
references specific to any one named gospel, even when
obviously citing from the written text of one in particular./32/

The second pericope (perhaps to be regarded as the
conclusion to the first) is more exclusively Johannine in
content, with parallels chiefly to 10:31, 7:30 and 10:39:

? ἔ]λκω[σιν] β[αστάσαν-]
[τες δὲ] λίθους ὁμοῦ λι[θάζω-]
σι[ν αὐ]τόν· καὶ ἐπέβαλον [τὰς]
25   χεῖ[ρας] αὐτῶν ἐπ' αὐτὸν οἱ [ἄρχον-]
τες [ἵ]να πιάσωσιν καὶ παρ[αδώ-]
σω[σι]ν τῷ ὄχλῳ· καὶ οὐκ ἠ[δύναντο]
αὐτὸν πιάσαι ὅτι οὔπω ἐ[ληλύθει]
αὐτοῦ ἡ ὥρα τῆς παραδό[σεως].
30   αὐτὸς δὲ ὁ κ(ύριο)ς ἐξελθὼν [ἐκ τῶν χει-]
ρῶν ἀπένευσεν ἀπ' [αὐτῶν·]

Koester notes that between John 10:31 and 10:39 is
interposed 'a typically Johannine discourse', and that the
vocabulary in *UG* 'shows several phrases paralleled in the
Synoptic gospels'. John has dispersed the parts of his source
'in order to give the impression of repeated attempts upon
Jesus' life'./33/ Koester passes over in silence both the
(secondary?) occurrence of ὁ κύριος (line 30) and more
significantly the incoherence of the pericope. The crowd were
attempting to stone Jesus, but the authorities sought to arrest
him...to hand him over to the crowd! Nor does Koester specify
any particular Synoptic phraseology. He simply refers to
Mayeda, pp. 27-31, who for this pericope makes no claim for
conspicuous Synoptic usage. Indeed, distinctive Johannine
features are to the fore:/34/ πιάζειν occurs solely in John,
and so too ἕλκω (if correctly reconstructed); βαστάζειν (again,
if correctly reconstructed) is used for stoning only in John;
ἀπονεύειν is not in the NT but ἐκνεύειν appears in John 5:13;
even ὁμοῦ is found only in John among the canonical gospels.
'They laid their hands on him' is a phrase with Synoptic
parallels, but in the context of this fragment it is perverse
of Mayeda (pp. 28-29) to refuse to see it as Johannine (cf.
7:30, 44). 'Tradition' is the meaning of παράδοσις everywhere
else in the NT (although the verb παραδίδωμι is frequent in all
the gospels and elsewhere in the NT in the sense of 'hand over,
betray'). Its addition for clarification to the pregnant
Johannine 'hour' is surely more likely than its omission by
John in taking over material from this source.

There is therefore no justification for Koester's
depiction of this pericope as 'language containing Johannine
elements but [revealing] a greater affinity to the Synoptic
tradition'. It is in fact the most markedly single-gospel
section of *UG*, and must correct the oft-repeated view that both
of *UG*'s Johannine passages are shot through with Synoptic
language and style. Little reason is left to doubt dependence
upon John's Gospel.

There follows immediately the story of a healing of a leper, in patently Synoptic dress:

> καὶ [ἰ]δοὺ λεπρὸς προσελθ[ὼν αὐτῷ]
> λέγει· διδάσκαλε ᾿Ιη(σοῦ) λε[προῖς συν-]
> οδεύων καὶ συνεσθίω[ν αὐτοῖς]
> 35 ἐν τῷ πανδοχείῳ ἐλ[έπρασα]
> καὶ αὐτὸς ἐγώ· ἐὰν [ο]ὖν [σὺ θέλῃς]
> καθαρίζομαι· ὁ δὴ κ(ύριο)ς [ἔφη αὐτῷ·]
> θέλ[ω] καθαρίσθητι· [καὶ εὐθέως]
> [ἀ]πέστη ἀπ' αὐτοῦ ἡ λέπ[ρα· ὁ δὲ κ(ύριο)ς]
> 40 [εἶ]πεν αὐτῷ]· πορε[υθεὶς ἐπίδει-]
> [ξον σεαυτὸ]ν τοῖ[ς ἱερεῦσι

The nearest parallel is the version in Mt 8:2-4 (par. Mk 1:40-44, Lk 5:12-14), but 'the leprosy left him' is close to Mark and Luke (Matthew 'his leprosy was cleansed'). Peculiar to *UG* is διδάσκαλε ᾿Ιησοῦ (Matthew and Luke κύριε), which also appears in line 45 (see below), and so may be regarded as an Egertonian distinctive. Double vocatives are very rare in the canonical gospels. Another (᾿Ιησοῦ ἐπιστάτα) occurs in Luke 17:13 in another account of healing from leprosy, which also has two other words in common with the pericope in *UG*: πορευθέντες ἐπιδείξατε (Matthew and Mark ὕπαγε, Luke ἀπελθών; all three δεῖξον). These complex affinities with the Synoptics are not of themselves conclusive indicators of any particular relationship between them and *UG*.

Perhaps of greater significance are *UG*'s differences from all three Synoptics: no parallel to the act of reverential supplication described in different terms by Matthew, Mark and Luke; καθαρίζομαι (Synoptics δύνασαί με καθαρίσαι); no parallel to the Synoptics' 'stretching out his hand he touched him'. Should the latter be regarded as one of the 'redactions or secondary expansions' in the Synoptic versions, whose absence from *UG* impresses Koester?/35/ Is it a 'more elaborate healing procedure'? It may be formally so without being secondary, for it cannot be thought inappropriate for Jesus to have touched lepers. Koester relegates to a footnote his notice of the incontrovertibly later addition of the reason for the leper's condition, but again he fails to remark on the occurrence of ὁ κύριος in the narrative./36/ The plural of 'priests' may, like the added explanation for the leprosy, reflect a non-Palestinian origin for the text, but since it is a further parallel with Luke 17:14, it is more likely a significant piece of evidence for *UG*'s dependence upon Luke. It must be

difficult, on the basis of this mixed crop of variations, to
argue strongly for *UG*'s independence of the Synoptics. Its
version is at once more folksy and more abrupt (cf. καθαρίζομαι).
Its silence about Jesus' touching the leper may be the omission
of an act distinctively eloquent of his care for such outcasts.

The fourth pericope in *UG* is the most complex in its
relations to the canonical gospels:

νόμενοι πρὸς αὐτὸν ἐξ[ετασ-]
τικῶς ἐπείραζον αὐτὸν λ[έγοντες·]
45 διδάσκαλε ᾽Ιη(σοῦ) οὕδαμεν ὅτι [ἀπὸ θ(εο)ῦ]
ἐλήλυθας· ἃ γὰρ ποιεῖς μα[ρτυρεῖ]
ὑπὲρ το[ὺ]ς προφ(ήτ)ας πάντας· [εἰπὲ οὖν]
ἡμεῖν· ἐξὸν τοῖς βα(σι)λεῦσ[ιν ἀποδοῦ-]
ναι τὰ ἀν[ή]κοντα τῇ ἀρχῇ; ἀπ[οδῶμεν αὐ-]
50 τοῖς ἢ μ[ή;] ὁ δὲ ᾽Ιη(σοῦς) εἰδὼς [τὴν δι-]
άνοιαν [αὐτ]ῶν ἐμβρειμ[ησάμενος]
εἶπεν α[ὐτοῖς]· τί με καλεῖτ[ε τῷ στό-]
ματι ὑμ[ῶν δι]δάσκαλον· μ[ὴ ἀκού-]
οντες ὃ [λ]έγω· καλῶς Ἠ[σ(αΐ)ας περὶ ὑ-]
55 μῶν ἐπ[ρο]φ(ήτευ)σεν εἰπών· ὁ [λαὸς οὗ-]
τος τοῖς [χείλ]εσιν αὐτ[ῶν τιμῶσίν]
με ἡ [δὲ καρδί]α αὐτῶ[ν πόρρω ἀπέ-]
χει ἀπ' ἐ[μοῦ· μ]άτη[ν με σέβονται]
ἐντάλ[ματά μου μὴ τηροῦντες]

Lines 45-46 are close to John 3:2 (cf. also 10:25), but the
rest to different parts of the Synoptics. Koester accepts that
the whole is a secondary composition, although he finds the
Synoptic accounts, reflecting 'the interest of the Christian
community in finding an accommodation to the Roman laws of
revenue', as themselves secondary compared with *UG*'s concern
with the understanding of Jesus' mission./37/ To this it
should be said with Mayeda that both the plural 'kings' and τὰ
ἀνήκοντα τῇ ἀρχῇ make *UG* 'viel allgemeiner und darum ethisch
verwendbarer' than the Synoptics./38/

The *UG* passage is again somewhat incoherent. The rebuke of
lines 52-59 is premature or out of place, for there has been no
word of Jesus to obey or disobey./39/ The parallel Koester
cites (Lk 12:13-14) is beside the point, for there Jesus'
response, if not a true answer, nevertheless relates explicitly
to the terms of the question ('divide' - 'divider'). Perhaps the
answer has been lost after line 59, in which case it would have
occurred rather awkwardly after a digression./40/

The vocabulary of this passage has some noteworthy
features: ἐξεταστικῶς is not found in the NT (once in Justin;
cf. ἀνεξέταστον, lines 4-5 above, if the correct reconstruction);
ἀνήκειν not in the gospels (three times in Paul); διάνοια only
in Luke 1:51, apart from citations of Deuteronomy 6:5 LXX;
τιμῶσιν agrees with LXX of Isaiah 29:13 (Mk 7:6, Mt 15:8 -
τιμᾷ). Perhaps most interesting is ἐμβρειμησάμενος, which
stimulates Mayeda to attempt to make consistent sense of the
varied uses of the verb in the canonical gospels./41/ Also to
be noted, however, is its occurrence in Mark 1:43 in the healing
of the leper to which *UG*'s third pericope discussed above is a
parallel. Is this another pointer to *UG*'s tendency to connect
verses by link-words,/42/ which would have an important function
in citation from memory? This question merits further
discussion below.

This fourth pericope, in Koester's judgment, is a
secondary framework for materials such as Luke 6:46 floating
freely in the sayings tradition. 'There is no reason to assume
that those materials were drawn from the canonical gospels.'/43/
Certainly not to 'assume', but also not to exclude this
possibility, or, as I would argue, this *a priori* probability.
The mere fact that we encounter the parallels to this pericope
dispersed in different places in the Synoptics of itself counts
for nothing. Nor can it be reasonably claimed that any of the
constituent sayings appears here in a more primitive form than
in the Synoptics. But it is possible to suggest that *UG*
assembled its materials by catchword connections. For example,
the introduction to the question διδάσκαλε, οἴδαμεν ὅτι,
(Mk 12:14 par.) is similar enough to John 3:2 (ῥαββί, οἴδαμεν
ὅτι .... διδάσκαλος) to explain how the latter came to be
prefaced to *UG*'s version of the tribute-money exchange. (Would
it be far-fetched to remark on the similarity between what
follows ὅτι - i.e., ἀληθής in Matthew and Mark, ἀπο θεοῦ
ἐλήλυθας in John? Note that ἀπο θεοῦ is reconstructed in *UG*
line 45.) As the pericope develops, διδάσκαλον recurs, στόματι
is picked up by χείλεσιν (some MSS of Is 29:13 LXX and Mt 15:8
have both στόματι and χείλεσιν), and perhaps ἐπροφήτευσεν
recalls προφήτας in line 47.

Such verbal connections are relevant to Koester's assertion
that 'it is hard to imagine that its author could have patched
his text together from half a dozen passages in John...and from
the three Synoptic Gospels'./44/ They can be discerned in other
pericope. In the first, for example, 'Moses' connects (the
parallels to) John 5:45 and 9:29, and κατηγορέω also functions as

a link. In the second, πιάζω and παραδίδωμι provide
connections. Perhaps catchwords even operate between pericope;
note, for instance, ἄρχοντες in the first two, and ἀνεξέταστον
and ἐξεταστικῶς in the first and the fourth. Jesus is
addressed as διδάσκαλε 'Ιησοῦ in the third and the fourth,
which also shows a special interest in Jesus as διδάσκαλος.
'Witness' is a concern of the first and fourth pericope, but
given its centrality in John this is not remarkable. Perhaps
the fourth is linked to the fifth (which is much more
fragmentary, and seems to contain a story of Jesus
miraculously foreshortening the time span from sowing to
harvest on the bank of the Jordan) by the motif of testing
questions. In the fifth, Jesus had apparently posed a ξένον
ἐπερώτημα which the miracle somehow clarified or resolved. If
UG's author worked by link-words, triggered partly by memory,
it might not be wholly fanciful to see significance in the
further use of χεῖλος 'bank', here in line 66 (cf. line 56
above), and in the occurrence of the phrase 'stretching out his
right hand' as an action in the miracle, recalling the phrase
in Mark 1:41 par. whose absence from UG's version of the
healing of a leper we noted above.

The remains of the third fragment of UG are much more
limited, but the recto seems to give ἔν ἐσμ[εν] (82), [λι]θους
(83/84) and [ἀπο]κτείνω[σιν] (84-85). The sequence obviously
recalls John 10:30-31, with ἀποκτείνω where John has λιθάζω./45/
The beginning of pericope two in UG, which parallels John 10:31,
shows UG's interest in this theme. Neither Mayeda nor Koester
considers the significance of ἔν ἐσμεν. Are we to conclude that
'il culmine della cristologia giovannea' (Gallizia, p. 223) was
found by John in this supposed source? Dodd (pp. 73-74) asks
the same rhetorical question about 'his hour' (line 29): is it
likely that John found this conception, which controls his
Gospel from 2:4 to 17:1, in a source like UG?

The only noteworthy word identifiable on the verso of the
third fragment is εἰδώς, which occurs in line 50 above (par.
Mk 12:15), and elsewhere in the canonical gospels, of Jesus'
knowing the dispositions of opponents (cf. Mt 12:25, Lk 11:17,
Jn 6:61).

Repetition of vocabulary may well point to the special
interests of the author, which Mayeda found in Jesus'
confrontations with opponents. But the healing of a leper
cannot be made to fit such a concentration, nor with any ease
can the apocryphal miracle in the fifth pericope. The fragments

may suggest that the complete *UG* consisted solely of miracle-
and controversy-stories, but this would be an insecure
deduction. Nor should we assume that *UG* was intended as a
gospel, to stand on a par with or in place of any other gospels
its compiler may have known, rather than as a selective
compilation for special purposes, such as catechesis or
apologia, much as a modern Bible Society might produce a
'selection' of gospel passages for a particular readership
without calling it a 'gospel'. Since we have no secure
knowledge of the intention of *UG*'s compiler, we cannot assume
anything about his handling of his sources. It is on the basis
of our knowledge of how other writers used their sources that
we regard it as most probable that he was writing from memory,
at least for the Synoptics, but such parallels may be
misleading, especially if Mayeda is correct in arguing that *UG*
was produced for private, domestic use and is in no way an official
or cultic writing./46/ We have no right to take for granted
that the distinctions and categories of form and tradition
established for Synoptic criticism apply to this text./47/

     An early date for *UG* is significant for Koester's thesis,
in rendering it less likely to be based on John's Gospel, and
conversely, if Jeremias' claim were sound, in making it 'a
spectacularly [i.e., unbelievably!] early witness for the four-
gospel canon of the NT'./48/ References by scholars to *UG*'s
date do not always distinguish clearly between the papyrus and
the composition of *UG*, but Koester obviously has the papyrus
itself in view. He cites the first editors' judgment that its
script aligned it with other papyri written before c.120, and
seems keen to make it as early as possible - 'into the
beginning of II CE...possibly shortly after 100'./49/ But if a
consensus obtains on the papyrus's date, it seems to lie
somewhere in the second quarter of the century. The original
editors' 'revised version' gives 130-165 and 140-160 (reported
by most cataloguers of Christian papyri as about the middle of
the century),/50/ Gallizia's discussion suggests a date nearer
125 than 150 and Jeremias says 'before 150'./51/

     Bell and Skeat went on to suggest a date of c.110-130 or
80/90-120 for the composition of *UG*, partly on the basis of
their assessment of the character of the work, and partly, on
the assumption that the papyrus was found at Oxyrhynchus, to
allow time for *UG* to have moved up country from Alexandria, its
likely place of origin./52/ But Bell goes too far in asserting
that 'we may quite certainly assume it is not the author's
autograph but is separated from it by repeated copyings'./53/

Perhaps more truly than they realised did he and Skeat call this
an 'unknown' gospel. It remains the solitary exemplar of its
text. There is no evidence that it ever existed beyond Egypt or
even beyond this one copy. No traces have been found of its
influence on later Christian literature, in Egypt or elsewhere.
Other apocryphal gospels survive only in fragments, but no one
has advanced any convincing identification of our text with any
of them./54/

If there is one thing that may with certainty be affirmed
about this text, it is, in Jeremias' words, that it 'shows no
historical knowledge that carries us beyond the canonical
Gospels'./55/ Vielhauer, who holds that it reflects the
influence of a continuing oral Jesus-tradition, nevertheless
reports that the question whether it contains older and possibly
more authentic tradition than the canonical gospels is answered
in the negative on both critical and conservative sides./56/
Mayeda himself held that it offered no new material for the
history of primitive Christianity and no new information for the
life of Jesus (p. 89). If Koester's case were sound, *UG* would
provide evidence of the kind of source materials John used and
of the way he used them. Even if this were so, it is doubtful
whether it would raise any new challenge to the historical worth
of his Gospel.

The Gospel of Peter (*EvP*)

EvP is a considerably longer text than *UG* and cannot here
be examined in such detail. Koester's summary is accurate:
'Until recently, the almost universal judgment of scholars saw
in this gospel secondary compilation on the basis of the
canonical gospels'./57/ The most recent editor concludes that
EvP follows, for its narrative, the Synoptics, and, for its
theology, the Gospel and Apocalypse of John./58/

Taking his cue from a Kiel dissertation of 1972 by Jürgen
Denker,/59/ Koester argues that, despite its obviously
secondary features (e.g., the exoneration of Pilate and
mythological elements like the speaking cross), *EvP* is 'an
independent witness of the formation of the passion narrative'
(p. 128). This judgment rests on his view of the general
development of the passion narrative, which grew up, not on the
basis of historical report, but as a kind of OT reflection on
the death of Jesus, finding 'both the rationale and the
content of Jesus' suffering and death in the memory of those
passages in the Psalms and the Prophets which spoke about the

suffering of the righteous' (p. 127). *EvP* provides, so he
believes, just such a composition of this 'scriptural memory'.
Its OT material lacks the apologetic interest of Matthew and
Justin in demonstrating precise correspondence between
prediction and fulfilment, and subject matter from any one OT
passage or text is found in only one place in *EvP*, and not
dispersed as often occurs in the canonical gospels (pp. 126-127).

A similar case is argued for *EvP*'s resurrection account.
Koester detaches a miraculous epiphany story which is 'well
preserved and could be very old' (p. 129). It was used intact
by *EvP*, but fragments of it were inserted by the canonical
evangelists into different settings in their narratives.

Before testing Koester's theses by examining one section
from the passion story, we must take note of a new papyrus MS
of *EvP*, P. Oxy. 41. 2949, published in 1972, but unfortunately
not known to Mara or Denker, and not considered by Koester./60/
The fullest study so far is by Dieter Lührmann in 1981./61/
The papyrus is dated c.200 and consists of two fragments, the
larger of which is clearly identifiable with *EvP* 2:3-5 in the
text of the eighth/ninth-century Akhmîm MS, hitherto our sole
witness to *EvP*. Lührmann sets out the text of this fragment and
its Akhmîm parallels as follows:

POx 2949 fr. I   EvPt 3-5 (Akhmim)

5   ]ὁ φίλος Π[ε]ιλά[τ]ου.[3 ὁ φίλος Πειλάτου καί
6   ].ς ὅτι ἐκέλευσεν[εἰδὼς ὅτι σταυρίσκειν
7   ἐλ]θὼν πρὸς Πειλᾶτο[ν   ἦλθεν πρὸς τὸν Πειλᾶτον
8   ]τὸ σῶμα εἰς ταφήν[τὸ σῶμα τοῦ κ(υρίο)υ πρὸς
                                                          ταφήν

9   'Ηρῴδ]ην ἡτήσα[το   4 πρὸς 'Ηρῴδην ἤτησεν
10]ηναι εἰπῶ[ν   5 ἔφη?
11]ητησα.[ἡτήκει?
12]αὐτόν[αὐτὸν ἡτήκει? αὐτὸν
                                                    ἐθάπτομεν?
13].ὅτι α[ἐπεί? γάρ?

The second, much smaller fragment gives only the beginnings of
five lines. Among these the appearance of πειλ[ᾶτος] suggests
that it belongs near to the first fragment, but the other line-
beginnings do not allow an obvious identification with any part
of the Akhmîm text./62/

The new papyrus contains a text of *EvP* 2:3-5 clearly
somewhat different from the one in the Akhmîm MS. Lührmann's
comparison shows that of the sixteen words more or less
confidently reconstructed in the larger Oxyrhynchus fragment,
ten are identical with Akhmîm. The others display some
variation, in two cases to a major extent. Lines 5-8 of the
fragment correspond more closely with Akhmîm than do 9-12.
What is identifiable from the smaller fragment also makes some
divergence from Akhmîm's text inescapable.

P. Oxy. 2949 should therefore be regarded as part of an
earlier version of *EvP* than the one given by the Akhmîm MS.
Unlike the canonical gospels, *EvP*'s text was obviously open to
considerable variation in transmission./63/ As a consequence,
any arguments based on the Akhmîm text for *EvP*'s relations to
the Synoptic and Johannine traditions must now be less secure.

Can any particular *Tendenz* be discerned from a comparison
of the parallel texts? The scope for a fruitful comparison is
strictly limited, but the following points may be made:

line 6 - ἐκέλευσεν (i.e., Herod; κελεύειν is twice used of Herod
in *EvP* 1:2);/64/ Akhmîm has σταυρίσκειν αὐτὸν μέλλουσιν
(σταυρίσκειν is a hapax legomenon). The variation is considerable. Ἡρῴδης is certainly required with ἐκέλευσεν. Did
P. Oxy. 2949 lack Akhmîm's unparalleled σταυρίσκειν? This seems
likely, for in 1:2 Herod ordered only that Jesus be 'taken off',
presumably for execution. But perhaps here Herod's instruction
had become more specific. The Syriac *Didascalia*, which has
affinities at points with *EvP*, says (in the Greek version of
Apostolic Constitutions) 'Herod the King ἐκέλευσεν αὐτὸν
σταυρωθῆναι'./65/ The text of Oxyrhynchus accords better with
the general apologetic thrust of *EvP* (see further below) than
does Akhmîm, for it makes quite explicit Herod's responsibility,
which in *EvP* 2:5 means Jewish responsibility, for the
crucifixion.

There is no canonical parallel to either text, but Akhmîm
is patently more divergent in vocabulary.

line 7 - ἐλ]θὼν πρὸς Πειλᾶτον; Akhmîm - ἦλθεν πρὸς τὸν Πειλᾶτον.
The parallels are: προσελθὼν τῷ Πιλάτῳ (Mt and Lk), εἰσῆλθεν
πρὸς τὸν Πειλᾶτον (Mk). Of the omission of the article before
'Pilate', nothing significant can be said. Akhmîm *EvP* has
Pilate with the article slightly more often than without, but
cf. φίλος Πειλάτου above. On several occasions *EvP* seems to

prefer simple to compound verbs,/66/ and Lührmann's suggestion
of εἰσελθών (p. 223) is questionable. It is not required by
the composition of the MS. The participle is parallel to
εἰδώς, and hence καί would have been omitted before ἤτησεν
(assumed reconstruction). Another marked stylistic feature of
EvP is the frequent use of καί, connecting clause after
clause./67/ The Oxyrhynchus text here linked two participles,
not two main verbs. Does this suggest it may have been less
popular in this stylistic respect than Akhmîm?

line 8 - lacks Akhmîm's τοῦ κυρίου between τὸ σῶμα and πρὸς
ταφήν; did it (or αὐτοῦ, as Lührmann, p. 223, suggests) precede
τὸ σῶμα? All the Synoptics have τὸ σῶμα τοῦ ᾿Ιησοῦ, but EvP
invariably has 'the Lord', never 'Jesus'. But was this feature
less prominent in Oxyrhynchus than it is in Akhmîm? Lührmann,
p. 222, like Coles, is inclined to reconstruct κ[αὶ τοῦ κυρίου
in line 5, but again the uncertain line-length cannot be said
to require it.

The εἰς/πρὸς ταφήν variation is probably without
significance. The four gospels provide no parallel here, but
cf. εἰς ταφήν (Mt 27:7), εἰς τὸν ἐνταφιασμόν (Mk 14:8; par.
Mt 26:12, πρὸς τὸ ἐνταφιάσαι με).

line 9 - probably ᾐτήσατο, to Akhmîm's ἤτησεν. Note that all
three Synoptics have ᾐτήσατο of Joseph's request to Pilate
(John ἠρώτησεν); here it is Pilate's to Herod. The Bauer-
Arndt-Gingrich-Danker Lexicon regards the active and the
middle as interchangeable in early Christian literature. If
Joseph's request influenced Pilate's in EvP, Oxyrhynchus is
nearer to the Synoptics. At this point Akhmîm's developed
text diverged further from the canonical gospels.

line 10 -]ηναι εἰπώ[ν cannot be further reconstructed from
Akhmîm. Coles (p. 16 n.10) suggests ἀποδοθῆναι from Matthew
27:58, which again would make EvP c.200 closer to the
Synoptics than is Akhmîm EvP.

line 11 - ᾐτήσα[το is a probable reconstruction, perhaps
parallel to Akhmîm's ᾐτήκει, but correlating the texts is
difficult. Lührmann (p. 224) suggests that P. Oxy. 2949 may
have had a repetition of Joseph's request in Pilate's mouth,
εἰπώ[ν, ᾿Ιωσὴφ αὐτοῦ τὸ σῶμα] ᾐτήσα[το, which would distance it
further from Akhmîm but in fact make good sense. Akhmîm says
that Pilate asked Herod for the body (2:4), and that Herod
replied, 'Even if no-one had asked...' (2:5), implying that

Pilate had named the source of the request, since Pilate could
scarcely have wanted it himself. At 6:23 the Jews gave the
body to Joseph.

line 13 - ὅτι is not paralleled in Akhmîm in this context. If
it represents the original of Akhmîm's ἐπεί or γάρ, the
following α is unexplained.

The following tentative conclusions may be drawn from this
investigation:

a)   the Oxyrhynchus text probably used less unusual vocabulary;
b)   at some points it may well have been closer to the
Synoptics;
c)   at one point it probably made smoother sense than Akhmîm;
d)   at another it accorded more definitely with the apologetic
thrust of EvP;
e)   at one or two points its linguistic and stylistic usages
may have been less marked than those of Akhmîm.

We will take up some of these pointers to the character of the
Oxyrhynchus text of EvP after the next stage in this
examination of the work.

Since the new papyrus has directed our attention towards
EvP 2:3-5a,/68/ we shall use the passage as a test-case for the
theses of Koester and Denker (even though Koester makes no
specific reference to it).

2:3. Ἱστήκει δὲ ἐκεῖ Ἰωσήφ, ὁ φίλος Πειλάτου καὶ τοῦ
Κυρίου, καὶ εἰδὼς ὅτι σταυρίσκειν αὐτὸν μέλλουσιν ἦλθεν
πρὸς τὸν Πειλᾶτον καὶ ἤτησε τὸ σῶμα τοῦ Κυρίου πρὸς ταφήν.

4. Καὶ ὁ Πειλᾶτος πέμψας πρὸς Ἡρῴδην ἤτησεν αὐτοῦ τὸ
σῶμα.
5. καὶ ὁ Ἡρῴδης ἔφη· "Ἀδελφὲ Πειλᾶτε, εἰ καὶ μή τις
αὐτὸν ἠτήκει, ἡμεῖς αὐτὸν ἐθάπτομεν, ἐπεὶ καὶ σάββατον
ἐπιφώσκει. Γέγραπται γὰρ ἐν τῷ νόμῳ ἥλιον μὴ δῦναι ἐπὶ
πεφονευμένῳ."

Denker (pp. 60-61) claims that EvP's sources here are the
OT and the 'Gemeindetradition', which itself kept close to the
OT. The passage relates a tradition similar to but
independent of the Synoptic version, but altered by being
combined by the author of EvP with a free citation of

Deuteronomy 21:23, which Denker believes was prominent in the
Jewish-Christian Jesus-tradition on which *EvP* drew. In
support of this view he cites Acts 5:30, 10:39, and Jerome's
references, in his commentary on Galatians 3:13, to Ebion's and
Symmachus's renderings of Deuteronomy 21:23./69/ Yet Denker
recognises that *EvP*'s interest in the verse is quite different
from Acts' and Galatians'. *EvP* is preoccupied solely with the
burial of the body before sunset, as is clear from the same
citation at 5:15 and an echo of the same motif at 6:23./70/

Mara (pp. 86-87) holds that *EvP*'s use of Deuteronomy at
5:15 comes from his following John 19:31, which, like the
preceding verse in *EvP* (4:14), refers to the breaking of the
legs. Although John, unlike *EvP*, relates the allusion to
Deuteronomy 21:23 specifically to the imminence of the sabbath,
EvP's citation here follows immediately upon a mention of the
sabbath's proximity. This seems a convincing interpretation.
It is difficult to envisage what role *EvP*'s very circumscribed
reference to Deuteronomy 21:23 could have played in the
development of a passion narrative along Koester's lines of OT
meditative recollection. On the other hand, its *secondary*
elaboration, for apologetic purposes, in the train of a more
kerygmatic use of the *testimonium* is historically quite
intelligible. Lührmann (p. 221 n.24) validly criticises
Denker's later attempt (pp. 80-81) to smuggle the curse (cf.
Gal 3:13) into *EvP*'s understanding of Deuteronomy 21:23 by
citing *EvP* 5:17, 'They...completed the measure of their sins on
their head'. *EvP*'s concern is simply that no πεφονευμένος
should remain unburied at sundown.

EvP's citation here is plainly apologetic. It may not be
prefaced by a Matthaean fulfilment-formula, but a formal enough
introduction is given, Γέγραπται γὰρ.... As Denker himself
puts it, 'steht im PE das ängstliche Bemühen im Vordergrund,
die Vorschrift des Gesetzes zu erfüllen' (p. 60). Mara may
well be right in suggesting (pp. 78-79) that the reason why
Joseph's request for Jesus' body comes so early in *EvP*'s
sequence of events is precisely in order to ensure the
certainty of burial before sunset. The construction of the
episode also serves to reinforce the central apologetic motif
of *EvP*, viz, the Jews' total responsibility for doing away
with Jesus, by demonstrating Pilate's subservience to Herod.

Denker (p. 61) maintains that *EvP* 2:3-5a is independent of
the canonical gospels, chiefly on the grounds that it does not
use the evangelists' common or special traditions. It does not

mention Arimathaea (all four gospels), but *EvP* seems
uninterested in topographical information, such as the place of
the crucifixion./71/ It makes Joseph not a disciple of Jesus
(Matthew and John; cf. Mark and Luke - 'looking for the
kingdom of God'), but a friend of both Pilate and the Lord.
In fact, when later (6:23) Joseph is given the body for burial,
EvP says that 'he had seen (θεασάμενος ἦν) all the good that
Jesus had done', which implies that Joseph had been a
follower of Jesus. So *EvP* does not, as Denker claims, tend to
present Joseph's relationship to Jesus in markedly neutral
terms. *EvP* also lacks, so Denker points out, Pilate's enquiry
of the centurion whether Jesus were already dead (Mk 15:44-45),
but this is hardly surprising, since *EvP* has chosen to place
the request for the body well before the crucifixion! In any
case, it is Herod, not Pilate, who in *EvP* has charge of the
crucifixion.

It is easier to demonstrate the secondary and tendentious
character of *EvP* 2:3-5a than its precise dependence upon the
canonical gospels. *EvP* here wears its apologetic *Tendenz* on
its face, which induces a quite unhistorical presentation of
political realities in Palestine./72/ We should also remember
that such hints as the Oxyrhynchus fragments provide, both
strengthen the apologetic *Tendenz* in this passage and align its
text more closely to the Synoptics.

Denker and Koester are right to stress the OT undergirding
of much of *EvP*, but wrong to deny the parallel undergirding of
the canonical gospels. More sensitive and accurate is Mara's
assessment of the work: 'Il semble donc que "l'apocryphe"
travaille sur un matériel de seconde main qu'il ne domine
qu'extérieurement; son intelligence historique paraît seulement
d'ordre théologique, elle ne part pas d'une expérience
d'événements vécus directement et interprétés, mais elle émerge
d'une lecture de textes médités religieusement, dans une
perspective qui situe au même niveau les prophéties
messianiques et le récit des Évangiles officiels' (pp. 31-32).

Notes

/1/ Raymond F. Collins, *Introduction to the New Testament*
(London, 1983), 28.
/2/ 'Apocryphal and Canonical Gospels', *HTR* 73 (1980), 105-130.
See also the relevant sections of his *Introduction to the New
Testament*, vol. 2: *History and Literature of Early
Christianity* (Philadelphia, 1982), and his brief foreword to
Ron Cameron's *The Other Gospels: Non-Canonical Gospel Texts*
(Guildford, 1983), 9-10. Cameron's introductions to the two
gospels under discussion here summarise Koester's views
(pp. 72-74,76-78).
/3/ *Art.cit.*, 130, 112.
/4/ In working on these texts for this study, I reached the
conclusion that the possibility of *UG*'s being part of the lost
pre-passion section of *EvP* has been too lightly dismissed. I
hope to reopen this question elsewhere. The present study,
however, treats them as unconnected texts, in accord with the
unanimous consensus.
/5/ (i) P. 37(P.Mich. 3.137), containing Mt 26:29-52, is dated
in the 3rd C. by most scholars; cf. K. Aland, *Repertorium der
Griechischen Christlichen Papyri*, vol. I: *Biblische Papyri
(Patristische Texte und Studien*, 18; Berlin and New York, 1976),
259, J. van Haelst, *Catalogue des Papyrus Littéraires Juifs et
Chrétiens* (Paris, 1976) 138-139.
(ii) A 2nd C. fragment of John to be published as P. Oxy.
50.3523 is recorded by C. H. Roberts and T. C. Skeat, *The
Birth of the Codex* (London, 1983) 41.
(iii) P. Ryl. 3.463 is a 3rd C. copy of part of a *Gospel of
Mary*; cf. E. Hennecke - W. Schneemelcher - R. McL. Wilson, *New
Testament Apocrypha*, vol. 1 (London, 1963) 340-341 (H. C.
Puech).
(iv) P. Doura 10, a 3rd C. fragment of Tatian's *Diatessaron*,
probably merits inclusion; cf. E. G. Turner, *The Typology of
the Early Codex* (Philadelphia, 1977) 150.
(v) P. Oxy. 41.2949 is a fragment of c.AD 200 'now plausibly
assigned to the banned Gospel of Peter' (Roberts and Skeat,
op. cit., 44; cf. Haelst, *op. cit.*, 209). See further below.
/6/ Cf. Hennecke etc., *op. cit.*, vol. 1, 115-116 (W.
Schneemelcher); Haelst, *op. cit.*, 208.
/7/ *Texte und Untersuchungen* 65; Berlin, 1957.
/8/ P. Vielhauer in Hennecke etc., *op. cit.*, vol. 1, 119.
/9/ The majority of scholars seems still to accept the
authenticity of the letter published by Morton Smith in
Clement of Alexandria and a Secret Gospel of Mark (Cambridge,
Mass., 1973). See his review of its reception in 'Clement of

/9/ Contd.
Alexandria and Secret Mark: the Score at the End of the First
Decade', *HTR* 75 (1982), 449-461.
/10/ 'He must have known the Gospel of John' - so Hans von
Campenhausen, *The Formation of the Christian Bible*
(Philadelphia, 1972) 160.
/11/ Campenhausen, p. 130 (with literature), is convinced that
Papias speaks of Matthew's Gospel.
/12/ *Synoptische Überlieferung*, 240.
/13/ See the study by D. A. Hagner in this volume.
/14/ 'No evidence...until the end of the second century' (*art.
cit.*, 110). But the Montanists and Irenaeus, whom Koester
cites, give a date no later than c.170.
/15/ R. M. Grant, *The Apostolic Fathers*, vol. 1: *An
Introduction* (New York, 1964), 60-62; Koester's article, p. 108,
lists only 'Free sayings and other materials' for Ignatius.
/16/ Campenhausen, *op. cit.*, 120 n. 61, accepts that the
Didache and *2 Clement* refer to written gospels.
/17/ *Das Leben-Jesu-Fragment Papyrus Egerton 2 und seine
Stellung in der urchristlichen Literaturgeschichte* (Berne,
1946). Cf. the careful assessment by one of the fragments'
initial editors, H. I. Bell, 'The Gospel Fragments P. Egerton
2', *HTR* 42 (1949), 53-63, concluding that, while Mayeda's
theory about the general character of the new text is
acceptable, his view of its use of sources independent of the
canonical gospels is more disputable.
/18/ *Art. cit.*, 123. He is more qualified in his *Introduction*,
vol. 2, 181-183, although he later says (p. 222) that *UG*
possibly provided some of John's source material.
/19/ Bell and T. C. Skeat, *Fragments of an Unknown Gospel and
Other Early Christian Papyri* (London, 1935) 34-38; Bell, *Recent
Discoveries of Biblical Papyri* (Oxford, 1937) 17.
/20/ In Hennecke etc., *op. cit.*, vol. 1, 95-96.
/21/ *Geschichte der urchristlichen Literatur: Einleitung in
das Neue Testament, die Apokryphen und die Apostolischen Väter*
(Berlin and New York, 1975) 637-638.
/22/ 'Il P. Egerton 2', *Aegyptus* 36 (1956) 29-72, 178-234.
Koester is incorrect (*art. cit.*, 119) in asserting that 'no
major attempt has been made to refute Mayeda's arguments'.
/23/ In Hennecke, *op. cit.*, vol. 1, 95.
/24/ *Unknown Sayings of Jesus*, 2nd edit. (London, 1964) 39-41.
/25/ *Art. cit.*, 120-121. Cf. *Introduction*, vol. 2, 182.
/26/ *Introduction*, vol. 2, 182.
/27/ *Art. cit.* (n. 9 above), 453.
/28/ Cf. Jeremias, *Unknown Sayings*, 40.
/29/ 'A New Gospel', *BJRL* 20 (1936) 56-92, at p. 70.

/30/ Mayeda points out, p. 24 n. 2, that ἦλθον καταλῦσαι occurs
in sayings of Jesus in both the *Gospel of the Ebionites* and the
Gospel of the Egyptians. John 4:7 has ἔρχεται.... ἀντλῆσαι of
the woman of Samaria. Dodd, *art. cit.*, 66, points to the
frequency of the ἦλθον + infin. construction in early Christian
usage to express the purpose of the incarnation.
/31/ Cf. H. Merkel, *Die Widersprüche zwischen den Evangelien.
Ihre polemische und apologetische Behandlung in der Alten
Kirche bis zu Augustin (Wissensch. Unters. zum NT*, 13; Tübingen,
1971), and *Die Pluralität der Evangelien als theologisches und
exegetisches Problem in der Alten Kirche (Traditio Christiana*,
III; Bern, Frankfurt, Las Vegas, 1978); O. Cullmann, *The Early
Church* (London, 1956), ch. III, 'The Plurality of the Gospels as
a Theological Problem in Antiquity'.
/32/ *Op. cit.*, 120 n. 61.
/33/ *Art. cit.*, 121; *Introduction*, vol. 2, 182.
/34/ As Gallizia, *art. cit.*, 65-68, effectively demonstrates.
/35/ *Art. cit.*, 121-122.
/36/ In this respect Koester may have been misled by an
extraordinary paragraph in Mayeda, p. 49 (cf. Gallizia, *art.
cit.*, 187), in which he draws special attention to the striking
fact that κύριος never occurs in the papyrus! He is referring
ad loc. to the appearance of διδάσκαλος in line 53 instead of
κύριος of Lk 6:46 (cf. Mt 7:21), but his comments on lines 30,
37 and 39 fail to notice the appearance of κύριος. Hence he
can say, 'Ob dieses Wort mit christologischer Tendenz in seiner
Quelle nicht vorhanden war, oder ob der Verfasser des Papyrus es
wegen des Zusammenhanges korrigiert hat, da er daran nicht
interessiert war, bleibt eine Frage. Jedenfalls ist es
auffallend, dass dieses für das Urchristentum spezifische Wort
nicht hier steht. Diese Tatsache gehört mit zu den Merkmalen
unseres Papyrus: er erzählt die Geschichten neutral und ohne
tiefe theologische Deutung'.
/37/ *Art. cit.*, 123; cf. Mayeda, 51 ('novellistischer').
/38/ *Op. cit.*, 44. Cf. Jeremias, in Hennecke etc., *op. cit.*,
vol. 1, 96: 'the question about tribute-money is robbed of its
typically Jewish tone through being worded in general terms'.
/39/ Koester, *art. cit.*, 122, says the text 'presents Jesus as
rejecting a secular affair', but this is far from obvious.
/40/ Dr. Richard Bauckham has plausibly suggested to me that
this pericope is modelled upon the sequence in Mark 10:17-19
par., where Jesus first picks up his questioner's form of
address ('Good Teacher') before answering his question. There
are, nevertheless, significant differences. Mark 10 contains
no reference to failure to fulfil Jesus' teaching, and hence
does not stray into gratuitous rebuke of the questioner.

/40/ Contd.
Furthermore, Jesus gave an answer after only a short digression.
In *UG*, if he did so at all, it must have been only after a
digression of such a kind as to nullify the value of any answer.
/41/ *Op. cit.*, 46-47.
/42/ Cf. Jeremias, *Unknown Sayings*, 41.
/43/ *Art. cit.*, 123.   'On the contrary, the Johannine parallel
would argue for a dependence of John upon the *Unknown Gospel*.'
This claim rests on conclusions reached from his consideration
of earlier pericope, especially the first.
/44/ *Introduction*, vol. 2, 182.
/45/ So Dodd, *art. cit.*, 85.
/46/ *Op. cit.*, 87-90. Bell, *art. cit.*, 62-63, finds this
account acceptable.
/47/ Koester's assumptions are crucial to his case: e.g., in
arguing that, because lines 7-14 are shorter than John 5:39-45,
their version is 'older in formal terms' (*Introduction*, vol. 2,
182).   There are clearly other possible accounts of the relation
between the two texts.
/48/ *Art. cit.*, 120. Koester makes his point in provocative
terms. Not only need not *UG*'s use of the four gospels imply
their canonical status, but it is certain that it used a source
or sources other than the canonical gospels.
/49/ *Introduction*, vol. 2, 182,222.
/50/ *The New Gospel Fragments* [by Bell and Skeat, although
unnamed], (London, 1935) 10, 17; cf. Bell, *Recent Discoveries*
(1937) 20 (the MS can hardly be appreciably later than the mid-
2nd C.); Haelst, *op. cit.*, 207 (also citing W. Schubart's date
of before 150); Aland, *op. cit.*, 376. Turner, *op. cit.*, 90, 144,
is no more precise than second century, as too are Roberts and
Skeat, *op. cit.*, 41.
/51/ Gallizia, 42-46; Jeremias in Hennecke etc., *op. cit.*,
vol. 1, 94.
/52/ *The New Gospel Fragments*, 16-19. Cameron, *op. cit.*, 74,
believes that *UG* was composed in the second half of the first
century, in Syria.
/53/ *Recent Discoveries*, 20.
/54/ Gallizia, 207-210. But see n. 4 above.
/55/ In Hennecke etc., *op. cit.*, vol. 1, 95.
/56/ *Geschichte*, 639.
/57/ *Art. cit.*, 126, referring to C. Maurer's treatment in
Hennecke etc., *op. cit.*, vol. 1, 179-182. Opinions earlier in
the century were much more divided; cf. Mara (next note), 17-20.
/58/ M. G. Mara, *Evangile de Pierre* (*Sources Chrétiennes*, 201;
Paris, 1973), 214. Koester does not mention this edition.

/59/ Die theologiegeschichtliche Stellung des Petrusevangeliums.
Ein Beitrag zur Frühgeschichte des Doketismus (Europ.
Hochschulschr. XXIII:36; Bern, Frankfurt, 1975). Denker was
able to take note of Mara only in a brief review at the end
(pp. 255-256). Cameron, op. cit., 78 suggests EvP was
composed as early as the second half of the first century.
/60/ Ed. R. A. Coles in G. M. Browne et al., The Oxyrhynchus
Papyri, vol. 41 (London, 1972), 15-16. Koester mentions it
en passant in his Introduction, vol. 2, 163, but not in his
article in HTR. It is not referred to in Vielhauer's
Geschichte, or by R. McL. Wilson in TRE III, 331-332.
See also n. 5 above. Cameron, op. cit., 76-77, refers to the
new MS, but merely as a recension different from the Akhmîm
text.
/61/ 'POx 2949: EvPt 3-5 in einer Handschrift des 2./3.
Jahrhunderts', ZNW 72 (1981), 216-226. Coles briefly compared
the fragment with EvP 2:3-5 in 1972.
/62/ Lührmann, 219-220.
/63/ Cf. Lührmann, 225-226.
/64/ Unless one is to make no reference at all to the text of
EvP beyond 2:3-5, one cannot avoid comparing the Oxyrhynchus
text with the Akhmîm text elsewhere.
/65/ Didascalia 21, tr. R. H. Connolly (1929), 190; Apost.
Const. 5:19:5, ed. F. X. Funk, 290-291. Cf. Denker, op. cit.,
12-14.
/66/ Cf. L. Vaganay, L'Evangile de Pierre (Paris, 1930),
144-145.
/67/ Vaganay, 145.
/68/ Denker, 34-35, rightly points out that EvP 2:5 (καὶ
παρέδωκεν κ.τ.λ.) belongs with 2:6 rather than with what
precedes it in 2:5.
/69/ PL 26, 387.
/70/ The Jews rejoiced that, after the darkness since noon
(5:15ff.), the sun shone again and it was only the ninth hour
(6:22), and so they happily gave Joseph the body for burial
(6:23).
/71/ Cf. Vaganay, op. cit., 126.
/72/ Cf. Mara, op. cit., 31, 79.

THE SAYINGS OF JESUS IN THE APOSTOLIC
FATHERS AND JUSTIN MARTYR

Donald A. Hagner
Fuller Theological Seminary
135 North Oakland Avenue
Pasadena, California 91001
U.S.A.

It is clear that after the resurrection, if not before, the authority of Jesus was indelibly impressed upon the earliest Christians. Thus, in the writings they produced, before the traditions about Jesus began to crystallize into our Gospels, the sayings of Jesus were already authoritative and influential, as essays in the present symposium will have shown./1/ This is also true, however, of the early Christian writings, later than the Synoptic Gospels, that did not become a part of the NT canon, at least the earliest of which (Clement of Rome, or '1 Clement') was written before some of the NT writings themselves (e.g., the Johannine literature).

The collection of these earliest writings outside the NT canon is a somewhat arbitrary one which was first designated 'The Apostolic Fathers' in the seventeenth century. They derive mainly from the second century and are often difficult to date precisely. Clement of Rome is probably to be dated at 95/2/ and the Didache and Barnabas, or at least parts of them, may also be from the first century,/3/ while the epistles of Ignatius are from very early in the second century, and Polycarp's epistle to the Philippians is not much later. The pseudonymous homily known as 2 Clement and the unusual apocalypse the Shepherd of Hermas (although parts of it may be earlier) are probably from the middle or just before the middle of the second century./4/ The writings of Justin Martyr come from about the same period and this justifies their treatment together with the Apostolic Fathers. We have little concern in the present article with other writings often included in the category of the Apostolic Fathers, viz., the enigmatic 'Epistle to Diognetus' (which may be as late as the third century), the Martyrdom of Polycarp (as well as the Martyrdoms of Clement and Ignatius), and the fragments of Quadratus and Papias./5/

The purpose of this paper is to examine the extent to which the Apostolic Fathers draw upon the written Gospels or the gospel tradition, the way in which such material is utilized, and the esteem in which it is held. This will in turn lead to an analysis of the transmission of the tradition about Jesus in the late first and second centuries and the drawing of some implications concerning the reliability of the tradition.

The study of quotation and allusion in the Apostolic Fathers and in Justin Martyr has been undertaken often in the past./6/ Although this literature has been consulted and will be referred to, the examination and evaluation of the data have been done afresh in the following study.

The Question of Dependence on the Written Gospels: the Data

In this section, rather than reviewing the evidence of each of our documents thoroughly and in order, we focus upon those passages which apparently have the strongest claim to direct dependence on the written Gospels and make only brief mention of those which have weaker claims. Since decisions concerning possible knowledge and use of a written Gospel can only finally be made by a consideration of the pattern of quotation or allusion within each individual document, allusions can hardly be ignored. Inevitably in a study such as this we must be prepared to be satisfied with varying degrees of probability rather than anything like certainty.

The passages that have the strongest claims are those that seem most like deliberate quotation, whether because of identical (or nearly identical) wording with a passage in the written Gospels, or because of the presence of an introductory formula. As we shall see, there are not many of these in the Apostolic Fathers.

1. Clement of Rome (1 Clement)

Two passages in Clement's epistle qualify for consideration in this category; both concern sayings of Jesus. In 13.2, Clement presents seven maxims drawn from the Sermon on the Mount, or from the tradition that eventually becomes that sermon in Matt 5-7 and Luke 6. These are given crisply and in a strong parallelism:

(1) ἐλεᾶτε, ἵνα ἐλεηθῆτε
(2) ἀφίετε, ἵνα ἀφεθῇ ὑμῖν
(3) ὡς ποιεῖτε, οὕτω ποιηθήσεται ὑμῖν
(4) ὡς δίδοτε, οὕτως δοθήσεται ὑμῖν
(5) ὡς κρίνετε, οὕτως κριθήσεσθε
(6) ὡς χρηστεύεσθε, οὕτως χρηστευθήσεται ὑμῖν
(7) ᾧ μέτρῳ μετρεῖτε, ἐν αὐτῷ μετρηθήσεται ὑμῖν

From a comparison with the Synoptic Gospels,/7/ the following conclusions emerge. Although none of the seven maxims is found verbatim in any of the Synoptics, three do find some close parallels. The seventh, which appears to be the only one found in all three Synoptics (Matt 7:2b; Mark 4:24b; Luke 6:38c), is the most closely paralleled. Maxims 4 (Luke 6:38a) and 5 (Matt 7:1-2) find parallels that are not so close, lacking the ὡς . . . οὕτως comparisons. Maxims 1 (Matt 5:7) and 2 (Matt 6:14; Mark 11:25b) find parallels, but these are not as close as in the earlier instances. Finally, maxims 3 and particularly 6 find no actual parallels although they are harmonious with other sayings in the Gospels (3 is possibly a version of the Golden Rule in Matt 7:12 and Luke 6:31; 6 finds at least an echo in Luke 6:35c).

From these data it can be seen that it is difficult to make a convincing case for dependence upon any of the Synoptic Gospels from this passage. Matthew has four of the maxims and Luke has but three (two of which parallel the same maxims as Matthew's). Two maxims thus remain unaccounted for.

The introductory formula with which Clement begins this passage must now be noted: μάλιστα μεμνημένοι τῶν λόγων τοῦ κυρίου Ἰησοῦ, οὓς ἐλάλησεν διδάσκων ἐπιείκειαν καὶ μακροθυμίαν· οὕτως γὰρ εἶπεν. The reference to 'remembering' the words of Jesus alerts us to the possibility that oral tradition is what is being cited in the maxims. And this, of course, is exactly what the terse, stylized form with its repeated parallelism suggests. The first two maxims utilize the imperative followed by a ἵνα and the passive of the same verb; the following five maxims consist of ὡς . . . οὕτως comparison, using in every instance the future passive of the same verb as in the ὡς clause. This is very obviously material that was designed for easy memorization.

Before we turn to the second passage in Clement, we must look at a passage in Polycarp's epistle to the Philippians that is closely related to the passage that has just been examined. Polycarp writes in 2.3,

(5) μὴ κρίνετε, ἵνα μὴ κριθῆτε
(2) ἀφίετε, καὶ ἀφεθήσεται ὑμῖν
(1) ἐλεᾶτε, ἵνα ἐλεηθῆτε
(7) ᾧ μέτρῳ μετρεῖτε, ἀντιμετρηθήσεται ὑμῖν

These four maxims are followed by the words καὶ (ὅτι) μακάριοι οἱ πτωχοὶ καὶ οἱ διωκόμενοι ἕνεκεν δικαιοσύνης, ὅτι αὐτῶν ἐστὶν ἡ βασιλεία τοῦ θεοῦ. Polycarp thus has four of Clement's seven

maxims (in the order 5, 2, 1, 7). Of these, however, only 1
agrees verbatim; 2 lacks the characteristic ἵνα with the
subjunctive; 5 is not in the ὡς . . . οὕτως form (but agrees
verbatim with Matt 7:1); and 7 uses the compound verb
ἀντιμετρηθήσεται (thus bringing it into virtually verbatim
agreement with Luke 6:38c)./8/

Although he does not mention it explicitly, Polycarp
appears to have been acquainted with Clement's epistle./9/ This
has led some scholars to conclude that Polycarp is dependent
upon Clement for the present passage./10/ Against this
conclusion, however, are the differences in the wording, number,
and order of the maxims. Moreover, Polycarp uses an
introductory formula for this passage which is very similar to
Clement's—although again, not similar enough to necessitate a
conclusion of direct dependence—and which may point to
memorized oral tradition as the source of these sayings of
Jesus: μνημονεύοντες δὲ ὧν εἶπεν ὁ κύριος διδάσκων. If it is
unlikely that Polycarp is dependent directly upon the Gospels
for the four maxims (despite the verbatim agreement of two of
them with the Gospel texts, two have only remote parallels), and
if it is unlikely for the above reasons that Polycarp depends in
this passage upon Clement, then we may be encouraged by this
introductory formula to conclude that this passage, like
Clement's, is drawn from oral tradition./11/ This conclusion is
further supported by the fact that the form of the maxims is
again stylized, as E. Massaux pointed out long ago,/12/ into the
form of a quatrain (with the first and third lines ending in
-θῆτε and the second and fourth in -θήσεται ὑμῖν), ideal for
memorization.

It is possible, of course, that Clement (and Polycarp) are
quoting the written Gospels from memory, as some have
claimed./13/ It is not necessarily the case that extracanonical
tradition is being cited in these passages. Nevertheless,
because of the form of the material, the probable independence
of Polycarp and Clement at this point, as well as the
introductory formulae, it seems most convincing to argue, as
several scholars have,/14/ that Clement and Polycarp are here
dependent upon oral tradition parallel to the Gospels./15/

It is not easy to explain the relationship between this
material in Clement and Polycarp to that in, say the Sermon on
the Mount material in Matthew (or Luke). The sayings as found
in the Synoptic Gospels also bear the marks of oral tradition.
Jesus himself may indeed have often delivered his teaching in

such striking, crisp, parallel forms for easy memorization. It
may be, given the earlier date of the written Gospels, that
they, rather than Clement and Polycarp, reflect more accurately
the original form of the sayings. But this cannot be known with
certainty. The same conclusion holds true for most, if not all,
of the material discussed below.

The second striking passage in Clement (46.8) is of a
somewhat different character:

(a) οὐαὶ τῷ ἀνθρώπῳ ἐκείνῳ. καλὸν ἦν αὐτῷ, εἰ οὐκ ἐγεννήθη,
(b) ἢ ἕνα τῶν ἐκλεκτῶν μου σκανδαλίσαι
(c) κρεῖττον ἦν αὐτῷ περιτεθῆναι μύλον καὶ καταποντισθῆναι
       εἰς τὴν θάλασσαν,
(d) ἢ ἕνα τῶν ἐκλεκτῶν μου διαστρέψαι./16/

Here two sayings occurring in different places in the
Synoptics have been put together. Neither agrees very closely
with the Synoptic parallels./17/ In the first saying, following
the words οὐαὶ τῷ ἀνθρώπῳ ἐκείνῳ, Clement lacks the clause δι'
οὗ ὁ υἱὸς τοῦ ἀνθρώπου παραδίδοται as well as the words ὁ
ἄνθρωπος ἐκεῖνος after ἐγεννήθη (cf. Matt 26:24b and Mark
14:21b). On the other hand, Clement's clause b does not occur
with this saying in the Synoptics. Clement's second saying is
even less like the Synoptic parallels (Matt 18:6 and Mark 9:42;
cf. Luke 17:2). It lacks the opening clause ὃς δ' ἂν σκανδαλίσῃ
ἕνα τῶν μικρῶν τούτων τῶν πιστευόντων (εἰς ἐμέ) as well as the
words περὶ τὸν τράχηλον αὐτοῦ, which are common to all three
Synoptic parallels.

Clement's passage is found in verbatim agreement in Clement
of Alexandria (Stromata 3.107.2). It is well known, however,
that the Alexandrian Clement refers to Clement's epistle by name
(Stromata 1.38.8; 4.105.1; 5.80.1)./18/ Here, therefore, we do
not have any independent attestation of the sayings that might
be appealed to as representing a common oral tradition. The
same must be said of other occurrences of the sayings in other
early Christian literature. In Shepherd of Hermas (Vis. 4.2.6)
we have at best an allusion to the same material as in Clement:
οὐαὶ τοῖς ἀκούσασιν τὰ ῥήματα ταῦτα καὶ παρακούσασιν. αἰρετώτερον
ἦν αὐτοῖς τὸ μὴ γεννηθῆναι. As can be seen, however, the words
differ considerably from both Clement and the Synoptics.
Marcion's Gospel (as witnessed by Tertullian's Adversus
Marcionem 4.35) appears to have conflated the same two sayings
as in Clement's passage, but the wording/19/ is again too
different to be able to conclude dependence upon a common
source. Although these passages/20/ do not provide evidence of

a source parallel to, but independent of, the Gospels, they do
at least point to the fact that the sayings were brought
together and given similar catechetical and homiletical
applications.

Again it is not impossible that the explanation of this
passage in Clement is to be found in quotation of the Synoptics
from memory./21/ But if Clement is dependent upon oral
tradition for the citation in 13.2, the possibility that he is
doing so here too should be considered seriously. The extensive
differences argue against literary dependence upon the
Synoptics, even if the quotation is made from memory. More
significant, however, is the fact that the passage in Clement
reveals a deliberate parallelism in the nearly verbatim lines b
and d, pointing perhaps to material designed for
memorization./22/ This lends support to the conclusion that
Clement here, as in 13.2, depends upon oral tradition. Further
to be noted is the introductory formula, which is similar to
that for 13.2: μνήσθητε τῶν λόγων τοῦ κυρίου Ἰησοῦ . The
emphasis here, as in 13.2, on 'remembering' is particularly
suitable for material derived from oral tradition./23/

It seems most probable then that the two important passages
in Clement together with the parallel in Polycarp point to oral
traditions parallel to the written Gospels. These traditions
may be said to be 'synoptic' in character, more closely
resembling Matthew than Luke. The tradition reflected in
Polycarp is similar to its parallel in Clement 13.2, but shows
interesting variations, also apparently designed to aid
memorization. Further confirming the correctness of this
conclusion is the fact that a similar introductory formula,
μνημονεύειν τε τῶν λόγων τοῦ κυρίου Ἰησοῦ, ὅτι αὐτὸς εἶπεν,
is used in Acts 20:35, introducing a saying of Jesus not found
in the Gospels: 'It is more blessed to give than to receive.'
Here is clearly a saying derived from the oral tradition that
was not picked up by the evangelists, a saying also introduced
with a formula that stresses 'remembering.'

In addition to the formal citations, Clement contains a
number of possible allusions to the Synoptic Gospels. The most
convincing of these is probably the reference in 24.5 to the
sower, which begins with the very words of the parable of the
sower as it is found in all three Synoptics: ἐξῆλθεν ὁ σπείρων
(Mark 4:3; Matt 13:3; Luke 8:5). Although Clement does not give
the parable, he uses its imagery in a homily based on
1 Cor 15:36ff. Here, as in other possible allusions to the
Synoptic Gospels found in Clement,/24/ it is difficult to

conclude that Clement depends upon any of our written Gospels.
The same must be said from the evidence of OT citations and
allusions common to Clement and the Synoptics, although in one
instance (15.2, quoting Isa 29:13; cf. Mark 7:6 and Matt 15:8)
the text of the quotation agrees so extensively with the
Synoptics against the LXX that dependence is a possibility./25/
Clement could derive the citation in this form from tradition or
even from a different Greek version of Isaiah./26/

The data of Clement taken together are best explained as
the result of dependence upon oral tradition similar to, but
separate from, the written Synoptic Gospels./27/

2. Ignatius

There are only a few possible allusions to the Synoptic
Gospels in the seven authentic letters of Ignatius. The
following are the stronger possibilities.

There is only one quotation of words of Jesus in Ignatius
that is introduced with an introductory formula (Smyrn. 3.2):
καὶ ὅτε πρὸς τοὺς περὶ Πέτρον ἦλθεν, ἔφη αὐτοῖς Λάβετε,
ψηλαφήσατέ με, καὶ ἴδετε ὅτι οὐκ εἰμὶ δαιμόνιον ἀσώματον.
Although these words are very similar to Luke 24:39, dependence
on Luke is made questionable by Jerome's attribution of the
citation to 'the Gospel according to the Hebrews' and Origen's
attribution of it to 'the Doctrine of Peter.'/28/

In the letter to Polycarp, 2.2, we have a possible allusion
to Matt 10:16: φρόνιμος γίνου ὡς ὁ ὄφις ἐν ἅπασιν, καὶ ἀκέραιος
εἰς ἀεὶ ὡς ἡ περιστερά. This is very close to the text in
Matthew, the main difference being that Matthew uses a plural
imperative and plural nouns and adjectives throughout.
Ignatius' singular forms may be accounted for by the fact that
he is addressing Polycarp and not a Christian community. This
appears to be fairly strong evidence for literary dependence,
but it must also be admitted that the saying has a proverbial
ring to it and that it is the kind of saying that could have
been part of an oral tradition available to Ignatius. Just
before these words (in the letter to Polycarp, 2.1) we find the
following possible allusion to Luke 6:32: καλοὺς μαθητὰς ἐὰν
φιλῇς, χάρις σοι οὐκ ἔστιν. Luke uses εἰ with the indicative,
ἀγαπάω instead of φιλέω and τοὺς ἀγαπῶντας ὑμᾶς as the object
clause. There is thus similarity of thought, but not of
wording. Again, however, the saying has a proverbial tone that
could cause us to regard it as derived from oral tradition.

A fourth important passage for our consideration is found
in the letter to the Smyrnaeans, 1.1: βεβαπτισμένον ὑπὸ Ἰωάννου,
ἵνα πληρωθῇ πᾶσα δικαιοσύνη ὑπ' αὐτοῦ, with which may be
compared Matthew's phrase in 3:15: πληρῶσαι πᾶσαν δικαιοσύνην.
This distinctive phrase in connection with the baptism of Jesus
by John looks very much as though it is derived from the Gospel
of Matthew, but could possibly be taken from the tradition
utilized by Matthew./29/

Other possible allusions can be mentioned,/30/ but in every
instance it is impossible to deny the possibility that oral
tradition rather than dependence upon the Gospels may explain
the words./31/ Ignatius' epistles also contain allusions to
Johannine material,/32/ but again this is perhaps mediated via
oral tradition./33/

3. Polycarp
We have already looked at one of the most important
passages containing gospel material in Polycarp's epistle to the
Philippians (2.3, parallel to 1 Clem. 13.1; see above, p. 235.
/34/   Another important passage which also contains an
introductory formula occurs in 7.2: δεήσεσιν αἰτούμενοι τὸν
παντεπόπτην θεὸν μὴ εἰσενεγκεῖν ἡμᾶς εἰς πειρασμόν, καθὼς εἶπεν
ὁ κύριος· Τὸ μὲν πνεῦμα πρόθυμον, ἡ δὲ σὰρξ ἀσθενής.   This is
very close to Mark 14:38 and Matt 26:41; indeed, the quotation
following καθὼς εἶπεν ὁ κύριος is in verbatim agreement with
both Gospels. The saying is again brief and pithy, however, and
may thus derive equally well from oral tradition as from the
written Gospels./35/ Polycarp 6.1-2 is an allusion to lines
from the Lord's prayer (Matt 6:12; cf. Luke 11:4), but such
common liturgical material as this rules out any decision on
literary dependence. Other possible allusions to the
Gospels/36/ are similar in nature and do not advance our
study./37/ There are furthermore a few possible allusions to
Acts/38/ and the Fourth Gospel./39/ These are again similar to
what we have looked at in the possible allusions to the
Synoptics.

4. Didache
The question of the Didache's dependence on the Gospels is,
if anything, more difficult than in the other Apostolic Fathers.
There is an abundance of material to consider, but it is not
clear what conclusions are to be drawn.

In only one place does Didache use an introductory formula
with gospel material. This is in 9.5, where in a discussion of
the Eucharist, the cryptic saying of Matt 7:6 is quoted: καὶ γὰρ

περὶ τούτου εὕρηκεν ὁ κύριος· Μὴ δῶτε τὸ ἅγιον τοῖς κυσί. This kind of saying, however, could as easily have been derived from oral tradition as from Matthew. In 8.1 the same general association between fasting and hypocrisy is made as in Matt 6:16. This is followed, however, by the Lord's prayer which agrees nearly verbatim with Matthew (Matt 6:9ff.) against the Lucan version. It is introduced with the words ἀλλ' ὡς ἐκέλευσεν ὁ κύριος ἐν τῷ εὐαγγελίῳ αὐτοῦ, οὕτω προσεύχεσθε. Despite the words 'his gospel,' we are probably not to think of dependence upon Matthew, but rather of Gospel tradition perpetuated in this instance through the liturgical tradition of the Church (as is confirmed by the minor variations and Didache's inclusion of the doxology at the end of the prayer, something not found in Matthew's version according to the earliest textual witnesses). We are probably again to think of liturgical tradition in 7.1, where the trinitarian baptismal formula occurs in agreement with Matt 28:19.

In 1.2, at the beginning of the description of 'the way of life,' two commandments are juxtaposed: πρῶτον ἀγαπήσεις τὸν θεὸν τὸν ποιήσαντά σε (cf. 19:2), δεύτερον τὸν πλησίον σου ὡς σεαυτόν. The same juxtaposition of Deut 6:5 with Lev 19:18b is found in Matt 22:37-39 and Mark 12:29-31 (cf. Luke 10:27), but since the combination probably had already been made in Judaism (cf. Pirke Abot 6.1) it is again difficult to conclude dependence upon the Gospels. Possibly a Jewish source is in view here (as might be suggested by the words τὸν ποιήσαντά σε, not found in the Gospels). The same is probably true of the negative form of the Golden Rule (cf. Matt 7:12) that immediately follows in 1.2 (cf. Tob 4:15; b. Shabb. 31a). The material that follows this (1.3-6), however, seems closely related to Synoptic tradition, finding parallels both in Matthew (5:39-47) and Luke (6:27-33), although it is again unlikely that literary dependence upon the Gospels is the explanation of this material.

Other passages that deserve mention are 11.7 (Matt 12:31; cf. Mark 3:28); 13.1-2 (Matt 10:10; cf. Luke 10:7; 1 Tim 5:18); 16.1 (Matt 24:42, 44) and 16.3-5 (Matt 24:10-13). There is no convincing allusion to Acts (cf. 4.8 with Acts 4:32),/40/ and in only one instance does an OT allusion (Ps 37:11) occur also in one of the Gospels (Matt 5:5) and the Didache (3.7)./41/ There is little evidence of a knowledge of the Fourth Gospel./42/

Although the Didache contains an abundance of material similar, and related in some way, to the Gospels, it is very interesting that the case for dependence upon the Gospels is so

particularly weak. The phenomena can be readily explained as
the result of dependence upon oral tradition./43/

5. Barnabas

Since the focus of Barnabas is upon OT texts, the amount of
material to be considered here is slight by comparison./44/ Two
passages are particularly important. The first (4.14) involves
the introductory formula ὡς γέγραπται, regularly used (with
slight variations) for OT citations in the Apostolic Fathers,
but used only here in introducing material found in a Gospel
(Matt 22:14; cf. Matt 20:16). The words in Barnabas, πολλοὶ
κλητοί, ὀλίγοι δὲ ἐκλεκτοὶ εὑρεθῶμεν, differ from the saying as
found in Matthew (where the first clause contains the verb εἰσιν
and the second lacks εὑρεθῶμεν). A similar saying in 4 Ezra 8.3
(cf. 10.57) together with the proverbial character of the saying
has discouraged many from concluding dependence upon the Gospel
of Matthew./45/ The γέγραπται naturally refers to a written
source, unless the author of Barnabas wrongly remembers the
saying as written somewhere; but this source, if it is not
Matthew, remains unknown to us. The second passage (5.9) again
consists of a brief saying, ἵνα δείξῃ ὅτι οὐκ ἦλθεν καλέσαι
δικαίους ἀλλὰ ἁμαρτωλούς, found (but with the first person
ἦλθον) in Matt 9:13. In Barnabas, unlike Matthew, the saying is
connected with the call of the Apostles. Here, as in the first
passage, it is not possible to conclude confidently that
Barnabas depends upon the Gospel of Matthew. This is again the
kind of saying that would have been transmitted orally.

In two places Barnabas contains OT material in common with
two or more of the Synoptic Gospels. In the first of these
(5.12; cf. Matt 26:31; Mark 14:27), Zech 13:7, whereas the
Synoptics quote Zechariah according to the LXX quite closely
(with introductory formula), Barnabas quotes more freely and
applies the passage not to the disciples, but to the Jews. In
12.10 Barnabas quotes Ps 110:1, in verbatim agreement with the
LXX (Barnabas has ὑποπόδιον, with Luke 20:43, and against
Matt 22:44 and Mark 12:36, which have ὑποκάτω in the best MSS).
That Barnabas here reflects at least Synoptic tradition is clear
from words in 12.11 (after a citation of Isa 45:1):/46/ ἴδε πῶς
Δαυείδ λέγει αὐτὸν κύριον, καὶ υἱὸν οὐ λέγει (cf. Matt 22:45;
Mark 12:37; Luke 20:44). It is more difficult, however, to
conclude from either of these quotations direct dependence upon
the Synoptic Gospels.

Other possible allusions to the Synoptic Gospels are less
convincing;/47/ there are no allusions to Acts and only a few

unconvincing possibilities concerning the Fourth Gospel./48/

6. Shepherd of Hermas

Although there are numerous allusions to Synoptic material
in Hermas, never is this material introduced with an
introductory formula./49/ Perhaps the strongest claim to
dependence upon a Gospel is found in Similitude 9.20.2: οἱ
τοιοῦτοι (i.e., πλούσιοι) οὖν δυσκόλως εἰσελεύσονται εἰς τὴν
βασιλείαν τοῦ θεοῦ. This agrees exactly with Matt 19:23 (cf.
Mark 10:23; Luke 18:24), except that the latter employs the
singular πλούσιος (with the correspondingly singular verb) and
οὐρανῶν in place of θεοῦ. This could well be a quotation from
Matthew, but is also capable of being explained as drawn from
tradition./50/ The same must be said of Similitude 9.29.1-3,
where several phrases are similar to Matt 18:3 (cf. 19:14 and
Mark 10:14). In Similitude 5.6.4, the words ἐξουσίαν πᾶσαν
λαβὼν παρὰ τοῦ πατρὸς αὐτοῦ could well be an allusion to
Matt 28:18. The parable of the sower (Mark 4:18f.; Luke 8:14)
may lie behind Sim. 9.20.1-2, and the parable of the wicked
husbandmen (Matt 21:33ff.; cf. 25:14) behind Similitude 5.2.

Luke 18:1 may underlie Mandate 9.8 (especially in the use
of the verb ἐγκακέω). Also to be noted are Mandate 4.1.1 (cf.
Matt 5:28) and Mandate 4.1.6 (Matt 19:9; cf. Mark 10:11). These
passages can be explained either by dependence upon the Gospels,
or by oral tradition paralleling the Gospels. Finally,
Vision 4.2.6 applies the saying of Matt 26:24 (cf. Mark 14:21),
found also in 1 Clem. 46.8 (see above), to the disobedient
generally. The wording here, however, differs considerably from
both the Synoptics and Clement.

Several other possible allusions to the Gospels could be
listed here,/51/ but they are not as convincing as those just
mentioned. Two possible allusions to Acts (Vis. 4.2.4; cf.
Acts 4:12; and Man. 4.3.4; cf. Acts 1:24) again fall short of
showing literary dependence. Possible allusions to the Fourth
Gospel are also doubtful (cf. Sim. 9.12.1 and 5-6 with
John 10:7, 9; 14:6; Sim. 9.15.3 with John 3:3-5).

Since the Shepherd of Hermas may date from as late as the
middle of the second century, the probability that the written
Gospels would be quoted seems proportionately higher than for
the earlier Apostolic Fathers. It is all the more striking,
then, to observe that the quotations do not yield any high
degree of confidence that Hermas used the written Gospels.
Instead, tradition can adequately account for the data examined.

It is worth noting that this is true despite the probability
that Hermas knew the Gospels./52/ The importance of the
memorized tradition is probably reflected in <u>Vis.</u> 1.3.2, where
Hermas is told to keep instructing his children and that "the
righteous word daily repeated (ὁ λόγος ὁ καθημερινὸς ὁ δίκαιος,
as translated by G. Snyder) becomes master of all evil." Hermas
himself a few lines later "remembered" the profitable and gentle
words of the Lady. (Conversely, the spirit-filled prophets,
though they speak "as the Lord wills," are never said to speak
the words of the Lord, perhaps indicating that this latter
designation was reserved for the Gospel tradition; <u>Man.</u> 11.9.)
It is further worth noting that all the material pertinent to
the Gospel tradition in Hermas consists of sayings of Jesus--
precisely what would have been cherished above all in the oral
tradition.

7. 2 Clement

In the case of 2 Clement we also have a document that
probably derives from the middle of the second century.
2 Clement contains many allusions to the Gospels and, unlike
Hermas, several that may be regarded as deliberate citations
(with introductory formulae), with every appearance of having
been derived from the written Gospels.

Probably the most striking introductory formula is that
which occurs in 2.4 where a saying of Jesus is introduced, after
a quotation from Isaiah, with the words, καὶ ἑτέρα δὲ γραφὴ
λέγει. The saying, οὐκ ἦλθον καλέσαι δικαίους, ἀλλὰ ἁμαρτωλούς,
agrees verbatim with Mark 2:17 and, except for the lack of γάρ,
with Matt 9:13 (cf. Luke 5:32). The same saying occurs in
<u>Barnabas</u> 5.9 (see above) and in Justin, <u>Apology</u> 15.8./53/ The
same formula (without ἑτέρα) is elsewhere used to introduce
quotations from Ezekiel (<u>2 Clem.</u> 6.8) and Genesis (<u>2 Clem.</u> 14.2;
cf. a similar formula in 14.1). Here then a Gospel, or some
other written/54/ collection of the sayings of Jesus,/55/ is
unequivocally put on a par with the OT scriptures and cited
formally with the typical formula./56/

Several other quotations are introduced by the formula 'the
Lord says' or some variant thereof. Thus, in 8.5 a quotation is
introduced with the words λέγει γὰρ ὁ κύριος ἐν τῷ εὐαγγελίῳ.
Although the last part of the quotation (introduced with λέγω
γὰρ ὑμῖν ὅτι), ὁ πιστὸς ἐν ἐλαχίστῳ καὶ ἐν πολλῷ πιστός ἐστιν,
agrees verbatim with Luke 16:10, the first part (εἰ τὸ μικρὸν
οὐκ ἐτηρήσατε, τὸ μέγα τίς ὑμῖν δώσει) is not found in the
Gospels. This material could be accounted for as a glossing of

Luke 16:11-12 or Matt 25:21, 23, but it could be derived from an
extracanonical source./57/ Whatever the case, ἐν τῷ εὐαγγελίῳ
here probably refers to gospel tradition/58/ rather than any
specific Gospel. Again the two sayings involve the kind of
terse parallelism that could easily be explained as the result
of oral transmission.

In 9.11 we have the following formula and logion: καὶ γὰρ
εἶπεν ὁ κύριος Ἀδελφοί μου οὗτοί εἰσιν οἱ ποιοῦντες τὸ θέλημα
τοῦ πατρός μου. This saying is not found exactly in any of our
Gospels,/59/ but could be explained as a mixture of Luke 8:21
and Matt 12:49f. (cf. Mark 3:35). On the other hand, that this
might be the material of oral tradition is supported by the
occurrence of a similar form in other early writers./60/

In 6.1f. material similar to that of the Synoptics is
introduced with the formula λέγει δὲ ὁ κύριος:
(a) οὐδεὶς οἰκέτης δύναται δυσὶ κυρίοις δουλεύειν
(b) ἐὰν ἡμεῖς θέλωμεν καὶ θεῷ δουλεύειν καὶ μαμωνᾷ, ἀσύμφορον
    ἡμῖν ἐστίν
(c) τί γὰρ τὸ ὄφελος, ἐάν τις τὸν κόσμον ὅλον κερδήσῃ, τὴν δὲ
    ψυχὴν ζημιωθῇ;
Here we again encounter the by now familiar problem. Whereas
the first line is found verbatim in Luke 16:13, and nearly so in
Matt 6:24, the second line is only similar to Luke 16:13 and
Matt 6:24, and the third is close to, but not identical with,
Matt 16:26 (cf. Luke 9:25; Mark 8:16)./61/ Are we to consider
this the fusion of material from Matthew and Luke, explained by
quotation from memory, or is this material drawn from tradition
that has similarities to the Gospels? The answer, it seems,
could go either way.

The final passage with introductory formula (λέγει γὰρ ὁ
κύριος) is 5.2-4, which again may be a combination and free
rendering of such passages/62/ as Luke 10:3 (cf. Matt 10:16) and
Luke 12:4f. or Matt 10:28. A close parallel is found in Justin,
Apology 19.7. This passage may be just as easily explained as
resulting from tradition material (in this case something like Q
may be in view).

At 13.4, what is possibly Gospel material is introduced
with ὅτι λέγει ὁ θεός. The passage is again in an interesting
parallel form:
οὐ χάρις ὑμῖν, εἰ ἀγαπᾶτε τοὺς ἀγαπῶντας ὑμᾶς,
ἀλλὰ χάρις ὑμῖν, εἰ ἀγαπᾶτε τοὺς ἐχθροὺς καὶ τοὺς μισοῦντας ὑμᾶς.

Since the resemblance to Luke 6:32, 35 is more in thought than
wording,/63/ it may be that the words are derived from oral
tradition. This conclusion receives support from a minor, but
perhaps significant, point: in <u>Didache</u> 1.3 and Justin,
<u>Apology</u> 1.15, the words τοὺς μισοῦντας ὑμᾶς (lacking in the
Lucan parallel) occur in the same logion about love. Some,
however, have been inclined to attribute this passage to the
same apparently apocryphal gospel cited in 12.2--a citation also
occurring in Clement of Alexandria (<u>Strom</u>. 3.13.92) and said by
him to be from the Gospel to the Egyptians./64/

       A number of other significant passages deserve mention
here, all leaving us with the same question about derivation:
3.2 (Matt 10:32; cf. Luke 12:8);/65/ 4.2, 5 (Matt 7:21ff.;
13:42ff.; Luke 6:46; 13:26ff.; cf. Justin, <u>Apol</u>. 16.9-12;
<u>Dial</u>. 76.5)./66/ The question is even more difficult in the
case of allusions./67/ In one place (3.4) an OT citation
(Deut 6:5) in common with the Gospels is given, where the text
agrees with Mark 12:30 (cf. Matt 22:37; Luke 10:27), in the
words ἐξ ὅλης καρδίας καὶ ἐξ ὅλης τῆς διανοίας, against any
single text of the LXX. This could reflect knowledge of Mark,
but could equally well be the result of dependence upon oral
tradition, of even upon a Greek translation other than our LXX.
There are no convincing allusions to the Fourth Gospel in
2 Clement.

       Since 2 Clement was written in the middle of the second
century, we are probably right to assume some knowledge of the
Synoptic Gospels. The large number of citations and allusions
may furthermore be thought to constitute a cumulative argument
in favor of dependence upon the Gospels./68/ It is also worth
noting that in 2 Clement introductory formulae are used only for
the sayings of Jesus and that one of these refers to ἑτέρα
γραφή. Nevertheless, it is interesting that very few citations
of the words of Jesus are in verbatim agreement with any of the
Synoptics. This raises the questions not only of apocryphal
gospels, but also the possibility of dependence upon oral tradition./69/ Perhaps the author of 2 Clement can sometimes depend
on a written Gospel quoted from memory, but other times depend
on the oral tradition containing the sayings of Jesus. It is
difficult to draw a more precise conclusion from the data.

8. Justin Martyr
       The amount of material to be considered in Justin is much
too large to deal with adequately in the limited space that can
be given to it here. Fortunately, this material has been

surveyed by others and we can draw upon their studies./70/ Here all we can do is to give some representative examples and to consider what conclusions may be drawn from the data.

To begin with, there can be no doubt that Justin uses written sources for the sayings of Jesus, at least some of the time, if not all the time. In Apology 1.67.3 he places what he calls 'the memoirs of the apostles' (τὰ ἀπομνημονεύματα τῶν ἀποστόλων) alongside 'the writings of the prophets' (τὰ συγγράμματα τῶν προφητῶν) and notes that one or the other was read in Christian gatherings on Sundays. These memoirs at one point (Apol. 1.66.3) are identified as 'gospels' (ἃ καλεῖται εὐαγγέλια). The formulaic use of γράφω occurs with τὰ ἀπομνημονεύματα in several places (e.g., Dial. 101.3; 103.6; 104.1; 105.6; 106.3; 107.1). What has puzzled scholars down to the present is the relationship between these written memoirs of the apostles/71/ and our canonical Gospels./72/

Sanday has conveniently summarized the data of the Gospel quotations in Justin: 'The total result may be taken to be that ten passages are substantially exact, while twenty-five present slight and thirty-two marked variations.'/73/ Examples of practically verbatim quotation can be seen in Dialogue 49.5 (Matt 17:10-13); Dialogue 76.4 (Matt 8:11f.); Dialogue 105.6 (Matt 5:20); Dialogue 107.1 (Matt 16:4); and Apology 1.19.6 (Luke 18:27). Most scholars have concluded that passages such as these depend upon our canonical Gospels. The real question of course involves the variant quotations. One of Sanday's 'slightly variant' quotations (Apol. 1.16.13, but partially found also in Dial. 35.3a) is close to several passages in Matthew (24:5; 7:15, 16, 19), with partial parallels in other Gospels (Mark 13:6; Luke 21:8; 3:9)./74/ This phenomenon is very common in Justin's gospel material. In this particular example, where the same citation is found in two places in Justin, there are some variants between the two passages (often with one or the other agreeing with the Synoptic parallels). Where, however, two passages in Justin agree in the same variant against the Synoptics, it is obvious that the use of another source containing that variant could explain the data. Thus in the present case, Justin's quotations agree in the words ἔξωθεν μὲν ἐνδεδυμένοι δέρματα προβάτων against the ἐν ἐνδύμασι προβάτων of Matt 7:15. Bellinzoni examines twelve passages containing citations of Jesus' words occurring more than once in Justin's writings and on the basis of such data makes a strong case for Justin's dependence on an extracanonical source./75/

The case for such a source can of course be argued even
more strongly from the quotations in Justin that vary more
substantially from the canonical Gospels. A number of these
occur in the large collection of sayings found in
Apology 1.15-17, where Justin says he will cite 'a few precepts
(διδάγματα) given by Christ himself' (Apol. 1.14.4), adding that
'brief and concise utterances fell from him, for he was no
sophist, but his word was the power of God.'/76/ Bellinzoni has
rightly emphasized the catechetical nature of this material/77/
and its similarity to the sayings of Jesus used in 1 Clement 13,
Didache 1-6, and Barnabas 18-20./78/ In Apology 1.15-17 some
citations appear to be derived from Matthew and some from
Luke./79/ Others, however, seem to show a harmonization of two
Gospels (e.g., Apol. 1.15.9; cf. Matt 5:46, 47, 44 and
Luke 6:32, 33, 27, 28),/80/ or combination of different parts of
the same Gospel (e.g., Apol. 1.15.12; cf. Matt 16:26 and 6:20).
Apology 1.19.7 seems to be a harmonization of Matt 10:28 and
Luke 12:4, 5, and is similar to 2 Clem. 5.4. Bellinzoni
concludes that it is 'quite possible that Justin and 2 Clement
are here based on the same harmony of Matthew and Luke.'/81/

Only three non-synoptic sayings are found in Justin
according to Bellinzoni (Dial. 35.3b; 47.5; and Apol. 1.61.4).
Bellinzoni denies that any of these depend on a noncanonical
gospel, opting instead for 'traditional sources' such as
handbooks or liturgies. Only in the last case, in all of
Justin's quotations, does Bellinzoni see 'a pre-gospel
tradition' (cf. John 3:3-5), in this case one that goes back to
a baptismal liturgy./82/

It seems fair to say that the amount and the complexity of
the data in Justin point to several possibilities. First,
unlike the Apostolic Fathers, Justin tells us of the
availability of written sources, 'the memoirs of the apostles.'
It is particularly interesting to note that the references to
the memoirs occur in a section devoted mainly to narrative
rather than to sayings of Jesus (Dial. 100-107). Where the
latter do occur in this section they are not of the didactic or
catechetical character as those of Apology 1.15-17. In two
cases, verbatim citation is evident (105.5; cf. Luke 23:46;
107.1; cf. Matt 12:38). In Dialogue 100-107, then, we have
dependence upon written sources. It is probable that these
sources are the canonical Gospels—at least some of the time.
The possibility that some of Justin's variant quotations can be
accounted for by quotation from memory cannot be totally
dismissed, as Bellinzoni does./83/ On the other hand, the

possibility of dependence upon extracanonical written sources
must also be allowed. Although Bellinzoni correctly points out
that no direct evidence for the use of such gospels exists, it
cannot be denied that such gospels existed and could account for
some of the gospel material in Justin./84/

Apology 1.15-17 is probably to be explained differently.
Bellinzoni rightly points to the catechetical nature of the
sayings of Jesus here. He concludes that this material is to be
explained as derived from written catechisms composed by Justin
in which he harmonized sayings drawn from the Synoptic
Gospels./85/ These short didactic harmonies anticipated to an
extent the proper harmony of the Gospels that was eventually
produced by Justin's pupil, Tatian. Bellinzoni's conclusion
that many of the sayings of Jesus in Justin owe their form to
written catechisms composed by Justin is highly speculative. If
written sources are in view, they could be earlier than Justin.
On the other hand, there is no reason that the material in
question could not be derived from oral tradition. It was
ethical catechesis above all that was committed to memory in the
early church./86/

If this analysis is fair, then Justin knew and made use of
the canonical Gospels, possibly one or more written
extracanonical sources (gospels, short harmonies, etc.), as well
as possibly oral tradition involving catechetical instruction
based on the words of Jesus.

A Multiplicity of Sources: Written and Oral

Having surveyed the use of the sayings of Jesus in the
Apostolic Fathers and Justin, albeit in a cursory manner, we
must now draw some conclusions concerning the way in which the
Jesus tradition was handed on in the early church. To begin
with, some comments must be made about the difficulty of
determining dependence.

All the writers we have surveyed probably wrote after the
Gospels, or at least the Synoptics, were written./87/ It can
hardly be doubted that many of our writers, if not all, had
access to one or more of the Gospels. It is perhaps at first
surprising, then, that there is practically no deliberate
citation of these documents as 'scripture' analogous to the use
of the OT by these writers, i.e., with introductory formulae.
(The exceptions would appear to be Barn. 4.14, 2 Clem. 2.4, and
a few references in Justin.)/88/ Moreover, when the sayings of

Jesus in these writers are compared with the canonical Gospels,
they only very seldom approach verbatim agreement. In the main
they exhibit an allusory character, with the largest number
varying the most.

How is this state of affairs to be explained? The attempt
to account for the 'variant' quotations or allusions as the
result of recalling the texts of the Gospels from memory--the
simplest explanation--should not be too quickly dismissed./89/
This accords with the way in which these writers often cite the
OT./90/ (It is hardly possible to argue that variant OT
citations derive from extracanonical sources in every instance.)
And if the OT is frequently cited by memory, not to mention the
letters of Paul, why may this not be true of the Gospels? This
initially appealing solution fails, however, to take seriously
the fact that particularly in the case of the sayings of Jesus
we are dealing with something that probably existed in several
written forms--pre-canonical, canonical, and extracanonical--as
well as in oral form, since the gospel tradition, and
particularly the sayings of Jesus were transmitted orally both
before and after the Gospels were written. Moreover, the
written Gospel texts had clearly not yet acquired the status of
absolute authority enjoyed by the OT writings. It is this
complex situation that makes the problem of identifying sources
so difficult.

Further calling our attention to the significance of oral
tradition for these early Christian writers is the form which
the sayings of Jesus often take. Thus we have seen the careful
use of parallelism, both in structure and euphony, used as a
mnemonic device (most conspicuously in 1 Clem. 13.2; 46.8; and
Polycarp 2.3). We may further note in the passages just
mentioned the use of the verb μνημονεύω in the introductory
formulae in all three cases. Throughout the writings we have
studied, the sayings of Jesus are often terse, epigrammatic, and
of a proverbial character that made them ideal for memorization.
That this is true even of the sayings of Jesus in the Gospels
reflects not only the transmission of the materials orally
before they were taken up by the evangelists, but probably also
the style in which Jesus himself taught--probably to facilitate
retention./91/

It is important to realize the continuing existence and
influence of oral tradition containing the sayings of Jesus long
after the production of written accounts. The importance of
oral tradition continues even after the canonical Gospels were

written and available. It took time for the Gospels to become
regarded as holy scripture and to supplant the oral tradition,
although this probably began to happen around the middle of the
second century. Indeed, Justin's 'memoirs of the apostles' is
probably an important transitional stage on the way to the
authoritative fourfold Gospel corpus championed by Irenaeus
around A.D. 180.

One of the important witnesses to this continuing
importance of oral tradition is Papias, who was bishop of
Hierapolis early in the second century. According to Eusebius
(Hist. eccl. 3.39.4), Papias, who wrote a five-volume work
entitled 'Interpretation of the Oracles (λόγια) of the Lord,'
preferred wherever possible the 'words of the presbyters,' or
disciples, as handed on by any who had followed them, because 'I
did not suppose that information from books would help me so
much as the word of a living and surviving voice' (τὰ παρὰ ζώσης
φωνῆς καὶ μενούσης). This provides evidence not only of the,
currency of oral tradition early in the second century, but also
of the high esteem in which it was held. Memory obviously
played a great role in handing on the tradition (cf. Papias'
reference to it a few lines earlier: οὐδὲ τοῖς τὰς ἀλλοτρίας
ἐντολὰς μνημονεύουσιν, ἀλλὰ τοῖς τὰς παρὰ τοῦ κυρίου, Hist.
eccl. 3.39.3).

Eusebius also records a similar comment, this time from
Irenaeus, bishop of Lyons, made more than fifty years after
Papias' remark. In this passage Irenaeus recalls proudly his
acquaintance with Polycarp, who had in turn been taught by John
and 'others who had seen the Lord.' He mentions how Polycarp
'remembered their words (ὡς ἀπεμνημόνευσεν τοὺς λόγους αὐτῶν)
and what were the things concerning the Lord which he had heard
from them, and about his miracles and about his teaching' (Hist.
eccl. 5.20.6)./92/ Irenaeus then adds, 'I listened eagerly even
then to these things through the mercy of God which was given
me, and made notes of them, not on paper but in my heart
(ὑπομνηματιζόμενος αὐτὰ οὐκ ἐν χάρτῃ, ἀλλ' ἐν τῇ ἐμῇ καρδίᾳ);
and ever by the grace of God do I truly ruminate on them.'
Irenaeus in this way testifies to the importance of oral
tradition even late in the second century and to the special
importance of the tradition about Jesus' words and deeds.
R. P. C. Hanson is thus essentially correct when he concludes,
'the situation of the Church in the years circa 60 to circa 160
A.D. is precisely this one, when written and oral tradition are
circulating in the Church side by side.'/93/

The transition from oral tradition to written tradition as
the authoritative source of information about Jesus was neither
sudden nor uniform. It took time for this transition to occur.
As Gerhardsson puts it, 'It appears unnatural to regard living
traditional material as something written, simply because
written versions have come into being.'/94/ This slowness in
the supplanting of oral tradition by written documents reflects
the milieu of the times, in which the careful handing down of
tradition by faithful individuals with highly practiced memories
was a common thing. But oral tradition eventually had to give
way to the written accounts of the ministry of Jesus. It is
true, as Westcott writes, that 'those who had heard the living
voice of the Apostles were unlikely to appeal to their written
words.'/95/ The 'living voice of the Apostles' could indeed be
perpetuated by those who had heard them, but it could not be
maintained much beyond this second generation of witnesses, and
hence the transition began to occur, inevitably, as the second
century wore on./96/

With the wide variety of sources available, both oral and
written, as well as the complicating possibility of quotation of
written sources by memory, it is an exceptionally difficult task
to determine the sources used by the Apostolic Fathers and
Justin Martyr. The number and complexity of possibilities are
such that it is impossible to decide consistently in favor of
one simple explanation of the data. In these circumstances, the
possibility of dependence upon the canonical Gospels cannot be
raised to probability, for example, merely by a cumulative
argument based solely on a large number of allusions.
Furthermore, because of the probable overlapping of oral
tradition and certain written sources, it may well be that some
of the early Christian writers are simultaneously dependent on
both written sources and oral tradition. In short, the
distinction between scripture and tradition, so clear and
important to us, is very much more difficult to make for
Christian writers up to the middle of the second century. In
that sense, our inability to determine whether written or oral
sources lie behind the sayings of Jesus in our writers is
unimportant. For the early Church it is the words of Jesus that
are important, whether they are transmitted in oral or written
form.

The Locus of Authority

For the first century and even longer, authority for the
early Church lay not in oral tradition or written sources, as

such, but preeminently in the person and hence the words of
Jesus, however mediated./97/ Jesus was the exalted Lord of the
Church and the words he spoke were of absolute authority.
Indeed, the authority of the words of Jesus was held to be equal
to, or even to surpass, the authority of the OT./98/ Thus Jesus
is sometimes said to be the speaker in OT texts (e.g.,
1 Clem. 22 [Pss 34:11-17; 32:10]). And at one point (13.2),
having just cited an OT passage, Clement writes 'most of all
(μάλιστα) remembering the words of the Lord Jesus.'

It is remarkable how frequently the words of Jesus are put
alongside OT quotations without differentiation (e.g., Did. 8.2;
Barn. 10.12; 2 Clem. 13.2ff.). Clement of Rome can refer
alternately to 'the commandments of Christ' (τὰ τοῦ χριστοῦ
παραγγέλματα, 49.1) and 'the commandments of God' (τὰ
προστάγματα τοῦ θεοῦ, 50.3). When exhorting his readers to be
subject to church authorities, Ignatius can on one occasion
refer to 'the law (νόμος) of Jesus Christ' (Magn. 2.1) and, on
another, refer to 'the command (ἐντολή) of God' (Smyrn. 8.1).
He can sometimes refer simply to 'the commandments (ἐντολαί) of
Jesus Christ' (Eph. 9.2; cf. 2 Clem. 17.6). Indeed, when these
early Christian writers refer to 'the commandments of the Lord,'
it is often difficult to know whether OT commandments or sayings
of Jesus are in view (e.g., Ignatius, Magn. 4.1; Trall. 13.2;
Phld. 1.2; Polycarp, Phil. 4.1; Did. 4.13; Barn. 19.2;
2 Clem. 17.3; Hermas, frequently; cf. the simple ἐντολή in
Did. 1.5). The author of Barnabas speaks about 'the new law (ὁ
καινὸς νόμος) of our Lord Jesus Christ' (2.6) and argues that
Christians understand the commandments 'righteously' (δικαίως)
and hence can 'announce the commandments (ἐντολαί) as the Lord
wished' (10.12). Justin also refers to keeping the commandments
(ἐντολαί) of Christ (e.g., Dial. 95.3; 116.2; 123.9; 134.4), and
at one point can say that 'an eternal and final law--namely
Christ--has been given to us' (Dial. 11.2). Another striking
example of the absolute authority of Christ, wherein he is
equated with truth, is found in Ignatius, Phld. 8.2. Here in
response to the argument that 'if I do not find it in the
charters (τὰ ἀρχεῖα, i.e., the OT), I do not believe in the
Gospel,' Ignatius' final appeal is to his conviction that 'the
charters are Jesus Christ, the inviolable charter is his cross,
and death, and resurrection, and the faith that is through him.'

All of this is in keeping with the view of these writers
not merely that God was in Christ, but--as these writers clearly
make explicit--that Christ is God (see, e.g., 1 Clem. 16.2;
Ign. Eph. 18.2; Smyrn. 1.1; Pol. 8.3; Justin, Apol. 1.63.15ff.;
Dial. 59.1; 126.2)./99/

Such an exalted view of Christ leads naturally to the
importance of those chosen by him to be Apostles. For they are
seen to partake of his authority in a special and unique way.
Clement of Rome states this viewpoint clearly: 'The Apostles
received the Gospel from the Lord Jesus Christ, Jesus Christ was
sent from God. The Christ therefore is from God and the
Apostles from the Christ' (1 Clem. 42.1f.). Ignatius reflects
the same view when he speaks of the subjection of the Apostles
to Christ and Christ to the Father (Magn. 13.3; cf. Smryn. 8.1;
Trall. 3.1) and when he speaks of Christian service 'to the
honor of the Father, of Jesus Christ, and of the Apostles'
(Trall. 12.2). According to Polycarp (Phil. 6.3) and Barnabas
(5.9), it is the Apostles who were appointed to preach the
Gospel. The special importance of the Apostles is also noted by
Hermas (Vis. 3.5.1), 2 Clement (14.2),/100/ and of course Justin
(e.g., Apol. 1.45.5; 50.12; Dial. 42.1; 110.2), who also refers
to 'God's voice spoken by the Apostles of Christ' (Dial. 119.6).
It is clear from these references that our writers carefully
distinguish themselves from the Apostles. On this point
explicitly, see Ign. Trall. 3.3; Rom. 4.3; and Polycarp,
Phil. 3.2.

The Apostles thus hold a special position as those
especially appointed by Christ to propagate the gospel. As
Jesus' words are put beside those of God in the OT, so the words
of the Apostles are put beside those of Jesus. Thus Ignatius
exhorts, 'Be diligent therefore to be confirmed in the
ordinances (δόγματα) of the Lord and the Apostles' (Magn. 13.1).
To his Apostles Jesus entrusts as a holy tradition the account
of his words and deeds. In short, the Apostles are entrusted
with 'the gospel' which they are called to proclaim in the
Church. The term τὸ εὐαγγέλιον is regularly used in referring
to this holy tradition./101/ 'Gospel' thus refers to the
tradition in its essential oneness--i.e., the tradition as a
whole, in any form, is regarded as the gospel./102/ Only later
does the εὐαγγέλιον come to be applied in an exclusive way to
particular written documents./103/ We begin to see this
unequivocally first in Justin, who not only refers repeatedly to
the written 'memoirs' of the Apostles (Dial. 100-106), but
identifies them explicitly as 'Gospels' (εὐαγγέλια,
Apol. 1.66.3). In his only two other uses of the word
εὐαγγέλιον, he also refers clearly to written sources. Thus
Trypho refers to 'the so-called Gospel' (τῷ λεγομένῳ εὐαγγελίῳ)
he has read (Dial. 10.2) and Justin refers to something written
in the Gospel (Dial. 100.1).

For the Apostolic Fathers and Justin, then, authority
resides in Jesus and particularly in his words (and deeds) as
mediated by the apostolic witnesses. Above all, the Apostles
held the responsibility of faithfully transmitting the
tradition. They were primarily 'witnesses' to the truth about
Jesus, as the NT puts it (cf. Acts 1:8, 22; 2:32; 5:32). Thus
it was finally the tradition that was holy and authoritative.
Only with the gradual passing of the Apostles and those who had
had contact with them, together with the concomitant threat to
the integrity of the tradition, did the authority of this
tradition come to lodge specifically in γραφή. Even then, there
was a transitional period wherein the tradition of Jesus passed
on in oral form retained authority alongside the written
Gospels. Although the tradition was 'one,' it existed in
multiple forms and undoubtedly contained variant elements. The
care with which the tradition was transmitted must next be
examined.

Variation and Care of Transmission

It seems obvious that words spoken by Jesus himself, and
handed on from the beginning by his special delegates, the
Apostles--thus, a holy tradition--should be carefully and
faithfully transmitted. The absolute authority of the words of
Jesus was, as we have seen, undisputed in the early Church.
Words of such unequalled authority, from the Lord of the Church,
were bound to have been treasured and regarded as of the utmost
importance.

We have, furthermore, in the first century of the Church a
milieu that was favorable to the transmission of material
orally. B. Gerhardsson has shown the importance of memory in
the ancient world, both in Hellenism and in Judaism./104/
Memories were particularly practiced in Judaism, of course,
where oral Torah was handed down with great care and skill.
Whether or not Jesus taught his Apostles in the way that a rabbi
taught his disciples,/105/ it seems hard to deny a basic
similarity in the transmission by memory of a holy tradition.
This is not to deny that some of the tradition may very early
have been committed to writing,/106/ but only to affirm that the
authority initially lay in the tradition and not in any written
sources. The fact that the form of certain sayings of Jesus as
found in both the Gospels and the Apostolic Fathers and Justin
seems especially designed to facilitate memorization itself
underlines the importance of oral tradition in the early stages
of gospel transmission. Thus the Apostles and their associates

functioned in an environment where the handing on of tradition
by memory was a finely practiced art.

But how is the variation encountered in the sayings of
Jesus as found in the Gospels and the early Christian writers
compatible with this argument about the effectiveness of memory
and the care exercised in the transmission of the tradition?
First it must be emphasized that although the sayings of Jesus
are reproduced freely and adapted to special purposes, the
amount of significant variation between the same sayings in our
sources is relatively small. It is particularly worth noting
that the sayings of Jesus, and especially his ethical teachings,
vary much less than the narrative materials about his deeds.
Ethical catechesis--the words of Jesus governing conduct--it
seems, perhaps because of the stress on its memorization by new
converts, is found with the lowest degree of significant
variation.

Undeniably, then, we encounter in our writers a variation
in the presentation of the words of Jesus, but this variation it
must be stressed is at least for the most part formal rather
than substantial. The situation is similar to what we encounter
in the Synoptic Gospels, in that sayings drawn from sources are
reproduced rather freely and with adaptation to new contexts.
The evangelists, however, use their sources, if anything, with
greater freedom, a greater degree of what might be called
interpretative adaptation, than do the Apostolic Fathers and
Justin Martyr./107/ The impact of this transmission of the
tradition orally is to be seen both in the Gospels and our
writers. Indeed, a possible explanation of the fact that the
sayings of Jesus in the Apostolic Fathers most often are closest
to the Gospel of Matthew could well be the result of the
latter's catechetical design. That is, so far as the sayings of
Jesus are concerned, Matthew is dependent upon tradition, probably oral and for the most part catechetical. To speculate
further, it may be that many of the textual variants in the
manuscripts of the Gospels were originally caused by a copyist's
knowledge of the same saying of Jesus through local oral
tradition. Q may have been oral tradition circulating in
different locales with minor variations. Somewhat later
noncanonical gospels and written collections of the sayings of
Jesus also eventually utilized the gospel tradition (both oral
and written) in varying degree, producing further mutations of
the tradition and introducing new, and sometimes alien,
material.

Notwithstanding the minor variations, the manner in which
our authors preserve the substance of the sayings of Jesus
points to the impressive tenacity of oral tradition in the
period of the Apostolic Fathers. We bring what is clearly an
improper and anachronistic standard to the subject of quotations
in this era when we expect verbatim agreement. Verbal exactness
was not a desideratum in that age as it has become in ours.
Occasionally, of course, much could be made to hinge on one
word. But in the main it was the substance, the meaning, that
counted, not the form or the detail--even when the authority of
the words was of the highest order. This attitude is apparent
in the free manner in which the OT is quoted by NT writers. This
prompted T. W. Manson to write the following: 'Odd as it may
seem to us, the freedom with which they handled the Biblical
text is a direct result of the supreme importance which they
attached to it.'/108/

Faithfulness to the tradition is not incompatible with
minor variations and alterations of form. The Apostles
perpetuated the tradition in faithfulness to Jesus' teaching;
those who followed the Apostles continued that tradition. The
situation was soon complicated, however, by not only corruptions
of the tradition, but also by the springing up of alien logia
that were attributed to Jesus. Cullmann rightly cautions that
by A.D. 150 oral tradition was hardly always reliable./109/ He
goes too far, however, when he implies that by 150 it was
totally unreliable and when he therefore restricts reliable oral
tradition to the time of the Apostles. Probably oral tradition
was reliable for another generation after the Apostles, although
as time passed it had to compete increasingly with counterfeit
traditions. And eventually, of course, as the second century
wore on, the canonical Gospels, Justin's 'memoirs of the
Apostles,' assumed a normative position, supplanting fully the
oral tradition.

Conclusions

To treat all of the Apostolic Fathers together with Justin
Martyr in a single article, as we have done, is difficult and
could be misleading. As well as writing in different contexts
and with different purposes, these writers span more than half a
century in an era of ferment and transition. The state of the
gospel tradition, not to mention the status of the Gospels
themselves, is different at the end of this period than it was
at the beginning. Nevertheless, the scope of this study may be
helpful in noting both the shifts that occurred and the

significant continuity of the gospel tradition in this period. Our conclusions may now be set forth in a summarizing way.

1. The question of the dependence of the logia Jesu upon our canonical Gospels, at least in the case of the earlier Apostolic Fathers (i.e., apart from 2 Clement and Justin), is virtually irresolvable. In some places it seems quite clear from the form of the sayings that oral tradition is the source of the sayings; in other places, however, it seems impossible to rule out the possibility of quotation of the Gospels from memory. Our inability to decide the issue is ultimately not important, for the reasons that follow.

2. The situation from the end of the first century to the middle of the second is that the gospel tradition concerning the words and works of Jesus exists side by side in the form of oral tradition and written Gospels. Thus, the two famous scholars who earlier discussed the question of the source of the sayings of Jesus in the Apostolic Fathers, Sanday and Westcott, were not without warrant in their respective conclusions./110/ Each, however, has overstated the case for his position, Sanday insisting exclusively upon literary dependence (but allowing noncanonical sources)/111/ and Westcott upon oral tradition./112/ In reality, a transition was slowly taking place. Oral tradition and the Gospels were both available, and the latter were slow in assuming the status of canonicity. But as the decades of the second century pass the probability increases that writers such as 2 Clement and Justin are dependent at least to some extent upon the written Gospels.

3. Throughout these writings it is clear that the sayings of Jesus are of the utmost importance. They, if anything, constitute a holy tradition mediated by the Apostles and their circle. It is in this tradition of the sayings of Jesus that authority finally resides. And it was accordingly a matter of indifference whether these sayings were derived from oral or written sources.

4. The oral tradition containing the ethical teaching of Jesus, particularly because of its value as catechesis for new converts, assumed the greatest importance in the early Church, and for our writers. The majority of allusions to the gospel tradition in our writers are to this material. This same material is taken up in the Gospels, especially in Matthew, and in extracanonical written sources, and thus may be said to be a widespread or common tradition.

5. Although this tradition is found with minor variations
in form, in its substance it remains essentially the same, thus
testifying to the general effectiveness of oral tradition in
faithfully preserving the content of the sayings. The
tradition, the gospel, remains one entity in a variety of
manifestations, a unified tradition, recognizably tracing back,
through the Apostles who preserved it, to the Lord who first
spoke it.

6. Finally, the implication of all of this for the
historical reliability of the words of Jesus as recorded in the
Synoptic Gospels is not insignificant. It may plausibly be
argued that, if the tenacity and relative stability of oral
tradition in the first half of the second century was as
impressive as we have seen it to be, the trustworthiness of that
oral tradition in the middle decades of the first century was,
if anything, even more substantial. The very fact that the oral
tradition reflected in the Apostolic Fathers and Justin Martyr
was so similar to the sayings of Jesus as contained in the
written Gospels thus, at the same time, confirms the reliability
of the latter which were of course themselves originally
dependent on oral tradition. The basic agreement between the
written accounts of Jesus' words and the oral tradition later
than the Gospels is evidence both that the words of Jesus were
treasured from the beginning and that they were handed down with
the utmost care. We may have a high degree of confidence, then,
that the sayings of Jesus in our Synoptic Gospels are true
representations of what our Lord himself spoke.

Notes

/1/See also especially D. Dungan, The Sayings of Jesus in the
Churches of Paul (Oxford: Basil Blackwell, 1971).
/2/J. A. T. Robinson has recently revived the view of
G. Edmundson, in the Bampton Lectures of 1913 (The Church in
Rome in the First Century [London: Longmans, Green & Co.,
1913]), that Clement's epistle is to be dated in early A.D. 70
(Redating the New Testament [London: SCM, 1976], 327-35). This
early date, however, is extremely unlikely because of certain
references in the epistle that presuppose the lapse of several
decades since the time of the Apostles (see especially chaps.
42-44).
/3/On the Didache, see J.-P. Audet, La Didaché, Études Bibliques
(Paris, 1958), who suggests a date as early as ca. 60. The
recent article by Peter Richardson and Martin B. Shukster,

'Barnabas, Nerva, and the Yavnean Rabbis' (JTS 34.1 [1983]:
31-55) dates The Letter of Barnabas just after the reign of
Nerva (A.D. 96-98). R. A. Kraft argues that the present form of
Barnabas dates from around the middle of the second century (The
Apostolic Fathers, vol. 3 [New York: Nelson, 1965]).
/4/We here assume the common dating of these writings, although
it is possible to date them earlier. Thus K. P. Donfried dates
2 Clement at the end of the first century, just after 1 Clement
(The Setting of Second Clement in Early Christianity, NovTSup 38
[Leiden: E. J. Brill, 1974]). R. M. Grant prefers a dating of
about 138-142 (The Apostolic Fathers, vol. 1 [New York: Nelson,
1964]). As for Hermas, Grant says that "none of it need be
dated much later than 140" (ibid., 85). Others prefer to date
the first four Visions during the reign of Trajan (e.g., S.
Giet, followed by G. Snyder). Giet puts the remainder late, but
Snyder argues that, except for Similitude 9, the remainder of
the Shepherd was written only a little later than Visions 1-4
(The Apostolic Fathers, vol. 6 [Camden, NJ: Nelson, 1968], 24).
The question of the precise dating of these documents does not
affect the substance of the arguments of this paper.
/5/The martyrdoms by their special nature have little to offer
us for the subject of our investigation. Papias and Quadratus
are only known to us indirectly and in a fragmentary way through
Irenaeus and Eusebius and a few later sources. Papias, who
wrote a multi-volume 'Exposition of the Dominical Oracles' that
has not survived, made remarks about the Gospels and the
transmission of the tradition which, because of their early
second century date, are interesting and significant for the
present study.
/6/The following are particularly relevant: The New Testament in
the Apostolic Fathers by A Committee of the Oxford Society of
Historical Theology (Oxford: Clarendon, 1905); W. Sanday, The
Gospels in the Second Century (London: Macmillan, 1876);
T. Zahn, Geschichte des neutestamentlichen Kanons, (2 vols.;
Erlangen, 1888-92); B. F. Westcott, A General Survey of the
History of the Canon of the New Testament (London: Macmillan,
1896); E. Massaux, Influence de l'Évangile de saint Matthieu sur
la littérature chrétienne avant saint Irénée, Universitas
Catholica Lovaniensis Series 2, Tomus 42 (Louvain, 1950); H.
Köster, Synoptische Überlieferung bei den apostolischen Vätern,
TU 65 (Berlin, 1957); R. M. Grant, The Apostolic Fathers, vol.
1: An Introduction (London; New York; Toronto, 1964); idem, The
Formation of the New Testament (London, 1965); D. A. Hagner, The
Use of the Old and New Testaments in Clement of Rome, NovTSup 34
(Leiden, 1973). (This last volume includes discussion of the
Apostolic Fathers and Justin Martyr, pp. 272-312.)

/7/For a full display of the Synoptic parallels, see D. A.
Hagner, ibid., 136. For a more complete discussion of this
passage in Clement, see pp. 135-51, of which the present
material is a summary.
/8/The modifications could be the result of Polycarp's
harmonizing the sayings with the written Gospel texts, although
this would entail knowledge of both Matthew and Luke. Cf.
Köster, op. cit., 121. On the other hand, it could be that
Polycarp reflects mutants of oral tradition that were either
caused by, or taken up in, the written Gospels.
/9/For a full list of allusions, see Lightfoot, The Apostolic
Fathers, vol.1, part 1 (London, 1890), 149-53.
/10/E.g., Lightfoot, op. cit., 1.2.52; 2.3.325; Köster, op.
cit., 115f. The later occurrences of Clement's passage in
Clement of Alexandria (Strom. 2.91.2), where all seven maxims
are quoted in practically verbatim form, is unquestionably
dependent upon Clement of Rome.
/11/Among scholars who conclude in favor of dependence upon oral
tradition are J. Knox, W. Sanday, and E. Massaux.
/12/Op. cit., 168f.
/13/E.g., Lightfoot, op. cit., 1.2.52; Zahn, op. cit., 1:917;
F. X. Funk, Patres Apostolici (Tübingen, 1901), 1:116f.
/14/E.g., V. H. Stanton, The Gospels as Historical Documents
(Cambridge, 1903), 1:7; E. Massaux, op. cit., 12f.; L. E.
Wright, Alterations of the Words of Jesus as Quoted in the
Literature of the Second Century, Harvard Historical Monographs
25 (Cambridge, MA, 1952); Köster, op. cit., 15; Köster is cited
approvingly by K. Beyschlag, Clemens Romanus und der
Frühkatholizismus, BHT (Tübingen, 1966), 30f.; R. M. Grant,
Formation, 79; idem, Apostolic Fathers, 1:40; 2:36. Other
scholars argue for an extracanonical written source. The
conclusion of the Oxford Committee (op. cit., 61) is worth
quoting in full: 'We incline to think that we have in Clem. Rom.
a citation from some written or unwritten form of 'catechesis'
as to our Lord's teaching, current in the Roman Church, perhaps
a local form which may go back to a time before our Gospels
existed.'
/15/'Extracanonical' is not quite the right word for this
tradition if it represents the same stream, allowing for natural
variations, from which the evangelists drew in composing the
Gospels.
/16/The two Greek MSS of Clement (A and C) read σκανδαλίσαι in
parallelism with line b. The reading of the early versions
(Latin, Syriac, and Coptic) and Clement of Alexandria, quoting
his Roman namesake, is to be preferred as the harder reading.
The Greek MSS have probably been altered to agree more closely
with the Synoptic Gospels.

/17/For a full display of the texts, see Hagner, op. cit., 152.
/18/In Stromata 4.105-119, Clement gives what is virtually a
précis of his namesake's epistle. Above (note 8) we have also
noted that the Alexandrian cites the maxims of 13.2.
/19/A reconstruction of the underlying Greek is available in
Harnack, Marcion: Das Evangelium vom Fremden Gott (Leipzig,
1921), 204.
/20/Others that are notable are Dialogue of Adamantius, De Recta
in Deum Fide, sec. 1, and Apostolic Constitutions 5.14.4.
/21/Several scholars draw this conclusion: e.g., Lightfoot, op.
cit., 1.2.141; Zahn, op. cit., 1:918f.; Funk, op. cit., 159f.;
and O. Knoch, Eigenart und Bedeutung der Eschatologie im
theologischen Aufriss des ersten Clemensbrief, Theophaneia,
Beiträge zur Religions- und Kirchengeschichte des Altertums 17
(Bonn, 1964), 72. Cf. above, note 11. Strangely, Massaux also
prefers literary dependence upon Matthew in this instance,
having argued for oral tradition in explaining 13.2. Op. cit.,
26. Cf., too, V. H. Stanton, op. cit., 13.
/22/Διαστρέψαι would appear to be stylistic variation,
substituting for σκανδαλίσαι. But it is worth noting that it
contains the same number of syllables and the same ending.
/23/Among scholars favoring this conclusion are the Oxford
Committee; R. Knopf, Die Apostolischen Väter, HZNT, 122;
E. Goodspeed, Formation of the New Testament, 9f.
/24/The following are the more conspicuous possible allusions:
23.4 (Mark 4:26-29); 27.5 (Matt 5:18 or 24:35); 30.3 (Matt 7:21,
but cf. James 2:14-26); 48.4 (Matt 7:13f.); 16.17
(Matt 11:29f.); 7.4 (Matt 26:28). For a discussion of these,
see Hagner, op. cit., 164-71.
/25/For the texts in parallel columns, see ibid., 172, and for
other such OT citations, 175-78.
/26/The same may be true of 1 Clement 18.1, which in quoting
Ps 88:21 agrees with the text of the same quotation found in
Acts 13:22. For an examination of the evidence concerning
Clement's knowledge of Acts, see ibid., 253-63. I am inclined
now to alter my estimate concerning dependence from probability
to possibility.
/27/Despite the claims of a few scholars, it is highly
improbable that Clement knew the Fourth Gospel. See ibid.,
264-68.
/28/Eusebius (Hist. eccl. 3.36.11), on the other hand, professes
not to know the source of the quotation.
/29/Köster (op. cit., 24-61) argues that Ignatius is dependent
only upon oral tradition for all three passages. R. M. Grant,
disagreeing strongly with Köster, concludes in favor of
dependence upon the Synoptics, which are cited from memory. (The

Apostolic Fathers, 1:60f.) The Oxford Committee similarly favor
dependence upon Matthew and Luke. Op. cit., 79f.
/30/Matt 15:13 may be alluded to in both Trall. 11.1 and
Phld. 3.1; cf. too, Smyrn. 6.1 (Matt 19:12); Eph. 5.2
(Matt 18:19, 20); Eph. 6.1 (Matt 10:40); Eph. 14.2 (Matt 12:33;
Luke 6:44); and Magn. 5.2 (Matt 22:19).
/31/Kümmel is thus much too confident about Ignatius' dependence
on Matthew. Introduction to the New Testament, rev. ed.
(London: SCM, 1975), 119. See the more cautious analysis of J.
Smit Sibinga, 'Ignatius and Matthew,' NovT 8 (1966):263-83.
Smit Sibinga denies that Ignatius knew the Gospel of Matthew,
arguing instead that Ignatius probably knew the M material in a
pre-Matthean form. Smit Sibinga refers to this as a written
document and does not consider the possibility that it could
well have been oral tradition.
/32/E.g., Phld. 7.1 (John 3:8); Magn. 7.1 (John 8:28f.); and
Rom. 7, which contains a number of apparent allusions (cf.
John 16:11; 4:10, 14; 7:38; 6:51). Westcott writes of this
chapter: 'It is, I think, quite impossible to understand the
Ignatian passage without presupposing a knowledge of the
discourse [John 6] recorded by St. John' (op. cit., 61). See,
further, C. Maurer, Ignatius von Antiochien und das
Johannesevangelium (Zürich, 1949).
/33/None of Ignatius' OT quotations reflects influence from the
Gospels.
/34/The question of whether this epistle as we know it was
originally two letters, with chapters 13 and 14 comprising an
earlier letter (as P. N. Harrison argued, Polycarp's Two
Epistles to the Philippians [Cambridge, 1936]), has no bearing
on our study. The last few chapters (10-14) survive for the
most part only in Latin translation.
/35/Cf. the opinion of the Oxford Committee (op. cit., 103):
'But this quotation might well be due to oral tradition; or it
might be from a document akin to our Gospels, though not
necessarily those Gospels themselves.'
/36/E.g., 5.2 (Mark 9:35; cf. Matt 20:28); 12.3 (Matt 5:44;
Luke 6:27).
/37/The few OT quotations in Polycarp are not paralleled in the
Gospels.
/38/E.g., 1.2 (Acts 2:24); 2.1 (Acts 10:42); 6.3 (Acts 7:52);
12.2 (Acts 26:18).
/39/Cf. 5.2 (John 5:21); 12.3 (John 15:16).
/40/The Western text (D) of Acts 15:20, 29 contains the negative
form of the Golden Rule (as in Did. 1.2). But the saying is
probably derived independently from oral tradition in both
cases.

/41/<u>Did.</u> 3.7: οἱ πραεῖς κληρονομήσουσι τὴν γῆν in verbatim
agreement with the LXX (Ps 36:11) except for δέ and the omission
of the definite article before γῆν.
/42/9.2 (John 15:1); 9.3 (John 17:3); 10.3 (John 6:45ff.)
/43/For a detailed study leading to a similar conclusion, see
R. Glover, 'The Didache's Quotations and the Synoptic Gospels,'
<u>NTS</u> 5 (1958-59):12-29. Glover argues that the Didache's sources
were those used also by Matthew and Luke.
/44/Although <u>Barn.</u> 18-21 is parallel to <u>Did.</u> 1-6, Barnabas lacks
the abundant Synoptic material found in <u>Did.</u> 1.
/45/Westcott, the Oxford Committee, Köster, and Kraft (<u>Apostolic</u>
<u>Fathers</u>, vol. 3 [New York: Nelson, 1965]; see too his 1961
Harvard dissertation, 'The Epistle of Barnabas, Its Quotations
and their Sources') incline away from the Gospel as Barnabas'
source here; Sanday and Grant, on the other hand, accept Matthew
as the source.
/46/This citation is made to refer to Christ, rather than Cyrus,
by reading κυρίῳ for LXX's κύρῳ.
/47/Some interesting allusions to details of the passion
narrative are found in Barnabas. E.g., 6.6 (cf. Matt 27:35;
Mark 15:24; Luke 23:34); 7.3 (Matt 27:34, 48); 7.9 (Matt 27:28;
26:63f.; Mark 15:17; 14:61f.; Luke 22:69f.).
/48/E.g., 6.3 (John 6:51, 58); 11.1-8 (John 19:34); 12.7
(John 3:14f.).
/49/Only one introductory formula (ὡς γέγραπται) occurs in this
long work, and that introduces a quotation from the
extracanonical Book of Eldad and Modad. Unlike most of the
other Apostolic Fathers, Hermas contains no OT citations.
/50/The Oxford Committee concludes, 'We can hardly doubt that
this is a quotation' (op. cit., 121). Grant also regards
dependence upon Matthew as 'possible.' <u>Apostolic Fathers</u>, 1:84.
Köster, on the other hand, sees no dependence upon the written
Gospels in Hermas; op. cit., 254f.
/51/See <u>The New Testament in the Apostolic Fathers</u>.
/52/C. Taylor was probably right that Hermas knew the four
Gospels, even if his argument about the references to 'four
feet' and 'four elements' (<u>Vis.</u> 3.13.3) and 'four tiers'
(<u>Sim.</u> 9.4.3) in this connection is dubious. <u>The Witness of</u>
<u>Hermas to Four Gospels</u> (London, 1892).
/53/For a display of the texts here (and throughout this
section), see K. P. Donfried, <u>The Setting of Second Clement in</u>
<u>Early Christianity</u>, NovTSup 38 (Leiden, 1974), 57.
/54/Donfried denies that γραφή necessarily refers to a written
source, arguing that it only suggests authority, op. cit., 58f.
But if authority were the concern, the author of 2 Clement could
have used λέγει ὁ κύριος, as he does so often, rather than

γραφή, especially if Donfried is correct that for the author,
the Lord, and not 'scripture,' was what was finally
authoritative.
/55/As Köster argues, but without good cause.
/56/The only comparable use of a formula with Gospel material is
Barn. 4.14, but there more uncertainty exists about the source
of the quotation. See above, 242.
/57/The Oxford Committee points to the same saying as found in
Irenaeus (Adv. Haer. 2.34.3), noting that Irenaeus does not use
his regular introductory formula and that his use of the
material presupposes a context such as that of Matthew 25. They
conclude that the saying had 'currency outside the Gospels' (op.
cit., 133). Donfried concludes in favor of 'a non-synoptic
source' (op. cit., 73).
/58/According to Donfried, εὐαγγέλιον means 'the oral message of
salvation' (op. cit., 72).
/59/The texts are displayed in Donfried, op. cit., 74.
/60/Epiphanius (Haer. 30.14.5), citing the Gospel of the
Ebionites: οὗτοί εἰσιν οἱ ἀδελφοί μου καὶ ἡ μήτηρ, οἱ ποιοῦντες
τὰ θελήματα τοῦ πατρός μου. Clement of Alexandria, Ecl.
Proph. 20: ἀδελφοί μου γάρ, φησὶν ὁ κύριος, καὶ συγκληρονόμοι οἱ
ποιοῦντες τὸ θέλημα τοῦ πατρός μου.
/61/For the second and third lines, see the display in Donfried,
op. cit., 83.
/62/Texts displayed in Donfried, op. cit., 69.
/63/For texts, see Donfried, op. cit., 78.
/64/Donfried, however, denies that 12.2 is dependent on the
Gospel of the Egyptians, pointing out that the Gospel of Thomas
(23) contains a much closer parallel. Donfried argues for a
source used in common by the Gospel of Thomas and 2 Clement (op.
cit., 77).
/65/Donfried displays these texts, op. cit., 60.
/66/Donfried displays these texts, op. cit., 64-65.
/67/E.g., 5.5 and 6.7 (Matt 11:28f.; 25:45f.); and 2.5, 7
(Luke 19:10).
/68/Grant, for example, allows knowledge of the three Synoptics
and an apocryphal gospel. Apostolic Fathers, 1:45. Westcott
seems to conclude in favor of free use of the Gospels, op. cit.,
185. Köster argues for a written collection of sayings other
than the Gospels, op. cit., 109f.
/69/Donfried seems to favor Gemeindetradition as the source for
the words of Jesus in 2 Clement (op. cit., 79ff., 93).
/70/The most recent full study is by A. J. Bellinzoni, The
Sayings of Jesus in the Writings of Justin Martyr, NovTSup 17
(Leiden, 1967). Convenient surveys are also available in
Sanday, op. cit., 88-137, and Westcott, op. cit., 98-181.

/71/This is extended to those who followed the Apostles in
Dial. 103.8.
/72/In one instance (Dial. 106.3) the memories of Peter are
specifically designated. No quote is given here; there is
simply a reference to the naming of Peter. This could refer to
Matt 16:18 or Mark 3:16, especially if Mark is believed to be
the reminiscences of Peter (cf. Papias, as recorded by Eusebius,
Hist. eccl. 3.39.15).
/73/Op. cit., 116. The passages falling into these three
categories are listed on 113-16. Sanday goes on to note that in
his handling of the gospel tradition Justin appears much freer
than in his quotation of the OT.
/74/The data are displayed in Bellinzoni, op. cit., 44f.
/75/Op. cit., 8-48.
/76/Bellinzoni lists ten introductory formulae in this section,
op. cit., 52f. It may be noted that none involves apparent
reference to a written source.
/77/Bellinzoni's conclusion is worth citing in full: 'It is,
therefore, quite probable from the foregoing discussion that
there is underlying Apol. 15-17 a primitive Christian catechism
in use in Justin's school in Rome, a catechism that was known in
similar form to Clement of Alexandria, Origen, and the author of
the Pseudo-clementine Homilies, a catechism based primarily on
the text of the Sermon on the Mount but that harmonized related
material from Mark, Luke, and from other parts of Matthew, and a
catechism whose tradition was of great influence in later
manuscript witnesses of the synoptic gospels' (op. cit., 100).
/78/Op. cit., 56f.
/79/For a careful examination of the texts, see Bellinzoni, op.
cit., 57-76.
/80/See Bellinzoni, op. cit., 76-88.
/81/Op. cit., 111.
/82/Op. cit., 138. For further possible Johannine echoes in
Justin, see Westcott, op. cit., 170.
/83/Bellinzoni draws the remarkable conclusion that in only one
place does Justin quote from memory (Dial. 122.1, νῦν δὲ
διπλότερον υἱοὶ γεέννης, ὡς αὐτὸς εἶπε, γίνεσθε; cf.
Matt 23:15). This conclusion appears to depend on the allusory
character of the words. 'There is no reason to believe from the
context of this verse that Justin was trying to quote exactly
the words of Jesus' (op. cit., 125). For the conclusion that
Justin often quotes the canonical Gospels from memory, see
Westcott, op. cit., 130ff.
/84/E. R. Buckley argued in favor of such a lost gospel.
'Justin Martyr's Quotations from the Synoptic Tradition,' JTS 36
(1935):173-76. See too, Sanday, op. cit., 109, 129.

/85/Op. cit., 141. Sanday also points out the harmonizing tendency of Justin's source, op. cit., 102. In an appended note he writes that he leans toward the hypothesis that Justin used a harmony, 136f.

/86/It is interesting in this connection to note that in Apol. 1.15-17 we have no reference to written memoirs as in Dial. 100-107. The introductory formulae used in Apol. 1.15-17 are 'he said,' 'he taught,' 'he commanded,' and many citations are joined simply by καί. See Bellinzoni, op. cit., 53. By contrast, Dial. 49.5 contains γέγραπται in the midst of material cited from Matt 17:10-13.

/87/Clement of Rome is probably the only one of our documents to be written before the latest of the Gospels, the Fourth Gospel.

/88/The noun γραφή is applied by our writers to NT writings only in Polycarp 12.1 (scripturis [Eph. 4:26]), and in 2 Clem. 2.4 (Mark 2:17), although it can be used for what are apparently apocryphal writings (1 Clem. 23.3; Barn. 16.5).

/89/In The Use of the Old and New Testaments in Clement of Rome I found most of the variant quotations (both from OT and NT) to be best explained by quotation of canonical texts from memory. Admittedly there I tried to see the extent to which literary dependence could be substantiated--without, I hope, distorting the most natural understanding of the evidence.

/90/Convenient summaries of these data can be found in Sanday, op. cit., 15-57. It is worth adding here that occasionally even OT quotations introduced with introductory formulae are freely rendered by early Christian writers.

/91/The use of a variety of mnemonic devices had been detailed in the Aramaic that underlies the teaching of Jesus. See. C. F. Burney, The Poetry of our Lord (Oxford, 1925); M. Black, An Aramaic Approach to the Gospels and Acts, 2nd ed. (Oxford, 1954); and J. Jeremias, New Testament Theology: The Proclamation of Jesus (London, 1971). The appearance of mnemonic helps in the Greek tradition of the sayings of Jesus would thus be in imitation of what already lay in the original Aramaic.

/92/Kirsopp Lake, whose translation is otherwise used here, wrongly translates 'about their teaching' (περὶ τῶν δυνάμεων αὐτοῦ, καὶ περὶ τῆς διδασκαλίας).

/93/Tradition in the Early Church (London, 1962), 21.

/94/Memory and Manuscript (Uppsala: C. W. K. Gleerup, 1961), 199.

/95/Op. cit., 47.

/96/R. P. C. Hanson is correct that 'the idea that the oral transmission of tradition continues indefinitely to retain a superiority over written transmission cannot be read into Papias' words' (op. cit., 38).

/97/See H. von Campenhausen, The Formation of the Christian
Bible, Eng. trans. (London: Adam and Charles Black, 1972), 121.
/98/'Die Autorität der Herrenworte war ebenso gross, in
Wirklichkeit vielleicht sogar grösser, als die Autorität des
Alten Testaments.' J. Leipoldt, Geschichte des
neutestamentlichen Kanons (Leipzig, 1907), 107.
/99/Note too, 2 Clem. 13.4 where what are very possibly words of
Jesus (cf. Luke 6:32, 35) are introduced with the words λέγει ὁ
θεός.
/100/The reference here to 'the books and the Apostles' as
parallel authorities may mean the OT writings and the writings
of the Apostles, but more likely it refers to the tradition
transmitted by them. In any event, the authority of the
apostolate is exalted here. See C. F. D. Moule, Birth of the
New Testament (London, 1962), 181.
/101/It may be something like this to which Clement refers in
the words 'the glorious and venerable rule of our tradition'
(τὸν εὐκλεῆ καὶ σεμνὸν τῆς παραδόσεως ἡμῶν κανόνα), 1 Clem. 7.2.
/102/See Westcott, op. cit., 119.
/103/See Friedrich, TDNT 2 (1964):735f.
/104/Memory and Manuscript, especially 123ff., and 56ff.
/105/As argued by Gerhardsson.
/106/A point emphasized by P. H. Davids, 'The Gospels and Jewish
Tradition: Twenty Years After Gerhardsson,' in Gospel
Perspectives, vol. 1, eds. R. T. France and D. Wenham
(Sheffield, 1980), 87, 90.
/107/This was already noted by Sanday, op. cit., 119f.
/108/'The Argument From Prophecy,' JTS 46 (1945):136.
/109/The Early Church (London: SCM, 1956), 89.
/110/Both men were interested in answering the attack of the
anonymous author of Supernatural Religion (W. R. Cassels) upon
the authority and reliability of the Gospels. This
controversial work was the cause of much discussion in the
middle of the nineteenth century. See the preface to Westcott's
fourth edition.
/111/Sanday writes, 'And I do not know that we can better sum up
the case in regard to the Apostolic Fathers than thus: we have
two alternatives to choose between, either they made use of our
present Gospels, or else of writings so closely resembling our
Gospels and so nearly akin to them that their existence only
proves the essential unity and homogeneity of the evangelical
tradition' (op. cit., 87).
/112/Westcott writes, '1) No Evangelic reference in the
Apostolic Fathers can be referred certainly to a written record.
2) It appears most probable from the form of the quotations that
they were derived from oral tradition' (op. cit., 63).

THE JESUS TRADITION IN THE DIDACHE

Jonathan Draper,
The Rectory,
Mtubatuba,
3935 Natal,
South Africa.

I.

Since it was rediscovered in a monastic library in Constantinople and published by P. Bryennios in 1883, the Didache or *Teaching of the Twelve Apostles* has continued to be one of the most disputed of early Christian texts. It has been depicted by scholars as anything between the original of the Apostolic Decree (c. 50 AD)/1/ and a late archaising fiction of the early third century./2/ It bears no date itself, nor does it make any reference to any datable external event, yet the picture of the Church which it presents could only be described as primitive, reaching back to the very earliest stages of the Church's order and practice in a way which largely agrees with the picture presented by the NT, while at the same time posing questions for many traditional interpretations of this first period of the Church's life. Fragments of the Didache were found at Oxyrhyncus (P. Oxy. 1782) from the fourth century and in coptic translation (P. Lond. Or. 9271) from 3/4th century. Traces of the use of this text, and the high regard it enjoyed, are widespread in the literature of the second and third centuries, especially in Syria and Egypt. It was used by the compiler of the Didascalia (C 2/3rd)/3/ and the Liber Graduum (C 3/4th), as well as being absorbed in toto by the *Apostolic Constititutions* (C c. 3/4th, abbreviated as Ca) and partially by various Egyptian and Ethiopian Church Orders, after which it ceased to circulate independently. Athanasius describes it as 'appointed by the Fathers to be read by those who newly join us, and who wish for instruction in the word of godliness'./4/ Hence a date for the Didache in its present form later than the second century must be considered unlikely, and a date before the end of the first century probable./5/

In the absence of external criteria for dating Didache
more closely, the problem resolves itself into a question
concerning possible sources, and especially concerning its
relation to the Jesus tradition in the Gospel and to the
Epistle of Barnabas, to which it presents extensive parallel
material in chapters 1-6. Robinson, Connolly and Muilenburg,
among others, saw Didache as having borrowed and re-arranged
the so-called 'Two Ways' material from Barnabas 18-20. This
would make Didache a second century work, whose object was to
codify and order material it considered to be 'apostolic', so
that any echo of the NT may be taken as evidence of literary
dependence. A. von Harnack had already taken such a position,
declaring Didache's purpose to be a harmony of the Gospel
material on the basis primarily of Matthew./6/ A number of
scholars preferred to see Barnabas as dependent on Didache,/7/
and the Didache as being thus contemporaneous with the
formation of the written Gospels. The 'Two Ways' material was
held to be derived from an earlier Jewish work of catechesis
for proselytes, which was taken up and modified by the
Christian community. The discovery of a Latin document
entitled *Doctrina apostolorum* consisting of Didache 1-6 without
1:3b-2:1, gave considerable weight to this argument./8/
However, it was not until the discovery of the Dead Sea Scrolls
that the study of the Didache was able to move out of the
impasse over its use of sources. The so-called *Manual of
Discipline* (IQS 3:13-4:26) proved to present a Two Ways teaching
remarkably close to the material in Barnabas, Didache and the
Doctrina, both in content and in structure. It was demonstrated
by J.-P. Audet/9/ that the Doctrina was closer in several
respects to IQS than either Barnabas or Didache. Hence, while
the recension of the Two Ways evidenced by these three works
may already have received Christian modifications, the teaching
as a block existed already as Jewish catechetical material.

This discovery led Audet to a radical re-assessment of the
relationship between the Didache and the Jesus tradition./10/
He argued for a composition of Didache in three phases:
1:1-11:2 (without 1:3b-2:1) written before the emergence of a
written Gospel; 11:3-16:8 written by the same author under the
pressure of changed circumstances in the knowledge of a written
pro-Gospel, and finally various additions (including 1:3b-2:1)
made at a later date by an interpolator, who nevertheless did
not have any Gospel as we know it today. Audet's theory sets
the origin of Didache entirely between 50 and 70 AD. This is
somewhat of a romantic over-simplification, since a closer
examination of the text shows signs of considerable redactional

activity, which defies any theory of a unity of composition,
even allowing for the activity of an interpolator./11/ Didache
is a composite work, which has evolved over a considerable
period, from its beginning as a Jewish catechetical work, which
was taken up and developed by the early Church into a manual of
Church life and order. The text was repeatedly modified in
line with changes in the practice of the communities which used
it. Thus the core of 1-6 is Jewish and pre-Christian (c. 100 BC
-50 AD) and the work as a whole had probably received its
present form by the end of the first century AD. However, the
full text of Didache, apart from its use in Ca and the various
fragments, is available only in a manuscript (H54) from the
eleventh century. It cannot be assumed that the text in H54,
accurate as it may be, does not contain alterations made
considerably later than the first or even second century.
Moreover the tendency in the transmission would always be
towards harmonisation with the written Gospels and with the
later practice of the Church. Thus divergence in Didache with
regard to the Jesus tradition in the Synoptic Gospels must be
held to be specially significant and indicative of an
independent witness, unless it can be demonstrated that a later
redactor would have had a motive in altering the form of the
text.

II.

Because Didache is a composite work, its evidence
concerning the Jesus tradition must be evaluated differently for
different sections of the work. The bulk of the tradition is
found in 1:3b-2:1; 8 and 15:3-4, which appear to represent the
latest redactional phase of the Didache, although still added
before the end of the first century. Here the concern is to
subordinate the teaching contained in the Didache to the
authority of the Gospel (καὶ πάσας τὰς πράξεις οὕτω ποιήσατε,
ὡς ἔξετε ἐν τῷ εὐαγγελίῳ τοῦ κυρίου ἡμῶν, 15:4), just as the
teaching of Jesus becomes the 'first teaching' of the Way of
Life (1:3), displacing the Torah to a 'second teaching' (2:1).
However it cannot be assumed without more ado that the
reference is to a written and not an oral Gospel, or that we
have to do here with our synoptic Gospels. Further important
material relating to the Jesus tradition is contained in the
'apocalypse' of chapter 16, although here the basis of the
teaching may well derive from the original schema of the Two
Ways and may not be simply equated with the Jesus tradition.
/12/ Apparent echoes of the Jesus tradition outside these
sections should be examined with great caution, since they may

well derive from a Jewish Urtext, and even if they are the
product of a Christian community, they may reflect the general
milieu of the earliest Christian communities rather than a use
of the Jesus tradition.

The possible parallels in the Two Ways (1-6) material prove
mostly to be independent of the Jesus tradition. 2:2 forms part
of midrashic expansion of the Decalogue; 3:7 forms part of the
'Tugendkatalog' from the earliest stratum of the Way of Life
(cf. IQS 4:3) which has been embellished from Psalm 36:11./13
The reference of 6:2 is to the yoke of the Torah and not the
'easy' yoke of Jesus, as the reference to the ritual food laws
in 6:3 shows./14/ Only in 1:2b does it appear that the teaching
of Jesus has influenced the text of the Two Ways. The original
reference in the Jewish tradition was in the first instance to
ἀγαπήσεις τὸν θεὸν τὸν ποιήσαντά σε, since a stress on God as
Creator is an essential part of the Two Ways, subordinating the
incipient dualism to the requirements of Jewish monotheism (as
in IQS 3:15f.; 9:26f.; 11:6, 11, 18; CD 2:21; 3:8). Then the
second component of the Way of Life referred to the keeping of
God's commandments, as in Deuteronomy 30:16. The combination of
these two elements survives in Barnabas 19:2: ἀγαπήσεις τὸν
ποιήσαντά σε.... οὐ μὴ ἐγκαταλίπῃς ἐντολὰς κυρίου. The use in
1:2b of πρῶτον and δεύτερον to describe God and neighbour love
as a summary of the Law seems to require the influence of
Matthew 22:37-39 or the tradition behind it, despite the fact
that a deep rooted Jewish tradition lay behind the teaching of
Jesus./15/

III.

In the liturgical instructions of Didache 7, 9-14, there
are few direct parallels with the Jesus tradition. The
trinitarian baptismal formula in 7:1 is probably a later
redactional retouch, since a slightly different formula is given
in 7:3, and the earlier formula εἰς ὄνομα κυρίου has survived
in 9:5. Both formulae are taken from current liturgical
practice and not from any written source./16/ The eucharistic
prayers of Didache 9-10 seem close to the language of John 6, 14,
but they are closer still to the language of the Jewish Berakoth
(see bBer. 35a) and to the Jewish hope for the eschatological
ingathering of the diaspora./17/ Moreover, the 'Johannine'
language of 'life' and 'knowledge' is now well attested in the
Dead Sea Scrolls, so that they can be seen to form part of the
milieu in which Didache originated. In any case, the
eucharistic prayers in Didache were likely already to have been

long an accepted part of the life of the Church and were
certainly not a literary composition of the Didachist. The
saying in 9:5 (μὴ δῶτε τὸ ἅγιον τοῖς κυσί) is attributed to the
'Lord', but the meaning is quite different to Matthew 7:6,
since it is used in a cultic purity sense to justify exclusion
of the unbaptised from the eucharist meal. A similar saying is
found also in MTem. 6:5, where it seems to be cited as an
authoritative saying, and it is matched by Essene practice
recorded by Josephus in *Ant*. XVIII.22 and by IQS 5:13. It may
thus represent a Jewish *mashal* which was re-applied by Jesus to
refer to his teaching in Matthew 7:6. The use of the saying in
Didache seems to argue against its having been taken from
Matthew, but rather from the Jewish milieu./18/ Although 11:3
refers specifically to τὸ δόγμα τοῦ εὐαγγελίου the only echoes
of the Gospel in 11-13 are very faint. In 11:7 there is a
parallel with Matthew 12:32, but the sense is different, since
it identifies blasphemy against the Holy Spirit with refusing
to accept the authority of a prophet speaking ἐν πνεύματι. On
the other hand 13:1, 2 is close to the wording of Matthew 10:10,
πᾶς προφήτης/διδάσκαλος.... ἄξιος ἐστι τῆς τροφῆς αὐτοῦ. This
saying of Jesus seems to have circulated independently of the
written Gospels as we know them today, since it is found also
in 1 Corinthians 9:13f., and 1 Timothy 5:18. It may also be
rooted in Jewish wisdom tradition. The instruction of 14:2 is
close to the sense of Matthew 5:23f., although the wording is
clearly independent. In all these examples, there is no proof
of a dependence on Matthew, rather a suggestion of
independence.

IV.

Turning now to the Jesus tradition in 1:3b-2:1, it is
important to notice first of all that the material is not
attributed to a written Gospel, indeed it is not even cited as
the teaching of Jesus. Moreover, it is interspersed with
material from the Wisdom tradition (1:5,6), given all together
as the distilled essence of the Way of Life. While the wording
of the sayings is closest to Matthew 5-7, they are given in a
quite different order, with significant differences of wording,
and interwoven with other material, some of which is found in
Luke 6, and some of which is independent of both Gospels. In
some respects Didache is closer to the collection of material
in Justin, *Apology* I.16 than to either Matthew or Luke. In
other words, this material in Didache 1:3b-2:1 draws on
material found also in the collection of sayings which is
often referred to as the source 'Q' in Matthew and Luke. The

question arises as to whether it derives the material from the
written Gospels and harmonises it, or whether it draws directly
on 'Q' or a similar source. For ease of reference, the material
is set out below:

A

Did 1:3b   εὐλογεῖτε τοὺς καταρωμένους ὑμῖν καὶ
                προσεύχεσθε ὑπὲρ τῶν ἐχθρῶν ὑμῶν, νηστεύετε δὲ
                ὑπὲρ τῶν διωκόντων ὑμᾶς. ποία γὰρ χάρις ἐὰν
                φιλῆτε τοὺς φιλοῦντας ὑμᾶς; οὐχὶ καὶ τὰ ἔθνη τὸ
                αὐτὸ ποιοῦσιν; ὑμεῖς δὲ φιλεῖτε τοὺς μισοῦντας
                ὑμᾶς, καὶ οὐχ ἕξετε ἐχθρόν.

Mt 5:44,46   ἀγαπᾶτε τοὺς ἐχθροὺς ὑμῶν καὶ προσεύχεσθε
                ὑπὲρ τῶν διωκόντων ὑμᾶς. ἐὰν γὰρ ἀγαπήσητε
                τοὺς ἀγαπῶντας ὑμᾶς τίνα μισθὸν ἔχετε; οὐχὶ
                καὶ οἱ τελῶναι τὸ αὐτὸ ποιοῦσιν;

Lk 6:27,28,32   ἀγαπᾶτε τοὺς ἐχθροὺς ὑμῶν, καλῶς ποιεῖτε τοῖς
                μισοῦσιν ὑμᾶς, εὐλογεῖτε τοὺς καταρωμένους
                ὑμᾶς, προσεύχεσθε περὶ τῶν ἐπηρεαζόντων ὑμᾶς.
                καὶ εἰ ἀγαπᾶτε τοὺς ἀγαπῶντας ὑμᾶς, ποία ὑμῖν
                χάρις ἐστίν; καὶ οἱ ἁμαρτωλοὶ τοὺς ἀγαπῶντας
                αὐτοὺς ἀγαπῶσιν.

Justin, *Apol*. I. εὔχεσθε ὑπὲρ τῶν ἐχθρῶν ὑμῶν, καὶ ἀγαπᾶτε τοὺς
   15:14   μισοῦντας ὑμᾶς, καὶ εὐλογεῖτε τοὺς
                καταρωμένους ὑμῖν, καὶ εὔχεσθε ὑπὲρ τῶν
                ἐπηρεαζόντων ὑμᾶς.

Justin, *Apol*. I. εἰ ἀγαπᾶτε τοὺς ἀγαπῶντας ὑμᾶς, τί καινὸν
   15:13   ποιεῖτε; καὶ γὰρ οἱ πόρνοι τοῦτο ποιοῦσιν.

B

Did 1.4a   ἀπέχου τῶν σαρκικῶν ἐπιθυμιῶν. ἐὰν τίς σοι
                δῷ ῥάπισμα εἰς τὴν δεξιὰν σιαγόνα, στρέφον
                αὐτῷ καὶ τὴν ἄλλην, καὶ ἔσῃ τέλειος.

Mt 5:39,48   ἀλλ' ὅστις σε ῥαπίζει εἰς τὴν δεξιὰν σιαγόνα,
                στρέφον αὐτῷ καὶ τὴν ἄλλην· ἔσεσθε οὖν ὑμεῖς
                τέλειοι.

Lk 6:29a   τῷ τύπτοντί σε ἐπὶ τὴν σιαγόνα πάρεχε καὶ τὴν
                ἄλλην.

Justin, *Apol*. I.   τῷ τύπτοντί σου τὴν σιαγόνα πάρεχε καὶ τὴν
  16:1   ἄλλην.

C

Did 1.4b   ἐὰν ἀγγαρεύσῃ σέ τις μίλιον ἕν, ὕπαγε
                      μετ' αὐτοῦ δύο· ἐὰν ἄρῃ τις τὸ ἱμάτιόν
                      σου, δὸς αὐτῷ καὶ τὸν χιτῶνα ἐὰν λάβῃ
                      τις ἀπὸ σοῦ τὸ σόν, μὴ ἀπαίτει· οὐδὲ γὰρ
                      δύνασαι.

Mt 5:41,40   καὶ ὅστις σε ἀγγαρεύσει μίλιον ἕν, ὕπαγε
                      μετ' αὐτοῦ δύο. καὶ τῷ θέλοντί σοι
                      κριθῆναι καὶ τὸν χιτῶνά σου λαβεῖν, ἄφες
                      αὐτῷ καὶ τὸ ἱμάτιον.

Lk 6:29b,30   καὶ ἀπὸ τοῦ αἴροντός σου τὸ ἱμάτιον καὶ
                      τὸν χιτῶνα μὴ κωλύσῃς, καὶ ἀπὸ τοῦ
                      αἴροντος τὰ σὰ μὴ ἀπαίτει.

Justin, *Apol*. I.   παντὶ δὲ ἀγγαρεύοντί σε μίλιον ἀκολούθησον
  16:2,1b.   δύο. καὶ τὸν αἴροντά σου τὸν χιτῶνα ἢ τὸ
                      ἱμάτιον μὴ κωλύσῃς. ὃς δ' ἂν ὀργισθῇ
                      ἔνοχός ἐστιν εἰς τὸ πῦρ.

D

Did 1:5a   παντὶ τῷ αἰτοῦντί σε δίδου καὶ μὴ ἀπαίτει.
                      πᾶσι γὰρ θέλει δίδοσθαι ὁ πατὴρ ἐκ τῶν
                      ἰδίων χαρισμάτων.

Mt 5:42   τῷ αἰτοῦντί σε δός, καὶ τὸν θέλοντα ἀπὸ
                      σοῦ δανίσασθαι μὴ ἀποστραφῇς.

Lk 6:30   παντὶ αἰτοῦντί σε δίδου.

Justin, *Apol*. I.   παντὶ τῷ αἰτοῦντι δίδοτε, καὶ τὸν
  15:15.   βουλόμενον δανείσασθαι μὴ ἀποστραφῆτε.

E

Did 1:5b   μακάριος ὁ διδοὺς κατὰ τὴν ἐντολήν· ἀθῷος γὰρ
            ἐστιν. οὐαὶ τῷ λαμβάνοντι· εἰ μὲν γὰρ χρείαν
            ἔχων λαμβάνει τις, ἀθῷος ἔσται. ὁ δὲ μὴ χρείαν
            ἔχων δώσει δίκην ἱνατί ἔλαβε καὶ εἰς τί.

            Cf. Acts 20:35.

F

Did 1:5c   ἐν συνοχῇ δὲ γενόμενος ἐξετασθήσεται περὶ ὧν
            ἔπραξε, καὶ ουκ ἐξελεύσεται ἐκεῖθεν μέχρις οὗ
            ἀποδῷ τὸν ἔσχατον κοδράντην.

Mt 5:25,26 καὶ εἰς φυλακὴν βληθήσῃ. ἀμὴν λέγω ὑμῖν, οὐ μὴ
            ἐξέλθῃς ἐκεῖθεν, ἕως ἂν ἀποδῷς τὸν ἔσχατον
            κοδράντην.

Lk 12:58f. καὶ ὁ πράκτωρ σε βαλεῖ εἰς φυλακήν. λέγω σοι
            οὐ μὴ ἐξέλθῃς ἐκεῖθεν, ἕως καὶ τὸ ἔσχατον λεπτὸν
            ἀποδῷς.

G

Did 1:6   ἀλλὰ καὶ περὶ τούτο δὲ εἴρηται· ἱδρωσάτω ἡ
            ἐλεημοσύνη σου εἰς τὰς χειράς σου, μέχρις ἂν
            γνῷς τίνι δῷς.

            Cf. Sirach 12:1.

        The peculiarities of Didache's version of these sayings
cannot be attributed to late glosses, since no doctrinal point
is implied in any of them, and the Greek of Didache is often
clumsier than that of the Synoptic Gospels, so that they cannot
be derived from stylistic corrections. The first group of
sayings (A) agrees first with the Lucan text, and then with
Justin against Matthew/Luke in the saying: (προσ)εύχεσθε ὑπὲρ
τῶν ἐχθρῶν ὑμῶν and presents a third member found nowhere else,
which forms a climax: νηστεύετε δὲ ὑπὲρ τῶν διωκόντων ὑμᾶς./19/
The connection between prayer and fasting (which is seen as
increasing the potency of prayer) is a common Jewish
understanding./20/ Didache gives φιλῆτε...φιλοῦντας...
φιλεῖτε against the Synoptic ἀγαπᾶτε... ἀγαποῦντας... ἀγαπᾶτε;
this reading is attested by the P.Ox. fragment and Ca., which

otherwise harmonises the text of Didache with Luke at this
point. The tendency of the tradition was inexorably towards the
use of ἀγαπάω, so this reading is important (cf. also IgPol.
2:1). The Didache uses ἔθνη for ἀμαρτωλοί in Luke and τελῶναι
in Matthew (cf. ἐθνικοί in 5:47) and πόρνοι in Justin. In this
Didache presents most clearly the Jewish perspective, which is
surprising in a work directed towards the Gentiles, as the
longer title of the work suggests: Διδαχὴ κυρίου διὰ τῶν
δώδεκα ἀπόστολων τοῖς ἔθνεσιν. It may well attest a very old
tradition. Finally Didache includes a puzzling sentence not
attested elsewhere: καὶ οὐχ ἕξετε ἐχθρόν. This is best taken
as a prohibition climaxing the teaching./21/ In this group of
sayings (A), Didache thus presents an independent text which
cannot realistically be viewed as a harmony of the Gospels.
It seems to have independent access to the traditions on which
the Gospels also draw.

     In the second group of sayings (B), Didache contrasts the
desires of the flesh/22/ with the way of perfection, which is
that of turning the other cheek. This sophisticated setting
for the saying is not to be found in other witnesses./23/
However, the form of the text, while close to Matthew, appears
the more primitive since ὃ ῷ ῥάπισμα is clumsy Greek compared
with Matthew's ῥαπίζει./24/

     In the third group (C), Didache presents a text close to
Matthew in wording, but following Luke in the order ἱμάτιον/
χιτῶνα against Matthew. As in Luke, this saying is followed by
the heightening saying ἐὰν λάβῃ τις ἀπὸ σοῦ τὸ σόν μὴ ἀπαίτει
(Luke ἀπὸ τοῦ αἴροντος τὰ σὰ ... μὴ ἀπαίτει) and it has a
further climax in οὐδὲ γὰρ δύνασαι (whose exact meaning is
problematic, perhaps, 'You are in any case not able to do so'
/25/). In this section, as in the others which have been
examined, Didache has the longest text. Glover sees in this
the sign of a greater faithfulness to a source which Matthew
and Luke abbreviate and refine./26/ Against this it may be
asserted that Didache arranges the material in a deliberately
climatic style to heighten its effectiveness as catechesis./27/

     The fourth section (D) in Didache turns to the question of
almsgiving, which preoccupies the rest of the material (E-G).
In doing so, Didache applies a saying to entreaty for alms
which in Luke applies to what is demanded by force (παντὶ τῷ
αἰτοῦντί σε δίδου). Matthew has a similar saying applied to
lending in 5:42 with quite different wording: τῷ αἰτοῦντί σε
δός καὶ τὸν θέλοντα ἀπὸ σοῦ δανίσασθαι μὴ ἀποστραφῇς. Didache

amplifies this saying with material drawn from the Two Ways:
πᾶσι γὰρ θέλει δίδοσθαι ὁ πατὴρ ἐκ τῶν ἰδίων χαρισμάτων.   (See
Doctrina 4:8, 'Omnibus enim dominus dare uult de donis suis'.
Cf. Hermas, *Mand*. II:4; Didsc. 4:3).   Its original reference, as
Doctrina shows, was to almsgiving within the community, but
Didache universalises its reference to include even one's
enemies, as the context suggests (1:4).   In this Didache
faithfully reflects the position of Jesus himself.   A further
saying attested also in *Mand*. II:5-6 is introduced (E) in the
form of a macarism.   It seems to be reflected also in Acts 20:35
and 1 Clem. 2:1, where it is attributed to the Lord Jesus
Christ./28/   Köster/29/ is sceptical of its origin as a saying
of Jesus, preferring to see in it a Jewish proverb.

        The short pericope concerning prison (F) has an
eschatological reference in Matthew and Luke.   Judgement is
coming and it is imperative to put one's affairs right while
there is still time.   The eschatological context is clearest in
Luke.   The same context probably lies behind Didache.   The
person who takes alms without needing them shall give account
not to a human court but to the heavenly judge before whom he
shall be examined (ἐξετασθήσεται περὶ ὧν ἔπραξε).   The use of
the word σύνοχη in Didache is striking, since it is a rare word,
meaning literally 'compression' and hence 'distress'./30/   Only
one possible instance of a use cognate with φυλακή is recorded
(P.Lond. 354.24) and even this is debatable.   The word may rest
on an Aramaic word such as מצר which could be rendered either
φυλακή or σύνοχη.   The wording differs considerably throughout
the pericope from that in Matthew/Luke.   The final saying (G)
draws on a version of Sirach 12:1 which is independent of LXX,
as a proof text from Scripture for the teaching./31/

        In none of these sayings from the Jesus tradition and the
wisdom tradition can a dependence on either Matthew or Luke be
demonstrated.   Rather, the variation in order and wording seen
in both Didache and Justin indicates an independence over against
the written sources in Matthew/Luke which is indicative of a
time when the Gospel tradition was still in the process of
formation.   It may be that such collections of material had
long been used in catechesis before they were finally inserted
into Didache, and indeed, such collections may well lie behind
the Sermon on the Mount/Plain in Matthew/Luke./32/   Most
important, for our purposes, is that all these parallels are
from what is traditionally called 'Q' material in Matthew/Luke,
and there is no trace of Markan material.   If Didache had our
synoptic Gospels in their present form, it seems hard to

understand how he could consistently have excluded Markan
material present in Matthew and Luke and only drawn on 'Q'
material. It would seem a more likely inference that Didache
had access directly to the so-called 'Q' material, either in a
written or an oral form.

V.

Didache 8 does seem to know a Gospel written or oral close
to the present text of Matthew. This is indicated by ὡς
ἐκέλευσεν ὁ κύριος ἐν τῷ εὐαγγελίῳ αὐτοῦ, as also by the
reference to the ὑπόκριται (cf. Mt 6:1-6) and by the closeness
of the text of the Lord's Prayer to that of Matthew 6:9-13.
Moreover Didache 8 appears to be a later addition to the
earliest text of Didache. It is inserted after the reference
to the baptismal fast in 7:4, but it has a quite different
reference to 'stationary fasts' and daily prayer. It breaks up
the natural flow in the catechetical manual from baptism to the
eucharist. Moreover, it is not introduced by the formula which
characterises the liturgical sections of Didache (περὶ δέ), and
in the Ethiopian version it is set after 11:3-13. Nevertheless,
the text of Didache 8 exhibits a certain independence with
regard to Matthew. The sense given to 'hypocrites' is quite
different to that in Matthew, where it is insincerity which is
under attack. Here the term simply designates the Jewish
opponents of the community. The differences in the text of the
Lord's Prayer, though minor, may be significant, since it is
clearly derived from the liturgy of the community, where it was
known by heart (it was to be repeated three times daily, 8:3).
Didache has ἐν τῷ οὐρανῷ for Matthew ἐν τοῖς οὐρανοῖς, and the
plural is characteristic of Matthew's editorial activity (5:12 =
Lk 6:23; 7:11 = Lk 11:3; 19:21 = Mk 10:21)./33/ Didache also
has the singular τὴν ὀφελήν for Matthew τὰ ὀφειλήματα where the
tendency in the tradition may be away from the more primitive
idea of collective 'debt' towards an understanding of the
number of particular sins (Lk τὰς ἁμαρτίας ἡμῶν). Finally
Didache has ἀφίεμεν for Matthew ἀφήκαμεν (Lk ἀφίομεν)./34/ Here
Matthew may be concerned to emphasise with the aorist the
requirement of forgiveness as a prerequisite to divine
forgiveness, in view of the logion which follows in Matthew
6:14f. The presence of the doxology in the Didache indicates a
liturgical use of the Lord's Prayer, and this usage gradually
began to invade the text of Matthew also./35/ Didache 15.3-4
seems to have been added at the same redactional stage as
Didache 8.

VI.

The 'apocalypse' of Didache 16 presents many parallels to
Matthew 24 and yet demonstrates a clear independence with regard
to its text. It is likely that the basis of Didache 16 was
formed by the original eschatological conclusion to the Jewish
Two Ways instruction of 1-6. Ethical parenesis is underscored
by the warning concerning the imminent judgement. This Two Ways
tradition appears most clearly in 16:2, which is paralleled by
Barnabas 4:9-10 almost verbatim, but may well be behind 16:1
also. Didache 16:1 uses material found in the Jesus tradition in
Matthew and Luke, but in a form which could hardly be a
harmonisation, since it agrees with neither in order or context.
/36/ Didache agrees with Matthew 24:42 in γρηγορεῖτε and 24:44
(= Lk 12:40) in γίνεσθε ἕτοιμοι. It is not likely that Didache
has drawn this material directly from Matthew, since the short
admonitions would be easily memorised and used in catechism.
/37/ There is a further agreement between Didache and
Luke 12:35 although the wording and the context are different:
/38/

Didache	Luke
οἱ λύχνοι ὑμῶν μὴ σβεσθήτωσαν καὶ αἱ ὀσφύες ὑμῶν μὴ ἐκλυέσθωσαν	ἔστωσαν ὑμῶν αἱ ὀσφύες περιεζωσμέναι καὶ οἱ λύχνοι καιόμενοι

Cf. Methodius, *Symposium* V. 2

This imagery seems to have been drawn in part from the
general fund of eschatological imagery from Exodus 12:11.
See Mekhilta Pis. VIII. 15-20 on this passage and jKil. IX,
32b.9; jKeth. XII, 35a. 9; New Year Amidah, Petition 3 in the
Jewish tradition, as well as Ephesians 6:11f. and 1 Peter 1:13
in the Christian tradition. B. C. Butler/39/ thinks that
Didache is here dependent on Luke, but this is unlikely.
Rather Luke is here drawing on 'Q' material. The same must be
said for the relation between 16:3-4 and Matthew 24:10-11, where
the sense is the same but the wording independent. The picture
of the eschatological woes is a common ingredient of Jewish
writings./40/ The only image which particularly calls for
comment is that of the sheep and the wolves.

Didache	Matthew 7:15

καὶ στραφήσονται τὰ πρόβατα εἰς
λύκους

Cf. Asc Isa 2:24f.

προσέχετε ἀπὸ τῶν
ψευδοπροφητῶν οἵτινες ἔρχονται
πρὸς ὑμᾶς ἐν ἐνδύμασιν προβάτων
ἔσωθεν δὲ εἰσιν λύκοι ἅρπαγες

Cf. Mt 10:16

ἰδοὺ ἐγὼ ἀποστέλλω ὑμᾶς ὡς
πρόβατα ἐν μέσῳ λύκων

Here the text of Didache could hardly be dependent on Matthew,
but the image is undoubtedly related. It may be that a Hebrew
saying lies behind these texts, such as ומסבב הצאן אל זאבים,
where the root סבב would explain στραφήσονται and ἐν μέσῳ as
well as the extended interpretation of the saying in terms of a
disguise.

There is a much closer relationship between the material in
16:5-8 and Matthew 24.

Didache	Matthew 24:10,13

καὶ σκανδαλισθήσονται πολλοὶ
καὶ ἀπολοῦνται

οἱ δὲ ὑπομείναντες ἐν τῇ
πίστει αὐτῶν σωθήσονται ὑπ'
αὐτοῦ τοῦ καταθέματος

καὶ τότε σκανδαλισθήσονται
πολλοί .....

ὁ δὲ ὑπομείνας εἰς τέλος
οὗτος σωθήσεται

Matthew 24:30,31

καὶ τότε φανήσεται τὰ σημεῖα
τῆς ἀληθείας

πρῶτον σημεῖον ἐκπετάσεως ἐν
οὐρανῷ

εἶτα σημεῖον φωνῆς σάλπιγγος

καὶ τὸ τρίτον ἀνάστασις νεκρῶν
οὐ πάντων δέ...

τότε ὄψεται ὁ κόσμος τὸν κύριον

καὶ τότε φανήσεται τὸ σημεῖον
τοῦ υἱοῦ τοῦ ἀνθρώπου ἐν
οὐρανῷ

καὶ τότε κόψονται πᾶσαι αἱ
φυλαὶ τῆς γῆς

καὶ ὄψονται τὸν υἱὸν τοῦ
ἀνθρώπου...

Didache	Matthew 24:30,31

ἐρχόμενον ἐπάνω τῶν νεφελῶν τοῦ οὐρανοῦ

ἐρχόμενον ἐπὶ τῶν νεφελῶν τοῦ οὐρανοῦ ... μετὰ σάλπιγγος μεγάλης καὶ ἐπισυνάξουσιν τοὺς ἐκλεκτοὺς αὐτοῦ ἐκ τῶν τεσσάρων ἀνέμων ἀπ' ἄκρων οὐρανῶν ἕως τῶν ἄκρων αὐτῶν

There are a number of details in Didache which show it to be independent of Matthew and perhaps even help to explain the background behind the text of Matthew. In 16:5 (cf. 4Esdr.6:25), for example, the difficult phrase ὑπ' αὐτοῦ τοῦ καταθέματος seems to be faithful to the tradition in which the faithful remnant is purged by suffering like a refiner's fire (Mal 3:2-4). The 'curse' which saves is the πύρωσις τῆς δοκιμασίας (16:5) as is seen in the closely parallel texts of Hermas, *Vis.* IV. 3,4 and 1 Peter 4:12. The σημεῖα of Didache are also true to the tradition on which Matthew 24:30f. depends. The meaning of Didache is somewhat obscured by the translation of two Hebrew words את and נס respectively by the same Greek word σημεῖον (as also in LXX). The σημεῖα τῆς αληθείας are the אותות האמת, true signs by which the heavenly Son of Man will be known, as opposed to the false signs given by the World Deceiver to pervert the world (16:4). The first sign (σημεῖον ἐκπετάσεως ἐν ουρανῷ) however is the נס פרש בשמים, the banner promised by Isaiah 11:10 which the Messiah would raise to rout the nations and gather in the exiles of Israel./41/ This is confirmed by the extensive commentary in the Targum to Isaiah whenever נס appears in the OT (e.g., Isa 10:11ff.; 18:3; 31:9). John 3:14 makes the same connection between the serpent set up as a נס (Num 21:4-9) and the cross as the sign of the Son of Man. The reason the nations mourn at the appearing of the sign of the Son of Man in Matthew is because the banner of the Messiah has been set up to rout the nations and gather in the diaspora. This banner was identified by the Church with the cross of Christ, and indeed even the word ἐκπετάσις, like the Hebrew פרש suggested crucifixion (cf. Didasc 26 [Lagarde p107.27-9)] Sib. Orac. V. 257; VIII.302; Od. Sol. 27:2f.; Gospel of Philip [NgH II.3] 63:21ff.). The trumpet and the rising of the dead follow the raising of the sign, the gathering in of the scattered tribes being held to include the saints who had died (see IQH 6:34; cf. 2:13). The whole schema is accurately reflected in the Jewish *Shemoneh Esreh*, Petition 10, which is widely regarded as being very ancient, probably going back to the late first or early second

century AD: תקצ בשופר גדול לחרותנו ושא נם לקבץ גליותינו'
וקבצנו יחד מארבע כנפות הארץ. Finally Didache in its present
form has the quotation from Daniel 7:13 found also in
Matthew 24:30. An older text of Didache may be represented by
Ca which has καὶ τότε ἥξει ὁ κύριος καὶ πάντες οἱ ἅγιοι μετ' αὐτοῦ
ἐν συσσεισμῷ ἐπάνω τῶν νεφαλῶν, since Ca usually harmonises the
text of the Didache with the Gospels. The H 54 text of Didache
like Matthew cites Daniel 7:13, but the survival of ὁ κύριος
indicates its independence of Matthew. Köster/42/ has argued
that Didache draws here upon the Ur text of a Jewish apocalypse
used also by Mark. However J. S. Kloppenborg has demonstrated
/43/ that Didache only uses the material parallel to Matthew's
special source 'M' and at no point cites Matthew where Matthew
can be seen to be using Mark. He concludes from this that
Didache represented an independent tradition under whose
influence Matthew altered his Markan source./44/ This
conclusion reached by Kloppenborg concerning Didache 16 is
similar to that reached by Glover,/45/ who goes so far as to say
that 'the case for the Didache being a witness to some source,
or sources, of our Lord's teaching more primitive than the
synoptic Gospels appears very strong indeed'./46/

                              VII.

    The above assessment of the Jesus tradition in the Didache
allows some tentative conclusions to be drawn. It suggests,
firstly, an independence over against the Synoptic Gospels which
often throws light on the Gospel material. Secondly, it shows
that firm dependence on the Jesus tradition, rather than what
can be attributed to the Jewish milieu, is limited to the
tradition which is found mainly in the Sermon on the Mount in
Matthew and the Sermon on the Plain in Luke, besides the
'apocalypse' of Matthew 24. Didache is usually closer to
Matthew but sometimes closer to Luke. While this might at first
suggest a knowledge of Matthew and Luke, in which the Synoptic
Gospels are harmonised on the basis of Matthew, this must be
unlikely. The context, order and wording of the sayings is
independent and cannot be derived from either. The material
Didache has in common with Matthew and Luke *never* includes
material these evangelists have drawn from Mark. It coincides
with what is normally described as the 'Q' Source in these
Gospels, and seems to confirm the hypothesis that sayings of
Jesus were collected and circulated in a more or less fixed
form, whether oral or written, before the collection was
incorporated into the Gospels as we have them. It may be that

these collections were already referred to as τὸ εὐαγγέλιον
(Did 8:2, 11:3, 15:3,4). The context of such a collection of
sayings in Didache 1:3-2:1 strongly implies the use to which the
collection was put - the instruction of catechumens: ταῦτα πάντα
προειπόντες./47/ Thirdly, the differences in wording and
context of the Jesus sayings in Didache, Matthew and Luke are
of the same kind. They indicate an independent use of a common
source at a time when that source was still fluid. Nevertheless
Didache largely supports the evidence of Matthew and Luke
concerning the teaching of Jesus./48/

Notes

/1/ E.g., Seeberg, *Die Beiden Wege und das Aposteldekret*
(Leipzig: 1906).
/2/ E.g., J. A. Robinson, *Barnabas, Hermas and the Didache*
(London: SPCK, 1902); R. H. Connolly, 'The Didache in Relation
to the Epistle of Barnabas', *JTS* 33 (1932) 327-353;
J. Muilenburg, *The Literary Relations of the Epistle of
Barnabas and the Teaching of the Twelve Apostles*, Yale
Dissertation (Marburg: 1929).
/3/ See R. H. Connolly, 'The Use of the Didache in the
Didascalia', *JTS* 24 (1923) 147-57.
/4/ *Festal Letter* 39:7.
/5/ A new consensus is emerging for a date c.100 AD. This is
represented for instance by W. Rordorf and A. Tuilier, *La
Doctrine des Douze Apôtres* (SC 248) (Paris: Les Editions du
Cerf, 1978).
/6/ *Die Lehre der zwölf Apostel* (TU 2), 1893, 63-88. Harnack
later changed his mind about the origin of the 'Two Ways',
seeing it as derived from a Jewish catechetical document. See
Die Didache und die jüdischen beiden Wege (Leipzig: 1896).
/7/ E.g., C. Taylor, *The Teaching of the Twelve Apostles*
(London: 1898); C. H. Turner, 'The Early Christian Ministry and
the Didache', in *Studies in Early Church History* (Oxford: 1912)
1-31; G. Klein, *Der ältestechristliche Katechismus und die
jüdischen Propaganda-Literatur* (Berlin, 1909).
/8/ The document was first published by J. Schlecht, *Doctrina
XII Apostolorum. Die Apostellehre in der Liturgie der
katholischen Kirche* (Freiburg i. Breisgau: 1901). Opponents of
the theory of a Jewish source held this to be an abridgement of
Didache.
/9/ 'Affinités littéraires et doctrinales du "Manuel de
discipline", *RB* 59 (1952) 219-38.

/10/ *La Didachè* (Paris: Gabalda, 1959) 166-186.
/11/ Note, for example, the fluctuation between the singular and plural of the second person in chapters 7 and 13. Although Audet notices this, he draws the wrong conclusion. It is the second person plural which is the mark of the later redaction, modifying the intimate tone of catechesis in favour of the collective plural of liturgical use in the community. See further my argument in *A Commentary on the Didache in the Light of the Dead Sea Scrolls and Related Documents* (unpublished Cambridge dissertation), 1983, 145-8; 258-9. J. A. T. Robinson (*Redating the NT*, London: SCM, 1976, pp. 322-7) agrees with Audet in his dating of Didache before 70 AD.
/12/ See E. Bammel, 'Schema und Vorlage von Didache 16', *Studia Patristica* IV (TU 79) (Berlin: 1961) 253-63.
/13/ The Doctrina makes it clear that it belongs within the context of Jewish hope by its addition of 'sanctam terram'.
/14/ See A. Stuiber, 'Das ganze Joch des Herrn (Didache 6:2-3)', *Studia Patristica* IV (TU 79) (Berlin: 1961) 323-9.
/15/ See K. Berger, *Die Gesetzesauslegung Jesu. Ihr historischer Hintergrund im Judentum und im Alten Testament* 1 (WMANT 40) (Neukirchen: 1972) 136f.; A. Nissen, *Gott und der Nächste im antiken Judentum* (WUNT 15) (Tübingen: 1974) 230-44.
/16/ The liturgical usage may well have influenced the text of Matthew also at this point, so that the original reference of Mt 28:19 was to 'the name' only as in most citations by Eusebius. See among others, F. C. Coneybeare, 'The Eusebian Form of The Matt 28:19 Test', *ZNW* 2 (1901) 275-288; E. Lohmeyer, 'Mir ist gegeben alle Gewalt!', *In Memoriam Ernst Lohmeyer*, ed. W. Schmauch (Stuttgart: 1951) 22-49. For a fuller bibliography see my thesis, *Commentary*, 146, 8.
/17/ See L. Clerici, *Einsammlung der Zerstreuten. Liturgiegeschichtliche Untersuchung zur Vor- und Nachgeschichte der Fürbitte fur die Kirche in Did. 9:4 und 10:5 (Liturgiewissenschaftliche Quellen und Forschungen 44)* (Münster i. Westf. 1966).
/18/ The 'Lord' referred to would then be the Lord of the OT and not Jesus.
/19/ H. Köster (*Synoptische Überlieferung be den Apostolischen Väter* (TU 65) Berlin: 1957, 224) sees this as a sign of a late date.
/20/ See Behm, 'NESTIS', *TDNT* IV, 928; Moore, *Judaism* II, 261; M. Mees, 'Die Bedeutung der Sentenzen und ihrer Ausesis für die Formung der Jesuworte nach Didache 1:3b-2:1', *Vetera Christianorum* 8 (1971) 55-76, esp. 68f.
/21/ Cf. Audet, *La Didache*, 264. R. Knopf (*Die Lehre der zwölf Apostel* (Hb. z. NT 1) (Tübingen: Mohr, 1920, 7) sees here a lost Gospel tradition.

/22/ καὶ σωματικῶν should be omitted since it is absent from
P. Ox. and Ca has a different reading also, καὶ κοσμικῶν.
/23/ Note however Gal 5:16f.
/24/ See R. Glover, 'The Didache's Quotations and the Synoptic
Gospels', NTS 5 (1958-9) 14f. It is interesting to note also
Jn 18:22, ἔδωκεν ῥάπισμα τῷ 'Ιησοῦ.
/25/ Cf. S. Giet, L'Enigme de la Didache (Paris: 1970) 59; Mees,
'Auxesis', 64.
/26/ 'The greater brevity and stylistic improvements of the
synoptics again recall the changes they made in the text of
Mark when he was their source', 'Quotations', 15.
/27/ Cf. B. Layton ('The Sources, Date and Transmission of
Didache 1:3b-2:1', HUCA 61 (1968) 343-83) who takes this
approach. However his assertion that Didache deliberately
disguised his 'plagiarization' of Scripture is absurd. The
tendency was not to disguise but towards harmony with the
Gospels, unless an author had theological motives. Moreover,
Layton's assumption that rhetorical climax is a mark of later
redaction is dubious. It is found already within the Gospels.
/28/ Cf. Glover, 'Quotations', 15f.
/29/ Überlieferung, 231-7.
/30/ Arndt and Gingrich, 799.
/31/ See P. W. Skehan, 'Didache 1:6 and Sirach 12:1', Bib 44
(1963) 533-6.
/32/ 'Nous sommes à l'intérieur d'une tradition du Sermon sur la
montagne, orale ou écrite relativement uniforme quant à
l'expression et relativement homogène quant au contenu', Audet,
La Didachè, 266.
/33/ See Köster, Überlieferung, 206.
/34/ Köster (Überlieferung, 208f.) sees this agreement between
Didache and Luke as indicating what lay in 'Q'.
/35/ Cf. Did 9:2,3; 9:4; 10:2,4,5.
/36/ See J. P. Audet, La Didachè, 180-2. B. C. Butler ('The
Literary Relations of Didache ch xvi', JTS ns 11 (1960) 265-83),
on the other hand, sees Didache as dependent on Luke.
/37/ See Köster, Überlieferung, 176f. On the other hand,
R. Bauckham ('Synoptic Parousia Parables and the Apocalypse',
NTS 23 (1976-7) 162-176, esp. 169) has seen the Didache saying
as a 'deparabolized' form of the 'Thief in the Night' saying.
/38/ Cf. Methodius, Symposium V. 2. See R. Bauckham, 'Synoptic
Parables Again', NTS 29 (1983) 129-43, esp. 131f. The wording
in Didache and Methodius may reflect LXX Job 18:5.
/39/ B. C. Butler, 'Literary Relations', 265-83.
/40/ See for instance IQH 4; IQS 3:21-24; 4QpFlor 1:8f.; Orac.
Sib. II. 165f.; Asc. Isa. 3:27ff.; Apoc. Pet. 1:1; Od. Sol. 38;
Rev 19:2; 16:13; 2 Pet 3:3; 1 Tim 3:1f.; 1 Jn 2:18; 4:1. See
further Köster, Überlieferung, 177-82.

/41/ See my thesis, *Commentary*, 319-25; also A. Stuiber, 'Die
Drei Semeia von Didache xvi', *Jahrbuch für Antike und
Christentum* 24 (1981) 42-4.
/42/ *Überlieferung*, 187-9.
/43/ 'Didache 16:6-8 and Special Matthean Tradition', *ZNW* 69-70
(1978-9) 54-67.
/44/ 'Tradition', 63. A reservation concerning Glover's
conclusion needs to be made, in that the Didache may reflect at
this point an underlying Jewish tradition rather than the Jesus
teaching in particular, which may draw on the same tradition.
/45/ 'Quotations', 25-28.
/46/ 'Quotations', 27.
/47/ The same explanation can be given for the collection of
sayings of Jesus in Justin, *Apol.*, I.15-16, which set out the
kernel of Christian teaching which was to precede baptism.
/48/ The differences are rather a matter of wording than of
substance, and the same authentic, challenging voice of Jesus
rings through the sayings.

JESUS IN JEWISH TRADITIONS

Graham H. Twelftree,
The Manse,
Main Road,
Houghton 5131,
South Australia.

Jewish writings, both Christian and non-Christian, can, with varying degrees of reliability, tell us something about the NT writers and their world, the world of Jesus and his immediate contemporaries./1/ For example, Josephus can tell us something about John the Baptist (*Ant*. 18:116-9, see below), and the Rabbinic writings are useful in reconstructing the milieu of the Palestinian origins of Christianity./2/ However the particular question this paper attempts to answer is, 'What light, if any, do the Jewish traditions shed on our knowledge of the historical Jesus?'.

There are a number of potential sources at our disposal. (a) The extant texts of the works of Josephus contain references to Jesus (*Ant*. 18:63-4; 20:200 and the 'Slavonic Addition' following *J.W.* 2:174 (see below)). (b) Within the body of Rabbinic literature/3/ Jesus is mentioned many times (see below). (c) Jewish traditions about Jesus are also preserved by pagan writers, for example by Celsus (*Origen: Contra Celsum* (hereafter *CC*), *e.g.*, I:28, 41, 62; II:34, 38, 55: V:52)./4/ Then (d) there are citations of Jewish traditions about Jesus in Christian literature (see, *e.g.* Justin, *Dial*. 17, 108, 117, Tertullian *Ad.Nat*. i:14)./5/ The focus of this paper is on Jesus in Josephus and in the Rabbinic literature ((a) and (b) above).

As will become obvious, a great deal of work has been done on these two traditions in relation to early Christianity./6/ Yet on their value to the historian of the origins of Christianity nothing like a consensus of scholarly opinion has been attained. There is then a need for continued study of these sources to clarify the issues as well as to bring to bear

upon them the historical-critical tools and methods that
continue to be developed. The Gospel traditions about Jesus
emerged in communities that were seeking to identify themselves
over against Jewish opponents./7/ The resulting *Tendenz* means
that the historian must carefully scrutinize the material in
recovering an 'historical' picture of say, the Scribes and
Pharisees./8/ Likewise some of the Rabbinic traditions arose
in a milieu that was hostile to Christianity,/9/ resulting in
a recognizable anti-Christian *Tendenz*./10/ Thus, as scholars
are recognizing, especially in the complicated field of Rabbinic
studies, critical tools need to be applied to these sources as
well as to the NT./11/

I. Josephus

Josephus ben Matthias was born in Jerusalem in the first
year of the reign of Caligula, AD 37-8 (*Life* 5)./12/ His
father was a priest and his mother was related directly to the
Hasmonean rulers (*Life* 2)./13/ He says, 'in my nineteenth year
I began to govern my life by the rules of the Pharisees' (*Life*
12)./14/ When he was 26 (c. AD 64) he went to Rome to gain the
release of some imprisoned priests. He says he was introduced
to Poppaea, Caesar's consort, who not only helped secure the
release of the priests but 'besides this favour received large
gifts from Poppaea' (*Life* 16), which, along with the visit
itself, was probably important in forming Josephus' pro-Roman
sympathies. At the beginning of the War (AD 66) Josephus was a
commander in Galilee (*Life* 28f.; cf. *J.W.* 2:566ff.), but after
a 47-day siege at Jotopata he gave himself up to the Romans.
His prophecy that Vespasian would rise to imperial power later
secured his release from Vespasian's camp at Caesarea in AD 68.
Josephus went with Vespasian to Alexandria (*Life* 415) and from
there to Jerusalem with Titus, where he witnessed the fall of
the city. Not surprisingly he was hated by his fellow Jews as
a traitor/15/ and he spent the rest of his life in Rome. He
became a Roman citizen, and was a court favourite. Under royal
patronage (see *Life* 361-6, 422-9/16/) Josephus set about writing
The Jewish War, The Antiquities of the Jews, his *Life* and
Against Apion. The date of his death is unknown, but he
outlived Agrippa II (*Life* 359) who died about AD 92/3./17/ In
view of even this very brief sketch of his life and situations
it will not be surprising for us to discover that, to say the
least, Josephus is 'pro-Roman' in his interpretation of events
in Palestine.

The two questions that will guide our discussion of the
relevant passages in Josephus are (1) Is it probable that
Josephus would have mentioned Jesus of Nazareth? (2) If he
did, in the light of the extant texts and what we know of
Josephus and Christian redactors and copyists, what might he
have said about Jesus? But before looking at any of the texts
it is necessary to ask some preliminary questions, for their
answers have implications for our procedure.

First, it is appropriate to begin with a discussion of the
question of the possible motive or perhaps range of motives/18/
that underlie these writings in order that we can uncover any
specific *Tendenz* in Josephus in relation to our study.

(a) Of his earliest work (*J.W.* c. AD 75-9) Josephus published a
first edition in Aramaic and a second in Greek (*J.W.* 1:3), both
apparently for Jewish readers (see 1:5 and 3:108). His concern
in this work is more with contemporary events than in a past
history. Along with Polybius (*Hist.* 9.2.1-2/19/) he censures
those erudite Greeks who reduce ancient wars to insignificance
and revile those who make a special study of current events
(*J.W.* 1:13). Rather he says:

> ... the work of committing to writing events which have
> not previously been recorded and of commending to posterity
> the history of one's own time is one which merits praise
> and acknowledgement. The industrious writer is not one who
> merely remodels the scheme and arrangement of another's
> work, but one who uses fresh material and makes the
> framework of the history his own. (1:15)

Over against previous inaccurate histories of the War, as
an observer and participant he intends 'to provide the subjects
of the Roman Empire with a narrative of the facts' (1:3)./20/
But later Josephus reveals, at least from our perspective, more
important moral motives behind his work. After describing the
Roman army at great length in an aside (3:70-107), he says,
'If I have dealt at some length on this topic my intention was
not so much to extol the Romans as to console those whom they
have vanquished and to deter others who may be tempted to
revolt' (3:108)./21/ Josephus recognized that there was a
possibility of Jews beyond the Euphrates joining the revolt in
the homeland (1:4ff.). Josephus is concerned to forestall such
an occurrence. Indeed he puts his point very forcefully in a
speech of Agrippa's./22/ An excerpt from the speech shows the

depth of Josephus' concern.

> Passing to your present passion for liberty, I say
> that it comes too late. The time is past when you ought
> to have striven never to lose it. For servitude is a
> painful experience and a struggle to avoid it once for all
> is just; but the man who having once accepted the yoke
> then tries to cast it off is a contumacious slave, not a
> lover of liberty. (2:355-6)

Agrippa goes on to explain how the great nations of the
world have submitted to Rome and that the Jews of Jerusalem can
expect no allies in war. The strength of Josephus' attitude is
summed up in the lines near the end of the speech: 'The only
refuge, then, left to you is divine assistance. But even this
is ranged on the side of the Romans, for, without God's aid, so
vast an empire could never have been built up' (2:390). His
full approval of this speech is in Josephus' comment, 'Thus for
the moment Agrippa dispelled the menace of war' (2:405).

Josephus, writing with the patronage of Vespasian,/23/ is
clearly on the side of the Romans and wants to use his history
of the Jewish war to support the moral that the Jews should not
rebel against the Romans but submit to their reasonable rule.
/24/ So in the introduction to the War (1:9) he says he cannot
conceal his personal feeling that the war just past was caused
by the Jews, though not the whole nation - which he describes
as mild and peaceful (4:397; 5:27-31, 265, 439) - but 'the
Jewish tyrants who drew down upon the holy temple the unwilling
hands of the Romans' (1:10; cf. 1:27-9; 5:442-5; 6:251).
Therefore when Josephus writes about those groups and
individuals whom he considers to be trouble-makers or
insurrectionists we would expect that he will do so in an other
than positive light.

(b) In his second work, *The Jewish Antiquities* (c. AD 93-4),
Josephus proposes not to deal with contemporary events as he
does in the *War*,/25/ but, as he says, with 'our entire ancient
history and political constitution' (*Ant.* 1:5)./26/ In this
way he believes 'that the Greek-speaking world will find it
(his history) worthy of attention' (1:5). This intention, set
out in his preface (1:1-26), has parallels with the preface of
Antiquitates Romanae by Dionysius of Halicarnassus (*Ant.Rom.*
1:8:2). The title as well as the division of the *Antiquities*
into twenty books suggests that Josephus was being influenced
by Dionysius./27/ One of the probable reasons for this

dependence on Dionysius for his historiography and programme
for the *Antiquities* is Josephus' desire to highlight the moral
implications of the history of the Jews. He states this
clearly in his preface,

> ...speaking generally, the main lesson to be learnt from
> this history by any who care to peruse it is that men who
> conform to the will of God, and do not venture to
> transgress laws that have been excellently laid down,
> prosper in all things beyond belief, and for their reward
> are offered by God felicity... (1:14)

A little further on in the preface, speaking of Moses who
was the lawgiver, he says,

> ... our legislator, ... having shown that God possesses
> the very perfection of virtue, thought that men should
> strive to participate in it, and inexorably punished those
> who did not hold with or believe in these doctrines. I
> therefore entreat my readers to examine my work from this
> point of view. For, studying it in this spirit, nothing
> will appear to them unreasonable, nothing incongruous with
> the majesty of God and his love for man. (1:23-4)/28/

Within this broader aim Josephus is able to pursue a more
specific objective in relation to the events of the recent past.
It is to show, as he says much later in his work, that the Jews
had been fairly treated by the Romans.

> ...our history is chiefly meant to reach the Greeks in
> order to show them that in former times we were treated
> with all respect and were not prevented by our rulers from
> practising any of our ancestral customs but, on the
> contrary, even had their co-operation in preserving our
> religion and our way of honouring God. (16:174)

Josephus has just quoted a number of royal decrees to
support his view.   For example, the first one he cites is a
decree of Augustus (ruling from 43 BC to AD 14).

> ...Since the Jewish nation has been found well disposed
> to the Roman people not only at the present time but also
> in time past, and especially in the time of my father the
> emperor Caesar, as has their high priest Hyrcanus, it has
> been decided by me and my council under oath, with the
> consent of the Roman people, that the Jews may follow

their own customs in accordance with the law of their
fathers, just as they followed them in the time of
Hyrcanus, high priest of the Most High God... (16:162f.)

It is noticeable that all of the decrees (16:160-73) are
recent, thus, with the recent war in mind, driving home his
point that the Jews were being fairly treated and had no cause
to revolt. On the other hand, as he has mentioned in *J.W.*1:10
(quoted in (a) above) it is his view that the wars and
misfortunes of the Jews were brought on by the Jews themselves
(cf. *Ant.* 14:77 'For this misfortune which befell Jerusalem
Hyrcanus and Aristobulus were responsible, because of their
dissension'). In view of all this, in relation to our inquiry,
we may expect Josephus at least (a) to justify the actions of
the Romans and (b) to be particularly critical of the actions
of any he would consider to be Jewish tyrants, insurrectionists
or leaders of revolts and their associates, for they had
destroyed the Jewish nation and the dominance of his
aristocratic class./29/

The second preliminary question is - Is it likely that
Josephus knew the Gospels? One way forward with this question
is to examine a passage where Josephus and the Gospels overlap
in subject matter - the pericope on John the Baptist. In
Josephus the passage is as follows:

But to some of the Jews the destruction of Herod's army
seemed to be divine vengeance, and certainly a just
vengeance, for his treatment of John, surnamed the Baptist.
For Herod had put him to death, though he was a good man
and had exhorted the Jews to lead righteous lives, to
practise justice towards their fellows and piety towards
God, and so doing to join in baptism... When others too
joined the crowds about him, because they were aroused to
the highest degree by his sermons, Herod became alarmed.
Eloquence that had so great an effect on mankind might
lead to some form of sedition, for it looked as if they
would be guided by John in everything that they did.
Herod decided therefore that it would be much better to
strike first and be rid of him before his work led to an
uprising, than to wait for an upheaval, get involved in a
difficult situation and see his mistake. Though John,
because of Herod's suspicions, was brought in chains to
Machaerus, the stronghold that we have previously
mentioned, and there put to death... (*Ant.* 18:116-9)

There are a number of points of agreement between this
account and those of the Gospels (Mt 3:1-12/Mk 1:1-8/Lk 3:2-17/
Jn 1:6-8, 19-28; Mt 14:1-12/Mk 6:14-29/Lk 9:7-9). For example,
Herod kills John, John is a preacher - a preacher of piety,
baptism is an action subsequent to an inner change, crowds
flocked to hear John and he had followers. Yet there are
significant points of contrast between the two traditions. For
example, Herod's fear of John's popularity and of an uprising
led to his death rather than John's condemnation of Herod's
marriage (Mt 14:3/Mk 6:17-19/Lk 3:19); Josephus says the
execution was at Machaerus, whereas Mark's Gospel seems to some
to suggest that it was at Tiberias (Mk 6:21); John is a 'good'
(*agathon*), rather than a 'righteous' (*dikaion*, Mk 6:20), man;
John exhorts his hearers to righteous or 'moral lives' (*aretēn*)
rather than to 'repentance' (*metanoias*, Mt 3:7-10/Lk 3:7-9;
Mk 1:4)./30/

Thus it is quite reasonable to conclude at a point where
the subject matter of Josephus and the Gospel traditions overlap
and where Josephus' dependence might be most obvious, no such
dependence - either way - seems likely./31/ This immediately
raises the question of Josephus' source(s) here. In short we
do not know what his source(s) were. He may have had
information from Agrippa II (see *Life* 366) and perhaps also
reports - oral or written - from Jews./32/

We can look at the question of Josephus' knowledge of the
Gospels from another perspective - the intended audience and
function of the Gospels. Many recent scholars have argued that
the Gospels were addressed specifically to the Christian
community./33/ If they are correct, then on this ground also it
is reasonable to suppose that Josephus did not know the Gospels.
/34/ It cannot even be shown that the different communities of
the early Church always knew about the writings of other
Christian communities./35/

Nevertheless, thirdly, is it likely that, even without
knowledge of the Gospels, Josephus would have known about or
written about Jesus? On the one hand, Paul's letter to the
Romans written in the mid 50's - our earliest witness to the
existence of Christian communities there - reveals that
Christianity was well established in the capital at least two,
perhaps four decades before Josephus wrote in the mid to late
70's and even before he first went there at the age of 26 (*Life*
13)./36/ Further there were Christians in high places in Rome,
at least towards the end of the first century (Marius Acilius

Glabrio, Flavius Clemens, Flavia Domitilla, see Dio Cassius
Hist. 68:13f.; Suetonius *Domitian* 10), so it is possible that
Josephus may even have come in contact with Christians in Rome.
Also, the Roman historians Suetonius (*Claudius* 25; *Nero* 16) and
Tacitus (*Annals* 15:44) make mention of the Christians. Even
though these are later writers than Josephus it suggests that
Christians were not unknown among the Roman intelligentsia.

On the other hand the decisive factor indicating that
Josephus would not only have heard of the Jesus movement but
have mentioned it or its founder is Josephus' interest in events
in Palestine at this time as well as his desire to show that
such movements, as he saw them, were futile. In Acts 5:34-9
the Jesus movement is compared to the popular messianic
movements of Theudas and Judas the Galilean. In Josephus Judas
and a Theudas (identified with the Theudas of Acts by most,
though not all, scholars) are roundly condemned. Theudas is
called a *goēs* (cheat, rogue or imposter) and he is said to have
deceived (*apataō*) many people by his talk (*Ant.* 20:97-9). In
Ant. 18:4-10 Judas is accused of causing factions among the Jews
which led to the slaughter of fellow citizens and eventually
even the destruction of the temple (18:8; see also *J.W.* 2:118,
433; 7:253; *Ant.* 18:23-5; 20:102)./37/ It would not be
surprising then if Josephus associated Jesus with these false
prophets and deceivers./38/ As it is one of Josephus'
principal aims in his major works, and brought into particularly
sharp focus in the *Antiquities* (see above), to show the
futility of and thereby condemn such men and movements it would
not be surprising if Josephus both mentioned Jesus or the
subsequent movement and also condemned Jesus and his followers -
perhaps as cheats or deceivers./39/

A number of factors would have contributed to Josephus'
attitude to these movements - including the Jesus movement.
(1) Josephus' life in Rome is unlikely to have altered, in fact
it probably confirmed, his attitude to the Jesus movement.
Attitudes in Rome can be gauged from the historians we have
mentioned. Suetonius (*Claudius* 25) said that as a result of
constant rioting at the instigation of 'Chrestus', that is
Christ, the Jews were expelled from Rome (AD 49). Then in his
Life of Nero 16 Suetonius said that Christians were 'a body of
people addicted to a novel and mischievious superstition'.
Tacitus, reporting Nero's attempt to blame the Christians for
the fire of Rome in AD 64 (*Annals* 15:44), describes the
Christians as 'a class of men loathed for their vices'. And the
Christians in high places, also mentioned above, were eventually

either banished or executed.

(2) Josephus was an aristocrat from Palestine and he describes his own situation in Rome as one of privilege and the envy of other Jews (*Life* 424). His being exempt from tax and his receiving pensions and protection from the emperors (*Life* 422-9) mean that he would most likely be out of sympathy with the masses and nationalistic movements.

(3) Another important factor in shaping Josephus' general attitude to movements in which he would have included the Jesus movement is that one of his sources, Nicolas of Damascus, a wealthy Syrian Greek minister of Herod's, had a profound aversion to nationalistic parties./40/

From these preliminary questions we can see that Josephus is quite likely to have known of the Jesus movement and its founder, whom he probably classed as one of the leaders of the Palestinian revolts; that Josephus was not dependent on the Gospels for information about Jesus and the Christians whom he may have known of in Rome (though knowledge of them is hardly likely to have changed his entrenched views).

(a) *Antiquities* 20:200/41/

> (Ananus, the high priest) convened the judges of the Sanhedrin and brought before them a man named James, the brother of Jesus who was called the Christ (*Iēsou tou legomenou Christou*), and certain others.

The text goes on to say that:

> He accused them of having transgressed the law and delivered them up to be stoned. Those of the inhabitants of the city who were considered the most fair-minded and who were strict in observance of the law were offended at this. (20:200-1)

We take this passage first because it is generally seen to be the most straightforward and because the reference to Christ here is thought to suggest that Josephus has mentioned him before. If this is the case then it would of course be of help in examining the possible previous reference (*Ant.* 18:63-4).

Our earliest witness to Josephus' mention of Jesus is Origen (*CC* 1:47).

...Josephus in the eighteenth book of the Jewish
antiquities bears witness that John was a baptist and
promised purification to people who were baptised. The
same author, although he did not believe in Jesus as
Christ, sought for cause of the fall of Jerusalem and the
destruction of the temple. He ought to have said that the
plot against Jesus was the reason why these catastrophes
came upon the people, because they had killed the
prophesied Christ; however, although unconscious of it, he
is not far from the truth when he says that these disasters
befell the Jews to avenge James the Just, who was a brother
of 'Jesus the so-called Christ', since they had killed him
who was a very righteous man.

Then further on Origen says (CC 2:13):

The siege began when Nero was still emperor, and continued
until the rule of Vespasian. His son, Titus, captured
Jerusalem, so Josephus says, on account of James the Just,
the brother of Jesus the so-called Christ, though in
reality it was on account of Jesus the Christ of God.

And in his Commentary on Matthew Origen also says:

And to so great a reputation among the people for
righteousness did James rise that Flavius Josephus, who
wrote the 'Antiquities of the Jews' in twenty books, when
wishing to exhibit the cause why the people suffered so
great misfortunes that even the temple was razed to the
ground, said, that these things happened to them in
accordance with the wrath of God in consequence of the
things which they had dared to do against James the brother
of Jesus who is called the Christ. And the wonderful
thing is, that, though he did not accept Jesus as Christ,
he yet gave testimony that the righteousness of James was
so great; and he says that the people thought that they
had suffered these things because of James. (10:17)

The mention of John the Baptist in CC 1:47 probably refers
to Ant. 18:116-9. Origen does not give a precise reference as
to where Josephus mentions Jesus. A difficulty in these two
passages is that Origen refers to Josephus saying that these
disasters - the fall of Jerusalem and the destruction of the
temple - befell the Jews to avenge the death of James. However,
in the texts we have Josephus nowhere connects the fall of
Jerusalem with the death of James. Thackeray's solution was to

propose that Origen confused Josephus' account of the death of
James with that of Hegesippus - for the names would have
sounded similar - an account which ends by saying 'And
immediately Vespasian besieged them' (quoted by Eusebius *H.E.*
ii.23.11-18).   However the reports of Josephus and Hegesippus
are considerably different and as Origen twice refers to
Josephus on this specific point - which would completely lose
its force if he had mistakenly quoted a Christian author - it
seems very unlikely that Origen would have confused the stories.

   The immediate question, then, is whether or not Origen is
using an older, more reliable version of Josephus.   In other
words did Josephus connect the death of James with the
destruction of Jerusalem or is it more likely that a Christian
redactor edited the passage to make this connection?   We know
Origen approved of the connection, though he would have
preferred the death of Jesus to have been more directly
connected.   Hegesippus also linked the fall of Jerusalem with
the maltreatment of the Christians.   Then in Mark 13,
Luke 19:43 and 21:20 we already have hints of such an
association.   Thus it seems that Christians would have been
anxious to make the connection if Josephus had not.

   On the other hand we can suggest why Josephus most
probably would not have made this connection between the
persecution of James and the fall of Jerusalem.   The cardinal
point to bear in mind (see above) is that Josephus wants to
condemn popular anti-establishment groups like the Christians
(see above and also *J.W.* 2:13).   However in this report (*Ant.*
20:197ff.) Josephus is critical not of James, or any associated
group, but of a heartless Ananus who had him stoned.   James is
described as having sympathies among those 'who were strict in
observance of the law' - precisely those whom Josephus saw as
helping to preserve the peace.   If he knows of James as a
Christian, that is, as associated with a messianic pretender,
then Josephus has here reversed all his sympathies.   Josephus
is contradicting his campaign against such popular leaders of
the Jews.   We may conclude, then, that Origen probably does not
have a reliable version of Josephus, but one in which Christian
copyists have connected the fall of Jerusalem with the
persecution of Christians.   This conclusion raises doubts about
the originality of the text associating James with 'Jesus who
was called the Christ'.   What then of the origin of this last
phrase?

We note, first, that Origen quotes this phrase exactly
from the extant texts each of the times he mentions it (*CC*
1:47; 2:13; *Comm.Matt.* 10:17). This certainly suggests that
what we now have in *Ant.* 20:200 was what Origen had before him.
/42/ And few scholars doubt the authenticity of the reference.
/43/ For example, Walter Bauer says that 'since the author
through the "so-called" clearly stands aside from the Christian
faith there is no reason for denying the words to Josephus.'/44/
However in Josephus *legomenos* very rarely,/45/ if ever, means
'alleged'. It is, rather, similar to *epikaloumenos* which can
be translated 'with the by-name', though *legomenos* introduces
an alternative name that can stand by itself./46/ The same
usage as here in *Ant.* 20:200 is also found in Matthew 1:16,
where it certainly does not mean 'alleged' (cf. 27:17; also,
e.g., 2 Macc 12:17; 14:6; 3 Macc 1:3). Thus the word should be
translated, according to its context, as 'said to be', or 'who
is spoken of as', or simply 'called'./47/ Nevertheless, the
construction *Iēsou tou legomenou Christou* is not characteristic
of Josephus, who usually places *legomenos* after the name in
question/48/ rather than before or between two names as here in
the text of *Ant.* 20:200./49/ On the other hand, it is a
construction Christians used when referring to Jesus (see
Mt 1:16; 27:17,22; Jn 4:25; 9:11/50/). Thus it can be argued
that the phrase under discussion is secondary. There being a
James in the NT known as the brother of Jesus (Mk 6:3; Gal 1:19),
who was a conservative in relation to the law (Acts 15:13ff.;
Gal 2:12), it can be understood how a Christian scribe -
sometime between the late first century, when Josephus published
the *Antiquities*, and the middle of the third century, when
Origen knew of a text containing the reference to Jesus - would
have entered this phrase here.

Brandon has suggested, because Origen says that Josephus
did not believe (*apistōn*, *CC* 1:47) or accept (*ou katadexamenos*
*Comm.Matt.*10:17) Jesus as Messiah, that Origen's text of
Josephus must have contained a further negative reference to, or
active rejection of, Jesus./51/ But Origen need not have seen
the phrase as a messianic confession, but rather as an
identificatory formula. *Apistōn* need mean no more than a lack
of faith/52/ and *ou katadexamenos* does not carry sufficient
force - that is the sense 'to actively reject'/53/ - for us to
follow this speculation of Brandon's.

On *Ant.* 20:200 we conclude by suggesting that the phrase
'the brother of Jesus who was called the Christ' did not
originate with Josephus. Rather, a Christian, anxious to

capitalize on the positive light in which an early Christian was
placed, took the opportunity of inserting these words. If the
James mentioned is that of Acts 15 and Galatians, we may have
here some light shed on earliest Christianity; but, if our
suggestion is correct, this passage offers no evidence in
relation to the historical Jesus. It is sometimes argued that
the way Josephus refers to Jesus here implies that he has
already spoken of him./54/ However the phrase does not need to,
and usually does not, mean that an earlier reference has been
made to the subject./55/ Either way we are not in a position to
draw any conclusions about the historical Jesus from *Ant*. 20:200.

(b) *Antiquities* 18:63-4/56/

> About this time there lived Jesus, a wise man, if indeed
> one ought to call him a man. For he was one who wrought
> surprising feats and was a teacher of such people as
> accept the truth gladly. He won over many Jews and many of
> the Greeks. He was the Messiah. When Pilate, upon hearing
> him accused by men of the highest standing amongst us, had
> condemned him to be crucified, those who had in the first
> place come to love him did not give up their affection for
> him. On the third day he appeared to them restored to
> life, for the prophets of God had prophesied these and
> countless other marvellous things about him. And the tribe
> of the Christians, so called after him, has still to this
> day not disappeared.

As with the passage with which we have already dealt scholars
are divided in their opinion of its value. For example Zeitlin
thinks that because of the vocabulary the passage was written by
Eusebius./57/ But the majority of scholars say either, that the
passage contains a genuine core that has been interpolated by
Christians,/58/ or, with Hahn, that it 'is so expressly
Christian in its content and language that we must consider it a
later interpolation'./59/ On the other hand a few writers take
the passage to be authentic./60/

We must begin our investigation by asking if it is likely
that Josephus would have mentioned Jesus here in this context.
Ant. 18:55-62 is paralleled in Josephus' earlier *J.W.* 2:169-77,
and it is noticeable that the so-called *Testimonium Flavianum*
is missing there. But we cannot use this point against the
authenticity of *Ant*. 18:63f., for Josephus has at times
considerably enlarged on his previous work:/61/ note
Ant. 14:156-17:199, which considerably enlarges, and, not without

inconsistencies, alters the picture of Herod already given in
J.W. 1:203-665.

However, Norden/62/ says that, when we look at the
sequence of reports in *Ant.* 18:55-87, pars. 63f. do not fit,
notably because of par. 65 which begins: 'About this same time
another outrage threw the Jews into an uproar'. This
introduces a story of the crucifixion of some priests of Isis
which took place not in AD 30, as the context suggests, but in
AD 19 (cf. Tacitus, *Annals* 2:85). Also, the Christ Passage is
the only one in the section (18:55-87) which does not have the
catchword 'riot' or 'disturbance' (*thorubeō*, 18:62,65;
thorubos, 18:85,88). Over against this argument it is to be
noted that even without the Christ Passage the reports are not
in sequence, for the crucifixion of the priests of Isis
(18:65ff.) is to be dated at AD 19 (see above), while the
earlier report (18:55) of Pilate making his winter quarters in
Jerusalem is probably the first year of Pilate's office (AD 26).
Then while the word 'riot' or 'disturbance' does not occur in
the *Testimonium* the Jesus movement probably was seen as a
disruptive faction and any such reference would have been
excised by a Christian copyist (see further on *ginetai de*
below).

Another potential difficulty in holding the authenticity
of this passage is that the earliest extant witness to it is
Eusebius, who quotes it almost exactly in his *History* 1:11
(AD 323). But Origen (c. AD 185- c.254), who refers to
Ant. 18:116-9 and 20:200 (see above), does not refer to this
passage. Instead he says that Josephus did not accept Jesus
as the Christ (*Comm.Matt.* 10:17, quoted above), whereas the
present passage has 'He was the Christ'. We probably ought to
conclude from this that, although it is likely that Josephus
referred to Jesus here in *Ant.* 18:63f., the passage - at least
as it stands - though quoted by Eusebius, was not known or
recognized by him as referring to Jesus of Nazareth. We would
have to say the same thing for Irenaeus and Tertullian, that,
although they knew of the writings of Josephus, they did not
refer to this passage, because it was not known to them or
recognized by them as referring to Jesus./63/

We need to look more closely at the extant text querying
the origin of its elements. As well as positively contributing
to the text it is also possible that later redactors and
copyists have also deleted offensive pieces from the passage.
Therefore we may be able to speculate on what may have been

excised from Josephus here. The redaction-critic's task in
Antiquities is made particularly difficult because the style of
the work is very uneven. Thackeray's suggestion - of two
scribes, one more able and one a 'Thucydidean hack' being
involved - may be too speculative in the light of the
evidence./64/ However, the general conclusion that *Ant.* 20 is
written in the 'normal' style of Josephus and also that in *Life*
'we get as near as we can anywhere to the *ipsissima verba* of
Josephus'/65/ will be part of our working assumptions. So also
will be the suggestion that *Ant.* 15-16 and 17-19 are two
separate units of style./66/

        The passage begins *ginetai de*. This is not uncommon in
Josephus, including *Ant.* 20 (51, 76, 118, 173, 230)./67/ And,
importantly, it is used by Josephus to introduce reports of
Jewish disturbances (*e.g.*, *Ant.* 18:310; 20:118; 20:173;
J.W. 1:99,648; 4:208). Thus Eisler may be justified in
inserting something like *archē neōn thorubōn* ('an occasion for
new disturbances') after *chronon* in the introduction.

        Following the name of Jesus one of the manuscripts of the
quotation of this passage in Eusebius' *Demonstratio Evangelica*
III:5:105 has *tis*/68/ which, with proper names, often carries a
sense of contempt or is deprecatory./69/   Thus the reading 'a
certain Jesus' is likely to be original, for no Christian would
introduce this to the text.

        Jesus is then described as a wise man (*sophos anēr*).
Eisler conjectured that the text once read *sophistēs anēr* (a
sophist), for Judas of Galilee who founded his own sect is
likewise described in *J.W.* 2:118./70/ But it is difficult to
suggest a reasonable motivation for such a change. Non-
Christian copyists are unlikely to wish to alter this
description. It is even more unlikely for Christians to make
this change; Jesus is nowhere described in the NT as a 'wise
man' - it is God who is wise (*e.g.*, Rom 16:27; 1 Tim 1:17), and
later Christians did not so title Jesus./71/ In Josephus it is
a term used of Solomon ('a wise man endowed with every virtue'
Ant. 8:53) and of Daniel ('a wise man and skilful in
discovering things beyond man's power and known only to God',
Ant. 10:237) and denotes a cleverness or mastery of skill./72/
In turn the phrase which we shall mention presently, 'For he
was one who wrought surprising feats...' is consonant with
this idea of Josephus thinking Jesus a 'clever' man. In the
context of the passage Josephus probably uses the description
with some suspicion or irony./73/

The parenthetical clause 'if indeed one ought to call him
a man' is taken by Thackeray to carry a ring of insincerity and
therefore authentic./74/ But, if, as we have argued, 'wise man'
is original to Josephus, this parenthetical clause may well be
from the hand of a Christian implying that Jesus was more than
a man./75/

The description 'For he was one who wrought surprising
(*paradoxos*) feats' may be from the hand of Josephus. *Paradoxos*
is relatively common in his writing (48 times excluding the
doubtful occurrence in *Ant*. 4:66; 17:330 and 18:63). It does
not often mean 'miraculous' (*e.g.*, *Ant*. 2:223,285,295,345,347;
3:1,30,38; 5:28; 9:58,60; 10:214,235), but can also be used for,
'strange' (*e.g.* *Ant*. 2:91; 5:125; 6:171,290; 9:14,182;
10:21,266; 15:379 and *Ag.Ap*. 2:114). On the other hand it is
used only once in the *NT* (Lk 5:26) and only occasionally by
early Christian writers./76/ 'Works' or 'feats' (*ergōn*) could
be evidence of a Christian hand (cf. the Fourth Gospel), but
poiētēs is not used in the NT, and when it is used in the early
Church in relation to Jesus it is usually connected with the
notion of him as participating in creation not with performing
miracles./77/ Eisler says that it is used in Josephus only of
poets (*Ant*. 1:16; 12:38,110,113; (18:63); *Ag.Ap*. 1:172; 2:14,
239,251,256), but as Thackeray suggests the amanuensis here
seems to have a predilection for resolving simple verbs into
two (*e.g.*, *Ant*. 17:155)./78/ On balance then we can probably
attribute this description of Jesus to Josephus, though in view
of the use of *paradoxos* in Josephus we ought not to equate it
too quickly with 'miracle'./79/

Jesus is then described as 'a teacher of such people as
accept the truth gladly'. A favourite description of Jesus for
the early Christians was 'teacher' (see Mark's Gospel).
However, when we examine Josephus' use of the word and
description of 'teachers' it is interesting to discover that of
the sixteen occurrences of the term seven of them/80/ refer
either to false teachers or teaching. That Josephus may have
described Jesus as a teacher and yet understood him to be a
false teacher is consonant with a suggestion that a slight
emendation of ΤΑΑΗΘΗ to ΤΑΛΗΘΗ has occurred in the text. It is
suggested that the middle bar of the capital letter 'A' has
been removed, so the ΤΑ ΑΗΘΗ ('the unusual') becomes ΤΑΛΗΘΗ
('the true')./81/ To postulate an emendation is somewhat
speculative and in relation to this case ΑΗΘΗΣ occurs in
J.W. 1:64; 4:587; 6:403; *Ant*. 3:81 and 13:276, but ΤΑΛΗΘΗ

occurs 36 times. On the other hand there are a number of things
to be said for the emendation of the text here. First in
J.W. 6:403 the manuscripts are not agreed whether or not to read
that the Roman soldiers were 'truly' or 'unusually' perplexed at
the lack of opposition./82/ Secondly that Jesus' followers are
said to accept the 'unusual' is in keeping with what has just
been said about him; that he did 'unusual' things. Thirdly,
Jesus has been described as doing 'works'. It is then more
likely that Josephus went on to talk about Jesus' followers
accepting the unusual rather than the truth. Finally here in
favour of this element being from Josephus and originally
referring to the unusual is the appearance of *hēdonē*
('pleasure'). It is very difficult to see a Christian using
this word here. 'Pleasure' did sometimes refer to the pleasures
of the Christian life./83/ However where it occurs in the NT it
is always in the negative sense of human pleasure (Lk 8:14;
Titus 3:3; Jas 4:1,3; 2 Pet 2:13) and in the early Church its
predominant use was to describe something incompatible with the
Christian life./84/ And in Josephus it is both common (127
times, 50 of them in *Ant.* 17-19, the section Thackeray isolated
as from a separate amanuensis/85/ and very often with the
negative connotations of an evil or sensuous desire (cf., *e.g.*,
Ant. 18:6,59,70 (in association with *dechomenos*), 77,85,176).

It is quite likely that Josephus wrote 'And he won over
many Jews and many of the Greeks'. *Epagō* ('to lead') is not
used in the NT of the relationship between Jesus and his
followers. (It is in the NT only at Acts 5:28; 2 Pet 2:1,5.)
In fact in 2 Peter it is used in connection with false prophets
'bringing' destruction on themselves. And later in the ancient
Church it is not a term normally used of the relationship
between Jesus and his disciples./86/ On the other hand the
repetition of 'many' is characteristic of Josephus, especially
here in the unit *Ant.* 17-19 (17:126,204,251,276; 18:38,353,366;
19:93,335). The neuter *to Hellēnikon* is not 'thoroughly
Josephan' as Thackeray thinks,/87/ for it occurs only here and
in *J.W.* 2:268. However Thackeray is right to point out that
there is a rough parallel to this description of the
'missionary' activity of Jesus in the pseudo-Alexander in this
section who 'was himself carried away with these tales... (that
he was Herod's son and)... he won the confidence (*epēgageto*) of
all the Jews with whom he came into contact' (*Ant.* 17:327).
Thackeray is also probably correct to suggest that Christians
are unlikely to say this in view of the strong Gospel tradition
that Jesus' ministry was confined to Palestine,/88/ and even in
some traditions to the Israelites (*e.g.*, Mt 10:5f.). Thus it

is unlikely that a Christian would have needed to enter this
element into Josephus' text./89/

The sentence of this passage which has been the centre of
much of the attention given to the *Testimonium* is: 'He was the
Christ' (*ho christos houtos ēn*). As these would not be the
words of a Jewish historian and as Origen says that Josephus
did not acknowledge Jesus to be the Christ, this statement
cannot be original - at least as it stands./90/ And in view of
Luke 23:35, John 7:26 and Acts 9:22 it may be more reasonable
to conclude that a Christian has inserted the messianic
confession./91/ On the other hand from what we have been able
to establish as probably coming from Josephus, it may be
expected that he would mention something about Jesus being
called or thought to be a messianic pretender./92/ But he
nowhere explains the term 'Christ'/93/ which may not have been
understood by his readers, and so it is reasonable to maintain
that 'He was the Christ' is secondary.

Then follows the sentence: 'When Pilate upon hearing him
accused by men of the highest standing amongst us, had
condemned him to be crucified, those who had in the first place
come to love him did not give up their affection for him.' The
objection has been raised that 'men of highest standing amongst
us' is not from Josephus because it does not show the
objectivity of the historian Josephus. But although in *J.W.*
Josephus does avoid speaking of the Jews in the first person he
abandons this in the *Antiquities* where his purpose is to
present the Jewish case./94/ 'Pilate... had condemned him to
be crucified' corresponds to Tacitus (*Annals* 15:44) 'per
procuratorem Pontium Pilatum supplicio adfectus erat', so that
the phrase may be a piece of Roman legal terminology./95/
Importantly Josephus uses a similar phrase in *J.W.* 2:183. We
may also take the remainder of the sentence as coming from
Josephus. The disciples are described as those who loved him.
This is not an expression characteristic of Christians
describing the disciples; 'followers' might have been expected
from a Christian. Further, in *Ant.* 18:60 and 242,245,361 'love'
has the deprecatory sense of 'to be content with' and in
J.W. 1:171 and *Ant.* 16:158 'admire'. A Christian copyist is
also unlikely to be responsible for *ouk epausanto* ('they did
not cease'), for it is in the style of Josephus, cf.
J.W. 2:494; *Ant.* 8:277; 15:80; 18:58./96/ The sentence in
Josephus ends rather clumsily (*hoi to agapēsantes*) so that it
may be suspected that an editor has deleted something, though
we cannot determine what it may have been./97/

There are some difficulties with the sentence which begins
'On the third day he appeared to them restored to life...'.
Although Josephus could have written the phrase 'on the third
day' (see *Ant.* 3:290; 7:1; 20:57/98/), this and the words
immediately following read very much like a Christian confession
(cf. (Mk 16:11); Lk 24:5,23; Acts 1:3; Rom 14:9; 2 Cor 13:4;
Rev 2:8), and are most likely from a Christian hand./99/ Thus
in Mark 16:9 a Christian has used *phainō* in the same way as it
is used here (cf. Jn 21:1,14)./100/ There is no textual
evidence to support the suggestion that *hōs elegon* or *hōs
legousin* should be read after the phrase *ephanē gar autois.*
/101/ The text says that 'these things' (*tauta*) were
prophesied by the holy prophets; yet only one thing has so far
been mentioned. However the *tauta* may be referring back to
things in previous sentences, or generalizing, or could be
plural by attraction to the following phrase. In any case
'countless other marvellous things' is a characteristic,
slightly derogatory, hyperbole of Josephus' (*e.g.*, *J.W.* 1:351,
540; 2:361; 4:121,240; 5:179,379; 6:2,271; 7:263; *Ant.* 1:228;
2:202; 4:114; 7:37,324; 8:113,127; 9:205; 13:382; 17:192,269;
19:1,3,67; *Ag.Ap.* 1:10; 2:131,228).

In the last sentence/102/ the word 'tribe' (*phulon*) is a
term Christians rarely used of themselves./103/ The word
Christianos here is of Latin formation, a nickname originating
in Antioch (Acts 11:26) and is used by other pagan authors.
/104/ Thus the last part of the *Testimonium Flavianum* is
probably from the hand of Josephus.

From the discussion of *Ant.* 18:63f. we can suggest that
Josephus did mention Jesus here, but that Christian redactors
and copyists have added to, subtracted from and altered what
Josephus wrote. The following is a possible reconstruction of
what he may have written.

About this time there lived (a certain) Jesus, a wise man
... For he was one who wrought surprising feats and was a
teacher of such people as accept the (unusual) gladly.
He won over many Jews and many Greeks. When Pilate, upon
hearing him accused by men of the highest standing amongst
us, had him condemned to be crucified, those who had in
the first place come to love him did not give up their
affection for him... for the prophets of God had
prophesied these and countless marvellous things about
him. And the tribe of Christians, so called after him,
has still to this day not disappeared.

What are the implications of this conclusion for the
historian in his search for the historical Jesus? The first
point to make is that although Josephus is most likely to have
mentioned Jesus and his followers at this point in *Ant.* 18,
Christians have so tampered with the text that what Josephus
wrote can only be recovered through reconstruction of the text.
Therefore, in turn, our conclusions can be only of the most
tentative kind. On the basis of our reconstructed text we have
evidence, independent of Christian traditions, not only of the
existence of Jesus, but of his reputation as a worker of
surprising feats (miracles?) and as a wise or clever teacher.
That Josephus thought that there was something distinctive
about Jesus' ministry is indicated by this vocabulary and also
by saying that it was the unusual that his adherents accepted
gladly. The reputation of the success of Jesus' ministry is
alluded to in saying that he won over many Jews and many
Greeks. That the ministry of Jesus ended with him being
crucified by the Romans is also supported by Josephus. The
mention of 'men of the highest standing among us' may be
support for the Gospel tradition that Jesus was tried before
the Sanhedrin (Mt 26:57-68/Mk 14:53-65/Lk 22:54-71/Jn 18:13-24)
before the matter came to the attention of the Roman
procurator of Judea. Josephus' remark - possibly slightly
derogatory - that 'the prophets of God had prophesied these
and countless other marvellous things about him' is probably
support for the importance of Scripture to Jesus and the early
Christians. Finally, that the Jesus movement continued and
that Josephus knew of Christians, perhaps in Rome, is suggested
by the last sentence of the *Testimonium*.

(c) *The Slavonic Addition* (after *J.W.* 2:174)/105/
     In 1929-30 Robert Eisler published a massive work *IHSOUS
BASILEUS OU BASILEUSAS* that argued that the Slavonic version
was dependent on a Greek or Aramaic manuscript more reliable
than those presently available. Initially there was
considerable discussion of Eisler's work. Some, like
Thackeray,/106/ were generous in their acceptance of it, while
others, such as Jack,/107/ rejected Eisler. The present state
of scholarly opinion is summed up by Rubinstein.

     While there is nothing in the O.R. (Old Russian/Slavonic)
     version of *Wars* to lead one to conclude that it is a
     translation of Josephus' original semitic version or a
     short Greek version intermediate between the semitic and
     the standard version, there is some evidence in the O.R.
     version of its ultimate dependence on a fuller Greek text.

There is also evidence in the O.R. version which seems to
point to deliberate additions either by the Byzantine
copyist or by the Russian translator or both./108/

Paul Winter had drawn attention to the difficulties in
numeration of the reports of 'disturbances' at this point in
J.W. (Slavonic). In the Slavonic text the disturbance is 'the
second riot', which corresponds to the sequence in the Greek
text but not in the Slavonic text itself where it is the third
disturbance. The conclusion which Winter rightly draws is that
the 'Slavonic Addition' 'is an addition composed even later than
the time at which the testimonium in its present form came into
existence'./109/

(d) *An Arabic Version* (of *Ant.* 18:63f.)/110/
     In an Arabic history of the world the Melkiti Bishop
Agapius of Hieropolis quotes the *Testimonium*.

> Similarly Josephus the Hebrew. For he says in the treatise
> that he has written on the governance of the Jews: At this
> time there was a wise man who was called Jesus. And his
> conduct was good, and (he) was known to be virtuous. And
> many people from among the Jews and the other nations became
> his disciples. Pilate condemned him to be crucified and to
> die. And those who had become his disciples did not abandon
> his discipleship. They reported that he had appeared to
> them three days after his crucifixion and that he was alive;
> accordingly, he was perhaps the Messiah concerning whom the
> prophets have recounted wonders./111/

The most noticeable feature of this text is that it lacks many of
the doubtful phrases that have been discussed in the 'vulgate
recension' and is perhaps, therefore, evidence that the
Testimonium is not a Christian interpolation but, as we have
argued, a Christianized version of what Josephus wrote./112/

David Flusser hailed the text as authentic./113/ However
the Arabic text is, according to Pines, in all probability a
translation from a Syriac version of a Greek text./114/ Further,
the words 'and to die' reflect an Islamic milieu where the
Christians had to contend with the view that Jesus had escaped
death and someone was crucified in his place./115/ Also,
although Pines favours the originality of the phrase 'he was
perhaps the Messiah',/116/ even with the circumspection of the
phrase it is unlikely that Josephus would even have gone this

far./117/ Ernst Bammel is probably correct in noting that this
hesitant expression about Jesus would be strange within the
confines of a Jewish-Christian controversy, but that it would
be quite appropriate and serviceable in a three-way contest
among religions. To quote Bammel, 'The qualified support given
by the representative of one religion could be used as an
argument *vis à vis* the other religion, whereas the claim of a
full support rendered by the one side to the other was bound to
be met by the disbelief of the third participant'./118/ Bammel
says that this kind of situation arose in the East after the
rise of the Sassanian Empire and again in the wake of Islam in
which the hesitant phrase 'he was perhaps the Messiah' could
have been appropriate in the arguments. Thus, to conclude
with Bammel, 'the characteristic features of the *Testimonium* in
the form rendered by the Arabic work of the Bishop of
Hierapolis point rather in favour of its having originated in
an Islamic environment than in an earlier one'./119/

      Our investigations have led to the conclusion that, so far
as it is possible to ascertain, only behind the report in
Ant. 18:63f. is there reliable evidence in Josephus for the
historian seeking to reconstruct a picture of Jesus of
Nazareth. Others may wish to call into question the
reliability of what Josephus knew of Jesus, but as well as
what we have already said above we can summarize his
understanding of Jesus as follows. From the context of
Ant. 18:63f., where Jesus is called a wise ('clever') man,
performing surprising or unusual feats, winning many followers
and being crucified, it seems that Josephus understood Jesus
to be a messianic pretender misleading or deceiving the people
and being part of the causes of the trouble in his homeland.
The text here does not say what Josephus thought Jesus would
have been charged with. However by comparing this report with
J.W. 2:55,258-60,403 and 434 Josephus may have understood
Jesus to have been accused of 'aspiring to sovereignty'
(cf. *J.W.* 2:55) or at least being responsible for preliminary
incidents leading to insurrection (cf. *J.W.* 2:258-60).

                    II. The Rabbinic Traditions

      Again the principal question which we will address in
discussing this literature is, 'What light, if any, do these
Jewish traditions shed on our knowledge of the historical
Jesus?' In particular, do we find in this material an
independent source of information about Jesus? If so, is it
reliable? Or, is this material a mere 'polemical and

tendentious misrepresentation'?/120/ As pointed out earlier
this literature is important not least because it is helpful in
filling out the background to the historical Jesus. However,
here we will restrict our discussion to seeing what the
historian can discover about Jesus in the Rabbinic traditions.
The material in these traditions which may possibly refer to
Jesus is collected in a number of places./121/ Potentially, at
least, there are many useful references. However there are
questions to be asked of them before the historian is able to
rely on their veracity and use them to help sketch a picture of
the historical Jesus.

        One of our greatest difficulties, shared by all involved in
Rabbinic studies, is the problem of dating. We will follow
Neusner where he takes 'very seriously attributions of a saying
to a named authority in a particular school and time'./122/
This approach is based on an assumption which, despite Neusner's
hesitation, is not without its force. That is, it is assumed
that the tradition has attempted to be faithful in its
assignation of sayings. This is a reasonable assumption for,
although the Mishnah attributes to a man words which the
Tosephta says were spoken by someone later, this is not a
common phenomenon./123/ But we need to proceed with three
further methodological principles also elucidated by Neusner.

        First, where a saying is in the name of an earlier
authority the attribution can be upheld 'if there is a
correlation between temporal attribution and traits of logic or
conception so that what is claimed in the attribution to be
early is shown in the character of what is attributed to be
relatively primitive'./124/ The second principle from Neusner
which helps us date and assign sayings is that if a later rabbi
refers to the substance and language of a pericope but stands
outside the substance and language we may suppose that the
pericope predates him or is contemporary to him in much of its
present form and wording./125/ Neusner's third principle is
that material which is early is generally more reliable than
that which is later: the order of reliability then being
(1) Mishnah-Tosephta, (2) Tannaitic midrashim, (3) baraitot in
the Palestinian Talmud, (4) baraitot in the Babylonian Talmud
and (5) traditions in later midrashim./126/

        Even after a saying has been assigned to its probable date
and/or creator the question still remains open as to how useful
it is for the historian in his task of sketching a picture of
Jesus. Thus we will need to go on and ask if the earliest form

of the tradition was intended as a reference to Jesus or was
only subsequently and incorrectly related to Jesus. We will
also have to exclude as possibly unreliable sayings and
material which have their setting in Jewish polemic against
Jesus, the tradition or early Christianity.

We shall begin by discussing the less useful material.

(a) *Toledoth Jesus*/127/
This Jewish 'Life of Jesus' is also known under other
titles, *e.g.*, 'Deeds of the One Who Was Hung' and 'Deeds of
Jesus'./128/ The beginnings of a Jewish life of Jesus may have
its roots in passages like those we will be discussing below
(*e.g.*, *b. Soṭa* 47a and *b. Sanh*. 43a; 67a; 107b)./129/ But it
is difficult to decide on a date for the complete or fully
developed 'Life' for, with the many different versions, it is
difficult to decide on what can be said to constitute the
Toledoth. The earliest witness to it is c. AD 826 in a mention
of elements of it by Agobard the Archbishop of Lyons./130/
However the consensus of scholarly opinion seems to be that
while a connected Toledoth-form may have been in circulation by
the end of the third century/131/ the developed Toledoth was
probably composed somewhere around the fifth and sixth
centuries AD./132/

For our purposes we will exclude the Toledoth from the
evidence for at least three reasons. First, even if with
Krauss an *Ur-Toledoth* is postulated we have a date probably no
earlier.than the fourth century AD for the creation of the
document./133/ Secondly the Sitz im Leben for the Toledoth is
a polemic against the Christians/134/ and, may be, as Krauss
suggested, a Jewish reply to the Gospel of the Hebrews./135/
In any case, thirdly, there is, throughout the Toledoth, what
seems to be prolific borrowing from the canonical Gospels and
Acts (for example elements in the passion narrative) as well
as Talmudic material (see above and note 129) and a heavy use
of the Old Testament. Indeed Klausner is probably correct to
conclude:

> The most superficial reading of this book serves to prove
> that we have here nothing beyond a piece of folklore, in
> which are confusedly woven early and late *Talmudic* and
> *Midrashic* legends and sayings concerning Jesus, together
> with Gospel accounts (which the author of the *Tol'doth*
> perverts in a fashion derogatory to Jesus), and other
> popular legends, many of which are mentioned by Celsus,

and Tertullian and later Church Fathers, and which Samuel
Krauss labels a 'folkloristische Motive'./136/

(b) There is another class of material that must also be set
aside as being of little value as an independent witness to
Jesus. That is *y. Ta'an.* 65b:

> R. Abbahu said 'If a man says to you "I am (a) God", he is
> a liar, "I am (a) Son of Man", he will regret it, "I go up
> to heaven", he has said it but he will not be able to do
> it"'./137/

And also Pesiq.R. 100b:

> R. Ḥija bar Abba said, 'If the son of the harlot says to
> you "There are two Gods", say to him "Face to face the
> Lord (singular) has spoken to you"' (Deut. 5:4)./138/

These are so obviously countering material in the Jesus
tradition (e.g., Mt 26:63-8/Mk 14:61-5/Lk 22:67-71; Lk 24:50-3;
cf. Acts 1:6-11; Jn 10:30-9) and the early Church (e.g.,
Phil 2:5-11; Col 1:15-20) that this Jewish tradition cannot be
relied upon to be an independent witness to the sayings of
Jesus, though it informs us about the debates between the Jews
and the Christians.

(c) We can also mention here passages regarding an unnatural
birth (*m. Yebam.* 4:13(49a)/gemera *b. Yebam.* 49b; *y.* gemera does
not have the passage; *t. Yebam.* 3:3f./*b. Yoma* 66b; *Kalla Rabbati*)
which have been taken to refer to Jesus./139/ It is not at all
certain that this material refers to Jesus, for his name is not
mentioned and an unnamed figure in even early material cannot,
without question, be taken as referring to Jesus. Importantly,
when the Amoraim discussed *t. Yebam.* 3:3 (see *b. Yoma* 66b) they
took it to refer to Solomon./140/ And, when we come to later
material in which the rabbis probably do mention Jesus'
unnatural birth (e.g., *b. Šabb.* 104) it is most likely to be the
result of the rabbis taking the opportunity of misusing a
tradition/141/ (cf. Mt 1:19,25) which perhaps even the
Christians found embarrassing (Mk 6:3/142/).

(d) A number of doubtful passages have been brought into the
arena of our study, because since the work of Abraham Geiger
/143/ some have found a reference to Jesus intended in the
mention of Balaam (*Yal. Shim.* par. 766; *b. 'Abod. Zar.* 10b-11a;
m. Sanh. 10:1f.; *b. Giṭ.* 56b, 57a; *b. B. Bat.* 14b; *b. Sanh.* 90a,

100b, 106a-b; b. 'Abot v. 19; y. Ber. i.18(3c)). This
connection between Balaam and Jesus is made because in the OT
Balaam is the chief corrupter of Israel's morality, so that he
might naturally be taken to be a type of Jesus, another
corrupter of Israel./144/ However the decisive evidence against
this identification is in two passages, b. Giṭ. 56b-57a and
b. 'Abod. Zar. 10b-11a/Yal. Shim. to Numbers 23:7./145/ We
need only quote one of the passages to make the point clear.

> The story is told of Onkelos son of Kalonymos, son of
> Titus' sister, that he wished to become a proselyte. He
> first called up Titus by means of spells. Titus advised
> him not to become a proselyte because Israel had so many
> commandments and commandments hard to observe; rather
> would he advise him to oppose them. Onkelos then called
> up Balaam, who said to him in his rage against Israel,
> Seek not their peace nor their good. Not till then did
> he go and raise up Jesus by spells and say to him: What is
> the most important thing in the world? He said to him,
> Israel. He asked, And how if I should join myself with
> them? He said to him, Seek their good and do not seek
> their harm; everyone that hurteth them is as if he hurt the
> apple of God's eye. He then asked, And what is the fate of
> the man? He said to him, Boiling filth. A Baraita has
> said: Everyone that scoffeth against the words of the wise
> is condemned to boiling filth. Come and see what there is
> between the transgressors in Israel and the prophets of the
> nations of the world. (b. Giṭ. 56b-57a) /146/

Here Jesus and Balaam are clearly distinguished and placed in
opposition. We must, therefore, exclude the Balaam passages
from consideration.

(e) A baraita in b. Sanh. 107b(/b. Soṭa 47a) reads:

> Our rabbis taught: Let the left hand repulse but the right
> hands always invite back: not as Elisha, who thrust Gehazi
> away with both hands (uncensored editions continue/147/)
> and not like R. Joshua b. Peraḥjah, who repulsed Jesus
> /148/ with both hands.

However, again, we must set aside this pericope for the grave
difficulty here is that this makes Jesus of Nazareth the
contemporary of R. Joshua b. Peraḥjah who lived a century before
Jesus./149/

(f) In *b. Sanh.* 103a there is a specific reference to Jesus.

> R. Ḥisda also said in the name of R. Jeremiah b. Abba:...
> 'There shall no evil befall thee' - thou wilt not be
> affrighted by righteousness and dread thoughts; 'neither
> shall any plague come nigh thy dwelling' - thou wilt not
> have a son or a disciple who publicly burns his food
> like Jesus of Nazareth.

The parallel saying to this pericope in *b. Ber.* 17b, if it is
by R. Joḥanan or his disciple R. Eleazar b. Pedat, is no earlier
than the last half of the third century. Here R. Ḥisda speaks
in the name of R. Jeremiah b. Abba, an Amora of the second
generation who was, in turn, an older pupil of Rab so that the
saying is not older than the third century. Thus even though
the reference to Jesus is in the uncensored text /150/ we must
exclude the pericope from consideration because of its late
origin./151/ To 'burn the food' is figurative, meaning to
spoil the teaching of Judaism./152/

(g) Also in *b. Sanh.* 107b (cf. (e) above) there is a passage in
the uncensored gemara of the Babylonian Talmud.

> What of R. Joshua b. Peraḥjah? - When King Jannai slew our
> Rabbis, R. Joshua b. Peraḥjah (and Jesus) fled to
> Alexandria of Egypt. On the resumption of peace, Simeon b.
> Sheṭach sent to him: 'From me, (Jerusalem) the holy city,
> to thee, Alexandria of Egypt (my sister). My husband
> dwelleth within thee and I am desolate.' He arose, went,
> and found himself in a certain inn, where great honour was
> shewn him. 'How beautiful is this Acsania!'/153/ Thereupon
> (Jesus) observed, 'Rabbi, her eyes are narrow.' 'Wretch',
> he rebuked him, 'dost thou thus engage thyself.' He
> sounded four hundred trumpets and excommunicated him. He
> (Jesus) came before him many times pleading, 'Receive me!'
> But he would pay no heed to him. One day he (R. Joshua)
> was reciting the Shema, when Jesus came before him. He
> intended to receive him and made a sign to him. He
> (Jesus) thinking that it was to repel him, went, put up a
> brick, and worshipped it. 'Repent', said (R. Joshua) to
> him. He replied, 'I have thus learned from thee: He who
> sins and causes others to sin is not afforded the means of
> repentance.' And a Master has said, 'Jesus the Nazarene
> practised magic and led Israel astray.'

But with this passage, we need to compare the more reliable
(see above on Neusner's third principle) *y. Ḥag.* 2:2.

> Yehuda b. Tabbai - the people of Jerusalem wished to
> appoint him as President (of the Sanhedrin) in Jerusalem.
> He fled and went to Alexandria. The people of Jerusalem
> wrote: From Jerusalem the Great to Alexandria the Little:
> How long doth my espoused dwell with you while I sit
> mournful for him? He embarked on a ship. He said: Debora,
> the hostess who received us, what was defective in her?
> One of his disciples said to him: Rabbi, her eyes were
> bad. He answered: There are two things lacking in you;
> one, that you suspected me, and the other that you
> inspected her closely. What did I say? that she was
> handsome to look at? (No) but that she was good in
> action. (The disciple was angry and went away) (cf.
> *y. Sanh.* 23c).

Thus the first problem with using *b. Sanh.* 107b for our
study is that *y. Ḥag.* 2:2 does not name the delinquent disciple.
Secondly, there is the problem of dating; King Janna lived
c. 103-76 BC (*Ant.* 13:320-3; *J.W.* 1:85/154/) and the pericope
(*b. Sanh.* 107b) comes from the post-tannaitic period./155/
Therefore we must exclude this pericope from our evidence./156/
As the Babylonians knew of Jesus b. Sirach, the translator of a
forbidden book (*b. Sanh.* 100a) who came out of Egypt in about
135 BC, we can see how another Jesus (of Nazareth), one who was
thought to have led Israel astray, could later have been thought
to be the referent in the tradition./157/ Also with Ben Stada
being connected with Jesus (see next point) it can be understood
how this passage has been thought to be concerned with Jesus of
Nazareth.

(h) As we have just said it is sometimes thought that the
references to Ben Stada are references to Jesus./158/ Two
important passages are:

> It was taught, R. Eliezar said to the Sages: But did not
> Ben Stada bring forth witchcraft from Egypt by means of
> scratches (in the form of charms) upon his flesh? (the
> uncensored text continues) Was he then the son of Stada;
> surely he was the son of Pandira? - Said R. Ḥisda: The
> husband was Stada, the paramour Pandira. But the husband
> was Pappos b. Judah? - His mother was Stada. But his
> mother was Miriam the hairdresser? - It is as we say in
> Pumbeditha: This one has been unfaithful to her husband
> (*b. Šabb.* 104b).

Also:

> And thus they did to Ben Stada in Lydda, and they hung
> him on the eve of Passover. Ben Stada was Ben Padira.
> R. Ḥisda said: The husband was Stada, the paramour
> Pandira. But was not the husband Pappos b. Judah? -
> His mother's name was Stada. But his mother was Miriam,
> a dresser of woman's hair? As they say in Pumbaditha,
> This woman has turned away from her husband. (*b. Sanh*. 67a,
> censored from the Oxford MS)/159/

Is this useful data for a study of the historical Jesus?
A number of points need to be considered. First, the
identification of Jesus and Ben Stada is late, by the Amoraim,
especially in sayings attributed to R. Ḥisda (AD 217-309, see
b. Sanh. 67b and *b. Šabb*. 104b./160/) Secondly, the more
reliable (see above on Neusner's third principle) *t. Sanh*. 10:11
(/*y. Sanh*. 7:16 (25c, d)) only says that Ben Stada was stoned.

> In the case of anyone who is liable to death penalties
> enjoined in the Torah, it is not proper to lie in wait for
> him except he be a beguiler. How do they lie in wait?
> Two scholars are stationed in an inner room, while the
> culprit is in an outer room. A candle is lit and so
> placed that they can see him as well as hear his voice.
> And so they did to Ben Stada in Lod. They concealed two
> scholars, and stoned him. (*t. Sanh*. 10:11)

Only the later *b. Sanh*. 67a (quoted above) has the idea
that he was hung on the eve of the Passover. Thirdly, still
later authorities did not identify Jesus and Ben Stada (*e.g.*,
Rabbenu Tam said that Ben Stada 'was not Jesus of Nazareth'
(Tosophoth *b. Šabb*. 104b) and *Toledoth Jesus* does not make the
identification)./161/ Fourth, the Talmud never actually has
the title 'Jesus ben Stada' as might be expected./162/ Along
with perhaps the majority of scholars we ought to conclude that
earlier reliable traditions did not identify Jesus and Ben
Stada and that we ought to disregard this later material. /163/
How some later Jewish traditions mistakenly came to identify
Jesus of Nazareth and Ben Stada is understandable in the light
of the traditions that Jesus' birth was unnatural (cf.
Mt 1:18-25; Lk 1:26-31; *b. Šabb*. 104b; *b. Sanh*. 67a); that he
had been to Egypt (cf. Mt 2:13-23; *b. Šabb*. 104b); that he was
a healer whose methods were questionable (cf. Mt 9:32-4/
12:22-30/Mk 3:22-7/Lk 11:14-15, 17-23; *b. Šabb*. 104b) and that
he had been condemned to death (cf. Mt 27:1-26; Mk 15:1-15;

Lk 23:1-25; Jn 18:19-19:1-16; *b. Sanh.* 67a)./164/ And in the
later Jewish-Christian polemic the Jews found in the Ben Stada
traditions elements readily to hand in the vendetta against
Jesus.

It is difficult to suggest and be sure of a more
reasonable identification for Ben Stada; a number of scholars
suggest the *planos* of Josephus (*J.W.* 2:261; *Ant.* 20:169ff.).
/165/

(i) On the other hand the designation 'ben Pandira'/166/
probably is an early name for Jesus. As early as Origen's
Contra Celsum (AD 248)/167/ there is the passage:

> Let us return, however, to the words put into the mouth of
> the Jew, where the mother of Jesus is described as having
> been turned out by the carpenter who was betrothed to her,
> as she had been convicted of adultery and had a child by a
> certain soldier named Panthera. (*CC* 1:32; cf. I:28)

Some of the interpretations of the origin of the term
Pandera/Pantera have been fanciful. For example it has been
suggested that the Jews sought a play on the word *parthenos*
('virgin') by saying that Jesus was the son of the lustful
panther./168/ Epiphanius (c. 315-403) has the lines 'This
Joseph was brother of Clopas, and was son of Jacob, surnamed
Panther; both of them were sons of him who was surnamed
Panther' (*Panarion* LXXVIII, 7, 5; cf. Eusebius *H.E.* 3:11). On
the basis of this Lauterbach suggests that Panther was Jesus'
family name./169/ However Epiphanius may well be rationalizing;
offering a rational explanation of Jewish tradition. The most
straightforward explanation is that the term Pandera/Pantera
derives from *parthenos*./170/ Perhaps some Jewish
controversialists took up the common Greek name *Panthēra*/171/
because it resembled *parthenos*./172/

There are two pieces of tradition in which this name
occurs that warrant our attention.

> The case of R. Eleazer ben Damah, whom a serpent bit.
> There came in Jacob, a man of Chephar Sama, to cure him
> in the name of Jesus ben Pandira, but R. Ishmael did not
> allow it. He said 'Thou art not permitted, Ben Damah'.
> He said, 'I will bring thee a proof that he may heal me'.
> But he had not finished bringing a proof when he died...

(*t. Ḥul.* 2:22f./*Koh. Rab.* 1:1:8/b. ʿ*Abod. Zar.* 27b)./173/

The second piece reads:

> The grandson (of R. Joshua ben Levi) had something stuck
> in his throat. There came a man and whispered to him in
> the name of Jesus Pandera, and he recovered. When he (the
> doctor) came out, he (R. Joshua) said to him, 'What didst
> thou whisper to him?' He said to him, 'A certain word'.
> He said, 'It had been better for him that he had died
> rather than thus.' And it happened thus to him...
> (*y.* ʿ*Abod. Zar.* 2:2(40d)/*y. Šabb.* 14:4(14d)/*Koh. Rab.*
> 10:5)./174/

R. Ishmael and his nephew R. Eleazer b. Damah lived in the
first half of the second century and R. Joshua ben Levi in the
first half of the third century AD,/175/ so that both stories
have a setting more than a century removed from the historical
Jesus. In any case, although using an early name for Jesus,
these stories tell us nothing directly about the historical
Jesus - only how his name was used/176/ and also forbidden to
be used in healing in the early second century./177/ Also in
view of its probable derivation, the use of the name Pandera/
Pantera and what Celsus says about Jesus (quoted above) shows
that at least by the later part of the second century/178/
Jewish tradition contained notions of an unnatural birth of
Jesus.

We come now to material that is generally argued to be
more reliable in providing data on the historical Jesus.

(j) The mention of the name Jesus and the hanging on the eve
of the Passover has meant that a section of *b. Sanh.* 43a is
often taken to be a valuable reference to Jesus of Nazareth.
/179/ In this section there are two short baraitot which
interest us.

> (1) It has been taught/180/ on the eve of the Passover
> Jesus/181/ was hanged. For forty days before the
> execution took place, a herald went forth and cried, 'He
> is going forth to be stoned because he has practised
> sorcery and enticed Israel to apostasy. Any one who can
> say anything in his favour, let him come forward and plead
> on his behalf'. But since nothing was brought forward in
> his favour he was hanged on the eve of the Passover./182/

The obvious difficulties here are with the trial and
execution and so we will discuss these first.

There are two problems with the mention of the heralding
of the execution for forty days before the event. First, this
heralding which, if it was originally intended to refer to
Jesus of Nazareth, was probably an attempt to show how
considered was Jesus' trial and condemnation, is in line with a
Jewish *Tendenz, viz.*, to justify Jewish actions against Jesus.
/183/ Secondly, the practice of a forty-day heralding and
period of appeal, is unknown in Jewish law,/184/ at least prior
to this baraita. The nearest thing to the practice mentioned
here is *b. Sanh.* VI(42b):

> When the trial is ended, he (the condemned) is led forth
> to be stoned... A man was stationed at the door of the
> court with the signalling flag in his hand, and a horse-
> man was stationed at a distance yet within sight of him,
> and then if one says, 'I have something (further) to
> state in his favour', he (the signaller) waves the flag,
> and the horse-man runs and stops them...

Even in the case of a false teacher, which might be thought
to apply here, the law mentions formal written warning, but not
a forty-day period (*b. Sanh.* 111b)./185/ Therefore we must
conclude that the forty-day period in which favourable
witnesses may come forward is unhistorical here. The Gospel
accounts that Jesus was hastily removed remain probable. Also
in view of the fact that Jesus was hung by Roman authorities
we are also probably justified in concluding that no herald
preceded Jesus to his execution./186/

But what of the charges here? Do they refer to Jesus of
Nazareth? The baraita says that Jesus was hung. In view of
Jewish law (*b. Sanh.* 45b) - 'All who are stoned are (afterwards)
hanged' - it would have been assumed that the subject of this
pericope had already been stoned. As F. F. Bruce says, for
the Jews, 'Hanging was not so much a method of execution in
itself as a form of treatment reserved in certain cases for the
corpses of people who had already been executed otherwise,
especially by stoning'./187/ There are a great number of
offences for which the capital punishment was by stoning./188/
Two offences that are seen to provide a basis for the
punishment by stoning are sorcery (*b. Sanh.* 67a; *Mek. Mishpaṭim*
17) and leading Israel astray (*b. Sanh.* 67a; *Sifre Deut* 90).
/189/ It is often assumed that the charge of sorcery in

b. Sanh. 67a is to be linked with the Beelzebul Controversy
(Mt 9:32-4/12:22-30/Mk 3:22-7/Lk 11:14-23/Jn 7:20; 8:48,52;
10:20)./190/   But the making of this direct link needs to be
questioned.   In the Beelzebul Controversy the charge is most
probably simply that Jesus was possessed by Satan for whom he
was accused of working, not a charge of magic./191/   If Jesus'
detractors had wished to lay a charge of magic against him we
would have expected them to accuse him of creating apparitions
rather than real miracles (cf. Quadratus in Eusebius
H.E. 4:3:2; *CC* I:6,68) or perhaps of insisting on exact
paraphernalia, that is, demanding particular properties for
different kinds of magic.   For in *b. Sanh*. 67b Abaye defines a
sorcerer as one who insists on exact paraphernalia.   The charge,
related in John's Gospel, that Jesus had a demon (7:20;
8:48,52; 10:20) is not understood as a charge of sorcery but,
as 10:20 implies, that Jesus was mad.   Further, this charge
relates not to Jesus' miracles, but is a response to words of
Jesus pertaining to his own status and relationship to God.
/192/   Thus, so far as we know from the Gospel accounts Jesus
was not accused of sorcery.   That Jesus led Israel astray is a
charge as old at least as the Gospel traditions (*e.g.*, Mt 27:63;
Jn 7:12,47; cf. Lk 23:5,14).   However, Jesus of Nazareth was not
the only figure over whom Jewish tradition placed some question
regarding their orthodoxy (*e.g.*, Ben Stada, see above;
t. Ḥul. 22f./*Koh. Rab*. 1:1:8/*b. 'Abod. Zar*. 27b; *y. 'Abod. Zar*.
2:2(40d)/*y. Šabb*. 14:4(14d)/*Koh. Rab*. 10:5; cf. *Ant*. 20:169ff.;
J.W. 2:261ff.).   Thus this tradition need not have originally
referred to Jesus of Nazareth.   Despite our conclusions, we
see from Justin's *Dialogue with Trypho* that by the second
century these charges were part of the debate between Jews and
Christians.   'But though they saw such works (*e.g.*, the
miracles) they asserted it was magical art.   For they dared to
call him a magician, and a deceiver of the people' (*Dial*. 69).

    It remains for us to mention the opening line of the
baraita - 'It has been taught, on the eve of the Passover Jesus
was hanged' (*b. Sanh*. 43a).   From our discussion of the context
of this text doubts are already raised about its value.   In
view of the Ben Stada tradition being taken as referring to
Jesus it is quite possible that this time reference in *b. Sanh*.
43a has been taken up in the oral tradition from the Ben Stada
text in *b. Sanh*. 67a - 'they hung him on the eve of the
Passover'./193/   Thus we would have to agree with Maier that
the agreement of *b. Sanh*. 43a with John 19:14 is probably an
accident rather than independent valuable source material for
the time of the death of the historical Jesus./194/

(2) Following this baraita (*b. Sanh*. 43a) there are the words:

> Our Rabbis taught: Jesus had five disciples, Mattha, Naqai, Neẓer, Buni and Todah.

Despite various attempts/195/ it is no longer possible to say why only five disciples are mentioned here. In turn there have been a number of suggestions as to the origin and meaning of the names./196/ The most reasonable suggestion is at least that Mattha is to be connected with Matthew and Todah with Thaddeus. /197/ From here much is conjecture. Naqai may be Nicodemus (John 3:1) or Nicanor or Nicolas (Acts 6:5) or the author of the Gospel of Nicodemus whom the Jews may have assumed had been a disciple of Jesus./198/ It is also possible that Naqai refers to the founder of the Nicolaitans (Rev 2:6/199/), since in Revelation Nicolaitan = Balaamite (Rev 2:14-15) and Balaam was in some Rabbinic traditions (see above) related to traditions about Jesus./200/ Neẓer is probably an allusion to the name Nazarene = Christian (cf. Acts 24:5)/201/ rather than a corrupted form from the name Andrew as Klausner suggested./202/ Buni may be Nicodemus, for *b. Ta'an*. 20a has 'His name is not Nakdimon but Buni. And why is his name called Nakdimon? - because the sun shone (*naq'da*) because of him'./203/ Buni may also be a corruption of 'Yuhonni' or 'Yuani' that is, John./204/

The value of this list is difficult to determine. The list is anonymous and so its early date is not decisive./205/ The number and order of the names in the list does not seem to rely on Christian tradition. It is possible then that we have a tradition independent from the Gospel tradition with echoes, at least in the case of Mattha and Todah, of disciples of Jesus or, with the other names, well known early Christians./206/

What follows the list of disciples is the mass condemnation of the disciples on the grounds of Scriptural interpretation (gezera shawa) of their names. For example, '"Yes", they (the judges) answered, "Todah shall be executed since it is written, Whoso offereth the sacrifice of Todah ('Thanksgiving') honoured me"'. This courtroom scene is most probably of little historical value for, as Klausner points out, a mass execution on the grounds of such Scriptural gymnastics in a court of law is highly unlikely./207/

These two baraitot are helpful to the historian only in so far as they witness to the reputation of Jesus as a miracle worker, and indicate that he had some (here said to be five) disciples, two of whom may be identifiable.

(k) The following story occurs in a number of places (*t. Ḥul.* 2:24; *b. 'Abod. Zar.* 16b; *m. Qoh. Rab.* on i:8; *Yal. Shim.* on Mic 1 and Prov 5:8).   In *b. 'Abod. Zar.* 16b the reference to Jesus is most clear.

> I (R. Eliezer) was once walking in the upper market of Sepphoris when I came across one (of the disciples of Jesus the Nazarene = MS. M) Jacob of Kefar-Sekariah by name, who said to me...   It is written in your Torah, 'Thou shall not bring the hire of a harlot... into the house of the Lord thy God'.   May such money be applied to the erection of a retiring place for the High Priest?   To which I made no reply.   Said he to me, 'Thus was I taught (by Jesus the Nazarene = MS. M) "For the hire of a harlot hath she gathered them and unto the hire of a harlot shall they return: they came from a place of filth, let them go to a place of filth"'.

It may be said in favour of the authenticity of the saying contained here/208/ that, although it may use what to us is an unpleasant metaphor,/209/ it is in keeping with sayings like Mark 7:18ff.   '... whatever goes into a man from outside cannot defile him, since it enters, not his heart but his stomach, and passes on...   What comes out of a man is what defiles a man'. /210/ However the oldest tradition does not have the saying:

> ...I (R. Eliezer) went out on a street of Sepphoris; there I encountered Jacob of Kephar-Sekhrim, who spoke a word of heresy in the name of Jesus b. Panṭera and it pleased me . (*t. Ḥul.* 2:24)

Therefore, despite the saying bearing some affinity with the sayings of Jesus in the Gospel tradition, we must reject the story in *b. 'Abod. Zar.* 16b as a later elaboration of *t. Ḥul.* 2:24.   And as can be seen there is some doubt, on textual grounds, about the saying used to elaborate the story.

Our analysis of two potentially important Jewish traditions, whose extant texts contain references to Jesus, has proved far less fruitful than might have been hoped in providing reliable data for the historians' search for the historical Jesus.   At the end of the section on Josephus we drew some conclusions about the value of *Ant.* 18:63f. for a study of the historical Jesus.   It remains for us to comment on our findings from the Rabbinic traditions.   What emerges from the last part of our study is that almost none of the

material stands up to careful scrutiny. In fact all we are
left with is the list of five disciples of Jesus in
b. Sanh. 43a ((j)(2) above) which possibly contains an
independent echo of at least two of the names of Jesus'
disciples. The Rabbinic literature is, then, of almost no
value to the historian in his search for the historical Jesus
(cf. Bornkamm, note 120 above). Probably in Jewish-Christian
debates the traditions have been confused so that Jesus' name
has been only later and incorrectly associated with stories of
other often unorthodox figures.

Notes

/1/ This conviction has motivated such publications as, e.g.,
W. Bousset, Die Religion des Judentums im neutestamentlichen
Zeitalter (Berlin, 1903); G. F. Moore, Judaism in the First
Centuries of the Christian Era (3 vols.; Cambridge, Mass.:
Harvard University, 1927-30); (note his 'Christian Writers on
Judaism', HTR 15 (1922) 41-61); H. L. Strack und P. Billerbeck,
Kommentar zum Neuen Testament aus Talmud und Midrasch
(6 Bänden; München: Beck, 1922-61); C. G. Montefiore, Rabbinic
Literature and Gospel Teachings (London: Macmillan, 1930);
E. Hennecke, NT Apocrypha (2 vols.; London: SCM, 1973, 1974);
James M. Robinson, The Nag Hammadi Library in English (Leiden:
Brill, 1977); George W. E. Nickelsburg, Jewish Literature
between the Bible and the Mishnah (London: SCM, 1981); George
W. E. Nickelsburg and Michael E. Stone, Faith and Piety in
Early Judaism: Texts and Documents (Philadelphia: Fortress,
1983).
/2/ See the previous note and the work of, e.g., J. Jeremias,
NT Theology (London: SCM, 1971) and The Parables of Jesus
(London: SCM, 1972) and G. Vermes, Jesus the Jew (Glasgow:
Collins, 1973).
/3/ See E. Schürer, The History of the Jewish People in the Age
of Jesus Christ, vol. 1 (revised by Geza Vermes and Fergus
Millar; Edinburgh: T. & T. Clark, 1973) 68ff. 'Rabbinic
Literature'.

/4/ M. Lods, 'Etude sur les sources juives de la polemique de
Celse contre les Chrétiens', *RHPR* 21 (1941) 1-33.
/5/ Further see H. L. Strack, *Jesus, die Häretiker und die
Christen* (Leipzig: Hinrichs, 1910); I. F. Baer, 'Israel, the
Christian Church and the Roman Empire from the Time of Septimus
Severus to the Edict of Toleration of A.D. 313', *Scriptura
Hierosolymitana* 7 (1961) 79-145, and W. Horbury, *A Critical
Examination of the Toledoth Jeshu* (Cambridge University:
Unpublished Ph.D. Dissertation, 1970) 308,340,345.
/6/ On Jesus in Josephus see, for the present, L. H. Feldman,
Josephus (Loeb Classical Library; Cambridge, Mass.: Harvard
University, London: William Heinemann, 1965) vol. 9 Appendix K;
H. Schreckenberg, *Bibliographie zu Flavius Josephus* (Leiden:
Brill, 1968, Supplement 1979); P. Winter, 'Bibliography to
Josephus, "Antiquities Judaicae" XVIII, 63,64', *Journal of
Historical Studies* (Princeton) 2 (1969-70) 292-6; Edwin M.
Yamauchi, 'Josephus and the Scriptures', *Fides et Historia* 13
(1980) 42-63. On Jesus in Rabbinic traditions see J. Klausner,
Jesus of Nazareth (London: George Allen & Unwin, 1928)
bibliography p. 18; *EncJ* 'Jesus'; F. F. Bruce, *Jesus and
Christian Origins Outside the NT* (London: Hodder and Stoughton,
1974); Johann Maier, *Jesus von Nazareth in der Talmudischen
Überlieferung* (EF 82; Darmstadt: Wissenschaftliche
Buchgesellschaft, 1978).
/7/ See, *e.g.*, G. D. Kilpatrick, *The Origins of the Gospel
According to St. Matthew* (Oxford: Clarendon, 1946); also E. P.
Sanders (ed.), *Jewish and Christian Self-Definition* (vol. 2;
London: SCM, 1981); R. E. Brown, *The Gospel According to John*
(2 vols.; London: Geoffrey Chapman, 1971) I. LXVII-IX.
/8/ Much modern Christian scholarship has accepted a view of
first century Judaism and its sects which has been based on an
insufficiently critical view of the canonical Gospels. Note
Moore, *HTR* 14 (1921) 197-254, and E. P. Sanders, *Paul and
Palestinian Judaism* (London: SCM, 1977) 33-62.
/9/ On the value of the Jewish-Christian debates in the
Rabbinic literature for identifying statements about Jesus see
Horbury, *Toledoth Jeshu*, 331 citing D. Daube, *The NT and
Rabbinic Judaism* (London: Athlone, 1956) viiif..
/10/ J. Neusner, *From Politics to Piety: The Emergence of
Pharisaic Judaism* (Englewood Cliffs: Prentice Hall, 1972), 'In
the study of nearly all other aspects of the history and
culture of antiquity - whether in Classics, or History, or
Biblical, or Ancient Near Eastern studies - one attitude
predominates: You do not take at face value what a source
purports to reveal. You ask *Cui bono?* Whose interest is
served by a story, a law, or a saying? What is the bias, the

polemical interest of an author? These things must be taken
into account in assessing the historical usefulness of every
source' (p. 7).

/11/ See, *e.g.*, J. Neusner, 'New Problems, New Solutions:
Current Events in Rabbinic Studies', *SR* 8 (1979) 401-18, esp.
408; and *The Rabbinic Traditions about the Pharisees Before 70*
(3 vols.; Leiden: Brill, 1971) III.3 and *Politics to Piety*, 7,
92f..

/12/ *Ant.* 20:267 - '... the present day, which belongs to the
thirteenth year of the reign of Domitian Caesar and to the
fifty-sixth of my life'. Cf. Schürer, *History* I.43 n.2.

/13/ There are further references to Josephus' family in *J.W.*
5:333,344,419,544; *Life* 204,414,416,426-7.

/14/ That Josephus was a Pharisee has gone unquestioned by some
(*e.g.*, Thackeray, *Josephus*) and argued for by others (*e.g.*,
A. Schlatter, *Die Theologie des Judentums nach dem Bericht des
Josephus* (Güttersloh: Bertelsmann, 1932)). B. Pick in 'A Study
on Josephus with Special Reference to the Old Testament',
Lutheran Quarterly 19 (1889) 325-46 and 599-616, following E.
Gerlach, *Die Weissagungen des Alten Testaments in den Schriften
des Flavius Josephus* (Berlin: Hertz, 1863) 10-11, argued for
Josephus being an Essene. However because the precise nature of
first century Palestinian Pharisaism still remains to be
clarified in the face of the anti-Pharisaic *Tendenz* of the NT
documents it is, as yet, not possible to be certain of the
precise religious affiliations of Josephus. Further cf. Harold
W. Attridge, *The Interpretation of Biblical History in the
'Antiquitates Judaicae' of Flavius Josephus* (Montana: Scholars,
1976) 176-9.

/15/ *J.W.* 3:355-92,438-42. Some still see Josephus as a traitor
see, *e.g.*, Martin Braun, 'The Prophet Who Became a Historian',
Listener 56 (1956) 53-7; Helgo Lindner, *Die Geschichtsauffassung
des Flavius Josephus im Bellum Judaicum* (Leiden: Brill, 1972)
13f.. Others see his writings as a means of self-justification;
see, *e.g.*, Wilhelm Weber, *Josephus und Vespasian* (Stuttgart:
Kolhammer, 1921); Clemens Thoma, 'Die Weltanschauung des
Josephus Flavius', *Kairos* 11 (1969) 39-52.

/16/ On Epaphroditus to whom Josephus dedicated his *Antiquities*
and *Life* (*Ant.* 1:8; *Life* 430) and for whom he wrote as patron
his apology for the Jews (*Ag.Ap.* 1:1; 2:1,296) see Bo Reicke,
The NT Era (London: A. & C. Black, 1969) 281.

/17/ See Schürer, *History*, I.481f. and n.47.

/18/ *Ant.* 1:1, 'Those who essay to write histories are actuated,
I observe, not by one and the same aim, but by many widely
different motives'.

/19/ On Josephus' use of Polybius see R. J. H. Shutt, *Studies in Josephus* (London: SPCK, 1961) 102-6 and Attridge, *The Interpretation of Biblical History*, 43ff.. On the historiography of Polybius see F. W. Walbank, 'Polemic in Polybius', *Journal of Roman Studies* 52 (1962) 5-12; P. Pedech, *La méthode historique de Polybe* (Paris: Les Belles Lettres, 1964); F. W. Walbank, *Polybius* (Berkeley/Los Angeles/London: University of California, 1972) 66-96.

/20/ On this intention in ancient historians - as opposed to writing poetry or tragedy for the gratification of their readers - see Attridge, *The Interpretation of Biblical History*, 47f. and notes.

/21/ Cf. H. St. J. Thackeray, *Josephus* (Loeb) II.608n.a.

/22/ On the sources Josephus may have used for this speech see Thackeray, *Josephus* (Loeb) II.457n.c.

/23/ That Josephus was officially 'inspired' in *J.W.* see R. Laqueur, *Der jüdische Historiker Flavius Josephus*, 126f.

/24/ Attridge (*The Interpretation of Biblical History*, 55f.) overlooks this moralizing aspect of *J.W.* and only attributes a moral intention to *Ant.* (see Attridge, *ibid.*, chap. IV and below).

/25/ On the different historiographical perspectives of the two major works of Josephus see A. Momigliano, 'Time in Ancient Historiography', *History and Theory*, Beiheft 6 (1966) 1-23 on which Attridge (*The Interpretation of Biblical History*, 56n.2) commented that Momigliano 'noted that two criteria were operative in the selection of historical material, qualitative importance and reliability. Polybius and Dionysius represent different ends of the spectrum in their judgements about what was qualitatively important. The two major works of Josephus also stand at the two different extremes'. More recently on the different purposes of Josephus' works see Shaye Cohen, *Josephus in Galilee and Rome: His 'Vita' and Development as a Historian* (Columbia University: Ph.D. Dissertation, 1975).

/26/ Josephus goes on to say that he will be translating the Hebrew records (*Ant.* 1:5). On the problem of the sources Josephus uses see the review by S. Rappaport, *Agada und Exegese bei Flavius Josephus* (Vienna: Kohut, 1930) and A. Schalit, 'Introduction' to the Hebrew Translation of the *Antiquities* (Jerusalem: Masad Bialik, 1967). For a brief summary of the problem see Attridge, *The Interpretation of Biblical History*, 29-38.

/27/ On the parallels between Josephus and Dionysius, and their importance, see Thackeray, *Josephus*, 56-8; F. J. Foakes-Jackson, *Josephus and the Jews: The Religion and History of the Jews as Explained by Flavius Josephus* (1931) 247f.; Shutt, *Studies*,

92-1Ol, and more recently Attridge, *The Interpretation of Biblical History*, 43-57.

/28/ With this can be compared Dionysius who says that he will include in his history of Rome 'infinite examples of virtue in men whose superiors, whether for piety or for justice or for life-long self-control, or for warlike valour, no city, either Greek or barbarian, has ever produced' (*Ant.Rom*. 1:5:3).

/29/ Cf. David M. Rhoads, *Israel in Revolution: 6-74 C.E., A Political History Based on the Writings of Josephus* (Philadelphia: Fortress, 1976) 13.

/30/ Further see V. Taylor, *The Gospel According to St. Mark* (London: Macmillan, 1959) 310.

/31/ So also A. E. J. Rawlinson, *St. Mark* (London: Methuen, 1947) 80ff.; Taylor, *Mark*, 310f.; D. E. Nineham, *Saint Mark* (Harmondsworth: Penguin, 1969) 172f.; Hugh Anderson, *The Gospel of Mark* (London: Oliphants, 1976) 166.

/32/ Norman Bentrick, *Josephus* (Philadelphia: Jewish Publication Society of America, 1914) 195; S. Safrai and M. Stern, eds., 'The Jewish People in the first Century', *Compendia Rerum Judaicarum ad Novum Testamentum* (Assen: Van Gorcum and Co., 1974) I.21ff.; Rhoads, *Israel in Revolution*, 15.

/33/ See on Matthew Günther Bornkamm, 'End-Expectation and Church in Matthew', in *Tradition and Interpretation in Matthew* (eds. Günther Bornkamm, Gerhard Barth and Heinz Joachim Held; London: SCM, 1963) 38. On Mark see Willi Marxsen, *Mark the Evangelist* (Nashville: Abingdon, 1969) 148; also Ralph P. Martin, *Mark: Evangelist and Theologian* (Exeter: Paternoster, 1972) 161; cf. his 'A Gospel in Search of a Life-Setting', *Exp Tim* 80 (1969) 361-4; also Howard C. Kee, *Christian Origins in Sociological Perspective* (London: SCM, 1980) 138. On Luke see Robert Maddox, *The Purpose of Luke-Acts* (Edinburgh: T. &.T. Clark, 1982) 180; cf. 14f. On John see discussion of John 20:31 in H. Riesenfeld, 'Zu den johanneischen 'hina'-Sätzen', *ST* 19 (1965) 213-20 cited by R. E. Brown, *The Gospel According to John* (2 vols.; London: Geoffrey Chapman, 1971) II.1056. Generally on the language of the gospels see A. D. Nock, 'The Vocabulary of the New Testament', *JBL* 52 (1933) 135f., also published in *Essays on Religion and the Ancient World* (ed. Zeph Stewart; 2 vols.; Cambridge, Mass.: Harvard University, 1972) I.344.

/34/ Contrast Thackeray (*Josephus* 126) who, arguing for Josephus' knowledge of Jesus, says that he cannot have been ignorant of the main facts of the life and death of Jesus because by the time Josephus was writing the Synoptic Gospels had been written.

/35/ Thus, *e.g.*, the Fourth Gospel is usually considered the latest, and it is by no means certain that the Synoptic Gospels were known to its author or his community. See J. A. T. Robinson, *Twelve NT Studies* (London: SCM, 1962) ch. VII; also R. E. Brown, *NT Essays* (New York: Image Books, 1968) and C. K. Barrett, 'John and the Synoptic Gospels', *Exp Tim* 85 (1974) 228-33.

/36/ On the dating see Thackeray, *Josephus* (Loeb) II.xii; Schürer, *History*, I.47f.

/37/ Cf. Josephus' description of the situation around Cyrene, *J.W.* 7:437-42.

/38/ Cf. H. Schreckenberg, *Rezeptionsgeschichtliche und Textkritische Untersuchungen zu Flavius Josephus* (Leiden: Brill, 1977) 15.

/39/ Cf. S. G. F. Brandon, *Jesus and the Zealots* (Manchester: University Press, 1967) 360.

/40/ See Safrai and Stern, eds. in *Compendium*, I.21ff.; also Morton Smith, 'The Description of the Essenes in Josephus and the Philosophumena', *HUCA* 29 (1958) 273-313. For an assessment of Josephus' portrayal of the Zealots see M. Hengel, *Die Zeloten* (Leiden: Brill, 1961) and S. G. F. Brandon, *Jesus and the Zealots* (Manchester: University Press, 1967) (on which see the critical article by W. Klassen, 'Jesus and the Zealot Option', *CJT* 16 (1970) 12-21); C. Roth, 'The Zealots in the War of 66-73', *JSS* 4 (1959) 332-55; S. Applebaum, 'The Zealots: The Case for Revaluation', *JRS* 61 (1971) 155-70.

/41/ On the extant MSS (the oldest being the fourteenth century R (Codex Regius Parisinus), see B. Niese, *Flavii Josephi Opera* (6 vols.; Berlin: Weidmannos, 1887-94) I.LXXVII; Thackeray, *Josephus* (Loeb) IV.xvii; G. C. Richards and R. J. H. Shutt, 'The Composition of Josephus' Antiquities', *Classical Quarterly* 33 (1939) 36-40; Shutt, *Josephus*, ch.6; H. Schreckenberg in *Theokratia* (Leiden-Köln) 2 (1970-2) 81-106, and *Die Flavius-Josephus-Tradition in Antike und Mittelalter* (Leiden: Brill, 1972) 32, and *Rezeptionsgeschichtliche*.

/42/ Schreckenberg, *Rezeptionsgeschichtliche*, 15.

/43/ Maier, *Jesus von Nazareth*, 45, also Schürer, *History*, I.430n.1 - 'Exceptions are B. Niese, *De testimonio Christiano quod est apud Josephum ant. Iud. XVIII, 63 sq. disputatio* (1893/4); E. Schürer, *Geschichte*, I (1901), 548,581f., n.45; J. Juster, *Les Juifs dans l'Empire romain*, II (1914) 139-41; and G. Hölscher, in *RE* [= PW] IX cols. 1934-2000, or col. 1993'.

/44/ Walter Bauer, 'The Alleged Testimony of Josephus', *NT Apocrypha* (ed. E. Hennecke and W. Schneemelcher, 2 vols.; London: SCM, 1963, 1965) I.436.

/45/ K. H. Rengstorf (*A Complete Concordance to Flavius Josephus* (Leiden: Brill, 1979) III.16), most probably incorrectly, says that in *Ag.Ap.* 2:34 *legomenos* has the meaning of 'alleged'.

/46/ Schürer, *History*, I.431. See also BDF 412:2.

/47/ See previous note and Maier, *Jesus von Nazareth*, 45.

/48/ Note *Ant.* 13:370. See also *Ant.* 1:38,80,95,123,126,133, 133,151,159,160,160,174,258,331,337; 2:6,317; 3:222,248,294, 295; 4:82,161; 6:28,71,274,310,360,370; 7:288,310; 8:95,100, 177,181,225,293,305,312,348; 10:23,70,175; 11:109,203,329; 12:6,125,259,340,369,397,408,429; 13:10,158,230, (309), 370, 418, (420); 14:8,131,342,415; (15:23); 17:87,171,319; 18:11,22, 315; 19:281; 20:2,24,118, (130), 197; *Ag.Ap.* 1:4,110,174; 2:21; *J.W.* (5:144); 7:180; *Life* 4,12,64,403,420.

/49/ See also *Ant.* 1:119,174,260; 3:162,172; 7:355; 8:92,145, 163; 9:11,271; 10:114; 11:31; 12:259,412; 13:338,394; 16:142; *Ag.Ap.* 2:48; *J.W.* 4:124; 7:226; *Life* 281.

/50/ It is a construction Christians also used of other people as well as objects - cf. Mt 4:18; 9:9; 10:2; 26:3,14,36; 27:16,33 (same construction as Josephus); see also Mk 15:7; Lk 22:1,47; Jn 4:5; 11:16,54; 19:13,17; 20:24; 21:2; Acts 3:2; 6:9; Col 4:11 - though it is by no means unique to Christians, see, *e.g.*, Pindarus, *Pythian*, 5:108; Thucydides, *History*, 7:68.

/51/ S. G. F. Brandon, *The Fall of Jerusalem* (London: SPCK, 1951) 111.

/52/ See, *e.g.*, Plato, *Gorgias*, 493c; *Phaedo*, 107b; 245c; Herodotus, *Historicus*, 3:66,80; Mt 17:17; Mk 9:19; Lk 9:41; 1 Cor 6:6; 7:15; 2 Clem. 17:5; 19:2; Diognetus 11:2; Mart. Pol. 16:1; Philo, *Leg. All.* 3:164; *Leg. ad Gai.* 3; Ignatius, *Eph.* 8:2; *Hom. Clem.* 7:7; Justin, *Dial.* 33:2; cf. R. Bultmann, *TDNT*, VI esp. 176,178,204f.

/53/ The natural meaning of *katadechomai* is to 'receive', 'accept', 'admit'. See, *e.g.*, Plato, *Republic*, 3:401E; 1 Clem 19:1; Chrysostom *hom. 20.5 in Mt* (7.267A); cf. *Ag.Ap.* 1:292.

/54/ S. Zeitlin, 'The Christ Passage in Josephus', *JQR* 18 (1928) 235f.; criticized by R. Eisler, 'Flavius Josephus on Jesus Called the Christ', *JQR* 21 (1930) 21f., on the grounds of the suggestion that *Ant.* 20:200 originally contained a fuller reference to Christ.

/55/ In, *e.g.*, the NT see Mt 1:16; Jn 9:11; Acts 3:2; 6:9; 9:36; Heb 9:2,3 where the construction is used to *introduce* the subject.

/56/ See n.41 above.

/57/ S. Zeitlin, *JQR* 18 (1928) 231-55 following (without acknowledgement) Tanneguy Lefevre (1655), Heinichen (1860) and

Goethals, see R. Eisler, *JQR* 21 (1930) 26 and previously in
IHSOUS BASILEUS OU BASILEUSAS (2 vols.; Heidelberg: Winters,
1930) I.123n.7 and n.8. (Scaliger in the sixteenth century was
the first to suspect the authenticity of *Ant.* 18:63f.; see
Feldman, *Josephus* (Loeb) IX.49 n.*b*.).

/58/ For example, K. Wieseler, 'Das Josephus Zeugnis über
Christus und Jakobus den Bruder des Herrn', *Jahrbücher für
deutsche Theologie* 23 (1878) 86-109; Thackeray, *Josephus*, 148;
A. Pelletier, 'L'originalité du témoignage de Flavius Josephe
sur Jésus', *RSR* 52 (1964) 177-203; 'Ce que Josephe a dit de
Jésus (Ant. XVIII 63-64)' *REJ* 4 (1965) 9-21; E. Bammel, 'Zum
Testimonium Flavianum (Jos Ant 18, 63-64)', *Josephus-Studien
für O. Michel* (ed. Otto Betz, Klaus Haacker und Martin Hengel;
Göttingen: Vandenhoeck & Ruprecht, 1974) 9-22; further see
Paul Winter, 'Bibliography to Josephus, 'Antiquitates Judaicae,
XVIII, 63, 64', *J.Hist.St.* 2 (1968-9) 292-6; Schürer, *History*,
I.429f.; and Walter Pötscher, 'Iosephus Flavius, Antiquitates
18, 63f. (Sprachliche Form und thematischer Inhalt)', *Eranos*
72 (1974) 26-42.

/59/ In F. Hahn, W. Lohff and G. Bornkamm, *What Can We Know
About Jesus? Essays on the New Quest* (Edinburgh: St. Andrews,
1969) 22. Though Hahn thought *Ant.* 20:200 to be authentic he
considered it unproductive (p. 23). See also E. Norden,
'Josephus und Tacitus über Jesus Christus und eine messianische
Prophetie', *Neue Jahrbücher für das Klassische Altertum,
Geschichte und deutsche Literatur* 16 (1913) 637-66; H.
Conzelman, *Jesus* (Philadelphia: Fortress, 1973) 13f.; and
Winter, *J.Hist.St.* 2 (1968-9) 292-6; Schürer, *History*, I.428f.;
Pötscher, *Eranos* 72 (1974) 26-42.

/60/ F. C. Burkitt, 'Josephus and Christ', *TT* 47 (1913) 135-44;
F. Dornseiff, 'Lukas der Schriftsteller, mit einem Anhang:
Josephus und Tacitus', *ZNW* 35 (1936) 129-55; 'Zum Testimonium
Flavianum', *ZNW* 46 (1955) 245-50; Shutt, *Studies*, 121. See also
Winter, *J.Hist.St.* 2 (1968-9) 292-6; Schürer, *History*, I.428;
Pötscher, *Eranos* 72 (1974) 26-42.

/61/ See Thackeray, *Josephus*, 51ff.,107f..

/62/ *Neue Jahrbücher für das Klassische Altertum Geschichte
und deutsche Literatur*, 16 (1913) 637-66.

/63/ P. Bilde ('Josephus' beretring om Jesus', *DTT* 44 (1981)
99-135) uses the fact that Irenaeus and Tertullian do not
mention the passages as evidence against the authenticity of
Ant. 18:63f.

/64/ Thackeray, *Josephus*, 108ff.; cf. the critical discussion
in Shutt, *Josephus*, 77, cf. 91.

/65/ Thackeray, *Josephus*, 115. See also Shutt, *Josephus*.

/66/ Thackeray, *Josephus*, 108.

/67/ Although the NT is only a very small part of the early
Christian literature it is perhaps noteworthy that, so far as I
can discover, the precise formula does not occur in the NT.
Egineto de occurs only in Acts 2:43; 4:5; 5:7; 9:19,32,37,43;
10:10; 14:1; 19:23; 22:6,17; 23:9; 28:8,17 and 2 Pet 2:1.

/68/ MS Paris Bibliotheque Nationale 1430 a Rom, Vaticana 399,
manuscript A.   See *Die Griechischen Christlichen Schriftsteller
der Ersten Drei Jahrhunderte: Eusebius* 2/1 (Leipzig, 1903) 78.
Cf. Thackeray, *Josephus*, 143 and *Josephus* (Loeb) IX. 63n.1.

/69/ Cf. BDF 301; LSJ 1796, and see, *e.g.* Homer, *Iliad*, 5:9;
Xenophon, *Anabasis*, 3:1:4; Sophocles, *Philoctetes*, 442; Rom 3:8;
1 Cor 4:18; 15:34; 2 Cor 3:1; 1 Tim 1:3,19; 2 Pet 3:9; and in
Josephus note *Ant.* 18:4 (codices MWE); *J.W.* 2:118,433.

/70/ See Thackeray, *Josephus*, 144.   See also J. S. Kennard,
'Judas of Galilee and his Clan', *JQR* 36 (1945) 281-6.

/71/ Concluded from G. W. H. Lampe (ed.), *A Patristic Greek
Lexicon* (Oxford: Oxford University, 1961); U. Wilckens, *TDNT* VII
esp. 514-28; cf. Bammel in *Josephus-Studien*, 'Die Ersetzung von
sophos durch *sophistēs* ist nicht notwendig', p. 18.   On Wisdom
Christology see F. Christ, *Jesus Sophia* (Zurich: Zwingli, 1970);
J. D. G. Dunn, *Christology in the Making* (London: SCM, 1980)
ch. VI.

/72/ See Pindar, *Pythian*, 5:115; *Olympian*, 1:9; Aristophanes,
Fragmenta, 390; Pindar, *Nemean*, 7; Euripides, *Alcestis*, 348;
Philo, *De Som.*, 2:8.

/73/ Cf. Bammel in *Josephus-Studien*, 18.

/74/ Thackeray, *Josephus*, 144.

/75/ Cf. Pelletier, *RSR* 52 (1964) 188; Bammel in *Josephus-
Studien*, 18; Yamauchi, *Fides et Historia* 13 (1980) 54.

/76/ Of the miracles of Christ, *e.g.*, *CC* 4:80; 5:8; 7:54;
Clement, *fragmenta*, 29; Hippolytus, *refutatio omnium haeresium*,
4:36.

/77/ Acts of Philip 73; Chrysostom, *hom.7.1. in Jo.* (8:46B).

/78/ Thackeray, *Josephus*, 144.

/79/ Cf. A.-M. Dubarle, 'Le témoignage de Josèphe sur Jésus
d'après la tradition indirecte', *RB* 80 (1973) 507, who sees
Josephus admitting the reality of the miracles of Jesus.   See
also *RSR* 52 (1964) 188f.

/80/ *Ant.* 1:61; 17:325,334; 19:172; 20:42; *J.W.* 7:442,444.   The
remaining references being *Ant.* 3:49; 13:115; 15:373; 18:16;
20:41; *Ag.Ap.* 1:176,178; 2:145; *Life* 247.

/81/ A. Heinichen (ed.), *Eusebii Historia Ecclesiastica* III[2]
(1870), 623-54; Thackeray, *Josephus*, 145; cf. Bammel in
Josephus-Studien, 19 and n.63.

/82/ L, R, C, read *alēthōs*, ν reads *aēthōs*.

/83/ See, e.g., Nemesius Emesensus, *de natura hominis*, 18;
Chrysostom, *expositiones in Psalmos quosdam*, 9:3; Pseudo-
Dionysius Areopagita, *de ecclesiastica hierarchia*, 4:3:4;
Maximus Confessor, *Ambiguorum liber*.

/84/ See, e.g., Ignatius, *Romans*, 7:3; Clement, *Stromateis*, 3/4;
see also Stählin, *TDNT*, II.909-26.

/85/ Thackeray, *Josephus*, 108ff.

/86/ Though perhaps see Chrysostom, *hom.31.1 and 42 in Jo*.

/87/ Thackeray, *Josephus*, 146.

/88/ For example J. Drury, *Tradition and Design* (London: DLT,
1976) 96ff. on the 'Great Omission' in Luke.

/89/ Thackeray, *Josephus*, 146.

/90/ This is the consensus of scholarly opinion; cf. J. Bloch,
'Josephus and Christian Origins', *Journal of the Society of
Oriental Research* 13 (1929) 135; Adolf Harnack and F. C. Burkitt
are the notable dissenters. See Bammel in *Josephus-Studien*, 19.

/91/ It has been suggested that Origen was the author of the
clause; see Pelletier, *RSR* 52 (1964) 191.

/92/ One MS has *ho christos legomenos* (see Shutt and Richards,
CQ 31 (1937) 176) so that Josephus may have written, 'He was the
one they called the Christ' (cf. Bruce, *Origins*, 37f.). But the
textual evidence is not sufficient to outweigh the suspicion
that we have a piece of Christian origins here. Note Schürer,
History, I.435n.15.

/93/ Further see M. de Jonge, *TDNT*, IX.520f.

/94/ Schürer, *History*, I.434.

/95/ Eisler, *IHSOUS*, I.74.

/96/ Cf. *ibid*.

/97/ Eisler suggests 'to create a tumult', see Thackeray,
Josephus, 147n.66.

/98/ Cf. Bammel in *Josephus-Studien*, 19 and also Eisler, *IHSOUS*,
I.76f. following van Liempt who also cites *Ant*.10:1; 15:89.
(Cf. Richards and Shutt, *CQ* 31 (1937) 176).

/99/ Contrast Pelletier who thinks the sentence too reserved to
be from a Christian hand, *RSR* 52 (1964) 195.

/100/ Christians used the *phainō* word group in a variety of ways
in relation to Jesus. See, e.g., Mark 1:45; John 1:31; 2:11;
7:10; *Barn*. 14:5; Cyril of Alexandria, *John* 6 (4:564E);
Diogn. 11:2,4; Eusebius, *d.e*. 3:7; Hegemonius, *Arch*. 8:4; Ign.,
Phld. 6:3; *Magn*. 6:1; Justin, *Dial*. 76:1; *T.Sim*. 6:5; *T. Benj*.,
10:7.

/101/ See Bammel in *Josephus-Studien*, 19. The suggestion has
been made by a number of scholars, e.g., G. A. Miller, *Christus
bei Josephus Flavius* (Innsbruck, 1895) 142 in Eisler, *IHSOUS*,

I.78; Richards and Shutt, *CQ* 31 (1937) 176; cf. L. H. Feldman,
Josephus (Loeb), IX.50n.7. A tenth century quotation in the
Arabic work by Agapius (see below) stands alone in 'they
reported' (*Dhakarū*). See Shlomo Pines, *An Arabic Version of
the Testimonium Flavianum and its Implications* (Jerusalem:
The Israel Academy of Sciences and Humanities, 1971) 10.
/102/ On the redundant accumulation of particles in this
sentence and in Josephus as a whole see Eisler, *IHSOUS*, I.80 and
n.3.
/103/ James 1:1 uses *phulē*, most probably referring to
Christians; cf. C. Maurer, *TDNT*, IX.249f.; M. Dibelius and H.
Greeven, *James* (Philadelphia: Fortress, 1976) 66f.; P. Davids,
James (Exeter: Paternoster, 1982) 63. S. Zeitlin in 'The
Christ Passage in Josephus', *JQR* 18 (1928) 238f. is correct in
saying that the term is not used of Christians. Christians
usually used the term for the twelve tribes of Israel, *e.g.*,
Mt 19:28; Lk 2:36; 22:30; Acts 13:21; Rom 11:1; Philip 3:5;
Heb 7:13,14; Rev 5:5; 7:4-8; 21:12; *Barn.* 8:3; 1 Clem 43:2;
55:6; Herm.*Sim.* 9:17:2. See also, *e.g.*, Justin, *Apol.* 52:12;
53:4. Cf. Theodorus Studia (AD 759-826), *epistularum libri duo*
1:7. Zeitlin argued that the use of *phulon* proves that the
entire passage was composed by Eusebius (see note 57 above and
Yamauchi, *Fides et Historia* 13 (1980) 55).
/104/ Lucian, *Alex.* 25; 38; M.Peregr. 11; 12; 13; Tacitus,
Annals, 15:44; Suetonius, *Nero*, 16; Pliny, *Epp.*, 10:96,97
(Trajan's reply). See J. H. Moulton & G. Milligan, *The
Vocabulary of the Greek Testament* (London: Hodder & Stoughton,
1930) 692f.
/105/ The Slavonic or Old Russian (O.R.) text and German
translation are in Eisler, *IHSOUS*, II.296-30; (cf. the English
translation, *The Messiah Jesus* (London: Methuen, 1931) 383-5).
There is an English translation of the German of A. Berendts
and K. Grass, *Flavius Josephus vom Jüdischen Kriege, Buch i-iv,
nach der slavischen Übersetzung* (Dorpot, Teil i, 1924-6, Teil
ii, 1927) in Thackeray, *Josephus* (Loeb) III 648f. and in G. A.
Williamson, *Josephus: The Jewish War* (Harmondsworth: Penguin,
1959) 404f. For secondary literature see Thackeray, *Josephus*
(Loeb), IX.419f.; Brandon, *Jesus and the Zealots*, 364ff. and
notes; S. Zeitlin, 'The Slavonic Josephus and the Dead Sea
Scrolls: an exposé of recent fairy tales', *JQR* 58 (1968) 173-
203.
/106/ *Josephus*, 34.
/107/ J. W. Jack, *The Historic Christ. An Examination of
Dr. Robert Eisler's Theory According to the Slavonic Version of
Josephus and Other Sources* (London: James Clarke, 1933); see

also M. Gougel, 'Jésus et le Messianisme Politique: Examen de
la Théorie de M. Robert Eisler', *Revue historique* 162 (1929)
217-67; J. M. Creed in *HTR* 25 (1932) 277-319.
/108/ A. Rubinstein, 'Observations on the Old Russian Versions
of Josephus' *Wars*', *JSS* 2 (1957) 348.
/109/ Excursus in Schürer, *History*, I.440; a revised version of
'Josephus on Jesus', *J.Hist.St.* 1 (1968) 289-302.
/110/ The texts have been edited by L. Cheikho, *Agapius: Kitāb
al-'Unwān/Agapius Episcopus Mabbugensis: Historia Universalis*
Corpus Scriptorum Christianorum: Scriptores Arabici (Louvain,
1954 reprint) and with a French translation, A. Vasiliev,
*Agapius: Kitāb al-'Unwān/Histoire Universelle, écrite par
Agapius (Maḥboub) de Menbibj*, Patrologia Orientalis, V, 4
(Paris: 1912). See the bibliography in Pines, *Arabic Version*,
83.
/111/ From Pines, *Arabic Version*, 16.
/112/ Cf. the review of Pines' *Arabic Version* by S. P. Brock in
JTS 23 (1972) 491f.
/113/ *Time* (Magazine), 28 February, 1972, 43.
/114/ Pines, *Arabic Version*, 23. The Syriac version may have
occurred in Theophilos of Edessa's historical work which may
have been Agapius' main source (*ibid.*, n.97; cf. 6n.5).
/115/ See S. M. Zwemer, *The Moslem Christ*, 1912, cited by E.
Bammel, 'A New Variant of the *Testimonium Flavianum*', *Exp.Tim.*
85 (1974) 146.
/116/ Pines, *Arabic Version*, 67f.
/117/ Cf. Bammel in *Exp.Tim.* 85 (1974) 146f.
/118/ *Ibid.*, 147.
/119/ *Ibid.*
/120/ G. Bornkamm, *Jesus of Nazareth* (London: Hodder and
Stoughton, 1973) 28; cf. Hahn, Lohf and Bornkamm, *What Can We
Know About Jesus?*, 23.
/121/ See, *e.g.*, H. Laible, *Jesus Christus im Talmud* (Cambridge:
Deighton Bell, 1983); J. Klausner, *Jesus of Nazareth* (London:
George Allen & Unwin, 1928) 18, and literature cited; M.
Goldstein, *Jesus in the Jewish Traditions* (New York: Macmillan,
1950); J. Z. Lauterbach, 'Jesus in the Talmud' in his *Rabbinic
Essays* (New York: Ktav Reprint, 1973) 473-570; Bruce, *Origins*,
chap. IV; Maier, *Jesus*. For early literature on Jesus in the
Rabbinic literature see S. Krauss, *Jewish Encyclopedia* 7 (1904)
173a; Maier, *Jesus*, and Sanders, *Paul*, 557-61.
/122/ Neusner, *Politics to Piety*, 94; see also his *Rabbinic
Traditions*, III.3, where Neusner takes post-140 AD attributions
as absolutely reliable, *i.e.*, he assumes they said what is written.
However while the later the attribution the more likely it is to
be reliable we need to exercise care with all attributions.

/123/ *Politics to Piety*, 93.

/124/ J. Neusner, 'New Problems, New Solutions: Current Events
in Rabbinic Studies', *SR* 8 (1979) 411.

/125/ *Politics to Piety*, 93. See also Neusner, *Rabbinic
Traditions*, III.3; C. G. Montefiore and H. Loewe, *A Rabbinic
Anthology* (London: Macmillan, 1938) 711.

/126/ As set out by Sanders, *Paul*, 63 from J. Neusner, *Eliezer
Ben Hyrcanus* (2 vols.; Leiden: Brill, 1973) II.225f.

/127/ For a list of manuscripts see W. Horbury, *A Critical
Examination of the Toledoth Jeshu* (Cambridge University:
Ph.D. Dissertation, 1970) 39-53; for a list of printed
editions see Ad. Jellenek, *Bet ha-Midrasch* VI (Jerusalem, 1967[3])
ixf.; and Horbury, *Toledoth*, 55-60; for a list of editions of
the Aramaic texts see William Horbury, 'The Trial of Jesus in
Jewish Tradition' in *The Trial of Jesus: Cambridge Studies in
honour of C. F. D. Moule* (ed. Ernst Bammel; London: SCM, 1970)
116 n.4 and 118 n.5. For an English translation see Hugh J.
Schonfield, *According to the Hebrews* (London: Duckworth, 1937),
'Its (the Toledoth Jesus) best representation is the Strasburg
Codex, with which Martin's thirteenth-century quotation
verbally agrees. The Bokhara fragment also is substantially
in agreement, and Wagenseil's text, together with a number of
others is closely allied. This is the document... of which we
give an English translation from Krauss' critical text', p. 32.
See S. Krauss, *Das Leben Jesu nach jüdischen Quellen* (Berlin:
S. Calvary & Co., 1902) 181-94. The first translation
into English of a version of Wagenseil's text was by Richard
Carlile, *The Gospel According to the Jews, called Toldoth
Jesu, the Generations of Jesus* (London: 1823). For secondary
literature see Krauss, *Das Leben Jesu*; B. Heller, 'Über Judas
Ischariotes in der jüdischen Legende', *MGWJ* 76 (1932) 33-42; and
'Über das Alter der jüdischen Judas-Sage und des Toldot Jeschu',
MGWJ 77 (1933) 198-210; S. Krauss, 'Neuere Ansichten über
"Toledoth Jeschu"', *MGWJ* 77 (1933) 44-61; Schonfield, *According
to the Hebrews*; Goldstein, *Jesus*, 260f. and Horbury, *Toledoth
Jeshu*. There is a précis of the contents of the *Toledoth* in
Klausner, *Jesus*, 48-51.

/128/ See Klausner, *Jesus*, 48; Goldstein, *Jesus*, 147 and notes.

/129/ Cf. Joseph Dan, *Enc.Jud*.15, 1208. See also H. L. Strack,
Jesus, die Häretiker, who juxtaposes passages relating to Jesus
in the Talmud and early Christian reports of Jewish statements
on Jesus showing their agreement. Cf. James Parkes, *The
Conflict of the Church and Synagogue* (London: Soncino, 1934).
On the suggestion that the Toledoth has its origin in Celsus
see E. Bammel, 'Origen *Contra Celsum* i. 41 and the Jewish
Tradition', *JTS* 19 (1968) 211f.

/130/ Maier, *Jesus*, 18 and n.10.

/131/ Horbury, *Toledoth Jeshu*, 433-8. Cf. James Parkes, 'Rome, Pagan and Christian', *The Contact of Pharisaism with other Cultures* (Judaism and Christianity, vol. II) (ed. H. Loewe; London: 1937) 115-44.

/132/ See, *e.g.*, Krauss, *Jesus*, 246-8; Paul Fiebig's review of Krauss in *TLZ* 29 (1904) 508; Krauss, 'The Mount of Olives in "Toledoth Jesu"', *Zion* 55 (1939) 175; Schonfield, *Hebrews*, 30. Without evidence Voltaire ('Lettres sur les Juifs' in *Oeuvres* i, 69, p. 36) thought that the Toledoth was written before the canonical Gospels. See Goldstein, *Jesus*, 304 n.82, and E. Bammel, 'Christian Origins in Jewish Traditions', *NTS* 13 (1966-7) 317. On the other hand some date the Toledoth late. For example, Klausner, *Jesus*, 53 (tenth century), and Jack, *The Historic Christ*, 19 (middle ages). Part of the evidence for a late date are the 6 Aramaic fragments from the Genizah of the Ezra Synagogue in Cairo found by Solomon Schechter. See Goldstein, *Jesus*, 147 and n.7, and Horbury in Bammel (ed.), *Trial*, 104.

/133/ Krauss, *MGWJ* 77 (1933) 57f.; cf. E. Bischoff, *Ein jüdisch-deutsches Leben Jesu* (Leipzig: 1895).

/134/ See Horbury, *Toledoth Jeshu*, 307-40.

/135/ Krauss, *MGWJ* 77 (1933) 54; cf. Schonfield, *Hebrews*, 27.

/136/ Klausner, *Jesus*, 51; cf. Krauss, *Das Leben Jesus*, 154-236 and notes; Bammel, *NTS* 13 (1966-7) 317.

/137/ See Laible, *Jesus*, 50f.; Herford, *Christianity*, 62f.; B. Pick, *Jesus in the Talmud* (London and Chicago: Open Court, 1913) 29f.; Maier, *Jesus*, 76ff.. Cf. *Yal. Shim.* par. 766 on Num 23:7 on which see Laible, *Jesus*, 34; Pick, *Jesus*, 30f.; Herford, *Christianity*, 63f.; Maier, *Jesus*, 87f.

/138/ See Pick, *Jesus*, 50f.; Laible, *Jesus*, 50f.; Herford, *Christianity*, 303ff.; Maier, *Jesus*, 244ff.

/139/ See references in Herford, *Christianity*, 47; and also Klausner, *Jesus*, 35f.; Laible, *Jesus*, 32,34ff.

/140/ See also Klausner, *Jesus*, 37.

/141/ See B. A. Fürst, 'Origenes wider Celsus', *Saat auf Hoffnung* 14 (1877) 45f.; Maier, *Jesus*, 256f.

/142/ See Maier, *Jesus*, 256 and n.582.

/143/ A. Geiger, 'Bileam und Jesus', *Jüdische Zeitschrift für Wissenschaft und Leben* 6 (1868) 31-7. Cf. Krauss, *Das Leben Jesu*, 32f.

/144/ See the discussion in Lauterbach, 'Jesus in the Talmud', 503ff.

/145/ On *Yal. Shim.* to Num 23:7 (text) see Herford, *Christianity*, 404; Klausner, *Jesus*, 34f.; Laible, *Jesus*, 10 (text), 34 (trans.); Lauterbach, 'Jesus in the Talmud', 501f.; Maier, *Jesus*, 87ff.

/146/ From Klausner, *Jesus*, 33.

/147/ On the censorship of the Rabbinic literature, primarily by Christians, see H. L. Strack, *Introduction to the Talmud and Midrash* (New York: Atheneum, 1978) 78, esp. n.20, and Maier, *Jesus*, 12f.

/148/ The Munich MS adds 'the Nazarene' which, on the principle of taking the most difficult reading, should probably be ignored. See Herford, *Christianity*, 52 n.2.

/149/ See *Jewish Encyclopedia* 7 (1925) 295 and *Enc.Jud*. 10, 284f. and literature cited there. On the problem of chronology see Goldstein, *Jesus*, 75.

/150/ Maier, *Jesus*, 63; cf. Lauterbach, 'Jesus in the Talmud', 501.

/151/ See further Herford, *Christianity*, 60ff.; Lauterbach, 'Jesus in the Talmud', 501; Maier, *Jesus*, 63ff.

/152/ See Lauterbach, 'Jesus in the Talmud', 500f.

/153/ 'The word denotes both inn and innkeeper. R. Joshua used it in the first sense; the answer assumes the second to be meant.' Note by I. Epstein *b. Sanh*. 107b *The Babylonian Talmud* (ed. I. Epstein; London: Soncino, 1961) Sanhedrin p. 736.

/154/ Schürer, *History*, I.219-28.

/155/ The means of excommunication which included sounding four hundred trumpets (cf. *b. Mo'ed Qat*. 16a) is later - from Amoraic times. See Goldstein, *Jesus*, 74ff. (cf. n.25) and Lauterbach, 'Jesus in the Talmud', 484f.

/156/ Goldstein (*Jesus*, 75 and n.22, following and citing Bacher, Strack, Klausner, Zeitlin, Frankel, Graetz and Lauterbach) says that the pericope looks like pure invention, especially Jesus' worshipping a brick, than which, as Klausner says, 'nothing could be more absurd' (*Jesus*, 26). Even R. Jehiel's suggestion (Paris, 1240) that the brick was cross shaped is of little help, for this is inexplicable, especially before the crucifixion. (See Lauterbach, 'Jesus in the Talmud', 483f.). In any case the worship of a brick is not Christian and is only found in the Hermes cult; see Goldstein, *Jesus*, 76 and n.26.

/157/ See the discussion in Lauterbach, 'Jesus in the Talmud', 489f.

/158/ For example, M. Jastrow, *A Dictionary of the Targumim, the Talmud, Babli and Yerushalmi, and the Midrashic Literature* (2 vols.: London; Trubner, 1886-1903) II p. 972; Herford, *Christianity*, 37ff., 344ff.; M. Smith, *Jesus the Magician* (London: Gollancz, 1978) chap. 4.

/159/ References to Ben Stada are *t. Šabb*. 11:15/*y. Šabb*. 12:4 (13d)/*b. Šabb*. 104b/*b. Sanh*. 67a (see the synopsis in Maier, *Jesus*, 207); *t. Sanh*. 10:11/*y. Sanh*. 7:16 (25c,d); *y. Yebam*. 16:6 (15d end).

/160/ Cf. Lauterbach, 'Jesus in the Talmud', 528f.
/161/ Cf. Laible, *Jesus*, 31; Klausner, *Jesus*, 20.
/162/ Herford, *Christianity*, 345n.
/163/ For example, Derenbourg, Joel, Chajes, Bacher, Kohler, Strack, Klausner, Ginzberg, Lauterbach, Soncino translators of the Babylonian Talmud all (favourably) cited by Goldstein, *Jesus*, 60 and notes. See also Bruce, *Origins*, 58; Maier, *Jesus*, 237.
/164/ See also Lauterbach, 'Jesus in the Talmud', 525ff.
/165/ Cf. Bruce, *Origins*, 58. In *b. Ketub.* 51b a robber, Ben Bezar, is mentioned. Without evidence a number of older scholars (*e.g.*, J. Levy, *Neuhebräisches und Chaldäisches Wörterbuch über die Talmudim und Midraschim* I (Leipzig: Brockhaus, 1876) 240) have seen in the name Ben Nezar an allusion to Jesus. Further see Herford, *Christianity*, 95f. Pappos ben Jehudah (*b. Git.* 90a) has also been considered as the father of Jesus (see Paulus Cassel, *Aus Litteratur und Geschichte* (Berlin und Leipzig: 1885) 241). However he was a contemporary not of Jesus but of R. Akiba (c.50–c.132 AD). Cf. Laible, *Jesus*, 18f.; Herford, *Christianity*, 40.
/166/ There are variant spellings - Pandera, Pantira, Pantera, Pantiri, Panteri; see Maier, *Jesus*, 264ff. and Jastrow, *Dictionary*, II p. 1186; also Krauss, *Das Leben Jesu*, 140ff.; Lauterbach, 'Jesus in the Talmud', 533; Goldstein, *Jesus*, 35 and n.23. The ben Panthera material is collected in Strack, *Jesus die Häretiker*, and also Maier, *Jesus*, 260ff.
/167/ On dating see H. Chadwick, *Origen: Contra Celsum* (Cambridge: Cambridge University, 1980) xiv-xv.
/168/ Cassel, *Aus Litteratur und Geschichte*, 334ff.; cf. Laible, *Jesus*, 23ff. and Lauterbach, 'Jesus in the Talmud', 533. For other explanations see, *e.g.*, Lauterbach, 'Jesus in the Talmud', 533ff. and Goldstein, *Jesus*, 35ff.
/169/ Lauterbach, 'Jesus in the Talmud', 536f.
/170/ F. Nitzch, 'Über eine Reihe talmudischer und patristicher Täuschungen...', *Theologische Studien und Kritiken*, 13 (1840) 116 followed by Klausner, *Jesus*, 23f.; and Laible, *Jesus*, 25.
/171/ Deissmann in Rahmer's *Literaturblatt* XIV (1885), No. 42, p. 165 cited by Lauterbach, 'Jesus in the Talmud', 537 and n.213.
/172/ Cf. L. Patterson, *JTS*, 19 (1917) 79f.
/173/ Translation from Herford, *Christianity*, 103. Cf. Klausner, *Jesus*, 40. Synopsis in Maier, *Jesus*, 182f.
/174/ Translation from Herford, *Christianity*, 108. Synopsis in Maier, *Jesus*, 193f.
/175/ For a discussion of dating see Goldstein, *Jesus*, 33f. and 42f.

/176/ H. H. Graetz, *Geschichte der Juden* I (Leipzig: Leiner, 1905[5]) 312f.; Klausner, *Jesus*, 47; cf. Goldstein, *Jesus*, 34.
/177/ In Ben Patura/Paṭira/Paṭire (*b. B. Meṣ*. 62a; Sifre to Lev 25:36) M. S. Rens (in 'Wer is Ben Patira?', *Das Jüdische Literaturblatt* 14 (1885) 165 and 193f.) mistakenly saw a reference to Jesus. See Lauterbach, 'Jesus in the Talmud', 537ff. and Maier, *Jesus*, 181f.
/178/ Chadwick, *Origen*, xxviii, assigns Celsus' work to the period 177-80 AD.
/179/ For example, Bruce, *Origins*, 55ff. Cf. Maier, *Jesus*, 225f. and 229.
/180/ 'It has been taught' - a cue-word designating a baraita tradition. Goldstein, *Jesus*, 269 n.2. Cf. Levy, *Wörterbuch* 4 (1898) 654.
/181/ The Munich MS adds 'the Nazarene', but it must be discounted on the principle of taking the most difficult reading. Cf. Goldstein, *Jesus*, 23.
/182/ A Florentine MS adds 'and the eve of the Sabbath' on which see Maier, *Jesus*, 219f. and notes. Cf. Klausner, *Jesus*, 27f.
/183/ Cf. Klausner, *Jesus*, 28. That immediately following our baraita (*b. Sanh*. 43a) Ulla (Palestinian amora of the last half of the third century) expresses surprise at there being a herald ('Did you suppose that he was one for whom a defence could be made?') is not evidence against the historicity of the herald for by this time there was little interest in rehabilitating Jesus.
/184/ Cf. Lauterbach, 'Jesus in the Talmud', 492.
/185/ *Ibid*.
/186/ See G. S. Sloyan, *Jesus on Trial* (Philadelphia: Fortress, 1973) chap. 2; Hans-Ruedi Weber, *The Cross* (London: SPCK, 1979) 1-29; H. Cohn, *The Trial and Death of Jesus* (New York: Ktav, 1977) chap. 8.
/187/ Bruce, *Origins*, 57n.8. On the method of hanging see *b. Sanh*. 46a.
/188/ Set out in *The Jewish Encyclopedia* 3 (1925) 555.
/189/ Also necromancy and pythonism (*b. Sanh*. 65a).
/190/ For example, W. L. Lane, *The Gospel According to Mark* (London: Marshall, Morgan and Scott, 1974) 142. Dunn and I also have made a direct link between *b. Sanh*. 43a and the charge in Mark 3:22 (James D. G. Dunn and Graham H. Twelftree, 'Demon Possession and Exorcism in the NT', *Churchman* 94 (1980) 213).
/191/ See Graham H. Twelftree, *Jesus the Exorcist* (Sheffield, JSOT, forthcoming) chap. III. Cf. L. Gaston, 'Beelzebul', *TZ* 18 (1962) 247-55.

/192/ Further see Twelftree, *Jesus*, chap. V.

/193/ Cf. Maier, *Jesus*, 229.

/194/ *Ibid*.

/195/ See, *e.g.*, those mentioned in Goldstein in *Jesus*, 32 and 111ff.

/196/ Goldstein, *Jesus*, 32 and 111ff. and Bruce, *Origins*, 63.

/197/ G. Dalman, *Die Worte Jesu* (Leipzig, 1898) 40; Krauss, *Das Leben Jesu*, 57; Herford, *Christianity, 92*; Klausner, *Jesus*, 30; Goldstein, *Jesus*, 32.

/198/ See Hennecke, *NT Apocrypha* I.444ff. See also Lauterbach 'Jesus in the Talmud', 557f.; Maier, *Jesus*, 234. On the Gospel of Nicodemus (*Acta Pilati*) see Hennecke, *NT Apocrypha* I.444ff.

/199/ Cf. Irenaeus, *Haer*. i:26:3; cf. iii:11:1; Hippolytus, *Refutat*. vii:36; Eusebius *H.E.* iii:29:1.

/200/ See Maier, *Jesus*, 234 and n.494. Cf. G. B. Caird, *Revelation* (London: A. & C. Black, 1966) 31 and also Lauterbach, 'Jesus in the Talmud', 557. On Krauss' view (*Das Leben Jesu, 57*n.3) that Luke is meant by Naqai see Lauterbach, 'Jesus in the Talmud', 558.

/201/ Cf. O. Cullmann, 'Nazarene', *IDB* III.523.

/202/ *Jesus*, 30.

/203/ Graetz, *Geschichte der Juden* III/I.303n. and Laible, *Jesus*, 70f.

/204/ Klausner, *Jesus*, 30.

/205/ *Ibid*.

/206/ Cf. Goldstein, *Jesus*, 31f. On the list of disciples in the Synoptic Gospels and Acts see J. Jeremias, *NT Theology* (London: SCM, 1971) 232f.

/207/ Klausner, *Jesus*, 29. Cf. Goldstein, *Jesus*, 111f.

/208/ Klausner, *Jesus*, 37ff. takes it as authentic.

/209/ Herford, *Christianity*, 143.

/210/ Cf. J. Jeremias, *Unknown Sayings of Jesus* (London: SPCK, 1957) 29. On the authenticity of Mark 7:18ff. see N. Perrin, *Rediscovering the Teaching of Jesus* (New York: Harper and Row, 1976) 150.

REFERENCES TO JESUS IN EARLY CLASSICAL AUTHORS

Murray J. Harris
Tyndale House
36 Selwyn Gardens
Cambridge
CB3 9BA

C'est peu et c'est beaucoup. With these apt words F. Prat concludes his brief discussion of the references to Jesus and infant Christianity contained in three Roman writers - Tacitus, Suetonius and Pliny./1/ Even if we add the testimony of the historian Thallus who wrote in Greek, we still have surprisingly few allusions to Jesus in early classical literature. This article will examine in some detail the references to Jesus in these four writers and then attempt to explain why there are so few references to him in that literature and yet how this 'little' is 'much'.

I. Thallus

Julius Africanus, who lived from about A.D. 160-240, was a Christian chronographer who composed a *History of the World* down to A.D. 217 in five books. Only fragments of his work survive, but in one fragment (preserved by the Byzantine historian Georgius Syncellus)/2/ which describes the earthquake and three-hour darkness that occurred at Jesus' crucifixion, he writes:

Τοῦτο τὸ σκότος ἔκλειψιν τοῦ ἡλίου Θάλλος ἀποκαλεῖ ἐν τρίτῃ τῶν ἱστοριῶν, ὡς ἐμοὶ δοκεῖ ἀλόγως·

In the third book of his history Thallus calls this darkness an eclipse of the sun - wrongly in my opinion./3/

According to Eusebius this Thallus wrote (in Greek) a chronicle of world history in three books from the fall of Troy possibly down to about A.D. 52./4/ If we accept a proposed textual emendation, Josephus also refers to a certain Thallus, a wealthy Samaritan freedman of Tiberius who had lent a million drachmas to the bankrupt Herod Agrippa I (*Ant.* 18.167)./5/

Whether the Thallus of Africanus and Eusebius is to be
identified with the (proposed) Thallus of Josephus must remain
uncertain, although E. Schürer,/6/ R. Eisler/7/ and M. Goguel
/8/ favour the identification. Nor can we determine precisely
when Thallus wrote his *Chronicle*. The outer limits would be
A.D. 29 (since Thallus refers to the fifteenth year of
Tiberius) and about A.D. 221 (the probable date of Julius
Africanus' *History*). Some scholars suggest the middle of the
first century,/9/ some opt more generally for the second half
of the first century./10/

     What may be inferred from the fragment of Julius Africanus
about the content of Thallus' statement? It is clear that
Thallus was not merely documenting an eclipse of the sun that
took place in the reign of Tiberius, as G. A. Wells alleges.
/11/ He was identifying 'this darkness' (τοῦτο τὸ σκότος),
viz. the preternatural darkness that accompanied the death of
Jesus (cf. Lk. 23:44-45), as a solar eclipse. If Africanus
were simply questioning the accuracy of Thallus in claiming
that an eclipse had occurred at a certain time, he would not
have rejected Thallus' view by an expression of *opinion* -
'(wrongly) it seems to me'. What he was rejecting was a
naturalistic explanation of the darkness, not an alleged
occurrence of a solar eclipse. He proceeds to point out that
Thallus' explanation was unsatisfactory because an eclipse of
the sun is impossible at the time of the full moon. Clearly
both Thallus and Africanus take it for granted that there had
in fact been an unusual darkness at the time of Jesus'
crucifixion./12/

     All this makes it virtually certain that Thallus had some
knowledge of the Christian tradition of the passion of Jesus
and that in his *Chronicle* he referred to the extraordinary
darkness which he accepted as a fact but regarded as a
phenomenon that could be explained without invoking the
category of miracle as the Christians did./13/ We may
reasonably infer that an historian who alluded to and accepted
as reliable the tradition (quite possibly a written tradition)
/14/ that Christ's death was accompanied by a preternatural
darkness also accepted the fact of Christ's existence. As far
as we know, then, Thallus was the first pagan writer to refer
to Jesus.

II. Pliny the Younger

Pliny the Younger (c. A.D. 61 - c. 112) trained in Rome as
a lawyer, practised in the civil courts, and held a succession
of administrative posts (including a praetorship and
consulship) before being sent by Trajan in c. A.D. 110 to the
province of Bithynia-Pontus as imperial legate to restore order
in that disorganised province. Between A.D. 100 and 109 he
published nine collections of literary letters which range in
form from personal notes to short essays. In the tenth book of
his letters, covering the years 110-112, is found his official
correspondence with the Emperor regarding various
administrative problems that arose in Bithynia-Pontus.

In Letters 96 and 97 of Book 10 we have the famous
correspondence between Pliny and Trajan regarding the
Christians. Pliny (*Ep.* 10.96, penned c. A.D. 111) found
Christianity to be spreading so quickly in his province, in
both town and country, that temples were 'well-nigh abandoned'
and sales of fodder for the sacrificial animals had fallen
dramatically. Formal accusations had been levelled against the
Christians, possibly by the aggrieved tradesmen, and Pliny had
presided at the trials. Because the number of accusations was
growing rapidly, he consulted with Trajan on several points:
whether discrimination ought to be made with regard to age;
whether the renunciation of Christianity should win indulgence;
and whether the very profession of Christianity should be
punished or only the 'disgraceful practices' that went along
with it.

As he reviewed his earlier procedure in dealing with
anonymous accusations, Pliny informed Trajan that some persons,
apparently falsely charged with being Christians, at his
dictation invoked the state gods, did reverence with incense
and wine to the emperor's image, and also 'cursed Christ'
(*maledicerent Christo*). Others, who claimed to have previously
renounced the Christianity they once professed, also did
reverence to the emperor's image and the statues of the gods
and 'cursed Christ' (*Christo maledixerunt*). Pliny continues:
'But they maintained that their guilt or error had amounted
only to this: they had been in the habit of meeting on an
appointed day before daybreak and singing a hymn antiphonally
to Christ as a god (*carmenque Christo quasi deo dicere secum
invicem*), and binding themselves with an oath - not to commit
any crime but to abstain from theft, robbery, and adultery,
from breach of faith, and from repudiating a trust when called

upon to honour it' (*Ep.* 10.96.7)

The authenticity of this letter is beyond doubt./15/ Both the style and the tone are unquestionably those of Pliny: the letter is written in his inimitable florid prose and he raises questions with Trajan in his characteristically obsequious, legal tone. It might be noted that the reply of Trajan (*Ep.* 10.97) is also true to form: it strikes at the heart of the issue with his customary terseness. As for the content of Pliny's letter, a Christian forger would be unlikely to testify to the apostasy of fellow-believers and the consequent revival of pagan worship, far less to predict that a 'multitude of people' would return to the state religion 'if an opportunity is granted them to renounce Christianity'. Nor would he have a Roman provincial governor speak so disparagingly of Christianity - as infatuation (*amentia*), as 'depraved and excessive superstition' (*superstitio prava, immodica*), as 'this contagious superstition' (*superstitionis istius contagio*).

It has been seen that the letter contains three references to *Christus*./16/ To suggest that this is a title ('Messiah') /17/ and not a proper name referring to a person ('Christ') is a counsel of despair. What would be the sense of asking any persons, Jews or otherwise, to curse a figure who was *ex hypothesi* simply an object of hope as proof of recantation? And why would Christians sing an anthem of praise to a Messiah who was merely an expected redeemer and not an historical personage? There is no evidence of a Jewish or Christian messianic cult whose object of worship was a purely mythical figure.

On the contrary, from the outset it was recognized among Christians that to 'curse Christ' was to repudiate an historical figure now exalted to universal lordship (1 Cor 12:3; Phil 2: 7-11). Further, the ascription of praise to the glorified Jesus of Nazareth ('singing to the Lord') was a characteristic of early Christian worship (Eph.5:19; cf.Jn.20:28; 1 Pet.3:15).

The Christians of Pontus were accustomed to 'sing a hymn' (or 'recite a poem') *Christo quasi deo*. Whatever this phrase meant to the one-time Christians who reported the matter to Pliny, Pliny himself would doubtless have understood the phrase in the sense 'to Christ as if to a god'./18/ If Pliny had regarded Jesus as a god comparable to Asclepius or Osiris, he would have written *Christo deo*, 'to the god Christ'. The

intervening word *quasi* ('as if') highlights the distinctiveness
of Jesus in relation to other known gods. In what did that
distinctiveness consist? In the fact that, unlike other gods
who were worshipped, Christ was a person who had lived on earth.
/19/

It is sometimes asserted that this reference to the worship
of Christ does not constitute 'independent evidence' since Pliny
is simply reporting Christian belief./20/ A crucial point,
however, is that this information about the worship of Christ
came from persons who had already abandoned the profession of
Christianity,/21/ people who would scarcely be likely to create
evidence that could prove incriminating, viz. the suggestion
that they had once worshipped a figure not recognised as a state
god. What is more, the two earlier references in the letter to
'cursing Christ' come from the pen of Pliny, who himself had
specified the cursing of Christ as one of the three ways in
which Christians might prove they had renounced their allegiance
to Christ.

Pliny, then, affords clear testimony to Jesus as an
historical figure whose influence was still being felt in the
Roman province of Bithynia-Pontus some eighty years after his
death.

III.   Tacitus

Cornelius Tacitus was born in c. A.D. 56 and may have lived
until Hadrian's reign (A.D. 117-138). He served as *consul
suffectus* in A.D. 97 under Nerva and as proconsul of Asia in
A.D. 112-113.

He authored two major historical works: the *Annals*, which
deal with the reigns of Tiberius, Gaius, Claudius and Nero
(A.D. 14-68) in eighteen books, of which about half is extant;
and the *Histories*, covering the period A.D. 69-96 in twelve
books, of which only Books 1-4 and a section of Book 5 have
survived.

In the course of describing the events of A.D. 64 in the
imperial city in Book 15 of his *Annals* (written c. A.D. 115),
Tacitus vividly recounts how ten of Rome's fourteen districts
were engulfed in disastrous fires that raged for more than
six days and outstripped every counter-measure (15.38-40).
Because people believed that Nero had grandiose plans to found
a new capital and give it his own name (15.40; cf. Suetonius,

Nero, 55), a rumour spontaneously arose that the fire had started at the instigation of Nero himself./22/ These sinister suspicions were not eliminated, Tacitus tells us (15.43-44), by the imperial munificence in rebuilding the city nor by the introduction of fire-regulations nor by Nero's elaborate appeasement of the gods. The emperor finally tried to scotch the rumour by diverting the blame for the disaster to the Christians as convenient scapegoats./23/ Self-confessed Christians (*qui fatebantur [se Christianos esse]*) were arrested and on the basis of information they gave (or some of them gave, perhaps under torture), many others were also convicted. All these were 'punished with the utmost refinements of cruelty' (15.44).

Tacitus seems to suggest two different reasons for the persecution: Christians were convicted as arsonists or they were persecuted merely for being Christians. It seems improbable, even with their view of an apocalyptic conflagration (2 Pet.3:7, 10-12), that the Christians were themselves incendiaries. More probably, as in Roman Pontus in A.D. 111 (Pliny, *Ep.* 10.96.2), Christians in Rome in A.D. 64 were guilty simply for bearing 'the name itself' (*nomen ipsum*), simply for the profession of Christianity,/24/ for being members of an unlicensed secret society that was regarded as a threat to public order, or was thought guilty of unspecified crimes.

After noting, then, that Nero 'punished with the utmost refinements of cruelty' a class of people 'hated for their vices' (*per flagitia invisi*) who were popularly styled 'Christians', Tacitus proceeds:

> *Auctor nominis eius Christus Tiberio imperitante per procuratorem Pontium Pilatum supplicio adfectus erat* (15.44)./25/

> They got their name from Christ who had been executed by sentence of the procurator Pontius Pilate in the reign of Tiberius.

There is no evidence to support the contention that the passage is inauthentic. Not only is the style of the whole episode thoroughly Tacitean; the particular references to Christians and Christ in the account of the Great Fire accord with the context. Tacitus is indicating Nero's final ploy to stifle scandal and regain popular approval. After he had poured the imperial riches into reconstruction, had formulated

rigorous building regulations and fire precautions, and had
tried to appease the gods, he finally 'fabricated scapegoats'
(*subdidit reos*,/26/ M. Grant's rendering). Also Tacitus is
suggesting that just as execution was the appropriate fate of
the founder of Christianity, so it is the fitting lot of his
followers. The repetition of the verb *adficere* underlines this
point: 'Nero ... punished them with the utmost refinements of
torture (*quaesitissimis poenis adfecit*) ... Christ had been
executed (*supplicio adfectus erat*) by sentence of the procurator
Pontius Pilate'. Finally, with his concern to trace cause and
effect in history and in particular to trace the origin of
momentous events in seemingly insignificant incidents, Tacitus
thought it appropriate to disclose the origin of this
contemptible religious sect that had gained such remarkable
imperial attention in A.D. 64. This 'pernicious superstition'
had in fact survived the 'temporary setback' (*repressa in
praesens*) of the crucifixion of its founder in Judaea in the
30's 'only to break out afresh, not only in Judaea, the home of
the disease, but in the capital itself' (15.44) in the 60's.
And for Tacitus, events in Rome, events involving the emperor,
were of universal significance, for Rome was the centre of the
world and the emperor the centre of Rome.

It must remain unlikely that an early Christian forger
would have fabricated a story that involved self-confessed
Christian informers whose treachery led to the conviction of
a 'vast multitude' of their fellow-Christians. Nor would he
have the foremost Roman historian speak of Christianity so
disparagingly (see below). /27/

But two problems remain in this discussion of authenticity.
First, why does Tacitus refer to Pontius Pilate as 'procurator'
of Judaea when we now know from an inscription discovered at
Caesarea in 1961 that his official title was in fact 'prefect'?
/28/ This alleged inaccuracy is taken by G. A. Wells as
evidence that Tacitus had not conducted a close inquiry into the
matter and did not gain his information from Roman records./29/

Now it may be that Tacitus is anachronising,/30/ either
consciously or unconsciously, and using in reference to Pilate
(as he does of Gessius Florus, *Hist*. 5.10) the title for an
equestrian governor (viz. *procurator* = ἐπίτροπος) common in his
own day. But since both Philo (*Leg*. 38) and Josephus (*War*,
2.169) use ἐπίτροπος ('procurator') of Pilate and Josephus
refers to the governor of Judaea as **either** ἐπίτροπος or ἔπαρχος
(= *praefectus*)/31/ it seems reasonable to suppose that there

was a certain fluidity of terminology regarding the titles of
the governor of Judaea, at least in popular usage, during the
period A.D. 6-66, but that from A.D. 6-41 the titles *praefectus*
or *pro legato* predominated, while after the reconstitution of
the province, from A.D. 44-66, the term *procurator* (=ἐπίτροπος)
became the common designation./32/ During both periods,
however, the unofficial term 'governor' (ἡγεμών) was also used,
as it is in the NT of Pilate (e.g., Mt.27:2; Lk.20:20; also
Jos. *Ant.* 18.55) and other Roman officials governing Judaea
(e.g., Acts 23:26; 26:30). We can scarcely accuse Tacitus,
then, of being inaccurate or ill-informed at this point.

The second question is this. It is sometimes affirmed that
if Tacitus' testimony were reliable we would expect some
official record of the trial and execution of Jesus of Nazareth
to have been sent by the prefect of Judaea to the Imperial
authorities in Rome. The absence of any such report casts
doubt on the accuracy of Tacitus.

We may agree with R. Eisler in his insistence that the rules
relating to the official records of the Roman bureaucracy
demanded that a record of proceedings be kept,/33/ but there is
no evidence that a prefect or procurator was obliged to send
to Rome a record of legal proceedings in all capital cases
involving persons not holding Roman citizenship. Now although
Justin Martyr and Tertullian refer to a report of Pontius Pilate
that existed in the imperial archives, neither writer gives
the impression that he was personally acquainted with the
document, whether it be the 'Acts of Pontius Pilate'(as in
the case of Justin Martyr, *First Apology*, 35.7-9; 48.3) or a
letter of Pilate to Tiberius (as in the case of Tertullian,
Apology, 21), while both apologists appeal to the record as
confirming their claims about the divinity of Jesus, which
suggests that apologetic interests may originally have
operated on the Gospel records and produced a bold conjecture.
These Christian apologists may have appealed to what they knew
to be customary practice, whether or not they had actually ever
seen the report.

It must remain uncertain, if not improbable, that if
Pilate had made a written record of the trial and execution of
Jesus he would have sent it to Rome. Eisler's view that the
sensitive political nature of the issues raised by the trial of
Jesus - suggested by the inscription on the cross *Jesus
Nazoraeus Rex Judaeorum* - and Pilate's concern for his own
safety would have dictated that a full report be sent to Rome

/34/ fails to reckon adequately with the barbarous and
unscrupulous character of Pilate's administration. A prefect
who was accused of numerous summary executions would be
unlikely to prejudice his reputation and to play into the hands
of his enemies at Rome by furnishing a compromising report to
the imperial chancery./35/

What we can affirm with confidence is that no official
records (*acta*) are extant that any Roman governor of Judaea sent
to Rome concerning any matter. Thus the absence of any report
from Pilate to Tiberius is patently inconclusive for the
question of the reliability of Tacitus.

What may be surmised about the source on which Tacitus
draws for his information about Jesus?

The absence of an expression such as *plerique tradidere*
('most have recounted') or *sunt qui ferant* ('there are some who
say') before the reference to Christ may suggest that Tacitus
is using a written source, not reproducing an oral tradition.
Certainly it indicates that Tacitus himself was convinced of
the accuracy of his statement as he records the origin of the
name *Christiani*. But we cannot rule out an oral source for this
snippet of information, for Tacitus is writing in about A.D. 115
shortly after he had been proconsul of Asia (probably
A.D. 112-113) during which time he must have known of the small
Christian congregations scattered throughout the province
(Rev.1:4). In addition, Tacitus was an intimate friend and
correspondent of the younger Pliny and was therefore probably
acquainted with the problems Pliny encountered with the
Christians during his governorship in Bithynia-Pontus (c. A.D.
110-112)./36/

Whether the source was oral or written, it was almost
certainly pagan rather than Christian or Jewish. We have seen
above that Tacitus' brief sentence about Jesus coheres with the
context and therefore stands or falls with the whole episode of
the Neronian persecution. But the description of Christians
throughout chapter 44 is uniformly scornful and hostile - they
are a people 'hated for their vices' (*per flagitia invisi*) who
have a 'hatred of the human race' (*odio humani generis*)/37/ and
whose guilt had earned the ruthless punishment it deserved.
Christianity was a 'pernicious superstition'(*exitiabilis
superstitio*) needing to be checked, a 'disease' (*malum*) to be
classed among 'all the degraded and shameful things in the
world'. Also the assertion of Tacitus that Christianity was

dormant between the death of Jesus and the time of the Great
Fire can scarcely derive from a Christian source. We cannot,
however, rule out the possibility that Tacitus has inserted
into a pagan source that dealt with the persecution of
Christians under Nero an item of information about Jesus that he
had gained directly or indirectly from Christians.

As for the possibility of a Jewish source, Goguel
succinctly comments

> What he (Tacitus) actually says about the 'detestable
> superstition' which reawakens simultaneously both in
> Judaea and in Rome, a little before the year 64, does
> not distinguish between the two forms of Messianism
> which were represented by Christianity and by Judaism.
> The words 'not only in Judaea' can only refer to the
> outbreak of nationalism which provoked the Jewish
> revolt and the Jewish war. Further, a Jewish
> document would never have represented Judaism as
> united with Christianity, nor would it ever have
> called Jesus 'the Christ'./38/

It is not impossible that Tacitus had access to some record
of the execution of Jesus under Pilate preserved in the imperial
chancery; however, these archives (*commentarii principis*) were
secret so that even the senate needed special permission to
consult them (Tacitus, *Hist*.4.40). Or Tacitus may have
depended on the *Histories* of the elder Pliny who probably served
as deputy commander of the general staff (ἀντεπίτροπος) during
the first Jewish war against Rome./39/

Our ultimate uncertainty about the precise origin of this
piece of information about Jesus may be frustrating but it
conforms with our general ignorance of Tacitus's specific sources
throughout the *Annals*.

Of the three main literary sources for the period of the
early principate, Tacitus surpasses Suetonius and Dio Cassius
not only in literary excellence but also in historical
accuracy./40/ We may therefore regard as being of special
importance his affirmation, registered with what R. Syme calls
'documentary precision',/41/ that Christ was executed under
Pontius Pilate and was the founder of a group of sectaries that
bore his name.

IV. Suetonius

Relatively little is known of the life and career of
Suetonius. He was probably from Hippo Regius in Numidia (now
Annaba in Algeria) and lived from c. A.D. 69-130's. For a
short period, perhaps A.D. 119-121, he served as secretary to
Hadrian. His voluminous writings range over the fields of
history, biography, natural history, antiquities, and grammar,
but the only work that has been nearly wholly preserved is his
Lives of the Caesars (*De vita Caesarum*), the biographies of
Julius Caesar and the first eleven Roman emperors down to
Domitian, published about A.D. 120.

Book Five of his *Lives* deals with 'The Deified Claudius'.
In the course of a rather prosaic enumeration of the
administrative acts of Claudius at home and abroad, which ends
with the comment that 'almost the whole conduct of his reign'
was determined by the desires and interests of his wives and
freedmen (*Claudius* 25.5), Suetonius makes the statement: *Iudaeos
impulsore Chresto assidue tumultuantis Roma expulit* .'He
(Claudius) expelled the Jews from Rome, because of the rioting
in which they were constantly engaging at the instigation of
Chrestus' (25.4).

Rarely has the authenticity of this passage been called
into question, for it contains two patent inaccuracies - the
spelling *Chrestus* for *Christus* (assuming the allusion is to
Christ); and the assumption that Christ, as the ringleader of
the rioters, was living in Rome during the reign of Claudius
(A.D. 41-54). What are we to make of these inaccuracies in
Suetonius or his source?

The word *Chrestus* is the Latin transliteration of the
Greek adjective χρηστός which could be applied to a propitious
god, a kind person, an upright citizen, a brave warrior, or a
useful slave (see *LSJ*, s.v. 1741-1742). Whereas for Greeks
Χριστός was a strange-sounding name drawn from medical or
building terminology and meaning 'anointed' or 'plastered',/42/
Chrestus (or Χρηστός) was a common personal name, particularly
apt for slaves ('useful one')./43/

If Suetonius were referring to some unknown Jewish
agitator/44/ or Christian leader called *Chrestus*, we might have
expected him to write *impulsore Chresto quodam,* 'at the
instigation of a certain Chrestus' (cf. *Claudius* 42.1, *cuidam
barbaro*)./45/ But in fact *Chrestus* was a common and natural

misspelling of *Christus*./46/   The substitution of 'e' for 'i'
is a common itacistic error in the popular spelling of proper
names. For example, the original hand of Codex Sinaiticus has
the spelling Χρηστιανός (*Chrestianos*) in the three NT uses of
the term 'Christian' (Acts 11:26; 26:28; 1 Pet.4:16). And
behind this frequent misspelling was a common mispronunciation.
Writing about A.D. 197, Tertullian observes that 'Christian'
(*Christianus*) is derived from 'anointing', but when it is
mispronounced as 'Chrestian' (*Chrestianus*) it is derived from
'sweetness' or 'kindness'. He concludes: 'So in innocent men
you hate even the innocent name' (*Apology* 3.5)/47/ It is
therefore reasonable to conclude that *Chrestus* in Suetonius is
simply a spelling variant for *Christus*.

   But is the term *Christus* here a title ('Messiah') or a
proper name ('Christ')? It is highly improbable that the
phrase *impulsore Chresto* means 'at the instigation of a Messiah',
far less 'because of disputes about the Messiah (or
messiahship)'/48/ or 'because of preaching about a Messiah'.
There is no evidence that *Christus* or *Chrestus* meant 'Messiah'
in current pagan Latin./49/ Moreover, would a Jewish
nationalism that resorted to violence (*tumultuantis*) against the
Roman power have survived for a prolonged period (*assidue*)?/50/
There are, however, several compelling considerations that
support the prevailing view /51/ that *Chrestus* refers to Jesus
Christ. First, the absence of *quodam* ('a *certain* Chrestus')
indicates that Suetonius expected his readers to be able to
identify the person to whom he was referring. Only one
Chrestus would fit that category in A.D. 120 - the *Chrestus*
whose followers were popularly known as *Chrestiani*. Secondly,
an unexplained passing allusion to the founder of Christianity
would be natural for a writer who elsewhere refers to
Christians./52/ Thirdly, Lactantius speaks (*Divine Institutes*
4.7.5, c. A.D. 311) of 'the error of the ignorant, who by the
change of a letter are accustomed to call him (viz. Jesus)
Chrestus'. Given the testimony of Tertullian cited above and
the widespread occurrence of itacism in the second century we
may fairly assume that what was true early in the fourth century
was also true early in the second when Suetonius was writing,
viz. that Jesus was frequently called *Chrestus*.

   The second inaccuracy in Suetonius is the erroneous
assumption that Christ was himself in Rome at the time of the
riots.

   Uncertainty persists concerning the nature of the riots

and the date of the expulsion edict.   The riots may have been
violent contention within Roman Jewry regarding messianic
expectations that was thought to have been fomented by Christ,
/53/ or violent demonstrations by Roman Jews against the
burgeoning Christian community in Rome, but more probably they
were violent disputes between Jews and Christians concerning
the claim being pressed by Christian missionaries that Jesus of
Nazareth was in fact the Jewish Messiah, disputes comparable to
those which also marked Paul's missionary activity./54/
Unlike his close friend Herod Agrippa I who saw a clear
difference between Jewish Christianity and normative Judaism
(Acts 12:1-4), Claudius evidently regarded the riots as a
purely Jewish affair or else did not deem it necessary to
distinguish between Christianity and Judaism in legal
proceedings and therefore directed his expulsion order against
'all the Jews' (Christian and non-Christian alike) (Acts 18:2)
in Rome./55/

As for the date of Claudius's edict, Dio Cassius recounts
that in the first year of his reign (A.D. 41-42) Claudius
decided not to expel the Jews from Rome (since they had
become so numerous that a riot would probably have ensued) and
instead deprived them of their right of association (*Historia
Romana* 60.6.6).   On the other hand, the fifth-century historian
Paulus Orosius, who cites and discusses the statement of
Suetonius, dates the expulsion in the ninth year of Claudius's
reign (A.D. 49-50)./56/ Although the dates of Orosius are not
always reliable, confirmation of the latter date may be found
in Luke's reference to the recent arrival in Corinth of Aquila
and Priscilla 'because Claudius had ordered all the Jews to
leave Rome' (Acts 18:2).   Paul arrived in Corinth towards the
end of A.D. 50 /57/ and promptly attached himself to this
refugee couple who had recently (προσφάτως, Acts 18:2) come
from Italy.

There are some who prefer the evidence of Dio Cassius and
who date an expulsion of the Jewish rioters (not one involving
all Roman Jews) in A.D. 41./58/ More satisfactory, however,
is the solution which delineates several stages in Claudius's
policy towards the Jews of Rome spanning the years 41-49.
Eager to reverse the effects of Gaius's restrictive policies,
Claudius first of all extended to Jews throughout the Empire
the freedom in religious matters that he had already restored
to the Jews of Alexandria and that they had enjoyed under
Tiberius (Josephus, *Ant*. 19.278-291).   But then, later in
A.D. 41, in order to curb Jewish unrest that had arisen in Rome

he denied Roman Jewry the right of assembly, although were it
not for the size of the Jewish colony and (possibly) the
intercession of Herod Agrippa I he might have expelled them from
the city (Dio Cassius). At some stage before A.D. 49 this edict
that forbad the Jews to associate was relaxed (this is implied
by Suetonius's statement) but because the arrival of Christian
missionaries had given fresh impulse to Jewish discord as well
as to Jewish proselytizing, Claudius, who did not distinguish
Christianity from Judaism, introduced a more drastic measure
(in A.D. 49) with which he may have threatened the Jews in
A.D. 41 - their expulsion from the capital./59/

If, then, we date the imperial edict mentioned in the
sentence of Suetonius in the year 49 the error regarding the
involvement of Christ remains, for we cannot argue that
Suetonius is alluding to the indirect or earlier influence of
Christ on the Jews, far less to the influence of the risen
Christ. Perhaps he is simply faithfully producing an unreliable
source, unaware of the Christian reference; it was typical of
Suetonius to quote his sources *verbatim*, whether they were in
Greek or Latin, in verse or in prose. Alternatively, 'if his
sources indicated that the riots which provoked Claudius's edict
of expulsion were due to the introduction and propagation of
Christianity in the capital, he could well have drawn the
mistaken inference that it had been introduced there by Christ
in person'./60/ But this error of fact does not invalidate the
reference to Christ. Clearly Suetonius or his source -
possibly an earlier historian's version of the riots, based on
local police records - viewed Christ as an historical person
capable of fomenting unrest.

For all its difficulties, this reference in Suetonius
points to Jesus as the leader of a band of dissident Jews, if
not the founder of Christianity.

V.   General Observations

C'est peu. Our four classical writers provide a modicum
of information about the life and influence of Jesus,
information that accords with the testimony of the New
Testament. We may summarise the data in six facts and indicate
a selection of the passages in the Gospels, the book of Acts
and the Epistles that are thus corroborated.

1. (i)   Christ attracted sufficient attention to be arraigned
          before the procurator of Judaea (ii) who condemned him

to death (Tacitus).

(i)   Luke 23:2-5; 1 Tim.6:13

(ii) Luke 23:20-24

2. (i)   Christ was executed by crucifixion (ii) while Pilate
was prefect of Judaea (A.D. 26-36) and Tiberius was
emperor (A.D. 14-37) (Tacitus). It may therefore be
assumed that he lived in Judaea early in the first
century.

(i)   Luke 23:33, 46

(ii) cf. Luke 3:1

3. (i)   At the time of the crucifixion there was a
preternatural darkness (ii) that called for special
explanation (Thallus).

(i)   Mark 15:24,33; Luke 23:33,44

(ii) Mark 15:34; Luke 23:45

4. (i)   Christ attracted a group of followers (ii) who by the
time of Nero were sufficiently numerous and despised
(iii) to be held accountable for the Great Fire of
Rome (Tacitus).

(i)   Luke 6:13-16; 10:1; 23:2, 14, 49; Acts 1:13-15

(ii) 1 Pet.1:1; 2:9,15; 3:9, 13-17; 4:14

5. (i)   Christ's followers derived their name 'Christians'
from him (Tacitus), (ii) which indicates his role as
founder (or 'instigator') of a distinctive sect
arising within Judaism (Suetonius).

(i)   Acts 11:26; 26:28; 1 Pet.4:14, 16

(ii) Luke 23:2-3; Acts 24:5

6.   Some eighty years after Christ's death Christians in
Pontus regularly addressed him as Deity (Pliny).
Cf. John 20:28; 1 Pet.1:1; 3:15

To summarise the data in more general terms, two of the
four authors describe certain circumstances of Jesus' death,
one referring to the responsibility of the local governor for
his execution (Tacitus), the other mentioning the extraordinary
darkness occurring at the time (Thallus). The other two
writers allude to Jesus' influence, either as leader of a
religious sect involved in rioting (Suetonius) or as the object
of his followers' worship (Pliny).

The relatively meagre nature of our findings prompts the question: why is the pagan testimony to Jesus so scanty?

It should be noted, in the first place, that our knowledge of any aspect of first-century history is dependent on comparatively few witnesses, witnesses that themselves are fragmentary. Secondly, Roman writers could hardly be expected to have foreseen the subsequent influence of Christianity on the Roman Empire and so to have carefully documented the beginnings of this new religion in the appearance of a Nazarene prophet. On the contrary, as M. Goguel observes,

> For the whole of Roman society in the first century, Christianity was merely a contemptible Eastern superstition. It was ignored, save when it proved the occasion of political and social ferment. It is from this point of view alone that the Latin authors speak of it, and it is natural that they should not take the trouble to collect and examine the real or fictitious traditions to which those whom they regarded as agitators referred./61/

Thirdly, for all its political turbulence, Judaea was in a remote corner of the Empire of little intrinsic importance to the imperial capital. The summary execution of a messianic agitator in Judaea would have been no exceptional occurrence. /62/ Josephus tells us that 'about two thousand' Jewish insurgents were crucified by the legate of Syria, Quintilius Varus, following the widespread disturbances after the death of Herod the Great in 4 B.C. (*War* 2.75)./63/

But not only are the pagan writers who refer to Jesus few in number; no one of them was a contemporary of Jesus, Thallus belonging probably to the second half of the first century and Pliny, Tacitus and Suetonius to the early second century. This indisputable fact does not, however, invalidate the testimony of these four writers or call into question the historicity of Jesus./64/ Our knowledge of the reign of the Emperor Tiberius, the best-known contemporary of Jesus, derives primarily from four Roman sources. The least satisfactory is in fact a contemporary record by the amateur historian Velleius Paterculus, penned about A.D. 30, whereas the most valuable sources for the life of Tiberius date from some 100-200 years later - the *Annals* of Tacitus (c.A.D. 115), the life of Tiberius by Suetonius (c.A.D. 120), and the Roman history of Dio Cassius (c. A.D. 230)./65/ We may add that none of the

Greek or Roman authors of the first century except Thallus would
have had reason to refer to Jesus, if we may judge from the
scope and purpose of their writings./66/ Thallus, on the other
hand, is distinctive in his effort to show the points of contact
between Graeco-Roman and Oriental history.

C'est beaucoup. Our four authors all witness to the
existence of an historical person called Christ./67/ We have
seen that whether they are based on specific or general
objections, claims that this evidence is not authentic or is
not valid cannot be substantiated./68/ The testimony clearly
cannot be dismissed as tendentious. True, the disinterestedness
of a writer (if such is possible) is no guarantee of the
reliability of his reporting, but the uniform testimony of four
'impartial' observers - two historians, a biographer, and an
epistolographer, none of them Christian - affords potent
confirmation of the uniform witness of some nine 'partial' New
Testament authors to the existence of Jesus and the influence
he exerted both during his lifetime and after his death.

If historical criticism were to pronounce the ultimate
verdict that Jesus never existed, a convenient or attractive
object for faith might not be lost but Christianity would be
reduced to fancy, for the Christ whom the apostles proclaimed
as the necessary object of faith was the resurrected Jesus of
Nazareth. If Jesus never lived, the validity of the Christian
faith is totally undermined, for Christians proclaim and
believe in Jesus as a person who once walked this earth. Such
a discovery would be no mere theological embarrassment or
inconvenience, but a religious catastrophe, the death-knell of
historic Christianity, for the Christian faith could not be
reinterpreted merely as a general metaphysical or religious
theory without ceasing to be Christian. Behind the speculative
hypotheses that discount the historical data we have analysed
is the wholly justifiable assumption that to establish that
Jesus was merely a mythical figure is to falsify Christianity.
/69/

We conclude that there are four early classical writers of
the first or early second century who make references to Jesus,
references that are, apparently, always made in passing and in
the two principal cases (Tacitus, Pliny) occur in descriptions
of measures taken to curb the influence of Christians.
Immensely significant though they be, these fleeting allusions
provide a geometrical point that has position but little
magnitude (to adapt a phrase of Giovanni Miegge). It is to the

four Gospels that one must turn to discover the full
magnitude of that point.

Notes

/1/ *Jésus-Christ. Sa Vie, Sa Doctrine, Son Oeuvre. I* (Paris:
Beauchesne, 1953, 21st edition) 3.

/2/ See F. Jacoby, *Die Fragmente der griechischen Historiker
II B* (Berlin: Weidmann, 1929) 1157, No. 256.

/3/ For all eight extant fragments of Thallus, see Jacoby,
Fragmente 1156-58. In the absence of any evidence to the
contrary, we shall be assuming that both Julius Africanus and
Georgius Syncellus have reported accurately the information
they relate.

/4/ *Eusebius Werke. V. Die Chronik* (ed. J. Karst) (Leipzig:
Hinrichs, 1911) 125. Eusebius in fact avers that the *Chronicle*
of Thallus covered the period from the fall of Troy down to the
167th Olympiad (112-109 B.C.). On the other hand Africanus
asserts that in his third book Thallus dates the darkness of the
crucifixion in the fifteenth year of Tiberius (A.D. 29). All
agree that Eusebius's date is in error and R. Eisler has
proposed (adopting a conjecture made by C. Müller in 1849) that
ρξζ (167th) should be corrected to σζ (207th Olympiad =
A.D. 49-52)(ΙΗΣΟΥΣ ΒΑΣΙΛΕΥΣ ΟΥ ΒΑΣΙΛΕΥΣΑΣ.ΙΙ *[*Heidelberg:
Winter, 1930*]* 140 n. 5).

/5/ This reference in the *Antiquities* to a certain Thallus
depends on correcting the reading ἦν ἄλλος Σαμαρεὺς γένος
(found in all manuscripts except E, a summarizing text that
eliminates the difficult ἄλλος by reading τὶς ἦν Σαμαρεὺς γένος)
into ἦν Θάλλος Σαμαρεὺς γένος. This seems an eminently
reasonable emendation since the context does not contrast one
Samaritan with 'another' and a certain Tiberius Claudius Thallus
is known from an inscription (see R. Laqueur, 'Thallus (1)' in
Paulys Real-Encyclopädie der classischen Altertumswissenschaft
*[*begun by G. Wissowa, ed. by W. Kroll and K. Mittelhaus*]*
*[*Stuttgart: Metzler, 1934*]* V.1 (9), col. 1226). But H.A. Rigg,
Jr., has defended the reading with ἄλλος which he construes as
a pronoun (equivalent to *quidam*), not an adjective: 'Now there
was another, namely a Samaritan by race' ('Thallus: The
Samaritan?', *HTR*, 34 (1941) 111-119). According to Rigg
(119 n.38), 'the context of this passage implies that Agrippa
has raised a sum of money in one direction and now borrows
another sum with which to pay off the former from another
source, viz., a certain Imperial freedman who happened to be
a Samaritan'.

/6/   *Geschichte des jüdischen Volkes im Zeitalter Jesu Christi.*
III.   Das Judentum in der Zerstreuung und die jüdische
Literatur (Hildesheim: Olm, 1964 reprint of 1909 edition) III,
495.
/7/   ΙΗΣΟΥΣ, II 140-141; *The Messiah Jesus and John the Baptist*
(Eng. tr. by A.H.Krappe) (London: Methuen, 1931) 298.
/8/   *The Life of Jesus* (Eng. tr. by O.Wyon) (London: Allen &
Unwin, 1933) 93; 'Un nouveau témoignage non-chrétien sur la
tradition évangélique d'après M Eisler', *RHR* 98 (1928) 6-7.
/9/   Eisler, ΙΗΣΟΥΣ, II. 141, 435; *Messiah Jesus*, 298; Goguel,
Life 93; F.F.Bruce, *Jesus and Christian Origins Outside the*
New Testament (Grand Rapids: Eerdmans, 1974) 30.
/10/   H.Windisch, 'Das Problem der Geschichtlichkeit Jesu: Die
ausserchristlichen Zeugnisse', *Theologische Rundschau*, n.f.1
(1929) 286; cf.B.Z.Wacholder, 'Thallus' in *Encyclopaedia*
Judaica, ed. C.Roth (Jerusalem: Keter, 1971), XV, col. 1045
('first century'). In holding to a second-century dating for
the *Chronicle* of Thallus,   F.Jacoby (*Fragmente*, II.D
[Berlin: Weidmann, 1930], 835) represents a minority opinion.
/11/   *Did Jesus Exist?* (London: Pemberton, 1975) 13.
/12/   Rigg, *HTR*, 34 (1941) 112 n.7, 114 and n.15.
/13/   'Aux chrétiens qui prétendaient que des ténèbres
miraculeuses s'étaient produites au moment de la mort de leur
Seigneur, Thallus opposait qu'il s'était agi d'un phénomène
tout naturel, d'une simple éclipse de soleil, qu'il n'y avait
donc eu qu'une coïncidence purement fortuite et qu'ainsi les
ténèbres qui ont couvert la terre au moment de la mort de
Jésus ne prouvent absolument rien pour le caractère de sa
personne ou l'origine de sa mission.   Thallus polémise contre
la tradition chrétienne, ou, plus exactement, contre
l'interprétation qu'elle donnait d'un fait qu'elle rapportait'
(Goguel, *RHR* 98 [1928] 4-5).
/14/   'It is of course evident that a man like Thallus would
never have taken the trouble to correct and criticize a
miraculous story existing only in oral tradition.   On the
contrary, he must have known a written source dealing with
the crucifixion and its attendant phenomena' (Eisler, *Messiah*
Jesus, 298; cf ΙΗΣΟΥΣ, II. 142).   But we need not follow
Eisler's conjecture (*ibid.*) that this written source was in
fact a collection of Old Testament prophecies (λόγια)
attributed to Matthew; it might equally well have been any one
of the synoptic Gospels (see Mt 27:45; Mk 15:33; Lk 23:44-45).
/15/   See the discussions of J.B.Lightfoot, *The Apostolic*
Fathers, Part II, Vol.I (London: Macmillan, 1885) 54-56;
E.C.Babut, 'Remarques sur les deux lettres de Pline et de

Trajan relatives aux chrétiens de Bithynie', *Revue d'histoire et de littérature religieuses,* n.s.1, (1910) 298-301; K.Linck, *De antiquissimis veterum quae ad Iesum Nazarenum spectant testimoniis* (Giessen: Töpelmann, 1913) 32-60, especially the careful linguistic analysis on pp 43-45; A.N.Sherwin-White, *The Letters of Pliny* (Oxford: Clarendon, 1966) 691-692, who lists the stylistic touches characteristic of Pliny, and asks (p 691) 'Where could a forger have learned about the special edict against *collegia*'('private associations') mentioned in 96.7?

/16/ From E.T.Merrill's critical edition of Pliny's letters it may be seen that there are no textual variants at these three points.

/17/ Thus P.L.Couchoud, *The Enigma of Jesus* (London: Watts, 1924) 24; G.A.Wells, *The Jesus of the Early Christians* (London: Pemberton, 1971) 185.

/18/ It is impossible to know the precise wording of the report given to Pliny. If the apostate Christians were accurately describing genuine Christian conviction, they may possibly have used the phrase *Christo Deo* ('to Christ who is God'; cf. the similar expressions in contemporary Christian documents, Ignatius, *ad Eph.* 18.2; *ad Rom.* 6.3; *ad Smyr.* 1.1), a sentiment Pliny then expressed in the more unassuming form *Christo quasi deo*, 'to Christ as if to a god'. If, on the other hand, these one-time Christians were reflecting a revised view of Christ that they presently held or if they were accommodating Christian language to pagan understanding, the phrase *Christo quasi deo* may have been used in the report they gave.

/19/ For a similar view of the significances of *quasi*, see Goguel, *Life* 94; *Jesus the Nazarene - Myth or History* (Eng. tr. by F.Stephens) (London: Unwin, 1926) 39-40.

/20/ Goguel, *Life* 94; G.Bornkamm, *Jesus of Nazareth* (Eng. tr. by J.M.Robinson) (London: Hodder, 1960) 28.

/21/ Pliny says (*Ep.* 10.96.6) that these defendants 'confessed themselves Christians but then denied it' (*esse se Christianos dixerunt et mox negaverunt*). Presumably they had misunderstood the nature of the charge, perhaps imagining that anyone who had ever espoused Christianity was obliged to confess to it. Pliny continues: 'they meant (they said) that they had once been Christians but had given it up (*fuisse quidem sed desisse*), some three years before, some many years previously, and a few as many as twenty years before.'

/22/ M. Grant suggests three further reasons why the rumour developed. (1) It was known that while Rome was burning Nero

had played the lyre and sung a song of his own composition
called *The Fall of Troy*. (2) Fire-fighting efforts met with
obstruction (*Ann*. 15.38). (3) A second fire broke out on the
property of Tigellinus, commander of the praetorian guard
(*Ann*. 15.40) (*Nero: Emperor in Revolt* [American Heritage:
New York, 1970] 152). Grant also proposes three reasons why
Nero cannot be deemed responsible for the Great Fire. (1) If
he had wished to make room for his projected Golden House, he
would not have started the fire some distance away. (2) His
own recently redecorated palace was destroyed in the
conflagration. (3) The fire took place at full moon - not an
ideal time to conceal arson (*Nero*, 154).

/23/ Nero chose the Christians of Rome, rather than the Jews,
as scapegoats, because Christians formed a relatively small,
defenceless group heartily despised by the people and
because the Jews enjoyed the favour of the empress Poppaea
Sabina and to attack Jews in Rome would have compromised Roman
administration in Judaea and other oriental provinces (see
Grant, *Nero*, 156, 158-9). Tacitus is the only ancient writer
who posits a connection between the Great Fire of Rome and
Nero's persecution of the Christians, although Suetonius,
Dio Cassius, Clement of Rome, Melito, Tertullian, Lactantius
and Eusebius discuss either the persecution or the fire, or
(as in the case of Suetonius, *Life of Nero*, 16.2, 38) both
episodes. (References in the other ancient authors mentioned
may be found in Smallwood, *Jews* 218 nn. 51-3). Some regard the
link between the fire and the persecution as a Tacitean
interpretation aimed at placing Nero in an unfavourable light -
thus A. Momigliano, *CAH*, X, 887, who suggests that Tacitus has
combined two sources which offer different explanations for
Nero's persecution; H. Mattingly, *Christianity in the Roman
Empire* (Dunedin: University of Otago, 1955) 32,39, who notes
that Tacitus tends to mislead, not in facts themselves, but
in their interpretation. Whatever view we take of this Tacitean
link, the twin facts remain intact: there was a Great Fire;
there was a Neronic persecution of Christians. It is the latter
fact alone, whatever its cause, that prompts the reference to
Christ.

/24/ Thus Momigliano, *CAH*, X, 887-8 (who also notes [p.725]
that, being extremely sensitive to popular opinion, Nero 'aimed
rather at directing the fury of the people upon a section that
was notoriously hated, and so winning back the favour of the
mob, than at attributing the charge of firing Rome specifically
to the Christians'); Mattingly, *Christianity* 33-34, 39. See
further, Sherwin-White, *Pliny* 772-787.

/25/ For the literature on this passage see H. Fuchs, *Vig Chr* 4

(1950)   66 n.1 and Smallwood, *Jews* 218 n.54.

/26/   On the expression *reum subdere* see Fuchs,*Vig Chr* 4,67 n.4.

/27/   On the difficulties of regarding this passage as a
Christian forgery, see Linck, *De antiquissimis ... testimoniis*
61-103, esp. 102-103.

/28/   The inscription reads *[*CAESARIEN*]*S(IBVS) TIBERIEVM*[*...
PON*]*TIVS PILATVS *[*...PRAEF*]*ECTVS IVDA*[*EA*]*E *[*... D*]*E*[*DIT*]*.
See A. Frova, 'L'Inscrizione di Ponzio Pilato a Cesarea',
Rendiconti 95(1961) 419-34, and the bibliography in Smallwood,
The Jews under Roman Rule (Leiden: Brill, 1976) 167 n. 79.

/29/   *Did Jesus Exist?* 14.

/30/   Thus A. N. Sherwin-White, *Roman Society and Roman Law
in the New Testament* (Oxford: Clarendon, 1963) 12;   C. H. Dodd
Historical Tradition in the Fourth Gospel (Cambridge: Cambridge
University Press, 1963) 96 n. 1.

/31/   For instance, Cuspius Fadus (c. A.D. 44-46) is given the
titles of ἔπαρχος (*Ant.* 19.363) and ἐπίτροπος (*War* 2.220; *Ant.*
20.2, 14), as is Porcius Festus (c. A.D. 59-61) (ἔπαρχος, *Ant.*
20.193; ἐπίτροπος, *War*, 2.271).   The term ἐπίτροπος
('procurator') predominates in Josephus, whereas ἔπαρχος
('prefect') is used only six times of the governors of Judaea
- of Valerius Gratus (A.D. 15-26) (*Ant.* 18.33), Cuspius Fadus
(*Ant.* 19.363), Porcius Festus (*Ant.* 20.193), and Lúcceius
Albinus (A.D. 61-65) (*War*, 6.303, 305; *Ant.* 20.197).

/32/   Similarly Smallwood, *Jews* 145, 256. See, however,
A. H. M. Jones, *Studies in Roman Government and Law* (Oxford:
Blackwell, 1960) 117-119.

/33/   ΙΗΣΟΥΣ I.   XXIX - XXXII; II. 164 n. 1; *Messiah Jesus* 4,
14, 591-592.

/34/   *Messiah Jesus* 3-4.

/35/   Cf. Goguel, *Jesus* 47-48; *Life* 100.

/36/   Cf. E. Meyer, *Ursprung und Anfänge des Christentums*
(Berlin: Cotta, 1923) III.505.

/37/   This phrase may allude to anti-social tendencies (cf.
Hist. 5.5) or to hostility to the Roman Empire; but it could be
translated 'because they were hated by the human race', *humani
generis* being a subjective genitive; see further Fuchs,
'Tacitus' *Vig Chr* 4 (1950) 82-87.

/38/   *Life*, 95.

/39/   *CIG* 3. 4536, cited by Couchoud, *Enigma* 25. But against
this see Linck, *De antiquissimis ... testimoniis* 82-84.

/40/   See further R. Syme, *Tacitus* (Oxford: Clarendon, 1958)
378-396.

/41/   *Tacitus*, 469.

/42/   The Greek for 'salves' is φάρμακα χριστά (literally
'medicine to be used as ointment'), as in Aeschylus, *Prom.* 480,

while in Diodorus Siculus (38.4) νεόχριστος means 'newly
plastered' (LSJ s.v. 1170, 2007).
/43/   See the list in Linck, De antiquissimis ... testimoniis
106 n. 2.
/44/   H. Janne gives a critique of H. Linck's advocacy of this
view ('Impulsore Chresto', in Annuaire de l'institut de
philologie et d'histoire orientales. Vol. 2. Mélanges Bidez
[Bruxelles: University Library of Bruxelles, 1934] 537-540).
/45/   It is significant that G. A. Wells actually translates
impulsore Chresto 'one Chrestus instigating' (Jesus 185).
/46/   In his Apology (1.4) (c. A.D. 152) Justin Martyr has a
sustained play on the words Χριστός and χρηστός: for example,
'we are accused of being Christians (Χριστιανοί) yet to hate
what is excellent (χρηστός) is unjust'.
/47/   See further F. Blass, 'ΧΡΙΣΤΙΑΝΟΣ - ΧΡΗΣΤΙΑΝΟΣ', Hermes,
30 (1895) 468-470; Fuchs, 'Tacitus' Vig. Chr., 4 (1950) 69-74.
Dr C. J. Hemer has drawn my attention to the common occurrence
of the spelling Χρηστιανοί in the third and fourth century
'Christians for Christians' inscriptions of Phrygia (see
E. Gibson, The 'Christians for Christians' Inscriptions of
Phrygia [Missoula, Montana: Scholars, 1978] 15-17).
/48/   Contra L. G. Rylands, Did Jesus Ever Live? (London: Watts,
1935) 17.
/49/   This fact, and the absence of quodam before Chresto, count
against M. Borg's vigorous defence of the view that 'Suetonius'
reference is to Jewish messianic agitation' ('A New Context for
Romans XIII', NTS 19 [1972-3] 211-213).
/50/   Janne, 'Impulsore Chresto', in Mélanges Bidez 544.
/51/   See, e.g., Schürer, Geschichte III.62-63; Janne,
'Impulsore Chresto', in Mélanges Bidez 537-546; H. J. Cadbury,
The Book of Acts in History (London: Black, 1955) 115-116;
A. Momigliano, Claudius the Emperor and his Achievement
(Cambridge: Heffer, 1961²) 32-33; F. F. Bruce, New Testament
History (London: Nelson, 1969) 281.
/52/   In his Life of Nero 16.2 Suetonius notes that under Nero
'punishment was inflicted on the Christians, a class of men
given to a new and mischievous superstition'.
/53/   A letter that may be dated 10th November, A.D. 41 and was
sent by Claudius to the Alexandrians provides evidence of Jewish
unrest not only in Alexandria but elsewhere. The emperor warns
the Alexandrian Jews 'not to bring in or admit Jews who sail
down the river from Syria or Egypt; such action will compel me
to redouble my suspicions. Otherwise I will by all means
take vengeance on them for fomenting a general plague that
infests the whole world.' For the full text see A. S. Hunt and
C. C. Edgar, Select Papyri, II (London: Heinemann, 1963) 79-89;

H. I. Bell, *Jews and Christians in Egypt* (London: British
Museum, 1924) 1-37.

/54/ E.g., Acts 13:32-39, 50; 14:1-6, 19; 17:1-8; 18:5, 12-16.

/55/ For the view that only the rioters (whether Jews opposing
Christianity or Christian missionaries and their converts) were
expelled, see Smallwood, *Jews* 216 and J. W. Drane, "Why Did
Paul Write Romans?" in *Pauline Studies. Essays presented to
Professor F. F. Bruce* (ed. D. A. Hagner and M. J. Harris)
(Exeter: Paternoster, 1980) 218. For a defence of the Lukan
statement, see Bruce, *History* 279-283, 286.

/56/ *Historia Contra Paganos* 7.6.15-16. Orosius cites Josephus
as his authority for the date, but the latter's extant works
contain no reference to this particular edict.

/57/ This date may be inferred from the combined evidence of
several facts: (a) the date of Gallio's proconsulship of Achaia
(Acts 18:12) viz. July A.D. 51 - June A.D. 52 (see G. Ogg, *The
Chronology of the Life of Paul* [London: Epworth, 1968] 104-111);
(b) Paul's residence of some eighteen months in Corinth (Acts
18:11); (c) the date of the next Isthmian games, viz. March
A.D. 51 (Paul was probably manufacturing tents for sale to
visitors at the games). For a contrary view, according to which
Paul began his ministry in Corinth about A.D. 41, see
G. Lüdemann, *Paulus, der Heidenapostel. I. Studien zur
Chronologie* (Göttingen: Vandenhoeck & Ruprecht, 1980) 195-198,
272.

/58/ See, e.g., H.J. Leon, *The Jews of Ancient Rome*
(Philadelphia: Jewish Publication Society of America, 1960)
23-27; Lüdemann, *Paulus* 183-195, 272; 'A Chronology of Paul' in
B. Corley (ed.) *Colloquy on New Testament Studies* (Macon,
Georgia: Mercer University, 1983) 292, 302-303.

/59/ Similarly Momigliano, *Claudius* 29-37; A. D. Nock, *CAH*,
X, 500-501; F. F. Bruce, 'Christianity under Claudius', *BJRL* 44
(1962) 314-315; *History* 279-283; Smallwood, *Jews* 211-216. The
expulsion order was perhaps the culmination of regular police
action aimed at quelling constant riots. For the view that the
edict applied only to the Jewish-Christian agitators but may be
dated in A.D. 49, see R. Jewett, *A Chronology of Paul's Life*
(Philadelphia: Fortress, 1979) 36-38.

/60/ Bruce, *History* 281.

/61/ Goguel, *Life* 98-99.

/62/ Cf. the oft-quoted statement of J. Weiss: 'Die Hinrichtung
des Zimmermanns von Nazareth war unter allen Ereignissen der
römischen Geschichte jener Dezennien für alle offiziell
Beteiligten das allerunwichtigste; sie verschwand unter den
ungezählten Supplizien der römischen Provinzialverwaltung

vollkommen' (*Jesus*   92).

/63/ For other examples of the summary administration of Roman
justice against Jewish insurrectionists, see *War* 2.241-242,
258-260.

/64/ G. A. Wells asserts 'that in the case of Jesus,
contemporary evidence of this kind [viz. extant letters of
contemporaries, such as demonstrate Faust to have been a
historical personage] , or indeed of any kind, is wanting'
(*Early Christians* 218). Although he freely admits that
'contemporary evidence ... does not always mean contemporary
documents' (*Early Christians* 220), he frequently seeks to
support his case for the non-historicity of Jesus by appealing
to the allegedly late date of the four gospels, which, he
believes, were all written eighty to a hundred years after the
events they purport to relate (*Early Christians* 218; *Did
Jesus Exist?* 3, 65, 78-92, 205-206). If this dating is correct
'Jesus is not linked with a recognizable historical situation
in any document (Christian, Jewish or pagan) that can be
proved to have originated before about A D 100' (*Did Jesus
Exist?* 205).

/65/ Cf. Sherwin-White, *Roman Society* 187-188.

/66/ T. R. Glover, *The Jesus of History* (London: SCM, 1927)
7; E. M. Blaiklock, *Who Was Jesus?* (Chicago: Moody, 1974),
11-17.

/67/ There is no special significance in the fact that the
three writers who actually name Jesus call him *Christus
(Chrestus),* Christ. In reference to Jesus this word had long
since become a personal name and it was natural for writers
(Pliny, Tacitus) who were speaking of Christians to refer to
the founder of their religion as Christ. A thorough treatment
of the documentary evidence for the historicity of Jesus (apart
from the testimony of the New Testament documents themselves)
would require that we evaluate the authenticity and
significance of the references to Jesus in Josephus, the Talmud,
Moslem tradition, the apostolic Fathers, the apocryphal gospels,
heretical writings, and the *Acta Pilati*; in the letter of Mara
bar Serapion to his son Serapion; and in the apocryphal letters
of Pilate to the emperor Tiberius and of Lentulus to the
Roman senate. Many of these texts are available in the
collection of J. B. Aufhauser, *Antike Jesus-Zeugnisse* (Bonn:
Marcus & Weber, 1913).

/68/ The view that these references to Jesus or the passages
in which they are found have been interpolated received its
classic formulation in P. Hochart's *Études au sujet de la
persécution des chrétiens sous Néron* (Paris: Leroux, 1885) 1-77,
145-257, 316-317 (on Tacitus), 79-143 (on Pliny), 281-282 (on

Suetonius). For Hochart's later views on Tacitus, see his
De l'authenticité des Annales et des Histoires de Tacite
(Paris: Thorin, 1890); *Nouvelles considérations au sujet des
Annales et des Histoires de Tacite* (Paris: Thorin, 1894).
/69/ Few, if any, doubts about the existence of Jesus were
expressed before the eighteenth century. But in the last two
centuries, particularly in the present century, there has been
a succession of writers who, for a variety of reasons, have
called into question this fundamental tenet of Christianity
and have sought to account for the rise of the Christian faith
without reference to its traditional founder. Most notable
among these have been B. Bauer (in his later writings),
J. M. Robertson, A. Kalthoff (in later works), W. B. Smith,
A. C. H. Drews, P. L. Couchoud, J. M. Allegro, and G. A. Wells.
Perhaps the most sophisticated attempt to counter the Christian
insistence on the historicity of Jesus is the most recent. In his
two books *The Jesus of the Early Christians* (1971) and *Did
Jesus Exist?* (1975), G. A. Wells propounds the thesis that
'Christian origins can be accounted for, with reasonable
plausibility, without recourse to a historical Jesus' (*Early
Christians* 313; cf. *Did Jesus Exist?* 205). One may surmise
that the denial of the existence of Jesus may have been
prompted - or at least was encouraged - by the tendency of
some radical critics to reduce the Jesus of the Gospels to 'a
shadow of a shade'. If it is affirmed that the historical
criticism of the Gospels tells us little more than that Jesus
existed, it is but a small step to deny any reality to that
insubstantial shadow. Moreover, the case for regarding
religion as a popular illusion would be strengthened if it
could be shown that the figure of Jesus was mythical.

THE STUDY OF GOSPEL TRADITIONS OUTSIDE THE CANONICAL GOSPELS:
PROBLEMS AND PROSPECTS

Richard Bauckham,
Faculty of Theology,
University of Manchester,
Manchester M13 9PL

1.   Introduction

The purpose of this concluding chapter is not to sum up
all of the important results of all the preceding chapters,
though I shall mention or discuss some of them. Rather my
intention is to offer some broader reflections on this field of
study, its importance for the study of the canonical Gospels
and the quest of the historical Jesus, the particular problems
it poses and the opportunities it provides for further study.
I limit the field to Gospel traditions in Christian literature
because this enables me to generalize to some extent, whereas
the pagan and Jewish sources, which are also the subject of
chapters in this volume, present quite distinct problems and
possibilities. I certainly do not mean to devalue their
importance./1/

Attentive readers of this volume will have noticed, as
well as some impressive areas of agreement among the authors,
other instances in which their conclusions point in somewhat
different directions. This is only to be expected, especially
in studies which are relatively exploratory and innovative.
Similarly my remarks in this chapter, though stimulated by
reading the other contributions and intended to follow some of
the directions in which they point, are very much my own
thoughts on the subject. I should be surprised if they met
with the complete agreement of all my fellow-contributors.

2.   The Importance of the Subject for Gospel Studies

The study of Gospel traditions outside the canonical
Gospels is the Cinderella of Gospels scholarship. Although
numerous articles have dealt with many particular aspects of

the subject, there have been few major book-length studies,
while most of the important work which has been done continues
to be largely ignored in mainstream Gospels scholarship. Some
of those who have championed the importance of the subject and
made major contributions to it, such as Alfred Resch in a
previous generation and Helmut Koester in this, have been
thought to make exaggerated claims for its significance which
have, rather perversely, tended to confirm more cautious
scholars in the conviction that it can safely be ignored. Only
the Gospel of Thomas seems to have acquired an assured place
in mainstream Gospels studies, as a document whose parallels to
Synoptic material must at least be discussed. The anomaly of
this concession, alongside the continued neglect of other
witnesses (such as the Apostolic Fathers) whose date is on
most estimates earlier than Thomas and whose claim to preserve
independent tradition is at least equally good, goes unnoticed.

I suspect that this situation results from a false
impression of the relationship between the canonical Gospels
and other early Christian literature in which the Gospel
tradition has been preserved./2/ It is assumed that almost all
other witnesses to the Gospel tradition are later in date than
the canonical Gospels and therefore of very little interest to
the student of the canonical Gospels. In fact, both parts of
this assumption are unwarranted. In other words, there is a
good deal of relevant material which is roughly contemporary
with the canonical Gospels, while the material which is later
is not necessarily unimportant because of its date. But
studies which demonstrate this in particular cases fail to
make a serious impact on Gospels studies because they fail to
shake the prevalent assumption in general. While the
assumption prevails as the general rule, too much notice need
not be taken of occasional exceptions to it. And while not
much notice is taken of the exceptions, the fact that they are
becoming so many as no longer to prove the rule but rather to
disprove it is not noticed either. Consequently the
assumption needs to be challenged directly and in general. The
following general reasons for Gospels scholarship to give
serious, sustained and detailed attention to Gospel traditions
outside the canonical Gospels seem to me to be valid on the
basis of the work which has been done in this field, both in
this volume and elsewhere.

2.1. Many early Christian works, within and outside the
New Testament, which contain allusions to and quotations from

Gospel traditions date from the period before and during which
the canonical Gospels were being written (i.e. up to c. 100 A.D.).
To this period belong the Pauline literature, Hebrews,
Revelation, the Didache, 1 Clement, and probably (though some
scholars date them later) James, 1 Peter and 2 Peter. In my
view, a good case can also be made for dating Barnabas, Hermas
and 2 Clement in the late first century. It should go without
saying that these works are relevant to the study of the
canonical Gospels. In some cases their independence of the
canonical Gospels is well established, but whatever their
relationship to the canonical Gospels, they provide much
important evidence about the extent to which Gospel traditions
were known and the ways in which they were used in the early
church before and during the time of writing of the canonical
Gospels.

2.2. The canonical Gospels were not the only Gospels
written during the first century. Scholars have often
postulated written sources, now lost, behind our canonical
Gospels. Moreover, there really is no good reason for not
taking seriously our one piece of explicit information on this
subject: Luke's statement that 'many' had written Gospels
before him (Luke 1:1)./3/ Most of these were probably smaller
collections of Gospel traditions, which passed out of use as
more comprehensive Gospels, including the canonical Gospels,
became known. Some may never have circulated beyond the church
in which they were produced. But there is no reason to suppose
that they all disappeared as soon as the canonical Gospels were
written. They very likely remained available to some second-
century writers who quote Gospel traditions, and they could
have been among the sources of those 'apocryphal' Gospels which
continued to be written throughout the second century. With
the exception of one or two papyrus fragments,/4/ it is not
likely that any of these other first-century Gospels have
actually survived,/5/ but the fact that they once existed means
that it is in principle quite possible that early Gospel
traditions have been preserved, independently of the canonical
Gospels, in extant writers of the second or even the third
century, who knew these works at first- or secondhand. Of
course, we must admit that in such circumstances the task of
identifying such traditions with reasonable probability is
usually likely to be hazardous, but it is not always
impossible./6/ Works later in date than the canonical Gospels
cannot be given priority over or equality with the canonical
Gospels as reliable means of access to first-century Gospel

traditions, but nor is their date alone sufficient reason for
considering them wholly dependent on the canonical Gospels for
their knowledge of early traditions. Careful study of them in
relation to the canonical Gospels can yield significant results.

2.3. That first-century Gospels other than the canonical
Gospels survived into the second century is intrinsically
likely, but lacks much firm evidence. Much better evidence,
however, is available to show that the oral tradition continued
well into the second century. Most recent scholars, including
Donald Hagner in this volume, have agreed on this.
Consequently, a considerable number of early second-century
Christian writers are likely either to have known, in a later
stage of transmission, the same cycles of oral traditions as
were known to the canonical evangelists and their sources, or
to have known parallel streams of oral tradition, whether or
not they also knew any of the canonical Gospels or any other
written Gospels. In my judgment these writings include the
letters of Ignatius, the Ascension of Isaiah, the Apocalypse of
Peter, and the Odes of Solomon, as well as several of the
apocryphal Gospels which survive in fragments. James, 1 Peter,
2 Peter, Hermas and 2 Clement would also have to be included
here, if they are not first-century works, and further
possibilities include the Epistle of the Apostles, 5 Ezra, some
of the apocryphal Acts, and the Apocryphon of James. Careful
study of these works could help us to understand the nature of
the oral traditions which were available to the canonical
evangelists and also to investigate the important question of
the relationship between oral and written forms of the Gospel
tradition and the transition from one to the other.

2.4. The tendency of Gospels scholarship, in practice if
not in theory, has been to treat the Gospel tradition as a
process which led up to and stopped with the canonical Gospels.
The above points 2.1, 2.2 and 2.3 require a quite different
picture of the Gospel tradition as a broader and longer
process, within which the canonical Gospels need to be located.
For some time and in some places other forms of the tradition,
oral and written, continued quite independently of the
canonical Gospels. We do not have much evidence to establish
how rapidly or how extensively throughout the church the
canonical Gospels came to be known and to be given a prominent
place within the tradition, but it is clear that when they did
so, the place they achieved was a place within the tradition.
They did not immediately replace all other forms of the

tradition, oral or written. Not until well into the second
century did the oral tradition largely give way to written
Gospels, and not until the third century did the canonical
Gospels virtually replace other written Gospels in most parts
of the church.

Thus the writing of the canonical Gospels neither brought
the Gospel tradition to a halt nor produced a radical change in
the nature of the tradition. The oral tradition covers a
period of at least a century, not only preceding but also
following the writing of the canonical Gospels. In ways which
have yet to be fully investigated it must have increasingly
interacted with its written products before giving way to them.
The writing of Gospels, which probably began before Mark,
continued unabated throughout the second century, and just as
Mark became a source along with other sources for Matthew and
Luke, so the canonical Gospels became sources, along with
other sources, for later Gospels. It is not clear to me,
though the matter deserves much more thorough study, that these
later evangelists treated the canonical Gospels differently
from their other sources or differently from the way in which
the canonical evangelists treated their sources. Of course,
there is an important sense in which increasing distance from
the origins of the tradition gradually made the production of
Gospels a qualitatively different matter from what it was in
the first century, and the recognition of this, along with the
theologically deviant character of many second-century products
of the tradition, forced the process of discrimination which
led to the exclusive canonical position of our four Gospels.
But the second-century Gospel tradition seems to have had a
momentum of its own, which was only halted by the imposition on
it of the need for discriminatory judgment./7/ Second-century
Gospels cannot really be understood from the perspective of the
canon.

It follows that the traditional task of Gospels
scholarship - the study of the canonical Gospels and their
sources - can only be adequately pursued as part of a much
larger task of studying the wider and longer process within
which the canonical Gospels historically belong. Otherwise a
serious distortion of perspective and neglect of important
evidence are bound to result. This was one of L. E. Keck's
concerns when he stated the methodological thesis: 'He who
studies only the canonical Gospels does not understand them.'
/8/ Though I disagree with many of Helmut Koester's
conclusions on this subject, it seems to me the great merit of

his *Introduction to the New Testament*/9/ that he has attempted
a broad description of the Gospel tradition in first- and
second-century Christianity without isolating the canonical
Gospels from this larger context. His work should be at least
a stimulus to the great deal of detailed study that needs to be
done before such a description can be attempted with real
confidence.

2.5. Although there are, of course, many valid reasons
for studying the Gospel tradition, the particular concern of
this *Gospel Perspectives* series has been with the historical
reliability of the canonical Gospels. The importance of the
Gospel tradition outside the canonical Gospels for this issue
needs to be considered with some care. It will not do to ask
questions about historical reliability too quickly. Rather our
first need is as accurate as possible an account of the whole
process of the Gospel tradition and the relationship of the
canonical Gospels to other parts of that tradition. Then it
will be possible to make informed assessments of the relative
historical value of various parts and phases of the tradition.
Nor will it do to approach this issue with the crude apologetic
desire to make the historical reliability of the canonical
Gospels apparent by contrast with the obvious unreliability of
the non-canonical material. Such a purpose is likely to be
self-defeating, for if the rest of the process of the Gospel
tradition produced only historically worthless material, how
are these four remarkable exceptions to be explained? My own
impression, necessarily provisional at this stage, is that the
studies so far available, including those in this volume, tend
to support the historical value of the canonical Gospels in
quite a different way: by showing that the earliest and most
plausible evidence for Gospel traditions outside the canonical
Gospels provides a wide-ranging set of independent parallels to
the kinds of material the canonical Gospels contain./10/ At
any rate, it must be conceded that the historical reliability
of the canonical Gospels can scarcely be adequately assessed
in isolation from the question of the reliability of the Gospel
tradition in general.

3. Some Particular Implications for Gospel Studies

In this section I shall discuss some particular ways in
which the study of Gospel traditions outside the canonical
Gospels can contribute to well recognized areas of Gospels
studies.

   3.1. The tendencies of the tradition.
   Craig Blomberg's study of the parables in the Gospel of
Thomas (in this volume) is an excellent example of the way in
which study of post-canonical phases of the Gospel tradition
can illuminate the tradition behind and in the canonical
Gospels, even when the post-canonical material in question is
judged wholly secondary to the canonical Gospels. Assumptions
about the way the tradition must have developed in the first
century can be tested against the evidence for the way it
continued to develop in the second century./11/ E. P. Sanders
already made considerable use of extra-canonical material to
throw doubt on common form-critical assumptions about the
tendencies of the tradition,/12/ but there is still room for
further work in this area./13/ The relevant second- and third-
century literature provides a long period and a large body of
material in which the tendencies of the tradition may come to
light more clearly than in the first-century evidence alone, as
well as providing some material whose relative dates and
literary relationships can be established more confidently than
those of the Synoptic Gospels. There are, however, problems
here about the relation of oral and literary forms of the
tradition, which will be mentioned in section 4.3 below.

   3.2. The *Sitz im Leben* of the tradition.
   Despite the form-critical interest in the settings of
Gospel traditions in the life of the early church, the value
and implications of the evidence of Christian literature other
than the Gospels on this subject has commonly been under-
estimated. In the New Testament letters, the book of
Revelation, the Didache, and the letters of Clement and
Ignatius, there is a great deal of contemporary evidence on how
the Gospel traditions were actually used in the church: in
catechetical instruction, apocalyptic teaching, and so on. At
the same time, in such literature we can see what happened to
Gospel traditions in such use: how they were adapted to needs
and circumstances, expanded and combined with a variety of
other types of material (Old Testament allusions and citations,
Jewish wisdom traditions, apocalyptic traditions, sayings of
Christian prophets, and so on), so that the Gospel traditions
in such literature would usually be indistinguishable to us if
we did not have the Gospels to help us identify them.

   From the study of this material, the conclusion, already
argued by Dodd,/14/ Piper,/15/ and Allison,/16/ is inescapable,
that the Gospel tradition itself and the paraenetic use of the

Gospel tradition by the teachers and prophets of the church
were relatively independent, just as the Gospel literature and
other kinds of literature (letters, apocalypses and the Didache)
which used Gospel traditions were distinct literary genres.
Who the tradents of the Gospel traditions were remains obscure,
but it is clear that they preserved the traditions, not of
course wholly without any influence from the circumstances in
which they were transmitted and the uses to which they were put
in the church, but nevertheless relatively independently of
these factors. What has happened to Gospel traditions in their
use in Christian literature other than the Gospels is only
occasionally analogous to what has happened to them in the
Gospels themselves. Clearly the Gospel tradition was not
understood to be the same thing as its interpretation and
application. In paraenesis, therefore, the influence of the
Gospel tradition was felt and its implications developed by
teachers and prophets, but the tradition was normally not
explicitly quoted. Since it was well known in its own right,
it did not need to be.

     Thus it happens that literature outside the Gospels
sometimes shows us how particular Gospel traditions were
understood and applied in the early church, whereas the form of
these traditions in the Gospels themselves has not been
affected by this use. For example, from 2 Pet 2:20 and Hermas,
Sim. 9:17:5 (cf. also Mand. 5:2:7; 12:5:4) we know that the Q
saying Matt 12:43-45 par. Luke 11:24-26 was applied to the
moral apostasy of Christians, whose post-Christian condition
was considered worse than their condition before conversion.
But this application has left no trace in the form of the
saying in the Gospels. In Luke, the saying itself seems wholly
unaffected by whatever significance may have been seen in it in
the tradition before Luke, while the evangelist himself
interprets it only by attaching it to the Beelzebul
controversy. In Matthew, an application quite different from
that to Christian apostates is given by means of the
redactional addition (if such it is) of 12:45b. Of course, it
could be argued that the application to Christian apostates was
peculiar to the tradition as used in the church of Rome in the
time of 2 Peter and Hermas, and was not known in the tradition
behind Matthew and Luke. But the point is that it was
precisely because such sayings were not themselves affected by
the uses to which they were put that they could be put to a
variety of uses at different times and places. Another example
is Matt 7:6, whose significance for Matthew can only be guessed
from the context he gives it, whereas Didache 9:5 gives it a

eucharistic application: but the saying remains verbally
identical. Such examples, of which more could be given,
illustrate the *relative* immunity of the tradition of the
sayings of Jesus from influence from the way in which they were
understood and the circumstances to which they were applied in
early Christian teaching.

3.3. The sources of the canonical Gospels.

If one takes seriously the general picture, suggested in
section 2 above, of the relation of the canonical Gospels to
the Gospel tradition as a whole, it should be apparent that the
conventional ways of discussing the Synoptic problem and the
sources of the canonical Gospels, may well be seriously
inadequate because they proceed as though the canonical Gospels
themselves were almost the only relevant evidence. Only within
the widespread assumption that a solution to the Synoptic
problem must result from study of the texts of the Synoptic
Gospels alone, could the recent tendency in some circles to
reduce or to dispense altogether with hypothetical Synoptic
sources, including Q, have arisen. Only within that assumption
could the extreme version of this tendency, Michael Goulder's
attempt to ascribe all non-Markan material in Matthew and Luke
to the creative compositional activity of the evangelists
themselves,/17/ have been suggested. Once the evidence for
Gospel traditions outside the canonical Gospels is
considered, it becomes clear that in the period of the
composition of the Gospels the Gospel tradition was known in
many forms, oral and written. Since the Apostolic Fathers
knew non-Markan traditions in oral form, it is inconceivable
that Matthew and Luke should not have done. Christian
literature outside the Synoptic Gospels provides so much
evidence of independent, varying forms of Synoptic material
that the *probability* is in favour of more, not fewer, Synoptic
sources. I am inclined to agree with Morton Smith's comment
that, 'From now on synoptic source criticism will have all the
classic simplicity of three-dimensional chess.'/18/

The possibility that Christian literature outside the
canonical Gospels provides us in some cases with independent
access to their sources needs to be taken entirely seriously.
This would, in effect, broaden the Synoptic problem into a
larger problem of literary (and oral) relationships among the
Gospels and other literature. Of course, it is important not
to jump to premature conclusions. Such critical studies as
David Wright's demonstration of the weakness of Mayeda's case

for the pre-Johannine character of Papyrus Egerton 2 (in this volume) and Christopher Tuckett's exposure of the lack of strong evidence for claims that Paul or the Corinthians knew Q/19/ constitute important warnings here. But they are warnings which establish the need for methodological rigour, not warnings which need deter us from investigating the relevance of any such material to the question of Gospel sources.

The following sections by no means exhaust the issues which arise in this area, but seem to me to be the most important issues which are raised by the studies of this volume and some other recent studies.

3.3.1. Pre-Synoptic blocks of tradition.

One of the most striking and surest results of studies of writers who probably knew Synoptic tradition independently of the Synoptic Gospels is that they knew, not simply independent *logia*, but particular 'blocks' of tradition. For example, the central part of the Sermon on the Mount/Plain material of Matthew and Luke seems to be independently attested as a connected series of *logia* by Paul,/20/ 1 Peter,/21/ James,/22/ Didache 1:3-6,/23/ 1 Clement 13:2, Polycarp, Phil. 2:3; 12:3, /24/ and perhaps Justin (1 Apol. 15-16). Though the precise range and form of the Sermon material attested by each of these writers differs, their common testimony to the fact that some such block of material was widely known in the early church is very impressive. It seems to suggest that such a block of tradition existed prior to and independently of its incorporation into any larger collection of Gospel traditions (such as Q), and a full study of all of this evidence together clearly needs to be made./25/ If, as I suspect, there are independent parallels to both Matthew and Luke at points where they differ in this material, the implications for the problem of Q and the evangelists' redaction of it could be of considerable interest.

Allison has argued that Paul also knew two other major blocks of sayings tradition: Mark 9:33-50 and the mission discourse (Mark 6:6-13; Matt 10:1-16; Luke 9:1-6; 10:1-12),/26/ and the latter is partly confirmed by Richardson and Gooch (in this volume). David Wenham has argued that Paul and the author of Revelation knew a pre-Synoptic version of the eschatological discourse,/27/ as Greg Beale also argues for Revelation and Gerhard Maier for 1 Peter (both in this volume). On the other hand, the implications of Didache 16:5-8, as discussed by Jonathan Draper (in this volume) and by Kloppenborg,/28/ seem to

be rather different, namely that the Didache is dependent on
something like the source of Matthew's special material in
Matt 24:10-12,30-31, as a separate block of eschatological
teaching.

Small collections of parables are a type of pre-Synoptic
block of tradition which has often been plausibly postulated.
/29/ That the Q collection of parousia parables (Luke 12:35-48)
was quite widely known in the early church, whether or not in
connexion with other eschatological material, seems to be
indicated by a variety of evidence outside the Synoptic Gospels.
/30/ That there were parable collections is also confirmed by
Apocryphon of James 8:6-10, which seems to presuppose a
collection of six or seven parables, though not a collection
known to the canonical evangelists.

3.3.2. Q.
In the literature on Gospel traditions outside the
canonical Gospels the suggestion is quite frequently made that
the early Christian author in question may have known Q
(independently of Matthew and Luke). In particular, the
suggestion has been made with reference to Paul,/31/ James,/32/
the Didache,/33/ and the Gospel of Thomas./34/ In my view,
such suggestions are sometimes too imprecise to be useful. In
the first place, they do not always distinguish between
allusions to one or two particular blocks of Q material (as
discussed in 3.3.1 above) and allusions to a wide range of Q
material. Although the former would have some relevance to the
Q hypothesis, only the latter could demonstrate a writer's
dependence on Q. Secondly, a general impression of dependence
on Q is sometimes given without a sufficiently careful
examination of each possible parallel to Gospel traditions.
Thus Allison,/35/ Wenham,/36/ and Tuckett/37/ have all
criticized the hypothesis of Paul's knowledge of Q, on the
grounds that Paul alludes to material which is found in a
variety of strands of the Synoptic tradition, not especially
to Q material.

Nevertheless, it seems to me that the independent
parallels to Q material are of considerable importance to the
question of the existence and nature of Q, which is regularly
discussed as though only the Synoptic Gospels were relevant
evidence. Independent parallels to Q material (whether they
indicate a writer's knowledge of Q as such or only of
particular sections of Q material) could help to substantiate
the Q hypothesis in its broadest and least dogmatic form,

i.e. the probability that the material common to Matthew and
Luke derives from one or more common sources, oral or written.
If, as I suspect may be possible, a significant number of
independent parallels agreeing with Luke against Matthew in Q
passages could be assembled, this would be important evidence
against the view that Luke derived his Q material from Matthew.
Study of the whole range of independent parallels to Q material
could help to establish whether Q material was known to
Matthew and Luke in the same or different forms. In any case,
the current reconsideration of the Synoptic problem needs to
break out of the traditional, but artificial restriction of its
evidence to the Synoptic Gospels alone./38/

3.3.3. Matthew's special source.
    In my opinion, of all the putative sources of the Synoptic
Gospels, the one for which there is the best evidence outside
the Synoptic Gospels is not Q, but Matthew's special source,
though that evidence has been little enough recognized and
studied.

    The best starting-point would be Ignatius' special
relationship to Matthean *Sondergut*, which led Smit Sibinga to
argue that Ignatius knew not Matthew, but Matthew's special
source M./39/ In section 5 below, I shall outline a fuller and
more rigorous method of testing and establishing that claim.
It is a claim of such significance for Matthean studies that it
at least deserves much closer attention than it has so far
received. Moreover, in a forthcoming study of Gospel
traditions in the Ascension of Isaiah I hope to show that a
similar claim can plausibly be made for the Ascension of
Isaiah (a work roughly contemporary with Ignatius). To these
two principal witnesses to Matthew's special source can be
added the Didache/40/ and the Gospel of Peter/41/. The result,
as I hope to argue elsewhere, is a cumulative case for seeing
Matthew's special material (or at least a large part of it) as
the tradition, probably oral, of the church of Antioch and
neighbouring churches, known in slightly varying forms to
Ignatius and the authors of the Ascension of Isaiah, the
Didache, and the Gospel of Peter. In this way the extracanonical sources should help to illuminate both the nature of
Matthew's special source and the way in which he uses it.

    Christine Trevett has recently used the issue of Ignatius'
relation to Matthew as an example of the way in which 'our
knowledge of the Synoptic Problem, of the form, date and
provenance of individual Synoptic sources and of the use of

Gospel traditions in Christian communities may be furthered by
means of an approach to the Gospels from the second century'.
/42/ Though by no means the only example, it is a particularly
good one, and I have therefore used it as a paradigm case in
section 5 below.

3.3.4. An Ur-Gospel?

Tending in a different direction from these suggestions
about Q and M is David Wenham's use of Gospel traditions,
especially in Paul and Revelation, as part of an argument
(which also depends considerably on his study of the Synoptic
material itself) for a kind of Ur-Gospel, i.e. a pre-Synoptic
source known to all three Synoptic evangelists and from which
they drew most of their material, including their special
material. Though he has argued this in detail primarily in
relation to a pre-Synoptic form of the eschatological
discourse,/43/ he has already suggested the extension of the
same approach to other parts of the Synoptic tradition and
proposed the thesis of a pre-Synoptic Gospel./44/ His
contribution to the present volume gives some examples of this
approach to other parts of the Synoptic tradition, with the aid
of Pauline evidence. It should also be noticed that Wenham's
approach is supported, in this volume, by Beale's study of the
eschatological discourse and Revelation, and to some extent
perhaps also by Maier's study of 1 Peter (see especially his
section A.III.5).

This approach not only represents a significant fresh
alternative within the current reconsideration of the Synoptic
problem. It is also reminiscent of Resch's use of Gospel
traditions outside the canonical Gospels to reconstruct a
Hebrew Ur-Gospel on which the Synoptic evangelists and many
other early Christian writers were dependent./45/ Wenham's use
of traditions outside the Synoptic Gospels is much more
limited and cautious than Resch's. However, perhaps it is time
that the conventional verdict that Resch's thesis was wholly
and conclusively refuted by Ropes/46/ should not be simply
taken on trust by those (like myself) who have not studied
either in detail.

3.3.5. Tradition and Redaction in the Gospels.

Synoptic redaction criticism has largely proceeded on the
unquestioned basis of the two-document hypothesis and the
assumptions of classical form-criticism, so that recent doubts
in both these areas make its results, as E. P. Sanders comments,
'by definition insecure'./47/ But it has also been conducted

as a wholly inner-Synoptic discipline, on the conventional
assumption that the Synoptic Gospels themselves provide all the
relevant material for their own criticism. Hence in the Markan
and Q passages of Matthew and Luke it is commonly assumed that
Matthean and Lukan redaction can be fairly easily distinguished
from their source simply by comparing the Synoptic parallels.
Large conclusions about the redactional intentions and
theologies of Matthew and Luke rest on this basis. It could be
that serious attention to parallels outside the Synoptic Gospels
could lead to different conclusions about what is redactional
in the Synoptic Gospels.

Thus - to take a small example from a critic who is in
general very cautious about the use of parallels outside the
Synoptic Gospels - Christopher Tuckett argues that, in the light
of 1 Cor 13:2, the Q saying Matt 17:20 par. Luke 17:6 may
already before Matthew have existed not only in the more
original Lukan form, but also in the Matthean form, so that
Matt 17:20 'is not simply due to Matthean redaction but reflects
a pre-Matthean development of the tradition'./48/ This is just
one example of the way in which consideration of parallels
outside the canonical Gospels can lead to the conclusion that
differences between the evangelists in parallel material are not
due to redaction by one of the evangelists, but to differences
in the traditions known to them. And if this conclusion is
sometimes necessary where independent parallels exist, it ought
to shake the confidence with which material is assigned to the
evangelists' redaction in other cases where, as it happens,
independent parallels do not exist.

Assuming the two-document hypothesis, the possibility that
what looks redactional may in fact be traditional applies not
only to Q passages but also to Markan passages in Matthew and
Luke. Matthew and Luke, even if working with a written source
in front of them, always had in their minds the oral traditions
of their own churches, and this mental familiarity with one
form of a tradition could easily influence their redaction of
another form of the tradition. The same would be true, of
course, of scribes, whose tendency in the *earliest* stages of the
transmission of the Gospels would not be to harmonize one
canonical Gospel with another, but rather to harmonize the text
they were copying with the oral tradition they knew by heart or
perhaps with some other, no longer extant, Gospel text which
they knew well. This point about scribal tendencies is a
somewhat disquieting consideration in view of the close
connexion between textual criticism and the practice of Synoptic
source- and redaction-criticism./49/

In view of these considerations, I would tentatively
suggest that Synoptic redaction criticism needs to adopt the
following two principles of method (in addition to other, well
recognized principles): (i) Parallels outside the Synoptic
Gospels which could plausibly be independent of the Synoptic
Gospels must always be considered before a judgment about what
is redactional in the Synoptic Gospels is reached, and such
judgments in cases where there are independent parallels must be
taken into account in cases where there are not. (Since the
relations between the Synoptic Gospels themselves are not known
with certainty, it is unreasonable to require conclusive proof
of the independence of a parallel before it can be considered.)
(ii) Textual variants must in some cases be treated as part of
the evidence.

4.   Problems

Some of the areas considered in section 3 seem to me to
offer very promising lines of research, but their promise is
unlikely to be fulfilled unless some progress is made towards
overcoming the peculiar problems that beset research in this
field, of which the following three are perhaps the principal:

4.1.   Establishing allusions.

In most of the literature with which we are concerned,
direct citations of Gospel traditions are the exception,
allusions the rule. This creates a problem which is apparent
in a great deal of work in this area: that of knowing how to
distinguish a real allusion to the Gospel traditions from a
coincidental resemblance. Frequently it seems a matter of
purely subjective judgment when one scholar detects an allusion
but another denies it, and readers of this volume may well have
noticed that some of its authors seem disposed to admit
allusions on fairly slender grounds, while others are evidently
working with more stringent requirements for what may count as
an allusion.

The problem arises because the judgments involved need to
be very complex. The degree of verbal resemblance is important,
but by no means decisive and cannot be applied as a mechanical
test. Agreement in an unusual idea, with minimum verbal
resemblance, may be more impressive than agreement in a
commonplace idea expressed in rather common and obvious words
and phrases, even if the degree of verbal resemblance is
relatively extensive. The relationship to the writer's own
style and vocabulary needs to be considered, but some writers
will be more likely than others to assimilate allusions to their

own style and vocabulary. Judgments are bound to be somewhat
affected, not unjustifiably, by prior judgments about the
general likelihood of a writer's familiarity with Gospel
traditions or with Gospel traditions of a certain category.
(For example, those who have strong reasons for thinking it
unlikely that Johannine traditions would be known to the author
of 1 Peter will probably require clearer allusions to convince
them than will those who would not find it surprising.) A
certain number of clear citations or allusions in a particular
writer may provide not unreasonable grounds for tipping the
balance in favour of more doubtful allusions, especially if
these show some kind of coherence with the clearer ones.
Furthermore, judgments are more complex than in the case, say,
of allusions to the Old Testament, because more allowance has
to be made for the possibility that allusions are being made to
a form of the Gospel tradition different from the forms we know.

Two developments in recent literature on the subject seem
to be useful steps towards dealing with this problem: (i) Both
Allison, in the case of Paul,/50/ and Davids, writing on James
in this volume, attempt to show that a particular writer knew a
particular block of Gospel traditions by arguing for a good
number of allusions to this one block of tradition. Such
allusions are more impressive in combination than they would be
singly. The same kind of principle can be used to establish a
writer's knowledge of a particular strand of the Synoptic
tradition or a particular Gospel. (ii) The method used long ago
in the Oxford Committee's work on the Apostolic Fathers/51/ is
used in this volume by Davids and Maier: that of classifying
allusions as more or less probable. If a table of a particular
writer's allusions is drawn up on a scale of probability, it
will be possible to base arguments (say, for his knowledge of a
particular Gospel) on the right kind of evidence: on very
probable allusions only, or on an impressive number of less
probable allusions, or on some appropriate combination of more
and less probable allusions, but not on a few rather uncertain
allusions alone.

These methods will be useful, but I think that some
valuable methodological work could be done in listing the kinds
of criteria which should count in establishing allusions and
arguing for their relative importance. In the end a degree of
subjectivity is bound to remain, but a more self-conscious and
disciplined use of clearly defined criteria could reduce the
subjective element considerably.

4.2. Establishing dependence.

Much of the literature with which we are concerned derives from a context in which Gospel traditions were known in many forms: oral and written, pre-canonical sources, canonical Gospels, non-canonical Gospels, some known, some no longer extant. The difficulty of telling from which of these sources a particular writer's allusions to Gospel traditions derive is considerable, as Donald Hagner points out in his chapter on the Apostolic Fathers. We have to recognize that a writer need not always allude to the same source, and that in a period when written and oral sources were both well known they might influence each other in his memory. Faulty memory and deliberate redactional adaptation of the material are also factors to be taken into account.

As in the case of allusions, prior expectations often seem to govern a scholar's judgment. It seems that for some scholars any allusion which could be to a canonical Gospel is, while for others any allusion which need not be to a canonical Gospel is not. Clearly we must become more selfconscious and reflective about method, and it is with the aim of beginning to develop more rigorous methods of determining dependence that I have added section 5 of this chapter.

4.3. Orality and textuality.

This whole area of study needs to become much better informed by thinking about the differences between orality and textuality and about what happens in a situation in which oral tradition and texts coexist.

For example, study of tendencies of the tradition (section 3.1 above) seems to make no distinction between the way oral traditions develop and the way a writer may use a written source. But Werner Kelber has strongly criticized E. P. Sanders' work (with its use of writings dependent on the canonical Gospels to establish tendencies which would have been at work in the pre-canonical tradition) on the grounds that studies of oral culture require a distinction between these two processes./52/ Craig Blomberg's contribution to this volume seems to be arguing that behind the Gospel of Thomas lies a period of *oral* tradition *dependent* on the Synoptic Gospels. Is this a plausible picture of how written and oral sources might have interacted in the second century? Donald Hagner in this volume plausibly uses mnemonic form as a criterion by which to distinguish an oral source for some Gospel traditions in the Apostolic Fathers. But to what extent might the forms of the sayings of Jesus in oral tradition and written Gospels have differed? Were some types of Gospel literature closer to the oral tradition than others?

The phenomena of allusions to Gospel traditions in much of the literature of the first and second centuries are unlikely to be properly understood unless they are deliberately related to the dynamics of a situation in which written Gospels functioned alongside oral tradition or (perhaps it would be better to say) within the context of oral tradition. What such a situation implies for the way in which written Gospels actually functioned in the churches, for the way in which their texts were transmitted,/53/ for the way in which people thought of, remembered and quoted the Gospel tradition, needs to be explored with the help of the modern studies of orality and textuality/54/ which are beginning to influence Gospels studies./55/ It would be a great pity if the growing interest in this subject confined itself to work on the canonical Gospels in the usual manner of trends in Gospels scholarship, since it is precisely outside the Gospels themselves, in writers who knew both oral and written traditions, that the interesting evidence for the way the two interacted and the way the transition from one to the other happened is likely to be found, once we have the methodological clues with which to detect and interpret it.

5. The Problem of Establishing Dependence: Ignatius and Matthew as a Paradigm Case

The relation of Ignatius to Matthew is a peculiarly interesting case of an early Christian writer's relationship to one of our Gospels. At least since Streeter/56/ the claim that Ignatius was dependent on Matthew has held an important place in Gospels scholarship, providing both the earliest firm *terminus ad quem* for Matthew and a possible indication of the Gospel's place of origin./57/ However, the confidence with which Ignatius' knowledge of Matthew is usually asserted in studies of Matthew is hardly justified by detailed studies of Ignatius' relation to Matthew. Though Massaux thought the evidence proved Ignatius' use of Matthew,/58/ Inge in the Oxford Committee's volume was much more cautious./59/ Koester denied that Ignatius knew any written Gospel, though he held that at one point he was indirectly dependent on Matthew./60/ Smit Sibinga, in the most recent detailed study, thought the evidence proves Ignatius' dependence not on Matthew, but on Matthew's special source./61/ Hagner, in the present volume, finds it

impossible to be sure that Ignatius is ever dependent on a
Gospel rather than on oral tradition. In a recent survey of the
issue, Trevett highlights 'the lack of consensus among scholars
on this topic and also the need for further work to be done'.
/62/
      This lack of consensus is not due to a lack of evidence.
Although there are few places where Ignatius could be held
simply to quote a Gospel tradition without adaptation, there are
a considerable number of certain or probable allusions, almost
all of which have some kind of parallel in Matthew. Trevett
provides a list of eighteen Matthean passages to which Ignatian
parallels are most commonly claimed in the literature on the
subject/63/ and a further list of eighteen other passages which
are sometimes cited./64/ (I should wish to add three more to
this latter list of possible parallels./65/) Naturally,
judgments vary as to which are the more probable allusions.
Most, but not all, of Trevett's 'top eighteen' seem to me
reasonably probable, and some are virtually certain. I myself
would regard six Matthean passages as having virtually certain
parallels in Ignatius,/66/ and about ten others as having
reasonably probable parallels./67/ Of course, the case for an
Ignatian allusion needs to be argued in detail in each case, and
an argument about Ignatius' relationship to Matthew ought to
give most weight to the most probable cases. But there are
enough probable allusions to provide a reasonable amount of
evidence for judging whether Ignatius used Matthew's Gospel or
relied on other sources for material parallel to Matthew.
Although the lack of scholarly consensus on this issue owes
something to the difficulty of deciding whether some possible
allusions really are allusions to the Gospel tradition, it seems
to me that it owes much more to the lack of a sufficiently
rigorous method for determining literary dependence or
independence.

      My present purpose is to develop a method by outlining the
stages which an argument needs to take. Although I shall reach
particular conclusions, I cannot in the space available provide
the full argument which would be needed to establish those
conclusions. Instead, I provide a skeletal argument in which
the main considerations which can help decide the issue will be
discussed and the way they need to be handled illustrated. The
skeletal argument is about Ignatius and Matthew, and the method
has been developed to suit this particular case,/68/ but my
hope is that it provides a paradigm argument which can be
adapted to suit other cases.

5.1. Dates and Places of Origin

The importance of these considerations is that they may provide us with an initial presumption that Ignatius is likely to have known Matthew or at least could have known Matthew. The letters of Ignatius are unusual among early Christian writings in that they can be dated and located with reasonable certainty: a date c. 107 is accepted by nearly all scholars,/69/ and Ignatius was undoubtedly from Antioch./70/ Matthew's Gospel has been very often thought to come from Syria in general or Antioch in particular, and is usually dated one, two or three decades before Ignatius' letters. So there seems a good case for expecting Ignatius to have known the Gospel. It should be noted that this case, based on both date and place, is much stronger than a case based on date alone, since we do not know how soon Matthew's Gospel is likely to have become known in places distant from its place of origin. But even a Syrian origin for Matthew would by no means ensure that Ignatius *must* have known it. Serapion, bishop of Antioch at the end of the second century, had never read the Gospel of Peter which was in use in the church of Rhossus, on the Syrian coast, only about twenty miles from Antioch (Eusebius, Hist. Eccles. 6:12:2-6).

It is also important to avoid the circular arguments which all too easily arise in this kind of discussion. Most arguments about the date and place of Matthew treat Ignatius' supposed dependence on Matthew as a very important piece of their evidence. But insofar as our conclusions about the date and place of Matthew are dependent on Ignatius' supposed knowledge of Matthew we cannot argue from them to Ignatius' knowledge of Matthew. Since, however, there are also other grounds for dating Matthew before Ignatius and for locating Matthew in Syria,/71/ the presumption that Ignatius is quite likely to have known Matthew remains reasonable, provided we are careful not to give it more weight than it can bear.

However, a degree of probability that Ignatius would have known Matthew cannot produce an equal degree of probability that Ignatius' allusions to Gospel traditions are to the text of Matthew's Gospel. Even if we could prove that Ignatius knew the Gospel, it would not follow that an Ignatian passage which could be dependent on Matthew is dependent on Matthew, since we do not know what place Matthew had in Ignatius' church or in Ignatius' own knowledge of Gospel traditions. Matthew need not yet have replaced other forms of the Gospel tradition in the church at Antioch. Ignatius himself might have memorized the oral Gospel traditions of his church long before

Matthew was known to him, so that his own allusions would still
be largely dependent on these, however prominent Matthew's
Gospel had more recently become in his church. Ignatius could
even have received Gospel traditions from the apostles. If
Matthew was written in Antioch, Ignatius could easily have been
as familiar with Matthew's sources as Matthew himself was. The
possibilities are such that we cannot assume, without argument,
that an Ignatian allusion which could be to Matthew is to
Matthew.

Thus, the relative dates and locations of Matthew and
Ignatius are a relevant consideration, but not in any way a
decisive one.

5.2. Evidence for unknown Gospel sources.
Good evidence that a writer knew a source (written or oral)
of Gospel traditions which is no longer extant is always
relevant to the question of that writer's dependence on the
canonical or other known Gospels, but is too often neglected in
studies which limit themselves to close parallels with the
canonical Gospels.

Three Ignatian examples will illustrate several kinds of
such evidence:

(a) Pol.2:1 is very likely an allusion to the Q saying
Matt 5:46 par. Luke 6:32. It is closer (in the words χάρις...
ἔστιν) to Luke than to Matthew, but even closer (in using
φιλέω where both Matthew and Luke have ἀγαπάω) to the form of
the saying in Didache 1:3 (where the best text has φιλῆτε).
That Ignatius' source used φιλέω rather than ἀγαπάω is
extremely likely, since Ignatius elsewhere uses ἀγαπάω twenty
times but φιλέω never. It therefore seems clear that
Ignatius knew a form of this saying different from the form(s)
known to Matthew and Luke. This example shows how important
it is to compare Ignatius not only with canonical but also
with extra-canonical parallels.

(b) Smyrn. 3:2 might be thought to be Ignatius' own
adaptation of Luke 24:39, were it not for other evidence that
these words of the risen Christ in the form which Ignatius
gives existed in a non-canonical source. Jerome's claim that
Ignatius was quoting the Gospel of the Hebrews may not be
trustworthy,/72/ but Origen (de princ. I prooem. 8) more
reliably informs us that this logion occurred in work called
the Petri doctrina./73/ Whether or not this was actually

Ignatius' source, it is much more likely that Ignatius does quote the logion from some source than that the *Petri doctrina* took the logion from Ignatius./74/ This conclusion is strengthened by the fact that Ignatius shows no other sign of dependence on Luke.

(c) Eph. 19:2-3 is unlikely to be Ignatius' own elaboration of the references to the star in Matt 2. He must be following a source other than Matt 2, but it could perhaps be a source which was itself dependent on Matt 2./75/

     In relation to Ignatius' possible use of Matthew, these three examples are of differing significance. (a) shows that Ignatius did know a source which contained material parallel to material in Matthew, but not dependent on Matthew. (c) shows he knew a source which contained traditions related to traditions in Matthew, but which could perhaps be dependent on Matthew. (b) shows that he knew a source of Gospel traditions with no parallel in Matthew.

     Even if (b) were our only evidence that Ignatius knew no longer extant sources of Gospel traditions, it would be important for our purposes. Since any considerable body of Gospel traditions is likely to have overlapped at some points with any other such body (as Mark and Q do), the possibility that an Ignatian parallel to Matthew derives not from Matthew but from the same source as Smyrn. 3:2 must always be considered. This point is often neglected in discussions of this kind. (To take another example, if the Gospel of Thomas can be shown to be dependent on our Synoptic Gospels in some instances, it is not therefore necessarily dependent on the Synoptic Gospels in all its parallels to them, since the Gospel of Thomas undoubtedly also had other sources of the sayings of Jesus and it remains possible that these sources preserved, independently of the Synoptic Gospels, sayings which also occur in the Synoptics.)

     In Ignatius' case, we know not only that he had another source or sources, but also, from (a) and (c), that this source or sources did in fact contain material parallel to Matthean material, both, as (a) shows, in Q passages, and, as (c) shows, in special Matthean passages. Consequently other parallels to Matthew cannot be assumed to derive from Matthew without argument. To distinguish an allusion to Matthew from an allusion to Ignatius' other source or sources will require rather stringent argument.

It is also important to notice that in cases (a) and (b) Ignatius' small variations of wording from the canonical Gospels can be shown, by means of extra-canonical evidence, to be derived from his sources, not due to his own free citation of the canonical text. This suggests that the same explanation should be seriously considered in other cases of Ignatian parallels to Matthew where there is significant variation of wording, even though extra-canonical parallels may not be available in these cases.

5.3. Distinguishing Matthew and other sources.

The difficulty of determining whether Ignatian parallels to Matthew are allusions to Matthew or to some other source is very considerable. The following attempt at an ideal method of deciding the issue will show the kind of evidence that is actually needed to prove specific conclusions. For the sake of relative simplicity, the argument in this section will not distinguish the various putative sources of Matthew, but that consideration will be introduced in 5.4.

The following explanations of Ignatian parallels to Matthew are possible:

A.   Ignatius knew and quoted Matthew.

B.   Ignatius knew and quoted Matthew's source.

C.   Ignatius knew and quoted not Matthew's actual source, but a closely related source.

D.   Ignatius knew and quoted a source dependent on Matthew.

To explain the full range of Ignatian parallels to Matthew, one of these explanations may be sufficient, or more than one may be necessary.

Study of the individual parallels could demonstrate one of the following in each case:

(1)   Ignatius agrees with Matthew and with Matthew's source (since Matthew here reproduces his source unaltered).

(2)   Ignatius agrees with Matthew against Matthew's source.

(3)   Ignatius agrees with Matthew's source against Matthew.

(4a) Ignatius disagrees significantly both with Matthew and with
     Matthew's source

   (4b)   while also agreeing with Matthew against Matthew's
          source

   (4c)   while also agreeing with Matthew's source against
          Matthew.

     In the case of many of the parallels it may not be possible
to decide at all confidently between some of these possibilities,
but if *some* clear cases of any of possibilities (2)-(4c) can be
demonstrated, then the following results can be obtained:

If there are clear cases of (2), but no clear cases of (3),
   (4a), (4b) or (4c), then A is proved.

If there are clear cases of (3), but no clear cases of (2),
   (4a), (4b) or (4c), then B is proved.

If there are clear cases of (4c), but no clear cases of (2) or
   (4b), then C is proved.

If there are clear cases of (3) and (4a), but no clear cases of
   (2) or (4b), then C is proved.

If there are clear cases of (4b), but no clear cases of (2) or
   (4c), then D is proved.

If there are clear cases of (2) and (4a), but no clear cases of
   (3) or (4c), then D is proved.

If there are clear cases of (2) and (3), but no clear cases of
   (4a), (4b) or (4c), then A and B are proved.

If there are clear cases of (2) and (4c), but no clear cases of
   (4b), then A and C are proved.

If there are clear cases of (3) and (4b), but no clear cases of
   (4c), then B and D are proved.

If there are clear cases of (4b) and (4c), then C and D are
   proved.

By this method it will not be possible to prove combinations B
and C or A and D, since B and C will be indistinguishable from
C alone, and A and D will be indistinguishable from D alone.

This method requires us to find clear cases of one or more of possibilities (2)-(4c), but this is difficult to do, for two reasons in particular: (i) Most Ignatian parallels to Matthew are to Matthean Sondergut (see section 5.4), where it is much more difficult to distinguish source and redaction than it is where (according to the two document hypothesis) Matthew is dependent on Mark or Q. (ii) Since Ignatius rarely, if ever, gives a straight quotation from Gospel tradition, there is the additional problem of distinguishing Ignatius' source from his redaction. These difficulties do not make the method impossible to use, but they do make it necessary to recognize the extent to which we are dealing only in relative probabilities. In particular, it will not be wise to assume, as unquestionable, judgments about what is redactional in Matthew which have been made in Matthean studies without reference to the parallel in Ignatius. Such judgments may have to be revised, since the Ignatian parallels may be part of our evidence for distinguishing source and redaction in Matthew (see section 3.3.5 above). The nature of the evidence also suggests that special importance be attached to cases where parallels outside Matthew and Ignatius help us to distinguish source and redaction (such as Pol. 2:1, discussed in section 5:2).

Sibinga, who provides the most sophisticated discussion of Ignatius' relation to Matthew, concentrates on discovering cases of (2) and (3) in order to prove either A or B. His discussion (which is deliberately not exhaustive, but covers only thirteen possible Ignatian parallels to Matthew) provides only one possible case of (2), and six cases which he judges to be cases of (3), and so he draws conclusion B.

However, it seems to me that Sibinga has neglected category (4) and possible explanation C. One of his six cases of (3) seems to me to be in fact a case of (4a), since his argument is that in Eph.14:2 Ignatius is dependent on a Greek translation of the Q saying (Matt 12:33 par. Luke 6:44) different from the translation known to Matthew and Luke. There seem to me to be at least three other cases of category (4): (i) Pol. 2:1 (discussed in section 5.2 above) is a case either of (4a) or, probably, of (4c). (ii) Eph. 19:2-3 (also discussed in section 5.2) is probably a case of (4a). (iii) Eph. 6:1 (cf. Matt 10:40; John 13:20) is a good case of (4a). These four cases of (4a) and (4c), together with at least some of Sibinga's remaining five cases of (3), point quite strongly to conclusion C.

Sibinga is also, in my view, mistaken in thinking that a selective discussion of only some Ignatian parallels to Matthew is sufficient to prove his case./76/ He seems to assume that if Ignatius knew Matthew, his allusions would normally be to Matthew./77/ But this is not necessarily the case. As I suggested in section 5.1, if Ignatius was already acquainted with another source or sources of Gospel tradition before he knew Matthew, he might continue to prefer this source, but could occasionally augment it from his knowledge of Matthew. Hence conclusions A and C are quite compatible, and if, in addition to cases of (3), (4a) and (4c), there were convincing cases of (2), then conclusions A and C would both be proved.

There seem to me to be only three arguable cases of (2): (i) Smyrn. 1:1, since the parallel words in Matt 3:15 are widely thought to be a Matthean composition; (ii) Eph. 17:1, which is Sibinga's only possible case of (2), since Ignatius' use of ἐπί puts him slightly closer to Matt 26:7 than to Mark 14:3 (unless D's reading with ἐπί is accepted); and (iii) Magn. 5:2, where again Ignatius is slightly closer to Matt 22:19 than to Mark 12:15. But (iii) may not be a true parallel at all, and (ii) hardly provides a very convincing case. The weight of the case for Ignatius' knowledge of Matthew therefore seems to rest on Smyrn. 1:1.

This is a difficult but very illuminating example for methodology. In the first place, a very good argument can be made for regarding it, not as a case of (2), but as a special case of (4b). It has commonly been recognized that in Smyrn. 1:1-2 Ignatius is dependent on a traditional form of kerygmatic summary,/78/ and there seems no good reason why Ignatius should have added the words about Jesus' baptism which are parallel to Matt 3:15. He probably found them in the traditional form he quotes. This would be a special case of (4b), because here Ignatius would have depended on a short, isolated source, not his usual source of Gospel traditions. Consequently a conclusion in this case would have no implications for other Ignatian parallels to Matthew. Thus Koester's position, which is that in this case Ignatius is indirectly dependent on Matthew/79/ but in no other case is he directly or indirectly dependent on Matthew, is a logical and defensible one, which does not deserve Grant's criticism./80/ If Matthew's Gospel were known in Ignatius' church it could have influenced a traditional kerygmatic summary which Ignatius quotes, but (as we have already suggested) it need not have been Ignatius' own preferred source of Gospel traditions.

However, Smyrn. 1:1 also illustrates another issue, by posing the question: How confidently can we know that Matt 3:15 is a Matthean composition? Koester's confidence on this point obliges him to regard Smyrn. 1:1 as the only Ignatian text influenced (albeit indirectly) by Matthew's Gospel, but Sibinga argues, on the contrary, that Smyrn. 1:1 reflects not Matt 3:15 but Matthew's source. The vocabulary and idea are certainly characteristically Matthean, appearing both in Matthean redaction of Markan and Q material and in passages which may derive from a special source. But the possibility cannot be entirely excluded that Matthean redaction, in Markan and Q passages, was influenced by Matthew's special source. If the special source were the oral traditions of Matthew's own church, this might even be considered rather probable. Thus the possibility that Matt 3:15 is based on Matthew's special source, which Smyrn. 1:1 also reflects, cannot be dismissed too easily.

Smyrn. 1:1 at most provides an isolated case of (4b), which which would permit conclusion D as the explanation of <u>this passage only</u>. For the rest of the Ignatian parallels to Matthew, we should be content with conclusion C. (The above argument is, of course, only a skeletal argument for conclusion C. A full argument would require detailed examination of all Ignatian parallels to Matthew.)

It will be remembered, however, that this method cannot prove conclusions B and C in combination, since the evidence for this would be indistinguishable from the evidence for C alone. The possibility therefore remains that other evidence could show that B and C are both true, and this must be borne in mind in the next section.

5.4.   The significance of the distribution of the
          parallels in Matthew.
Ignatius' parallels to Matthew are very predominantly to Matthew's special material, and are scattered quite widely through that special material. This is true whatever one's judgments as to the most probable parallels. In Trevett's list of the eighteen Matthean passages most commonly cited as parallels to Ignatius, twelve are in M material, four in Markan material, and two in Q material. In my judgment, there are sixteen very or reasonably probable parallels, of which twelve are in M material, two in Markan material, and two in Q material.

Sibinga rightly points out the importance of this
distribution for the question of Ignatius' sources. Matthew's
special material 'may make up roughly 25% of the whole Gospel;
so one could normally expect that if Ignatius were using
Matthew, the quotations from his special source would amount to
a similar percentage'./81/ Sibinga concludes that Ignatius
must have known Matthew's special source M, and that for him
this was a much larger percentage of all the Gospel traditions
he knew than it was for Matthew.

Some caution is required here. Sibinga has not asked
whether Ignatius' interests might have determined this
particular pattern of allusion to Matthean material. Ignatius
does have a special interest in Gospel sayings which he can
apply to his enemies the false teachers, and would have found
more of these in M material than elsewhere in Matthew. This
interest accounts for five passages in Trevett's list of twelve
M parallels and for four passages in my own list of twelve M
parallels. It therefore goes a little way, but only a little,
towards accounting for Ignatius' selectivity. I cannot discern
any other possible reason for Ignatius' preference for M
material, if he were equally familiar with all of Matthew or
with all of Matthew's sources. Those who take Ignatius'
parallels to Matthew to be proof of his dependence on Matthew
do not seem to have noticed this problem.

Sibinga's argument therefore seems a sound one, though
compatible with conclusion C as well as with his own
conclusion B. But before discussing further the form in which
Ignatius knew the M material, we must consider the explanation
of the fact that Ignatius does have a small number of probable
parallels to the Q material and the Markan material in
Matthew. The main possibilities are two: (a) The M traditions
known to Ignatius overlapped at these points with Q and Mark.
This is quite probable not only in general terms, but also
specifically in relation to the passages in question. We have
already noticed (sections 5.2, 5.3) that the two Q passages
which were very likely known to Ignatius (Pol. 2:1 par.
Matt 5:46; Eph. 14:2 par. Matt 12:33) were known to him in
forms different from those in Matthew's and Luke's source(s).
The story of Jesus' anointing (Eph. 17:1; cf. Matt 26:7 par.
Mark 26:7) was evidently a very popular Gospel story, known
also in Luke's special source and in Johannine tradition.
Other possible parallels with Markan material are with the kind
of *logia* which could easily have been duplicated in another
stream of Gospel tradition.

(b) The Ignatian parallels with *Markan* material could
derive from his knowledge of Matthew or Mark. Although he was
mainly familiar with the M material, independently of Matthew,
he may have read Matthew or Mark and absorbed some Gospel
traditions from that source. If it was Mark that he knew, this
could also explain the one plausible (though far from certain)
instance of an Ignatian parallel to a Markan passage without
parallel in Matthew (Smyrn. 10:2; cf. Mark 8:38)./82/ On the
other hand, if more weight were given than I am inclined to
give (see section 5.3) to the fact that in Eph. 17:1 and
Magn. 5:2 Ignatius's wording agrees very slightly with Matthew
against Mark, then we should conclude that it was Matthew,
rather than Mark, which served as Ignatius' minor source.

It seems to me most probable *either* that Ignatius knew the
M traditions only, independently of Matthew, *or* that he knew the
M traditions, independently of Matthew, and also Mark's Gospel.
It would be hard to make a case for his knowledge of Q.

However, it is now necessary to reconsider the conclusion
to 5.3, which was reached without distinguishing Matthew's
sources. If we decide that Ignatius knew Mark as well as some
form of the M traditions, then we can affirm conclusion B (in
relation to Mark) as well as conclusion C (in relation to the M
material). (This combination B and C could not, by the method
used in section 5.3, be distinguished from conclusion C alone.)
But conclusion C in relation to the M material now needs to be
checked. In section 5.3, we reached conclusion C rather than
Sibinga's conclusion B   because of the evidence of four texts
in category (4). But two of these (Eph. 14:2; Pol. 2:1) were
the two parallels with Q material, and a third (Eph. 6:1) *may*
also be a parallel with Q material (if Matt 10:40 derives from
Q). We can now see that these three passages could be
attributed to the overlap between M and Q, so that Ignatius
follows the M form but Matthew preferred the Q version. They
would not then be evidence that M as known to Ignatius differed
from M as known to Matthew. To establish this we would need
cases of (4) in Ignatian parallels to M material in Matthew.
But our fourth case of (4) was such a case: Eph. 19:2-3 (cf.
also Eph. 19:1) does seem to suggest that Ignatius knew a
source related to, but different from the source of Matthew's
infancy narrative.

Thus conclusion C may still stand in relation to Ignatius'
knowledge of the M traditions, but we have very little evidence
to indicate *how* different they were in the form known to

Ignatius from the form known to Matthew.   The difference would
be readily explicable if in both cases M was the oral tradition
of the church of Antioch, on which Matthew drew some twenty or
thirty years before Ignatius wrote./83/

Notes

/1/ Though the facts that may be known about Jesus from non-
Christian sources may seem meagre, A. E. Harvey has recently
demonstrated (*Jesus and the Constraints of History* [London:
Duckworth, 1982] chap. 2; p. 41 n. 23; p. 98) that they can be
combined with broader historical information about the first-
century world in order to yield a surprising number of
implications about Jesus, which can then be compared with the
Gospels for consistency.
/2/ This impression is probably to some extent due to the way in
which the canon has functioned to delimit the area of early
Christian literature to which New Testament scholars pay close
attention.   For those, like myself, who hold a high view of the
canon, it is important to distinguish the proper function of
the canon, as a theological norm which delimits the Gospel
traditions which have normative authority for the church, from
an improper intrusion of the canon into the purely historical
question of determining the range of early Christian literature
which is relevant to or important for the study of early Gospel
traditions.   If the Gospel of Thomas were in fact the earliest
extant Gospel (I do not think it is) or if a papyrus copy of Q
were discovered in the sands of Egypt, the relevance for Gospel
studies would be very considerable, but I do not think the
canon would need to be extended or the normative authority of
the four Gospels for the church's life and thought affected.
/3/ See the careful discussion in L. C. A. Alexander, *Luke-Acts
in its Contemporary Setting with Special Reference to the
Prefaces (Luke 1:1-4 and Acts 1:1)* (D.Phil. thesis, Oxford,
1977) 88, 90-91; cf. 144-49.
/4/ In my opinion, neither Pap. Oxy. 840 (on which see J.
Jeremias, *Unknown Sayings of Jesus* [London: SPCK, 1957] 36-49;
and the doubts expressed by F. F. Bruce, *Jesus and Christian
Origins outside the New Testament* [London: Hodder & Stoughton,
[2]1984] 159-60; O. Hofius, 'Unbekannte Jesusworte', in P.
Stuhlmacher ed., *Das Evangelium und die Evangelien* [Tübingen:
J. C. B. Mohr, 1983] 372-73) nor Pap. Oxy. 1224 (see Jeremias,
op. cit., 85-86; Hofius, art. cit., 378; E. Hennecke, W.
Schneemelcher and R. McL. Wilson ed., *New Testament Apocrypha* I

[London: SCM Press, [2]1973] 113-14) can be shown to be dependent
on the canonical Gospels or necessarily later in date than the
first century.
/5/ In my view, David Wright's careful study in this volume
establishes the probability that Pap. Egerton 2 is dependent on
the canonical Gospels. I am not convinced that the Gospel of
Thomas is a first-century Gospel, but it may be dependent on one
or more such writings.
/6/ For a cautious attempt to identify an early tradition in the
third-century Acts of Thomas, see my article, 'The Parable of
the Vine: Rediscovering a Lost Parable of Jesus', forthcoming
in *NTS*. See also Bruce Chilton's treatment of 'kingdom' sayings
in the Gospel of Thomas in this volume.
/7/ In the patristic period it was never *entirely* halted.
/8/ L. E. Keck, *A Future for the Historical Jesus* (Philadelphia:
Fortress Press, [2]1981) 26.
/9/ I refer to vol. 2: *History and Literature of Early
Christianity* (Philadelphia: Fortress Press/ Berlin & New York:
W. de Gruyter, 1982).
/10/ Cf. the final paragraph of Donald Hagner's contribution to
this volume.
/11/ Cf. Keck, *Future*, 27.
/12/ *The Tendencies of the Synoptic Tradition* (SNTSMS 9;
Cambridge: CUP, 1969).
/13/ For a few examples, see my article, 'Synoptic Parousia
Parables Again', *NTS* 29 (1983) 129-34.
/14/ C. H. Dodd, 'The Primitive Catechism and the Sayings of
Jesus', in A. J. B. Higgins ed., *New Testament Essays* (T. W.
Manson Festschrift; Manchester: MUP, 1959) 106-18.
/15/ J. Piper, *'Love your enemies': Jesus' love command in the
synoptic gospels and in the early Christian paraenesis* (SNTSMS
38; Cambridge: CUP, 1979) 136-39.
/16/ D. C. Allison, 'The Pauline Epistles and the Synoptic
Gospels: The Pattern of the Parallels', *NTS* 28 (1982) 1-32.
/17/ M. D. Goulder, *Midrash and Lection in Matthew* (London:
SPCK, 1974) and other writings.
/18/ Quoted in B. Corley ed., *Colloquy on New Testament Studies:
A Time for Reappraisal and Fresh Approaches* (Macon, Georgia:
Mercer U. P., 1983) 85.
/19/ C. M. Tuckett, '1 Corinthians and Q', *JBL* 102 (1983) 607-19.
/20/ Allison, 'Pauline Epistles', 11-12, 18-19; Wenham in this
volume; Piper, *'Love your enemies'*.
/21/ See G. Maier in this volume.
/22/ See P. Davids in this volume.
/23/ See J. Draper in this volume.

/24/ For these passages in 1 Clement and Polycarp, as well as
Hagner's contribution in this volume, see his fuller
discussion (with references to other literature), in D. A.
Hagner, *The Use of the Old and New Testaments in Clement of Rome*
(Suppl. Nov. Test. 34; Leiden: E. J. Brill, 1973) 135-51.

/25/ Other probably independent parallels to particular *logia*
would also need to be included in such a study: e.g. Ignatius,
Pol. 2:1; Pap. Oxy. 1224.

/26/ Allison, 'Pauline Epistles', 12-15; cf. also D. L. Dungan,
The Sayings of Jesus in the Churches of Paul (Oxford: Blackwell,
1971) 41-75.

/27/ *The Rediscovery of Jesus' Eschatological Discourse* (*Gospel
Perspectives* 4) (Sheffield: JSOT Press, 1984), with summary on
pp. 366-67.

/28/ J. S. Kloppenborg, 'Didache 16$^{6-8}$ and Special Matthean
Tradition', *ZNW* 70 (1979) 54-67.

/29/ The common view (e.g. R. Bultmann, *The History of the
Synoptic Tradition* [Oxford: Blackwell, ^{2}1968] 325; Koester,
Introduction II, 150) that Mark 4 contains a pre-Markan parable
collection is questioned by J. Lambrecht, *Once More Astonished:
The Parables of Jesus* (New York: Crossroad, 1981) chap. 4.

/30/ See my article, 'Synoptic Parousia Parables and the
Apocalypse', *NTS* 23 (1976-77) 162-76; and Wenham, *Rediscovery*,
chap. 1. Wenham extends the collection to include all the
parables in Matt 24:42-25:30; Mark 13:33-37.

/31/ Richardson and Gooch in this volume; cf. Tuckett's useful
survey of claims that either the Corinthians or Paul in
1 Corinthians used Q: '1 Corinthians', 607-10.

/32/ P. Davids in this volume.

/33/ J. Draper in this volume.

/34/ H. Koester argues, not exactly that Thomas is dependent on
Q, but that both have a common origin in early collections of
logia: 'Apocryphal and Canonical Gospels', *HTR* 73 (1980) 112-19;
Introduction II, 47.

/35/ 'Pauline Epistles', 19.

/36/ In this volume.

/37/ '1 Corinthians'.

/38/ For this reason, H. Koester's interaction with proponents
of the Griesbach hypothesis, in Corley ed., *Colloquy*, 31-122,
is important and interesting. Cf. Koester's remark (in
discussion) on p. 77: 'the problem of the Synoptic Gospels I
don't think can be solved as such anymore.... Because the
synoptic problem is also a small part of a larger problem'.

/39/ J. Smit Sibinga, 'Ignatius and Matthew', *NovT* 8 (1966)
263-83.

/40/ For the Didache's relationship to M material, see J. Draper
in this volume, and Kloppenborg, 'Didache 16[6-8]'.
/41/ See Koester, 'Apocryphal and Canonical Gospels', 129-30;
B. A. Johnson, *The Empty Tomb Tradition in the Gospel of Peter*
(Th.D. thesis, Harvard, 1965). I do not deny that the Gospel of
Peter probably shows some signs of dependence on the canonical
Gospels, but I think it can also be shown to have had
independent access to something like Matthew's special source.
However, as David Wright shows in this volume, the new fragment
of the Gospel of Peter in Pap. Oxy. 41.2929 throws doubt on the
reliability of the Akhmim MS. as an accurate witness to the
original second-century text of the Gospel, and therefore makes
arguments about the relationship to the canonical Gospels
hazardous.
/42/ C. Trevett, 'Approaching Matthew from the Second Century:
The Under-Used Ignatian Correspondence', *JSNT* 20 (1984) 59-67.
/43/ *Rediscovery*.
/44/ Ibid., 367-71. He allows that this may have been an oral
'Gospel'.
/45/ A. Resch, *Aussercanonische Paralleltexte zu den Evangelien*
(TU 10; Leipzig: Hinrichs, 1894); idem, *Agrapha:
aussercanonische Schriftfragmente* (TU 30; Leipzig: Hinrichs,
²1906).
/46/ J. H. Ropes, *Die Sprüche Jesu* (TU 14; Leipzig: Hinrichs,
1896).
/47/ In Corley ed., *Colloquy*, 18.
/48/ '1 Corinthians', 614.
/49/ Cf. Koester in Corley ed., *Colloquy*, 76-77.
/50/ 'Pauline Epistles'.
/51/ A Committee of the Oxford Society of Historical Theology,
The New Testament in the Apostolic Fathers (Oxford: Clarendon
Press, 1905).
/52/ W. H. Kelber, 'Mark and Oral Tradition', *Semeia* 16 (1980)
19-20.
/53/ Cf. Ong's comments on the way in which manuscripts are less
'final' than printed books: W. J. Ong, *Orality and Literacy:
The Technologizing of the Word* (London/ New York: Methuen, 1982)
132. A manuscript copied within a living oral tradition of its
subject-matter could well be regarded as anything but final.
/54/ Ong, *Orality and Literacy*, is a stimulating introduction to
the subject.
/55/ W. H. Kelber, *The Oral and the Written Gospel: the
Hermeneutics of Speaking and Writing in the Synoptic Tradition,
Mark, Paul, and Q* (Philadelphia: Fortress Press, 1983), which I
have not yet been able to see, is clearly an important
pioneering study in this area. From the reviews in *Bib* 65

(1984) 279-81 (D. J. Harrington) and *CBQ* 46 (1984) 574-75
(T. L. Brodie), it seems that Kelber may be overstressing the
contrasts between orality and textuality in a situation where
texts belonged in an oral context.
/56/ B. H. Streeter, *The Four Gospels: A Study of Origins*
(London: Macmillan, 1924) 16, 504-7.
/57/ One of the latest writers in this tradition is J. P. Meier
in R. E. Brown and J. P. Meier, *Antioch and Rome* (London:
Geoffrey Chapman, 1983) 24-25. His brief argument for
Ignatius' dependence on Matthew evades the real complexity of
the issue.
/58/ E. Massaux, *Influence de l'Évangile de saint Matthieu sur
la littérature chrétienne avant saint Irénée* (Louvain:
Publications Universitaires/ Gembloux: Éditions J. Duculot,
1950) 106-7.
/59/ *The New Testament in the Apostolic Fathers*, 79.
/60/ H. Koester, *Synoptische Überlieferung bei den apostolischen
Vätern* (TU 65; Berlin: Akademie-Verlag, 1957) 59. The passage
is Smyrn. 1:1.
/61/ J. Smit Sibinga, 'Ignatius and Matthew', *NovT* 8 (1966) 61.
/62/ Trevett, 'Approaching Matthew', 64.
/63/ Ibid., 62-63.
/64/ Ibid., 67 n. 22.
/65/ Matt 5:39 (Eph. 10:2); Matt 9:12 (Eph. 7:2); Matt 26:40-41
(Pol. 1:3).
/66/ Matt 3:15 (Smyrn. 1:1); Matt 10:16 (Pol. 2:2); Matt 12:33
(Eph. 14:2); Matt 15:13 (Trall. 11:1; Philad. 3:1); Matt 19:12
(Smyrn. 6:1); Matt 26:7 (Eph 17:1).
/67/ Matt 2:2 (Eph. 19:2-3); Matt 5:45-46 (Pol. 2:1); Matt 7:15
(Philad. 2:2); Matt 8:17 (Pol. 1:2-3); Matt 10:40 (Eph. 6:1);
Matt 10:42 (Rom. 9:3; Smyrn. 10:1); Matt 13:24-25, 36-43
(Eph. 9:1; 10:3); Matt 18:19-20 (Eph. 5:2); Matt 23:8
(Eph. 15:1; Magn. 9:1); Matt 27:52 (Magn. 9:2-3).
/68/ My indebtedness especially to Smit Sibinga's discussion of
Ignatius and Matthew will become apparent.
/69/ For a recent dissenting opinion, see C. Munier, 'A propos
d'Ignace d'Antioche: Observations sur la liste épiscopale
d'Antioche', *RevSR* 55 (1981) 126-31.
/70/ The letters were not, of course, actually written in
Antioch.
/71/ See Meier, *Antioch and Rome*, 22-24; J. Zumstein, 'Antioche
sur l'Oronte et l'évangile selon Matthieu', *Studien NT Umwelt*
5 (1980) 122-38.
/72/ See *New Testament Apocrypha* I, 128-29.
/73/ The dismissal of Origen's evidence here by R. M. Grant,
'Scripture and Tradition in St Ignatius of Antioch', *CBQ* 25

(1963) 327, is irresponsible. The *Petri doctrina* may be the same work as the *Kerygma Petrou* known to Clement of Alexandria.

/74/ As Vielhauer in *New Testament Apocrypha* I, 130, thinks.

/75/ P. Borgen, 'Ignatius and Traditions on the Birth of Jesus', in *Paul Preaches Circumcision and Pleases Men and other essays on Christian origins* (Trondheim: Tapir, 1983) 160, has a useful, but I think not wholly conclusive argument against this. See also Koester, *Überlieferung*, 31-32.

/76/ 'Ignatius and Matthew', 266.

/77/ Ibid., 265.

/78/ Most recently, Borgen, 'Ignatius', 156-58. Ignatius' use of similar traditional forms in Eph. 7:2; 18:2; Trall. 9:1-2, provides a cumulative argument.

/79/ Koester, *Überlieferung*, 58-61.

/80/ Grant, 'Scripture', 325.

/81/ Smit Sibinga, 'Ignatius and Matthew', 282.

/82/ See Massaux, *Influence*, 107-8.

/83/ The argument of section 5.4 assumes a theory of Synoptic sources. If this assumption is disallowed, the argument would have to proceed rather differently, and could become part of a larger argument *for* a theory of Synoptic sources.

A BIBLIOGRAPHY OF RECENT WORK ON GOSPEL TRADITIONS OUTSIDE THE
CANONICAL GOSPELS

Richard Bauckham,
Faculty of Theology,
University of Manchester,
Manchester M13 9PL

Bibliographical resources for this field of study (with
the exception of the Nag Hammadi literature) are not easily
available, and so this bibliography may prove useful to future
researchers along some of the lines suggested in the previous
chapter. It may also help to indicate the potential scope of
the field. I have limited it to works published since 1970.
References to earlier literature can usually be found in these
more recent works, and some which contain especially full
bibliographies are marked *. The studies included in this
volume are not listed. Otherwise I have tried to make the
bibliography as complete as possible, but I am sure it is far
from exhaustive.

One area of the field which I have excluded is the Infancy
Gospels, on which there is a large literature, but whose
relevance to the study of the canonical Gospels is rather more
limited than most of the literature included here.

General Works

Bruce, F. F. *Jesus and Christian Origins outside the New
Testament* (London: Hodder and Stoughton, 1974, [2]1984).

Koester, H. *Introduction to the New Testament. Vol. 2. History
and Literature of Early Christianity* (Philadelphia: Fortress
Press/ Berlin and New York: W. de Gruyter, 1982).

Mees, M. *Ausserkanonische Parallelstellen zu den Herrenworte
und ihre Bedeutung* (Bari, 1975).

*Wilson, R. McL. 'Apokryphen des Neuen Testaments.'
Theologische Realenzyklopädie 3 (1978) 316-62.

Acts of Pilate

Lampe, G. W. H.   'The trial of Jesus in the *Acta Pilati.*'   In
    E. Bammel and C. F. D. Moule ed., *Jesus and the Politics of
    His Day* (Cambridge: Cambridge University Press, 1984) 173-82.

Agrapha
(Only items not listed under other headings are included here.)

Bauer, J. B.   'Agraphon 90 Resch.'   *ZNW* 62 (1971) 301-3.

Bauer, J. B.   'Unverbürgte Jesusworte.'   *Bibel und Liturgie* 54
    (1981) 163-66.

Delobel, J.   'The Sayings of Jesus in the Textual Tradition:
    Variant Readings in the Greek Manuscripts of the Gospels.'
    In J. Delobel ed., *Logia* (Mémorial J. Coppens; Bibliotheca
    Ephemeridum Theologicarum Lovaniensium 59; Leuven: University
    Press, 1982) 431-57.

*Hofius, O.   'Agrapha.'   *Theologische Realenzyklopädie* 2 (1978)
    103-110.

Hofius, O.   'Unbekannte Jesusworte.'   In P. Stuhlmacher ed.,
    Das Evangelium und die Evangelien (WUNT 28; Tübingen:
    J. C. B. Mohr, 1983) 355-82.

Karawidopulos, J.   'Ein Agraphon in einem liturgischen Text der
    griechischen Kirche.'   *ZNW* 62 (1971) 298-99.

Mees, M.   'Formen, Strukturen und Gattungen ausserkanonischer
    Herrenworte.'   *Augustinianum* 14 (1974) 459-88.

Stroker, W. D.   'The Source of an Agraphon in the Manichean
    Psalm-Book.'   *JTS* 28 (1977) 114-18.

Stroker, W. D.   'Examples of Pronouncement Stories in Early
    Christian Apocryphal Literature.'   *Semeia* 20 (1981) 133-41.

Apocalypse of Peter

Bauckham, R. J.   'The Two Fig-Tree Parables in the Apocalypse of
    Peter.'   *JBL*, forthcoming.

Apocryphal Acts of Apostles

Bauckham, R. J.   'The Parable of the Vine: Rediscovering a
    Lost Parable of Jesus.' *NTS*, forthcoming. (On the Acts of
    Thomas.)

Leloir, L.   'La Version Arménienne des Actes Apocryphes d'André,
    et le Diatessaron.' *NTS* 22 (1976) 115-39.

Apocryphon of James (CG I,2)

Cameron, R. *Sayings Traditions in the Apocryphon of James*
    (Harvard Theological Studies, 1984)

Hedrick, C. W.   'Kingdom Sayings and Parables of Jesus in the
    Apocryphon of James: Tradition and Redaction.' *NTS* 29 (1983)
    1-24.

Perkins, P. *The Gnostic Dialogue* (New York: Paulist Press, 1980)
    145-54.

Perkins, P.   'Johannine Traditions in the *Ap. Jas.* (NHC I,2).'
    JBL 101 (1982) 403-14.

Rouleau, D. 'Les paraboles du Royaume des cieux dans l'*Épître
    apocryphe de Jacques.*' In B. Barc ed., *Colloque
    internationale sur les Textes de Nag Hammadi (Québec, 22-25
    août 1978)* (Québec: Laval University Press/ Louvain: Éditions
    Peeters, 1981) 181-89.

Sevrin, J.-M.   'Paroles et paraboles de Jésus dans les écrits
    gnostiques coptes.' In J. Delobel ed., *Logia* (Mémorial J.
    Coppens; Bibliotheca Ephemeridum Theologicarum Lovaniensium
    59; Leuven: University Press, 1982) 517-28.

Ascension of Isaiah

Bauckham, R. J.   'Synoptic Parousia Parables Again.' *NTS* 29
    (1983) 129-34.

Norelli, E.   'La resurrezione di Gesù nell'Ascensione di Isaia.'
    Cristianesimo nella storia 1 (1980) 315-66.

Book of Thomas (CG II,7)

Sevrin, J.-M.   'Paroles et paraboles de Jésus dans les écrits
   gnostiques coptes.'   In J. Delobel ed., Logia (Mémorial J.
   Coppens; Bibliotheca Ephemeridum Theologicarum Lovaniensium
   59; Leuven: University Press, 1982) 517-28.

Tuckett, C.   'Synoptic Tradition in Some Nag Hammadi and
   Related Texts.'   Vigiliae Christianae 36 (1982) 173-90.

Turner, J. D.   The Book of Thomas the Contender from Codex II
   of the Cairo Gnostic Library from Nag Hammadi (CG II,7) (SBL
   Dissertation Series 23; Missoula, Montana: Scholars Press,
   1975).

Clement of Alexandria

Mees, M.   Die Zitate aus dem Neuen Testament bei Clemens von
   Alexandrien (Rome: Istituto di Litteratura Christiana Antica,
   1970).

Quispel, G.   'Jewish-Christian Gospel Tradition.'   ATR Suppl.
   Ser. 3 (1974) 112-16.

1 Clement

*Hagner, D. A.   The Use of the Old and New Testaments in Clement
   of Rome (Supplements to Novum Testamentum 34; Leiden: E. J.
   Brill, 1973).

2 Clement

Baarda, T.   '2 Clement 12 and the Sayings of Jesus.'   In J.
   Delobel ed., Logia (Mémorial J. Coppens; Bibliotheca
   Ephemeridum Theologicarum Lovaniensium 59; Leuven:
   University Press, 1982) 529-56; reprinted in T. Baarda,
   Early Transmission of the Words of Jesus (Amsterdam: Free
   University Press, 1983) ch. 13.

Donfried, K. P.   The setting of Second Clement in early
   Christianity (Supplements to Novum Testamentum 38; Leiden:
   E. J. Brill, 1974).

Clementine Literature

Kline, L. L. 'Harmonized Sayings of Jesus in the Pseudo-
Clementine Homilies and Justin Martyr.' *ZNW* 66 (1975)
223-41.

Kline, L. L. *The Sayings of Jesus in the Pseudo-Clementine
Homilies* (SBL Dissertation Series 14; Missoula, Montana:
Scholars Press, 1975).

Strecker, G. 'Eine Evangelienharmonie bei Justin und
Pseudoklemens?' *NTS* 24 (1978) 297-316.

Dialogue of Timothy and Aquila

Birdsall, J. N. 'The Dialogue of Timothy and Aquila and the
Early Harmonistic Traditions.' *NovT* 22 (1980) 66-77.

Dialogue of the Saviour (CG III,5)

Koester, H. 'Gnostic Writings as Witnesses for the Development
of the Sayings Tradition.' In B. Layton ed., *The
Rediscovery of Gnosticism: Vol. I: The School of
Valentinus* (Studies in the History of Religions 41; Leiden:
E. J. Brill, 1980) 238-61.

Koester, H. 'Apocryphal and Canonical Gospels.' *HTR* 73 (1980)
105-30.

Pagels, E. and Koester, H. 'Report on the *Dialogue of the
Savior* (CG III,5).' In R. McL. Wilson ed., *Nag Hammadi and
Gnosis* (Nag Hammadi Studies 14; Leiden: E. J. Brill, 1978)
66-74.

Sevrin, J.-M. 'Paroles et paraboles de Jésus dans les écrits
gnostiques coptes.' In J. Delobel ed., *Logia* (Mémorial J.
Coppens; Bibliotheca Ephemeridum Theologicarum Lovaniensium
59; Leuven: University Press, 1982) 517-28.

Didache

Bauckham, R. J. 'Synoptic Parousia Parables and the
Apocalypse.' *NTS* 23 (1976-77) 162-76.

Court, J. M. 'The Didache and St Matthew's Gospel.' *SJT* 34
(1981) 109-20.

Kloppenborg, J. S.   'Didache 16[6-8] and Special Matthean
    Tradition.' *ZNW* 70 (1979) 54-67.

Mees, M.   'Die Bedeutung der Sentenzen und ihrer Ausesis für
    die Formung der Jesuworte nach Didache 1:3b-2:1.' *Vetera
    Christianorum* 8 (1971) 55-76.

Montagnini, F.   'Echi del discorso del monte nella Didaché.'
    Bibbia e Oriente 25 (1983) 137-43.

Trevijano Etcheverría, R.   'Discurso escatológico y relato
    apocalíptico en *Didakhe* 16.' *Burgense* 17 (1976) 365-93.

Epistle of the Apostles

Alsup, J. E.   *The Post-Resurrection Appearance Stories of the
    Gospel Tradition* (Calwer Theologische Monographien A5;
    Stuttgart: Calwer, 1975) 128-30.

Bauckham, R. J.   'Synoptic Parousia Parables Again.' *NTS* 29
    (1983) 129-34.

5 Ezra

Stanton, G. N.   '5 Ezra and Matthean Christianity in the Second
    Century.' *JTS* 28 (1977) 67-83.

Freer Logion

Haacker, K.   'Bemerkungen zum Freer-Logion.' *ZNW* 63 (1972)
    125-29.

Lane, W. L.· *The Gospel according to Mark* (NICNT; London:
    Marshall, Morgan and Scott/ Grand Rapids: Eerdmans, 1974)
    606-11.

Schwarz, G.   'Zum Freer-Logion - ein Nachtrag.' *ZNW* 70 (1979)
    119.

Gospel of Bartholomew

Beeston, A. F. L.   'The *Quaestiones Bartholomae*.' *JTS* 25
    (1974) 124-27.

Brock, S.   'A New Testimonium to the "Gospel according to the
    Hebrews."' *NTS* 18 (1971-72) 220-22.

Cherchi, P. 'A Legend from St Bartholomew's Gospel in the Twelfth-Century.' *RB* 91 (1984) 212-18.

Gospel of Peter

Craig, W. L. 'The Guard at the Tomb.' *NTS* 30 (1984) 273-81.

Denker, J. *Die theologiegeschichtliche Stellung des Petrusevangeliums*: *Beitrag zur Frühgeschichte des Doketismus* (Bern, 1975).

*Fuchs, A. *Das Petrusevangelium* (SNTU B2; Freistadt: Plöchl, 1978).

Koester, H. 'Apocryphal and Canonical Gospels.' *HTR* 73 (1980) 105-30.

Lambiasi, F. 'I criteri di autenticità storica dei vangeli applicati ad un apocrifo: il vangelo di Pietro.' *Bibbia e Oriente* 18 (1976) 151-60.

Lowe, M. ''Ιουδαῖοι of the Apocrypha.' *NovT* 23 (1981) 56-90.

Lührmann, D. 'POx 2949: EvPt 3-5 in einer Handschrift des 2./3. Jahrhunderts.' *ZNW* 72 (1981) 216-26.

*Mara, M. G. *Évangile de Pierre* (SC 201; Paris: Éditions du Cerf, 1973).

McCant, J. W. 'The Gospel of Peter: Docetism Reconsidered.' *NTS* 30 (1984) 258-73.

Neirynck, F. *Evangelica* (Bibliotheca Ephemeridum Theologicarum Lovaniensium 60; Leuven: University Press, 1982) 436-38.

Gospel of Philip

Lagrand, J. 'How was the Virgin Mary "Like a Man"? A Note on Mt. i 18b and Related Syriac Christian Texts.' *NovT* 22 (1980) 97-107.

McNeil, B. 'New Light on Gospel of Philip 17.' *JTS* 29 (1978) 143-46.

Segelberg, E.   'The Gospel of Philip and the New Testament.'
    In A. H. B. Logan and A. J. M. Wedderburn ed., *The New
    Testament and Gnosis* (R. McL. Wilson Festschrift; Edinburgh:
    T. & T. Clark, 1983) 204-212.

Tuckett, C.   'Synoptic Tradition in Some Nag Hammadi and
    Related Texts.'   *Vigiliae Christianae* 36 (1982) 173-90.

Gospel of Thomas

Arthur, R. L.   *The Gospel of Thomas and the Coptic New
    Testament* (Ph.D. thesis, Graduate Theological Union,
    California, 1976).

Baarda, T.   'Jesus said: Be Passers-by. On the meaning and
    origin of Logion 42 of the Gospel of Thomas.'   In *Early
    Transmission of the Words of Jesus* (Amsterdam: Free
    University Press, 1983) ch. 10.

Davies, S. L.   *The Gospel of Thomas and Christian Wisdom* (New
    York: Seabury, 1983).

Dehandshutter, B.   'Les paraboles de l'Évangile selon Thomas.
    La Parabole du Trésor caché (log. 109).'   *ETL* 47 (1971)
    199-219.

Dehandshutter, B.   'L'Évangile selon Thomas: témoin d'une
    tradition prélucanienne?'   In F. Neirynck ed., *L'Évangile de
    Luc* (Gembloux: Duculot, 1973) 287-97.

Dehandshutter, B.   'La parabole des vignerons homicides (Mc.,
    XII, 1 -12) et l'évangile selon Thomas.'   In M. Saabe ed.,
    L'Évangile selon Marc (Leuven: LUP, 1974).

Dehandshutter, B.   'La parabole de la perle (Mt 13,45-46) et
    L'Évangile selon Thomas.'   *ETL* 55 (1979) 243-65.

Dehandshutter, B.   'L'Évangile de Thomas comme collection de
    paroles de Jésus.'   In J. Delobel ed., *Logia* (Mémorial J.
    Coppens; Bibliotheca Ephemeridum Theologicarum Lovaniensium
    59; Leuven: LUP, 1982) 507-15.

Dehandshutter, B.   'The Gospel of Thomas and the Synoptics:
    The Status Quaestionis.'   *TU* 126 (1982).

Fitzmyer, J. A. 'The Oxyrhynchus *logoi* of Jesus and the Coptic
    Gospel of Thomas.' In *Essays on the Semitic Background of
    the New Testament* (London: Geoffrey Chapman, 1971) 355-433.

Glasson, T. F. 'The Gospel of Thomas, Saying 3 and Deuteronomy
    xxx.11-14.' *ExpT* 78 (1976-77) 151-52.

Kaestli, J.-D. 'L'Évangile de Thomas: son importance pour
    l'étude des paroles de Jésus et du gnosticisme chrétien.'
    ETR 54 (1979) 375-96.

Klijn, A. F. J. 'Christianity in Edessa and the Gospel of
    Thomas.' *NovT* 14 (1972) 70-77.

Koester, H. 'Gnostic Writings as Witnesses for the
    Development of the Sayings Tradition.' In B. Layton ed.,
    *The Rediscovery of Gnosticism: Vol. 1: The School of
    Valentinus* (Studies in the History of Religions 41; Leiden:
    E. J. Brill, 1980) 238-61.

Koester, H. 'Apocryphal and Canonical Gospels.' *HTR* 73 (1980)
    105-30.

Koester, H. 'Three Thomas Parables.' In A. H. B. Logan and
    A. J. M. Wedderburn ed., *The New Testament and Gnosis* (R.
    McL. Wilson Festschrift; Edinburgh: T. & T. Clark, 1983)
    204-12.

Lagrand, J. 'How was the Virgin Mary "Like a Man"? A note on
    Mt i 18b and Related Syriac Christian Texts.' *NovT* 22 (1980)
    97-107.

Lincoln, B. 'Thomas-Gospel and Thomas-Community: A New
    Approach to a Familiar Text.' *NovT* 19 (1977) 65-76.

Lindemann, A. 'Zur Gleichnisinterpretation im Thomas-
    Evangelium.' *ZNW* 71 (1980) 214-43.

Ménard, J.-É. *L'Évangile selon Thomas* (Nag Hammadi Studies 5;
    Leiden: E. J. Brill, 1975).

Ménard, J.-É. 'La tradition synoptique et l'Évangile selon
    Thomas.' In F. Paschke ed., *Überlieferungsgeschichtliche
    Untersuchungen* (TU 125; Berlin: Akademie-Verlag, 1981).

Morrice, W. G. 'The Parable of the Dragnet and the Gospel of
    Thomas.' *ExpT* 95 (1984) 269-73.

Perkins, P.   'Pronouncement Stories in the Gospel of Thomas.'
    Semeia 20 (1981) 121-32.

Peterson, W. L.   'The Parable of the Lost Sheep in the Gospel of
    Thomas and the Synoptics.'   *NovT* 23 (1981) 128-47.

Quispel, G.   'Jewish-Christian Gospel Tradition.'   *ATR* Suppl.
    Ser. 3 (1974) 112-16.

Quispel, G.   *Tatian and the Gospel of Thomas* (Leiden: E. J.
    Brill, 1975).

Quispel, G.   'The *Gospel of Thomas* Revisited.'   In B. Barc ed.,
    *Colloque internationale sur les Textes de Nag Hammadi
    (Québec, 22-25 août 1978)* (Québec: Laval University Press/
    Louvain: Éditions Peeters, 1981) 218-66.

Schoedel, W. R.   'Parables in the Gospel of Thomas: Oral
    Tradition or Gnostic Exegesis?'   *CTM* 42 (1972) 548-60.
    Translated as: 'Gleichnisse im Thomasevangelium: Mündliche
    Tradition oder gnostische Exegese?' In W. Harnisch ed.,
    *Gleichnisse Jesu: Positionen der Auslegung von Adolf
    Jülicher bis zur Formgeschichte* (Darmstadt: Wissenschaftliche
    Buchgesellschaft, 1982) 369-89.

Snodgrass, K. R.   'The Parable of the Wicked Husbandmen: Is the
    Gospel of Thomas Version the Original?'   *NTS* 21 (1974-75)
    142-44.

Suarez, P. de.   *L'Évangile selon Thomas* (Marsanne: Métanoia,
    1975).

Tripp, D. H.   'The Aim of the "Gospel of Thomas."'   *ExpT* 92
    (1980-81) 41-44.

Ignatius

Borgen, P.   'Ignatius and Traditions on the Birth of Jesus.'
    *Paul Preaches Circumcision and Pleases Men and other essays
    on Christian origins* (Trondheim: Tapir, 1983) 155-63.

Trevett, C.   'Anomaly and Consistency: Josep Rius-Camps on
    Ignatius and Matthew.'   *Vigiliae Christianae* 39 (1984)
    165-71.

Trevett, C. 'Approaching Matthew from the Second Century: The
    Under-Used Ignatian Correspondence.' *JSNT* 20 (1984) 59-67.

James

Harvey, A. E. '"The Workman is Worthy of His Hire": Fortunes
    of a Proverb in the Early Church.' *NovT* 24 (1982) 209-21.

Minear, P. S. 'Yes or No: the Demand for Honesty in the Early
    Church.' *NovT* 13 (1971) 1-13.

Jewish Christian Gospels

Alsup, J. E. *The Post-Resurrection Appearance Stories of the
    Gospel Tradition* (Calwer Theologische Monographien A5;
    Stuttgart: Calwer, 1975) 126-28.

Bertrand, D. A. 'L'*Evangile des Ebionites*: Une Harmonie
    Evangélique antérieure au *Diatessaron*.' *NTS* 26 (1980) 548-63.

Brock, S. 'A New Testimonium to the "Gospel according to the
    Hebrews."' *NTS* 18 (1971-72) 220-22.

Mees, M. 'Das Paradigma vom reichen Mann und seiner Berufung
    nach den Synoptikern und dem Nazaräerevangelium.' *Vetera
    Christianorum* 9 (1972) 245-65.

Mees, M. 'Herrenworte und Erzählstoff in den judenchristlichen
    Evangelien und ihre Bedeutung.' *Augustinianum* 23 (1983) 187-
    212.

Quispel, G. 'Mani et la tradition évangelique des
    judéochrétiens.' *Rech.Sci.Rel.* 60 (1972) 143-50.

Stroker, W. D. 'Examples of Pronouncement Stories in Early
    Christian Apocryphal Literature.' *Semeia* 20 (1981) 133-41.

Justin Martyr

Abramowski, L. 'Die "Erinnerungen der Apostel" bei Justin.'
    In P. Stuhlmacher ed., *Das Evangelium und die Evangelien*
    (WUNT 28; Tübingen: J. C. B. Mohr, 1983) 341-353.

Kline, L. L. 'Harmonized Sayings of Jesus in the Pseudo-
    Clementine Homilies and Justin Martyr.' *ZNW* 66 (1975)
    223-41.

Mees, M.   'Form und Komposition der Herrenworte in Justin,
    Apol. 1,15-17.' Augustinianum 17 (1977) 283-306.

Strecker, G.   'Eine Evangelienharmonie bei Justin und
    Pseudoklemens?' NTS 24 (1978) 297-316.

Nag Hammadi Literature
(See also separate headings for Book of Thomas, Dialogue of the
Saviour, Gospel of Philip, and Gospel of Thomas. Fuller
bibliography is available in D. M. Scholer, Nag Hammadi
Bibliography 1948-1949 (Leiden: E. J. Brill, 1971) and
Scholer's annual supplement in NovT.)

Dubois, J.-D.   'L'Apocalypse de Pierre (NHC VII,3) et le
    Nouveau Testament.' In Écritures et Traditions dans la
    Littérature Copte (Cahiers de la Bibliothèque Copte 1;
    Louvain: Éditions Peeters, 1984) 117-25.

Janssens, Y.   'The Trimorphic Protennoia and the Fourth Gospel.'
    In A. H. B. Logan and A. J. M. Wedderburn ed., The New
    Testament and Gnosis (R. McL. Wilson Festschrift; Edinburgh:
    T. & T. Clark, 1983) 229-44.

Koester, H.   'Dialog und Sprachüberlieferung in den gnostischen
    Texten von Nag Hammadi.' EvTh 39 (1979) 532-56.

Tuckett, C.   'Synoptic Tradition in Some Nag Hammadi and
    Related Texts.' Vigiliae Christianae 36 (1982) 173-90.

Tuckett, C.   'Synoptic Tradition in the Gospel of Truth and the
    Testimony of Truth.' JTS 35 (1984) 131-45.

Odes of Solomon

Charlesworth, J. H.   'Tatian's Dependence upon Apocryphal
    Traditions.' Heythrop J. 15 (1974) 5-17.

Lagrand, J.   'How was the Virgin Mary "Like a Man"? A note on
    Mt. i 18b and Related Syriac Christian Texts.' NovT 22
    (1980) 97-107.

McNeil, B.   'The Odes of Solomon and the Scriptures.' Oriens
    Christianus 67 (1983) 104-22.

Tosato, A.   'Gesù e gli zeloti alla luce delle Odi di Salomone.'
    Bibbia e Oriente 19 (1977) 145-53.

Tosato, A.   'Il battesimo di Gesù e le Odi di Salomone.'
    Bibbia e Oriente 18 (1978) 261-69.

Papias

Deeks, D. G.   'Papias Revisited.'   *ExpT* 88 (1976-77) 296-301,
    324-29.

Delclaux, A.   'Deux Témoignages de Papias sur la Composition de
    Marc?'   *NTS* 27 (1981) 401-11.

Körtner, U. H. J.   'Markus der Mitarbeiter des Petrus.'   *ZNW* 71
    (1980) 160-73.

Körtner, U. H. J.   *Papias von Hierapolis: Ein Beitrag zur
    Geschichte des frühen Christentums* (FRLANT 133; Göttingen:
    Vandenhoeck & Ruprecht, 1983).

*Kürzinger, J.   *Papias von Hierapolis und die Evangelien des
    Neuen Testaments* (Regensburg: F. Pustet, 1983).

Perumalil, A. C.   'Papias.'   *ExpT* 85 (1973-74) 361-66.

Perumalil, A. C.   'Are not Papias and Irenaeus competent to
    report on the Gospels?'   *ExpT* 91 (1979-80) 332-37.

Siegert, F.   'Unbeachtete Papiaszitate bei armenischen
    Schriftstellern.'   *NTS* 27 (1981) 605-14.

Pauline Literature

Achtemeier, P. J.   'An Apocalyptic Shift in Early Christian
    Tradition: Reflections on Some Canonical Evidence.'   *CBQ* 45
    (1983) 231-48.

Allison, D. C.   'The Pauline Epistles and the Synoptic Gospels:
    The Pattern of the Parallels.'   *NTS* 28 (1982) 1-32.

Catchpole, D. R.   'The Synoptic Divorce Material as a Traditio-
    Historical Problem.'   *BJRL* 57 (1974) 92-127.

Dungan, D. L.   *The Sayings of Jesus in the Churches of Paul:
    The Use of the Synoptic Tradition in the Regulation of Early
    Church Life* (Oxford: Blackwell, 1971).

Fjärstedt, B. *Synoptic Tradition in 1 Corinthians: Themes and*
    Clusters of Theme Words in 1 Corinthians 1-4 and 9 (Uppsala:
    Uppsala Teologiska Institutionen, 1974).

Harvey, A. E. '"The Workman is Worthy of His Hire": Fortunes
    of a Proverb in the Early Church.' *NovT* 24 (1982) 209-21.

Stuhlmacher, P. 'Jesustradition im Römerbrief.' *Theologische*
    Beiträge 14 (1983) 240-50.

Tuckett, C. M. '1 Corinthians and Q.' *JBL* 102 (1983) 607-19.

Wenham, D. 'Paul and the Synoptic Apocalypse.' In R. T.
    France and D. Wenham ed., *Gospel Perspectives: Vol. II:*
    Studies of History and Tradition in the Four Gospels
    (Sheffield: JSOT Press, 1981) 345-75.

Wenham, D. *The Rediscovery of Jesus' Eschatological Discourse*
    (Gospel Perspectives Vol. 4) (Sheffield: JSOT Press, 1984).

1 Peter

Best, E. 'I Peter and the Gospel Tradition.' *NTS* 16 (1970)
    95-113.

Gundry, R. H. 'Further *Verba* on *Verba Christi* in First Peter.'
    Bib 55 (1974) 211-32.

2 Peter

Bauckham, R. J. *Jude, 2 Peter* (Word Biblical Commentary 50;
    Waco, Texas: Word Books, 1983) 148, 199-201, 205-12, 253,
    273, 277.

Revelation

Bauckham, R. J. 'Synoptic Parousia Parables and the
    Apocalypse.' *NTS* 23 (1976-77) 162-76.

Smitmans, A. 'Das Gleichnis vom Dieb.' In H. Feld and J.
    Nolte ed., *Wort Gottes in der Zeit* (K. Hermann Festschrift;
    Düsseldorf: Patmos, 1973) 43-68.

Wenham, D. *The Rediscovery of Jesus' Eschatological Discourse*
    (Gospel Perspectives Vol. 4) (Sheffield: JSOT Press, 1984).

Secret Gospel of Mark

Koester, H. 'History and Development of Mark's Gospel (From
    Mark to *Secret Mark* and "Canonical" Mark).' In B. Corley
    ed., *Colloquy on New Testament Studies: A Time for
    Reappraisal and Fresh Approaches* (Macon, Georgia: Mercer
    University Press, 1983) 35-57, followed by seminar dialogue
    (59-85) and response by D. Peabody (87-132).

*Smith, M; 'Clement of Alexandria and Secret Mark: The Score
    at the End of the First Decade.' *HTR* 75 (1982) 449-61.

Tiburtine Sibyl

Flusser, D. 'An early Jewish-Christian Document in the
    Tiburtine Sibyl.' In A. Benoit, M. Philonenko and C. Vogel
    ed., *Paganisme, Judaïsme, Christianisme: Influences et
    affrontemonts dans le monde antique* (M. Simon Festschrift;
    Paris: Éditions E. de Boccard, 1978) 153-83.